Poli Sci

6⁵⁰

WAR
AND
POLITICS

WAR
AND
POLITICS

Bernard Brodie

MACMILLAN PUBLISHING CO., INC.
New York
COLLIER MACMILLAN PUBLISHERS
London

Macmillan Publishing Co., Inc.
866 Third Avenue, New York, New York 10022

Collier Macmillan Canada, Ltd.

Library of Congress catalog card number: 72–78607

PRINTING   91011   YEAR   123456

To Fawn

après trente-six ans

Preface

The central idea of this book I have borrowed from Clausewitz who, as a seventeenth-century writer said of Machiavelli, "hath been too often taxed for his impieties." It is a simple idea, and the novice would justly imagine it to be a commonplace—that the question of *why* we fight must dominate any consideration of means. Yet this absurdly simple theme has been mostly ignored, and when not ignored usually denied.

Though I had long thought of writing this book, it required the special agonies of Vietnam to bring a sense of urgency to the matter. To attempt to put war in its political context is to observe inevitably that war is characterized by men killing on a grand scale for reasons that are usually foolish and often wicked; and Vietnam, besides being recent, presents more than its share of both foolishness and wickedness.

The word *politics* in the title of this book is used in the broadest possible sense; on the whole it more often refers to the international than to the domestic variety. I may here perhaps also reassure the reader that the difference between the two parts of the book is more a matter of structure than of essence. The first part reads rather like a historical resumé of four wars, but it has in it more generalization than a historian would own to. Conversely, in the second part there is a good deal of history along with the theory, and in any case my purpose is exactly the same in both parts.

vii

An earlier version of Chapter 7, "Some Theories on the Causes of War," appeared in the two-volume *Festschrift* published in Paris in 1971 in honor of a friend and a great contemporary contributor to insight on matters of war and peace—*Science et conscience de la société; mélanges en l'honneur de Raymond Aron* (Calmann-Lévy). I have, however, entirely rewritten it and greatly expanded it for this book. The rest is almost entirely new.

Most of the persons whose assistance I most gratefully acknowledge here read only a small portion of the manuscript, usually because I desired to tap some special knowledge that each of them represents. First I must thank Professor Michael Howard of All Souls College, Oxford, who was especially helpful with the first chapter. The following colleagues of my own political science department at the University of California, Los Angeles, were helpful mostly in giving their responses to the two chapters on Vietnam: Professors Hans H. Baerwald, Irving Bernstein, William P. Gerberding, Simon Serfaty, Richard Sklar, and David O. Wilkinson. Those of the history department at UCLA who gave valuable assistance, especially with respect to Chapter 6, "Changing Attitudes Toward War," were Professors Jere King, Andrew Lossky, and Arthur J. Slavin. Another member of the latter department is my wife, Fawn M. Brodie, who, as always, assisted in a multitude of ways. I must also mention Konrad Kellen of the RAND Corporation, whose special gifts of insight I tapped for the Vietnam chapters.

I am happy to mention my indebtedness to Mrs. Arvella Powell, who typed and retyped the entire manuscript, and to the Ford Foundation, which allocated to me a most useful grant that was benignly administered by Professor David A. Wilson and Mrs. Clare Walker.

Finally, I would like to pay my grateful respects to the memory of my greatest teacher, Jacob Viner, who at the time I was his student in graduate school over thirty years ago was Professor of Economics at the University of Chicago. Whatever is good in my work owes something to him, and I was especially conscious of his eye over my shoulder in writing Chapter 7. I also offer my respects to another dedicated and scholarly teacher of whom I was very fond, Quincy Wright, formerly Professor of International Law and

Political Science at the University of Chicago. Both were friends and colleagues as well as former teachers, and both died not long ago.

B. B.

viii

Contents

PART I

xi

Contents

PART II

CHAPTER

1

De quoi s'agit-il?

The quarrel is a very pretty quarrel as it stands; we should only spoil it by trying to explain it.

Sheridan, *The Rivals,* Act IV, sc. 3.

"War," said Clausewitz, "has its own language but not its own logic." We may extend this metaphor slightly by adding that the language is most cruelly obscene but that the logic it serves may at times give it some redeeming social value. In any case, Clausewitz is here expressing the single most important idea in all strategy. It is the idea expressed in the question that Marshal Ferdinand Foch used to ask, *De quoi s'agit-il?*—"What is it all about?"

By "language" Clausewitz refers to the means or methods of conducting war, and his "logic" relates to the purpose for which the peculiarly foul language is adopted. He is underlining the point that war takes place within a political milieu from which it derives *all* its purposes. He proceeds to argue forcefully and unequivocally that the influence of the purposes upon the means must be continuing and pervasive. His originality is not in his reassertion of what must really be an old idea but rather in the clarity and insistence with which he hews to it and develops it. It is an accomplishment against perennial resistance, indicated by the fact that this understanding has never fully got across to the great majority of those people who think or write about war, and even less to those who fight it.

It is in making this point that Clausewitz several times uses his often quoted but constantly misrepresented dictum: "War is a continuation of policy by other means." He is very far from intending this remark cynically, as is often supposed, as though war merely added violence to perfidy. It is a conviction that he develops in the first and only truly finished chapter of his great work, to which he returns in the last of his eight major sections or books, and which we know he intended to make, had he lived, the central organizing thesis of the whole.

To appreciate the idea, one must first observe that war is an act of choice. A small state may have no influence over the events that lead to its being invaded, but it does choose whether or not to resist. In 1940 Belgium chose again to resist German invasion, as it had in 1914, but Denmark did not. A large nation will not only be more nearly certain to resist so direct an offense as invasion of its own borders, but, depending on its sense of power and importance, it will also commit itself to war or warlike acts over a broader spectrum of what it asserts to be provocations, which is to say simply that it interprets more expansively its "vital interests."

Vital interests, despite common assumptions to the contrary, have only a vague connection with objective fact. A sovereign nation determines for itself what its vital interests are (freedom to do so is what the term *sovereign* means), and its leaders accomplish this exacting task largely by using their highly fallible and inevitably biased human judgment to interpret the external political environment. To save wear and tear on their always overburdened and frequently limited analytical powers, they cling obsessively to commonly accepted axioms, some of which may be old enough to have the aura of "traditional" policy. As such they help to warn other powers where they may be trespassing. Britain's concern both with the "balance-of-power" in Europe and with the freedom of the Low Countries insured her commitment to war in 1914, but as British "vital interests" they were not new in Louis XIV's time. The United States for a century or more had its Monroe Doctrine and its disdain for "entangling alliances."

Traditional views on vital interests may, like other old ideas, outlive whatever usefulness they once had. Sir Anthony Eden must have had "lifelines of Empire" and a variety of associated ideas in mind when he induced his French colleagues to join him in the Suez fiasco of 1956, an affair that struck most of the world, including and especially a large proportion of the British people, as being simply anachronistic.

Axioms need not always be old in order to be powerfully entrenched. Those that triggered United States involvement in Vietnam were largely born out of World War II. In any case, when political leaders decide that some vital interests of their country are threatened enough to warrant resort to war or warlike measures, they are making contingency predictions, the basic one being that more evil to the state will ultimately result from not going to war than from doing so. This means, among other things, that they think the military action will be successful, and the costs tolerable. Viewed historically, the relevant predictions have normally reflected much more ignorance about related conditions than is necessary, far more confidence in the correctness of the key assessments than is warranted, and astonishing levity about leaving the gravest decisions to chance. They also reflect preoccupation with the image of the state functioning solidly as a unit, rather than as an organized collection of citizens with highly individuated private interests.

Nevertheless, the decision to go to war has not always in retrospect appeared wrong, the alternative in some instances being submission to unmitigated lawlessness, tyranny, and other evils. Those to whom Hitler is a live memory cannot be in doubt about that. On the other hand, it is right to cultivate skepticism, because this is an area of consideration too much cluttered with obsessive symbols, and clear thinking does not flourish in it. Men have fought and bled for values held too sacred to question and yet in fact juvenile.

The world has never been in want of theories about how wars may be avoided, and no doubt the human race could do very much better in this respect than it has done. However, the advocates of the various theories have tended in common to expose simplistic notions of the causes of war—which, as we shall see in another chapter, is a field full of pitfalls. They also often show (for example, in theories advocating "world government") an ignorance or intolerance of various deep-felt human desires and attachments, like the common desire of peoples everywhere to be ruled by persons who, whatever their shortcomings, are at least not felt to be foreigners.

As we shall also see in another chapter, the idea is not new that war has consequences that are hideous and evil. What is relatively new is the idea that war is *intrinsically* evil, though with the exception of the thoroughgoing pacifist, who is a quite rare species, the general view is that it may still occasionally prove necessary. Ambivalence has always characterized man's view of war. In the past, what was recognized as evil or at least unfortunate was seen also to provide a unique and magnificent setting for something superlative about man. That was certainly the ancient and the medieval idea, and it has lasted well into modern times. Also, the idea that a nation engages in war for some distinctive political end could hardly have been overlooked—and we have had at least since St. Augustine the conception of the "just" as distinguished from the "unjust" war. Nevertheless, with that recognition went a simple "stop-go" approach, so that the actual outbreak of war was the occasion for instituting completely new sets of values and objectives, especially the objective of winning the war for the sake simply of winning. One remembers the eloquent simplicity of the late General Douglas MacArthur's famous remark, apropos the then current negotiations for a peace in Korea: "There is no substitute for victory!" [1]

The disposition towards this attitude is especially a mark of the military profession—though certainly not confined to it—and is no doubt necessary if the object is to produce good fighters. All the more reason for genuine civilian control. For as Raymond Aron has noted: "The history of the twentieth century suffices to remind us that there are many ways to win a war, that the various

---

[1] Admittedly General MacArthur's statement, used first in his letter of March 20, 1951 to Congressman Joseph W. Martin, can be interpreted in a manner that makes it eminently reasonable, that is, that prolonged and frustrating pseudo-negotiations that the enemy uses as a delaying tactic can be avoided by defeating him unequivocally, or at least by establishing a clear military ascendancy and showing a readiness to use it. If he had so meant it, his words could have been called prophetic in view of what followed. However, all the contextual indications are that MacArthur had a less sophisticated meaning in mind—that victory produces a satisfaction and a fulfillment not obtainable in a negotiated settlement. He repeated the same phrase in his speech to Congress on April 19, where he also said: "But once war is forced upon us, there is no other alternative than to apply every available means to bring it to a swift end. War's very object is victory. . . ." The letter to Congressman Martin and the speech to Congress are reproduced respectively in *New York Times* for April 6 and April 20, 1951.

ways are not equivalent, and that the final victory does not necessarily belong to the side that dictates the conditions of peace." [2] Also, as has been abundantly clear from the French and American experiences in Vietnam, decisive military victory may simply not be attainable even by the nation enjoying an overwhelmingly military superiority, except by means that the circumstances make unacceptable or at a price that its people are unwilling to pay and which it makes no sense to try to pay.

When General Maxwell Taylor admonished the Senate Foreign Relations Committee in 1966 that France had lost its Vietnam war not in Vietnam but in Paris,[3] which he considered to be an important object lesson to the United States, the proper reply might well have been: "Of course; where else should they have made the appropriate decision?" The French army, which is to say its professional officer corps, was outraged by its government's decision after Dien Bien Phu to liquidate the war, and these feelings were to accentuate the subsequent bitterness over Algeria. However, Premier Pierre Mendes-France agreed with the common judgment that whatever benefits accrued to France from keeping Vietnam as a colonial dependency were in no sense worth the cost. This was certainly from any nonromantic point of view a correct judgment. Anyway it was the average citizen who was paying the bill and he wanted out. Significantly, Mendes-France remained under the Fifth Republic the most respected of the political figures of the preceding regime, an attitude shared even by so nationalistic and imperious a figure as Charles de Gaulle, who in fact followed his example under the more difficult circumstances of Algeria.

As American citizens we expect and desire that our own nation will involve itself in war only under rare circumstances of impelling need, and then only for political ends that are reasonably consistent with its basic political philosophy. That basic philosophy is discernable, despite wide variations in political beliefs, in some few principles that command almost universal concurrence, and which are most clearly visible in the appeals that government leaders make in defending their policies with respect to interven-

---

[2] Raymond Aron, *War and Peace: A Theory of International Relations,* trans. by Richard Howard and Annette Baker Fox (New York. Doubleday, 1966), p. 577.

[3] With an Introduction by J. William Fulbright, *The Vietnam Hearings* (New York: Random House, Vintage Book V-354, 1966), p. 176. The official Senate publication is cited on p. 120, footnote 4.

tions like that of Vietnam. (For example, we are *not* imperialistic; we do *not* support repressive governments; we *are* fighting for objectives that ultimately affect our own survival.)

We should also expect that the ends for which we fight are reasonably to be sought through the kind of war that it is reasonable to fight. This requirement also invokes the question of the possibility of success—a markedly elastic consideration in view of the very different kinds of threat to which we might think it necessary to respond. Whatever happened at Tonkin Bay in 1964, it was not the same as what happened at Pearl Harbor in 1941.

All this may seem quixotic. The pertinence of the rule of reason is readily accepted for much lesser issues, but where war is concerned we are usually guided by faith, tradition, and passion. It is inescapable, however, that unless it is in pursuit of a reasonable political objective, any nation resorting to war is simply perpetrating wanton destruction of life and goods on a vast scale. The appearance of order imposed on the process by the use of military organization and method only makes the destruction greater and more efficient.

War inevitably includes enormous wanton destruction anyway, and just as inevitably it includes the slaughter of innocents, by which I mean not only noncombatants but also the armed young men on both sides. They have not willed the war nor do they usually understand its purposes, and it is not greatly material whether they were drafted or induced by propaganda and other pressures to volunteer. These evils taint even those wars that have come closest to being "just" wars,[4] or which have resulted in marked improvements in the political conditions that provoked them—like the abolition of slavery in our own Civil War and the destruction of Hitler and his abominations in World War II.

These are sufficient reasons for regarding war as inherently hideous, and not ever to be accepted as anything else. Now, with nuclear weapons and other latter-day improvements in the efficiency of killing, resort to it can also pose unprecedented danger

---

[4] As I have indicated, the effort to distinguish morally between "just" and "unjust" wars goes back at least to St. Augustine. However, in the development of modern international law such distinctions were abandoned until recently—that is, until after World War I, when the effort was made to distinguish, legally as well as morally, between the aggressor and the victim of aggression. One of the charges made against the Nazis who were tried and hanged at Nuremberg was that they were guilty of perpetrating wars of aggression. However, the older concept has recently been revived in several writings. See, for example, Robert W. Tucker, *The Just War: A Study in Contemporary American Doctrine* (Baltimore: Johns Hopkins Press, 1960).

to the state and its people. Thomas Paine, certainly no pacifist, wrote in 1778 in a letter to General Sir William Howe:

If there is a sin superior to every other, it is that of wilful and offensive war. Most other sins are circumscribed within narrow limits, that is, the power of *one* man cannot give them a very general extension, and many kinds of sin have only a mental existence from which no infection arises; but he who is the author of a war, lets loose a contagion of hell, and opens a vein that bleeds a nation to death.[5]

Writers on strategy, and certainly its practitioners, have almost always rejected from their conscious concern those characteristics of war that to ordinary folk are its most conspicuous ones. In the treatises on strategy, battlefields rarely have the smell of death. Weapons produce "fire-power," but no searing din and uproar. Men in battle and on the march feel triumph and sometimes panic, but rarely are they described suffering pain, cold, sweat, exhaustion, and utter misery. Certain standard and conventionalized euphemisms conceal or dissipate the cruder, unhappy images. Among them are many phrases in which the word *military* serves as a descriptive adjective, concealing with a certain air of punctilio and correctness the raw fact of violence, as in *military action, military necessity,* or *military justification.* The words *casualties were heavy* deliberately leave much to an unresponsive professional imagination and have a very different ring from any of a number of nonextravagant and more graphic phrases that could be used. True, the military phrasing uses only three words to communicate the message that large numbers of young men were killed, maimed, or disabled by wounds, but economy is not the main reason for it.

Up to a point, certainly, this kind of glossing over by verbalization is necessary. But like any other kind of deliberate insensitization or self-deception, it has its price. In war the manipulators use a jargon that the man in the front lines—or the reporter observing the latter—can hardly consider relevant to his condition. In a very real way it is not, and sometimes the discrepancy flies back into the face of the astonished commander, like the mutiny in the French army following the disastrous failure of General Robert Nivelle's extraordinarily ambitious offensive in the spring of

---

[5] William M. Vander Weyde (ed.), *Life and Works of Thomas Paine,* 10 vols. (New Rochelle, New York: National Historical Association, 1925), vol. III, p. 28.

7

1917. Nivelle in the preceding year had commanded during part of the nine-months-long Battle of Verdun, possibly the most terrible battle in history and futile to both sides as well. What kind of language could have befuddled *him*?

The United States even in wartime allows fairly unfettered speech, and its press, radio, and television go uncensored. Also, like other advanced countries it has left the age of chauvinism mostly behind it—though the laggards sometimes include politicians of the highest rank. Thus, in any war marked by something well short of full and unified commitment of the people, the considerations that guide the military commanders and the top political leadership of the country will be tested not only against individual private self-interest but also against various sensibilities of the community, including what in a few will be moral sensibilities. This is one of the lessons that have already emerged out of Vietnam.

In such a situation, axioms and clichés derived from old patterns of *Realpolitik*, already out of harmony with modern times, sound doubly hollow. Those who talk abstractly of national prestige and national honour, and of other interests that inevitably differentiate the state from its people, find themselves matching their discourse with those who speak of dead bodies, burnt villages, My Lai massacres, and other ugly matters that are highly visible in the field, noted by reporters, and sometimes picked up on television screens. The language of the latter group is not more sentimental or less real than that of the former—quite the contrary—and we have now had two opportunities, including Korea, to see how with time and in the absence of unequivocal success the language of lesser abstraction tends to prevail. Clearly then, the euphemisms of the strategists can be counterproductive from their own point of view.

If the last several paragraphs go somewhat beyond the point Clausewitz was making a century and a half ago, it is because we speak from a position in time that has behind it two world wars, the advent of nuclear weapons, and for the United States a particularly perplexing and tragic involvement in a distant and hitherto obscure peninsula in Southeast Asia. The wars he knew of were limited to a history culminating with Napoleon, and the bitterest disaster in his experience was the campaign of Jena in 1806, topped off by two battles that by modern standards were brief and of small dimensions. It discomfited the Prussian army and dynasty far more than it did the Prussian people. If, despite these differences, we see him warning against errors that are relevant to our experience, and we also notice that despite his great authority these warnings have been completely ignored, it is worth our while to consider how and why they were ignored.

It is really marvelous how modern is the ring of what Clausewitz has to say on this subject! In a chapter near the end of his towering work, he returns to the statement on war being a continuation of policy by other means, which he has presented with some preliminary explanation in his opening chapter, and proceeds further to illuminate its meaning. He points out first that political intercourse with the enemy does not cease through the onset of war but continues to exist, "whatever may be the means which it uses. . . . The main lines along which the events of the war proceed and to which they are bound are only the general features of policy which run on all through the war until peace takes place." Accordingly, he says, "war can never be separated from political intercourse, and if, in the consideration of the matter, this occurs anywhere, all the threads of the different relations are in a certain sense broken, and we have before us a senseless thing without an object." [6]

It is true, he admits, that the political element does not penetrate deeply into the details of war—"patrols are not sent out on political considerations"—but "its influence is all the more decisive in regard to the plan of a whole war, or campaign, and often even for a battle." "There is, on the whole," he continues, "nothing more important in life than to find out exactly the point of view from which things must be regarded and judged, and then to keep to it, for we can only apprehend the mass of events in their unity from *one* standpoint, and it is only the keeping to one point of view that can save us from inconsistency." [7]

And as he warms to the subject: "That the political point of view should end completely when war begins would only be conceivable if wars were struggles of life or death, from pure hatred." Clausewitz has indeed already acknowledged, at the very beginning of his book, the inevitable and indeed necessary involvement of aggressive emotions in any act of force, an involvement that grows with "the importance and duration of the hostile interests";

---

[6] Karl von Clausewitz, *On War*, trans. by O. J. Matthijs Jolles (New York: Modern Library, 1943), p. 596.
[7] Ibid., p. 597.

9

but it is not compatible with statecraft to permit such emotions to dominate the choice of means, let alone ends. Therefore, he goes on: "The subordination of the political point of view to the military would be unreasonable, for policy has created the war; policy is the intelligent faculty, war only the instrument, and not the reverse. The subordination of the military point of view to the political is, therefore, the only thing which is possible." [8]

Clausewitz pursues this last point with special avidity, because experience has told him how readily it is ignored or rejected:

> According to this view, it is an unpermissible and even harmful distinction, according to which a great military event or the plan for such an event should admit a *purely military judgment*; indeed, it is an unreasonable procedure to consult professional soldiers on the plan of war, that they may give a *purely military* opinion, as is frequently done by cabinets; but still more absurd is the demand of theorists that a statement of the available means of war should be laid before the general, that he may draw up a purely military plan for the campaign in accordance with them. . . . [Italics in original.]
>
> None of the principal plans which are necessary for a war can be made without insight into the political conditions, and when people speak, as they often do, of the harmful influence of policy on the conduct of the war, they really say something very different from what they intend. It is not this influence, but the policy itself, which should be found fault with. . . .
>
> It is only when policy itself promises a wrong effect from certain military means and measures, an effect opposed to their nature, that it can exercise a harmful effect on war by the course it prescribes. Just as a person in a language which he has not entirely mastered sometimes says what he does not intend, so policy will often order things which do not correspond to its own intentions.
>
> This has very often happened and shows that a certain knowledge of military affairs is essential to the management of political intercourse.[9]

The message could hardly have been clearer (and I have quoted only a very small portion of what Clausewitz has to say on the

---

[8] Ibid., p. 598.
[9] Ibid., p. 599.

subject), but if it was ever taken to heart and remembered at all, it could not have been for very long. Shortly corrupted editions were to appear that would veil or delete passages like those just quoted. Soldiers usually are close students of tactics, but only rarely are they students of strategy and practically never of war! It is not their function, after all, to study history creatively or to concern themselves with the economic, social, and political costs of war. Anyway, who but Germans of his own and closely succeeding generations could read Clausewitz, and who of these could do so with understanding? [10]

It would not even be the elder Helmuth von Moltke—who spent an incredible sixty years on the Prussian General Staff with over thirty years as its chief, and who led the Prussian forces in the wars of German unification culminating in the Franco-Prussian War of 1870–1871. He was in his own right a productive scholar as well as a practical war leader. We know he read Clausewitz avidly. Bismarck, however, did not find him particularly deferential to political leadership. On the contrary, he is known to have declared: "The politician should fall silent the moment that mobilization begins." And after Moltke? Well, there was Schlieffen, the creater of the famous plan that the younger Helmuth von Moltke (nephew to the elder) was charged with executing in 1914.

The Blood Test: World War I

It has long been an article of faith among many historians that the Schlieffen Plan was a work of genius, vitiated in execution by the incompetent Moltke, who lacked the courage of the convic-

---

[10] I am referring here not only to the language problem and to the issuance of abbreviated and corrupted editions but more especially to the dialectical character of Clausewitz's presentation. He often starts out saying very nearly the opposite of what he concludes with, following the Hegelian pattern of thesis, antithesis, and synthesis. This trait he conspicuously demonstrates in the opening chapter, where he first insists that the use of force is theoretically without limits and then goes on to explain why it must in fact be limited. He also frequently invokes the images of philosophical idealism, no doubt also derived from Hegel, as when he speaks of "absolute war," meaning an abstract idea akin to Plato's ideas and not something to be witnessed on earth. These tendencies have made for much misunderstanding and especially misquotation. So far as language is concerned, German has always been less accessible to English-speaking readers than French, the language of Clausewitz's famous but much lesser contemporary, Antoine Henri Jomini; translations were late in arriving and were usually done inadequately from corrupt texts. The 1943 translation by Jolles cited in footnote 6 (this chapter) was the first generally satisfactory translation into English, though it, too, was from a faulty German text. However, Professor Peter Paret of Stanford University together with Professor Michael Howard of Oxford have used the original text to make a new and superior translation that is not yet published.

tions that inspired the plan. Perhaps so, but it was an unavoidable element in the plan that the projected attack through Belgium and Luxemburg would assure the entry of Great Britain into the war, because it would confront the British with a gross violation of the Five Power Treaty of 1838 mutually pledging defense of Belgian-Luxemburg neutrality. Besides, Britain had been known for something like three centuries to regard the freedom of the Low Countries as a "vital interest" affecting its own security. Had not the Duke of Parma waited there for the Armada to carry him to England? Chancellor Theobald von Bethmann-Hollweg's famous "scrap of paper" remark in August 1914 indicates that the Germans were not as clear about these matters as they should have been.

The Germans reasoned that if the British were going to enter the war they would not need the violation of Belgium as an excuse—a conclusion that had the defect of being quite possibly wrong (Britain was *not* unequivocally allied with France), and besides, why give them the excuse? To be sure, it was the aim of the Schlieffen Plan to produce a German victory over France and Russia so speedily that there could be no time for possible British intervention to produce its effect. Even so, the Plan had enormous built-in political penalties. Was the outflanking of the French border fortresses (having none of the continuity of the later Maginot Line) worth the price? One even wonders whether Schlieffen kept in mind that foot soldiers carrying heavy packs, especially reservists, become dead tired after a long succession of forced marches, which the crucial right-wing enveloping maneuvers required. Curiously, for the troops in that wing it was a little more distance and very nearly the same route that Napoleon had traversed in the opposite direction in coming up to Waterloo.

However, Schlieffen was clear in his own mind, and he set it down on paper, that if his plan miscarried, which is to say if it failed to produce a decisive German victory at least in the west in the opening weeks of the war, Germany should seek at once to negotiate a termination of the war.[11] To that extent he was infinitely wiser than most of his successors.

One would be tempted to say that most other German generals

---

11 See the chapter by Hajo Holborn, "Moltke and Schlieffen: The Prussian-German School," in Edward M. Earle (ed.), *Makers of Modern Strategy* (Princeton: Princeton University Press, 1943); the present standard critique, with original memoranda, is Gerhard Ritter's excellent *The Schlieffen Plan* (London: Oswald Wolff, 1958).

have been the worst students of their own Clausewitz—whose bloodier passages they were everlastingly quoting, while forgetting his own modifications. In World War I, however, they had formidable competition from British and French generals, who were not at all behind the Germans in demonstrating supreme improvidence and recklessness. The Germans did manage, when they were about to win in the east, to bring the United States into the war against them through the reimposition in February 1917 of unrestricted submarine warfare (a final disastrous echo of the spent Schlieffen Plan, for without British participation there would have been no U-boat problem and thus no occasion for American entry). With the French and British generals' unflagging appetite for offensives that continued to fail at enormous cost one after the other; with their disdain of the politicians who appeared to them squeamish over the terrible casualty rates; with their notions about war objectives being summed up quite simply in the conviction that they had to "defeat the Hun" at whatever cost, it is difficult to surpass them historically in willfulness and arrogance, as well as sublime disregard of the Clausewitzian ideas that would marry strategy to a political purpose.

It is, however, understandable that the soldiers of World War I should reject these ideas, if they were indeed acquainted with them, which is doubtful. To the soldiers the idea of civilian domination of military planning and operations, especially during wartime, was simply anathema. It represented "interference" by people who were in their eyes incompetent to wage war, and whose motives they distrusted as being too much bound up with the winning of elections. Field Marshal Sir Douglas Haig noted in his diary that Prime Minister Herbert Asquith was too concerned with votes and he regarded Asquith's successor, David Lloyd George, as a "thorough imposter." [12] The latter he did not hesitate to deceive with regard to casualty rates and to his own plans.

What about the politicians? Among the western powers constitutional government guaranteed civilian supremacy. Why did they not in World War I seize firmly the control of events, giving meaningful overall direction to the military campaigns as well as to efforts on the home front?

The answer is not simple. World War I from the start took on a

---

[12] Robert Blake (ed.), *The Private Papers of Douglas Haig, 1914–1919* (London: Eyre & Spottiswoode, 1952), p. 139.

character wholly different from that of any previous European war. Thus, the civilian leaders were lost in a confusion even deeper than that of the generals, who were at least armed with their unyielding military axioms and clichés. In order to oppose an idea effectively, one needs more than superior authority—one needs in addition one or more alternative ideas. These were lacking. The civilians shared almost equally with the soldiers an obsession with victory for its own sake.

Also, the politicians were captives of the vast prestige surrounding their own appointed generals, a prestige that they were obliged themselves to help build up. The French political authorities had a difficult enough time getting rid of General Joseph Joffre, who, after being credited with the "miracle of the Marne," sat solidly entrenched for over two years carrying out the most unrelenting spendthrift and futile shedding of French blood. After him the French civilian leaders were quicker to punish failure. Lloyd George on his part reciprocated fully Haig's distrust of him, but he never dared move against the prestigious commander of the British Armies in France, perhaps because he lacked an alternative man as well as an alternative idea. Haig had indeed replaced Sir John French after the first year of the war, mostly because the latter had been too pessimistic about the way the war was going. Optimism is what the politicians asked for, and that is what they got from then on. Perhaps it mattered too that the King was known to like Haig and to have confidence in him.

There was also the unhappy example of the Dardanelles campaign of 1915, which the civilian Winston Churchill, as First Lord of the Admiralty, had pushed upon a somewhat uneager staff. Its failure was no more monumental than those occurring regularly on the western front, but the "meddling civilian" had been quickly sacrificed. It was this same Churchill, later returned to the Cabinet as Minister of Armaments after an intervening stint as a field officer in France, who sponsored, while still in the Admiralty, the development of the tank as a tactical answer to the machine gun. Then too, it was Lloyd George who pressured the reluctant Admiralty under First Sea Lord Admiral Sir John Jellicoe to adopt the convoy system, which proved the key to success in coping with the awful menace of the German U-boat.[13] The promotion of such technical ideas did not, of course, signify the kind

---

[13] A. Temple Patterson (ed.), *The Jellicoe Papers, Vol. 2, 1916–1935* (London: Navy Records Society), pp. 111-263.

of leadership that Clausewitz demanded and expected of the civil power in wartime; it merely demonstrated once again what ingenuity untrammeled by rigid adherence to service doctrine can accomplish.

Even as World War I recedes in time, all the dismal and hideous events that mankind has suffered since cannot diminish our dismay in looking back at it. It lies, in Michael Howard's words, "like a dark scar across the history of Europe." It was a vast effusion of blood for purposes that could hardly be discovered, let alone commended, by those who survived it and by the generations following. Military ineptitude, itself nothing new, had an unparalleled opportunity to display how much harm it could do. There was never before such fruitless sacrifice of such huge numbers, who struggled and died in drearily stagnated positions under conditions unimaginably monstrous. If there is any other abyss of horror to rival Verdun, it is likely to be found in the same war, perhaps Passchendaele or the Somme. Thus, if we seek historical examples of a failure to match military design with political purpose, with measureless unhappy consequences, World War I is exhibit number one. No other war comes close—which is saying much, considering what other wars have been like.

There is also perhaps room for a fresh approach. We owe much to those scholars in all the involved countries whose patient and tireless work has given us our existing illumination on the origins of the war. Usually, however, they have tended to accept the ritualistic values of the times they were interpreting. Diplomatic historians, like the diplomatists themselves, have spoken all too naturally of countries being diplomatically "isolated" or "humiliated" and of their opponents as scoring diplomatic "triumphs." What the real costs were of the one category or the real gains of the other have not usually been considered. Neither has it often been asked why presumably mature men should have played with such ardor an extraordinarily dangerous game for tokens that seem to have been so largely fetishistic.

Symbols do indeed often reflect real values, accepting "real value" to mean something that commands the respect if not always the concurrence of deeply considered judgment. Some measures taken in the name of "national prestige," for example, may in fact work towards efficient achievement of a greater measure of security and tranquillity. They may make other nations more respectful of one's power and thus less willing to challenge it. Yet as these same measures become stereotyped, or are pushed too avidly, they begin to have the opposite effect. Thus, smaller nations that cannot afford the luxury of worrying too much about their national prestige often manage to achieve their public tranquillity at much lower cost. In any case, in the realm of diplomacy and war the more emotionally evocative symbols have usually not borne any just proportion to real values. Few would question the reasonableness of pursuing national security, but how often have we seen irrelevant or grossly self-defeating measures perpetrated in its name!

It is easier to observe these things in the past than in the present, because we can see the blundering policy of the past only by gazing at it across the years that contain its disastrous consequences. The latter are indeed responsible for directing our attention towards the policies that produced them, just as World War I provoked an enormous amount of research into its origins. Even so, to say that it is less difficult to analyze these things retrospectively is not to say that it is easily done or usually done well. It is a misplaced faith that holds that the story will somehow come out right in the history books—that the mere flow of time will bring clarification, much as the flow of water in a stream is supposed to cleanse it of pollution and make it pure again.

American historiography, for example, is just beginning to emerge from over three decades of domination by what has been called the "revisionist" interpretation of the origins of the American Civil War, an interpretation that combined a complete inversion of the values that our society is supposed to cherish with various gross distortions of historical fact. For, inasmuch as it threw the blame overwhelmingly on those "hotheads" who were abolitionists, revisionism could not flourish unless slavery could be made to look somewhat bland. It is by now clear, from the new current of writings, that this phase is passing.[14] Still, it is more

---

[14] The landmark writings in establishing the "revisionist" school—the term is obviously a relative one, and is now occasionally applied to those books that mark the retreat from earlier revisionism—were especially: George Fort Milton, *The Eve of Conflict: Stephen A. Douglas and the Needless War* (Boston: Houghton Mifflin, 1934); and James G. Randall, *The Civil War and Reconstruction* (New York: Heath, 1937). Also important was the pamphlet by Avery O. Craven, *The Repressible Conflict, 1830–1861* (Baton Rouge: Louisiana State University Press, 1939). In 1949 Arthur M. Schlesinger, Jr. wrote a brilliant and eloquent rebuttal of the revisionist view in the *Partisan Review*, entitled "The Causes of the Civil War," but the time was not ripe for stemming the revisionist tide. Recently, however, the turning of that tide has been demonstrated in the writings of Fawn M. Brodie (on Thaddeus Stevens), Bruce Catton, Dwight L. Dumond, Richard Hofstadter, Winthrop D. Jordan, Allan Nevins, Russel B. Nye, Oscar Sherwin, Kenneth Stampp, and C. Vann Woodward.

than a hundred years since the Civil War, which means that it has been taking a very long time to get some elementary points straightened out—including the realization that man is by nature deeply emotional, and that the real issue is not his inclination to feel and express indignation but rather what it is that he becomes indignant about.

Even with the most neutral spirit in the world, it is not a simple matter, in considering the origins of such a catastrophe as World War I, to distinguish the sheer blunder from the reasonable though ill-starred response. Some major idiocies were so conspicuously such as to solve the problem of classification, but not of explanation. How did they happen? How, for example, could a generation of Germans believe before 1914 that building up a great High Seas Fleet would be more likely to make Great Britain a passive partner than an enemy? Obviously, some of them wanted to believe it because they wanted the fleet, but what were the mechanisms by which they succeeded so well in deceiving themselves and others? How could the entire diplomacy of Germany following the dropping of Bismarck in 1890 be so clumsily and yet so surely designed to produce disaster? We have acquired relatively recently the psychological and sociological tools to enable us to examine and appreciate these issues in greater depth, but historians as a group have proved tenaciously resistant to utilizing those tools. In any case, theories of international relations that assume certain motivations to be rational, or at least perennial, merely because they are familiar are likely in a swiftly changing era like our own to fall very wide of the mark.

In this chapter, however, we have to content ourselves with lesser issues. One of these, the most compelling of the conflicts between the French and British military chieftains on the one side and the civilian leaders on the other, continued not only throughout World War I but also for years afterward in various contentious writings. It centered upon the enormous blood-letting of the futile offensives that French and British generals pursued with such ardor and with far greater persistence than their German counterparts. All were failures but the last, launched when the war was entering its fifth year and after the German army had spent itself with a supreme effort of its own. In an earlier book I dwelt at length upon the prewar exaggeration of the mystique of the offensive, especially among the French military leaders; I shall not repeat here the story of that strange and

17

horribly costly aberration.[15] I shall, however, touch upon the relevant debate during and following the war.

Hope springs eternal in the human breast, at least that breast which is not being pierced by bullet or shell fragment. World War I involved an unprecedented separation of the senior commanders in the field from the men in the front lines. There is impressive documentation to prove that the former often did not know what was going on during their great offensives or pushes. Each time they were sure that they had the formula that would work and redeem the previous failures. Each time but the last —at least on the western side—they were wrong. The attendant awesome casualty lists were passed off as contributing to the "attrition" that would at last critically weaken the enemy but presumably not themselves.

The fact that under prevailing tactical conditions the attacker almost invariably took far heavier losses than the defender was simply rejected by the British and French generals because it did not conform with doctrine. As late as the Passchendaele offensive of the autumn of 1917, after three years of terrible experience that should have proclaimed the near certainty of the opposite conclusion, Haig was sure that his forces wearily attacking in a sea of mud had the Germans "so near the breaking point," as he expressed it in a letter of October 8 to the Chief of the Imperial General Staff, General Sir William Robertson, that he thought a continuance of the offensive might achieve that break "at any moment." The Germans, after months of fighting, merely yielded up some 10,000 yards of territory while exacting well over 300,000 British casualties, producing also a vast depression in the British survivors. Today at Ypres there stands a monument to 56,000 British soldiers whose bodies were ground into the mud in that area and never found.

The politicians tended for a variety of reasons to be more sensitive to the human costs. No doubt one reason was that they were more accustomed to identifying the state with its people. Another important reason was that they had escaped the special military indoctrination that sufficed, as indoctrination usually does, to make those subjected to it largely oblivious to contrary indications from new experience. But during the war they felt nearly helpless.

---

[15] See my *Strategy in the Missile Age* (Princeton: Princeton University Press, 1959), pp. 42–61.

After the war, however, they were not so constrained. Winston Churchill, for example, in an extraordinary chapter entitled "The Blood Test," part of his four-volume history of World War I, eloquently excoriated the western military chieftains for their insensate and obstinate follies that produced such frightful losses.[16] None could charge Churchill with lacking understanding of the necessity for offensive action to achieve success in war, but he demanded as a precondition for any offensive a tactical basis for success, without which heroism and resolve merely increase the terrible human costs of failure.

This chapter (and others, including one of the naval battle of Jutland, where Churchill chided Admiral Sir John Jellicoe for not having been offensive-minded enough) provoked strong hostile responses, including a volume entitled *The World Crisis by Winston Churchill: A Criticism*, by Lord Sydenham of Combe, Admiral Sir Reginald Bacon, General Sir Frederick Maurice, General Sir W. D. Bird, and Sir Charles Oman.[17] This was a group of men distinguished for their scholarship on military subjects, and thus as qualified as any to provide any needed rebuttal. They argued first that Churchill was wrong in attributing persistently greater casualties during the offensives to the attacking Allies than to the defending Germans. The official tables of casualty figures had indeed been doctored enough to permit them to make so remarkable a misreading of results,[18] but as the picture evolved in the postwar years, it became obvious that it was Churchill's critics who were wrong, by a wide margin. Germany's sum of war fatalities was considerably less than the total for Britain and France, and Germany had also been fighting a major (and successful) war against Russia in the East!

More pertinent, however, is the basic argument of Churchill's critics, which was that it is the politicians who make the choice for or against war, and that if they opt for war they must be ready to accept all the attendant consequences including very high casualty rates. It is not for them to interfere in the military

---

[16]Winston S. Churchill, *The World Crisis* (New York: Scribners, 1929), vol. 3, chap. 38.

[17] London: Hutchinson, 1928.

[18] They were deliberately doctored by the official historian, Brig. Gen. Sir James E. Edmonds, out of loyalty to a senior Army commander. Edmonds nevertheless privately expressed the opinion that Haig was "really a stupid man," and that he could not "grasp anything technical." See the important article by B. H. Liddell Hart, "The Basic Truths of Passchendaele," *Journal of the Royal United Service Institution* (London), vol. 104, no. 616 (November 1959), pp. 1–7.

direction of the war, which must be left to the professionals. If they are too faint-hearted to accept heavy bloodshed, they should avoid going to war.

To the last sentence one may wish to say "Amen," but unfortunately it touches but a small part of the problem. Presumably the statesman's choice between war and peace is not usually a free one—though it is certainly less determined than is often made out. The part the military play in the choice has not usually been inclined towards peace, and certainly it was not in 1914. But the main thesis of Churchill's critics—which we bother to consider only because it has been so widely shared, and remains with many until this day an article of faith—is that once war breaks out the politicians have little or no role to play in overseeing military operations. They have, according to this view, their own duties to perform, which involve doing supporting chores on the home front and in diplomacy.

Even the most civilized and enlightened of modern military men, supported by not a few civilians who should be experienced enough to know better, have protested *in principle* the intervention of the political leader in the realm of military strategy or policy. One scholarly French general of our time, eschewing examples from the country whose military history he knows too well for one whose comparable history he does not know, has chosen as a particularly unfortunate and unwarranted case the intervention of President Abraham Lincoln in the plans of his generals! Actually, Lincoln's interventions with such modestly endowed men as McClellan, Burnside, Hooker, and Meade were not the least of his contributions to saving the Union. It was Lincoln who decided after Gettysburg that Meade, despite his victory there, had erred grievously in allowing Lee to escape over the swollen waters of the Potomac, which had held him up for thirteen days, and that Meade therefore had to be put under the command of the more competent and aggressive general who had just taken Vicksburg. It was a wise, necessary, and courageous decision, the mark of a great leader, and only one among a number of his military interventions that could be so characterized.

This brings us back to Churchill's critics, who obviously did not worry about the civilian leader's responsibility for determining whether and when the top military leader should be replaced. On this sovereign issue the politician may have to act without the advice of the military aides, or against their advice, for it is frequently their collective and common commitment to error that he needs to guard against. The Germans in the latter stages of World War I turned their backs on this problem by letting General Erich Ludendorff become virtual dictator, but the example does not commend the practice.

Why Could the War Not Be Stopped?

There is another and much greater problem with respect to World War I, one so utterly confounding that we can here do little more than state it and record its dimensions. Why, over more than four long and ghastly years, did it prove impossible to stop it? One sees exposed in this question the ultimate failure of the idea that political purpose should dominate military action.

It was clear within weeks of the war's outbreak, or should have been, that the Schlieffen Plan on which the Germans had staked all had utterly failed; so too had the French Plan XVII, which is less well known to the world than its German counterpart only because it was so utterly banal; and completely disintegrated in disaster too was the Russian plan for coming to the aid of France with the invasion of East Prussia. Within a very few months it was clear, or should have been, that the war was going to be exceedingly costly in life and resources and that it would be extraordinarily difficult for either side to prevail over its opponents.

Neither side regarded the other as led by governments with which it would be impossible to live in the future—as was to be true in the later war against Hitler and his associates. All the major governments involved had the quality of legitimacy, and, with some qualifications of which neither side was in a position to take much notice, of general decency. None had been intolerably aggressive. Why then was it necessary for each side to seek a victory that, as became increasingly clear with the war's progress, had to result in the overthrow of the governments of the vanquished states? The Czar's Finance Minister, Sergei Witte, was convinced of this as early as September, 1914, and expressed his views to the French ambassador.[19]

The orthodox historians help us relatively little on this prob-

---

[19] Ambassador Paléologue reports Witte's words as follows:
    Even if we assume a complete victory for our coalition—the Hohenzollerns and the Hapsburgs reduced to begging for peace and submitting to our terms—it means . . . the proclamation of republics throughout Central Europe. That means the simultaneous end of Tsarism. I prefer to remain silent as to what we may expect . . . on our defeat.
Maurice Paléologue, *An Ambassador's Memoirs*, trans. by F. A. Holt, 3 vols. (New York: G. H. Doran Co., 1924), vol. I, p. 123.

lem, mostly because they believe they are explaining it when in fact they are only delineating its symptoms. They tell us of various territorial ambitions within Europe, ambitions whetted by secret treaties concluded during the war itself, and in some instances reinforced by conceptions of "unredeemed" fellow nationals under foreign governments. For some countries there were demands for restoration of territories (for example, France, with its "gap in the Vosges," resulting from the loss of Alsace and part of Lorraine in 1871); for other countries unification, and for all countries security. But all these requirements had existed before the war began, at which time the respective hopes of fulfillment were never separated from considerations of the costs and risks attending their attainment. Why did that separation become total and conclusive the moment hostilities broke out, after which the conception that dominated absolutely over all others was simply that of achieving victory?

We know that both sides had always expected that the war, when it came, would be violent but short. The whole concept of the Schlieffen Plan was based on winning a lightening decision in the west, and had it worked as intended—and, some would say, as it almost did—the campaign there would have been over in four to six weeks. Then the Germans could have turned their whole attention to the destruction of Russian power, which they considered far the more important long-term goal. We know that at the beginning of August 1914 Bethmann-Hollweg assured his predecessor, Prince Bernhard von Bülow, that he was reckoning on "a war lasting three, or at the most, four months . . . a violent, but short storm." [20] The Entente Powers had comparable but less well-focused ideas. The German General Staff naturally did not inform the political leadership of the real consequences of the reverse on the Marne in early September.

Moltke knew well enough what had happened, and faced it clearly; few of his colleagues did. On September 8, while the Battle of the Marne was still in progress, Moltke wrote to his wife:

> It is going badly. The Battle to the east of Paris will go against us. One of our armies must withdraw, the others will have to follow. The opening of the war, so hopefully begun,

---

[20] Fritz Fischer, *Germany's Aims in the First World War* (New York: Norton; London: Chatto & Windus, 1967), p. 92. Originally published in Germany in 1961 under the title *Griff nach der Weltmacht*, this book, based on extensive new documentation, effectively displaces most of the older writing on the subject of its English title.

will turn into the opposite. I must bear whatever befalls and shall stand or fall with my country. We must suffocate in the fight against east and west—how different it was when we opened the campaign a few weeks ago—the bitter disillusionment now follows. And we shall have to pay for everything that is destroyed. . . .[21]

Naturally a general of such clear insight must go, unless everyone concerned is prepared to pay the consequences of an admission of failure. But the Germans, being deep into France and having destroyed the Russian armies that had invaded East Prussia, found it much simpler to sack Moltke, whose health was indeed breaking under the strain. On September 14, General Erich von Falkenhayn replaced him, though this was not immediately announced to the German people. On the day after Moltke wrote that despairing letter to his wife, Bethmann-Hollweg drew up some "provisional notes" for the conclusion of a peace in the West that provided, among other things, for the annexation of Luxemburg, of large parts of Belgium and the reduction of the rest to a vassal state, of absorption of considerable parts of France, including the iron ore fields of Briey, plus a heavy indemnity designed to prevent French rearmament for years. The provisions concerning France might be modified if France agreed to join Germany against Russia, the main enemy! The stalemate that developed thereafter left the Germans bemused over the fact that they were in occupation of all of Luxemburg and Belgium and of one-tenth of the territory of France. This was a heavily industrialized area that included also the major part of the French coal and iron ore deposits. Germany remained confident of ultimate victory, and the aspirations contained in Bethmann-Hollweg's "provisional notes" of September 9, 1914 remained intact into 1916, helped along, no doubt, by such events as the feelers early that year of King Albert of the Belgians for a separate peace.[22]

The western Allies knew, on the other hand, that temporary loss of the invaded territories, though an impairment to their industrial war effort, could in no way be decisive. The French and British could now guess how much the Germans had gambled

---

[21] Quoted in Harvey A. DeWeerd, *President Wilson Fights His War* (New York: Macmillan, 1968), pp. 72 f.
[22] Fischer, *Germany's Aims*, pp. 98–105, 215–224.

and lost on the Schlieffen idea. Therefore, their goals, too, had to be considerably better than the *status quo ante bellum*. For the French it was utterly unthinkable that they should not regain the territories lost in 1871, but beyond that they yearned for the ultimate defeat and humiliation of the German Empire whose birth had been declared at Versailles in that same year. In short, war aims on the part of the French were couched as much in terms of retribution as restoration—just as those of the Germans were couched in terms of total supremacy on the Continent.

The British for their part did not enter the war to gain or regain territories. They interpreted restrictively the commitments they thought to be owing to allies, especially those inherited with the war itself. Thus, it was at first taken for granted that France should have restored to her only the French-speaking parts of Alsace and Lorraine, but this attitude naturally changed with time. There was indeed some tea-time talk about what might be acquired for Britain. Churchill's biographer describes a meeting of the War Council in March 1915, during the early part of the Gallipoli operations, when conversation casually shifted to how the Turkish Empire should be carved up not only for giving the Russians their hearts' desire in the Dardanelles, but also for British benefit. They would, however (at least at that early date), avoid taking too many of the German colonies because, as Field Marshal Lord Kitchener put it, that "would more than anything else interfere with the future establishment of goodwill between Germany and ourselves after the war."[23] Naturally such an idea could not be allowed to interfere with the conclusive destruction of German naval power.

It was, perhaps curiously, mostly the military, with General Robertson at their head, who tended to press their unwilling civilian colleagues to turn their thoughts to peace aims, but the military tended also to be generous in their intentions for the enemy after the war. Most of them were convinced that a strong Germany was necessary for the future balance of power in Europe, which of course could only mean against their current allies. During the Somme offensive of 1916 Robertson assured the War Council that the Germans were suffering more than twice the casualties of the British and that the end might be close. He expressed the fear, therefore, "that we may be caught unprepared and find that we

23 Martin Gilbert, *Winston S. Churchill, Vol. III, 1914–1916* (London: Heinemann, 1971), pp. 321 f., 332–334.

have mobilized for Peace as we did for war—inadequately and subordinate to France." [24]

It is thus easy enough to see on both sides, during the terrible fury of fighting that reached full crescendo from the outset, thoughts of territorial gain mixed with various other thoughts including conciliation—and also extraordinary naivety about the opponent. But all this deflects our attention from something more important and more persistent, something that dwarfs all other considerations—fierce dedication to the goal of victory, which none in power will permit to be even slightly shaken. Hope of gain mattered far less than the feeling that one's own side must and will win, at whatever price and however long it might take. We are, in short, confronted not with simple greed but with some deep psychological need expressed on the national rather than the personal level. The obsession from first to last was with winning, with vanquishing the foe, with showing that one's own strength and will were greater than his—or at least not less. The obverse of this obsession, and indeed the stronger motivation, was the fear of losing, of being the defeated, and thus of paying consequences that were in a very real sense unimaginable. Feeding the latter fear was the need, growing rapidly more intense as the losses mounted, for the governments to prove to their peoples that the sacrifices had not been in vain. It was this need on each side that was the insuperable one, for it made compromise impossible. Compromise would represent for each side a significant absence of gain, and hence admission of failure.

Compared to these needs, the object of acquiring more territories appears as hardly more than a search for a vivid and permanent demonstration that one has won and not lost. The same was true of many other so-called war objectives or goals. If, for example, one seeks to gain more security through war, then success at accomplishing that gain will cast at least some doubt on the preexisting need for it. This object blends into that of "preventive war," the undertaking to destroy now an already strong rival whose power one fears *may* grow faster than one's own. It

---

[24] V. H. Rothwell, *British War Aims and Peace Diplomacy, 1914–1918* (Oxford: Clarendon Press, 1971), p. 40. For the interesting related views of Field Marshal Sir Douglas Haig, among others, see my *Strategy in the Missile Age*, pp. 61–64. Unlike Robertson, Haig was generally distrustful of people who tried to think ahead about the peace. Like Robertson and almost everybody else, the one thing Haig was clear about was the need for absolute victory. When he finally got it, however, he was all in favor of generous terms.

was mostly for this reason that Germany went to war, especially against Russia. The very commitment to war naturally enhances this motivation. But the rationalization for it, which is all too familiar historically, has some suspicious qualities, especially the prominence of an attitude that is normally most uncharacteristic of politicians: a willingness to gamble *now* at unlimited stakes for what is a highly speculative long-term gain. Normally the politician is given to taking the cash and letting the credit go, to making provisions for the short term and abjuring anything costly that promises possible long term gains. Why should a weakness for unjustified certainty be most easily evoked by that most uncertain of pursuits, war, where mischance and miscalculation reign?

The opening weeks of World War I provide spectacular demonstrations that the best laid plans of general staffs can go awry. Usually one side sees its plans fail utterly; this time both sides did. One is forced to conclude that confidence in victory is as often due to the fear of relinquishing the test as to the presence of any proof that the judgment is correct.

No doubt the problem we have been seized with in these paragraphs—that of discovering why it proved impossible to stop an infinitely bloody and senseless war—has not stood out as prominently as it should because it has become too familiar in modern times. It therefore involves elements that we are too accustomed to taking for granted. The waging of modern war on any scale approximating total national commitment necessitates so huge and unwavering an effort that the first casualty is not so much "truth" as simply reason. To attempt to express reason is, under a wide variety of wartime circumstances, to risk the label of "defeatist," the penalties for which are always unpleasant and sometimes extreme. The military commanders who in adversity can feel and exude optimism are the ones who inspire confidence. If in addition they have an overriding "will to win," coupled with insensitivity to huge personnel losses, they are marked as great commanders—until they lose, and sometimes even if they lose. It was, as we have noticed, because he had these qualities that Haig replaced French, whom he surpassed mostly in possessing an obtuse callousness combined with an irrepressible and totally unrealistic optimism.

That Haig lacked imagination is hardly to be wondered at, inasmuch as imagination was not what was asked of him but rather a complex of characterstics that effectively ruled it out. He was overwhelmingly dedicated, like his colleagues elsewhere, to a goal that was at once abstract and wholly simplistic, that of "winning." In order to win he was willing to pay any cost that it was possible for Britain to pay, and in that respect he was always ready to stretch the conception of what was possible. That he lacked compassion or empathy for the men in the front lines is only to say that he had the absolutely required insensibilities to carry out his function. He could surely have used much more tactical insight and discrimination than he possessed, and he seems not to have demanded really professional standards of performance on the part of his staff. He could thus have been far more effective in his job, but not by giving up those of his traits that were demanded of him.

However, with respect to our main problem, we must avoid putting the blame primarily on the military commanders. The responsibility for their selection and their retention or dismissal is and was ultimately the politician's. What we saw during World War I in those countries that possessed any degree of political fluidity was a flow of power towards those who were conceived to be uncompromising with respect to the war. An opposite effect was produced only in politically congealed Russia by the second revolutionary explosion of 1917, which brought the Bolsheviks to power. Anyone who, like Lord Lansdowne in Britain and the historian Hans Delbrück in Germany, raised his voice in the name of reason against the prevailing tempest of fiery passions had some measure of that storm directed at once upon him. Nations have not always conducted themselves in that way, but we have to go back to something like the brief Austro-Prussian War of 1866 to find behavior that is markedly different.

World War I was not unique with respect to the insuperable difficulties it exposed in accomplishing what Woodrow Wilson called (but only before he entered the war): "a peace without victory." It only demonstrated that the most conspicuously profitless and costly war will see these difficulties not diminished but increased. World War I was to prove the foresight of the elder Moltke, who wrote in 1890, when he was already a very old man:

It the war which has hung over our heads, like the sword of Damocles, for more than ten years past, ever breaks out, its duration and end cannot be foreseen. The greatest powers of Europe, armed as never before, will then stand face to face. No one power can be shattered in one or two campaigns so completely as to confess itself beaten, and conclude peace on hard terms. It may be a Seven Years War; it may be a Thirty Years' War—woe to him who first sets fire to Europe. . . .[25]

What followed was actually worse. It did not last thirty years, nor even seven, but its ghastliness over more than four years could not have been within Moltke's power to imagine. The urge to prevail, fed initially by what seemed an unlimited supply of frenzied national rage, managed afterwards with tragic impressiveness to survive a long time on a diet of despair.

---

[25] Quoted in R. J. Sontag, *European Diplomatic History, 1871–1932* (New York: The Century Co., 1933), pp. 5 f. I suspect that in this statement the elder Moltke is showing very markedly the influence of his Polish contemporary, Ivan Bloch, whose work is discussed in Chapter 9. On earlier occasions Moltke had betrayed very different sentiments, being one of those who was dismayed at the rapid recovery of France after 1871 and who had urged at various times a preventive war.

CHAPTER

2

The Test of World War II

Wars then must sometimes be our lot; and all the wise can do, will be to avoid that half of them which would be produced by our own follies, and our own acts of injustice; and to make for the other half the best preparations we can.

> Thomas Jefferson, *Notes on the State of Virginia.*

. . . this evil man, this monstrous abortion of hatred and defeat.

> Winston S. Churchill on Adolf Hitler.

The second of the two world wars is separated from the first by only twenty-one years, but in terms of the issues we are exploring its complexion was completely different. It was a war that on the Allied side had a purpose—one that more than thirty years later still commands, at the very least, respect. With but few exceptions, only those too young to remember and not given to reading the record have questioned that conclusion. On both sides it was a war that the people accepted grimly, without the enthusiasm and the demonstrations in the capitals of Europe that had marked the coming of the war in 1914. It was not simply that the earlier war was still too vivid a memory—though that it surely was to many. It was rather that a basic historical change had occurred in the attitudes of the European (and American) peoples towards war. There were no pretenses to glory and few illusions about easy victory. These changes were not enough to prevent the war, not with a Hitler in being, but they were real and deeply significant. Insofar as they have been intensified by the experience of World War II and the coming of nuclear weapons, they are tremendously important to us today.

Then, too, the whole social climate had changed. Gone were the monarchical and aristrocratic regimes, especially of central and eastern Europe, whose way of life had centered around the dignity of the officer caste. Their influence had helped to keep alive similar traditions in republican France as well as in Britain. Under such social systems the military during wartime are highly resistant to civilian control. However, the social revolutions that swept Europe between the wars inevitably changed the status of the military in each major country of Europe.

There were other reasons for the changes in the status and prestige of the military. The political revolutions in Russia, Italy, and Germany had produced dictators with the ruthlessness and will to put themselves unequivocally in charge. In these countries there was never the slightest question who was boss, and it was not the military. In the Soviet Union Stalin had even indulged himself in the Great Terror, which had wiped out, among innumerable others high and low, practically the whole of the higher command structure of the military forces, and that on the very eve of the outbreak of World War II.[1] Hitler purged far fewer officers, but the viselike character of his grip on their corporate body was no less pronounced. In Japan there had been a very different kind of revolution. There political power had fallen increasingly into the hands of a tightly knit military clique, whose mores and values derived with little modification from feudal times, and whose every goal was oriented towards enhancing the military prestige, power, and glory of Japan.[2] Britain, France, and the United States had not gone through such awful upheavals and had made, in their various ways, gradual progress in a rather con-

[1] See Robert E. Conquest, *The Great Terror: Stalin's Purge of the Thirties* (New York: Macmillan, 1968), especially chap. 7.

[2] See Robert J. C. Butow, *Tojo and the Coming of the War* (Stanford: Stanford University Press, 1961).

trary direction—towards democracy that was greater for being less class-structured than before.

The three great democracies had also undergone another change that affected the military profession. The post-World War I writers, including those of poetry and fiction, who had so belabored the wartime chieftains for their incompetence, arrogance, and insensibility, had succeeded overwhelmingly in making their point.[3] The Churchillian view as opposed to that of his critics had won the day, and this triumph was bound in time to permeate the officer class. Brigadier General Giulio Douhet, the Italian prophet of air power, proved in his brilliant *Command of the Air* to be a critic of his World War I military brethren easily comparable in severity and pointedness to Churchill.[4] The result was a considerably more chastened officer corps and, no doubt partly for that reason, a markedly more competent one. In the distinction made famous long ago by Dr. Alfred Vagts in his *History of Militarism,* the British and American officer corps had become more military (that is, professionally competent) and less militaristic (that is, obsessed with the prestige and prerogatives of their class).[5]

In France a general staff formerly wedded to the most extravagant conceptions of offensive élan had in one generation become content to adapt itself to the Maginot Line. There was some disposition to be behindhanded in tactical doctrine as compared with the Germans, especially with respect to the dispositions of tanks, but it is hazardous to make generalizations about levels of competence. Too much of the swift French collapse in 1940 is attributable to bad luck in the choice of key commanders and above all to the general social malaise in France. That malaise was certainly in large part a consequence of the terrible blood-letting of World War I, which at that time looked so recent and—with the country again at war with the same enemy even more formidable than

---

[3] One must have lived through that postwar period to appreciate fully how the anti-war and antimilitary attitudes engulfed all forms of literature and, in time, the movies. See especially Brian Gardner (ed.), *Up to the Line of Death: The War Poets, 1914–1918* (London: Methuen, 1964). It is also significant that the play (and later movie) popular in the mid-1960s, "Oh, What a Lovely War!" is a commentary not on World War II but on World War I, which it treats with biting satire.

[4] Giulio Douhet, *The Command of the Air,* trans. by Dino Ferrari (New York: Coward McCann, 1942). This translation includes, besides the original *Il Dominio dell' Aria* (1921 and 1927), the cited long polemical article, originally published in the *Rivista Aeronautica* for November 1929.

[5] Alfred Vagts, *A History of Militarism* (New York: Norton, 1937; revised ed., New York: Meridian, 1959).

before—so obviously futile. Thus, in a very real sense, the strategy that had "won" World War I for France lost her World War II —or would have done so had she not been rescued by her English-speaking allies.

Following the armistice of 1940 there was among the French forces outside the area of German occupation, especially in North Africa, a posture of exaggerated obedience to the Vichy regime, with Marshal Henri Philippe Pétain as its Chief of State. By a curious twist of fate, he was the one surviving Marshal of France of World War I days, and he had stood out from the others in his opposition to the offensive ardor at the time. *"Le feu tue"* ("fire kills"), he had said. He was the hero of the defense at Verdun who had been pushed upstairs during that long agony because he was not eager enough to waste lives in constant use of counter-attack, who had been appointed head of the French army to restore ·it to health during the mutinies following the terrible failure of the Nivelle offensive in the spring of 1917, and who had saluted detachments of troops with the words *mes enfants*. General Charles de Gaulle had not only dedicated to him his first professional book, *La France et son armée*, but had also named his son after him.

Above all Pétain represented French "unity," the preservation of which justified for the French military the capitulation of France. It was this combination of attitudes that de Gaulle had to contend with until the last stages of the war. It was also for this reason that the American forces under General Dwight D. Eisenhower, which landed in French North Africa in November 1942, did not even apprise de Gaulle of its plans, and also went to considerable lengths to keep British participation muted and preferably invisible. Eisenhower in his memoirs of the war describes with some awe the entire planning and handling of this operation in the following words:

> Our concern over these affairs illustrates forcibly the old truism that political considerations can never be wholly separated from military ones and that war is a mere continuation of political policy in the field of force. The Allied invasion of Africa was a most peculiar venture of armed forces into the field of international politics; we were invading a neutral country to create a friend.[6]

---

[6] Dwight D. Eisenhower, *Crusade in Europe* (New York: Doubleday, 1949), p. 93.

It is also in respect to this operation that the United States Chiefs of Staff intervened to oppose omitting Casablanca from the original attack plan, for reasons that had to do with the presumed possible intervention of Franco's Spain. Eisenhower has the following to say on this matter:

> As far as I can recall, this was the only instance in the war when any part of one of our proposed operational plans was changed by intervention of higher authority. We cheerfully accepted the decision because the governing political estimates are the function of governments, not of soldiers. However, we did point out that the early capture of Tunis was, by this decision, removed from the realm of the probable to the remotely possible.[7]

Eisenhower's sensitivity to these matters is refreshing, but what is most curious about the portion just quoted is the first sentence. As we shall see, the American Joint Chiefs, speaking for President Franklin D. Roosevelt, were always most reluctant to intervene in an operational plan for any reasons that might be called "political." Actually, the exception just noted is hardly a good example of such intervention, because the dominant motive was simply the safeguarding of the pending operation.

Another episode related by Eisenhower is interesting on several counts, one being that de Gaulle was to keep the story of it alive in speeches long after the war. At the end of 1944, during the latter stages of the Battle of the Bulge, and when the Allies were already resuming the offensive in the Ardennes, the Germans began diversionary attacks to the south in Alsace where American forces had been thinned out. General Eisenhower ordered the American commander in that area, Lieutenant General Jacob L. Devers, to withdraw from any salients rather than permit sizeable portions of his forces to be cut off. This order accentuated French fears that the Germans might retake the important city of Strasbourg, ancient capital of Alsace, which had only recently been liberated from German occupation and annexation.

> On January 3, de Gaulle came to see me. I explained the situation to him and he agreed that my plan to save troops in that region was militarily correct. However, he pointed out that ever since the war of 1870 Strasbourg had been a symbol

---

[7] Ibid., p. 84.

to the French people; he believed that even its temporary loss might result in complete national discouragement and possibly in open revolt. He was very earnest about the matter, saying that in extremity he would consider it better to put the whole French force around Strasbourg, even at the risk of losing the entire Army, than to give up the city without a fight. He brought a letter saying that he would have to act independently unless I made disposition for last-ditch defense of Strasbourg.[8]

After reminding de Gaulle that the French army would get no supplies unless it obeyed his orders, Eisenhower agreed that he would modify his orders to Devers to assure the protection of Strasbourg. "This modification," he says, "pleased de Gaulle very much, and he left in a good humor, alleging unlimited faith in my military judgment." But at one point in his narration of the episode, Eisenhower has the following revealing remark:

At first glance de Gaulle's argument seemed to be based upon political considerations, founded more on emotion than on logic and common sense. However, to me it became a military matter because of the possible effect on our lines of communication and supply, which stretched completely across France, from two directions. Unrest, trouble, or revolt along these lines of communication would defeat us on the front. Moreover, by the date of this conference the crisis in the Ardennes was well past.[9]

The revelation of priorities is instructive. To be sure, a major military defeat is always a serious matter, and if not redeemed in good time can have its own political consequences. A failure of the landings on the Normandy beaches in June of 1944 would have had extremely grave consequences. But Eisenhower was not describing anything like that kind of risk. He recognized that the most the Germans could do against Devers' front was not much. The telltale clause is where he speaks of political considerations, in this instance important ones, as likely to be "founded more on emotion than on logic and common sense." Where he can impute a military value to changing his orders, he feels himself on firmer ground.

Winston Churchill happened by chance to be at Eisenhower's

[8] Ibid., p. 384.
[9] Ibid., p. 384.

headquarters when this meeting with de Gaulle took place. Listening without comment to the interchange, he remarked quietly to Eisenhower after de Gaulle's departure, apropros the promised change in orders: "I think you've done the wise and proper thing."

As the final collapse of Germany drew near, Eisenhower, referring to the Allied political agreements concluded in February 1945 at Yalta that marked out posthostilities occupational zones, commented:

> This future division of Germany did not influence our military plans for the final conquest of the country. Military plans, I believed, should be devised with the single aim of speeding victory; by later adjustment troops of the several nations could be concentrated into their own sectors.[10]

This turns out to be by way of preface to an explanation of why it made sense to let the Russians take Berlin. The Russians were, indeed, much closer to Berlin at the time the Yalta agreements were concluded, but Eisenhower omits mentioning a fact of which he must have been aware—that the German military commanders, knowing that Berlin must fall anyway, were desperately eager to have it fall to the Western Allies rather than to the Russians. Their passive and tacit collaboration could have guaranteed that result. However, it would have involved collaborating with the enemy against an ally—a notion that was deeply offensive to Eisenhower and also to his civilian superiors.

One must not demand too much in the way of foresight; it is too easy to be unreasonable in this respect. Still, the word *statesman* has no meaning except as it describes one whose gifts prominently include foresight. He is one who makes good policy decisions, and doing so is inevitably a predictive process because it involves projections into the future. A good decision is one likely to prove more successful, or at least less disagreeable in its consequences, than one or more alternatives. There are sophisticated ways of dealing with prediction, which include among other things a proper regard for the character and dimensions of uncertainty. These are the province of the technical expert, whom the statesman should know how to use appropriately. Of the latter, however, we expect something more intuitive, something that

---

[10] Ibid., p. 419.

tells us he has incorporated experience to good effect in sharpening his insights. We hold the political leader accountable for a blunder, which almost by definition reflects a gross failure of foresight, and the persistent blunderer is the opposite of a statesman. On the other hand, a statesman like Bismarck has stood out historically because besides being ruthless and lucky he was also cunning and shrewd in a manner that expressed a really awesome endowment of political prescience.[11]

Today we have good reason to suppose that if the line of demarcation across Germany had been so drawn as to include at least western Berlin as an integral part of West Germany, an enormous amount of trouble in the score of years following World War II could have been avoided. Our postwar experience proved that the proposition advanced by Eisenhower in the passage last quoted—that military plans should be devised "with the single aim of speeding victory"—is simply not true. One could say that in view of the limitations always besetting our predictive capacities (and perhaps also our political and analytical skills), speeding victory, which is to say terminating the war successfully at the earliest possible time, is not a bad aim to have. But it cannot be the "single aim" of military plans.

Incidentally, in another part of his war memoirs Eisenhower casually remarks:

> I always felt that the Western Allies could probably have secured an agreement to occupy more of Germany than we actually did. I believe that if our political heads had been as convinced as we were at SHAEF of the certainty of early victory in the West they would have insisted, at Yalta, upon the line of the Elbe as the natural geographic line dividing the eastern and western occupation areas. Although in late January 1945 we were still west of the Rhine, and indeed had not yet demolished the Siegfried Line, my staff and I had informed our superiors that we expected to proceed rapidly to great victories. Except for a fear that we could advance no farther eastward, there would seem to have been little reason for agreeing to an occupational line no deeper into Germany

---

[11] For an opposing view stressing the futility of political prediction see Klaus Knorr and Oskar Morgenstern, "Political Conjecture in Military Planning," Policy Memorandum No. 35, Princeton University Center of International Studies, November 1968, especially the section entitled: "The Hopelessness of Prediction." See also Raymond Aron's rebuttal to an earlier similar statement by Morgenstern, in his *Peace and War: A Theory of International Relations*, trans. by R. Howard and A. B. Fox (New York: Doubleday, 1966), pp. 767 ff.

than Eisenach. This, however, is pure speculation. I have never discussed the matter with any of the individuals directly responsible for the decision.[12]

In World War II the most interesting contest between, on the one hand, supporters of the Clausewitzian ideal of keeping political aims always at the forefront of strategic consideration, and, on the other hand, those inclined to the traditional military preference for keeping them out altogether, was played out in a tug of war between Prime Minister Churchill and President Roosevelt.

Churchill, who in this respect was the follower of Clausewitz, surely by instinct rather than by learned precept, embodied to a degree unique in contemporary times the experience and insight of the profound student of war combined with the experience and qualities of a great politician and statesman. To imply that he ran true to form is to suggest that there were others with whom to compare him. Even if there had been one or two others of like stature, individual traits of temperament and personality would surely have made each case distinctive. De Gaulle comes closest, and is *very* distinctive. Generalizations must be based on broader statistics.

President Roosevelt, the artful politician, also had a long-standing interest in military affairs, having served enthusiastically during World War I as Assistant Secretary of the Navy, and none can say he did badly in overseeing for the American side the main strategic planning of World War II. On certain basic and critical issues, he was certainly better than his Joint Chiefs. For example, Roosevelt insisted on holding them to the original decision that Germany was the number one enemy and must be defeated first.[13]

---

[12] Eisenhower, *Crusade in Europe*, p. 503.

[13] There was almost constant pressure against this decision from Admiral Ernest J. King, and in the summer of 1942 when the British withdrew their support from the proposed Operation SLEDGEHAMMER (a cross-channel attack that would certainly have been premature), General George C. Marshall joined King in proposing to the President that the United States go "all out" in the Pacific, a proposal that Roosevelt flatly and correctly rejected. This controversy, it should be noted, concerned not a marginal issue but the most fundamental (and clearly correct) Allied decision of the war. Similarly, in 1940 Roosevelt had correctly perceived, as his Joint Chiefs most emphatically had not, that assisting beleaguered Britain with American aircraft production on a 50–50 basis was of the first importance, even at the cost of slowing American air rearmament. See Kent Roberts Greenfield, *American Strategy in World War II: A Reconsideration* (Baltimore: Johns Hopkins Press, 1963), especially pp. 71 f.; also William Emerson, "Franklin Roosevelt as Commander-in-Chief in World War II, *Military Affairs*, vol. 23, no. 4 (Winter 1958–59), pp. 181–207. A view somewhat different from Emerson's is presented by Robert A. Divine, *Roosevelt and World War II* (Baltimore: Johns Hopkins Press, 1969). For the British side see, above all, Michael Howard, *Grand Strategy*, vol. IV of *History of the Second World War* (London: H.M. Stationery Office, 1972).

But he was deeply committed throughout to the idea that "winning the war" was and should be kept a quite separate function from what he called "winning the peace." Naturally if one insists on so exclusive a distinction, all priorities must go to achieving that "strictly military" aim. In Roosevelt's case it must be added that inasmuch as he expected that the United States would refuse to become involved in European affairs after the war—that is, would return to something like its historic isolationism—his disinclination for elaborate peace planning was partly an adjustment to what he conceived to be political realities.

From the examples we have thus far considered, one thought already comes through clearly. The distinction between "fighting for a political purpose" and "fighting to win" is only tangentially a question of whether it is the soldiers or the politicians who rule. The constitutional question must be distinguished from the philosophical one. At the time of World War II there was not the slightest question in either the United Kingdom or the United States that the head of government was in command and that the soldiers were his subordinates. In any overt sense there never had been in either country any question of this. However, the supremacy in authority of the civilian leader merely favors the possibility, but certainly does not guarantee, that political purpose will dominate strategy. Soldiers through their training and conditioning will, with rare exceptions like Clausewitz himself, be insensitive if not hostile to the idea that it should. But that does not mean that the ordinary politician will be readily receptive to it. The politician may be psychologically freer than the soldier to adopt the Clausewitzian view, and under the right circumstance he is significantly more likely to do so. But all too often he has adapted himself to "the exigencies of war" in a manner indistinguishable from the soldier's.

World War II did have one distinctive and important characteristic that helps to justify Roosevelt's attitude. Among the two or three most important decisions agreed upon by Roosevelt and Churchill after the United States' entry into the war was that which made it the overriding war aim of the coalition to accomplish the *complete defeat* of their enemies. This basic understanding later occasioned Roosevelt's utterance of the "unconditional surrender" theme, which borrowed a phrase famous in American military history because of its use by General Grant before Vicksburg. Although Roosevelt's flaunting of this phrase has been criticized as flippant and possibly costly, no other military goal was possible. Such a goal was *not* necessary in World War I, and the Armistice of 1918 did in fact leave a mostly uninvaded Germany and a fairly intact German Army. If the Allies had insisted in 1918 on going to Berlin, that aim would have resulted in a probably substantial prolongation of a purposeless war. Getting rid of the Hohenzollern dynasty was hardly an essential war aim, and the fact that the Germans did it themselves was simply a bonus —or at least appeared to be so when the replacement was for a time a democratic republic. The Nazi regime of Adolf Hitler, however, had to be completely and utterly crushed in order to be also totally discredited, thus leaving no room for the later revival of some version of the *Dolchstoss* or "stab-in-the-back" theory by which Hitler had "explained" the defeat in World War I.

In World War II the Western Allies were fighting not for the return of some lost provinces, or to give a salutary lesson in humility to an opponent grown too arrogant, or for some abstract conception of maintaining the balance of power, or for whatever else was conceived to be the justification for their going to war with Germany in 1914. In World War II Britain and the United States could have no meaningful attainable objective that did not include the utter extirpation of the Nazi tyranny and all its works. Even the German people were shortly thereafter to agree with their victors in the West upon the propriety of this aim, and they have remained so agreed by hugely preponderant majorities down to the date of this writing.[14] The cases of Italy and Japan were not quite the same, but neither were they profoundly different.

To insist upon a goal that means utter defeat of the enemy, as symbolized by the complete occupation of his territories, is normally to add a heavy additional burden upon the military commitment. Historically, this kind of uncompromising goal has been characteristic of civil wars rather than international wars. In World War I a Germany prepared to yield up Belgium and the lost French provinces as well as the territories wrested from Russia in the Treaty of Brest-Litovsk of 1918 had to be a nation quite unambiguously defeated. Still, it was very different from insisting on the crushing of all resistance. The aim of complete victory obviates any negotiations with the enemy other than those providing for the capitulations of his armies in the field. It re-

---

[14] An attitude culminating in October 1969 in the election as Chancellor of the Federal Republic of Willy Brandt, who had not only left Germany prior to World War II but had worn during that war the uniform of an enemy army, that of Norway.

quires him to expose to risk to the detested conqueror, whose humanity and sense of justice he has been vehemently denying, everything conceivably precious.

Because of these special burdens in World War II, almost every major decision made jointly by Churchill and Roosevelt was and had to be based fundamentally on military expediency. As Kent R. Greenfield puts it, "Political considerations affected the debates, but had a minor effect on their outcome."[15] The great exception was Operation TORCH, the decision to invade North Africa, where Roosevelt overruled his Chiefs of Staff and his Secretary of War and went along with Churchill. Roosevelt justified his decision on the ground that it was desirable to have large American forces heavily and sucessfully engaged in offensive action at least on the periphery of Europe before the end of 1942. Besides, the possibility of winning over to the Allied side the French forces in North Africa offered a considerable prize militarily as well as politically.

In the later stages of the war, however, a persistent tug-of-war developed between Churchill and Roosevelt concerning the degree to which strategic decisions should be affected by the common political interest of both their nations against the Soviet threat. In Greenfield's words, "Mr. Roosevelt decided that the interests of the United States would best be served by letting the judgment of his military advisers prevail, and these invariably closed ranks in favor of decisions that could be justified by military ends as against those that could not."[16] In the earlier stages of the coalition, when the German and Japanese power had looked so formidable, there had been simply no question that military considerations must dominate. After the success of the June 1944 landings in Normandy was assured, however, the defeat of Germany was only a question of time, and it could not be a long time. Even so, no question developed of letting military decisions deviate from conformity with strictly military purposes until near the very end of the European war.

A good deal has been written of Churchill's yearning to go into the Balkans to anticipate the Russian presence there. It was, however, General Eisenhower rather than President Roosevelt whom Churchill approached on this subject, and with Eisenhower he would naturally have to argue his case primarily even if ficti-

---

[15] Greenfield, *American Strategy*, p. 15.
[16] Ibid., p. 16.

tiously on military grounds. Eisenhower relates that after the Saint-Lo "breakout" of July 1944, the new situation brought up one of the longest-sustained arguments that he had with Churchill throughout the period of the war. Churchill held that the imminent Allied landing at Marseilles in the Mediterranean planned as a followup to the successful landings in Normandy was no longer necessary, and that the forces allocated to this task should instead be pushed through Italy into the Balkans. This, he argued, would bring a new threat to Germany from the south in addition to the already established threat from the west. Eisenhower, who relates the military arguments offered by both Churchill and himself in some detail, goes on to say,

> Although I never heard him say so, I felt that the Prime Minister's real concern was possibly of a political rather than a military nature. He may have thought that a post-war situation which would see the Western Allies posted in great strength in the Balkans would be far more effective in producing a stable posthostilities world than if the Russian armies should be the ones to occupy that region. I told him that if this were his reason for advocating the campaign into the Balkans he should go instantly to the President and lay the facts, as well as his own conclusions, on the table. I well understand that strategy can be affected by political considerations, and if the President and the Prime Minister should decide that it was worth while to prolong the war, thereby increasing its cost in men and money, in order to secure the political objectives they deemed necessary, then I would instantly and loyally adjust my plans accordingly. But I did insist that as long as he argued the matter on military grounds alone I could not concede validity to his arguments.
>
> I felt that in this particular field I alone had to be the judge of my own responsibilities and decisions. I refused to consider the change so long as it was urged upon military considerations. He did not admit that political factors were influencing him, but I am quite certain that no experienced soldier would question the wisdom, strictly from the military viewpoint, of adhering to the plan for attacking southern France.[17]

It is interesting that at that stage of affairs Churchill did not

---

[17] Eisenhower, *Crusade in Europe*, pp. 301 f.

see fit to bring his argument to Roosevelt. One can only guess at the reason. Perhaps he did not expect Roosevelt so early in the campaign to see as clearly as he did either that Germany was militarily finished, and that the Western Allies had some latitude in deciding how to administer the final blows, or that Stalin's intentions were far from benign and that he really could not be controlled simply with joviality and gestures of goodwill. As Herbert Feis has shown in his book, *Churchill, Roosevelt, and Stalin*, it was difficult for both Allied leaders, including Churchill, to convince themselves how thoroughly unscrupulous and treacherous Stalin was, but Churchill did see the light before Roosevelt.

Shortly it became impossible for any informed person to remain blind to the rude and bloody opportunism that Stalin was displaying or to fail to guess his purposes. For example, after the Warsaw uprising of August-September 1944, obviously timed by the Polish Resistance to coordinate their efforts with those of the advancing Red Army, Stalin halted the Soviet forces ten to twelve miles out of Warsaw and held them there until the Germans had liquidated the uprising—and with it the Warsaw resistance and its non-Communist leaders.[18] Clearly, Stalin was satisfied to let the Germans save him the trouble of dispatching those leaders himself. It is difficult to think of a comparable example in modern history of a political leader using the hated enemy for so hateful a purpose, but we have to note in passing that Stalin was indeed following the Clausewitzian dictum we have been discussing. However disgusting and insensate his goal and his means of accomplishing it, Stalin did not have to be told that war is fought for political ends.

However, even when Roosevelt was ready to agree with Churchill about Stalin's aims, he was not ready to risk military estrangement from the latter, especially because he felt until his death—quite mistakenly we know now and should have known then—that Soviet intervention in the war against Japan remained extremely desirable even if no longer critical.[19] Thus, differences

---

[18] See Herbert Feis, *Churchill, Roosevelt, Stalin* (Princeton: Princeton University Press, 1967), pp. 378–389. Feis ostensibly leaves open the question whether the Russian halt was deliberate or not, but the evidence he produces confirms the conviction, which he appears to share, that it was in fact deliberate.

[19] See ibid., pp. 405 f. Also Greenfield, *American Strategy*, pp. 21 f. The United States Joint Chiefs remained persuaded throughout 1944 and until August 1945, despite their great naval and air victories and the forthcoming availability of the nuclear bomb, that it would still be necessary to launch a full-scale invasion of Japan, which they predicted would be terribly costly. They therefore wanted the Soviet armies to tie

between Churchill and Roosevelt concerning methods of exerting leverage against Stalin continued to be resolved, as Roosevelt insisted, according to the presumed dictates of "purely military" considerations. The disproportion in military contributions between the two Western Allies deprived Churchill of an adequate platform for comparable insistence on his own contrary views.

However, in the last six weeks of the war in Europe, Churchill, now in desperate anguish, urged the new President, Harry S Truman, to agree to having their armies in Europe rush forward in Germany to meet the Russians, with the idea of withdrawing them into the prearranged zones of occupation only if and when Stalin relaxed his grip on eastern and central Europe. Truman refused, on the grounds that such action would sacrifice the last chance to get the Soviet Union to join in founding the United Nations. Although Truman, like Woodrow Wilson before him, was greatly exaggerating the feasibility of coming out of the war with an international organization really capable of keeping the peace, he at least was appealing to what he presumed to be a profoundly important political goal. Still, it is suspicious that the political goal should accord so nicely with objectives congenial to the American Joint Chiefs, who resisted any deviation from a strictly military strategy until victory was complete.

As Greenfield sums it up:

> Both presidents consistently gave the green light to their military chiefs, and these consistently rejected decisions on grounds other than military effect. General Marshall, surely one of the most statesmanlike of them, wrote to General Eisenhower when Mr. Churchill, in late April, 1945, was urging the political advantages to be gained by liberating Prague, and as much of Czechoslovakia as possible, before the Russians arrived on the scene: "Personally and aside from all

---

down as much Japanese force as possible on mainland Asia. In 1946 this writer had occasion to ask the late Vice Admiral Russell Willson, who during the war had been a member of the United States Joint Strategic Survey Committee, why the conviction had prevailed until the end that Soviet intervention in the war against Japan remained desirable and even necessary. Willson's reply was a frank admission that the answer lay simply [as is so often the case] in the sheer inertia of a prevalent view that had outlived all its justification. At the very end Stalin insisted that he be formally *invited* to enter the war, which the United States government did by drawing up a document making fictitiously legal claims on the basis of the United Nations charter, which had not yet been ratified. See Robert J. C. Butow, *Japan's Decision to Surrender* (Stanford: Stanford University Press, 1954), pp. 155–158.

logistical, tactical or strategical implications I would be loath to hazard American lives for purely political purposes." [20]

To avoid hazarding American lives is bound to be commendable, but if it was not to be done for "purely political purposes," what then was that or any other war all about? *De quoi s'agit-il?* This same General George C. Marshall was before long to become President Truman's Secretary of State, in which office he seems to have functioned admirably. But by then hostilities were well over, and the soldier-turned-statesman never had to concern himself in that post with finding the appropriate amalgam of strategy and politics.

We need not assume that Churchill was always right and his American colleague correspondingly wrong in their respective appraisals of the extent to which Western Allied power could or should be used to curb Stalin and his designs in that region. Feis and others think that Roosevelt was convinced, rightly, that there was nothing the Western Allies could do to keep the Soviet Union from controlling affairs in eastern Europe, and that it would be folly to try. Some also argue that our willingness to cooperate faithfully with Stalin had to be proved with utter conclusiveness to the wartime and postwar world. The latter argument is not without merit, but it does not justify much sacrifice because there always remain in any case those who will be unsatisfied. The number of the latter indeed increases with time, less from development of objectivity than from forgetfulness, from sheer ignorance of past events including even recent ones, and from the inevitable revival of that double standard which holds the ruthless authoritarian regime less accountable than the responsible democratic one.

In any case, the issue for us is not who was right or wrong in his assessments or predictions, but rather: What kind of criteria and attitudes were held relevant and brought into play? In this respect there can be no question that the American attitude differed profoundly from that represented by Churchill—who after all was just as interested in seeing the war ended and whose country had been longer and much more desperately engaged in it. We cannot know what would have happened in the postwar world if Churchill's urgings had prevailed. It seems clear, however, that some of our conduct does not in retrospect look very

---

[20] Greenfield, *American Strategy*, p. 19.

clever, especially with respect (a) to leaving Berlin an enclave deep within Soviet-controlled East Germany, and (b) to inducing the Soviet Union to enter the war against Japan, long after it should have been obvious that such intervention would be of little or no military value. The tribulations resulting directly from the former error are quite familiar, though by extension they probably include even the Cuban missile crisis of 1962.[21] The latter error had among other effects that of leaving Korea divided at the 38th parallel. It was therefore to be a major direct cause of the Korean War, which broke out within five years of the end of World War II, and which was to leave a menacing situation for many years thereafter.

These and related later events enormously affected American military budgets as well as military and diplomatic propensities —and, at least by reaction if not otherwise, Soviet budgets and propensities as well. Naturally, imaginary reconstructions of what might have been must assume neither perfect foresight nor a total absence of errors in any alternative policy. It is always possible to imagine how we could have done worse. But that is an utterly nihilistic consideration if it is supposed to bar us from designating as wise or unwise those decisions that in retrospect appear to have been clearly one or the other.

The Decision to Drop the A-Bomb: A Question of War Morality

Another decision that some would hold of equal or greater importance than those just discussed was that of President Truman to use the newly developed nuclear weapon against Japan, specifically against two heavily populated Japanese cities. The alternative most strongly urged, by some of the scientists who produced the weapon, was to use it against some unpopulated target in a manner designed simply to demonstrate our possession of this new power.

Much has been said and written on this subject, most of it centering around the question of the morality of the American action. The morality or immorality of acts of war is not a popular subject among the military and their civilian associates, nor for that matter among writers on strategy. It makes the military

---

[21] This is on the likelihood that Khrushchev's main purpose in placing the missiles in Cuba was to gain leverage for a showdown with the United States over Berlin. See Adam B. Ulam, *The Rivals: America and Russia Since World War II* (New York: Viking, 1971), chap. 10.

uneasy and defensive, ready to dismiss the troubling issue whenever it arises, either by asserting its irrelevancy or by falling back on some convenient sophistry. The soldier, we repeat again, is trained to the conviction that the all-important goal is to win—if at all possible, and at (almost) any cost. Whatever contributes to his quick victory usually diminishes overall casualties, especially his own. It is therefore self-evident to him that any device or tactic that hastens victory represents the highest morality.

There is really nothing to wonder at or to reproach in such an attitude. Given the premise, which apotheosizes victory, the conclusion is anything but preposterous. The premise goes with being a soldier, that is, with achieving the particular form of character integration necessary to his professional effectiveness. He is far from perceiving himself as a monster. Much of the ceremony and punctilio that go with the profession, for example, the peculiarly frequent use of the word *gentlemen* in addressing or referring to brother officers, appear designed to ward off the disturbing thought that one belongs to a trade devoted to slaughter.

As for writers on strategy, who today are mostly civilians, they seek naturally to connect with that profession which provides them with most of their readers, and especially those readers through whom they may have a modest chance of being effective upon policy.[22] The frame of reference of the strategic thinker is strictly pragmatic. He is not interested, as the scientist is, in discovering ultimate truths, but rather in helping the military leaders, and through them the political leaders, to prepare their minds and their equipment for contending efficiently and successfully with an adversary, one who at the time of crisis will be a specific and not a generalized adversary. He may view objectives more comprehensively than the soldier, but not differently. He must, after all, win the confidence of the soldier and persuade him that he has some useful insights to offer, which he will not succeed in

---

[22] Actually, most contemporary writers on strategy seem to be ambivalent on this score. They certainly get far more visible attention from military officers, especially those functioning as students at the war college level (usually rank of colonel, age about 40). Still, as the era of McNamara proved, the strategic writer can sometimes have important influence directly through his civilian readers, the more so as he tends to challenge long-accepted shibboleths. Today we have the phenomenon of Henry A. Kissinger, whose reputation was of course originally made by his writings. However, his great influence is due to President Nixon's becoming persuaded, not necessarily from reading any large portion of Kissinger's writings, that their author had gifts that would be useful to him. Inasmuch as that persuasion clearly grew with the actual services, Kissinger's great influence on affairs must be said to stem from his gifts as an adviser and an operator rather than as an author.

doing if the soldier senses an essential divergence between them in purpose. Thus, the strategic writer, too, will normally regard moral considerations as tiresome impediments to the flow of one's thoughts.[23] Even the philosophical Clausewitz was strongly negative on the relevance of moral issues.

Another reason why moral considerations do not progress very far in discourses on military methods is that very few people are equipped emotionally as well as intellectually to deal with them. Nuclear weapons arouse special anxieties, as well as the understanding that the social environment is deeply sympathetic to the denial of any possibility of their utility, even as a deterrent. It is therefore greatly tempting for anyone discussing the issues publicly to establish that he is on the side of the angels. And appallingly often those who persuade themselves that they are on that side feel themselves thereby licensed to indulge in behavior that is ill-mannered, dishonest, or worse.[24]

Certainly there is no intrinsic reason why moral issues should not be raised concerning those decisions of men that are expressed in acts of war, as we raise them concerning all other actions of men. True, there is a hoary convention that holds that morality ends at the threshold of affairs of state, not to speak of war. It is expressed in many well-spoken aphorisms or quotations, like the remark of Talleyrand on Napoleon's execution of the Duc d'Enghien: "It was worse than a crime, it was a blunder!" Thus wit establishes immunity, and the man who spent a million lives to make himself and his family royal has gone down in history as a genius who committed no crimes, only a few costly blunders.

---

[23] Including, rather oddly, even such a writer as the distinguished Professor Raymond Aron of France, whose renowned works are largely in the field in which politics borders on strategy. Despite the fact that he has also made important contributions to philosophy, he tends *explicitly* to shut out moral considerations from his political-strategic realm of discourse. See, for example, his "The Evolution of Modern Strategic Thought," in *Problems of Modern Strategy*, with Foreword by Alastair Buchan (London: Chatto and Windus, 1970), p. 18 n.

[24] A particularly unedifying example occurred in a meeting of the A.A.A.S. in December 1970, where some young scientists who disapproved of Dr. Edward Teller (because of his special contributions to the development of nuclear weapons) demonstrated against him in an especially nasty manner. Dr. Teller then defended himself by revealing that he, too, had been on the side of the angels concerning the first use of the A-bomb. He, too, he said, had wanted to see the bomb used over an unpopulated target in a strictly demonstration manner, but he had been dissuaded by the late Dr. J. Robert Oppenheimer, who had ulterior motives, from signing the relevant petition. Thus Dr. Teller was able at the same time to show his essential goodness and to strike yet another blow at the deceased man from whom he clearly suffered some deep sense of betrayal. See *New York Times*, Dec. 28, 1970; also *Science*, Jan. 8, 1971, pp. 47 ff.

Even so, the language of morality is ever on the lips of politicians, though it is left for the greatest of them really to mean it.

The main difficulty about discriminating with respect to acts of war is that everything seems to be caught up in a vast savagery of destruction, in which essentially nothing can be done, even in the strictest defensive stance, without in some way violating what in peacetime would be a moral code to which most of us would be sensitive. Every soldier who lays down his life in battle does so in response to orders. These orders, often given in the expectation that the loss rate will be high, are naturally always meant to achieve the killing and maiming of at least as many in the ranks of the enemy. The saving grace is that the commander does not specifically select those among his command who are to be killed or maimed, he simply feeds the whole lot into a statistical chopper. No one expects him to feel the slightest hesitation about giving such orders or any remorse or guilt from observing the consequences; on the contrary, any such inclination would be a mark of absolute unfitness for combat command.[25] And these reflections concern only that portion of war activities which has the clearest mark of legitimacy—the mutual slaughter of armed, military personnel. Small wonder that so many, both hawks and doves, dismiss the problem with the remark that war itself is basically immoral and that all efforts to discriminate between acts of greater or less morality are bound to be vain and useless, possibly even harmful.

Still, there is always the difference between more and less. If destruction is bad, then greater destruction is worse. We have already noted that the conception of *wanton* destruction has long been absorbed into the international codes that seek to distinguish between permissible and impermissible acts of war. If the common insistence on military success will brook no interference, then we do well to derive from that overweening purpose some standard of discrimination: Do what you must to secure your military aim, but avoid destruction that contributes little or noth-

---

[25] That commanders should have the toughness or insensitivity to give commands that will result in casualties is worthy of observation but hardly of reproach. Quite another matter, however, is the spectacle of commanders being preoccupied with the future of their own military careers even while they are presiding over the deaths of hundreds or even thousands, sometimes cultivating reputations for ruthless aggressiveness in order to favor those careers. The late Humphrey Cobb, in his novel *Paths of Glory* (New York: Viking Press, 1935), brilliantly portrayed such a situation in the French Army during World War I, but the command attitudes he described are not confined either to that army or to that war.

ing to achieving that aim. It is not much to go on, but it is at least something; if we cannot significantly build upon it, we should at least preserve it.

With these few observations to assist us, we may now return to the issues raised by the use of two nuclear weapons over Hiroshima and Nagasaki in August 1945.

The question divides into two parts: first, whether so-called strategic bombing itself may be considered legitimate, especially that part of it characterized by terror raids against civilian populations, and second, what in 1945 was distinctive about the new atomic bombs that made them so much more awful to use than conventional air-dropped weapons. The latter in 1945 included incendiary bombs and napalm as well as various kinds of high-explosive bombs. Also, we should consider this question with respect not only to the moral issues but also to long-range political considerations.

The various attempts to outlaw strategic bombing, beginning with the Hague Convention of 1899 which prohibited the dropping of bombs from balloons, may now be regarded as having plainly failed. The basic cause of the failure is that too many people regard such bombing as being militarily desirable or even indispensable—for those who have the means to wage it. The lesson here is that rules made with too much disregard of the issue of military utility are not likely to survive. Any legal rule, on the basis of its own authority as law, can bear only so much weight of contrary interest. If the burden upon it is heavy, it needs some support from pragmatic mutual-self-interest considerations.

We may also recall that the trail-blazing treatise of General Douhet, first published in 1921, made much of the fact that strategic bombing would avoid that hideous and horribly life-consuming stalemate of the trenches that marked the war of 1914–1918. It was therefore in his eyes a more moral or at any rate less immoral way of conducting war. As for the distinction between so-called military targets and civilian populations, Douhet and others refused to regard it as valid. The various axioms about "total war" that sprang from the experience of World War I held that these populations, significantly called the "home front," were indistinguishable from the military forces because of their efforts in producing war materials. This was fortified by the strictly pragmatic consideration that, at least in Douhet's eyes, the civilian front was so vulnerable to attack that the desirable and commendable goal of shortening the war—and thus reducing its overall cost—necessitated and justified such an attack.[26] Bombing of civilian populations had already been practiced in World War I, and it was again brought into use by the Franco forces in the Spanish Civil War of 1936–1938, by the Germans against the Poles in 1939 and against the Dutch and others in 1940, and, after some initial hesitation, mutually between the Germans and the British beginning later in 1940.

A great deal of debate ensued, following World War II, about how effective strategic bombing really was in achieving significant military goals. A fairly vociferous school of thought charged that the British-American strategic bombing of Germany produced few if any real military results, certainly too few to be worth the cost. Others have disputed this view concerning even Germany; but whether or not strategic bombing accomplished its intended objectives against Germany (in the net it did, but too tardily) it certainly succeeded against Japan.[27] The Japanese military who were holding out against surrender knew they were beaten even before the atomic bombs were dropped.

Our military chieftains expected their planned invasion to be extremely costly in lives, and our present knowledge gives us no reason to assume they were exaggerating. It is true that by the middle of 1945 the Japanese war fleet and air force had been pretty nearly totally destroyed, and that large numbers of Japanese troops were stranded on isolated islands of the western Pacific and on the mainland of Asia. Still, there were enough ground forces left on the main islands of Japan, coupled with a sufficiently unquestioned conviction among the military of the inadmissibility of surrender, to make it appear certain that there would be gross carnage on both sides if American forces had to fight their way ashore.

As it turned out, owing entirely to the bombing, which had reached a savage crescendo from the time American forces had established themselves in the Mariana Islands in the late autumn of 1944, it was possible for the Japanese Emperor by his personal intervention to defuse the spirit of the military diehards. The

[26] See my *Strategy in the Missile Age* (Princeton: Princeton University Press, 1959), chap. 3, "The Heritage of Douhet." See also footnote 4, this chapter.

[27] See ibid., chap. 4, "Strategic Bombing in World War II." That chapter relies heavily on the results provided in the extensive *United States Strategic Bombing Survey*, as well as a few other sources.

entry of the Soviet Union into the war could not by itself have had that result, because the Russians could attack only the Japanese ground forces on mainland Asia. They had no naval or air means of carrying the war to Japan.

But were the two nuclear weapons necessary to produce that result? This question has to be answered in terms of what we knew then as well as what we know now. Would the same effect have been accomplished by the demonstration urged by a group among the scientists who had produced the bomb? And what really was their objection to using nuclear weapons in view of the lack of objection from the same people to the fiery horror that was already pouring down on Japan, especially in the last three months preceding the use of the nuclear bombs?

That last question may be taken first. Undoubtedly the worst city attack of the war, and thus the worst of all time, was that which occurred on the southwest portion of Tokyo during the night of May 23, 1945. Within a period of little more than two hours, some 520 bombers dropped almost 4,000 tons of incendiary bombs on an area of about eleven square miles. This created the phenomenon known as a "fire-storm" (encountered previously at Dresden and later at Hiroshima), in which the flames create their own strong winds to fan them into greater intensity. Estimates of the number of Japanese people of all ages who perished in that storm range from 83,000 to over 100,000. Many of them died from asphyxiation in the vicinity of the Meiji Shrine to which they were running for protection. We can say about Hiroshima that it was a comparable horror, accomplished more efficiently by one airplane with one bomb, but we can hardly say it was a worse one, the number of fatalities being substantially less. People were killed and disfigured by radiation as well as by fire; but to the survivors as to the dead, it is the degree of injury that matters and not the way in which it was inflicted.

Today, it is precisely the efficiency of the nuclear bomb that makes it matter so much, the fact that there can be as many vast fire storms as there are target cities to create them and that all can be ignited within the space of half an hour. But that is not the way it looked at the beginning of August 1945. The bomb that had been tested at Alamagordo in mid-July and the two that were destined for Hiroshima and Nagasaki were all that existed in the United States stockpile. If the war had not terminated so soon after the Nagasaki bomb was dropped, it would have taken weeks before another bomb would have been ready for delivery on target.[28] Dropping the only two available bombs a mere two days apart, combined with the somewhat fortuitous circumstance that their delivery coincided with the entry of the Soviet Union into the Pacific war, made for the maximum morale effect on the Japanese government.

As seen from Washington, it was a combination that might work promptly to terminate the war. True, President Truman had been personally informed by Stalin at Potsdam that the Japanese government had already twice requested Soviet mediation to seek the same end, a request that the Soviet government rejected, allegedly on the ground that it contained no specific proposals. Anyway, on the same day that Truman received this news (July 28) Radio Tokyo rejected as "absurd" and "presumptuous" the Potsdam Declaration of July 26, which stipulated terms on which the Japanese were again called upon to surrender—and which stated that the might converging on Japan was "immeasurably greater" than that which had devasted Germany.[29]

President Truman had appointed a committee to advise him on the use of the bomb. It was chaired by the highly respected Secretary of War Henry L. Stimson and had the assistance of at least four scientists who had played a prominent part in the development of the bomb: Drs. J. Robert Oppenheimer, Arthur H. Compton, E. O. Lawrence, and Enrico Fermi. President Truman in his *Memoirs* reports their advice as follows:

> It was their recommendation that the bomb be used against the enemy as soon as it could be done. They recommended further that it should be used without specific warning and against a target that would clearly show its devastating strength. I had realized, of course, that an atomic bomb explosion would inflict damage and casualties beyond imagination. On the other hand, the scientific advisers of the committee reported: "We can propose no technical demonstration likely to bring an end to the war; we see no acceptable alternative to direct military use." It was their conclusion that no technical demonstration they might propose, such as over a deserted

---

[28] This fact was related to me orally, in December 1950, by the late Dr. J. Robert Oppenheimer. Herbert Feis thinks a third bomb could have been dropped before August 20, but has no information about a fourth bomb. See his *The Atomic Bomb and the End of World War II* (Princeton: Princeton University Press, 1961, 1966), p. 198.

[29] Harry S Truman, *Memoirs, Vol. 1, Year of Decisions* (New York: Doubleday, 1955), pp. 390–397.

island, would be likely to bring the war to an end. It had to be used against an enemy target.[30]

Looking back at this recommendation more than a quarter century later, it is difficult to fault it. A demonstration over a deserted island would have been anything but impressive, and there were too few bombs in hand to use one in that manner. This writer has witnessed from a trench 1,000 yards away the explosion over a portion of Nevada desert of a nuclear bomb of some 50 kilotons yield, that is, more than twice the size of the Nagasaki bomb, which had half again as much yield as the Hiroshima bomb.[31] The extreme intensity of the light was eerie but of exceedingly brief duration. It was something to look down the length of a trench and see it wobbling from ground shock, but one has to be close in for that. After the mushroom cloud had begun to dissipate and the sand had settled, which took very little additional time, the floor of the desert looked relatively unchanged. Some sheep that had been tethered within one mile of the bomb looked uninjured except for the scorching of their wool on the side that had faced the fireball (some may indeed have had lethal doses of radiation, which takes some time to show its effects). Only a few airplane wing structures that had been placed at various distances from the bomb site showed the hammer-blow effects of the blast.

The thought of the unimpressiveness of a test carried out over an uninhabited area had of course occurred to the members of the panel. As Dr. Oppenheimer later testified: "We did say that we did not think exploding one of these things as a firecracker over a desert was likely to be very impressive. This was before we had actually done that [at Alamagordo]. The destruction on the desert is zero." [32] There was also the fear that a bomb announced in advance as a test might not work. Actually, the type of bomb used at Hiroshima (gun-type detonation, as contrasted with implosion) had never previously been tested; if it had not worked the Japanese would never have known it. The type used at

---

[30] Ibid., p. 419.

[31] Journalists and others constantly refer to the Hiroshima bomb as having been of 20 kilotons yield, though Dr. Willard L. Libby stated publicly, while he was a commissioner on the AEC, that the yield had been about 12-14 kilotons. The 20 kilotons are about correct for the more efficient Nagasaki bomb, which like the one tested at Alamagordo was of the implosion type, as contrasted with the gun type used at Hiroshima. The designations *implosion* and *gun* refer only to the method of nuclear ignition.

[32] Quoted in Feis, *The Atomic Bomb*, p. 55.

Nagasaki had been tested at Alamagordo, but that test did not prove indisputably that a second bomb of the same kind would work, especially under the very different conditions of airplane delivery and drop. However, as Herbert Feis points out:

> speculation on this subject may be regarded as a professional indulgence. For, in fact, even if the decision-makers had not feared a possible failure in demonstration, they would not have tried it. For they deemed it most unlikely that a demonstration could end the war as quickly and surely as hurling the bomb on Japan, and that was their duty as they saw it. No matter what the place and setting for the demonstration, they were sure it would not give an adequate impression of its appalling destructive power, would not register its full meaning in human lives. The desired explosive impression on the Japanese, it was concluded, could be produced only by the actual awful experience.[33]

The destruction that did result from the Hiroshima and Nagasaki bombs, especially the former (a smaller bomb, but achieving more destructive effect because of the flatter terrain) left Japan and the whole world awed, appalled, and unequivocally convinced that a terrible new revolution had occurred in the means of waging war. They were the most extraordinarily effective demonstrations possible. The Japanese residents of those two cities paid a terrible price, but if the war had lasted even a few weeks longer they or others would have paid a comparable price from more of the kinds of raids that had devastated Tokyo and most other cities of Japan.[34] And lurking only three months in the future was the planned invasion of Japan, which, had it taken place, would have been a blood bath for Japanese and Americans alike.

One writer has argued—what he could not possibly prove—that the two atomic bombs played little or no part in inducing the Japanese to surrender.[35] Even if that had been true, we should have to acknowledge that the President and his advisers could certainly not have predicted with confidence so negative a result.

---

[33] Ibid., p. 199.

[34] Almost certainly Hiroshima and Nagasaki would have been included quite soon in a continuing program of conventional bombing. One of the chief reasons for their selection as nuclear bomb targets was that they were among the very few cities of any size left in Japan that had not already been heavily bombed.

[35] Paul Kecskemeti, *Strategic Surrender: The Politics of Victory and Defeat* (Stanford: Stanford University Press, 1958), pp. 199–206.

We now know it is not true. The two bombs heightened the Emperor's determination to end the war as soon as possible. Several cabinet ministers, affected the same way, moreover felt that they now had a powerful new leverage for persuading the Army diehards in and out of the cabinet to acquiesce in a surrender. It is true that the Emperor and some cabinet members, including Prime Minister Admiral Kantaro Suzuki and Foreign Minister Shigenori Togo, had been convinced from at least the previous autumn that Japan had to quit the war. Yet in view of the difficulty—and near failure—to bring it off even after the two nuclear disasters and the Soviet declaration of war, it is obvious that these men had no leverage to spare.[36] In any case, the delicacy and intricacies of the maneuvering in Tokyo were certainly beyond the vision and quite probably the comprehension of the President in Washington, who, incidentally, also had the support of Prime Minister Churchill in making the decision to use the bomb.

One may feel some sympathy for the scientists who professed themselves shocked at the decision to use the bomb and who subsequently made great public protestations of their feeling of guilt.[37] Still, it was unreasonable to expect Harry Truman to be moved by arguments that the bomb was different because it represented a *cosmic* force. His *Memoirs* show that he undertook his responsibility most soberly, and that he probably did not underestimate the effects of the bombs at the two cities. Nevertheless, he was eager to end the war as soon as possible, he was totally committed to ending it through a Japanese surrender, and he could not see that the two atomic bombs had worse effects than the raids that General Curtis LeMay had already been hurling upon the Japanese for the previous three or four months.

Where is his error? If it was politically and morally wrong to use the new bomb, it was surely equally wrong to do the "conventional" kind of bombing that was already succeeding very well in laying waste the cities of Japan. The scientists and others who have railed against the Truman decision on the use of the bomb

---

[36] See John Toland, *The Rising Sun* (New York: Random House, 1970), pp. 806–855.

[37] They had been working on the bomb for a long time, certainly in full knowledge of what they were doing. Apparently their consciences had been kept quiescent by their erroneous belief that the Nazis were also working on a nuclear bomb, and that it was imperative not to be outdistanced by them. This motivation of course tended to collapse with the surrender of Germany in May 1945. It was then that some committees were formed, especially among the Chicago group of scientists headed by Drs. James O. Franck and Leo Szilard, to try to alter the government's intentions about using the bomb over Japan. Their liaison with the government panel was through Dr. Arthur Compton. See Feis, *The Atomic Bomb*, pp. 50 ff.

actually seem not to be aware that there was already another kind of bombing going on that was producing just as evil results for the people in the target cities as did the nuclear bombing. Actually, in this writer's experience in conversations with such people, including some who were already adults at the time of the events in question, they usually are not aware of these matters, which means that they once knew but have allowed themselves to forget.

Lately a typically "revisionist" kind of speculation has developed to the effect that the government that the President really wanted to impress was not so much that of Japan as that of the Soviet Union. It is impossible to hold that the thought never crossed the minds of the President or his advisors. What we can say, however, is that to the extent that it did cross their minds, it could not have been a critical consideration. It seems not to have been mentioned in the relevant councils, and the people pondering the question apparently found quite enough incentive for using the bomb in their great desire to end as quickly as possible the war with Japan. Moreover, at that time the cold war had not yet begun to throw its chill upon the relations between the two superpowers.[38]

The cold war was to develop soon enough, in a mood of soberness deepened by the knowledge that war, that is, what we have come to know as "general war," had entered a wholly new and hitherto unbelievable dimension of horror. In any new war between the superpowers, the terrible devastation of the two world wars would be at once immeasurably surpassed. Certainly the clarity of this realization was heightened and made more acute by the knowledge of what had happened at the two Japanese cities that had been struck, accounts of which were soon widely published with no want of detail.[39] After more than a quarter of a century they are still the only nuclear weapons to have been used in war, and their use has not made one iota more likely any future use. One would suspect that quite the contrary is the case. Though the people of the two cities paid bitterly for it, their sacrifice unquestionably contributed to the significance and the effectiveness of the "balance of terror," which thus far has shown itself to be an exceedingly stable balance.

[38] A leading "revisionist" view is presented by Gar Alperovitz, *Atomic Diplomacy: Hiroshima and Potsdam* (New York: Simon and Schuster, 1965).

[39] The best and most important is still John R. Hersey's *Hiroshima* (New York: Knopf, 1946). For strictly physical effects there have been a number of official publications, the most useful being Samuel Glasstone, *The Effects of Atomic Weapons* (Washington: Government Printing Office, revised 2nd ed., 1964).

CHAPTER
3

The Test of Korea

In simplest terms, what we are doing in Korea is this: We are trying to prevent World War III.

President Harry S Truman

Never, never, never believe any war will be smooth and easy, or that anyone who embarks on that strange voyage can measure the tides and hurricanes he will encounter.

Winston Churchill, from *A Roving Commission*

In the more than quarter century since World War II, the United States has engaged in two wars of a nature totally different from that titanic struggle. By any of a number of reasonable criteria, especially American casualties, each deserves to be considered a major war. Each has also been called a "political" war (as though World War II was supposed not to be such), and indeed each has been characterized on the American side by a relatively large degree of conscious intrusion of political considerations upon strategy. Under the circumstances, however, which

57

include a distaste in some quarters for such intrusion and inevitably a lack of relevant experience among the civilian leaders, the result in each case has been conspicuous confusion and disappointment. Korea was less costly and less complicated than Vietnam, though with some 40,000 American troops still there at this writing, it is not quite yet time to close the books on Korea.

The issues concerning Korea that are most relevant here are (a) the reasons for our entering the war, (b) the reasons for our exercising a kind of restraint that made it the first important limited war of the nuclear age, and (c) the confusion concerning war objectives, especially as they centered round the question of whether or not we should accept continuing division of Korea at about the 38th parallel. On a quite different level of interest and importance there was also the President's dismissal of General Douglas MacArthur. The General differed from President Truman with respect to items (b) and (c) above; he was dismissed, however, not for his differences but for his insubordination in repeatedly making them public in a manner clearly designed to exert pressure upon the President. The dismissal triggered intensive public questioning, including a prolonged congressional investigation of the President's action and of his Korean policies generally. Politically hostile opinion naturally revived the timeworn denunciation of politicians who "meddle" in strategy, and the hearings demonstrated the political pitfalls hedging about the President's constitutional prerogatives in replacing a national hero like MacArthur.

More appropriately subject to question, and indeed becoming increasingly a domestic political issue as time went on, was the President's constitutional authority to wage war in the absence of an appropriate pronouncement by Congress. The Korean War was the first large foreign war fought by the United States without congressional authorization, and as such would have been inconceivable before the changes wrought by World War II in the American people's conception of their nation's world role. The questioning on this score was, however, muted by a number of factors, especially (a) the relative popularity of the intervention in the early stages of the war, a popularity enhanced by the protective coloration afforded by significant United Nations participation; (b) the relative brevity of the intensely active phases, which lasted about one year and ended with the onset of armistice negotiations at Kaesong on July 10, 1951; and (c) the dramatic quality of the action during those active phases, with swiftly moving fronts that left no question at any time of how the war was going and, for that matter, why it was going the way it was. In these respects it differed markedly from the Vietnam War that was to follow; though after it entered the period of stagnation that coincided with the long drawn out armistice negotiations, public attitudes towards the war moved in a direction that anticipated the later war.

The prompt American intervention in the war that broke out on June 25, 1950 was not in response to any direct United States treaty obligation. President Truman's decision pleased but also surprised General MacArthur and those other senior American military officers stationed in Japan and in adjoining seas who were ordered to conduct the appropriate operations. It also followed by little more than five months a widely publicized speech at the National Press Club on January 12, 1950 by Secretary of State Dean Acheson, in which, with the prior approval of the Joint Chiefs and the President, he drew what he called the American "defense perimeter" in the Pacific along a line that left Korea clearly outside of it.[1]

Acheson was later to point out that the "defense perimeter" aspects of his speech had only echoed a speech that General MacArthur had given one year earlier, on March 1, 1949.[2] Indeed we know that it had long been axiomatic among the American military that the United States should not become involved in ground warfare on the Asian mainland. If the somewhat gratuitous declaration in the Acheson speech had any effect in triggering the aggression of the North Koreans and their sponsors, which quite possibly it did, the latter no doubt came to regard it as additional evidence of United States treachery and, in the peculiarly Communist sense of that term, *provocation*. Insofar as the American intervention was able to take on the attribute of being

---

[1] To save needless footnotes, we may point out here that almost all the speeches referred to in this chapter were reported, mostly in full, in the *New York Times*, usually on the date following the release or presentation of the speech. Those by the Secretary of State or the President will also normally be found in the *Department of State Bulletin* for the appropriate date, and repeated in part in their respective memoirs, cited below. In addition, many relevant letters, speeches, and other statements were reprinted or excerpted in vol. 5 of the Senate hearings on the MacArthur dismissal, the full title of which is given in footnote 11, this chapter.

[2] He quotes the relevant portions of the MacArthur speech as well as of his own, in his *Present at the Creation: My Years in the State Department* (New York: Norton, 1969), pp. 355–357.

a United Nations "police action," one needs to recall (a) that President Truman committed the United States to air and naval intervention *before* the U.N. Security Council was able to take any action,[3] and (b) that the June 27 decision of the Security Council supporting and implementing the American action was entirely adventitious. This was made possible by the fact that the Soviet delegate had, beginning in the previous January, deliberately absented himself in protest at the Chinese representation on the Council being of Nationalist rather than of Communist China. The one thing that can be said with certainty about such an event is that it was bound not to happen again.

An important lesson may be derived from our rushing in where we had said or implied we would not. It concerns the frequent inability of governments to predict, let alone guarantee, what their own behavior will be on important issues, in this instance as little as six months in advance. The reasons are several, but one is the tendency of people in office to use formulae rather than imaginative rumination in projecting their own behavior into the future. Emotions are not supposed to be considered, and it is not a normal human attribute to comprehend the true dimensions of uncertainty. President Truman and his Secretary of State had endorsed the well-known and obviously rational opposition of the military to becoming involved on mainland Asia. When the crisis came, all, including the military, immediately reversed their position. Apparently few had asked themselves: How will we *feel,* and how will we in consequence respond, if there is a flagrant attack upon this state and this government that we have ourselves set up and but recently withdrawn from on the now disproved

---

[3] The confusion on this score shown by some writers is due to a number of circumstances, including the fact that June 25 in Washington and New York was a day later than June 25 in Korea. Thus, the U.N. Security Council meeting of June 25 occurred the day after the attack. In announcing his decision to intervene with American air and sea power at noon on June 27, President Truman found it convenient to say that he was acting in support of the June 25 resolution of the Security Council, which in fact had not called for such action but had simply called upon North Korea to withdraw its forces and had invited members "to render every assistance to the United Nations in execution of this resolution and to refrain from giving assistance to the North Korean authorities." It was the Security Council resolution of the afternoon of June 27 that stated that "urgent military measures are required" and recommended that "Members of the United Nations furnish such assistance to the Republic of Korea as may be necessary to repel the armed attack and to restore international peace and security in the area." The text was identical with the draft resolution submitted by the American delegate. See *United Nations, Security Council, Official Records,* 473rd and 474th meetings; also, Raymond Dennett and Robert K. Turner (eds.), *Documents on American Foreign Relations,* vol. XII, 1950.

assumption that they were no longer in danger? Will we really stand by and let them go down?

This kind of issue arises again and again. What is predictable is that high government leaders will not usually ask themselves searching questions about what they will really do under a variety of circumstances, some of which will deeply engage their emotions. They are content to accept for themselves the facile assurances they give to others.[4]

Why We Entered the War

Why *did* President Truman decide that it was a responsibility of the United States to intervene in South Korea, first with air and naval power and almost immediately thereafter with ground forces as well? And why enter with such conclusiveness as to commit the United States not simply to the gesture of aiding South Korea but actually to the defeat of North Korean aggression? It could not have been because the Korean peninsula, being close to Japan, was thought to have special strategic significance; if it had been so regarded, Secretary Acheson would not have put that unfortunate remark in his speech. Acheson, incidentally, was among those who, upon the outbreak of hostilities, was all for intervention and encouraged the President in his relevant decisions.[5]

The reasons for our intervention were, in considerably more pristine form, much like those that some fifteen years later were to determine our intervention on a combat basis in Vietnam. In Korea the decision was made easier by the brusqueness and arro-

---

[4] Another example can be cited from my own experience. As a staff member of the RAND Corporation during the mid-1950s, I undertook to persuade officers of the U.S. Air Force that they could not rely upon President Eisenhower's assurance to the armed forces that in future military crises they could count on receiving his sanction to use nuclear weapons. However sincerely he meant it, I argued, the president of the day certainly lacked the freedom from other cares and possibly also the capacity really to think through (or to realize his own uncertainty about) his own behavior in various kinds of crisis situations that might arise in the future. The Air Force officers quite refused to believe this, partly because the President represented to them ultimate authority, but also because in this instance they *wanted* to believe the President's assurance. As a result the Air Force removed from its bombers all shackles for conventional bombs and thus deprived itself of a conventional bombing capability. Later events (that is, the Quemoy-Matsu and Lebanon crises of 1958), and then a new president caused the Air Force to restore the old bomb shackles. See on the Lebanon crisis Col. Albert P. Sights, Jr., "Lessons of Lebanon: A Study in Air Strategy," *Air University Review*, vol. 16 (July–August 1965), pp. 28–43, especially pp. 42 f.

[5] See Glenn D. Paige, *The Korean Decision, June 24–30, 1950* (New York: Free Press, 1968); Acheson, *Present at the Creation*, pp. 402–413; and Harry S Truman, *Memoirs, Vol. 2: Years of Trial and Hope, 1946–1952* (New York: Doubleday, 1956), p. 334.

gance of the North Korean attack, which among other things swept away all ambiguity about the fact of aggression and the identity of the aggressor, and which therefore helped make it possible for the United States to convert its intervention into a United Nations "police action"—a matter of great importance both abroad and within the United States. The basic reason is to be found in the attitude in this country that easily combined "containment" of Communism, regarded as especially an American obligation, with what Professor Arthur Schlesinger, Jr. was later to call "Stimsonianism," that is, the conviction that peace in the world is essentially indivisible. However, the indivisibility of the peace everywhere depended very much on *who* was breaking it somewhere. Communist aggression unquestionably rang bells of alarm that would not have been sounded by other kinds of aggressors.

As President Truman was later to put it in his radio address of April 11, 1951, explaining the relief of General MacArthur:

> If history has taught us anything, it is that aggression anywhere in the world is a threat to peace everywhere in the world. When that aggression is supported by the cruel and selfish rulers of a powerful nation who are bent on conquest, it becomes a clear and present danger to the security and independence of every free nation.

A conception so absolute and so far-reaching had to find its stimulus in experience that was both recent and deeply traumatic. World War II was the cataclysm that seemed to justify the principle, but its special application to the Soviet Union stemmed from later events. The outbreak of the war in Korea came less than a year after the signing of the North Atlantic Treaty, which had been a reaction to the "rape of Czechoslovakia" in 1948 and to the "blockade" of Berlin that had been defeated that same year. It was indeed the culmination of a long series of frustrating and unhappy events dating back at least to Stalin's deeply disturbing speech of February 9, 1946, when he had openly recommitted the Soviet Union to inexorable conflict with the capitalist West. It was, in short, the early flood tide of the cold war.

The conviction that the Soviet Union now had to be regarded as a powerful, unrelenting, and aggressive enemy, and that it was undoubtedly responsible for the brutal and cynical attack in

Korea that it proceeded at once to support, was at the time entertained unquestioningly and almost universally not only within the United States but elsewhere as well. A view similar to President Truman's had been expressed by Labour Prime Minister Clement Attlee in the House of Commons when the House greeted with cheers the announcement that the United States had decided to intervene in Korea.

There had to be, naturally, an additional supporting reason for the quick American intervention. Nations doubtful of their power, or sure of the lack of it, will sadly regret deplorable events abroad, but they will not take the lead in doing something about them. The United States, however, had very good reason, only recently confirmed in World War II, to consider itself a nation capable of extraordinary military feats, and North Korea looked puny by comparison. We were to learn more on that subject, especially some years later in Vietnam.

The First Modern Limited War

The United States *backed* into a limited war in Korea, because the kind of doctrine about limited war that is so completely familiar today not only did not then exist but would have been utterly incomprehensible. Public discussion of and rumination upon limited war did not begin until about 1954.[6] The prevailing axiom among the American military at the time the Korean War began, existing since World War I and reinforced by World War II, was: "Modern war is total war!" This doctrine actually persisted in full force throughout the period of most active fighting in Korea, and for one very good reason. The Joint Chiefs in Washington were utterly convinced that the Russians were using Korea as a feint to cause us to deploy our forces there while they prepared to launch a "general" (total) war against the United States through a major attack in Europe. In early December 1950, they were actually persuaded—for reasons that may some day be revealed and thus enlighten us further about the dangerous extravagances in intelligence analysis that derive from the *idée fixe*

---

[6] The best available discussion of the development of limited war doctrine in the 1950s, based entirely on openly published materials, is offered in Morton Halperin's *Limited War: An Essay on the Development of the Theory and an Annotated Bibliography* (Cambridge: Harvard Center for International Affairs, Occasional Paper No. 3, May 1962).

—that a Soviet initiation of a general war was only two or three weeks away![7]

There were other reasons, subsidiary to the major one just mentioned, why the United States chose a limited form of engagement, mostly having to do with attitudes towards the American nuclear stockpile. What was limited about the United States military effort in Korea was mainly the nonuse of nuclear weapons, and it should be remembered that at that time there was (in Thomas C. Schelling's phrase) no "tradition of non-use" of such weapons. It was only five years since we had used the only two nuclear weapons then existing.

The reasons why nuclear weapons were not used in Korea seem to have been, in descending order of importance:

1. The stockpile was limited, and earmarked entirely for the European theatre, especially the Soviet Union. Production had been remarkably low-keyed before the Korean War, largely for reasons of economy,[8] and the United States had accumulated only about three hundred fission bombs, each having a yield roughly twice that of the 20 kiloton bomb used at Nagasaki. The fear of imminent major war in Europe was quite enough to keep this scarce and terribly important military resource untouched.

2. The U.S. Joint Chiefs generally concurred with the view of General Curtis LeMay, then commanding officer of the Strategic Air Command (SAC), that the one appropriate purpose for the still very limited United States nuclear stockpile was strategic bombing. The Chiefs earmarked a miniscule portion of that stock-

---

[7] The intensity of that fear during the first week of December 1950, and the measures of readiness taken with respect especially to the Mediterranean Fleet, were first publicly disclosed at the end of May 1951 by Admiral Forrest P. Sherman, Chief of Naval Operations, in his testimony before the Senate hearings on the MacArthur case. However, though this testimony was published verbatim in the *New York Times* (May 31 and June 1, 1951), it was omitted from the published version of the hearings! At the time of greatest fear this writer happened to be working as Special Assistant to the Air Force Chief of Staff, the late General Hoyt. S. Vandenberg, and was aware of that officer's intense anxiety.

[8] The Atomic Energy Commission was apparently concerned lest a fast rate of production should cause too heavy a demand on supplies of uranium ore and thus push up its price! This exemplified the antithesis of systems-analysis thinking. The cost of the raw materials represented a small fraction of the cost of the finished bomb, and the cost of the latter was a small fraction of the cost of delivering a bomb to target, besides which the nuclear bomb represented the only real capability we then had for curbing the aggressive designs we were so ready to attribute to the Soviet Union. As it happened, the high price of uranium ore stimulated a vast prospecting effort that resulted in large supplies being discovered within the United States, especially in southern Utah, as well as elsewhere in the world.

pile to interdiction targets *in Europe*, but Air Force officers generally scoffed at the idea of using such weapons tactically. Army officers were less skeptical of the tactical utility of nuclear weapons, but were not in a position to press their views. They shared completely the fear of the imminent general war.

3. Our U.N. allies, especially the British, did not wish to see nuclear weapons used in Korea. When President Truman in December 1950 casually remarked, in answer to a question at a press conference, that of course the United States was giving consideration to the use of nuclear weapons, just as it was giving consideration to all sorts of possibilities, Prime Minister Attlee rushed to Washington to dissuade him.[9] No doubt this anxiety refortified existing American misgivings, which should not be underestimated, about using the bomb. However, in the absence of the other factors described above it would probably not have been effective. Insofar as it was supposed to be a United Nations action, the United States was carrying a hugely disproportionate share of the burden of the war and of the casualties. In the first weeks of the war, and again in November-December 1950, our military position had approached desperation.

4. The Soviet Union had tested its first nuclear device in October 1949, and although the chances of the retaliatory use of one or more Soviet-made weapons at a place like Pusan were extremely slight, they were nevertheless considered to be no longer quite zero. On the other hand, it is again doubtful that these Soviet capabilities, trivial at most, would have been sufficient in themselves to deter our use of nuclear bombs.

5. There was even talk at the time about the racist overtones of our using nuclear weapons against Koreans and Chinese, in addition to having already used them against their racial brothers, the Japanese, but not against the Germans. It is not likely that this consideration really affected Administration decisions. Still, governments do like to appear sophisticated in the refinements of their policies, even when the basic decisions are of the most simplistic sort.

Whether or not it was a "good thing" that the United States refrained from using nuclear weapons in Korea is a question to which the answer is not readily obvious. It is not really separable from the question whether it was correct policy for the United

---

[9] The conversations with Attlee are well described in Acheson, *Present at the Creation*, 478–485; and Truman, *Memoirs*, 2, pp. 395–413.

States to intervene in Korea at all. If it was correct policy to intervene, then one has to accept what is generally called "philosophically" the loss of almost 34,000 American lives plus more than ten times that number of Korean lives, and much other suffering and bitterness from the prolongation of the war, to conclude without question that we were "right" not to use nuclear weapons. That is assuming, as there is good reason for assuming, that use of nuclear weapons tactically would have enormously shortened the war and probably forestalled Chinese intervention. However, this question is so large and so important that we must give it separate treatment in a later chapter.

Another important kind of self-imposed restraint practiced in the Korean War (and later again in Vietnam) was that which revived the ancient term *sanctuary*, and which applied to a practice conspicuous on the part at least of the United States. The term as used today may indicate the avoidance of all kinds of attack upon specific enemy-held areas, or it may apply to the withholding of ground forces from such areas while not sparing them air or naval bombardment. But whether the sanctuary be partial or complete, it designates an area or region enjoying specially favored treatment in view of the belligerent status of its occupiers. In the Korean War, all of China throughout the whole period of fighting was accorded complete sanctuary privilege by the United States, despite the huge intervention of the Communist Chinese armies. American military aircraft were severely enjoined not to let any bombs fall on the north side of the center channel of the Yalu River, even when bridges on the river itself were to be attacked.[10]

It is not at all clear that the enemy accorded us similar sanctuary privileges on a tacit *quid pro quo* basis, though many quite knowledgeable Americans were entirely persuaded that they did. Our tactical airfields were never struck, nor were our aircraft carriers ever brought under attack either by aircraft or submarines. However, it appears likely that this immunity simply reflected awareness by the enemy of his insufficient capabilities. Considering the hugely disproportionate losses their inadequately trained pilots in Russian-built fighter aircraft suffered in aerial combat with American fighters (on the order of twelve or fourteen to

---

10 This provision was in accord with the well-established principle in international law that wherever a river forms the boundary between two states, the exact line of division runs along the center of the navigable channel of the river.

one), they must surely have considered it prohibitively costly to attempt to raid American tactical airfields protected with radar warning. Aerial attacks upon our naval vessels, especially carriers, would have presented still greater risks. An effective submarine attack upon those vessels could not have been carried out except by the Russians, who would thereby have demonstrated their direct participation—something they appeared most anxious to avoid. Thus, in the Korean War, and even more clearly in the Vietnam War, the granting of sanctuary privilege seems to have been a unilateral practice of the United States. This does not, of course, establish it as an error.

The principle of sanctuary is a vital one in the whole concept of limited war. Nevertheless, it is too easy to gloss over the heavy military disadvantage that may result from applying it as we did in Korea and even more so in Vietnam. One major dilemma is pointed up by the question: If the enemy is already doing virtually all he *can* do against us, what kind of sanctuary does it make sense to grant him and why? One major reason might be to induce the enemy to do likewise, that is, to make some comparable gesture of restraint, perhaps as a token of willingness to cooperate in winding down the war. A second reason might be that we grant him sanctuary because we wish not to provoke his powerful ally to come to his assistance or to increase the assistance already being given.

The first reason would normally demand some visible *quid pro quo*, which when forthcoming might be adequate payoff for the restraint. If it is not forthcoming, the sanctuary privilege could presumably be withdrawn. The second motivation for granting sanctuary, however, seems to indicate a condition beyond the control of the belligerent who does so. He may be giving up a large military advantage, and he does not know whether he is getting anything in return. The enemy's ally, the feared nonbelligerent, can gain great advantages for his partner by merely making occasional menacing noises. He may have neither the capability nor the desire to do or risk anything more under any circumstances. And the sanctuary granted out of this kind of concern or fear is logically irrevocable—unless the formerly quiescent partner makes a full scale commitment to the war.

Specifically, in the Korean War, after the Chinese entered in full force, what did we gain by scrupulously avoiding hitting any interdiction targets, that is, channels of reinforcement or supply, within Chinese territory? Did it make the Chinese less ill-disposed towards us, or less ready to fight to the limits of their logistic capabilities? Did it keep the Russians from coming in more overtly on the Chinese side? Probably not, but there was certainly a great fear in Washington of what the Russians might do, not so much in eastern Asia as elsewhere.

To be sure, any general interdiction campaign might have been a failure. There is always the question whether we are really giving up something militarily substantial by our caution. Also, the U.S. Air Force was generally far less interested in interdiction than in strategic bombing, and there were important reasons for the Joint Chiefs as a body maintaining tight control from Washington of the target categories of all our Far East air power.[11] Nevertheless, it was certainly important if not vital to knock out at least the bridges across the Yalu as soon as we saw that China had committed large forces to the war. Yet the strict prohibition of bombing of *any* Chinese territory, which included about half the length of each bridge, made for totally ineffective bombing of those bridges. Less important but easily within sight from the air space above those bridges were tactical airfields from which Chinese and North Korean aircraft regularly made their sorties. Restraint in the use of force is, under a wide spectrum of circumstances, a most commendable inclination, but, like other virtues, it can go to excess.

[11] Since well before World War II the U.S. Air Force had been doctrinally wedded to Douhet's hierarchy of values concerning the three categories of bombing. To "understand airpower" was to place an almost exclusive emphasis on strategic bombing. Interdiction bombing was in second place but far down the course, and close-support bombing was hardly worth the attentions of a first-rate air force, inasmuch as it fulfilled functions best left to the artillery. The latter two categories, it may be noticed, are always in support of ground forces while the first is "independent." In his testimony before the Senate hearings on the MacArthur dismissal, the Chief of Staff of the Air Force, General Hoyt S. Vandenberg, exposed the hold of this orthodoxy on his thinking even while explaining why MacArthur's desire to bomb China did not make strategic sense. To "lay waste all of Manchuria and the principal cities of China" would do no good because it was Russia and not China that was the major source of the war material used by the Communists in Korea. And the "shoe-string air force" that the United States then had (the bomber force) must be kept intact for the greater threat—from Russia. To use bombers for selected interdiction targets in China or on its frontiers was presumably to risk scarce and high-value military means for low-value targets. The Air Force did in fact engage in interdiction and even close-support bombing within Korea, but almost entirely with smaller aircraft. For General Vandenberg's testimony, see *Hearings Before the Committee on Armed Services and the Committee on Foreign Relations, United States Senate, 82nd Congress, 1st Session: To Conduct an Inquiry into the Military Situation in the Far East and the Facts Surrounding the Relief of General of the Army Douglas MacArthur from his Assignments in That Area*, part 2, pp. 1375–1406, 1408–1506, hereafter in this chapter referred to as the *MacArthur Hearings*.

It is necessary to clarify these issues. Restraint as a demonstration of "goodwill" to the opponent is preposterous when we are at war with him and killing his people. It may be a manifestation of "good faith" connected directly with some ongoing negotiation, but in such instances it should normally be conditioned upon visible reciprocity. Where, however, it is applied as a permanent condition regardless of enemy responses, we have to be clearly aware that it may be costing us a great deal in military effectiveness—hence also in casualties to our own and friendly troops. When General MacArthur learned that even after the massive intervention of Chinese forces in November 1950 our aircraft were kept under strict orders not to drop bombs one foot within Chinese territory, he recommended that Washington consider total evacuation from Korea. It may well have been a loss of nerves in the face of humiliating and costly defeats, or it may have been a soldier's simple judgment that this was carrying restraint too far. It was quite probably some of both.[12]

Strategic generalizations are helpful for particular situations only if they help prepare our minds to find the particular solutions that are right for those situations. It is the same in strategy as Justice Holmes said of the law: "General propositions do not decide concrete cases." That restraints may be dictated by valid political considerations is truistic, though insisting upon the point serves to prepare our commanders in the field for what may be to them onerous orders. Only slightly less truistic, but obviously neglected, is the admonition that to give advance consideration to the cost in military effectiveness of a particular kind of restraint may save the government from making a hopeless or unduly costly commitment of forces. The consciousness of being a great power may impel us to moves that we then proceed to disable ourselves from executing like a great power. The restraints may in specific instances be excessive, but it is also likely that the intervention that has to bear such critical restraints was wrong in the

---

12 When in reply to the Joint Chiefs' directive of December 29, 1950 MacArthur referred to the bad morale of his troops, General George C. Marshall, then Secretary of Defense, remarked to Dean Rusk that when a general complains of the morale of his troops, the time has come to look into his own. Acheson, *Present at the Creation*, p. 515. There is no doubt that MacArthur was severely shaken emotionally by the defeats in the northern provinces that had so exposed his own fallibility, and it is likely that his initial references to the possible necessity of evacuation from Korea were mostly a reflection of the state of his nerves. On the other hand, as the weeks went by and he continued to insist on the probable necessity of evacuation unless his demands were met, his motivation seemed to become more and more one of exerting pressure on Washington in order to get his way.

first place. Naturally, if the intervention was wrong, the practice of restraints will not make it right, though they may provide a saving grace for what would otherwise be a totally atrocious performance.

The War Aims

The war aims of the United States in Korea have to be considered in both general and specific terms. In general terms they were, as already indicated, covered by two slogans, which despite ambiguities carried powerful emotional charges: (a) we must contain Communism, and (b) we must oppose or resist aggression occurring anywhere. The latter notion—derived from the ideology of League of Nations days and strongly enforced by the experiences leading up to World War II, especially the futility of the "sell-out" or appeasement at Munich—was, as we have seen, powerfully refortified by the former. The idea had to be still quite new in 1950 that the central issue around which American foreign policy must revolve was resistance to the spread of Communism. Nevertheless, it was already a virtually undisputed article of faith among those who managed American foreign policy. Naturally, once the United States fully committed herself to the defense of South Korea, the latter also became a client state entitled to very special benefits, and the entire military prestige of the "leader of the free world" was on the line.

In specific terms, the issue came to center around the following question: Should the United States, acting also for the United Nations, settle for the restoration of a boundary line at or near the 38th parallel, that is for the *status quo ante bellum*, or should it reunify Korea under a non-Communist regime with its northern boundary at the Yalu? The latter goal could be justified under the slogan that "resistance to aggression" was better served if it meant also "punishment of aggression," and punishment required something beyond the mere frustration of an offensive. It also seemed to make sense to cancel out the situation that had caused the war.

After General MacArthur's brilliant Inchon landing of mid-September 1950, which rolled up the entire enemy line and sent the surviving fragments of the North Korean army into a headlong retreat tantamount to flight, President Truman and his advisors slipped somewhat uneasily into concurrence with MacArthur's view that the forces led by the United States should ignore the former status of the 38th parallel and proceed on to the Yalu.[13] The time accorded them for deciding on this radical change in policy was exceedingly short, not more than two or three weeks, and it had to be made during a period of enormous euphoria at the dramatic reversal in our military fortunes. Where we had earlier been hanging on by our fingernails at Pusan, now suddenly the enemy army had been virtually destroyed, with its remnants offering no significant resistance to our northward push. We had indeed, once again, proved to ourselves and to the world what a great military power was the United States. Still, there were misgivings.

The instructions sent to MacArthur via the Joint Chiefs on September 27 declared that his objective should be "the destruction of the North Korean Armed Forces." To attain this objective he was authorized "to conduct military operations . . . north of the 38th parallel in Korea, provided that at the time of such operations there has been no entry into North Korea by major Soviet or Chinese Communist Forces, no announcement of intended entry, nor a threat to counter your operations militarily in North Korea." He was most strongly enjoined against any kind of military operations against the Chinese or Soviet territories beyond Korea. It was also stipulated "as a matter of policy," that, as he approached the boundary between Korea and China, he should use only Korean forces. Thus we see that the whole tone of the instructions indicated a restrictive interpretation of the permission granted him to proceed north. They also included the request that he "submit [his] plan for future operations north of the 38th parallel to the JCS for approval." [14]

The latter request MacArthur fulfilled promptly, but the force of making it was somewhat tempered by what seems to have been a simple gesture of personal consideration (and fraternal military feeling towards a very senior commander) on the part of General George C. Marshall, who had been recalled from retirement, after having served as Secretary of State, to replace Louis Johnson as Secretary of Defense. On September 29, the same day on which MacArthur's plan was approved, General Marshall addressed an "eyes only" telegram to MacArthur saying "We want you to feel

---

[13] See especially General J. Lawton Collins, *War in Peacetime: The History and Lessons of Korea* (Boston: Houghton Mifflin, 1969), pp. 155 ff.
[14] Acheson, *Present at the Creation*, pp. 451–455.

unhampered tactically and strategically to proceed north of the 38th parallel." No one would have been less likely than Marshall to suggest a contravention of the approved instructions. He no doubt desired simply to sooth the imperious MacArthur's sensibilities at being asked to submit his plan for the approval of the Joint Chiefs, whom MacArthur must have regarded as being very much his juniors in age, rank, and experience, and certainly his inferiors in talent. This telegram was later to cause trouble. MacArthur mentioned it in his defense, not for the last time, when questioned about his orders to his commanders on October 24. Upon arrival close to the northern borders of Korea, they were ordered to "drive forward with all speed and full utilization of [their] forces," in direct disregard of that part of his instructions stipulating that "only Korean forces" be used in the border provinces.

Meanwhile, on October 7 the United Nations, acting now through the General Assembly instead of the Security Council, passed a resolution that in effect approved the decisions made in Washington. The stated object was to achieve conditions "insuring conditions of tranquility throughout the country" and subsequently permitting the holding of elections under U.N. auspices. Dean Acheson considered that this resolution simply "revived the dormant United Nations plan of 1947." He felt, though it is a little difficult to see just why, that MacArthur immediately exceeded the intentions of the resolution, while using its authority, in broadcasting a new surrender demand to the North Korean forces.

Some cautioning voices were raised in Washington against attempting to go too far in Korea, including that of George Kennan. The original author of the term *containment*, Kennan had by now amply demonstrated his extraordinary gift for prophetic insight. Our action in Korea had been right, he said in a memorandum to Secretary of State Acheson, because the aggression had to be defeated and discredited. But he was disturbed at the emotional and moralistic conclusions that were being drawn from this fact. Still, one must notice that the memorandum warned not against a Chinese reaction but against a Russian one.[15]

Actually, the spirit of one crucial part of the September 27 in-

---

[15] Ibid., pp. 445 f.

structions seems to have been violated most of all in Washington. Approval of operations north of the 38th parallel had been made contingent upon there being at the time of such operations, no entry or "announcement of intended entry" by the Soviet or Chinese Communist Forces. After the Inchon landings, however, Chou En-lai, Foreign Minister of Communist China, proceeded to give precisely such an announcement of intended entry. On October 3 he called in the Indian Ambassador, K. M. Panikkar, and informed him that if American troops crossed the parallel China would enter the war. Acheson in his memoirs makes the following remarkable statement: "Chou's words were a warning, not to be disregarded, but, on the other hand, not an authoritative statement of policy." [16] What, indeed, would have been an authoritative statement of policy? Lieutenant General Walton Walker leading the Eighth Army in Korea took Chou's words very seriously, but he could be only as cautious as MacArthur permitted him to be.

President Truman reveals in his own memoirs that Chou's statement was partly responsible for his decision early in October to meet General MacArthur on Wake Island in the middle of that month and have a "heart-to-heart talk" about prospects in Korea.[17] At this meeting MacArthur, when asked by the President of the possibility of a Communist Chinese intervention, gave the following unfortunate reply:

> Very little. Had they interfered in the first or second months it would have been decisive. We are no longer fearful of their intervention. We no longer stand hat in hand. The Chinese have 300,000 men in Manchuria. Of these probably not more than 100–125,000 are distributed along the Yalu River. They have no air force. Now that we have bases for our Air Force in Korea, if the Chinese tried to get down to Pyongyang there would be the greatest slaughter.

He also told the President that he expected North Korean resis-

---

16 Ibid., p. 452; see also Robert Leckie, *Conflict: The History of the Korean War* (New York: Putnam, 1962), pp. 162–165. Leckie's is probably the best one-volume account available on the subject. His book also includes (pp. 431–434) an excellent bibliography of works on the Korean War published prior to the date of his own publication. A somewhat later work, equally useful and authoritative, is David Rees, *Korea: The Limited War* (London: Macmillan, 1964; reissued by Penguin Books, 1970).

17 Truman, *Memoirs*, 2, p. 363.

tance to end by Thanksgiving and that it was his hope "to be able to withdraw the Eighth Army to Japan by Christmas."

It must be said that Truman did have means for an independent judgment, which on this occasion he did not exercise. The General's self-confidence and enthusiasm were now at flood tide, as a result no doubt of his truly fabulous success at Inchon. Truman cannot be blamed for stifling his doubts and going along with one so successful and so glowingly confident. Still, the difference in accomplishment between an excellent president and a great one—and, in the case of another president some fifteen years later, between extraordinary success and dismal failure—may lie in knowing when not to believe a general.

On October 25, some leading South Korean and United States forces encountered large concentrations of Chinese troops, and in the next six days of fighting the South Korean II Corps completely collapsed; among U.S. forces the 1st Cavalry and the 2nd Division were badly mauled. Also, on November 1 the first MIG-15 jets appeared in the skies over Korea. These events ought to have established the presence of large Chinese forces south of the Yalu, but something seems to have remained in doubt. As late as November 4 General MacArthur, responding to the President's request for more information, sent an evaluation intended to calm him and warning against "hasty conclusions which might be premature." However, on the next day MacArthur ordered his Air Force commander, General George E. Stratemeyer, to hurl continuing sorties, flying the crews "to exhaustion if necessary," against the North Korean forces "and their allies," *to knock them out of the war.* Among the objectives designated for Stratemeyer was that he take out all the Yalu bridges.

An information copy of this order went back to Washington, where it caused another severe disturbance. Only twelve days earlier the Joint Chiefs had eased the restrictions on the U.S. Fifth Air Force to allow bombing up to five miles from the border. When Washington intervened to remind him of the five-mile restriction, MacArthur cabled back: "Men and material in large force are pouring across all bridges over the Yalu from Manchuria. This movement not only jeopardizes but threatens the ultimate destruction of the forces under my command. . . ."

This plea gained MacArthur permission to bomb only the Korean ends of the Yalu bridges, the bombers involved being confined strictly to the air space over Korean territory. Such an order was a military impossibility, and, in Stratemeyer's view, must have been known in Washington to be such.[18]

MacArthur throughout this period revealed to the full his peculiarly mecurial temperament, sending a stream of messages that alternated between deep alarm and high confidence. However, his dispositions during this period reflected only the latter mood. The man who had insisted on going forward with the Inchon landing despite his own assertion that the odds were "five thousand to one" against his success—a mark only of the MacArthur flamboyance, for if that evaluation had been even remotely correct the act would have been sheer idiocy—now decided to continue moving all his forces northward. Yet he was completely ignorant of the position of the Chinese forces. After their initial heavy and highly successful fighting with the U.N. groups they had on November 6 and 7 broken contact and disappeared.

MacArthur now had to determine what they were up to. Certainly any sober consideration of the range of possibilities would have had to include the likelihood that the number of Chinese troops in Korea was rapidly growing. The bridges over the Yalu were intact, and the Chinese could without difficulty be pouring across them at night—which is indeed what they were doing. These were troops skilled in concealment, accustomed to long night marches, and they had already demonstrated their remarkable capabilities in these respects by starting forest fires to conceal with smoke their initial penetrations into Korea.

MacArthur, however, after recovering from the shock and gloom occasioned by the recent reverses, apparently reverted to his earlier conviction. That his prediction to the President could

---

[18] Bridges were at best difficult to take out with pre-1970 conventional bombs. From the air a bridge represents an exceedingly narrow target, and because of its strong structure it must be dealt direct hits with heavy bombs. Important bridges will usually be well protected by anti-aircraft weapons, as were the Yalu bridges at the time of the Chinese intervention. Under Korean War conditions this meant forcing the bombers up to altitudes of at least 18,000 feet, and from this altitude strong winds will greatly affect the bomb trajectory and thus reduce accuracy. The order from Washington to bomb only the southern portions of the bridges was a military impossibility for at least two reasons: (a) under the conditions imposed, bombing could not be accurate enough to assure that bombs aimed at the bridge could be confined to the permissible portion, and (b) because of the bridge's profile as a target, bombing runs must usually be along the length of the bridge rather than cross-wise, but a length-wise run would greatly increase the chances of bombs falling on proscribed portions. Also, the order required that "extreme care be taken to avoid violation of Manchurian territory *and air space* [italics added]," thus prohibiting a length-wise run and making *any* bombing of the bridges impossible so long as the wind was from a northerly quadrant.

have been basically wrong was a realization not yet possible for him. The Chinese were indeed committing troops to Korea, but he seemed to feel that their numbers had to be limited by both caution and logistic restraints. His intelligence officer, Major General Charles Willoughby, responsive as MacArthur staff members were ever wont to be to the moods of their chief, accommodated him by estimating 60,000–70,000 Chinese "volunteers" in Korea—thus adopting the term that the Chinese government had used in acknowledging on November 7 the presence of some of its troops in Korea. The number of Chinese actually present at the time of Willoughby's estimate was about 300,000, and far from being volunteers they were there in organized divisions from the best field armies in China—a tough veteran force "with a tradition of victory."

MacArthur's forces were in two main bodies, the larger being the Eighth Army under General Walker, and to the east of it, separated by a high mountain ridge, was the independent X Corps under Lieutenant General Edward M. Almond, with various allied contingents distributed among them. Moreover, each major grouping was perforce divided into several columns committed to the roadways in order to achieve maximum speed of movement. Among the senior officers conducting these operations, several besides General Walker had the most intense misgivings. What could have been in MacArthur's mind we cannot quite know; his own subsequent explanations simply do not accord with the facts.[19] It was most likely the idea that the sooner he reached the bridges of the Yalu the sooner would his victory be conclusive and thus further impress the Chinese, and the more quickly he would be able to stop the flow of any new forces that might attempt crossing the river and to cut off and encapsulate whatever Chinese contingents had already entered Korea. The latter could then be destroyed at leisure.

On November 17, MacArthur cabled the Joint Chiefs that he would launch a general offensive on November 24 to reach the line of the Yalu. He was pushing the odds again, but this time his luck had run out. The Chinese in Korea had other plans, and

---

[19] General MacArthur later tried to describe his advance to the Yalu as "a reconnaissance in force," and his aide, Major General Courtney Whitney, described it as a spoiling attack, designed to reach up and spring "the Red trap." Neither explanation is compatible with the orders issued by MacArthur at the time and especially with the fact that it was the whole of the United Nations forces that were making a headlong movement northward. See Leckie, *Conflict*, pp. 232 f.

they were then already superior in numbers to the whole of the United Nations ground forces. In this mountainous terrain, they had taken to the hills alongside the roads, preparing a perfect ambush for the American and allied forces moving up those roads. On the day after MacArthur began his offensive, they struck.

The ensuing fighting was not, as some have made out, the worst disaster that has ever overtaken American arms.[20] Pearl Harbor still has that distinction. But it was bitter in the extreme. In this high northern plateau, winter cold and winds had already descended upon the battlefields, with temperatures as low as 30 below zero. It was under such conditions, with aggressive, well-trained enemy troops exploding all around them, that our forces with their allied contingents fought desperately to escape entrapment and destruction. This they mostly managed to accomplish, though at heavy cost. After running a gantlet of ambushes, they escaped to the south, badly hurt and defeated, but not broken. They were able to make their swift and long retreat as organized forces. However, General MacArthur had provided one more historical proof that admirable boldness in a commander is distinguishable from gross incaution and self-deception mostly by the results. On November 28, when he cabled the famous estimate that began: "We face an entirely new war," the situation was more changed than he knew.

It is not our purpose here to summarize the military events of the Korean or any other war. The military historians have done their work well. However, it is necessary to establish the military background for the mood or moods that prevailed in Washington from then on to the end of the war and that accounted for the immediate restructuring of our war aims. It is also worthwhile indicating that MacArthur's subsequent dismissal, though it was in no way provoked by the military defeat in the north, would have been justified on that ground alone. An overweening, bombastic, and arrogant man, brilliant but also intensely narcissistic, he had unnecessarily converted a triumph—his own triumph, it must be acknowledged—into a disaster. In so doing he had stretched or disobeyed his orders. He had misled the President and himself about the likelihood of Chinese intervention, and when that intervention became plain for all to see he attempted after the first

[20] It is so described in S. L. A. Marshall's excellent and detailed account, *The River and the Gauntlet, Defeat of the Eighth Army by the Chinese Communist Forces* (New York: Morrow, 1956).

shock to make it conform to his preconceptions, trusting to his star as a guide to his action. It is an old and good rule that, regardless of previous performance, generals who err so badly usually have to be replaced.[21]

He had been created a hero by President Roosevelt in 1941 when the country desperately needed one, and he did indeed have the qualities to enable him to play the part well, including a flair for the theatrical and an intense concern with public relations.[22] His role in World War II can hardly be summed up in a sentence, but was no doubt in the net commendable. His role as the head of the occupation of Japan has been unconscionably inflated. He had at no time been indispensable, as General U. S. Grant had been indispensable when Lincoln chose him to lead the federal armies or as General Dwight D. Eisenhower had been indispensable, in a very different way, in leading what was quintessentially an allied enterprise.[23] On the contrary, it was clear at the beginning of December 1950 that he had cost the country and the forces under his

---

[21] Among the reasons that usually justify such action are the following: (a) the defeat or failure may expose the general as being incompetent, or at least less competent than previously supposed; (b) it may result in a serious loss of confidence in his leadership among the troops; and (c) the general himself is affected by his disaster, so that he either loses confidence in himself, tries to find scapegoats, or seeks in his subsequent actions to find justification for his failure. It is (c) that appears especially applicable to MacArthur. If left to his own devices, he would hardly have attempted the counteroffensive launched by Ridgway in mid-January, the successes of which he seemed, in his public statements, not to accept too graciously. They did, after all, contradict all his basic arguments of the preceding six weeks. There was clearly no diminution in the morale of the Eighth Army as a result of MacArthur's relief. One wishes always to spare the feelings of any senior officer, but the cost may very easily go too high.

[22] Many generals are given to hyperbole in their communiqués, especially when announcing victories, but MacArthur's hyperbole was always in a class by itself. See, among numerous possible examples, his special communiqué of November 6, 1950, in which he announces the intervention of the Communist Chinese as a kind of postscript to a claim that the Korean War has been "brought to a practical end with the closing of the trap on enemy elements north of Pyongyang," and that "the defeat of the North Koreans and destruction of their armies was thereby decisive." Quoted in Leckie, *Conflict*, p. 181. See also Richard H. Rovere and Arthur M. Schlesinger, Jr., *The General and the President, and the Future of American Foreign Policy* (New York: Farrar, Straus and Young, 1951).

[23] Concerning General Eisenhower, I was brought to this conclusion, somewhat surprising to myself, in reviewing some years ago the diaries of Field Marshal Lord Alanbrooke, Chief of the Imperial General Staff during the latter part of World War II. If the supreme commander of the combined British-American forces in Europe had been British, it would almost certainly have been Alanbrooke, and he bitterly resented the fact that the choice had gone to an American. His diaries prove how ill-suited he would have been for that command, partly because of his habitual pessimism but mostly because of his intensely nationalistic jealousies and dislikes. It also seems clear that on the American side there was no one of sufficiently elevated rank better suited than Eisenhower to command British as well as American armies. See Arthur Bryant, *The Turn of the Tide, 1939–1943*, and *Triumph in the West 1943–1946, Based on the Diaries of Field Marshal Viscount Alanbrooke* (London: Collins, 1957 and 1959).

command more than he was worth militarily, even if he had refrained from the intolerable political maneuvers that finally obliged the President to replace him.

This needs saying because the ubiquitous refrain from some quarters in times of war crisis that "the military know best" naturally rose to a shriek when the military man concerned was the much-authenticated hero MacArthur, and when a president as unpopular in those same quarters as Truman had the gall to fire him. Even real geniuses are often in some way deeply flawed, sometimes in a manner that directly impairs their effectiveness; and if MacArthur was indeed a military genius, which is quite possible, his flaws were of the deepest, and to any discerning man obvious. It is essential, but also probably sufficient, for military leaders to be competent. When they win great national acclaim they tend to become high risks, possibly difficult to control and certainly difficult to replace.

By mid-December our forces were back below the 38th parallel, where they established a new line that few felt they could hold. Meanwhile, in Washington the fear of the aggressive designs of the Soviet Union had been reaching its apex. By early December the Joint Chiefs had convinced themselves that an outbreak of general war in Europe was both probable and imminent. No doubt the fact that China, then closely allied to Russia, had dared to engage the United States in war greatly contributed to that fear. In any case it created in Washington, and most especially and profoundly in the Pentagon, an atmosphere of gloom and foreboding. The Joint Chiefs had already raised on December 3 the question of requesting a cease fire, with all its implications of surrender and withdrawal. General J. Lawton Collins, Army Chief of Staff, who had been dispatched to Tokyo to confer with MacArthur, sent back in his first report the dismal intelligence that MacArthur felt he would have to evacuate his forces unless conditions were met that no one in Washington had any intention of meeting. The conditions were very heavy reinforcements, including the troops offered by Chiang Kai-Shek some months earlier, and the blockade and unrestricted bombing of China, probably supported by some use of nuclear weapons in North Korea. At just this time Prime Minister Attlee made his visit to Washington and added his voice to those counseling a cease fire.[24]

While staunchly rejecting this advice, President Truman and

---

[24] The Attlee visit is well described in Acheson, *Present at the Creation*, pp. 478–485; also Truman, *Memoirs, 2*, pp. 394–413.

his closest adviser, Acheson, nevertheless automatically and totally revamped their war objectives for Korea. Acheson and his State Department aides considered exaggerated the dejection of the military, and clearly did not share their fear that general war with the Soviet Union was impending. These views they must have communicated to the President. Nevertheless, there was no going back to the attitudes of late September and October. From then on any settlement that approached the *status quo ante bellum* would be quite good enough. And, as often happens in these matters, this attitude was to survive changes in circumstance that might have well prompted a reconsideration.

With a new Chinese offensive launched on January 1, 1951, our line in Korea continued to be pushed back, though more slowly, to where on January 15 it lay some distance below Seoul and nearby Inchon. This was still considerably north of the Pusan perimeter from which the U.N. forces had broken out only three months earlier, and it was to be the end of the retreat. Ten days later, on January 25, Lieutenant General Matthew Ridgway—who had been sent out from Washington to replace General Walker as commander of the Eighth Army when the latter was killed in a road accident—felt strong enough, after his own personal aerial survey of the battlefield ahead, to begin a counteroffensive.

The ensuing fighting was not without some serious Communist counterstrokes. Nevertheless, by mid-February the Chinese and North Koreans were in full retreat, and by the end of the month had been ousted from all their positions south of the Han River. Now United Nations soldiers began, as Robert Leckie puts it:

> to find evidence of how cruelly the winter and American firepower had treated the armies of Red China. The hills were littered with their dead; shallow mass graves were uncovered everywhere around Wonju and Chechon. The People's Volunteers who had been fresh and strong and close to home when they attacked the Eighth Army in the hills near Manchuria, had not been able to withstand the climate and the failures of a supply line running back 260 miles to the Yalu. Many of these dead had perished of cold or hunger, or of inadequate treatment for their wounds.[25]

A further offensive begun by Ridgway on March 7 achieved quick success. Seoul, the capital, changed hands for the fourth

---

[25] Leckie, *Conflict*, p. 261.

time, and by the end of the month United Nations forces were back along the 38th parallel and preparing to cross it a second time. The object now was not to try to unify Korea following a complete victory but rather to keep up pressure on the Chinese in order to prevent them from organizing a new offensive and also to force them to negotiate. At least, that was Washington's intention and also that of Ridgway, who, though now under MacArthur's orders, had sat in on White House conferences during the darkest days of the defeats in the north. He was known not to have unlimited appreciation for MacArthur's methods, and this could have played a part in his being chosen to replace Walker.[26] Naturally, as a subordinate to MacArthur he had obvious limitations on his freedom of action, but his mind was nevertheless attuned to the considerations current in Washington rather than to those of Tokyo. Fortunately, MacArthur had concluded their first meeting in Tokyo with the words: "The Eighth Army is yours, Matt. Do what you think best."

A further push in late March and early April was again achieving conspicuous successes when, on April 11, Ridgway was ordered to Tokyo for the purpose of relieving General MacArthur of all his commands. Thus, it should be noticed, MacArthur was dismissed not during the awful morass following the defeats of four months earlier but rather when the forces under his command had been brilliantly successful for more than two months of offensive action. Ridgway clearly had a freer hand as commander of the Eighth Army, which now included the X Corps, than did his predecessor. Still, MacArthur as supreme commander was receiving due credit for Ridgway's successes, which had incidentally been accomplished despite the restrictions that MacArthur had continued to consider intolerable.

The Dismissal of a Hero
The President's difficulties with his proconsul in Tokyo had begun from the very onset of the Korean War. When Generalissimo Chiang Kai-shek offered 33,000 troops for Korea and Washington decided that it must decline, MacArthur volunteered to go to Taiwan to explain the decision in person. This seemed quite

---

[26] Ridgway in a White House conference had expressed himself concerning the defeats in the north in a manner that prompted Acheson later to write: "This was the first time that someone had expressed what everyone thought—that the Emperor had no clothes on." Acheson, *Present at the Creation*, p. 475. See also Matthew B. Ridgway, *The Korean War* (New York: Doubleday, 1967), p. 62.

unnecessary and undesirable to the President, and MacArthur was so informed. Nevertheless, hardly more than a month later, on August 1, 1950, he showed up in Taiwan anyway. Later on in that month, in a message to the annual convention of the Veterans of Foreign Wars, he included a strong statement about the need for preserving Taiwan (then still being called Formosa) for eventual offensive purposes, and showered sarcasm on those who were of a different opinion. This became known in Washington only when it appeared on an Associated Press ticker tape report, though the publication date was to be two days later. The idea that so important a policy statement from so important a person should have been coordinated with Washington seems never to have occurred to the General—or perhaps it did and he knew it would not be cleared.

The President ordered MacArthur to withdraw the statement because it was contrary not only to United States but even more to United Nations policy, and MacArthur had after all just been appointed a U.N. commander. The statement was withdrawn but also, naturally, unofficially published. President Truman was later to say he should have fired MacArthur then, and saved the country and himself a good deal of trouble. Incidentally, it was on this occasion that Secretary of Defense Louis Johnson asked Acheson whether "we dare send [MacArthur] a statement that the President directs him to withdraw his statement?" This attitude no doubt helped to confirm in the President's mind the conviction that he needed a new Secretary of Defense.[27]

That was but the beginning of a series of policy statements vouchsafed by MacArthur to the press and to public personages without his first troubling to coordinate them with Washington. Specific and unequivocal orders that obliged him to desist from such behavior were called to his attention several times. Each period of obedience would be abruptly terminated by some outrageous example of disregard for these instructions. The final and culminating event was a letter he wrote on March 20, 1951 to Republican Congressman Joseph W. Martin, Minority Leader of the House of Representatives, in reply to Martin's request for comment on a speech the latter had given on February 12. In that speech Martin had called for "opening a second front in Asia" by using Chiang's forces, had said that he had "good reason to believe that General MacArthur favors such an operation." Martin had

---

[27] Acheson, *Present at the Creation*, pp. 423 f.

offered the following judgment on the morality of the Administration's policy: "If we are not in Korea to win, then this Administration should be indicted for the murder of thousands of American boys." [28]

MacArthur's reply expressed admiration for Martin's "old-time punch," stated that he had submitted his own like-minded recommendations to Washington "in most complete detail," and indicated that his views were generally well-known and understood, "as they follow the conventional pattern of meeting force with maximum counterforce as we have never failed to do in the past." Then he saw fit to add, in direct attack upon the President:

> It seems strangely difficult for some to realize that here in Asia is where the Communist conspirators have elected to make their play for global conquest, and that we have joined the issue thus raised on the battlefield; that here we fight Europe's war with arms, while the diplomats there still fight it with words; that if we lost the war to Communism in Asia the fall of Europe is inevitable; win it and Europe would most probably avoid war and yet preserve freedom. As you point out, we must win. There is no substitute for victory.

On March 24, after he had written the letter to Congressman Martin but before the latter had released or perhaps even received it, MacArthur issued a statement in Tokyo that directly attacked, without specifically mentioning their sources, some views expressed in a message sent him from Washington concerning a possible initiative to obtain a cease fire. Acheson justly says of this statement: "It can be described only as defiance of the Chiefs of Staff, sabotage of an operation of which he had been informed, and insubordination of the grossest sort to his Commander-in-Chief."[29] MacArthur was again reminded, in quite plain language, of previous orders to coordinate with Washington statements of the kind he had just delivered. His letter to Martin was already on the way or perhaps already delivered, but he still had ample opportunity, of which he did not avail himself, to ask the recipient to hold it confidential. Lacking such instructions, Martin on April 5 released the letter and read it in the House.

---

[28] A long excerpt from the Martin speech is included in *MacArthur Hearings,* part 5, pp. 3176–3179. The MacArthur letter to Martin on this speech is reprinted in many places, including the *New York Times,* April 6, 1951, and *MacArthur Hearings,* part 1, p. 185.

[29] Acheson, *Present at the Creation,* pp. 518 f.

President Truman waited several days, during which he solicited the recommendations of his top advisers. On April 9, he learned that the Joint Chiefs of Staff, including their chairman General Bradley, unanimously recommended that General MacArthur be relieved of all his commands, and that Secretary of Defense Marshall concurred in that recommendation. Although the President had already made up his mind what he had to do, it was politically useful for him to have this firm support, which included two five-star generals. He then proceeded to action.

From the time Communist China had entered the war, General MacArthur had been completely and vehemently at odds with the government's policy of limiting the war. Already past seventy, he had lived and fought through two world wars, and had spent much of his life and all the previous fourteen years in the Far East. The events in which he had played so conspicuous a role during those fourteen years had been important enough, and he was hardly one to undervalue any sector of affairs identified with himself. It is therefore not remarkable that he should have lacked empathy with the view prevailing in Washington that not China but the Soviet Union was the supreme enemy. The latter view was summed up in the well-known words that General Bradley was shortly to use before the Senate committee investigating the MacArthur dismissal: "Red China is not the powerful nation seeking to dominate the world. Frankly, in the opinion of the Joint Chiefs of Staff, this strategy [enlarging the conflict with China] would involve us in the wrong war, at the wrong place, at the wrong time, and with the wrong enemy." [30] According to that conviction nothing should be permitted to increase the American commitment to fighting China beyond what the Chinese themselves made necessary *in Korea*—and even the American commitment in Korea was not sacrosanct. During the December defeats and into mid-January MacArthur had talked darkly of the probable necessity of evacuating Korea unless China were directly and heavily attacked. The President, through the Joint Chiefs, had left him in no doubt of the Administration view: that however serious and unfortunate would be such an event, it was definitely not as unacceptable as full-scale war with China.

Whatever else might be said about that view, it was rational —in the sense of being based on a reasoned though no doubt imperfect evaluation of the relevant circumstances—and it was internally consistent. It was also more than a little remarkable in

---

[30] *MacArthur Hearings*, part 2, p. 732.

the degree to which it rejected the age-old need to save face in order to cleave to what was construed to be the basic imperative of the times. Among its premises was an attribution of aggressiveness to the Soviet Union that in retrospect appears greatly exaggerated. Yet, there could be no question then or now that that nation was and would remain far more powerful than China, that it had already solved the secret of nuclear weapons, and that on the doorstep of Russia lay Europe while on that of China lay the poverty stricken countries of Asia—and the Soviet Union. The Administration was also showing a proper concern for the views of our United Nations associates and especially of our new NATO allies.

There was besides a deep impression of Japan's failure in China in the years before World War II and of Chiang's failure after it. Viscount Montgomery once said, with Napoleon and Hitler in mind, "The first principle of war is not to try to walk to Moscow"; so in the American view the first principle of war was not to try to walk to Peking. This attitude of renunciation may indeed have been carried too far—halting the war absolutely at the center of the channel of the Yalu was carrying restraint pretty far—but that was a strictly tactical decision when viewed against the overwhelming strategic concept that determined it. The price of a wrong tactical decision is usually limited and allows for recovery. The price of a wrong decision in basic strategy will likely be far more serious.

MacArthur's view, besides being specifically China-directed, was exactly what he had called it in his letter to Martin, the conventional one "of meeting force with maximum counterforce as we had never failed to do in the past." Communist China had hurled down the gauntlet and that was enough. There should now be no stopping short of a complete victory. One almost has visions of another surrender ceremony on the deck of the battleship *Missouri*, which was after all still available for the purpose and in fact just then doing heavy work off the coasts of Korea.

It could conceivably be said for MacArthur that what he abhorred most was not defeat but rather stalemate and indecision. He underrated the ability of the forces under his command to recoup their losses and to regain the upper hand despite the restrictions that so irked him. The stalemate that did follow in Korea was, as we shall see, the result of a major mistake of judgment on the part of Truman and his aides and by no means preordained by the military circumstances. Nor did the stalemate in Korea ever become remotely so bad as that which we were to know in Vietnam. One feels he would have protested at least as hard at the restrictions imposed in Vietnam as he did with respect to Korea; but if we could take him at his word, if he really meant it when he said that "the worst of all choices," that is, worse than acknowling failure or defeat, is "to go on indefinitely, neither to win nor to lose in that stalemate," then we have special reason today to be respectful of that view. Actually, we cannot take MacArthur at his word. His stated preference for defeat over stalemate is clearly a forensic ploy in view of his constant diatribes against the whole concept of limited war, which he identified with "the concept of appeasement."

These vehement, reiterated protests he directed first of all repeatedly to the Joint Chiefs, which was his right and indeed his duty so long as he kept it confidential. Still, it raises the question whether a commander should be kept in a position requiring him to execute orders with which he is so completely out of sympathy, the more so as he insisted for a month and a half that these restrictions probably made it impossible for him to realize even his minimum task of maintaining a bridgehead in Korea. He was chagrined, and his public comments showed it, when Ridgway began to prove in late January 1951 that he was able to take the offensive and suceed in it spectacularly despite those same restrictions, about which Ridgway expressed no misgivings whatever. Indeed we have the curious spectacle of Ridgway attempting on March 12 to allieviate through his own press conference what he conceived to be the blow to Eighth Army morale of MacArthur's press conference of March 7, in which MacArthur had reiterated publicly his old themes of hopelessness under existing restrictions. Ridgway opened that conference with a statement that began: "We didn't set out to conquer China. We set out to stop Communism." The same statement ended: "This war is positive from beginning to end, and the potentialities are positive." [31]

Keeping a general in command when he is completely out of sympathy with his orders usually argues the absence of an available alternative general. But Ridgway was clearly such an alternative. Actually, in their memorandum justifying their recommendation that MacArthur be relieved, the Joint Chiefs gave as their first reason precisely this lack of sympathy for the basic

---

[31] Leckie, *Conflict*, pp. 265–267.

strategy adopted in Washington. However, the Chiefs did not initiate this recomendation, but offered it only upon request. Again it is obvious that what kept MacArthur in his post not only after the defeats due to his rashness but also after his total rejection of the concept basic to his orders was his status as a national hero of much acclaim. And again one must say, such men are dangerous. One almost has to be grateful to MacArthur for finally making himself so flagrantly and publicly insubordinate as to provoke dismissal from his patient and too-long-abused President.

The explosion of indignation from the Republican side, culminating in hearings that are the longest on record for any Senate committee (taking up five large volumes of print), open up a number of questions concerning the American body politic that we can here only touch upon. One notices, not for the first time nor the last, the existence of several syndromes in United States party politics, one being the familiar but nevertheless curious identity of right-wing views with hawkishness in matters of war. It is not an invariable identity; some "liberals" make good hawks too, like today's Senator Henry M. Jackson of Washington, and the true conservative is likely to be as appalled as any by the outbreak of war or any extension of it. But the politician who becomes especially noted as a "conservative," which is nowadays usually a euphemism for "reactionary" or "radical right," is likely to be a fire-breather, impatient of restrictions both in Korea and later in Vietnam. The reasons for this are undoubtedly deeply psychological, probably having to do with unconscious urges that include a strong compulsion to punish.

Another syndrome was the identification of the "conservative" group with what came to be called the "China Lobby." In the mythology of this group Chiang Kai-Shek was rather a saintly figure, and the always-perfidious British influence in Washington (with Dean Acheson the especially receptive figure) was allegedly responsible for the apparent willingness of a Democratic Administration to sell Nationalist China down the river. Senator William F. Knowland, who was then Minority Leader in the Senate, and Congressman Martin were two among many stellar examples of this view, which combined a general distaste for Europe and things European with an obsessive hatred of Communism. To them, as to General MacArthur, it was putting things upside down to say that the Soviet Union was more important than Communist China partly *because* the former menaced Europe and the latter did not. This group had been ardently isolationist, at least about Europe, before World War II.

There is also the question of the legitimate limits of political maneuvers during wartime. This is largely a subjective matter, partly ethical and in part simply practical. Often heard in the past during periods of international crisis or war was the cry that "politics should stop at the water-line!" Insofar as this opinion would proscribe political debate and dissension on critical matters of foreign policy and especially of war, it is plainly absurd. It offers to hold open to debate all public issues except those that matter most. Usually the recourse of an administration in trouble wishing to call upon feelings of patriotism for support, this appeal is not as often heard as it once was, though both the Johnson and the Nixon Administrations have made attempts to utilize it concerning Vietnam.

On the other hand, it is generally true that unprincipled partisan politics can do more harm in these areas than they normally do on domestic issues, and certainly this was the case in the Great Debate, with the Senate hearings at its core, which revolved about the MacArthur dismissal. Hardly raised at this time was the question whether it had been right for the United States to enter this war. Administration opponents were already beginning to call it "Truman's War," yet they seemed not to question the original decision to intervene, which apparently in their opinion had been the only correct decision the Administration had made concerning the war. Naturally, with a martyr-hero like MacArthur available for the purpose, almost all the opposition centered on special advocacy of his side of his controversy with his superiors. Not that anyone really wanted to see the much greater mobilization and far higher taxes that would attend anything approaching a full-scale war with China, and certainly no one wanted to see World War III. But the Republican minority report on the hearings found it quite safe to say: "We believe a policy of victory must be announced to the American people in order to restore unity and confidence. It is too much to expect that our people will accept a limited war."

With over 21,000 Americans already dead in Korea by the time the hearings started (the total was to be close to 34,000), enough blood had been spilled to provide fuel for passions. Arguments opposed to the war itself would have been honest. Arguments that criticized the handling of the war, rarely based on anything other than malice or ignorance—such as the resurgence of the perennial charge that our allies were not doing enough—helped to make the war itself deeply unpopular even with those who seemed to favor a larger war.

However, what anyone with real commitment to democratic processes finds most disturbing in reading the Senate hearings was the reckless disregard by so many Administration opponents of that basic principle of democracy: subordination of the military to civilian rule. It is bizarre to see men like Generals Bradley and Collins repeatedly reminding U.S. senators that under our form of government the President and his appropriate lawfully appointed aides are and ought to be supreme over the military, and that the designation of "commander-in-chief," which the Constitution accords the President, must have meaning in this respect if in no other. The second and third of the three reasons that the Joint Chiefs wrote into their memorandum justifying their recommendation to dismiss MacArthur concerned precisely this point. The second mentioned MacArthur's failures "to comply with the Presidential directive to clear statements on policy before making such statements public," and other such unwarranted actions, and the third stated simply that "they, the Joint Chiefs of Staff, have felt and feel now that the military must be controlled by civilian authority in this country." [32]

The three Joint Chiefs and their chairman were quizzed closely and repeatedly concerning all the circumstances leading up to their unanimous recommendation for the dismissal. Among things the senators wanted to know: Were they totally free of pressure? Did they make their decision on *strictly military* grounds? Was any measure of personal pique involved? And so forth, and so forth. These questions are not irrelevant to the historian and cannot be regarded as a waste of the Committee's time, but in the aggregate they reflect a preoccupation and a structure of thinking

---

[32] General Bradley in his testimony described in detail the Joint Chiefs memorandum and quoted portions of it. *MacArthur Hearings*, part 2, pp. 878 f. We have noted above that President F. D. Roosevelt more than once went against the unanimous advice of his Joint Chiefs on matters that could be considered predominantly military (see p. 37). One may also recall that on a later occasion President John F. Kennedy was to reap the following bitter lesson from the Bay of Pigs fiasco: "The experts were unanimous, and they were wrong!" Undoubtedly included among the experts referred to were the Joint Chiefs, who had approved the plan for an invasion that could not possibly succeed considering the pitifully small number of men involved in it. President Kennedy was not trying to divest himself of blame in that remark—made in his television interview on New Year's eve at the end of 1961—but was definitely making a mental note for the future.

among some senators that suggest no great allegiance to the most fundamental and cherished of the democratic principles laid down by the Founding Fathers. *No one* ventured the opinion that even if the Joint Chiefs had recommended unanimously against the dismissal, it would still be the President's prerogative and duty to go through with it if he considered it to be in the country's interest. Military opinion may easily be uniform on a particular issue and yet unacceptable. The President might, for example, consider a political issue paramount which the military felt was not their affair—like the manifest loss of confidence in MacArthur felt by those fourteen allies other than Korea who had made enough military contributions to suffer significant casualties. And he should be free to follow his own judgment against the advice of the Joint Chiefs even on matters that some would consider "strictly military." They are after all not infallible, and a man of shrewd insights can often detect error among the experts. Not only is this the philosophy of democracy, it was also the Clausewitzian principle expounded in Chapter 1; it was a principle that at the time of the Korean War had not made much headway in the United States Senate.

It is sobering to think what could have happened if there had been a high-level cabal among the military determined to support MacArthur and his views—if officers like Bradley and Collins and others on the Joint Chiefs, instead of being the honest, intelligent soldiers they were, with deep attachment to their country's institutions, had staged a "generals' revolt" on the side of MacArthur. Would the Senate have closed ranks on the side of Constitutional principle as against partisan advantage? Unfortunately, there is nothing in the record to indicate they would have done so. It is likely that there would have been a Republican move to secure the impeachment of the President, which, however, would not have succeeded because of Democratic majorities in both houses.

A brief extract from the questioning of General Bradley by Republican Senator Styles Bridges of New Hampshire will convey some of the flavor of the hearings. After pressing the General on the importance of "the best military judgment of our military leaders" wherever that judgment may be in conflict with political judgment, the Senator goes on:

Senator Bridges. If it reaches the time in this country where you think the political decision is affecting what you believe to be basically right militarily, what would you do?

General Bradley. Well, if after several instances in which the best military advice we could give was turned down for other reasons, I would decide that my advice was no longer of any help, why, I would quit. I feel that is the way you would have to do. Let them get some other military adviser whose advice apparently would be better or at least more acceptable.

Senator Bridges. Would you speak out, tell the American public?

General Bradley. No, sir.

Senator Bridges. Don't you think that is your duty, your loyalty to your country, to do that?

General Bradley. No, sir; I don't think so. I have been brought up a little differently.

Senator Bridges. Where does the loyalty to your country come in?

General Bradley. I am loyal to my country, but I am also loyal to the Constitution, and you have certain elected officials under the Constitution, and I wouldn't profess that my judgment was better than the President of the United States or the administration.

Senator Bridges. Would it not be on a military subject?

General Bradley. Yes.

Senator Bridges. Should not you speak out?

General Bradley. I would; yes, to the constituted authorities; yes.

Senator Bridges. But you would stop there?

General Bradley. Yes.[33]

The Decision to Halt the Offensive

Upon Ridgway's being posted to Tokyo to relieve MacArthur, command of the Eighth Army, which also included control of the Republic of Korea (ROK) Army, passed on April 14 to the highly competent Lieutenant General James Van Fleet. A week later the Communists tried an offensive of their own, which made some small progress, largely because of the resilient tactics used by Van Fleet, but which was stopped within the next seven days.

After some further see-saw movement, the Communists made their final big bid. On the night of May 15–16, they attacked with a force that incorporated twenty-one Chinese divisions in the center with nine North Korean divisions distributed on both flanks. Van Fleet, who had meanwhile called for vastly greater than normal artillery support in order to "expend steel and fire,

---

[33] *MacArthur Hearings*, part 2, pp. 752 f.

not men," stopped this offensive within five days, and then on May 23 resumed his own offensive across a 140-mile front. The Chinese and their allies, terribly bloodied from the events of the previous month, were in no condition to withstand the powerful United Nations force that now began to push northward, supported by a large and completely dominant airpower and by naval gunfire on both flanks of the peninsula.

Throughout the end of May and into June the United Nations armies made rapid progress, parts of them pushing again through the 38th parallel. Van Fleet remarked that that parallel "has no significance in the present tactical situation . . . The Eighth Army will go wherever the situation dictates in hot pursuit of the enemy." By mid-June he held a line that on the west coast lay some ten miles below the parallel, but which ran thence northeastward with a center and eastern section well above it. Now Van Fleet proposed to Ridgway a combined amphibious and overland operation towards Wonsan on the east coast, which he was confident the enemy could not effectively oppose, and which would pinch off and destroy a large fraction of the Chinese and North Korean forces in the area. Although Van Fleet unquestionably had the forces necessary to execute this plan, Ridgway, acting under prior directives of the Joint Chiefs, rejected it.

Separation from the battlefield undoubtedly meant that the Joint Chiefs and their civilian superiors in Washington, and for that matter also Ridgway in Japan, could not easily appreciate the terrible state to which the erstwhile triumphant enemy had been reduced. It is questionable whether even Van Fleet knew *at the time*, though as he put it later: ". . . in June 1951 we had the Chinese whipped. They were definitely gone. They were in awful shape. During the last week in May we captured more than 10,000 prisoners." [34] What that last comment really meant was significantly amplified in reports coming up—though with considerable delay—from prisoner interrogation units. That large numbers of prisoners had come in despite the fact that the Chinese commanders were doing everything possible to make it difficult for their troops to surrender, including resort to treacherous fake surrenders that would put American and ROK troops on their guard against any enemy troops or units waving white flags. Those

---

[34] Quoted in Malcolm W. Cagle and Frank A. Manson, *The Sea War in Korea* (Annapolis: U. S. Naval Institute, 1957), pp. 308 f. General Collins, it should be noted, presents a very different view of the situation, and points out also that General Van Fleet's "estimate of the situation" sent to Ridgway on June 9, 1951, does not jibe with his later comments. See Collins, *War in Peacetime*, pp. 306 ff.

commanders knew that the morale among their men was collapsing, and that all the latter needed to induce them to surrender was the opportunity. The enormous American fire power—air, naval, and field artillery—and the fighting skill and spirit of the veteran ground forces in the United Nations command, well supplied and well equipped, had done its work. The North Korean army had been virtually destroyed, and the Chinese had lost in their eight months of fighting about half a million men. Their supply situation was desperate, with all of North Korea behind them in a shambles.

There can hardly be any doubt that the Communist forces were ripe for destruction, that Van Fleet sensed it more than his superiors did, and that even without the amphibious operations called for in his plan, any continuation of the United Nations offensive would have pushed them further towards collapse. However, Van Fleet *at the time* did not appear to press this view, despite his subsequent protestations. He and Ridgway toured the front together on June 22, and agreed not to advance north of what was called the "Kansas-Wyoming" line. This decision accorded with an Administration and Joint Chiefs directive that the Eighth Army and the ROK Army should halt more or less where they were, though Ridgway in transmitting these orders gave Van Fleet permission to conduct local advances to seize better ground. Here they were to await the enemy's bid for a cease-fire, while maintaining an "active defense."

I have hitherto in this book been stressing the all-important idea that politics must control strategy, but this conception does not exclude the need for responsiveness to feedback from the fighting fronts. In this case the military situation could not have been better. When the U.N. forces had first pushed north of the 38th parallel, the Chinese Communists had not yet committed themselves to the war. Now, some eight months after they had entered the war, they had shot their bolt. It was no doubt possible for them to send reinforcements, but the prospect, logistically and otherwise, for any large new commitment of forces was decidedly uninviting. They had sent in their two best field armies, and despite their initial heady successes these had been smashed. United States air and naval dominance was complete, and this meant for the Chinese, among other things, a difficult and precarious line of supply to the fighting front. The best the Chinese could hope to do was send in enough reinforcements to hold a new line somewhere north, perhaps considerably north, of the 38th parallel. But in mid-June of 1951 their immediate problem was to save their existing force in Korea from annihilation. This we accomplished for them simply by halting our offensive.

General Ridgway in his memoirs describes the decision in a manner that clearly suggests he has missed the point. After acknowledging that there might be some debate on the wisdom of "stopping that proud Army in its tracks at the first whisper that the Reds might be ready to sue for peace," he argues that a drive back to the Yalu would not have been worth the cost. Then he says: "The seizure of the land between the truce line and the Yalu would have merely meant the seizure of more real estate." And he mentions again the point so much stressed by MacArthur, that pushing the Chinese back to the Yalu meant shortening their supply lines and lengthening our own. It is curious that he is able to write this even in the knowledge of what happened subsequently.

The reason for continuing the extraordinarily successful enterprise that the U.N. offensive had become had nothing to do with the acquisition of more real estate. Its purpose should have been to continue maximum pressure on the disintegrating Chinese armies as a means of getting them not only to request but actually to conclude an armistice. The line they finally settled for two years later, or something like that line, might have been achieved in far less time if we had meanwhile continued the pressure that was disintegrating their armies. Even allowing for the possibility that they might have been able to reform and hold somewhere further to the north, they would have had every inducement to seek an early end to hostilities if we could offer the bait of handing back territories they had lost. Or if we were determined to stop voluntarily somewhere short of the Yalu, the narrow waist of Korea between Tongjoson Bay on the east and Sojoson Bay on the west, some 100 miles north of where we did stop, would have been a better place to do it. With our complete command of the sea and air, it can hardly be true that pushing northward significantly lengthened our supply lines. We could always seize and use new ports as we moved, should they indeed be necessary.

Granting that our chief objective was, correctly, to bring the war to an early end, in pursuit of which we had come around to considering acceptable something like the *status quo ante bellum*, the only way to insure getting it was to continue our markedly successful offensive. The Chinese willingness to begin discussing terms, the hint of which caused us to stop that offensive, was certainly not signaled out of charity. In deciding to halt we decided inadvertently on a continuance of the war.

Naturally, no one then knew that the talks would drag on with maddening futility for more than two years, during which more than 12,000 additional Americans would lose their lives, as well as untold thousands among our Korean and other allies. But we should have known that by suddenly relieving all pressure on the Chinese and granting them an undreamed-of chance to recover, we were depriving them of any incentive to agree to our terms, however generous, without testing us to see if they could squeeze out more. It is easy enough to cry "hindsight" and to excuse every blunder ever committed on that basis, but surely one must ask: Why was this decision on our part so much without precedent?

At the close of World War I, the Allies were not trying to get to Berlin, but they did not pause in their offensive when the Germans first communicated to President Woodrow Wilson on October 4, 1918 an interest in discussing an armistice. Terms had to be clarified and associated powers consulted, and meanwhile the offensive that had forced the Germans to seek those terms went relentlessly on, until the Germans signed the armistice on November 9 to become effective 36 hours later. The terms of the armistice included the continuation of the blockade conditions and various other measures that would make certain that the Germans would sign the peace treaty that was put in front of them. The harshness of that blockade and even more of the peace treaty itself have been much criticized, and no doubt justly so. But the Allies had not denied themselves the option of being magnanimous simply because they had known enough to continue their pressure in order to get the kind of armistice they wanted at the earliest possible date. If they had stopped that pressure, the Germans might have changed their minds (Ludendorff *did* change his mind after first informing his government that the German cause was hopeless). An *agreed upon* armistice, one that would not have disarmed the Germans unilaterally, was unfortunately not in the cards at that time, and the chances for it would not have improved as the American armies in France increased in numbers. At any rate, the Allied leaders knew that war is not a game in which one makes gentlemanly gestures in the hope of getting like treatment in return. In World War II the same requirement for conclusive action was fulfilled even more decisively by demanding and receiving unconditional surrender from each one of the major enemy states.

95

The situation in Korea was of course much different. Each new war situation is always different in important respects from all previous war situations (just as Vietnam is again completely different from Korea). The Chinese armies in the field were entirely beaten, but China itself was untouched. She had other forces in reserve ready to be sent into Korea *if she was willing to pay a heavy price for continuing the war.* What we did by halting our offensive was to make that price dirt cheap. The army that was about to be destroyed we accorded gratuitously a chance to recover. The Chinese were not obliged to replace it but simply to reinforce it. The quieting of the front lines, even if only temporarily, meant that the strain upon their supply lines was much relieved. Above all they knew, in the many months of stalemated war that were to follow, that the Americans were not again likely to mount the kind of offensive that had so nearly overwhelmed them. It was not a question of resources but of will. Positions could be held. Limited attacks or counterattacks could still be carried out. Any new attack meant heavy fighting, not a pursuit of a defeated horde. Therefore something of the magnitude of the spring 1951 offensive was not likely to happen again. In short, the Communists were left without incentive to come to terms. If they felt they might gain by procrastinating and delaying, it would cost them relatively little to do so.

On June 23, 1951 the Soviet Ambassador to the United Nations, Jacob Malik, in a United Nations radio broadcast devoted mostly to denouncing the United States, finished off with a hint that it was possible that discussions might now begin between the belligerents "for a cease-fire and an armistice providing for the mutual withdrawal of forces from the 38th parallel." After a Peking newspaper endorsed Malik's proposal two days later, President Truman directed American Ambassador Alan Kirk to contact the Soviet government for additional information. The reply was that the proposed armistice would not discuss political or territorial matters but only a cease-fire, and that political settlements might come later. On this basis the President directed General Ridgway to send by radio in clear to the commander-in-chief of the Communist forces in Korea a message that included the following sentence: "I am informed that you may wish a meeting to discuss an armistice providing for the cessation of hostilities and all acts of armed force in Korea, with adequate guarantees for the maintenance of such an armistice." Ridgway then went on to propose as a meeting place the Danish hospital ship *Jutlandia* in Wonsan Harbor.

The following night he received a reply from Premier Kim Il Sung of North Korea, and General Peng Teh-huai, commander of the Chinese armies in Korea, agreeing to the meeting but rejecting the proposed meeting place. They suggested rather the town of Kaesong, which because it was on the west end of the line could be a mile below the parallel and still well within Communist-held territory. Ridgway, upon sending a patrol into Kaesong to check that there was little enemy activity there, agreed to it as an acceptable neutral site. And thus the talks began.

Talks Interminable and a Military Stagnation

By succeeding in choosing a meeting place in territory controlled by them, and by showing extraordinary arrogance even in the first meetings, the Chinese tried to make it appear that the United Nations had requested an armistice. This was a matter not simply of face but of important tactical advantage. Their conduct was the usual Communist probing to see how far they could get. Our response told them at once that their abusive behavior, very soon to take the form also of wilful procrastination, did not greatly risk the stability of their lines.

It is pointless to attempt here even to outline the dreary course of those talks as well as nontalks, or of the attendant military operations and nonoperations, except where events occur to throw in relief the relationship between the two. However, the story of the meetings at Kaesong, and later and much longer at Panmunjom, provide much insight into the methods of Communist negotiators, particularly when they be Chinese. It has been well narrated and the story should be read, especially by those who insist that Communists are simply reasonable people like everybody else and will in negotiations respond to courtesy and consideration with reciprocal treatment.[35] They are indeed capable

---

[35] Concerning the negotiations at Kaesong and Panmunjom, see especially Admiral Turner C. Joy, *How Communists Negotiate* (New York: Macmillan, 1955) and William H. Vatcher, Jr., *Panmunjom, The Story of the Korean Military Armistice Negotiations* (New York: Praeger, 1958). An excellent account of the opening weeks of the negotiations at Kaesong and of the qualities and characteristics of the chief American negotiators, which I have been privileged to read, has been prepared by Dr. Herbert Goldhamer, of the RAND Corporation, who served unofficially as adviser of the American delegation during the first four months of its work. Unfortunately, however, as of the date of this writing, Dr. Goldhamer's report is still highly classified.

of being reasonable when they consider it to their advantage to be so, or at least useless to be otherwise. However, the kind of Communists likely to be encountered in anything as serious and important as armistice negotiations are people who have been specifically trained to regard such procedures as a continuation of war by other means with the imperialist enemy and therefore to reject as useless impediments bourgeoise notions of gentlemanliness and common courtesy. If, in other words, they seem to be playing a strange kind of game, it is partly because they are so determined not to be playing games.

We may be sure they took the Korean armistice negotiations with the deadliest seriousness, and that they were determined not to yield up one iota of advantage that they could gain or retain. This aim had to entail constant probing to see just what they could obtain. For them to have behaved otherwise would have been to betray their faith as good Communists and serious revolutionaries. Engaged as they were with people who, especially at the outset, were novices in the business, they had some considerable advantage, which of course they played to the hilt. This is not to say that they made no mistakes even by their own lights, but their lights were different from ours. The greatest single difference was that so long as the war was "under control" from their point of view, they were in no hurry to end it.

After six weeks of quite useless talks about the agenda and about an armistice line of demarcation, the Communists made one of their many charges of U.N. military violation of the neutral area, this one allegedly a bombing from the air of Kaesong with the intention of murdering the Communist delegation. This allegation was made at midnight, on August 22, by a Chinese colonel, who demanded that the American officer in charge examine the evidence immediately. The American, an Air Force colonel, was able to point out at once that the "evidence" had been quite clumsily fabricated. Upon this rejection of his charge, the Communist colonel announced forthwith that the armistice negotiations were suspended indefinitely! Obviously, so junior an officer could not have made so momentous a decision unless authorized

---

Dr. Goldhamer, incidentally, was engaged in prisoner interrogation before he was assigned to Kaesong, and he was responsible for sending forward a memorandum, which went as far as Ridgway in Tokyo, detailing the desperate morale conditions of the Chinese army just prior to the onset of armistice negotiations. This memorandum is said to have created a sensation in Van Fleet's headquarters as well as Ridgway's, but by this time the decision to halt the offensive had been made and acted upon.

in advance to do so, and the use by his superiors of this means of breaking off negotiations provided a nice example of the tactical use of the studied insult. It reflected the conviction that the Americans were very eager to have the negotiations continue and make progress, and this attitude on our part could perhaps be exploited for some concessions.

The Communists must also have felt they could break the truce without suffering any new United Nations offensive. Charging us with attempts at "murder," they could blame us for any move to renew the hostilities—as they were already blaming us for lack of progress in the talks. Meanwhile they could go on reinforcing and strengthening their military position.

A week later some of their own troops strongly attacked an ROK division and punched through it, but were contained. Thereupon Van Fleet obtained permission to renew his offensive in a limited fashion, which he did on August 31. There was much hard fighting during September, considerably harder than it would have been two or three months earlier, but the U.N. forces nevertheless succeeded wherever they attacked in moving up substantially and holding their new positions. This brought the Communists back to the conference table, even though the U.N. Command, who had learned their lesson, had meanwhile announced that any resumption of the negotiations would have to be at a new site. Ridgway had suggested on the radio the bridge at Panmunjom as a place to discuss the selection of a new site. Liaison teams, meeting on October 8, needed two weeks of meetings to insure the neutrality of Panmunjom itself as the site, after which, in late October, two months after the talks had been broken off, the delegations again sat down together.

Progress, though not entirely lacking, was no more rapid than before. Agreements were reached only on issues that both sides regarded as relatively unimportant or innocuous. By mid-December 1951, the major stumbling block became the question of the repatriation of war prisoners in U.N. hands. A large number of these, almost half, were anxious not to be returned to Communist control, and indeed many of them were from South Korea and had been impressed into the North Korean forces only when the later overran the southern territories. The United States was adamant on "no forced repatriation," offering repeated suggestions for devices to allow the prisoners to make a free choice in the presence of representatives of neutral states, while the Commu-

99

nists insisted equally stubbornly on total "repatriation" of all prisoners, forced or otherwise. The latter notion was deeply repugnant to President Truman, as it was also to be to his successor, and here Truman knew he had a moral issue that he could stand upon, both domestically and abroad, though the continuation of the war was rapidly becoming more unpopular.

American enthusiasm for the war took a sharp drop from the moment the Chinese entered, especially after the heavy defeats of the end of November 1950. The opening of the MacArthur controversy and the debates centered on the Senate hearings in May and June 1951 further eroded support. It was not only that the General was a hero; the people could understand his simple theme better than they could the somewhat complex counter-arguments of the Administration. After firing MacArthur the President had appeared on the radio and said: "In simplest terms, what we are doing in Korea is this: We are trying to prevent World War III." He had gone on to stress why it was desirable not to extend the war, inevitably at the cost of reinflating the question why we were there in the first place. The argument that a war that is not important enough to win is not important enough to fight is indeed a catchy one, not easy to answer satisfactorily to an electorate to whom the war has already caused some deep anxieties and which is experiencing increasingly some of the pains and inconveniences that go with fighting any war.

In the later Vietnam War we were to learn of the tribulations of fighting a limited war in a distant land with a conscript army. In the earlier stages of the Korean War we had no adequate conscript army, and had to call back into service many veterans of World War II who had stayed in the National Guard or otherwise retained their reserve status. Many of these had already fought a long and hard war, and had since married and started to raise families. They and their families were naturally bitter at their being called away again when many who had not served at all were spared, at least until Selective Service might catch up with them. Also because of the nearness in time to World War II, there were certain inconveniences that were not to be repeated in the Vietnam War, such as shortages in various materials. What was indeed to see repetition later was the Korean stimulus to another round, following that of World War II, of serious inflation.

But it was the dashing of the hopes raised in June and July 1951 that triggered the sharpest decline in support of the war.

What had appeared to be the start of serious armistice discussions was followed by interminable acrimonious confrontations between the delegations, punctuated by outright breaks in the talks and by the occasional resumption of serious fighting. And casualties continued, fewer per week than what the first year had known, but seemingly interminable.

It is not always easy to gauge public attitudes towards a war, especially a limited war. The Korean War also had its Gallup and other polls, and while these provide a generally reliable reflection of trends in attitudes, their usefulness is limited by certain factors intrinsic to polls and by others intrinsic to war. Polls are usually not good at measuring *intensity* of feeling (they can be improved in that respect, but only by making the questioning more intensive and therefore more costly). When the questions are about support of a war, people feel they ought to be or at least appear to be patriotic, and they therefore tend to keep to themselves their negative feelings. Besides, the normal attitude towards any condition or event that one supports in principle but which causes anxiety, pain, or inconvenience is one of ambivalence. The person concerned can support the war rather more by word than by deed, and he wishes desperately it would go away. Untoward events will provoke a sharp breakthrough of the suppressed negative feelings.

One event that strikingly brought out the national feeling about the Korean War was the steel strike that began in April 1952. On the day the mills were to shut down, President Truman seized them with the intention of keeping them producing, justifying his action in a radio speech by stressing the needs of the war. This appeal had little effect on anybody. The Supreme Court found that the President had not the power to seize the mills, the press applauded this decision, the Congress refused to grant the President the appropriate powers, and the mills were therefore returned to the owners and struck by the workers for fifty-three days. The strike was settled only by an agreement that resulted in a severe and inflationary rise in the price of steel. The President knew very well how to interpret these events, and he was also aware that 1952 was a Presidential election year. He was more than ever eager to see the war ended.

The meeting place at Panmunjom became increasingly a battle ground for propaganda warfare. The prisoner issue was now a symbol of irreconcilable differences. It was impossible for Communists to admit publicly that any sizeable group of men formerly theirs would resist being returned to their rule. Then the charge and stigma of biological warfare was raised against the United States. This charge ultimately collapsed from total want of evidence, but meanwhile it was played as far as any fiction could be. Also exposed to charge and countercharge between the two parties were the "confessions" of American prisoners in Communist hands, the result of what came to be known as "brain-washing" and in some instances of simple, low-intensity but prolonged torture.

In the summer of 1952, on the eve of the elections in the United States, the Communists opened a powerful offensive designed to take back the ground won by Van Fleet in the previous year. Heavy rains interrupted this offensive in July and August, but it was resumed in September, at which time the Communists were able for the first time to use a large amount of Russian-made artillery. However, the offensive failed utterly to make any progress, and the coming of winter put an end to it. The air fighting, on the other hand, was never interrupted except for the period of heavy rains; the American pilots in their Saberjets continued to demonstrate their awesome superiority in fighting quality to their opponents.

Meanwhile, on October 8, 1952, General Mark Clark—who had replaced Ridgway when the latter had gone to NATO to relieve the Presidential candidate, General Eisenhower—decided with the approval of Washington to call a halt to the travesty going on at Panmunjom. There had also been a brief interruption in June of that year, but this time the American delegation told the Chinese and North Koreans that talks would resume only when the latter were prepared to accept one of three plans offered by the Americans for return of war prisoners or to offer a constructive alternative. The talks were thus recessed, and six months passed before they were resumed.

During that six months the United States elected a Republican President for the first time since 1928. Dwight D. Eisenhower's popularity was such as to give him an excellent chance for election anyway in a country grown weary of Democratic and especially of Truman rule. Still, the stagnated Korean War unquestionably played an enormous part in the campaign and contributed heavily to the Eisenhower plurality. It could indeed have been the decisive factor. Certainly it was the main one. We know that Eisenhower's famous remark during the campaign, that if elected, "I will go to Korea," had an astonishing effect. During the campaign the New York *World Telegram and Sun* began printing the weekly American casualty lists under headlines of the size known as "scareheads." The war had become a heavy incubus to the nation and certainly to the Democratic party.

On February 11, 1953, with Eisenhower already in office, General Van Fleet was relieved as commander of the Eighth Army in order to go into retirement, his replacement being Lieutenant General Maxwell Taylor, who was later to play a key part in our Vietnam involvement. Upon his retirement Van Fleet announced to reporters that until his last day in command he had been confident of his capacity to launch a new and successful offensive against the Communists in order to end the war. He had long been bitter at being denied permission to do so, and one of his letters to his wife reflecting this bitterness was placed by her in Eisenhower's hands during the campaign.

On the eve of the resumption of talks on April 27, the fiery ROK President Syngman Rhee declared he would be no party to any armistice that left Chinese troops on Korean soil, and he also threatened to release unconditionally the prisoners in control of ROK troops. Rhee's agitation and threats continued, and may well have sparked the very strong Communist attack launched on the night of June 13–14 against a portion of the line held by the ROK 5th and 8th Divisions, as though to demonstrate the punishment invited by Rhee's threats. Three days later, on June 17, the truce line was finally fixed at Panmunjom and preparations were being made for the final conclusion of the armistice agreement, when Rhee astounded and shocked the world by carrying out his threats about releasing prisoners, some 27,000 Korean POW's being freed in a well-planned operation. The Chinese reply was again to break off the talks and to address a letter to General Clark asking whether he could really control the South Korean government and army. However officially indignant he was with Rhee (and personally he sympathized with him), Clark had to bargain with him to get his acquiesence.[36] The result was terms assuring Rhee of, among other things, a U.S.-ROK mutual security pact after the armistice, long-term economic aid, of which the first installment would be $200 million plus an additional $10 million for immediate food relief, and an agreement to expand the ROK Army to twenty divisions. No doubt much of this would have been contributed by the United States anyway, but Rhee was using his

---

[36] See Mark W. Clark, *From the Danube to the Yalu* (New York: Harpers & Row, 1954), chap. 18.

capacity for obstruction in order to get a hard and fast agreement. This gained, he promised no longer to hinder the armistice.

On July 10, 1953, the second anniversary of the start of truce talks at Kaesong, the plenary sessions were resumed and were proceeding well when the Communists made what General Clark has called a "politically inspired" offensive. Five Chinese armies struck at three ROK divisions, in order again to prove to Rhee how futile it was to cherish notions of besting the Communists on his own. To make their point they were apparently willing to lose what by American estimates were 72,000 men, of whom some 25,000 were presumed killed, to make gains that had virtually no effect on the truce line established by the armistice. Though these figures are undoubtedly exaggerated, the idea still holds.

Then, on the morning of July 27, 1953, two lieutenant generals, one American (General William Harrison) and the other North Korean, led their respective delegations to the special hut that had been constructed for the purpose at Panmunjom, and, without speaking a word to each other, signed eighteen copies of the armistice agreement and departed. Twelve hours later the armistice took effect. The guns were silenced and the Korean War was over.

Termination and Aftermath

Why after impeding matters so long did the Chinese and their North Korean junior partners finally settle for terms not substantially different from those we had been prepared to offer at the outset? Even General Clark in his memoirs professed to being mystified.[37] If we were basing our answer on surmise, we might guess that they had played out every last card they had, every conceivable maneuver and occasion for delay, and saw no chance for additional gain from delaying further. They, too, were suffering casualties and other costs and had some incentive for ending the fighting. They had tested to the full the use of their singular negotiating techniques for extracting every possible advantage. The direct returns had not been great, but the two year delay in itself won them the inestimable advantage that they had come

---

[37] Ibid., pp. 241, 258. However, Clark does indicate (p. 267) that on May 23 he was authorized, if the Communists rejected the United Nations final offer, to break off the talks and to "carry on the war in new ways never yet tried in Korea." He did not at the time of writing feel free to disclose what those "new ways" were. As indicated in the text, however, this was later disclosed by Eisenhower to mean the use of nuclear weapons.

back from imminent collapse and defeat—a condition now forgotten even by most of that very small segment of the world that had originally been conscious of it—and were able to sign the armistice as established equals. Again we must stress that prestige is not merely a matter of face; there is a great advantage in having the world, especially one's erstwhile opponent, treating one's arms with respect. One could also guess that they felt that a new President in the White House who did not have to face a Presidential election for another four years and who could not be blamed for initiating the American intervention would not be nearly so vulnerable to pressure as his predecessor.

So much for surmise; and, indeed, some or all of these suppositions may accord with the facts. But we also now know, from a few paragraphs in his published memoirs of his White House years, that President Eisenhower during February 1953 let it be made known to the other side that if they did not swiftly end the charade, large-scale United Nations offensive action would be resumed, *with the use of nuclear weapons.*[38] It is quite clear that he meant it; reliance upon nuclear weapons and upon the "massive retaliation" principle later to be proclaimed by Secretary of State John Foster Dulles were to be the hallmark of the entire Eisenhower defense policy.

If President Eisenhower's threat really played the part that he thought it did in bringing the other side to an appropriate negotiating attitude—willing to treat reasonably, and as eager as ourselves to bring the fighting to an end—it casts some light again on what might have been if the United Nations Command had not prematurely stopped its swiftly-moving offensive two years earlier.

One of the few unequivocally sound lessons of history is that the lessons we should learn are usually learned imperfectly if at all. Concerning what I do not hesitate to call the "blunder" of halting the June 1951 offensive, there is little indication that any of the major public figures involved, other than General Van Fleet, ever recognized it to be such. We have noted Ridgway's comment, which seems to have been widely shared. There is no hint in the memoirs of either Mr. Truman or Mr. Acheson that they had a different opinion. In view of the many pressures put upon them at home and from abroad, they had plenty of grounds for excusing themselves for their error if they were ready to ac-

---

[38] Dwight D. Eisenhower, *The White House Years, Vol. I: Mandate for Change* (New York: Doubleday, 1963), pp. 178–181.

knowledge it as such, but they seemed to feel no need for such excuses. Dean Acheson, some years after the event, when questioned about the painful Communist procrastination in the talks and how it might have been avoided, exclaimed: "Who would have thought that the Chinese would make so much fuss over war prisoners!" [39]

Shortly after the Korean War ended, the theory of limited war became increasingly a subject of discussion and development. Except for recognizing the fact that Korea had provided the first important instance of limited war, at least with respect to United States capabilities and efforts, almost all the relevant lessons that it might have provided were overlooked or ignored. Among these potential lessons were the following:

1. What is a limited war to us, limited in terms of emotional as well as material commitments, may be total war to our opponents and to one or more of our allies; thus, their demonstration of "resolve" may well exceed ours.

2. Limited wars, while very much less terrible than general war in a nuclear age, may nevertheless be exceedingly costly and prolonged. American battle losses were officially registered as 33,629 dead and 103,284 wounded. Those of our South Korean allies were recorded as 415,004 dead and 428,568 wounded, not counting many missing, and not counting civilian casualties. Other U.N. allies suffered over 3,000 dead and over 12,500 wounded and missing.

3. The capacity of the American public to support a limited war is likely to be precarious, and certainly not to be counted upon if that war be prolonged. Limited wars are those in which the threat to our own national security is usually admitted to be minor or indirect, and in view of the inevitable casualties and other costs and the prevalence of various inconveniences, sustained support is too much to expect. Moreover, in a democracy cherishing free speech, there will be important voices opposing the government's action, and the influence of these voices will grow as the war endures in time and becomes more costly.

4. The United States is indeed a very great military power, but when it fights in a limited manner it automatically

---

[39] In a conversation with this writer during a British-American conference at Ditchley House, Oxfordshire, England, in September 1963.

cuts itself down to a size that the opponent may be able to cope with, even if only temporarily, thus raising our costs and prolonging the war.

A word on the Korean War as a United Nations "police action." It was the first to be such, and will very likely be the last. Minor forces have been and may continue to be raised under U.N. auspices to *patrol* (not fight) along such truce lines as those obtaining until June 1967 between Israel and its Arab neighbors. But the kind of enforcement action envisaged in Chapter VII of the United Nations Charter has had its day in Korea and will not likely have another. It is not only a matter of the voting rules in the U.N. Security Council, but rather that the whole character of the United Nations has changed, and even more the attitudes towards it of those member nations who would have to support a police action. To go into these changes would be too long a dissertation and lead us too far afield. The most important difference is that the United Nations is now more than twenty-five years old rather than only five. Various hopes and expectations originally raised have since been dashed, and the world has greatly changed.

The part played by our United Nations allies (other than the Republic of Korea) has been both underestimated and misunderstood by most Americans who have commented on it. None of these allies made military contributions at all proportionate to ours in size, but some did send significant forces that fought exceedingly well. The British Commonwealth provided a division of over 15,000 men, mostly from the United Kingdom. The Turks, the French, and others contributed forces of brigade, regimental, or battalion size, with even little Luxemburg sending a company, and all suffered casualties proportionate to those suffered in the American forces.[40] During the war many in the United States criticized our allies for contributing so little. But the latter regarded it, with good reason, as an American war at least as much as it was a United Nations one, and certainly every aspect of it was controlled and directed by United States authorities. The allies felt they were making an important contribution that ought to be appreciated rather than condemned, and, considering how they would be missed in the Vietnam experience, it was a justified attitude.

---

[40] See Clark, *From the Danube to the Yalu*, pp. 222 f.

The Presidential Powers and the Congress

A note finally on the constitutional and political aspects of President Truman's decision not to seek congressional authorization of his decision to intervene in Korea. The action naturally needed and received congressional support in the form of money grants and various other kinds of legislation, which, however, is not the same as explicit approval. Such support derives from the attitude that one cannot let down soldiers already in the field however much one may disapprove the decision that put them there.

The issue arises from the Constitutional provision that gives to Congress alone authority to declare war but says nothing about undeclared wars. The Constitution also designates the President as "commander-in-chief" of the armed forces, but does not delimit the authority that role entails. At minimum it means superior in command functions to any military officer, and that is important enough. But how far does it stretch? We might note that this question does not arise in some sister democracies like the United Kingdom. There the Prime Minister with the support of the cabinet has the constitutional authority to declare war and even to enter, with the concurrence of the appropriate ministers but not the whole cabinet, into military understandings with other countries that may be secret and that commit the country to military action in certain contingencies. But the Prime Minister is always leader of the majority party in Parliament and in theory the agent of Parliament, which puts him in an altogether different position from the President of the United States.

The experience of the United States with undeclared wars is not new. There was such a war with republican France, our erstwhile ally, in 1798–1799, but hostilities were confined to some ship actions at sea. The Civil War by its nature could not be a declared war, inasmuch as its whole purpose was to deny the opponent recognition as a sovereign state. It became legally a war, with respect to such matters as the observance under international law of belligerent and neutral rights, by virtue of President Lincoln's proclamation of April 19, 1861 declaring a blockade of southern ports, a blockade being a legally defined mode of warfare in which both belligerents and neutrals have specified priviliges and obligations. Still, this proclamation was an executive action. If one also counts such actions as the numerous so-called "Indian wars," which were in large part forays of extermination by the United

States Cavalry, then the number of undeclared wars in American history becomes quite considerable.

Our intervention in Korea could not legally be a declared war. We were assisting a government recognized by us in what was essentially a civil war, at least a war against an opponent that we had not recognized as a separate state, let alone as a legitimate government.[41] The same was true even after Communist China entered the war, but now we had an additional motivation for avoiding the legal status of war in that our government was anxious to limit the scope of the conflict and bring it to a close as soon as possible.

So much for the legal aspects, which while not unimportant are rarely the dominant considerations. The President's prerogative as commander-in-chief to carry out military actions that may amount to a good-sized war has never been challenged by the U.S. Supreme Court, which has refused to hear relevant cases on the ground that the Court has no jurisdiction to question such "political" decisions. However, that does not keep Congress from growing restive when it feels the President has grossly exceeded the powers that the framers of the Constitution intended him to have —or that reasonable people today would want him to have. This will naturally vary with the partisan structure of the Congress of the day and with the character and popularity of the war. The President may not need it legally, but it will assist him in Congress and with the country if he succeeds at some early stage in the military operations in getting some form of specific congressional approval—as President Lyndon B. Johnson did in 1964 by obtaining the Tonkin Bay Resolution from the Congress. President Richard M. Nixon was later, in 1970, to acquiesce in congressional abrogation of that resolution (he really had no choice) on the ground that his authority as commander-in-chief gave him all the authority he needed, but by that time he was committed to

---

[41] International law distinguishes between the recognition of a state as a national entity and the recognition of a government with which we are ready to enter into normal diplomatic relations. Thus, after the Communist revolution of November 1917, the United States recognized the continuing existence of the nation previously called Russia, but it did not officially recognize until 1933 the Communist government of that nation, now called the Soviet Union. Similarly, the United States has never failed to recognize the existence of a nation formerly called China of which Taiwan formed an integral part, but even after President Nixon's visit to Communist China in February 1972, we continued to withhold *de jure* recognition from the Peking government (and still do at this writing).

winding down the American participation in the Vietnam War. Still, he was not winding it down anywhere near fast enough to suit many members of a Congress that throughout his Administration was controlled by the opposition party. A declaration by Congress is no guarantee that the war will stay popular with the body concerned, just as the legal declaration of war against Great Britain in 1812 did not keep that war from becoming exceedingly unpopular, but it helps not to have the opposition maintain that the President's action, besides being misguided, is also illegal.

A few days after the Korean War broke out, and a few hours after President Truman had committed ground troops in addition to the already committed air and naval support, he met with leaders of both parties and of both houses of Congress to report on the situation and on his actions. As Acheson reports it:

> A general chorus of approval was interrupted by, I think, Senator Kenneth Wherry questioning the legal authority of the executive to take this action. Senator Alexander Smith suggested a congressional resolution approving the President's action. The President said that he would consider Smith's suggestion and asked me [Acheson] to prepare a recommendation. The meeting ended with Representative Dewey Short stating that Congress was practically unanimous in its appreciation of the President's leadership. Short was a Republican from the President's home state of Missouri and ranking minority member of the Armed Services Committee.[42]

However, after thinking the matter over for another three or four days, Acheson recommended that the President make a full report on the Korean situation to a joint session of Congress but refrain from asking for a resolution of approval, resting on his constitutional authority as commander-in-chief. It happened also that the Congress had recessed for a week, and the President was reluctant to call it back for either purpose. A few other informal advisers, including Senate Majority Leader Scott Lucas, concurred with Acheson's recommendation about not asking for congressional approval, and the President so decided.

Acheson adds:

> There has never, I believe, been any serious doubt—in the sense of non-politically inspired doubt—of the President's

---

[42] Acheson, *Present at the Creation*, p. 413.

constitutional authority to do what he did. The basis for this conclusion in legal theory and historical precedent was fully set out in the State Department's memorandum of July 3, 1950, extensively published. But the wisdom of the decision not to ask for congressional approval has been doubted. To have obtained congressional approval, it has been argued, would have obviated later criticism of 'Truman's war.' In my opinion, it would have changed pejorative phrases, but little else. . . . Nevertheless, it is said, congressional approval would have done no harm. True, approval would have done none, but the process of gaining it might well have done a great deal.[43]

In this writer's opinion Acheson was clearly wrong on both counts. A State Department memorandum written under his direction can hardly be considered an unbiased or even authoritative statement of the constitutional issues. In a nation that prides itself on being ruled by a government of laws and not of men, the constitutional issue on so weighty a problem as the President's authority to wage war without congressional approval is bound to be a nagging one. Acheson tells us that the President, in agreeing to the recommendation, was moved by the following "passionately held" conviction: "His great office was to him a sacred and temporary trust, which he was determined to pass on unimpaired by the slightest loss of power or prestige." This pronouncement will be consoling to future holders of that office (as it clearly has been to Richard Nixon), but not to very many others.

It is of course necessary for the President to be able on his own authority to repel an attack on this country, or to reply to such attacks and to attacks on *bona fide* allies, or to carry out certain military actions in situations that develop overnight or in which the American preparations must be carried on in great secrecy —like the preparations for the confrontation with the Soviet Union in October 1962 concerning the presence of Soviet missiles in Cuba. But for military actions big enough to be called wars, which may endure for months or years, it is hard to see the

---

[43] Ibid., pp. 414 f. The memorandum referred to by Mr. Acheson is reprinted in the *MacArthur Hearings*, part 5, pp. 3198–3204, 3373–3381. See also the speech by Senator Robert A. Taft of June 28, 1950 protesting, among other things, "a complete usurpation by the President of authority to use the Armed Forces of this country." Senator Taft nevertheless asserts "that if a joint resolution were introduced asking for approval of the use of our Armed Forces already sent to Korea and full support of them in their present venture, I would vote in favor of it." Ibid., pp. 3210–3217.

slightest justification for the President's unwillingness to share his responsibility as well as his authority with Congress. True, too small a majority even in a favorable vote may be an embarrassment, but if the President has no more support than that, it is better he not be at war. There is also the danger, certainly realized later in the case of Vietnam, that the President will begin to identify his own personal prestige with that of the United States.

On the political side, it seems curious that both Acheson and President Truman could have questioned the likelihood of a swift and overwhelmingly favorable vote of support from the Congress during the earliest days or weeks of the war, despite the current anxieties about the retreats attending our initial commitments and the precariousness, for a time, of our hold on the Pusan perimeter. An élitist to the core, Acheson could not feel that the Congress, and Americans generally, would share his conviction of the rightness of the act and his complete confidence in our military capability to remedy the situation. On the contrary, the confidence of the uninformed might well have exceeded his. That the United States, which had but recently won World War II—despite incomparably greater initial reverses—could be bested by some small thing called the Army of North Korea was an idea that could not then have made any imprint on the minds of the great majority of Americans, including members of Congress. The above-described meeting (on June 30, 1950) with congressional leaders should have been a sufficiently reassuring demonstration of congressional support. The situation then was very different from what would obtain later in the war.

Actually, the constitutional issue and the question of congressional support did not become really key issues during the Korean War, because events during the critical first year moved too rapidly and dramatically. It did not become "Truman's War" until after we had already started armistice negotiations, and nothing was clearer, perhaps too clear for the opponent, than the President's desire to terminate that war. And, as we have seen, the fact that it was the first United Nations police action in the net greatly helped President Truman's domestic position.

All this was to be changed, enormously changed, in the war that was already in its first stages and that was to become an American war some fifteen years later.

CHAPTER

4

Vietnam:
How We Became
Involved

When Rostow came home early one morning . . . in the mingled exhilaration and exhaustion of crisis, his wife said to him, "You know what you all are? You are the junior officers of the Second World War come to responsibility."

Arthur M. Schlesinger, Jr., in *A Thousand Days*

At a conference sponsored by the Adlai Stevenson Institute of International Affairs in Chicago in June 1968, the proceedings were challenged at the outset by one of the participants who, turning upside down Santayana's famous warning, protested that "if we remember the past, we are condemned to misread it!" Professor Samuel P. Huntington went on to utter what he called "the subversive idea that this conference may well mark the formal beginning of the misreading of the Vietnam experience." As if that were not enough, he added: "It is conceivable that our policymakers may best meet future crises and dilemmas if they simply blot out of their minds any recollection of this one."

Conceivable yes, but one would have to add, most unlikely. Yet before voices of dissent could take hold, another participant had rushed forward to support Huntington. Professor Albert Wohlstetter expressed himself as "painfully aware that, of all the disasters of Vietnam, the worst may be the 'lessons' that we'll draw from it." Those lessons would have to be terribly distorted indeed to fulfill *that* description, and yet, it is again conceivable that such a thing could come to pass. But what is *not* conceivable? There is surely more plausibility in Stanley Hoffmann's retort to Wohlstetter: "Of all the disasters of Vietnam the worst could be our unwillingness to learn enough from them." [1]

What could account for this attitude of two university professors? Is it better not to think at all than, thinking under emotional stress, to risk coming out with the wrong answers? Both indeed had favored and supported our intervention in Vietnam and both were no doubt troubled at finding themselves within a smaller and smaller minority of those within the intellectual community who were not yet ready to acknowledge they had been wrong. Both were now implicitly calling upon all the old shibboleths with which the layman approaches history: Time will clarify all, will straighten out all distortions, or at least will let us know the final results. In something like the Vietnam War, current at the time of the conference and still current even now at this writing over four years later, our reactions, according to Wohlstetter, "tend to be visceral rather than reflective." If by visceral he means that in matters concerning Vietnam we tend to think under some strain of passion, he is surely right; but to wait for some cool moment in the future is to wait for apathy and forgetfulness on the part of all but a few professional historians. As we have seen, the latter, too, have their problems coming out with the right answers, and anyway, the right answers in the remote future may sell at a steep discount today. New policy is being made day by day, and if we cannot profit now from so searing a national experience as that of the United States in Vietnam, then the cause of rational policy-making is really hopeless.

So far as concerns the influence of our viscera, the effort of thinking is never easy, and human beings are rarely induced to engage in it deeply without some motivation that has an emotional basis. Anyway, it is not the felt emotions that distort our

---

[1] Richard M. Pfeffer (ed.), *No More Vietnams?* (New York: Harper & Row, 1968). The statements of Huntington, Wohlstetter, and Hoffmann are on pp. 1–6. This book purports to be a reporting of the conference, but it is a good deal more than that, containing as it does carefully edited papers that go much beyond the conference discussion.

thinking so much as the repressed ones. That observation of Samuel Johnson's that "it marvelously clarifies a man's mind to know he is to be hanged in a fortnight" was surely not intended to suggest that the person concerned was indifferent to his condition or felt in the net benefited by the clarification. Similarly, the events in Vietnam have marvelously clarified our thinking about many things on which we were previously wrong or indifferent, and this change has inevitably followed from the fact that to many of us these events have been deeply disturbing or distressing.

As Professor Hoffmann so eloquently and trenchantly characterized our national behavior, in the retort just referred to:

> the very attempt, indeed the massive and often frenzied effort, at pursuing goals, applying notions, and devising strategies that turned out to be irrelevant, self-defeating, and dangerous in so unrewarding an area with such persistence in wishful thinking and self-delusion, tells us a great deal about what ought to be discarded in the future. It reveals flaws that come from the depths of our political style and machinery, but had never been so clearly brought to light in any previous operation.

That is Vietnam, a story of virtually unmitigated disasters that we have inflicted on ourselves and even more on others. It could have been worse, naturally, had we taken on a more powerful and dangerous enemy, but that we had already largely learned to avoid. The Korean War was one long story of earnest desire to disengage from China. The Vietnamese situation seems to have been peculiarly constructed to entice us ever deeper into a morass of error, and essential to that treacherous construction has been the puny quality of the opponent, against whom two Presidents have found it temperamentally beyond their powers to admit failure.

How the United States Became Involved

The question of how the United States became involved in Vietnam has not lacked for earnest, informed, and insightful explorers, moved by a sense of tragedy and a feeling that the sum of many transparent parts is nevertheless a mystery. The relevant items can be described, tagged, put together, and still we are left with a question mark. It is not an unfamiliar question mark. The persistence of presumably rational men in what is conspicuously irrational behavior seems to have been an essential ingredient in most wars, and we have already observed it operating on a far higher level of pain and tragedy in World War I. Still, there is an extra dimension of unreality in American behavior in the Vietnam War. There may for that reason be a special opportunity here to find those ingredients in the mix that are too infrequently noted and which may help reduce the mystery.

In the same Chicago conference Arthur Schlesinger, Jr. presented his view of our Vietnam intervention as stemming from two traditional strands of American thinking about our role in the world and one newer one. The two older strands were responsible in times past "for some of the most splendid moments of our international behavior." One of them, as we noticed in discussing the American intervention in Korea, he called "Stimsonianism," because it was "the basis of Secretary of State Stimson's reaction [in 1931] to the Japanese incursion into Manchuria." This is the idea "that an orderly world requires a single durable structure of world security, which must everywhere be protected against aggression: if aggression were permitted to go unpunished in one place, this by infection would lead to a general destruction of the system of world order." This was the familiar conception associated with "collective security" under the League of Nations and greatly refortified by the events leading up to World War II.

The second strand is "the concept that the United States has a saving mission to the world. It is an old idea, rekindled by Woodrow Wilson in 1917-20 and enlarged by World War II into a kind of global New Dealism. Global New Dealism meant that we have an obligation to deal with poverty, repression, and injustice 'everywhere in the world.'" Among the numerous undertakings that stemmed from this "honorable tradition" was the Marshall Plan, which played so vital a role in restoring Europe to health after the ravages of World War II.

This "liberal evangelism . . . was reinforced by a third factor: the impact of Stalinism." Stalinism gave rise to an anti-Communism in the United States that embraced virtually all political viewpoints including the most liberal. "For many people in the 1940's this necessary and correct anticommunism hardened into a series of conditioned reflexes which continued to guide their thoughts after communism itself was beginning to be transformed under the stress of nationalism." [2]

In other words, the thinking that ascribed monolithic aspects to world Communism not only failed to take account of important

[2] Ibid., pp. 7-9.

changes within the Soviet Union, but also survived the recognition, itself tardy, of the split between the Soviet Union and Communist China. It therefore accorded to each of the two great Communist capitals a degree of dominion over neighboring Communist regimes that they really did not have. We now know that Hanoi was never a mere outrider in a carriage driven by Peking, though the United States State Department with Dean Rusk at the head of it considered it so for much too long a time. Containment of Hanoi might not have been regarded as sufficiently important to warrant our intervention, but containment of Communism's eastern empire headed by Peking definitely was.

These ideas, recalled rather than discovered by Schlesinger, incidentally tell us why in matters concerning Vietnam the younger generation of today find it so difficult to understand or believe what they consider the hypocritical protestations of their elders. Of all the charges levelled against President Lyndon B. Johnson and serving in the end to harry him from office, the one that must have pained and bewildered him most was the repeated insistence that what the United States was doing in Vietnam was "immoral." We shall presently see that there is much to justify that charge, the more so as our government moved gradually into a position where we were continuing a war, at vast cost to the Vietnamese people if not to our own, for little purpose other than to save face. But the events leading up to and including the shift to an open combat commitment in 1965 were undertaken for motives that to President Johnson as well as to his predecessor—and to all the many idealists in their retinues—seemed to be of the purest. We need not ask whether they actually were so at any time, and even less is it necessary to ask whether, starting pure, they remained so for very long. Motivation, as Freud taught us long ago, is that concerning which human beings are capable of the greatest self-deception.

One can of course exaggerate the degree to which the traditions described by Schlesinger have been distinctively American. Other western nations, too, have at various times shown a strong commitment to collective security and to the idea that their mission in the world was to do good, not only without gain but possibly at some cost. France for a long time conceived of itself as having a colonial policy inspired by its *mission civilisatrice,* and Britain carried proudly its "white man's burden." It is all too easy for cynics to make fun of these mottoes and to find an explanation for everything in avarice, but they thereby deprive themselves of an important part of the understanding of the foreign policies of great nations. There is little doubt that whatever gain Britain and France derived from their colonial policies in the nineteenth and twentieth centuries was in national pride rather than economic advantage, and it is clear too that many if not most of their national leaders were aware of that.[3]

Even so, the United States did have certain qualities, or rather advantages, which enabled it to pursue "global New Dealism" with a quite special verve. First, it enjoyed until World War II, as compared with all the other great powers of the world, what can be described as a surplus of security. It was also committed to an anticolonial policy, or at least what could be called that if one ignored a few aberrations like the Philippines and Puerto Rico. It was also very powerful and very rich. There was no compelling reason why for self-interest we needed to oppose Japanese expansionism in the Far East, but we did so, and the result was Pearl Harbor and our engagement in World War II.

As we have noted, the conviction that peace and security in the world were indivisible was strongly refortified by the events leading up to World War II. People who do not remember these events find it difficult to recapture the tremendously traumatic impact of the Munich Agreement on the thinking of the postwar world, especially in the United States. Why the United States, which was not a party to that agreement? It was Britain and France that had "sold the Czechs down the river" in 1938, but the experience of these two countries in the war that came only one year later showed that they had had very little choice. And because of what they went through in that war, their postwar attitudes had little room for guilt about Munich. The United States, however, by its aloofness at that time from the affairs of Europe had made the agreement necessary; it had been dragged into the war anyway, and it had then demonstrated by its performance in the war that it had the means to make a vast difference in those affairs from which it had previously abstracted itself. And the fact that we had not actually been a party to the pact meant that it was less embarrassing for American leaders to mention it, which we see them doing over and over again in the postwar years.

Thus, the motives that propelled us into the Vietnam War were basically the same as those that had precipitated our Korean intervention some fifteen years earlier. Still, there were differences,

---

[3] This subject is treated in some detail in Chapters 6 and 7.

some of which were reflected in the nearly total absence of support for our Vietnam intervention among those nations (especially of Europe) that had warmly supported us in Korea. One conspicuous difference was that in the Korean case the aggression had been abrupt and across a line and therefore unambiguous, while in the case of Vietnam the action of the northern Communist regime against the southern non-Communist one was, at least initially, hidden and somewhat indirect. The difference was important throughout the world and also with respect to a minority of American opinion. However, the Administrations of Presidents Kennedy and Johnson deemed this difference to be superficial. Camouflaged aggression, they held, was no less blameworthy and dangerous than the more overt kind, and anyway it just as inexorably meant the spread of Communism. Still, it seems odd that a subterfuge that was so transparent to the American leaders should fool the rest of the world. The major differences must be found elsewhere.

The United States appeared to have been affected differently from Europe simply in the lapse of time. In 1950 our government was imbued with the *new* notion that Communism must be "contained," naturally by the only nation capable of doing so, with whatever help it could marshal under the aegis of the new United Nations and the newer NATO. There is something about an ideology being new that helps to lend it vigor amounting at times to religiosity. There has been no opportunity for experience to deaden the excitement, or to show that the world is after all more complex than any single formula allows for, or to indicate that circumstances are really not altogether what they first appeared, or to suggest that even if they were so they could yet change substantially, or to qualify our estimate of our own infallibility, or to let any of a number of things occur that can happen only over time. Thus, a few simplistic ideas could have a kind of thrust in 1950 that, to the rest of the world at least, would seem somewhat bizarre by 1965. Certainly in the decade following 1950, European opinion substantially led official American opinion in becoming more relaxed about the dangers of Soviet aggression.

The United States, however, appeared caught in the toils and ecstacy of its role of *leadership*. Other nations might relax their vigilance; we dared not, either for ourselves or for them. Moreover, the fact that only fifteen years separated the two crises meant also that many of the same people were around and in power during the second of them who had been very much in evidence during the first. Dean Rusk, for example, who was to play so significant a role as Secretary of State during the years in which we were escalating the Vietnam War, had been Assistant Secretary of State for Far Eastern Affairs during the Korean War; General Maxwell D. Taylor, whom we last saw as commander of the Eighth Army in the final stages of the Korean War, was on hand to exert a powerful influence upon our involvement in Vietnam. The inflexibility of these two men and of those of whom they were representative cannot be ascribed to their respective ages. The policy-makers who propelled us into the Vietnam War were, on the average, young for the offices they held. One figure before the public who opposed our intervention from the beginning, Walter Lippmann, was older than any of them. It is simply that some people are more inflexible than others, regardless of their years, and those who held important policy-making posts in the Eisenhower, Kennedy, and Johnson Administrations were all children of the cold war. Some of them, especially Rusk and Taylor and the less important Walt Rostow, were also extraordinarily rigid.[4]

But all this still fails to account for the fact that the American response to Vietnam was basically different from that of the rest of the western world. Some have added the ingredient of hubris, the ancient Greek equivalent to the pride that goeth before a fall.[5] That pride had been engendered by our performance in World War II and also by those tremendous postwar accomplishments in Europe, such as the hugely successful Marshall Plan, success in forestalling Communist take-overs in Greece and in West Berlin,

---

[4] Dean Rusk's inflexibility on Vietnam is by now legendary, a good example of it being his testimony before the Senate Committee on Foreign Relations on January 28, 1966. Compare his testimony with that of one at least equally experienced in foreign affairs, George F. Kennan, delivered on February 10, 1966. Rusk speaks in terms of moral imperatives implying open-ended obligations; Kennan in terms of objectives that bear a sensible proportion to the means and exertions necessary to achieve them. Their testimony, plus that of General Maxwell Taylor on February 17, 1966, is published in the usual Senate hearings series, and also in *The Vietnam Hearings*, with an Introduction by J. William Fulbright (New York: Random House, Vintage Book V-354, 1966). The official publication, more complete, is entitled: *Supplemental Foreign Assistance Fiscal Year 1966—Vietnam; Hearings Before the Committee on Foreign Relations, United States Senate, 89th Congress, 2nd Session, on S. 2793*; Jan. 28; Feb. 4, 8, 10, 17, and 18, 1966. As for General Taylor, one of the most urbane and presumably gifted military officers of our time, the publication six years later of his memoirs, *Swords and Plowshares* (New York: Norton, 1972) confirmed the fact that in all matters relating to Vietnam his mind was set in concrete.

[5] See comments of Adam Yarmclinsky, *No More Vietnams?* pp. 22–25.

and the political unity represented by that NATO of which we were the undoubted leaders—and in the Far East the astonishing economic and political recovery of Japan as an American protegé. China had indeed been lost, in what looked in retrospect like a fit of American absent-mindedness, but South Korea had been saved.

For the reader of this book the Korean War is only a few pages back, and to read about it reveals triumphs mixed with heavy American losses, defeats, and periods of desperation as well as of agonizing frustration. But few people read about past wars, especially small ones, and the number of American dead in Korea could not make a lasting impression upon a nation that loses considerably more than that number on its highways each year. After a dozen years, the pain was forgotten and only the triumph remained. We had certainly turned back the march of Communism in Korea. The subsequent economic development of South Korea had made it into an Oriental showcase of prosperity nearly on a par with Japan.

The heady consciousness of leadership of what we delighted to call "the free world" had been held partly muted during the somewhat stodgy stewardship of President Dwight D. Eisenhower. Our policies militarily were committed mostly for economic reasons to the doctrine of "massive retaliation," which was in large measure a doctrine of noninvolvement. The government refused to build up conventional forces for the purpose of carrying on Korean-type wars. We would depend on our nuclear power to deter not only great wars but also lesser ones like Korea, and if some disturbance or aggression occurred that did not warrant the use of nuclear weapons, it probably would not warrant intervention at all. And, at least for the limited time of the Eisenhower Administration, it worked. The intervention in Lebanon in 1958 was not a shooting affair; neither was our partial intervention in the Quemoy-Matsu crisis of the same year. As for Dien Bien Phu in 1954, the net result after some maneuvering was a decision not to intervene.

The events surrounding Dien Bien Phu and President Eisenhower's reaction to them are instructive. He was deeply concerned with the possibility of a Communist victory in Vietnam, and his Administration, with congressional approval and support, had been continuing the considerable material aid to the French begun under President Truman early in 1950 and accelerated at the outbreak of the Korean War. When the fate of the garrison at

Dien Bien Phu became desperate and the French called upon him for more direct aid, President Eisenhower wrote to Prime Minister Winston Churchill urging the formation of a coalition that would include, indispensably in his mind, some Asiatic nations as well as France, Britain, and the United States. The cold British response caused Eisenhower to drop the idea of intervention—partly because he knew that the absence of broad international collaboration would dampen congressional support for our intervention, but also because he was entirely in accord with the presumed congressional attitude. He himself almost instinctively opposed any kind of intervention that would not involve "a concert of powers," and his attitude towards the need for congressional support was summed up in the following declaration: "Part of my fundamental concept of the Presidency is that we have a constitutional government and only when there is a sudden, unforeseen emergency should the President put us into war without congressional action." [6]

Eisenhower was also sensitive to the crucial importance of the political situation within Vietnam in determining the success of the military operations. In his memoirs he reports a conversation between French Foreign Minister Georges Bidault and Walter Bedell Smith in which Bidault expressed the opinion that General Navarre ought to be replaced in Vietnam because the French seemed to be suffering defeat after defeat despite their great material superiority. Bedell Smith, also a former general it might be noted, "gave a straightforward answer: he told Bidault that any second-rate general should be able to win in Indochina if there were a proper political atmosphere." In another place, after stressing again the importance of the poor political leadership within

---

[6] Dwight D. Eisenhower, *Mandate for Change: Vol. 1: The White House Years* (New York: Doubleday, 1963), p. 345. Concerning the need for a "concert of powers," see his letter to General Alfred M. Gruenther, p. 352. His memoirs, however, tend to understate his eagerness to intervene, which is revealed in *The Pentagon Papers: The Defense Department History of United States Decisionmaking on Vietnam, Senator Mike Gravel Edition*, 4 vols. (Boston: Beacon Press, 1971), vol. 1, pp. 98–107. The Pentagon Papers, in three different editions, powerfully supplement or effectively supersede much previous source material on U.S. involvement in Vietnam. In addition to the Gravel edition, there is the official U.S. government edition in 12 volumes, *United States-Vietnam Relations, 1945–1967: A Study Prepared by the Department of Defence; Printed for the Use of the House Committee on the Armed Services* (Washington: Government Printing Office, 1971). There is also the one-volume edition, *The Pentagon Papers*, which prints only the portions originally published by the *New York Times* (New York: Quadrangle Books, 1971; paperback: Bantam Books, 1971).

Vietnam, Eisenhower quotes with approval what an unnamed Frenchman had said to him. "What Vietnam needs is another Syngman Rhee, regardless of all the difficulties the presence of such a personality would entail." [7]

It is also revealing that Eisenhower saw fit to mention that his Vice President, Richard M. Nixon, had made a "not for attribution" speech ("and thereafter widely attributed") before the American Society of Newspaper Editors indicating much greater readiness than his chief to intervene at Dien Bien Phu. He quotes Nixon as saying: ". . . if to avoid further Communist expansion in Asia and Indochina, we must take the risk now by putting our boys in, I think the Executive has to take the politically unpopular decision and do it." [8] This language appears to reflect a willingness to contemplate such a move without too much regard for congressional or foreign support, and Eisenhower seems to indicate that his own view was different. Eisenhower, incidentally, was also able to lean upon his own military knowledge and experience to persuade himself—in opposition to Admiral Arthur W. Radford, then Chairman of the Joint Chiefs of Staff—that a few strikes by small American aircraft operating mainly from two aircraft carriers in the western Pacific would be of no help against the forces beseiging the French garrison. At least they would be of no help without nuclear weapons, which the President had no intention of using.

Eisenhower's conclusion should indeed not have required his degree of experience. Whether Radford really believed the air strikes would have so much effect or whether he simply wanted to intervene is not clear. The Joint Chiefs disagreed with their chairman on the desirability of intervening and presumably also on the efficacy of the air strikes. It is worth noting that Senator Lyndon B. Johnson was one of the congressional leaders consulted, and he agreed with his colleagues in opposing intervention except in concert with other powers. At this stage Senator Johnson registers as definitely less keen on intervening than Vice President Nixon.

It was indeed Eisenhower who provided us with the unfortunate domino analogy, and who cherished in Dulles an aggressive Secretary of State who was at least as eager as Nixon to intervene at

---

[7] Eisenhower, *Mandate for Change*, pp. 360, 372.

[8] Ibid., p. 353 n.

Dien Bien Phu. But on this matter he kept Dulles under firm control. The latter put in a testy appearance at the Geneva Conference in April 1954, just long enough to indicate his distaste for the proceedings, he being an anti-Communist of the most fundamentalist sect.[9] Eisenhower also started the practice of providing "military advisers" to the Ngo Dinh Diem regime, and he and his Secretary of State hastily created in September 1954 the somewhat equivocal commitment represented by the Southeast Asia Treaty Organization (SEATO). Still, all this was playing on the edges. Although SEATO might be a potential embarrassment, we were certainly not irrevocably committed to Vietnam by the time Eisenhower left office.

At that time he seemed for some reason to be more concerned with Laos than with Vietnam. In a briefing that he gave to his successor and a few members of the latter's staff on the eve of the Kennedy inauguration, Eisenhower scarcely mentioned Vietnam in dwelling on his preoccupation with Laos. He seemed to be advising the President-elect that if all else failed in Laos, that country was important enough to warrant United States intervention even if we had to "go it alone." This was an extraordinary view, and contrasted sharply with one that Eisenhower was supposed to have expressed within the National Security Council only a few months earlier.[10]

The Administration that came to power in January 1961 under President John F. Kennedy presented an attitude towards American responsibilities for "leadership" of the free world that one could call either "vigorous" or "frenzied," depending on how one felt about it. Our NATO allies were quickly apprised of the fact that the Americans had many new ideas for the defense of Europe, and that the Europeans would have to make some endeavor to understand and implement them. These ideas were themselves

---

[9] He did leave behind Undersecretary of State Walter Bedell Smith. A good brief description of the Geneva Conference of 1954 is given in a chapter by Donald Lancaster, "Power Politics at the Geneva Conference of 1954." Originally published in his *The Emancipation of French Indochina* (London: Oxford University Press, 1961), it is reprinted in Marvin E. Gettleman (ed.), *Vietnam: History, Documents, and Opinions on a Major World Crisis* (New York: Fawcett, 1965), pp. 118–137. The latter book includes also the texts of the agreements issuing from that conference, ibid., pp. 137–159. See also *The Pentagon Papers*, Gravel ed., vol. 1, pp. 108–178, 499–573.

[10] Clark Clifford, later Secretary of Defense, was present at the briefing of December 1960, and it is his impressions of that event that Townsend Hoopes cites in his indispensable *The Limits of Intervention* (New York: McKay, 1969), pp. 167 f. The discerning British journalist, Henry Brandon, seems to be using independent sources in describing the same briefing, as well as the earlier NSC meeting. See his *Anatomy of Error* (London: Andre Deutsch, 1970), pp. 14 f.

significant for what was to happen in the Far East, because they involved a complete dismantling of the "massive retaliation" concept in favor of a whole new complex of ideas stressing the use of conventional forces in limited wars. The man who as a true believer presided intimately over this change was the new Secretary of Defense, Robert S. McNamara. However, the President also brought back from retirement to serve as his personal military adviser (and later as Chairman of the Joint Chiefs of Staff and then Ambassador to South Vietnam) General Taylor, who had been Army Chief of Staff during part of the Eisenhower years. During his retirement Taylor expressed in a much read book his indignation over the emphasis on massive retaliation at the cost of *more usable* forms of power, including conventional as well as tactical nuclear weapons.[11] Though his book was not significantly original, all the ideas in it being considerably in vogue by that time, he had coined the term "flexible response."

Anyone who worked at the strategic theory-building of that day must recall with how much enthusiasm one's colleagues (and perhaps also oneself) spoke of "putting out brush fires" wherever they occurred.[12] A *brush fire*, according to the usage of the time, was of somewhat vague definition but was clearly less than a world war. Perhaps the term *brush fire*—like the term *firebreak*, to stress the difference between nuclear and conventional weapons —was chosen because so much of this thinking went on originally at the RAND Corporation, which was surrounded by the arid hills of southern California. Anyway, there seemed to be no doubt in anyone's mind that it was the complete responsibility of the United States to put out these brush fires wherever they might occur. Neither did there appear to be any doubt of the capability of the United States to do so quickly and easily, regardless of what

---

[11] Maxwell Taylor, *The Uncertain Trumpet* (New York: Harper & Bros., 1960), p. 24. In this book he says of the Dien Bien Phu crisis and our reasons for not intervening in it: "*Unfortunately,* such forces [conventional] did not then exist in sufficient strength or in proper position to offer any hope of success." [Italics added.] I leave for the next chapter a brief consideration of General Taylor's outlook on affairs. One should also notice, however, the quotation from Robert Kennedy in Chapter 10 referring to Taylor as the most restrained of the military chiefs advising President J. F. Kennedy during the Cuban missile crisis.

[12] I was involved in this theorizing, and contributed something to it in its earliest stages, which began at the RAND Corporation early in 1952. I continued in this endeavor until the publication of my *Strategy in the Missile Age* (Princeton: Princeton University Press, 1959); see especially chap. 9, "Limited War." However, when limited-war theorizing went into its rococo stage during the McNamara period at the Pentagon, I published some articles and one book in opposition to what I then considered the absurd excesses of the school. This subject is treated in greater detail in Chapter 9.

sanctuaries it allowed the enemy, provided it built up and maintained not only substantial conventional forces (including the "Special Forces" that so engaged the fancy of the President himself), but also the means of quickly delivering them and their equipment to places where they might be needed.

Of the several heavily overworked terms in the McNamara lexicon, none suffered more use than the term *options*, normally in the context of stressing the laudibility of expanding one's options, or keeping one's options open, or the like. By the end of his term in office Robert McNamara was very likely of the opinion that it had been far better had some options not been so sedulously developed. One effective way of keeping out of trouble is to lack the means of getting into it. In his protest cited at the beginning of this chapter, Professor Wohlstetter mentioned among the obviously absurd "wrong lessons" that we might derive from analyzing the Vietnam War such conclusions as "that we are better off reducing the choices available to us . . ." Actually, if we approach the matter with an open mind, determined not to bar any finding that our experience seems to warrant, then one does indeed have to entertain such a thought. What greater objection could there be to heavier reliance on nuclear weapons (which Wohlstetter does object to) than the fact that fallible political and military leaders have given us all too much indication that they cannot be wholly trusted with their use? We have had to learn that the same lesson also applies, naturally with important differences, to the possession of large conventional capabilities. In any case, it was undoubtedly to be a factor in President Johnson's decision to send combat forces to Vietnam beginning in March, 1965 that in the preceding four years we had considerably expanded the number of American combat-ready divisions and related forces.

The Nature of the Decision-Maker

An issue of at least comparable moment to those just considered, one would think, is the personality and character of the President in power when the basic decisions were made. The essential question is: Given the circumstances prevailing, did it matter much or relatively little who was President? What the journalist and usually the historian take for granted we have to discuss seriously, because this issue is rather deliberately evaded in some learned discussions of what got us involved in Vietnam. At the Adlai Stevenson Institute conference already mentioned, all sorts of reasons for our intervention were mustered for review—save the special nature of the man who made the critical decisions. One participant, Professor Richard J. Barnet, referred to the President's role only to discount its relevance! First giving lip service to *New York Times* editorialist Tom Wicker's idea that "the President's role is crucial," he went on to argue his well-known special position: "but he operates within limits set by the vast foreign-policy machinery of government. The President may decide, but the bureaucracy structures the decisions by setting out the choices." Yet even that appraisal seemed in his opinion to give the President too much latitude, because he continued with the following: "If the basis of the American commitment to take on revolutionary movements around the world is institutional, then we cannot hope to avoid future Vietnam-like adventures in other places merely by shifts in personnel [including, he means, the President!] or even by changes in general policy pronouncements." [13]

Barnet's comments were strongly challenged on the spot, especially by Schlesinger, who had served on the White House staff during President Kennedy's "thousand days."

> The great trouble with [Barnet's] argument is that it concentrates on those who give the advice rather than on those who take it. Kennedy did not escalate at the time of the Bay of Pigs, and after the Bay of Pigs he never again took the advice of the Joint Chiefs of Staff on a serious issue. . . . The useful area of concern for us is who makes the decisions, who takes the advice, and why.[14]

There exists today a strong movement in academia bent on creating a "theory" of international relations in which events conform to models that have the virtue of being simple. In order to accomplish this end, nations have to be conceived as units (or at least there are "superpowers" that are units and lesser powers that are other units). Time periods of equal length also have to be conceived of as units, even though one such period may occupy a decade before World War I and the other a decade after, and of course governments or heads of government, too, have to be conceived of as units. This school thus effectively depersonalizes all the decisions that go to make up the subject matter of interna-

---

13 Pfeffer, *No More Vietnams?* pp. 50–74; the quoted remarks are on p. 51.
14 Ibid., p. 85.

tional relations. The major acts of any nation and of whole groups of nations are held to be ruled by certain institutional principles —subject, perhaps, to minor deviations that can be handled in terms of statistical probabilities—and so entirely governed by laws that appropriate study can easily disclose.

A striking example is found in the same Chicago conference, when Professor Huntington rose to remind his colleagues of the cyclical theory of American interventionism advanced by Frank L. Klingberg some sixteen years earlier. Based on his own historical perceptions of American "introversionist" and "extraversionist" moods, Klingberg had charted United States behavior back to 1776, and had found that periods of introversion had averaged some twenty-one years, and those of extraversion about twenty-seven years. Softly reproaching Klingberg for being, "if anything, a little too unsure of his own theory," Huntington triumphantly noted that the current disillusionment on Vietnam had come back promptly on schedule! In making his point he peremptorily asserted, among other things, that "the American outrage at the war reflected less the war than it did the impact of TV. . . ." The frequency with which the latter assertion has been uttered obscures the fact that it has never been in the slightest degree tested, let alone proved—only one indication among many of how scientific is this self-styled "scientific approach." The assertion also leaves us wondering what could possibly have caused the often violent domestic opposition to such other American wars as the War of 1812 and the Mexican War of 1846–1848.

What the United States of 1968 had in common with the colonies of 1776 other than language is infinitely debatable, but surely we are in the absence of anything like a controlled test for a theory that utterly negates not only the consequences of personal leadership but of vast sociological and political change. It was incidentally an economic theorist shortly to become widely known, Dr. Daniel Ellsberg, who at the conference promptly gave the Huntington intervention the retort it deserved.[15]

Ellsberg in his turn was later to develop a theory that also went very far in depersonalizing the workings out of the Presidential power. His argument is somewhat radically summed up by Dr. Leslie H. Gelb, who directed the task force that prepared the Pentagon Papers, in an article entitled "Vietnam, The System

---

[15] Ibid., pp. 38–43. For the Klingberg article see "The Historical Alternation of Moods in American Foreign Policy," *World Politics*, vol. IV (Jan. 1952), pp. 239–273.

Worked." By this provocative title Gelb means that the Presidents who involved the country in Vietnam were not stumbling into a quagmire unawares. As he puts it, "U.S. involvement did not stem from a failure to foresee consequences." Each President, according to him and Ellsberg, was intent simply on avoiding blame for losing South Vietnam to Communism and did what he construed to be the minimum necessary for passing the burden on to his successor.

Though Gelb and Ellsberg succeed in demonstrating that the interventionist moves, especially of President Johnson, did *not* stem mainly from optimism about what those moves would accomplish, they fall into the opposite error of implying that the President knew very well what he was getting into. The implication that in 1965 Lyndon B. Johnson foresaw anything like 1968 is on the face of it an absurdity. It is a fairly safe guess that if Johnson had had the necessary foresight, he would have much preferred in 1965 to take his chances with the electoral penalties he allegedly feared from letting South Vietnam go. Ellsberg makes clear in a later paper what he thinks those penalties were. They turn out to be the fury of the radical right and a recrudescence of McCarthyism.[16] I shall consider this view in greater detail in the next chapter. The only point I wish to make here is that both Gelb and Ellsberg tend to wash out completely the distinction between those whom they refer to as "the Presidents." Their thesis represents the triumph of ideology over evidence, for the Pentagon Papers, to which both appeal, can be just as strongly cited on the other side. Moreover, it is pretty much contradicted by Gelb himself in a later review-article on ex-President Johnson's memoirs, where he is obliged to confront directly the relevance of the very special character of Lyndon Johnson.[17]

It would be simply absurd to depreciate the fundamental effects

---

[16] Gelb's article appears in *Foreign Policy*, no. 3 (Summer 1971), pp. 140–173. This article was in part a reflection of some views expressed by Ellsberg in "The Quagmire Myth and the Stalemate Machine," *Public Policy* (Harvard), Spring 1971. A debate ensued concerning it, mostly in the pages of the *New York Review of Books*, in which Gelb and Ellsberg were joined by Morton H. Halperin, all in opposition to Arthur M. Schlesinger, Jr. See *New York Review of Books*, Oct. 21, Dec. 2, and Dec. 16, 1971, and a final "letter to the editor" by Halperin in the issue of Jan. 27, 1972. Ellsberg greatly expanded his argument in a long chapter entitled "The Quagmire Myth and the Stalemate Machine," in his *Papers on the War* (New York: Simon and Schuster, 1972).

[17] "The Pentagon Papers and *The Vantage Point*," *Foreign Policy*, no. 6 (Spring 1972), pp. 25–41.

upon national policies and conduct of institutions and traditions, as well as of changing currents of thought. But surely something has to be left to the nature of the chief decision-maker. Europe in the sixteenth century was no doubt ripe for the Reformation, but it took a Luther to trigger it, and the manner in which it swept over Christiandom depended largely on such caprices as, in England, the feelings of a petulant and ruthless king about his wife.

There are always important latitudes of choice within existing patterns of thought. And there can be few decisions more crucial than that of deciding whether or not to go to war. Within any given climate, one man may decide for one course and another man for the opposite course, and surely it should be redundant to say that it matters which of them is in control. Why each makes his choice the way he does depends in large part on things internal to him, including significantly the unconscious aspects of his motivation. To adopt this conception means to be ready to accept the notion that caprice may play a significant part in the destinies of great nations and thus of the world—for when a man like Lyndon B. Johnson can become President of the United States by virtue of the fact that an otherwise insignificant person full of rage happened to be able to fire a rifle bullet accurately, or another some five years later can achieve the authority because he won by a majority of 313,000 popular votes with only 43 per cent of the electorate, that victory being partly the result of a second assassination, then surely we are dealing with a large measure of caprice. This is hard on "theorists." Actually the point of view I am expressing is itself only a different kind of theory, but with much less accent on tidiness. It is significant that in one of the previously mentioned debates, it was Schlesinger the historian who accepted without question the importance of the man in charge, while it was political scientist John McDermott who defended Barnet's thesis as "intellectually more interesting. . . . *even if wrong.*" [Italics added.] [18]

We have already paid our respects to the currents of thought and of doctrine that would have affected the judgments of any United States President holding office in the 1950's and 1960's and that certainly influenced deeply those who did hold that office. However, it is also necessary to observe the relevant differences in insight as well as other aspects of personality and character among those who held it.

---

[18] Pfeffer, *No More Vietnams?* p. 98.

There were, as we saw, important differences between Eisenhower and his successor, but we might also speculate briefly on whether it would have made a substantial difference to the decisions made in 1964 and thereafter had President Kennedy stayed alive to make them (in view of his great and growing popularity there can be small doubt that he would have been reelected in 1964). It is not an easy thing to do. We have to make judgments on the basis of deeply conflicting evidence, relying only on intuition to tell us which is the most significant among several widely varying indications of how a man's mind inclines. We feel the frustration of forever lacking any final and decisive proof. Also, we can have no idea at all how a third or a fourth or a fifth person in the same post would have acted. Presidents Kennedy and Johnson were each in his own way very special persons, and as examples of possible Presidential behavior they offer at best limited statistics. These are among the reasons why some rationalize away the importance of the problem. We shall never know conclusively how President Kennedy, had he lived, would have acted differently from his successor. Nor is there publicly available anything like an adequate body of insight into the psychological makeup of either of these two men, and there may never be one. The personality and character of some of the greatest figures of our national history have until now persistently eluded their biographers.[19]

The waters would be muddied enough, but we now are additionally blessed with something called the "New Left," which differs from the old left mostly in that it seems to lack entirely any integrating doctrine and that its adherents insist on the absence of any significant differentiation among any politicians outside their own vaguely defined camp. They naturally find it excessively easy to wipe out *any* distinction between Lyndon Johnson and his 1964 electoral opponent Senator Barry Goldwater, though the public statements that the latter was continuing to make into 1972 suggest strongly that had he won that election the levels of

---

[19] I am particularly sensitized to this point by the biographical work of my wife, Fawn M. Brodie, who is currently engaged on a volume on Thomas Jefferson aimed at recapturing his essential personality and character—which have been entirely blanked out by all his major biographers thus far. The basic reasons for the latter phenomenon appear to be two-fold. First, biographers of great national heroes like Jefferson tend to be primly protective of the man who is their subject, apparently feeling that a child-like adulation is the only right attitude with which to approach him. Second, all but a very few of them live in a world unsullied by any of the psychological notions developed by Freud and others.

violence in Vietnam would have gone sharply higher than they did, quite possibly including the use of nuclear weapons. With the New Left marches also the new "cold war revisionism," according to which Harry Truman and his successors were guilty not simply of errors of judgment, which included exaggerated fears of Soviet intentions, but of a conspiratorial villainy! In a sudden Vietnam-induced paroxysm of disillusionment with former hero John F. Kennedy they suddenly discover that the very words they had been wont to quote approvingly from his inaugural speech demonstrate his commitment to the cold war, as indeed they do. His "missile-gap" warnings in his 1960 campaign speeches are paraded as wilful deception when we know they were due to an error in intelligence shared by the Administration in power. Such is the environment in which we must attempt a tentative appraisal.

The record is not simple and one-sided, but we do have many important hints. We notice one in Schlesinger's earlier quoted statement concerning Kennedy's behavior during and after the Bay of Pigs fiasco. We know from others, too, that he immediately admitted to his friends and staff members and shortly thereafter to the world at large that he had made a tragic mistake: "Not only were our facts in error, but our policy was wrong because the premises on which it was built were wrong." [20] One cannot remotely imagine President Johnson saying any such thing, publicly or privately. Does this reflect merely a difference in personal style, or does it go much deeper? There is quite enough known publicly about both men to suggest that we are dealing with a basic and vital character difference.

We know from many sources, including the books he had written when he came to office (for example, *Why England Slept; Profiles in Courage*), that Kennedy was deeply affected by the thinking of his time on international affairs. We know also that he immensely admired dynamism of character and personal courage, both physical and moral. Partly for those reasons he yielded to what he felt to be massive pressures shortly after his inauguration in permitting to go into execution that hare-brained plan

---

[20] Clark Clifford quotes the late President as using these words to him just after the Bay of Pigs disaster. See his article, "Set a Date in Vietnam . . ." in *Life*, May 22, 1970. But see especially Arthur M. Schlesinger, Jr., *A Thousand Days* (Boston: Houghton Mifflin, 1965), pp. 265–273.

developed and implemented under his predecessor by the CIA and approved by the Joint Chiefs to have some 1,200 refugee Cubans invade their native land against Castro's 200,000; but he determined after its failure that he would never again so yield. Eighteen months later he carried off, without violence, the tremendous triumph of the missile crisis, the "Cuban Trafalgar" of October 1962. He was profoundly concerned with what was happening in Indochina and in his somewhat less than three years in office he increased the number of "military advisers" in Vietnam from about 600 to almost 17,000. We can also charge Kennedy with responsibility for appointing those officials who were to guide his successor down the path of major military intervention in Vietnam, including Secretary of State Dean Rusk, Secretary of Defense Robert McNamara, General Maxwell Taylor, McGeorge Bundy, and Walt W. Rostow—none of whom, it should be noticed, projected himself in 1960-1961 as a particularly warlike character. In October 1961 he sent Taylor and Rostow to Vietnam to report on the situation there. Their report elicited from J. Kenneth Galbraith, then Ambassador to India, the following remark: "It is a curious document. The recommendations are for vigorous action. The appendices say it cannot possibly succeed given the present government in Saigon." [21]

This looks rather like a man who could easily have done what President Johnson did in early 1965, and naturally the data on this side could be greatly expanded. However, there is another large side to the story. Kennedy had toured Indochina in 1951 and 1953, had also read considerably about it, and had expressed the belief that Communism could be defeated in Asia only by the force of nationalism. "Without the support of the native population," he had stressed, "there is no hope of success in any of the

---

[21]·See Galbraith's *Ambassador's Journal: A Personal Account of the Kennedy Years* (Boston: Houghton Mifflin, 1969), p. 254. Galbraith saw the Taylor-Rostow report in Washington, but after stopping off in Saigon on his way to his post at New Delhi, he sent President Kennedy on November 20 and 21, 1961 cables eloquently and cogently urging against further escalation of our action in Vietnam and specifically against commitment of combat forces. See *The Pentagon Papers*, Gravel ed., vol. 2, pp. 121–125. See also Galbraith's memorandum to the President of April 4, 1962, reproduced in part in *Ambassador's Journal*, pp. 342–344. The compilers of the Pentagon Papers in their connecting narrative seem to me to be quite in error when they interpret Galbraith's view as being "optimistic" and as seeing "no alternative to continuing to support Vietnam." Galbraith could not, after all, wholly condemn the President's existing policy in his communications to him; the obvious thrust of his remarks was for holding back.

countries in Southeast Asia." To attempt to halt Communist advance "apart from and in defiance of innately nationalistic aims spells foredoomed failure." [22]

When in office he impressed those around him with the conviction that he did not approve the commitment of American ground troops. However, Roger Hilsman, who expresses this thought, also adds: "In an interesting example of one type of gambit in the politics of Washington policy-making, the President avoided a direct 'no' to the proposal for introducing troops to Vietnam. He merely let the decision slide, at the same time ordering the government to set in motion all the preparatory steps for introducing troops." [23] The latter remark is not too reassuring, but we also learn that the President frequently remarked concerning the Vietnamese: "In the final analysis, it is their war." And in one of his statements of that opinion he added, ". . . I don't think the war can be won unless the people support the effort." [24]

More directly significant, no doubt, is the fact that although the Taylor-Rostow report of November 1961 specifically urged a "hard commitment to the ground" made persuasive by the immediate introduction into Vietnam of some American combat forces, and although this recommendation was supported by the Joint Chiefs and by Rusk and McNamara—the latter in his memorandum talked of going as high as 205,000 men—the President flatly refused to do it. The statement that Kennedy approved omitted the key opening sentence of the Rusk-McNamara recommendations, that "we now take the decision to commit ourselves to the objective of preventing the fall of South Viet-Nam to Communism . . ." Schlesinger reports the President as telling him at that time:

> They want a force of American troops. They say it's necessary in order to restore confidence and maintain morale. But it will be just like Berlin. The troops will march in; the bands will play; the crowds will cheer; and in four days everyone will have forgotten. Then we will be told we have to send in more troops. It's like taking a drink. The effect wears off, and you have to take another.

---

[22] From a Senate speech, quoted by Roger Hilsman, *To Move a Nation* (New York: Doubleday, 1967), p. 423.

[23] Ibid., p. 424. See also pp. 504, 536.

[24] In a televised interview with Walter Cronkite of CBS, on September 2, 1963, reported in the *New York Times* for the following day.

The war in Vietnam, the President added (and here the words are Schlesinger's, no longer using the direct quote), "could be won only so long as it was their war. If it were ever converted into a white man's war, we would lose as the French had lost a decade earlier." [25]

It is also interesting that his brother, Attorney General Robert Kennedy, in whose judgment the President reposed much confidence, was dubious throughout about the wisdom of introducing American fighting forces. He was sure that a Communist takeover could not be successfully resisted with the Diem government then in power, and he felt that no one had enough information to answer the question whether it could be successfully resisted with *any* government.[26]

Hilsman also records a most significant conversation with President Kennedy early in 1962 in which the President, taking up the former's statement that it would be impossible to cut off the infiltration routes completely in Vietnam, added an extraordinarily penetrating and prophetic observation. The President thought it was really worse than that. In Hilsman's words:

> Even if the flow was choked down to a trickle, he went on to say, we would still have to carry a political burden. It was not that anyone would actually lie, but every time things went badly in the future, there would be more reports about increased use of the trails, and people in Saigon and Washington would take them seriously. "No matter what goes wrong or whose fault it really is, the argument will be that the Communists have stepped up their infiltration and we can't win unless we hit the north. Those trails are a built-in excuse for failure, and a built-in argument for escalation." [27]

What is revealed here is not only exceptional insight but also a confidence in his own judgment and in his understanding of both foreign and military affairs that his successor completely lacked. Even in the Bay of Pigs disaster, he had intervened in the existing plan at the last minute to eliminate the air strike that would have made United States participation too open and blatant—a decision that has been absurdly charged with being responsible for the

[25] Schlesinger, *A Thousand Days*, p. 505. On the Taylor-Rostow report and the follow-on Rusk and McNamara memoranda and recommendations, see *The Pentagon Papers*, Gravel ed., vol. 2, pp. 84-120.

[26] Hilsman, *To Move a Nation*, p. 501.

[27] Ibid., p. 439.

failure of a plan that had no possibility of success even with a hundred times the originally planned air strikes. After that affair, and after experiencing the highly variable estimates of the Joint Chiefs of Staff concerning the requirements for an intervention in Laos, he was not again prepared to stake very much politically on what is sometimes called (usually by those who acknowledge themselves to possess it) "mature military judgment." Apart from his own direct experience in World War II as a junior naval officer, he had served on the Senate Armed Services Committee at a time of great ferment in strategic thinking and had been an avid reader in the considerable literature expressing that new thought. He thus had some basis for being properly critical or skeptical of military advice that he felt to be illogical or presumptuous—as it all too often is—and this is a marvelous quality for any President to have.[28] It served him well in the Cuban missile crisis of 1962.

Schlesinger relates one episode in the discussions over Laos that eloquently portrays this quality. Having earlier recommended that 60,000 men would be sufficient to guarantee success in Laos, the Joint Chiefs were chastened by the Bay of Pigs disaster and were now implying that they did not want to intervene at all "unless they could send at least 140,000 men equipped with tactical nuclear weapons." They were also trying to set down "the impossible condition that the President agree in advance to every further step they deemed sequential, including, on occasion, nuclear bombing of Hanoi and even Peking." At this point there occurred a meeting of the National Security Council with the President, at which General Lyman L. Lemnitzer, Chairman of the Joint Chiefs,

> outlined the processes by which each American action would provoke a Chinese counteraction, provoking in turn an even more drastic American response. He concluded: "If we are given the right to use nuclear weapons we can guarantee victory." The President sat glumly rubbing his upper molar saying nothing. After a moment someone said, "Mr. President, perhaps you would have the General explain to us what he means by victory." Kennedy grunted and dismissed the meet-

---

[28] In using the word *presumptuous* I mean that the military are wont to speak with an unwarranted certitude of prediction. No doubt it is partly because it is expected of them.

ing. Later he said, "Since he couldn't think of any further escalation, he would *have* to promise us victory." [29]

Kennedy apparently assumed in 1961 and 1962 that the war in Vietnam was going well, but, according to Henry Brandon

at the end of 1962, in a conversation with Roswell Gilpatrick [Deputy Secretary of Defense], he talked in a restless and impatient way about how the U.S. had been sucked into Vietnam little by little. By the autumn of 1963 he seemed sick of it, and frequently asked how to be rid of the commitment. He began talking about the need to reduce the size of American forces in Europe and extricate the U.S. from Southeast Asia. Just before his death he gave Mike Forrestal [of McGeorge Bundy's staff], in private conversation, odds of a hundred-to-one that the U.S. could not win. But he also knew that he could not get out of Vietnam before the elections in November 1964 without inviting his own political eclipse.[30]

Perhaps the clinching point, confirmed in the Pentagon Papers but hardly mentioned in the voluminous discussion of those papers, is the fact that shortly before his death President Kennedy approved a plan for the phased withdrawal of U.S. military personnel from Vietnam. They were supposed to be reduced to about 12,000 by the middle of 1964, bottoming out by the middle of 1968 at the level of 1,500, which would simply provide for a headquarters for the Military Assistance Advisory Group (MAAG). The functions of the men removed were to be taken over by the Vietnamese. The removal of the first 1,000 was to be completed before the end of 1963, and almost that number were in fact withdrawn in the month following Kennedy's assassination on November 22 of that year.[31] To be sure, this withdrawal plan was drawn up and approved during a period when things seemed to be going well, and it is possible that Kennedy might have been as willing

---

[29] Schlesinger, *A Thousand Days*, pp. 315 f. General Lemnitzer was shortly thereafter sent to Paris to relieve General Lauris Norstad as Supreme Commander, Allied Forces Europe (SACEUR).

[30] Brandon, *Anatomy of Error*, p. 30. The sources for this important statement obviously include Gilpatrick and Forrestal. The reference to marking time until the next election will no doubt shock some readers, but we are not here dealing with the question of moral issues in domestic politics, or of the divergence between Kennedy and Johnson in *this* respect.

[31] *The Pentagon Papers*, Gravel ed., vol. 2, pp. 160–200.

to reverse the process as his successor was when things began to turn ill again in March 1964. But, again, the assumption that he would in fact have done so is based on the doubtful premise that with respect to Vietnam, Kennedy and Johnson would respond to any new situation in practically identical fashion.

It is clear, however, that John F. Kennedy had a basically different comprehension as well as temperament, in various ways that deeply mattered, from the man who succeeded him. It was not that the latter was originally bellicose about Vietnam, anxious to prove his virility and muscle. The bellicosity developed later, after he felt himself fully committed and under attack. As a politician President Johnson was at home in domestic affairs. Foreign affairs were indeed foreign to him, and so for that matter were military affairs. Nor was he one to buck the opinion of experts, the latter being rather narrowly defined as the persons holding appropriate office.

When in May 1961 Kennedy had sent him as Vice President to Vietnam, Lyndon Johnson, influenced no doubt by Ambassador Frederick Nolting, Jr., among others, returned uttering the clattering sounds of falling dominoes.[32] Time was running out, he said, and, with characteristic exaggeration, added that if we did not go ahead with a full, forward strategy, the United States would have to "pull back our defenses to San Francisco and a 'Fortress America' concept." [33] His succession to the Presidency did not find him eager to rush into war, but he was not one to question seriously the unanimous recommendations of people like McGeorge Bundy, General Taylor, and Secretaries Rusk and McNamara, as well as numerous others at the Pentagon and the State Department. When he made the fateful decision to send combat forces to Vietnam, beginning in March 1965 with some battalions of Marines, he publicly stressed the *continuity* of his action with what his three predecessors had been doing and emphasized that nothing was really changed. In this he was of course either deceptive

---

[32] Of the four ambassadors we have had in Vietnam during the critical years since the early days of the Kennedy Administration—Frederick Nolting, Jr., Henry Cabot Lodge, Maxwell Taylor, and Ellsworth Bunker—only Lodge can be regarded as having served his President with even a relatively detached view of events in Vietnam. The others were strongly prointervention and generally supported in their reports and behavior the government in power in Saigon. Nolting had been sent out early in 1961 because his predecessor was considered too anti-Diem, and he in turn had to be relieved by Lodge in 1963 because he was clearly too pro-Diem.

[33] *The Pentagon Papers*, Gravel ed., vol. 2, pp. 55–59.

or enormously wrong. Up to that point a retreat and a liquidation of commitment would have been relatively easy. From then on retreat would have been difficult for any man, and for a Lyndon B. Johnson close to impossible.

Early in his administration he gave instructions for everyone in his entourage to ask himself each day what he had done toward victory and reminded everyone "that Vietnam was 'the only war we've got.' " [34] When he got well launched into the war he became obsessed, as was to be true also of his successor, with the attitude that he was not going to be the first American president to lose a war. Then, as more and more troops were needed, as casualties mounted, as month followed month without a definitive improvement in the situation, he became increasingly the man at bay, insisting not only on the absolute rightness of the decisions he had made but also on having around him none who might cause him even a moment's self-doubt. Thus he brought Walt Rostow back from the State Department to become a constant shield between him and reality and to give every untoward turn of events its optimistic interpretation. Those about him who became doubters left of their own accord or were cast out. As James Reston of the *New York Times* put it in late 1967: "The President is being told by a shrinking company of intimates that the Communist aggression in Vietnam is the same as the Nazi aggression in the Rhineland, Austria and Czechoslovakia, and he is holding the line; as Churchill defended freedom in Europe, so Johnson is holding the bridge in Asia . . . ." [35]

It took much more than the shock of the Tet offensive of February 1968, mounted after three years of American combat and of troop buildup to numbers reaching over half a million, to jar his confidence in the rightness of his course. He was quite ready to fulfill General William C. Westmoreland's request for more troops, a request actually initiated by General Earl Wheeler, Chairman of the Joint Chiefs, who wanted a global total of 206,000 additional troops, which would have necessitated what

---

[34] Hilsman, *To Move a Nation*, p. 534.

[35] Quoted in Hoopes, *The Limits of Intervention*, p. 100. Though it would have been of no help to inform them so, neither Johnson nor Nixon could possibly have been the first American President to lose a war. That was James Madison's distinction. The War of 1812 cannot by any stretch of the imagination be considered as having been won by the United States. That war ended with American ports under tight blockade, and none of the reasons for which we ostensibly went to war were mentioned in the peace treaty signed at Ghent in 1815.

Wheeler had long been pressing for—the calling up of the reserves.[36] President Johnson's instructions to outgoing McNamara and incoming Clark Clifford were simply to look into how it should be done. Things began to break only when a certified hawk like Clifford, after undergoing his own profound conversion, set about in a real saga of determination and forensic skill to induce the President *not* to escalate further and to agree to a halting of the bombing of North Vietnam. Even so, Clark Clifford could not have done it alone. He needed and received the support and assistance of dedicated and gifted subordinates like Paul Nitze, Townsend Hoopes, and others, as well as the concurring opinion of several others of credentials similar to those he originally possessed, notably Dean Acheson, whom the President, in Hoopes' words, "held in the highest regard as a brilliant mind, a courageous and distinguished former Secretary of State, and the toughest of Cold Warriors." Hoopes reports a conversation in February 1968 between the President and Acheson concerning some briefings the latter had been given by JCS officers: " 'With all due respect, Mr. President, the Joint Chiefs of Staff don't know what they are talking about.' The President said that was a shocking statement. Acheson replied that, if such it was, then perhaps the President ought to be shocked." [37]

That was not yet the end. The President continued "to lash out in a kind of emotional tantrum." In mid-March he flew to the Midwest to deliver two thoroughly truculent speeches, in the drafting of which Rostow and fellow hawk Abe Fortas (whose position on the Supreme Court did not prevent his doubling as the President's alter-ego) had had a major hand. The battle continued to the very end of March, with the President sustaining continued shocks from the obvious defections among his Senior Advisory Group on Vietnam, an *ad hoc* group of the country's

---

[36] Wheeler went to Saigon and apparently cautioned Westmoreland not to let the outcome of the Tet offensive look too much like an American victory, which was the latter's inclination. Wheeler wanted to use the event as leverage to get his way finally on the matter of calling up the reserves. See John B. Henry II, "February, 1968," *Foreign Policy*, no. 4 (Fall 1971), pp. 3–33. Note especially that Henry received the approval of the person quoted for each of his direct quotations as published, which is astonishing in view of what they reveal. From this article (part of a bachelor's thesis at Harvard!) it is difficult to escape the conclusion that Wheeler engaged in some deception of his superiors, the Secretary of Defense and the President of the United States. If so, the results backfired on him.

[37] Hoopes, *Limits of Intervention*, pp. 204 f.

most distinguished Presidential advisors with Acheson at their head. Finally, at the very last minute before the President was to give his major speech of March 31, 1968, the break came. The President had been presented with two drafts—a war speech and a peace speech. He used the latter, announcing the halting of the bombing north of the 20th parallel—and his own withdrawal from the forthcoming Presidential election.

From all this, and of course much more of like nature than can be included here, the following judgments seem reasonable. Although it is most unlikely that Kennedy would have followed the path that led Johnson in March 1965 to lay on the "Rolling Thunder" bombing program of North Vietnam and in the same month to land Marines in South Vietnam, thereby making it an American war, one cannot deny the possibility that he would have done so.[38] What seems to this writer next to impossible to imagine, however, is President Kennedy stubbornly escalating the commitment thereafter and persisting in a course that over time abundantly exposed its own bankruptcy, not only in its failure to accomplish the desired results and in its fantastically disproportionate costs to the United States, but also in the fact that it completely betrayed what he knew to be the basic principle of guerrilla warfare: that the object is not the killing of enemy soldiers but rather the winning of the allegiance of the people. Neither can one imagine him continuing to believe the unvaryingly optimistic reports and constantly disproved predictions of a General Westmoreland, or permitting a Walt Rostow to be a monitor for the kind of uniformly biased reports that the latter thought appropriate for the President's eyes,[39] or long outlasting in hawkishness a McGeorge Bundy and a Robert McNamara, or

---

[38] It is somewhat unclear just when President Johnson took the most decisive step in shifting to a combat role. The Administration leadership seemed to feel the critical date was April 2, 1965, with the issuance of National Security Action Memorandum (NSAM) 328, directing that the Marine battalions already deployed to South Vitenam be shifted from a static defense role to one of active combat operations. See *The Pentagon Papers*, Gravel ed., vol. 3, pp. 345–354. It is, incidentally, quite wrong to assume, as the *New York Times* encouraged its readers to assume in its publication of a portion of the Pentagon Papers, that when he was campaigning as the peace candidate in the 1964 election against Senator Goldwater, President Johnson had already made up his mind to commit the nation to a combat role in Vietnam.

[39] When he sent Rostow to the State Department in late 1961, President Kennedy said of him to some intimates: "Walt has ten ideas every day, nine of which would lead to disaster but one of which is worth having, and this makes it important to have a filter between the President and Rostow." Brandon, *Anatomy of Error*, p. 28.

giving Clark Clifford so difficult a time in accomplishing as late as 1968 the mere beginning of deescalation of what was by then a wholly catastrophic war.

The last point above is especially important. If we ask who in government supported intervention in 1964 and 1965, the answer is almost everyone. At least, the opponents were neither many nor conspicuous. The Tonkin Bay Resolution in the Senate in August 1964 had but two negative votes, those of Wayne Morse and Ernest Gruening, both of whom were to lose their seats in the 1968 election. (Other reasons may have contributed; Gruening was over 81 years old; nevertheless, both lost.) The floor manager for putting through the Resolution was Senator J. William Fulbright (who reassured doubting senators with his own firm belief that it would not be used in the way it subsequently was used). Among those associated with the Executive at the time of the March 1965 intervention, we find opposing that intervention only Vice President Hubert Humphrey, Undersecretary of State George W. Ball, W. Averell Harriman, and Ambassador to the Soviet Union Llewellyn Thompson. Outside the government, but distinguished former members of it, were ex-Ambassadors George F. Kennan and J. Kenneth Galbraith. These were persons who might be listened to, but none was in a commanding position (Humphrey was in fact quickly brought to heel). Also, they were exceedingly few against many. The significant story lies in the subsequent steady erosion of support at the top, marked by a series of quiet defections. Whether or not they stayed in the Administration—most of them did who were not in the White House—former supporters of subcabinet rank became first doubters, then alarmed disbelievers.[40] President Johnson thus has to be placed among the very last to give way.

When even McNamara began in late 1966, and increasingly through 1967, to feel disenchantment with what his revered statistics had been telling him, President Johnson surely had reason to

---

[40] In government circles doubters and opponents of current policy do not normally beat drums to call attention to their opposition, and may thus remain in part unknown to each other. Townsend Hoopes, who was Undersecretary of the Air Force at the time, speaks thus of the events of February 1968: "In the Pentagon, the Tet offensive performed the curious service of fully revealing the doubters and the dissenters to each other, in a lightning flash." Among the civilians these turned out to be numerous and to include officials of high rank, including Paul H. Nitze, then Deputy Secretary of Defense. See Hoopes, *Limits of Intervention*, p. 145.

suspect that he, too, needed desperately to reconsider the whole situation. Instead, he concluded automatically that McNamara had to go. He thought he had a reliably hawkish replacement for him in Clark Clifford, but as we have seen, the latter's accession to office coincided with the Tet offensive of February 1968. Johnson rewarded Clifford for his noble and difficult accomplishment with what seems to have been a massive bitterness, which he subsequently revealed publicly to his own discredit.[41]

The conclusion is unavoidable that Kennedy had a far more subtle intelligence than his successor, that he was decidedly less naive with respect to the advice of "experts," military and otherwise, and especially that he was free of the personal pigheadedness and truculence that Johnson so markedly betrayed. There can thus be little doubt that his conduct concerning Vietnam would have been critically and basically different.

Johnson was himself succeeded in the Presidency by a man who as Vice President had favored our intervention at the time of Dien Bien Phu, along with John Foster Dulles, Admiral Radford, and practically no one else, and who in early 1961 had called on the newly inaugurated Kennedy to urge intervention in Laos.[42] In 1965 Richard Nixon had written a letter to the *New York Times* with the astounding declaration that "victory for the Vietcong . . . would mean ultimately the destruction of freedom of speech for all men for all time, not only in Asia but in the United States as well." [43] The same man as President referred in his speech of November 3, 1969 to the "great stakes involved in Vietnam," asserting that they were no less than the maintenance of the peace "in the Middle East, in Berlin, eventually even in the Western Hemisphere." We are hearing here the crashing fall of dominoes to the last syllable of recorded time.

In the 1968 election Nixon won by a hair's breadth over Vice President Hubert Humphrey, a man of very different feelings

---

41 I am referring here to the second of the two television interviews, that of February 6, 1970, which former President Johnson had with Walter Cronkite of CBS. In it the former President tried to give to Dean Rusk the credit that should have gone to Clark Clifford. See, regarding that interview, Townsend Hoopes, "Standing History on Its Head: LBJ's Account of March, 1968," *The New Republic*, March 14, 1970.

42 See Schlesinger, *A Thousand Days*, p. 314.

43 This sentence is quoted in Clark Clifford's article in *Life* (footnote 20, this chapter). It perhaps explains the extreme waspishness of President Nixon's reference to Clifford in a press conference shortly after publication of the article.

about Vietnam,[44] and if Robert Kennedy, who by then was totally opposed to the Vietnam War, had not been felled by an assassin a few months earlier, he would very likely have won the Democratic nomination and also the election. One may conclude, therefore, that the United States at a crucial stage in its history has been the victim of cruel and capricious chance, that two small bullets have cost the American and the Vietnamese people exceedingly dear—the rifle bullet that killed President John F. Kennedy and the .22 calibre pistol bullet that five years later took the life of his brother. Those two bullets, too well aimed, have to be accounted an important part of the reason why we made the 1965 commitment to the war in Vietnam and why we are still there at this writing some seven years later.

The Domino Theory

We have several times in the preceding pages referred or alluded to what has come to be known as "the Domino Theory." The term comes from an analogy used by President Dwight D. Eisenhower concerning Vietnam in a press conference of April 7, 1954, in which he said the following: "You have a row of dominoes set up, you knock over the first one, and what will happen to the last one is that it will go over very quickly. So you have a beginning of a disintegration that would have the most profound influences."

We may also give his own translation into policy terms of his domino formulation. In a speech of August 4, 1953 at the annual governors' conference, he said the following: If Indochina fell to

---

[44] Hoopes has the following to say about Humphrey's position early in 1965: "Immediately following the February attack on Pleiku, but before retaliatory action had been ordered, Vice-President Humphrey returned urgently to Washington from a trip to Georgia, to make a last-ditch attempt to prevent escalation. He gave the President his view that bombing the North could not resolve the issue in the South, but that it would generate an inexorable requirement for U.S. ground forces in the South to protect airfields and aircraft. . . . His views were received at the White House with particular coldness, and he was banished from the inner councils for some months thereafter, until he decided to 'get back on the team,'" *Limits of Intervention*, p. 31. Brandon supports this view of Humphrey, see *Anatomy of Error*, pp. 35, 50 f. Humphrey was perhaps too anxious to "get back on the team," but as a Vice President he could have little choice and anyway this kind of dissent was not in his temperament. Besides, it must have been no help to the independence of his thinking to sit regularly in the meetings of the National Security Council. During the 1968 election campaign he freely expressed in semiprivate meetings his opposition to the ABM, but, knowing President Johnson's feelings on the matter, was markedly guarded about references to Vietnam. At a decent interval after he lost the election Humphrey began in his public utterances, especially as an occasional newspaper columnist, to attack the slowness of President Nixon's rate of deescalation.

Communism the Malay Peninsula "would be scarcely defensible"; he added that other parts of Asia would be "outflanked" or "in no position for defense." In such a situation, Eisenhower asked, "how would the free world hold the rich empire of Indonesia?" It was evident, therefore, that "somewhere along the line, this must be blocked, and it must be blocked now. . . ." He warned that success to what he considered the Communist Chinese supported movement in Vietnam must be regarded as "something that would be of the most terrible significance to the United States . . . ." [45]

The analogy has here been translated only into metaphor, in which this excerpt is exceedingly rich—much more so than in thought. They are, we have to remember, the remarks of a man with the professional credentials to claim authority as a distinguished strategist, so that when he uses words or phrases like "outflanked" and "in no position for defense," we should ordinarily assume that he knows what he is talking about.

In diplomacy as in life generally, one thing leads to another, and in important decisions we try to consider ultimate as well as near-term consequences. Many decisions are of a kind that aim directly at producing a special ultimate result, as when we initiate a task and persevere in it in order to achieve its fulfillment— which, depending on the task, may be years away. If the task is finally accomplished, one will tend to forget that chance also intervened, at least in a negative sense, by refraining from throwing insuperable obstacles in the path of accomplishment. In any case we know that final accomplishment cannot occur without the initiation and the perseverence, which usually mean a great many related actions that in the aggregate cause the fulfillment.

With most events, however, we can say only that they succeed each other in time, and because the earlier ones produce some of the conditions out of which the later ones grow, we also tend to see certain causal relationships between them, even where the factor of intention is missing. That may be reasonable enough depending on how much we have really taken into account the various relevant factors that have intervened. Often that will depend largely on the time interval between event A and event B; a longer interval obviously allowing for the intervention of additional factors that may be quite extraneous to event A. Also, insofar as we want to plan ahead wisely, it does little good to be able

---

[45] Quoted in Melvin Gurtov, *The First Vietnam Crisis* (New York: Columbia University Press, 1967), p. 31.

to say in retrospect that event B was directly caused by event A unless event B was reasonably predictable at the time of event A, or would be now with our further experience. The whole accident insurance business is a monument to the fact that frequently this element of predictability is lacking except in a statistical sense.

In looking back at a long sequence of events, there is often a temptation to exaggerate the causal links between them. The temptation comes from a variety of reasons, one being merely that we may find the imputed connection intriguing. That old and possibly familiar sequence of lines which begins with a lost horseshoe nail and ends with a lost kingdom is intriguing because of our sense of disproportion between cause and effect.[46] We know that in real life many other factors would have to operate to make it possible for a lost nail to result in a lost kingdom.

The historian as a human being is also affected by the fact that certain links are intriguing to contemplate. But he is affected more seriously by something else. His data come to him in a vast chaotic mass, and his function as a historian requires above all his organizing this data into meaningful patterns. There is thus a built-in bias in the profession in favor of discovering such patterns. This tends to mean, inevitably, an exaggeration of the causal relationship between events that succeed each other in time. And because in no profession is there an abundance of originality, certain conceptions of cause-and-effect relationships become established as orthodoxies. There are orthodoxies enough among *bona fide* historians, but when we come to politicians who are all too ready to begin speeches with some remark presuming to state what "history teaches," then all sorts of weird fantasies can be elevated to orthodoxies.

Thus we are told over and over again, among the things "history teaches," that some broad category of actions that was given the name *appeasement* was not only useless but actually *caused* the war it was designed to avoid. The reference is to a sequence of events beginning in Europe in 1936 and in the Orient about

---

[46] I last heard it in childhood, but it runs something like this:

> For want of a nail a shoe was lost,
> For want of a shoe a horse was lost,
> For want of a horse a rider was lost,
> For want of a rider a battle was lost,
> For loss of a battle a war was lost,
> For loss of a war a kingdom was lost.

The message to little children was to take care of their things.

1931. Insofar as the events in Europe concerned Hitler, we have to consider first, that people quite like Hitler are mercifully not very common among heads of government. Thus, a kind of concession that turned out to be useless when made to a Hitler need not have the same result when made to a different kind of political leader. Also, the various concessions to Hitler that are grouped together under the term *appeasement* were very different from each other. The earlier ones, like effectively ignoring the German remilitarization of the Rhineland in 1936 or doing nothing about the *Anschluss* with all-too-willing Austria in 1938, were indeed permitting violations of the Versailles Treaty of 1919. In terms of doing direct and immediate harm to others they were nothing like the dismemberment of Czechoslovakia that followed from the Munich Pact of September 1938 and especially from the German invasion of the remainder of that country in the spring of the following year. But by then the outbreak of World War II was very close.

The Munich Agreement was no doubt a stain upon the diplomacy of France and Britain, and even more so was their ignoring the invasion of the following spring; but after the latter event even a Neville Chamberlain was ready to accord a guarantee to Poland. At any rate, none of these events *caused* World War II but at most changed the time and occasion for its outbreak. The relevant question was whether the delay gained by each successive act of appeasement, including Munich, was worth the price it cost. The answer lies mostly in what was done with the time (for example, in the construction of British fighters) and also in what *might* have been done with better leadership.

It is in any case clear that the British and French (and American) people still needed more persuasion than they had in October 1938 that Hitler was essentially unappeasable. Perhaps it was a pity that they needed so much persuasion, but their experience with World War I, only twenty years in the past, had given them plenty of reason for pause. It is not obvious that *in the net* the British and French lost anything by waiting until September 1939. To determine whether or not they did requires making judgments, upon which reasonable experts might differ, based upon a good deal of historical research. How much more difficult the problem is—indeed usually impossible—when the task is not to make an appraisal of some sequence of events of the past but rather to make a prediction about some course of events in the future! And if the decision that is to be affected by this prediction is whether or not *to go to war now*, well, going to war is a pretty serious course of action. We know from a long and much too war-abundant past that nations on the whole have been too ready rather than too loath to go to war. Wars avoided are sometimes only wars postponed, and postponement, as Machiavelli tells us, may sometimes be a bad thing and sometimes a good thing. Wars avoided, however, are sometimes totally avoided, which is almost always a good thing.

To return now to the specific application of the "domino theory" to the situation in 1964, we must note, first, that it required a good deal of presumption about the infallibility of one's predictions —especially on the part of people who were unaware even of their ignorance of the role that Peking was playing in Hanoi's decisions —to predict that if South Vietnam fell to the Communists, states X, Y, and Z would also inevitably fall; X, Y, and Z often being filled in by the names of nations rather far away. That South Vietnam itself was going to fall was fairly obvious in 1964 and early 1965—for reasons that should have argued strongly *against* our intervention, that is, that the government was collapsing out of its own inadequacy. That Laos would then go too was also a pretty safe prediction, but Laos contains only about 3 million of the most primitive people in Indochina. Cambodia at that time was under Prince Norodom Sihanouk, who had made some shrewd accommodations to the Communists, and it was not at all necessary to write him off.[47] No doubt the basic consideration was that Ho Chi Minh's regime was quite demonstrably inspired far more by the nationalistic urge to achieve the reunification of an independent Vietnam than by a desire to spread Communism abroad. Their slogans for resistance to American "imperialism" had to be primarily nationalistic rather than Communist, or they would never have elicited such sacrifices from their people. And if it be argued that this betokened merely a cynical displacement of symbols, one would have to explain why, if it were a war primarily to spread Communism, the Chinese did not play a bigger role in it, especially in terms of sharing the awful rate of casualties. Later, China was to receive a visit from President Nixon in March 1972 on the eve of a great new North Vietnamese offensive. To Hanoi the

---

[47] See Prince Sihanouk's remarkable statement, "What Can Be Done in Southeast Asia," in *Ramparts*, July 1965, reproduced in Marcus G. Raskin and Bernard B. Fall (eds.), *The Vietnam Reader* (New York: Random House, Vintage Book V–309, 1965), pp. 357–362.

regime in Saigon was not simply capitalist-reactionary and corrupt; it also kept half of the single and integral state of Vietnam under the dominance of the major imperialist power of the West.

The only other country in Indochina was Thailand, which in modern times had not been under French or any other foreign dominion, and thus had not had to suffer the travail of "emergence" from colonial status into independence. Thailand, one of the original signatories in the Southeast Asia Treaty Organization (SEATO), had its own problem with Communist guerrillas, not yet serious but perhaps ultimately threatening, and its conservative government naturally appreciated the willingness of the United States to guarantee its future as a non-Communist state.

However, even if one concedes as a possibility that all of Indochina, being formed of contiguous states, might within a decade or so follow Vietnam into the Communist fold, the next question should be: What difference would this make to the security and power of the United States? These are all countries at a low level of industrial development, normally successful during peacetime in feeding themselves and having a modest surplus of agricultural commodities for export—until their population growth eventually catches up with their resources—but in no way capable of being a threat abroad or of adding significantly to the military-threat potential of Communist China. However, our present concern is still with the notion of falling dominoes, and therefore let us for the sake of argument concede all of Indochina.

The moment we leave Indochina, however, assertions about what must happen as a result of what we do or fail to do in Vietnam are totally without serious analytical foundation and therefore simply brazen. So, too, have been certain allegations about what *has* happened as a result of our intervention in Vietnam, especially in Indonesia. It has, for example, been stated emphatically that those Indonesians who put down with much bloodshed the attempted Communist coup in October 1965 could not have succeeded and probably would not even have acted except for the fact that the United States had demonstrated its resolve to keep Communism in check by sending an army to fight in Vietnam. Professional students of Indonesia who have most closely followed events there deny any basis for such a claim.[48] Our Seventh Fleet

---

[48] I am assured of this by one of the foremost American authorities on Indonesian politics, Dr. Guy Pauker of the RAND Corporation, who made a special study of the October 1965 rising.

was in the western Pacific to indicate that we had not forsaken the area, besides which considerable American forces were stationed in Japan and Korea. If the Indonesians really were so much keyed to respond to our manifest intentions about keeping Communism from spreading throughout the western Pacific, we did not need to go into Vietnam in order to reassure them.

What is really difficult to imagine is a political situation that actually approximates the mechanically simple and totally predictable one suggested by the row of dominoes. "Politics," as Einstein noted, "is much harder than physics." When China went Communist, it involved a huge land mass and approximately one-fifth the human race. What other country, contiguous or otherwise, toppled as a result? Tibet, of course, which the Chinese claimed as part of their ancient domain and which departed the roster of the "free countries" without being much noticed. It is also likely that the Korean War would have been avoided if we had prevented the fall of China, but the Korean War might have been avoided in other and simpler ways as well. In any case it is not a foregone conclusion that if we had to fight the Communists somewhere in Asia, China before 1949 was a better time and place to do it.

At the beginning of 1948 Chiang had a three-to-one superiority in troops, easily a five-to-one superiority in basic weapons, a near monopoly of heavy equipment and transport, and total mastery of the air. Yet he lost. By 1949 some 75 per cent of the material that the United States had furnished to the nationalist forces during and after the war with Japan had been captured by the Communist forces. Chiang lost because, as American Ambassador Leighton Stuart put it in mid-1948, the nationalistic government was

> no longer capable of changing and reforming or discarding inefficient associates in favor of competent ones . . . it ignores competent military advice and fails to take advantage of military opportunities offered, due . . . to the fact that . . . the Generalissimo selects men on the basis of personal reliability rather than military competence.[49]

At about the same time the head of the American military mission

---

[49] From Ambassador Stuart's report to Secretary Marshall, August 10, 1948, reprinted in *The China White Paper* (Stanford: Stanford University Press, 1967), pp. 885 f. Originally issued as *United States Relations With China*, Department of State Publication (Washington: Government Printing Office, August 1949).

called it "the world's worst leadership." The only kind of additional intervention by the United States that could have made a difference would have been the commitment of hundreds of thousands, perhaps millions, of American troops under American leadership, committed for an indefinite period of time. This seemed unnecessary at the beginning of 1948, useless a year later, quite unattractive in both cases, and, especially with World War II but recently terminated, almost surely politically impossible.

The new government in China turned out to be more hostile to the United States than seems to have been expected, but it was difficult to assess—and was no doubt easy to exaggerate—the inevitability of that hostility (that is, the role in it of American provocation, for example, our continuing support of Chiang Kai Shek on Taiwan), its durability into the future, and above all the real danger that it meant to us or to our legitimate interests. In the last dozen years or so the Chinese have redeemed themselves considerably for their hostility towards us by directing some of it also towards their Soviet neighbor, which has made both parties a good deal more tractable for the United States. Finally, there appears to be very little basis for connecting what was going on in China with the Communist revolution under Ho Chi Minh in Vietnam. His struggle against the French had begun well before the Communist takeover in China, and there is no evidence that he was ever receptive to direction from Communist China; indeed there is considerable evidence to the contrary.

We could go on indefinitely with examples, but the essential fallacies of the domino theory must already be clear. They are basically two-fold. First, events are not remotely as predictable, let alone as irremediable, as those people pretend who glibly assure us that all sorts of dire consequences will result from our failure or refusal to intervene in some current disagreeable situation. Whatever develops from that situation will probably allow for a broad range of new policy choices on our part, few of which need involve hostile and therefore costly and risk-filled action.

Second, even if we possessed the magical property of being able to determine that hostilities in some distant area involve an enemy on the march who will very likely require our ultimate intervention to stop him (something that in real life might take quite some time to determine), it is not obvious that the most convenient and effective time and place for that intervention is always *now*, wherever the fighting happens to be. It is a strategic truism that some territories are far easier to defend than others; a water barrier, for example, gives our powerful navy and our air force a chance to be fully effective—though the enemy may not even have the transport capability for ferrying his army across that water. More important, a country led by a strong and solidly supported government is more worthy of support by us and can profit more from it than a country led by a despised and ineffective government. Few conclusions are more proved by experience or more obvious to reason, but alarmists pay no attention.

We have described Clark Clifford's personal conversion following the Tet offensive and its remarkable consequences. What had readied him for this conversion was his disturbing discovery, in the course of a trip as President Johnson's emissary through some of the SEATO capitals in 1967, that those countries that by domino-theory lights were far more immediately threatened than we from events in Indochina showed unconcern for their danger. Certainly the few that had made token contributions to the forces in Vietnam were not in a mood to increase them significantly.[50] Clifford then reached the somewhat un-American conclusion that the leaders of these goverments might be just as good judges of their own interests as we were.

The above treatment is no doubt brief enough for an idea that has played such an extraordinary part in our national destiny over at least the last quarter century. Yet in a sense it is a long way around when one considers how much the inherent fallacy of that idea is exposed by the very exaggeration by which it is normally, and perhaps *necessarily*, uttered. We have already noticed how two men who were later to become President expressed it. Vice President Johnson in 1961 was certain that a failure to intervene in Vietnam meant a pulling back of our defenses to San Francisco and a "Fortress America" concept. Private citizen Richard Nixon

---

[50] Australia, New Zealand, Korea, Thailand, and the Philippines had provided forces. By the time of Tet the Koreans had 48,000 tough combat soldiers in Vietnam, whose expenses were of course entirely underwritten by the United States on very generous terms. Thailand had contributed 2,200 men, and as a result of Clifford's trip in 1967 had agreed to add 10,000. Not only were these completely subsidized by the United States, but the Thais had asked and received as compensation a substantial increase in U.S. military equipment to Thai forces remaining at home. Under similar terms the Philippines had provided a noncombatant engineer battalion of about 2,000 men, but refused to entertain requests for additional forces. Australia had provided at its own expense a brigade of 6,000 troops, and after much American pressure, an additional artillery unit and an air squadron, bringing the total to about 8,500 men. New Zealand, which in World War II had raised 157,000 men, had made a contribution, which it subsequently refused to enlarge, of but 450 men. Hoopes, *Limits of Intervention*, pp. 167–171. By 1972 all these forces had been removed except for some Koreans.

was sure in 1965 that a victory of the Vietcong "would mean ultimately the destruction of freedom of speech for all men for all
time, not only in Asia but in the United States as well." Can these
men have been serious? Alas, yes. They seem to have been deadly
serious. Also preposterous. So was President Eisenhower in his
1953 statement quoted at the beginning of this section. And even
in February 1971 a journalist who wrote books on the Far East was
able to say the following: "Clearly, if the United States had not
intervened when it did, the Commonwealth position to the south
would have become untenable. A consolidation of the 'Axis' [that
is, China and Indonesia] would have confronted the United States
and its allies with a line of hostile, militant, and authoritarian
states from Korea to New Guinea." [51] All this is introduced by the
word *clearly*, which in this context means *unquestionably*. But if
the assertion is questioned, it immediately topples of its own
weight. Yet it is this kind of dogmatic pronouncement that over
and over again in history has plunged some part of the world into
bloody war.

Did We Have Treaty Obligations to Intervene?

We are usually accustomed to regarding a treaty obligation for
military intervention, wherever it exists, to be sufficient justification for such intervention. This is the occasion for using such
adjectives as *sacred* or *solemn* to describe the obligation, for alliances have indeed formed the basic cement of international security systems since the beginning of recorded history. Actually, it is
not as simple as all that. If we want to know why a nation is at
war, it is surely not enough to reply that it is in that condition
because of a treaty obligation. We should want to know why and
under what circumstances the treaty was concluded, whether it
actually required the action taken, what assurances were given in
pursuance of it, and so on. Nations are rarely trapped because of
treaty obligations into wars they would otherwise be unwilling to
fight. However, in the present instance, we are first concerned with
whether we actually were obliged by some international commitment to intervene in the fashion that we did in Vietnam.

The only treaties or conventions that could possibly be relevant
would be the United Nations Charter and that treaty which forms
the basis for SEATO. Secretary Rusk invoked both treaties in a

---

[51] Arnold C. Brackman, in an editorial-article, "Why We Escalated," the *New York Times*, February 6, 1971.

speech before the American Society of International Law on April 23, 1965.[52] About our obligations under the United Nations, the most we can claim is that we have thus far escaped censure. There can be no obligation to use military force in support of the United Nations Charter except by an affirmative vote of the Security Council (though we have in the past used the Assembly as a by-pass for action properly belonging to the Security Council but blocked by veto in that body). There has been no affirmative vote in the Security Council to sustain our conduct in Vietnam, and under the present membership there can be none. Neither can there be under the present membership and voting rules a resolution that finds the United States the aggressor. The security enforcement provisions of the Charter do not make the Assembly a legitimate body for sanctioning the use of force anywhere, but of course the Assembly can pass any resolution it pleases. Thus far it has not passed one that either supports or condemns our Vietnam policies.

We must consider SEATO more seriously, because both President Johnson and Secretary Rusk alleged from time to time that we were in Vietnam in pursuance of SEATO obligations. If that were true, we should simply have to conclude that our major intervention in Vietnam began not in 1965 but in 1954 with the signing of that treaty, and that it was an unabashed submission to the "domino theory" that accounted for our taking that step. Otherwise there could be no conceivable justification for the United States looking to Thailand and to the so-called "protocol states," which include Vietnam, to assist it in achieving its own security.

We may suspect that Johnson and Rusk knew these allegations to be of slight foundation or else they would have made them in a more forthright and sustained manner. When the issue arose during Secretary Rusk's testimony before the Senate Committee on Foreign Relations on January 28, 1966, Senator Fulbright observed that as he read the Southeast Asia Treaty, ". . . the obligation is to consult with our allies in the case of these non-overt aggressions. We have no unilateral obligation to do what we are doing. Now you say we are *entitled* to do it. That is different from saying we have an *obligation* under this SEATO Treaty." [Italics added.] To this Rusk could reply only that he felt it was "an obli-

---

[52] *Department of State Bulletin*, LII (May 10, 1965), pp. 694–700.

gation of policy," that is, something that was "rooted in the policy of the Treaty." What this could possibly mean he did not indicate.[53]

The Southeast Asia Treaty was signed in September 1954 and ratified in February 1955. The signatories were Australia, France, New Zealand, Pakistan, the Philippines, Thailand, the United Kingdom, and the United States. By a protocol appended to the Treaty at the time of signing the following was stated: "The parties to the Southeast Asia Collective Defense Treaty unanimously designate for the purpose of article 4 of the Treaty the States of Cambodia and Laos and the free territory under the jurisdiction of the State of Vietnam." Hence, these became the "protocol powers."

Article 4 contains, in three paragraphs, the security enforcement provisions. Paragraph 1 provides that in the event of "armed attack in the treaty area against any of the parties" each party will "act to meet the common danger in accordance with its constitutional processes." It provides further that measures taken under this provision "shall be immediately reported to the Security Council of the United Nations."

By common agreement Section 1 is intended for the kind of overt armed attack that marked the beginning of the Korean War, and such had not occurred at the time of our combat-force intervention in 1965. The more relevant section is therefore Section 2, which reads as follows:

> If, in the opinion of any of the Parties, the inviolability or the integrity of the territory or the sovereignty or political independence of any Party in the treaty area or of any other State or territory to which the provisions of paragraph 1 of this Article from time to time apply is threatened in any way other than by armed attack or is affected or threatened by any fact or situation which might endanger the peace of the area, the Parties shall consult immediately in order to agree on the measures which should be taken for the common defense.

The third paragraph merely provides that no action shall be

---

[53] *Senate Foreign Relations Committee Hearings of 1966 on Vietnam*, p. 45. It is incidentally noteworthy that one of the signers of the treaty for the United States was Senator Mike Mansfield, who must therefore be regarded as an authority on the treaty's interpretation and who has long opposed our Vietnam intervention.

taken "except at the invitation or with the consent of the government concerned." [54]

We notice that even if Paragraph 1 were deemed to apply, it describes no specific action as being the required one, and it would be difficult to find any reason why the United States had a degree of obligation not fully shared by the other parties in proportion to their resources. Under Paragraph 2 the requirement is only for consultation and agreement on the measures to be taken. The United States has consulted only informally and individually with the other parties in order to secure some kind of assistance, but France, Pakistan, and the United Kingdom have never contributed any forces. France was no doubt never asked. The others have contributed what either amounted to forces hired by the United States (for example, Thailand) or token forces. After the United States the largest forces have been contributed, on essentially a basis of hire, by Korea, which is not even a party to the treaty. Also, the Korean forces would not have been able to depart their native land if it had not been for the continuing presence there of two American divisions.

---

[54] The text of the Southeast Asia Treaty is contained in numerous places, including the appropriate issue of the *Department of State Bulletin*; Richard P. Stebbins (ed.), *Foreign Relations of the United States* (Washington, 1954); and Eisenhower, *Mandate for Change: Vol. 1: The White House Years*, appendices. See especially, however, Richard A. Falk (ed.), *The Vietnam War and International Law* (Princeton: Princeton University Press, 1968), part IV.

CHAPTER

5

Vietnam:
Why We Failed

Allow the President to invade a neighboring nation whenever *he* shall deem it necessary to repel an invasion . . . and you allow him to make war at pleasure. . . . If today he should choose to say he thinks it necessary to invade Canada, to prevent the British from invading us, how could you stop him? You may say to him, "I see no probability of the British invading us"; but he will say to you, "Be silent; I see it, if you don't."

> Reply of Abraham Lincoln to the argument of his law partner, William Herndon, that President Polk had invaded Mexico for a defensive purpose.

In one of his many, long, wide-ranging, and insightful "Letters from Vietnam" published in the *New Yorker*, this one dated November 1, 1971, Mr. Robert Shaplen starts out as follows:

Now that President Nguyen Van Thieu's "reelection" in a one-man race and his lavish inauguration ceremony are both over with, it is obvious that the whole ludicrous performance has left his government in a more precarious political position than ever, both internally and in relation to the Communists. It is equally obvious that United States policy-makers are largely devoid of ideas about how to cope with the situation, beyond suggesting once again that Thieu should broaden the base of his government and live up to his repeated promises to make other reforms. The remoteness of the chance that these hopes will be realized opens another dreary, repetitious chapter in the case-book of American-Vietnamese relations, emphasizing again on our side an almost total misunderstanding of Vietnamese mores, methods, and political attitudes, and on theirs a parallel misunderstanding, along with a growing resentment of our clumsy involvement in the life of their nation.

After going on to describe how the election was conducted ("In many instances, torn—and thus invalid—ballots were counted for Thieu, and in others local officials, in obedience to orders, got the ballot boxes filled early in the day with the votes of soldiers and government workers, and then simply extrapolated the results to obtain the desired final figures"), Shaplen goes on to describe the feelings expressed to him of one Vietnamese:

> "We have accepted the man sent us by the American gods," a former high-ranking Vietnamese official cynically observed to me, illustrating the obsessive insistence of many Vietnamese that we are pulling all the strings and also their failure to observe that the puppets seldom perform as directed.

If we now go back more than six years, which means also some 45,000 American deaths and six million tons of American bombs earlier, we can single out the date of February 10, 1966, when our intervention with combat forces in Vietnam was less than one year old. On that date George F. Kennan in his testimony before the Senate Foreign Relations Committee made the following statement:

> The first point I would like to make is that if we were not already involved as we are today in Vietnam, I would know of no reason why we should wish to become so involved, and I could think of several reasons why we should wish not to. Vietnam is not a region of major military, industrial importance. It is difficult to believe that any decisive develop-

ments of the world situation would be determined in normal circumstances by what happens on that territory. If it were not for the considerations of prestige that arise precisely out of our present involvement, even a situation in which South Vietnam was controlled exclusively by the Viet Cong, while regrettable, and no doubt morally unwarranted, would not, in my opinion, present dangers great enough to justify our direct military intervention.

Then he added:

From the long-term standpoint, therefore, and on principle, I think our military involvement in Vietnam has to be recognized as unfortunate, *as something we would not choose deliberately, if the choice were ours to make all over again today.* [Italics added.][1]

The italicized portion of this statement is interesting mainly because the manner of its utterance seems, even at that early stage, to reflect on Kennan's part an expectation of general concurrence from his listeners. His several preceding sentences, however, not only bear on the italicized conclusion but also express a conception that ought to be utterly commonplace in strategic discourse and in related national policy decisions but that seems on the contrary to be often neglected or omitted. It is the conception simply of reasonable price, and of its being applied to strategy and national policy—the idea that some ends or objectives are worth paying a good deal for and others are not. The latter include ends that are no doubt desirable but which are worth attempting to achieve only if the price can *with confidence* be kept relatively low.

Can it really be that such a simple and obvious idea is often neglected or overlooked? The answer is, most decidedly, yes. Consider the following exchange, by no means an unusual one. Secretary Rusk, when asked by Senator Claiborne Pell during his appearance of January 28, 1966 before the Senate Foreign Relations Committee whether he saw any end to the "corridor we are following" answered, "No, I would be misleading you if I told you that I know where, when, and how this matter will be

---

[1] *Supplemental Foreign Assistance Fiscal Year 1966—Vietnam; Hearings Before the Committee on Foreign Relations, United States Senate, 89th Congress, 2nd Session, on S. 2793,* pp. 331 ff. Also reproduced in *The Vietnam Hearings,* with an Introduction by J. William Fulbright (New York: Random House, Vintage Book V–354, 1966), pp. 108 f.

resolved." Shortly he added, "The nature of a struggle of this sort . . . is, of course, substantially determined by the other side." [2] With these words Secretary Rusk neatly summed up his own unwavering determination and also echoed the convictions of the President he then served. "We will stay the course." "We will persevere." "We will not tire." "Nothing will deflect us from our purpose"—including the most preposterously disproportionate and steadily mounting costs.

What can account for this attitude? The answer has to be found in either or both of two ideas. One is that in the opinion of Rusk and others the passage quoted from Kennan gave a poor assessment of the real United States interest in Vietnam, which is to say not that the intrinsic military and industrial importance of Vietnam is greater than he allowed—which no one pretended to believe, including the Joint Chiefs—but rather that the objective of frustrating Communist aggression overrides awesomely the question of the intrinsic importance of the territory concerned, as it presumably did also in Korea. The other idea, too, is contained in the same quoted passage, where Kennan apparently concedes that "considerations of prestige" arising "precisely out of our present involvement" do hinder our freedom to withdraw.

We may dismiss the first of these two ideas as not of much relevance to the problem except as support to the second. The main reason for saying this is that, despite some assertions to the contrary noted in the previous chapter, we know from the Pentagon Papers and other sources that the price of intervention rather quickly went beyond what President Johnson thought it would be when he made his decisions of March and April 1965.[3] The Administration leaders clearly expected that an infusion of strong American ground forces combined with a program of sustained bombing of North Vietnam would change the situation drastically, and soon. Thus they expected the price to be moderate. At least we know that they did not remotely expect what came to pass. It is impossible to imagine anyone not absolutely bereft of his senses sitting in the President's chair in early 1965 who would if he could but look ahead only one or two years, let alone five or six, repeat the decision then made by Lyndon Johnson. Concern for his own political skin would force him to do otherwise; and the more he took into account values of im-

---

[2] *Senate Hearings on Vietnam,* pp. 32, 36.

[3] The reference to contrary assertions is mainly to the position argued by Daniel Ellsberg and Leslie H. Gelb, and discussed above, pp. 128 f.

portance to the larger community, the more certainly would he avoid any semblance of intervention.

We may therefore assume that even as the price multiplied immeasurably beyond the whole range of his original expectations, the President stuck to his commitment because of what Kennan called "considerations of prestige." This would naturally not be the reason announced publicly; it would sound too much like "saving face," deep concern for which is always supposed to be a cultural trait of others, especially Orientals, but not of ourselves. Thus our political leaders would continue to beat the drums for the necessity of saving South Vietnam from Communism, usually couched in terms of preserving for the people of that country freedom of choice about their political destiny; but only obliquely would we admit that we continued the war and escalated it because the fact of success was far more important to us than its specific fruits. The United States simply could not afford, the general opinion went, to let its military forces be defeated in its purpose by the likes of North Vietnam.

"Considerations of prestige" are a complex aggregate. It is difficult for any President, and obviously much more so for some than for others, to separate considerations of national prestige from those of personal prestige. To be responsible for a national humiliation is inevitably a great personal humiliation, and may be paid for at the polls. Even where the latter consideration is suppressed, elements of personal combativeness may come to the fore. The culture in which we live and breathe also plays its part in conditioning us to respond favorably to symbols that hold up fortitude, stubbornness, and tenacity as transcendant virtues so long as the adversity against which they are contending takes a military form and engages something we can call "the enemy." For that subculture representing the military profession, these symbols take on an even more intensified power. The soldier is trained, as we have seen, to seek to win at all costs if at all possible, and he will cry out against inhibition of effort or any withholding of resources that may diminish the possibility. He is not alone in this; many civilians will be caught up with the same ardor. But taken as a group, his profession exhibits a certain purity in its devotion to victory. We have also observed it operating in other wars.

If considered rationally, prestige, too, is an elastic value to which it is pertinent to apply the conception of reasonable price. Occasionally it is so treated. A good and perhaps rare example of such treatment is seen in the decision of President Kennedy not to send good money after bad in the Bay of Pigs operation when its failure became apparent:

> But he did not propose to send in the Marines. Some people, he noted, were arguing that failure would cause irreparable harm, that we had no choice now but to commit United States forces. Kennedy disagreed. Defeat, he said, would be an incident, not a disaster. . . . But would not United States prestige suffer if we let the rebellion flicker out? "What is prestige?" Kennedy asked. "Is it the shadow of power or the substance of power. No doubt we will be kicked in the can for the next couple of weeks, but that won't affect the main business." [4]

He was of course proved right. Actually, it was not United States prestige that suffered at the Bay of Pigs so much as Kennedy's, and he knew that, too. In the early days of his Administration he had let himself appear reckless and foolish, but he knew that new appraisals would shortly be forthcoming and that they would take into account subsequent behavior. In any case, at the moment of decision Kennedy knew that whatever prestige loss he would suffer at the Bay of Pigs did not warrant actions far more injurious to the good name either of the United States or himself. He therefore was able to end the operation and cut his losses. It is amazing how constantly the lesson is rejected that few things are more evanescent in their effects than some real or fancied injury to the prestige of a great nation.

Kennedy's conduct was indeed unusual, but not entirely novel. The pattern of limited war in older times usually involved a readiness by one side or the other to put an end to the business whenever it became too patently unprofitable to continue it. That situation might be manifested by a major defeat in battle, which proved that one had resisted, in vain, and thus had satisfied the requirements of honor. Whether the defeated party was physically *able* to continue the war was deemed irrelevant. Prestige considerations were not ignored; they were simply given measured and largely ceremonial value. To be sure, the opposite behavior also has its many ancient and modern antecedents. Nevertheless, there is something distinctively aberrant about the compulsion to plunge on and on in some profitless and clearly

---

[4] Arthur M. Schlesinger, Jr., *A Thousand Days* (Boston: Houghton Mifflin, 1965), p. 258.

disastrous course in order to preserve and redeem something called "prestige" or, more recently, "credibility"—thereby jeopardizing among many other things the very values designated by those terms, for prestige has to include a reputation for reasoned judgment.

No doubt it is now clear what we mean by calling United States intervention in Vietnam a failure, even though at this writing it is not yet over. We mean that from at least as early as the beginning of 1968 even the most favorable outcome, from within that spectrum of outcomes that one could reasonably regard as possible, could not remotely be worth the price we would have paid for it. Moreover, "prestige" and "credibility" were bound to be among the items of cost rather than of gain. Other nations will evaluate our prestige in their own way rather than in the way we would like them to, and it will very likely appear to them that our failure to achieve our objectives in Vietnam is far from representing the worst aspect of our performance there. So far as credibility is concerned, our capability for supportive action to an ally has been diminished by the experience rather than enhanced, and everyone will know that. Whether or not it has been diminished seriously over the long term we still do not know, and other nations may possibly exaggerate the degree to which our enthusiasm to make the world secure has suffered contraction. But in any case, our "credibility" will not have been improved.

Nor is it irrelevant to consider whether the objective that President Johnson and his associates hoped and expected to attain was worth even the relatively modest price they expected to have to pay (assuming these things were thought out with any clarity, which is a large assumption). If the government of the United States can embrace that of Franco Spain, as well as the junta of colonels in Greece, not to mention that brace of reactionary governments in Latin America with whom our official relations have long been more than cordial, and if it can take without the slightest apparent concern the overthrow (in November 1971) of constitutional government by a military junta in allied Thailand, and the more serious action of Philippine President Marcos a year later, then we are obviously not really interested in fighting to protect any other people's constitutional liberties or their freedom to "choose their own destinies." For that is denied them as much by the radical right as by the radical left. Nor is there any reason—now that we have found officially that the world Communist movement is far from monolithic and that we can enjoy quite amicable relations with virtually all Communist regimes, not even excluding China—why we have to regard a Communist takeover in a country that is certainly not democratic to begin with as producing inevitably and implacably a government that is hostile to us and to our interests. Of course, if we continue as a matter of national policy to support with arms and other aid all governments that are anti-Communist, regardless of how reactionary and at odds with their own people they may be, and to oppose with force as we have in Vietnam all nationalistic movements that are also Communist, then we can indeed expect hostility from the latter.

All this is highly relevant to determining *why* we failed in Vietnam. Of the two or three reasons that dominate all the others, the one that is clearly of greatest importance, and no doubt sufficient in itself to explain the failure, is that we attempted to support a government that our leaders knew to be both inept and corrupt and, in President Kennedy's words, "out of touch with the people." This government changed its face from time to time but not its essential character. Diem's assassination, which preceded Kennedy's by only a few weeks, was followed after a period of chaos by the regime of Major General Nguyen Khanh. The latter was superseded in June 1965, just after our combat intervention had begun, by the ineffable Brigadier General Nguyen Cao Ky. Ky in turn was superseded in the Presidency in the election of 1967 by Major General Nguyen Van Thieu, with Ky staying on as Vice President. Though there were undoubtedly significant differences between these men, they had in common the fact that their major ambition seemed to be that of being the heirs, with respect to the perquisites of power, of the old colonial governors who ruled for France. They tended to be severe and vindictive with political opponents or dissenters and utterly corrupt in their management of the government, and thus, one should hardly need to add, ineffective in dealing with their own people.

We have noted in the preceding chapter President Eisenhower quoting approvingly someone's words to the effect that what South Vietnam needed was a Syngman Rhee. Now Rhee was hardly a paragon among democratic rulers. He was finally overthrown in 1960, in extreme old age, allegedly because he controlled the ballot boxes and was authoritarian—though General Park Chung Hee, who ultimately took control, proved to be far more so. Nevertheless, Rhee had established his credentials as a Korean patriot during the era of Japanese colonial rule by serving several years in a Japanese prison. The Vietnamese whose life career did have astonishing parallels with Syngman Rhee, including education abroad (Rhee was a Princeton Ph.D.) was Ho Chi Minh, but he forfeited official American approval by his choice in economic and social philosophy. Anyway, genuine patriots and effective leaders like either Syngman Rhee or Ho Chi Minh have been rare among the governments that have emerged from colonial domination since World War II, and South Vietnam has not had any who remotely resembled either one.

The extraordinary degree of corruption in the country has been described in detail, especially in the writings of David Halberstam and Robert Shaplen, and admitted even by so ardent an apologist for the regime and for our role in supporting it as Robert S. Elegant.[5] Sometimes it surfaces in the most bizarre fashion, as when the wife of Vice President Ky claimed as "abandoned waste land" some 3,500 acres of choice land in the central highlands that had belonged for generations to a tribe of Montagnards who had been forced to leave it temporarily because of the war. The Vice President defended his wife's claim on the ground that it furthered "the land development policy of the government," but did not seem to consider that, apart from the questionable legitimacy of the claim, asking for 3,500 acres for one person might be a bit much.[6] Similarly, when American military service men were given the right under "Operation Reunion" to have two-week leaves in the United States so long as they paid the round-trip fare themselves on charter flights, the Vietnamese officials partially sabotaged the operation by rescinding landing rights in order—according to U.S. Congressman Lester L. Wolff, who chanced to be in Saigon at the time—to

---

[5] See especially David Halberstam, "Return to Vietnam," *Harper's*, December 1967, pp. 47–58. Shaplen's long "Letters from Vietnam," published irregularly in the *New Yorker*, have already been referred to; in them the corruption is often mentioned and sometimes graphically described. Robert S. Elegant in his brief article on corruption in Vietnam (*Los Angeles Times*, April 16, 1971) could not forebear to add: "Vietnamese should not be encouraged to strive toward the perfection of graft that the United States has occasionally attained." From the information conveyed by Halberstam and Shaplen, and partly though grudgingly confirmed by Elegant, the United States has never remotely been in the running.

[6] *New York Times*, January 6, 1971, and *Los Angeles Times*, January 7, 1971. Madame Ky may also be remembered as the woman who, during Vietnam's agony, thought it necessary to go to Japan to have an operation performed to remove the epicanthic fold from her eyelids, thus making her look less oriental.

blackmail the charter companies into leasing a Boeing 727 jet-liner to Air Vietnam, the national airline, and into turning over some $1 million in ground equipment to Tan Son Nhut Airport at Saigon.

It was entirely characteristic of our United States Ambassador in Saigon, Ellsworth Bunker, that when Congressman Wolff raised the matter with him he had been unwilling to interfere for fear of offending the Vietnamese. "He went on," according to Wolff, "about how we were guests in a host nation and how we mustn't offend our hosts." [7] There was not the slightest reason for suspecting Congressman Wolff of any exaggeration, because we have numerous such stories concerning Ambassador Bunker, a businessman turned diplomatist. Despite his advanced age, he had been sent to Saigon in 1967 by President Johnson precisely because he was known to entertain the feelings he expressed to Wolff and, of course, to be ardently in favor of our war objectives in Vietnam and reliably given to sending home the most optimistic of reports.

Later the Nixon Administration, which kept Ambassador Bunker at his post, knowing well his convictions, wanted very much that Thieu win reelection in 1971, and by a clear majority. In the 1967 election President Thieu and Vice President Ky had got less than 35 per cent of the votes cast, over 60 per cent going to civilian candidates who had some kind of peace plank in their platforms, and this in an election that was already markedly "managed." The man who had the second largest number of votes in the 1967 election, Truong Dinh Dzu, was shortly thereafter thrown into prison and remains there at this writing.

Then came the notorius case of Tran Ngoc Chau, who in the 1960s made a name for himself as a province chief in the Mekong Delta where, because of the character of his administration, he succeeded in winning over to support of the government what had been an overwhelmingly pro-Viet Cong population. In 1967 he ran for deputy in the Lower House, collecting one of the largest votes received by any elected deputy. His troubles began in October 1969 when he rashly accused Nguyen Cao Thang, Thieu's liaison man with the Lower House, of buying votes. (Meanwhile Chau also became identified with a movement aimed at negotiations to secure peace and at seeking to provide a political alternative to Thieu.) Thieu asked the National Assembly to

---

[7] *New York Times,* December 31, 1970.

strip Chau of his immunity to prosecution, a move allowed by the Constitution only if three fourths of the Assembly approved. The vote failed to carry, whereupon a paid mob of several hundred was unloosed to riot in the legislative chambers. Still the lower House refused to remove the immunity. At that point Thang circulated among the deputies an undated petition asking for Chau's prosecution, and later boasted to friends that he had spent ten million piasters (about $80,000) getting signatures, an outlay supplemented, according to numerous deputies, by blackmail and intimidation.

By February 1970, Thieu had a document authorizing the trial of Chau. In March a military field court created by Diem to try political dissidents sentenced Chau to ten years of imprisonment at hard labor. In May the Supreme Court ruled that Chau's conviction was unconstitutional as was the whole military field court system. After further investigations into the Chau case, the Supreme Court ruled in October that Chau should be freed. Thieu's response was to replace the Chief Justice of the Supreme Court and to get the legislature to pass new laws effectively renewing the military field court. Chau remained in prison under increasingly severe conditions.

The behavior of the American Embassy throughout this case is interesting. Although the Americans who knew Chau best were among his most ardent supporters, the Embassy imposed a gag rule upon them. No official of the United States government was permitted to see Chau, or to discuss the case with any outsider, whether Vietnamese official or American journalist. According to one member of the Embassy, Ambassador Bunker personally delivered an ultimatum to the late John Vann, an ex-Army colonel in Vietnam, then the American head of pacification in the Mekong Delta, and a staunch defender of Chau. If Vann talked to one more reporter about Chau, he was told, he would be summarily fired.[8]

In August 1972 Thieu removed even the facade of democracy by a decree that not only stifled the opposition press but wiped it out. The action was unique in form, but with enough deviousness about it to make it characteristic. Each newspaper was required to put up a large sum of money as a bond against future fines that might be levied against it for expressing senti-

---

[8] On the Chau case see especially Elizabeth Pond, "South Vietnam: The Tran Ngoc Chau Affair," *Atlantic*, May 1971, pp. 19–29.

ments that could be construed as being antigovernment. The sum was large enough to be prohibitive for very nearly all newspapers, which therefore went out of business. The following month another decree ended the selection by local elections of over 10,000 hamlet chiefs. Democracy, Thieu said, had been "too disorderly."

One could expand indefinitely on instances of governmental corruption and repression in South Vietnam, but this is enough for our purposes. We are after all interested in the question *why* the United States failed in Vietnam, not whether it deserved to fail. It is obvious that the government we have described, necessarily briefly but by overwhelming evidence fairly—a government composed of men who had previously sided with the French against their own nationalists and who inevitably identified their own interests with those of the landowners and the urban middle-class—have not been in good position to win the allegiance of the people, especially of the peasantry. The peasants of Asia, including those of relatively democratic India as well as those of Communist China, cannot in any case be expected to share our sense of priorities concerning the fundamental freedoms of democracy.[9] But they could not have those freedoms under the Thieus of this world.

Whether the United States could have used its influence effectively to help bring into power a more representative government having a better chance of competing with the Viet Cong and with Hanoi for the support of the people is another question. There is normally not much leverage for a foreign government, especially one of different race and culture and inevitably identified with those countries responsible for the colonialism of the past, to improve significantly the character of the government with which it finds itself allied. Yet the influence of the United States government on the internal politics of South Vietnam has indeed been

---

[9] The view stated in this sentence has been expressed many times, but I especially like its formulation by John Kenneth Galbraith, as follows: "The Third World consists, by definition, of poor rural societies—that is what undeveloped or underdeveloped countries are. It follows that whether such countries call themselves free, free enterprise, capitalist, socialist or Communist, has, at the lowest levels of development, only terminological significance. They are poor and rural however they describe themselves. For the appreciable future, they will so remain. Even by the crudest power calculus, military or economic, such nations have no vital relation to the economic or strategic position of the developed countries." Then he adds, "It is hard now to see why so much tension developed in the fifties and early sixties over whether such countries would follow the Communist or non-Communist patterns of development." From "Plain Lessons of a Bad Decade," *Foreign Policy*, no. 1 (Winter 1970–1971), p. 37.

substantial—as evidenced, for example, by the fact that the generals did not move against Diem in 1963 until the American disenchantment with him had become manifest. However, what influence we had has been thrown consistently on the side of those whose chief claim to our favor was that they appeared the most staunchly anti-Communist. This usually meant that we supported military leaders over civilians and "conservatives" over those of more liberal persuasion, for the latter in each case might seek to end the war through some measure of accommodation with the Communists. It meant, therefore, inevitably helping to remain in power governments that continued to be "out of touch with the people."

These characteristics of American diplomacy in Vietnam remained unchanged whether the government in power in Washington was relatively liberal, as the Johnson Administration clearly was in domestic affairs, or quite emphatically conservative, like the Nixon Administration. The clue seems to be that in both instances hawks were favored over doves, not only with respect to those Vietnamese with whom we preferred to deal, but also with respect to all senior American personnel in Vietnam including those of the American Embassy in Saigon.

The alienation especially of the rural population from the government of South Vietnam is an old story. We know that President Eisenhower supported Diem in the latter's refusal in 1956 to hold the elections called for in Paragraph 7 of the "Final Declaration" of the Geneva Conference of 1954—or at least refrained from exerting any pressure on him to hold them.[10] Eisenhower's reasons were no doubt anticipated by the views he held in 1954 and communicated to his memoirs: "I have never talked or corresponded with a person knowledgeable in Indochinese affairs who did not agree that had elections been held as of the time of the fighting, possibly 80 per cent of the population would have voted for the Communist Ho Chi Minh as their leader rather than Chief of State Bao Dai."[11] Bao Dai, the playboy Emperor

---

[10] The United States did not officially join in the "Final Declaration" of the Geneva Conference, which was approved by a voice vote on July 21, 1954. However, on the same date W. Bedell Smith reminded the conference that the United States supported such an election as that called for in the Declaration so long as they are "supervised by the United Nations to ensure that they are conducted fairly." See Mervin E. Gettleman, *Vietnam: History, Documents, and Opinions on a Major World Crisis* (New York: Fawcett, 1965), pp. 151–157.

[11] Dwight D. Eisenhower, *Mandate for Change: Vol. I: The White House Years* (New York: Doubleday, 1963), p. 372.

established by the French, had in 1954 summoned Ngo Dinh Diem from a Catholic monastery in the United States to be his Prime Minister, Diem having been a Minister of the Interior under the French in the 1930's. In an election in October 1955 the people of South Vietnam were permitted to choose between the absentee Emperor and his Prime Minister, and they overwhelmingly chose the latter. However, as Eisenhower well knew, this vote (in another typically "managed" election) did not mean that the people had a higher regard for Diem than for Ho Chi Minh.

The alienation grew rather than diminished. Halberstam, in his insightful and illuminating *The Making of a Quagmire*, relates an event that happened eight years after Diem came to power. Following a battle at Go Cong in August 1963, which Saigon claimed as a considerable government victory:

> a friend of mine, a non-American who was an expert on guerrilla warfare, took me aside and told me why he felt it was hardly a victory, why in fact it was a sign of imminent disaster. The action had taken place very near a district capital outside of My Tho, he noted, and at least five hundred Vietcong had participated. Yet this large a force had been able to gather near a major center in a heavily populated area, without one single peasant warning the Government. Therefore, my friend said, it was not a victory, but rather a grim lesson in making it clear which side controlled the population and could move freely in the countryside. The war, he said, was closer to being over than anyone realized.[12]

Under the circumstances then prevailing, this prediction was quite correct. For the government did move steadily closer to collapse, and it was chiefly to keep it going that President Johnson, who succeeded to office within a few months of the event just described, made his decisions first to increase aid considerably and then to send in combat forces.

When the American forces came in steadily increasing numbers, they could hardly avoid presenting an aspect to the people much like that presented by the French in their last days—only even more foreign, English being a new language. What the

---

[12] David Halberstam, *The Making of a Quagmire* (New York: Random House, 1964), p. 183.

French had looked like to the Vietnamese in the last days of the colonial war is also described by Halberstam:

> The French controlled the highways and the cities; the Vietminh controlled the people. The French moved during the day, and the face they presented was always a military one; the Vietminh moved at night, lecturing the people, distributing medicine, promising land reform, reducing rents, teaching some of the youngsters to read and write, promising a better society.[13]

It may have been possible for Americans to do better than the French in some ways, but they were bound in other ways to do much worse. Having far greater resources, and being for political reasons eager to get the job over with and also sensitive about casualties in a conscript army (the French had sent no conscripts to Vietnam) the American forces were bound to rely heavily on their enormous firepower. This was to mean, by the end of 1971, over six million tons of bombs and other munitions dropped from the air on Indochinese territory, or about three times the total tonnage dropped by American air forces in all theatres throughout World War II. The major part of this total, or 3.6 million tons, was dropped on the country we were "defending," South Vietnam.[14] Such a rain of destruction could at the same time fail to be decisive and yet tear up a great many bodies, including a high proportion of noncombatants. With the bombs and napalm went a huge program of defoliation through the spraying of herbicides from the air, ruining by the end of 1971, apparently permanently, over 5 million acres of hardwood forests. Even more injurious to the peasant economy was the vast destruction caused by deep craters left by 500-pound antipersonnel bombs.[15] This does not take into account the comparable weight of munitions fired by heavy guns. And 1972 saw a great increase in the rate of bombing in both North and South Vietnam.

The Americans also could and did undertake a vast population removal program, displacing people from the countryside to refugee camps. They also set up "free-fire zones," where our bombers and artillery could bomb and fire without restriction,

---

[13] Ibid., p. 35.

[14] Raphael Littauer and Norman Uphoff (eds.), *The Air War in Indochina* (Boston: Beacon Press, 1972), chap. 1.

[15] See Arthur H. Westing and E. W. Pfeiffer, "The Cratering of Indochina," *Scientific American*, May 1972, pp. 20–29.

among areas where the people could not or would not be displaced. They could sense the hostility of the rural people, and would respond to it in kind—sometimes with gross atrocities like that at My Lai. They inundated Saigon and other cities with a population accustomed to living well and overwhelmed the Vietnamese economy, contributing among other things to a galloping inflation. Above all, they could and did keep the war going long after it would otherwise have ended. The Vietnamese people were supposed to be grateful for that, but there was nothing they could hope for more profoundly than the coming of peace.

The insensitivity possible among military men with respect to the moral and political effects of what they are doing is illustrated by the following incident. The American Association for the Advancement of Science sent into Vietnam to investigate the effects of the military use of herbicides a team that included a social scientist to interview samples of the population. Samuel Popkin, Assistant Professor of Government at Harvard, who directed the interviewing, reported that the spraying had had "a very negative psychological impact" on the farmers, many of whom felt that the Americans were deliberately trying to destroy the rural economy to make the farmers dependent on the United States. This section of the report evoked a commendably honest but also shocking response from Brig. Gen. William W. Stone, Jr., who had recently retired as director of chemical and nuclear operations for the U.S. Army and who had sought to rebut the remainder of the report. General Stone told *Science* (the organ of the AAAS) that he found the psychological results reported by Popkin and his team on the basis of interviews with Montagnards to be the most dramatic finding of the AAAS study. "They're saying the herbicides have had a negative impact that detracts from our overall program rather than adds to it," he said. "I had frankly never realized there was this psychological impact." [16]

Anyway, the government in Saigon could not but be identified with everything done by the Americans. They need not have been quite so degraded as to seek to deny, when the story of the My Lai massacre first broke, that anything untoward had happened there. But they had their commitments, too. The terrible impact of American power had indeed also hurt the Viet Cong in the South. The kind of cozy and touching activities of the Vietminh described in the quotation from Halberstam on the last days of

---

[16] "Herbicides in Vietnam: AAAS Study Finds Widespread Devastation," *Science*, January 8, 1971, pp. 43–47, quotation on p. 47.

the French presence were no longer possible. The peasants were no longer pleased to see the Viet Cong arrive, because they knew what retribution could be visited upon them. But this situation simply created a no-man's-land into which the Saigon government was incapable of moving. The Viet Cong's loss, probably only temporary, could not be their gain.

Thus, the main reason we failed in Vietnam was also the reason why it was impossible from the beginning to succeed. We were supporting a government that not only did not deserve that support but which could not benefit from it. It could only be kept in place for as long as we were there in force. Nor was this an insight available only after the fact of failure had been established —the usual pure vision of hindsight. President Eisenhower had in a rather confused way been aware of it; President Kennedy had seen it somewhat more clearly. Both had therefore managed to stand off, though the force of the slogans of the time caused both to move the country toward full intervention while avoiding it themselves. President de Gaulle of France had also warned that the United States would find Vietnam a "rotten country," and that the war would therefore be impossible to win. We could, he agreed, bring more power to bear than France, but he insisted that the power to destroy the whole country would still not enable the United States to prevail. It was sage advice, and it was an ex-general as well as a great politician who was offering it. But what American could accept as well-intentioned advice proferred to America by Charles de Gaulle? Not even George Ball, the American emissary to whom de Gaulle vouchsafed it personally, though Ball was one of the few prominent Americans with the same convictions.[17]

Later we were to learn, when the last memoirs of de Gaulle were finally published, what he had fantasied himself saying to President Kennedy on the occasion of the latter's visit to him at the end of May 1961. When Kennedy told the French President that he aimed to establish a bulwark against the Communists in Indochina, the latter, according to Ambassador James M. Gavin who was present, merely passed off with a typical Gallic shrug the comment that France had had enough of Southeast Asia. However, in his memoirs he dressed up the scene significantly:

> You will find, I said to him, that intervention in this area will be an endless entanglement. Once a nation has been aroused, no foreign power, however strong, can impose its

---

[17] Henry Brandon, *Anatomy of Error* (London: Andre Deutsch, 1970), pp. 36 f.

will upon it. You will discover this for yourselves. For even if you find local leaders who in their own interests are prepared to obey you, the people will not agree to it, and indeed do not want you. The ideology which you invoke will make no difference. Indeed, in the eyes of the masses it will become identified with your will to power. That is why the more you become involved out there against Communism, the more the Communists will appear as champions of national independence, and the more support they will receive, if only from despair. . . . Now you want to take over where we left off and revive a war which we brought to an end. I predict that you will sink step by step into a bottomless military and political quagmire, however much you spend in men and money.[18]

Not all such sage warnings were imaginary, but it is easy to forget the background noise in which they could be all too easily lost. One part of this noise is recalled in a point made by J. Enoch Powell, the well-known British Conservative M.P., which is more intriguing than important but not unimportant. Writing early in 1971, he expressed puzzlement at the lack of really serious parliamentary criticism in America of what had been happening in Vietnam. "The military futility of the operations," he said, "so glaringly obvious and even predictable from the other side of the world, was apparently invisible to the Americans." Then he added the following:

> After lately reading "At War With Asia" by the distinguished professor of linguistics, Noam Chomsky, I think I begin to understand what happened. Communism and the movements to leftward of it ate up the other critics: they so monopolized and identified with themselves the critique of American policy and operations in Southeast Asia that they rendered the position untenable to anyone who did not want to risk being found dead in such company.

He goes on to quote some passages from the book to illustrate what he calls the "Marxist brew" out of which it is possible, if one tries hard enough, to distill a reasonable position.[19]

---

[18] Charles de Gaulle, *Memoirs of Hope: Renewal and Endeavor*, trans. by Terence Kilmartin (New York: Simon & Schuster, 1971), p. 256.

[19] "America's Moral Egocentrism," the *New York Times*, March 1, 1971. It should be said that Professor Chomsky is intellectually one of the most respectable of the Marxian interpreters of the American intervention, on which he has by now provided a considerable literary output.

It may not be a good justification for anyone's position on an important public issue that he did not want to be found dead in certain company, but it is frequently the reason for it. When one recalls who were the most vociferous among the few who during 1964–1965 opposed our intervention in Vietnam, one understands marginally better why it was possible to be so obtuse about the course upon which our government was embarking. In 1971 one still heard some of the same noise. The notoriety given early that year to oil explorations off the coast of South Vietnam and to the fact that certain American industrialists had begun to show an interest in building industrial plants in South Vietnam gave new life to the hue and cry about the "military-industrial complex" and the greed that was allegedly responsible for all our evils. However, by that time there was no longer any danger that such a view would monopolize the criticism.

The new mood had been well expressed early in 1968 in another set of hearings by the Senate Foreign Relations Committee at which Secretary Rusk was testifying. After Republican Senator Clifford Case of New Jersey asked Rusk whether the United States commitment really called upon us to persevere to the point of destroying South Vietnam in order to save it, Rusk made a reply rejecting the premises of the question and then archly commented that all would be well in the end if only the faint-hearted would show steadfastness. This nettled the normally gentle Case, who responded:

> Mr. Secretary, you don't have to persuade this committee, or even me, that it is good to meet commitments, that a nation like the U.S. has responsibilities in the world. You really do not. But there is a line to be drawn between the honorable meeting of commitments and pigheaded pushing in the direction of a course which has become more and more sterile. We are trying to find out which is which. . . . For myself, it seems that a course which more and more is producing agony and destruction for the people we are trying to help, and degradation at home, requires more justification than has been made and presented for it.[20]

The Military Problem

In 1964, when General Earle G. Wheeler succeeded General Taylor as Chairman of the Joint Chiefs of Staff, he had the

---

[20] Quoted in Townsend Hoopes, *The Limits of Intervention* (New York: McKay, 1969), pp. 197 f.

following to say on the Vietnam question: "It is fashionable in some quarters to say that the problems in Southeast Asia are primarily political and economic rather than military. I do not agree. The essence of the problem in Vietnam is military." [21] This was also the attitude of the man he replaced, who then became for a year U.S. Ambassador to Saigon. After a second tour of duty by Lodge, who both preceded and followed Taylor in Saigon, the new Ambassador was Ellsworth Bunker. We know that Bunker also shared Wheeler's opinion, as did the Joint Chiefs of Staff. It seems to have been the conviction of every high American official intimately concerned with Vietnam, with the possible exception of Henry Cabot Lodge.

This view explains, among other things, the attachment in Washington to someone like Thieu, and previously even to Ky. The dominant view was: whoever holds supreme office in Saigon is the one to work with so long as he is cooperative with the American military—and let us not fuss about in a search for reformers; in fact, we must avoid the latter because they may cause difficulties, and anyway their anti-Communism is suspect.

It would no doubt be the duty of an officer in Wheeler's position to admonish his government that however much the situation in South Vietnam was a political problem, it was also inevitably a military one. Whatever the inducement offered the peasant to support and cooperate with his government, he could not do so unless he were also assured some reasonable measure of security, and to give him that security might entail considerable military effort. To say, on the other hand, that "the essence of the problem is military" was to show a fateful misapprehension of that problem. For then the peasant became not someone to be won over but quite literally someone in the way. He might provide soldiers for the South Vietnamese army but too often the Viet Cong got to him first. The enemy could also shelter in his hovels and his villages. Even the rice he raised was not really necessary; it might provide a supply for the enemy, and what one needed oneself could be imported. Thus, whatever happened to him or his family, or his few animals, or the dykes by which he irrigated his fields—assuming we did not displace him entirely—could be laid simply to the harsh fortunes of war. Moreover, where villages or districts seemed to show some partiality for the Viet Cong, they became enemy territory, or "free-fire zones," into which bombs or shells could be dropped indiscriminately.

---

[21] Quoted in Brandon, *Anatomy of Error*, p. 23.

De quoi s'agit-il? The old question returns. And we see General Wheeler and all his colleagues answering it in a manner calculated to make the whole American effort not only futile and wasteful but in addition terribly destructive to the Vietnamese society and territory, and thus to our own goals. Stopping Communism in Vietnam was not a matter of stopping an enemy line, as it had been in Korea, where the attack was open and quite conspicuously military, and where the people being fought over were already sympathetic to one's ends, or at any rate not hostile.

But there was a further objection, and a major one. To accept the Wheeler view at face value meant that one should then recognize a terrible impediment to success. Militarily we operated at too grave a disadvantage. However puny North Vietnam might be as a military opponent to the United States, so long as we granted sanctuary to its territory against our own and South Vietnamese ground forces, its forces were essentially invulnerable until they chose to attack.

To grant this sanctuary seemed clearly necessary. The first premise of our intervention was that the resulting war would remain strictly limited, that it would not again involve us directly with Red China. The chances of the Chinese intervening if we invaded North Vietnam could not be rated low. We know that they stationed some 50,000 troops in North Vietnam from 1965 to 1968, and that these forces included two antiaircraft divisions "whose regular exchanges of fire with attacking American aircraft drew casualties on both sides." When our bombing stopped, the troops went back across the border—but they could have returned at any time, and in far greater numbers.[22]

We thought we had had sufficient experience with granting sanctuary in the Korean War. There China had been immune not only to invasion by ground forces but even to air attack, yet this granting of sanctuary on our part had not proved crippling to us. The Chinese forces *in the Korean peninsula* were exposed totally to our armed might, and suffered terribly for it. They could not retire from Korea without giving it up and finding themselves unable to return. Their home base was immune from attack, but not their lines of communication within Korea. Although it was not planned that way, one can say looking back that the Chinese ground forces suffered the more heavily *because*

---

[22] The information and quotation are in a letter to the editor, in the *New York Times*, March 9, 1971, by Professor Allen S. Whiting, author of *China Crosses the Yalu* (New York: Macmillan, 1960), and formerly Director of Far East Research and Analysis in the U.S. Department of State.

we left the Yalu River bridges intact as well as the Chinese territories beyond. Because we left those bridges intact, a crack Chinese army was offered up to our forces and came very near to being destroyed.[23] However, the lesson that impressed itself upon most American students of strategy was simply the following: When fighting an inferior enemy, granting sanctuary to his home grounds is not necessarily crippling even when the sanctuary is total, that is, interdicted to air attack as well as ground invasion. Those who drew the lesson paid too little attention to possible variants.

The military apparently expected a comparable situation in Vietnam, and did not fear granting sanctuary to North Vietnam, the more so as heavy bombing would not be interdicted. However, the key difference between Vietnam and Korea was that in Vietnam there was no large-scale open warfare in the South, no movement of lines to determine success or failure and thus no commitment to take or hold positions at heavy cost. The Viet Cong could melt into the landscape or be sacrificed, but the units of the North Vietnam Army operating in South Vietnam could come and go as they wished, falling back into their sanctuary protection as the situation required.

In the kind of war the North Vietnamese could impose upon us because of their sanctuary status, there was something reminiscent of what Francis Bacon had said about the nation that commands the sea, one of the sagest remarks in all the literature of strategy: "But this much is certain, that he that commands the sea is at great liberty, and may take as much and as little of the war as he will." [24] It was England's strategy from the time of the Hundred Years War to World War II, to sit behind her Channel barrier and to bide her time against her enemies, putting an army on the Continent only when and where it suited her. The coming of air power had only modestly modified this strategy, as we saw in World War II, unless that air power could be truly overwhelming.

Perhaps our military expected that our air power would indeed overwhelm North Vietnam. The Air Force naturally expected it. The Navy, fearing no serious attack upon its own ships, could participate fully from its carriers, and could add the firepower of

---

23 This is discussed in Chapter 3, pp. 74–76, 80 f.

24 In his essay, "Of Greatness of Kingdomes and Estates." I have modernized the spelling.

its guns and missiles, and was therefore also enthusiastic. The Army, being prohibited from invading North Vietnam, was glad to have it raked over with bombers. And by the time the bombing was suspended in 1968 the amount of destruction heaped on North Vietnam, including even Hanoi and the harbor at Haiphong, was really tremendous.[25] But it did not make the North Vietnamese government yield, and it did not reduce appreciably the power of the Communist forces fighting in South Vietnam.

However much the war in Vietnam was a limited one for the United States, it was a total war for our opponents. They were emotionally and in every other way committed to the hilt. They could send their people to air raid shelters—often individual man-holes—and the industrial equipment of the state was expendable. The reason the bombing had so little effect on the fighting in South Vietnam was simple: prior to the spring offensive of 1972, the amount of materiel being expended in that fighting was quite small. It involved mostly small arms and mortar fire, with no large and prolonged battles being fought to cause a high rate of consumption. Much the same thing had happened in Korea during the two-year period of spasmodic fighting that ran concurrently with the prolonged armistice negotiations; the so-called "Operation Strangle" mounted during that period by United States combined Air Force and Navy bomber operations had simply failed. Not enough munitions were being used up at the front to make the supply lines vulnerable.[26] The situation in Vietnam was even more unfavorable to the attempts at interdiction or strategic bombing, because until April, 1972 the consumption of munitions was at a far lower rate than in Korea. Any heavier armaments or munitions needed could be imported from China or the Soviet Union.

No doubt if we had been willing to follow the prescription of retired General Curtis LeMay to bomb the North Vietnamese "back into the stone age," or that of California Governor Ronald Reagan to "flatten the country and pave it over," something could have been accomplished that some would call victory. With nuclear weapons it was technically feasible. But there was no real consideration of using nuclear weapons. American armed forces in Vietnam had never been in the position of desperation that

---

[25] See interview with M. Pierre Darcourt, *U.S. News and World Report*, Dec. 22, 1969, pp. 39 f.

[26] M. W. Cagle and F. Manson, *The Sea War in Korea* (Annapolis: U.S. Naval Institute, 1957), chap. 8, "The Struggle to Strangle."

they had several times experienced in the Korean War, where nuclear weapons had also not been used. The extirpation of North Vietnam through nuclear bombing, besides being dangerous in a nuclear-armed world, was in any case felt to be incompatible with our goals. This amount of rationality did prevail.

Some among the military have argued that the job could have been done properly even without nuclear weapons if President Johnson had simply waived the restrictions concerning the center of Hanoi and especially the harbor at Haiphong. For reasons already suggested, this conclusion does not appear warranted. Townsend Hoopes, who as Undersecretary of the Air Force was in a good position to know, describes a careful investigation of the situation at Haiphong that produced strong evidence that there was simply not enough transshipment of war goods in that harbor to make any strategic difference whether it was bombed or not, yet the military persisted in their demands that it be bombed.[27] These were the same people, General Westmoreland and Admiral Ulysses S. Grant Sharp among them, who were publicly making claims after the bombing had been terminated a year or more that if only it had been continued, "the war would be won by now." [28] Inasmuch as they completely lacked evidence with which to support these claims, their remarks deserved to be denounced as plainly irresponsible.

Why *did* President Johnson terminate the bombing of most of North Vietnam with his speech of March 31, 1968 and abandon it totally 'in the following November? Certainly it was hurting the North Vietnamese; the common notion that anyone's morale is improved by bombing is an absurdity that was amply exposed as such by the strategic bombing surveys following World War II.[29] The pressure upon Johnson to stop the bombing, from sources both at home and abroad, was tremendous. The usual allegation

---

[27] Hoopes, *Limits of Intervention*, pp. 80 f.

[28] The views of General Westmoreland were given in secret testimony before the House Appropriations Subcommittee in October 1969 but released by that subcommittee on December 1, 1969. Westmoreland's statement was: "It is my opinion that if we had continued to bomb, the war would be over at this time—or would be nearly over." *Los Angeles Times*, Dec. 2, 1969. I heard Admiral Sharp make a similar, less qualified assertion on national television at about the same time, but I have no record of the date.

[29] See my *Strategy in the Missile Age* (Princeton: Princeton University Press, 1959), pp. 131–143, where I analyze the relevant items among the extensive official publications.

was that only through halting it could the North Vietnamese be brought to the conference table, a conviction that the latter naturally did their best to encourage. It was, however, clear that three years of the bombing had not produced the results hoped for. Another year of it conceivably might, but there was little enough to warrant the presumption that it would. We have already seen also how the Tet offensive of February 1968 created a crisis in Washington that demanded a resolution, and the change in policy on bombing was indispensably a part of that resolution.

Anyway, inasmuch as the bombing of North Vietnam prior to March 31, 1968 proved not to be decisive, and inasmuch as it was greatly restricted after that date and then virtually halted in November of that year, which naturally permitted some recovery from the damage done, North Vietnam became a true and complete sanctuary for the Communist troops. Bacon's precept was now in unqualified operation. The Communist troops were at great liberty, and could take as much or as little of the war as they wished. Later it would be obvious that they had made good use of this advantage. In the autumn of 1969 and continuing through 1970 and 1971 the feeling in Washington, fed as usual on official and invariably optimistic reports from Saigon, was that the Viet Cong and the North Vietnamese Army had been very seriously hurt, perhaps decisively so. Certainly they were engaging in much less activity in the South. However, Robert Kleiman of the *New York Times*, whose views may indeed have reflected his steady opposition to American involvement in the war, wrote in a November 17, 1969 article the following sentence about the "progress" proclaimed from Washington: "Some analysts—skeptical of any basic shift—have noted that all the indicators of progress would be the same if the enemy forces, instead of being beaten, had withdrawn of their own volition."

The strength of the North Vietnamese counterattack against the Laos offensive of early 1971 seemed to suggest that this skeptical interpretation was correct. More to the point, there was no reason why it should not be correct for the longer term. Even forces badly hurt, if given rest, will recuperate and recover. There had been very heavy attrition among the North Vietnamese forces in the several years of fighting, though we know also that the "body counts" that had been so prominent a feature of our estimates of enemy damage had been enormously exaggerated. The My Lai incident, where the victims were at first reported as slain

Viet Cong, gave only one among many hints about the identity of the bodies counted. There was no doubt great hurt and war-weariness in the North as there certainly was in the South, but no solid indication that forces in North Vietnam would not be able to surge back into the South at any time they pleased. And they would have been foolish not to wait until the withdrawal of American forces had proceeded further than it had by mid-1971.

The resurgence came in the following year, with the great North Vietnamese offensive that began in early April 1972. Despite long months of American bombing of the "Ho Chi Minh trail" and of what were said to be storage depots for enemy arma-ments, it was quickly apparent that the South Vietnamese forces could nowhere sustain themselves without the massive American bombing support accorded them, supplemented near the coasts by the 5-inch guns of U.S. destroyers. Even with that help, how-ever, it appeared at the beginning of May that they were not succeeding in holding their own.

It was again obvious that the allegedly defused issue could still sputter hotly. President Nixon's speech of April 26, in which he committed himself anew to the maintenance of the Saigon regime in power—"We will not be defeated and we will never surrender our friends to Communist aggression"—though as skillfully wrought as such a speech could be at such a late date, rallied no one who was not utterly locked into the President's support. It was now more clearly than ever "Nixon's war." Shortly before that speech a Democratic caucus in the House voted for the first time by an overwhelming majority to join the Senate in demand-ing a terminal date for U.S. participation in the war. And on the day before the speech was given, Senator George McGovern, leading antiwar Presidential candidate, swept the Democratic primaries in Massachusetts by a 52 per cent majority, despite the presence of eleven other candidates on the ticket.

However, the power of the air and naval forces always at the command of a President of the United States must never be underestimated, even apart from nuclear weapons, and before long it became clear that the North Vietnamese had seriously underestimated it. They had, apparently, overplayed their hand in Paris in late April, when Dr. Kissinger, on his way home from Moscow where the Soviet leaders had encouraged him to resume direct personal negotiations with the North Vietnamese emis-saries, tried to reach with the latter some last minute understanding. The huge success of their offensive up to that time apparently betrayed their comprehension of what it meant to scorn the desires of an American President who happened to be capable of great ruthlessness, and who was determined, especially in this election year, that he or at least his office should be accorded proper "respect." They thought they had understood what American air power could do to their troops in the field, and they had chosen to defy it. So did many Americans misapprehend what air power could do, because they thought that the record showed nothing but wanton destructiveness combined with military ineffectiveness.

There can be no question about the destructiveness, but the effectiveness depends on many variables. Now, by attacking in large conventional forces with tanks and other accoutrements, the North Vietnamese attackers had made themselves as never before a great and vulnerable military target. That mode of attack with its heavy dependence on munitions and other commodities, also made them much more vulnerable to an interruption of supplies from China and especially the Soviet Union. Another critical variable is always the weight and mode of the attack. Besides enormously increasing the amount of air power over Vietnam (with eight aircraft carriers stationed in nearby seas and almost two hundred B-52's operating from bases in Thailand and elsewhere) President Nixon on May 6 took the step theretofore sedulously avoided by himself as well as by his predecessor: he ordered the mining of Haiphong and other North Vietnamese harbors, which was accomplished in a few hours by aircraft operating from carriers. He also ordered the resumption of the bombing of North Vietnam on a far heavier scale than ever before, and it was soon additionally revealed that our forces now had available two new kinds of guided bombs or "smart bombs," which enabled our aircraft to bomb with unprecedented accuracy and effectiveness such hitherto difficult but important targets as bridges.

In announcing in a speech of the same date the steps he was taking, President Nixon also restated his war-termination aims in a manner that highlighted omission of reference to his commitment to maintaining the Saigon regime, last enunciated less than six weeks earlier. He still called for "an internationally supervised cease-fire throughout Indochina," a requirement that could be interpreted by Hanoi as demanding surrender, but he coupled this for the first time with a promise that if such a cease-fire were concluded and American prisoners of war released (always mentioned as though it were a serious obstacle to peace, which it certainly was not), the United States would "proceed with complete withdrawal of all American forces from Vietnam within four months." The same speech contained an appeal to the Soviet Union, whom "we respect . . . as a great power," to recognize the legitimacy of American defensive interests in Vietnam.

There can be no doubt that the President won his gamble on all fronts. Under the extraordinary pounding the North Vietnamese field forces received from the air, their long-prepared offensive collapsed. The destruction of railroad bridges connecting North Vietnam with China and the mining of the harbors effectively cut off Hanoi from any large scale military resupply, and the destruction of power stations and other industrial targets within North Vietnam did not halt but much reduced domestic production for both war and peace. At the same time the Soviet Union, with no effective means for challenging the blockade and desiring above all to preserve the scheduled summit meeting —thereby showing that its fear of and animosity toward China were considerably greater than any comparable feelings toward the United States—proceeded to conduct itself as though nothing had happened. The Moscow summit in the latter part of May was held with the usual bravura and with the signing of the arms limitation treaties.

This meeting followed by little more than two months the President's epoch-making trip to Peking, where nothing was signed and where diplomatic relations were not even established (a nicety inhibited by the 1954 alliance treaty with Taiwan), but where a demonstration was made to all the world that the United States military actions in Vietnam were as unlikely to cause a war with China as with the Soviet Union. Rarely has a great power— or at least its ruling figure in the conduct of his policies—benefited as much from the mutual hostility of its two erstwhile major enemies.

The following months saw an extraordinary reaffirmation of the political utility of success. After sputtering on into July 1972, the peace movement in the United States virtually collapsed as a vital force. Votes in the Congress that had seemed to be building up to demanding a specific war termination date began to go the other way even in the Senate, the only chamber in which relevant amendments to authorization bills had ever carried a majority. Street demonstrations of militant university students and other young people practically disappeared, and that at the very time a peace candidate was running for the Presidency at the head of one of the two major parties. As for Senator McGovern, who had marched triumphantly to the Democratic nomination primarily on his unequivocal stand for immediate withdrawal from Vietnam, his campaign began to flounder in an effort that looked so hopeless as to induce only apathy. Subsequently beset by both mishap and blunder, McGovern went down to one of the most overwhelming defeats in U.S. electoral history, deserted contemptuously by large sections of his own party.

We are obliged to speculate on what caused the marked shift in sentiment. The three most important reasons are quite undeniable. Other possible contributing factors are both less important and less certain.

First was the fact that the removal of American troops from the battle fronts and indeed from Vietnam itself reduced American casualties almost to zero. There were still large American forces in the area, at Air Force bases in Thailand, and on naval vessels afloat, but these were no longer mostly conscripts and they were not in danger. Vice Admiral William P. Mack was able on his last day in command of the Seventh Fleet (May 23, 1972) to boast to newspaper reporters that out of the 75,000 men in that fleet, including pilots, losses in the preceding month had been only seven men, which was statistically about half the number that would have been lost back at home out of the same number of men in a comparable age group. "It's less dangerous here," he said, "than it is in New York." The number of brown people ashore who had been killed by that force over that same period could not be expected to be causing him distress. Neither was it causing any to the great majority of American citizens at home in whose name and with whose financial support it had been done.

In these matters we have to take account not only of callousness but also of ignorance. Most of the essential data about the war are fairly recondite. Few Americans, for example, were aware that a B-52 flying such short distances as were required of it in Indochina could carry about thirty tons of bombs, which meant over one hundred 500-lb antipersonnel bombs each sortie—the primary reason why the huge tonnages of bombs dropped in Vietnam are even believable. One could say that the people did not know because they did not care, but the habits of the public have to be accepted for what they are. The major part of the American public—like the major part of any other public—does not read whatever foreign news may be carried in its newspapers, or listen to news reports on television or radio, and the minority that does is likely to lose interest in a war that has gone on too long and that is no longer taking the lives of any appreciable number of Americans. Thus the despairing cry of editorialist Tom Wicker in the *New York Times* (September 12, 1972) concerning what the current election campaign was failing to bring out: "The American people do not seem to realize that their air power is carrying out one of the most terrible mass exterminations in history, not only in the North but in the South Vietnam that it is supposed to be defending and over which the squalid Thieu has been given such dictatorial sway."

The message signaled by the popular outcry (at about the time of the Laos offensive) against the conviction of Lieutenant William Calley, Jr. for his leading part in the My Lai massacre had been too clear to miss. The murder of brown people far away, concerning whom we seem to have had nothing but trouble, does not really count. Besides, how many had any real notion of what had happened? *Life,* a magazine of quite exceptional circulation, had carried vivid color pictures of the victims both before and after their murder, but it was nevertheless only a minute proportion of the American public that had seen them. Anyway, the pursuit of the good, the true, and the beautiful, as Plato pointed out long ago, has nothing to do with popular majorities.

Second, the lurking fears that our involvement in Vietnam might sooner or later entrap us into serious difficulties with China (as the Korean War had done) or with the Soviet Union, or with both, were laid to rest by the President's visits to Peking and to Moscow, and especially by the fact that the Russians had welcomed him *after* he had ordered the mining of the North Vietnamese ports. What had been undoubtedly a gamble looked after the event like a demonstration of the President's extraordinary sagacity in these matters, and the common tendency to believe that in such affairs the President always has the most knowledge and the best advice received a Herculean boost. The same factor of diminished fears of a larger war undoubtedly also affected public opinion abroad, and the resumption and then continuation of the American bombing of Vietnam on a far larger scale than had ever been chargeable to President Johnson aroused nothing like the protest throughout Europe and Asia that he had known.

Third, the conventional Communist offensive that began in March 1972 had all the outward trappings of aggression, and could be successfully so labeled. Just as the Laos offensive the year before on the part of South Vietnamese forces had aroused what subsequently proved to be the last huge wave of indignation in the United States at the President's war policies, at least until December 1972, so it was the other side now that seemed conspicuously to bear the major responsibility for the continuation of the war. To most of the American public the President's peace terms appeared reasonable enough. After all, who was in favor of seeing the United States "humiliated?" It is difficult to measure the importance of this factor, but it undoubtedly helped to contribute to a mood revealed in a Harris poll published in mid-September 1972. It showed 55 per cent of the American people in favor of our bombing in Vietnam and only 32 per cent opposed to it. The others did not know what to think, and obviously could not much have cared.

There is a fourth and more speculative factor. The candidacy of George McGovern no doubt alarmed many people because of his alleged radicalism, including a good proportion of those who would normally have voted Democratic. It is likely that with many voters the rejection of this candidate and the resulting shift to Nixon prompted also a corresponding shift in sentiments about the war. There is something in what William James once said: One runs (from a bear) not because one is frightened; one is frightened because one runs. Similarly, to some extent at least, the way one votes determines the way one feels.

Still, in the last weeks of an electoral campaign in which the victory of the Republican candidate was all but assured, the stock market was ailing again and it was once again limiting its favorable response only to rumors of an imminent peace in Vietnam. Such rumors were constantly recurring and as constantly being denied. It still seemed to matter. Well, the war was still costing money—at least $7 billion annually before the Communist spring offensive, and probably twice that amount afterward. This meant continued inflationary pressure and continued governmental moves to repress inflation. But one should not assume that the money was the important factor. There was a great longing to have the whole sorry business over with, and with the Communists shifting back to the guerilla tactics in which they had been so successful, and doing very well indeed in the Mekong delta area, there was simply no telling when the business would be over with. The Communist offensive had been contained, but not through any spectacular demonstration of the success of our Vietnamization policy.

The Role of the American Military Leaders

In a book dedicated to exploring the intimate and pervasive connections between politics and strategy, there is little point in attempting to analyze or criticize United States military operations as such in the Vietnam theater, except insofar as those operations reflected various political considerations. We have already observed that the premise on which these operations proceeded was one that downgraded basic political issues that should have operated as controlling parameters. The amount of damage done to the people and environment of all Vietnam, and especially of South Vietnam, is all-too-eloquent testimony of the fact that both General Westmoreland and his successor, General Creighton W. Abrams, though the latter less so than the former, were committed to the notion that the only way to win the war was to kill a sufficient number of Viet Cong and North Vietnamese soldiers, and that every other goal must yield place to this one.

Others having better opportunities than I to investigate the facts in the field have written valuable critiques, and there will no doubt be more.[30] In general they tend to confirm the impression that not only were political considerations downgraded in importance but the war itself was for a long time downgraded in relation to other wars the United States might be called upon to fight. Thus, the Army remained highly resistant to any kind of organizational change that might enable it better to cope with a war that was considered to be aberrant in character. Senior commanders also tended to look upon the Vietnam War as having a special function for training, screening, and decorating career officers. A journalist in a special study of General Westmoreland reported in the following language one of his remarks:

---

[30] I have in mind especially the outstanding work of Brian Jenkins, of the RAND Corporation, who was a participant and later an observer of the American military effort in Vietnam and who has written several memoranda on the subject. However, at this writing they have not yet been cleared for public distribution or even quotation.

I bet that Russian Army is jealous as hell. Our troops are here getting all this experience, we're learning about guerilla warfare, helicopters, vertical envelopment, close artillery support . . . Those Russian generals would love to be here . . . Any true professional wants to march to the sound of gunfire.[31]

Some writers, notably Henry A. Kissinger (before he became the President's assistant) severely criticized our military for going after the wrong objectives. The chief objective, Kissinger said, should have been not attrition of enemy troops but rather full protection of as much as possible of the population: better 100 per cent control of 60 per cent of the country than 60 per cent control of 100 per cent of the country. As he put it: "The North Vietnamese used their main forces the way a bullfighter uses his cape—to keep us lunging in areas of marginal political importance." [32] All this is perhaps true, but it is subsumed in General Wheeler's basic appraisal that the problem in Vietnam was mainly military, not political. A strategy of protecting population instead of seeking out enemy forces would have run counter to all the proudest traditions of the American military, especially that of maintaining an offensive rather than a defensive stance. "Search and destroy" meant going after the enemy, that is, maintaining the initiative, which in turn meant concentrating one's own forces against enemy detachments rather than letting them be spread out in a defensive posture in a manner likely to make them vulnerable to enemy concentrations. Apart from tradition, there is much to be said for the Army view.

One is reminded of the World War I controversy in Britain, touched upon in Chapter 1, between the Admiralty and the government concerning the merits of hunting for U-boats with destroyer forces as against devoting the same forces to protective escort of convoys. The Admiralty urged all the traditional arguments in asserting the superiority of the "search and destroy" strategy; the government, under Lloyd George, finally insisted

---

[31] Ernest B. Furgurson, *Westmoreland: The Inevitable General* (Boston: Little, Brown 1968), p. 27. Israeli General Moshe Dayan visited Vietnam in 1968 and wrote a series of newspaper articles, published throughout the world, in which he described his observations and also his interviews with American military officers. The Israeli newspapers carrying his accounts—but not the American ones—included his comment that senior American officers had spoken with evident satisfaction of the training being afforded the younger officers by the Vietnam experience.

[32] "The Vietnam Negotiations," *Foreign Affairs*, vol. 47, no. 2 (January 1969).

on the convoy strategy, on the grounds that the U-boats had to seek out the transport ships in order to carry out *their* mission. Lloyd George turned out to be right, and spectacular results followed from adopting in 1917 the practice of convoying with escorts. Again we see that the ruling question is not: What are the right principles? It is rather: What is the problem? What is it all about?

On the other hand, it would clearly be wrong to assume that protecting villages in Vietnam is anything like protecting maritime convoys. The latter are relatively few, each presents a requirement for protection for only a brief period, and the war itself gets resolved in other ways. What Kissinger was asking for would at best be an endless war—and thus, again, one not to be entered into.

In any event, it does not appear that the Vietnam War will stand out historically for the United States armed forces as one of their finest hours. In this respect it contrasts markedly with the Korean War. The reasons are several. First, the Korean War was much more "conventional," in every sense of the term, falling entirely within the traditions and the training of the officers called upon to wage it. Second, in the case of Korea, as we have seen, officials in Washington, especially the Joint Chiefs of Staff, considered a war with the Soviet Union to be imminent. This fear, however unwarranted, was quite enough to assure a somewhat detached view about Korea and a lively unwillingness to become too deeply committed there. In the Vietnam business, unfortunately, we were undeterred by such fears. The "detente" with the Soviet Union appears in this respect to have had an ill effect, and for that matter there was confidence that so long as we avoided invading North Vietnam, Communist China, too, would stay out of the war. Thus did growing sophistication contribute to the error of our ways. The military in this case had little incentive to rein in their usual obsession with winning whatever ball game they happen to be playing.

Third and last, we are confronted again with the element of chance that always operates with respect to the selection of the military officers that are found at the pinnacles of authority in the moment of crisis, as is true of Presidents as well. In the Korean War we had men like Omar Bradley as Chairman of the Joint Chiefs of Staff, George C. Marshall, as Secretary of Defense, J. Lawton Collins, Chief of Staff of the Army (whose fine intelligence and sensitivity to political constraints have not thus far been adequately recognized), and Matthew L. Ridgway.

As early as December 1954 Collins reported after a mission to Saigon that Diem was incapable of leading South Vietnam—which was contrary to the opinions both of Senator Mike Mansfield and of the State Department—and recommended the return of Bao Dai. If Bao Dai proved inadequate or inacceptable, he went on, the United States should consider "re-evaluation of our plans for assisting Southeast Asia with special attention (to an) earlier proposal." This earlier proposal was that the U.S. gradually withdraw from Vietnam. Collins said this was the "least desirable [but] in all honesty and in view of what I have observed here to date this may be the only sound solution." [33] No military successor to Collins in Saigon was to show anything like such sensitivity and insight.

When the United States became fully committed in Vietnam General Ridgway, then in retirement, publicly urged withdrawal, as did Lieut. General James M. Gavin, Ambassador to France under President Kennedy; but these officers were not listened to. They have, however, served a permanently useful purpose. In view of their outstanding combat records no one could ever accuse Generals Collins, Ridgway, and Gavin of lacking gallantry. They have proved that patriotic and courageous officers, fully representative of the best traditions of the service in which they spent their life careers, could remain detached from the constricted, win-at-any-cost attitudes of officers like Generals Wheeler and Taylor.

General Maxwell Taylor, Chairman of the Joint Chiefs until 1964, Ambassador to Saigon during the critical period when President Johnson was making his crucial decisions to shift to a combat role, and thereafter informal advisor to the latter and to his successor bears as much responsibility as any other military man for the sad story of our commitment to Vietnam. Tall and strikingly handsome, urbane, a dedicated acquirer of languages, possessor of a splendid war record from World War II, and the author of *The Uncertain Trumpet* which sought to knock nuclear weapons out of their then favored place in U.S. strategy, he

---

[33] *The Pentagon Papers: The Defense Department History of United States Decision-making on Vietnam, Senator Gravel Edition*, 5 vols. (Boston: Beacon Press, 1971), vol. 1, pp. 222–227.

was certain to captivate President Kennedy. He seemed really to fulfil the latter's well-known passion for "excellence" in every sphere, or at least what seemed like it.

The story of Taylor's interventions concerning Vietnam is told mostly in the Pentagon Papers. His memorandum to President Kennedy of November 3, 1961 strongly urged intervention with combat forces, though during his ambassadorship in Saigon in 1965 it appeared as though he might be having some second thoughts about such intervention at the moment it was actually beginning. However, if he did have reservations then, which is not at all clear, it was for the last time. After that he was consistently a zealous advocate of the win-at-any-price commitment.

One was perhaps forewarned about his views from various passages in *The Uncertain Trumpet,* published in 1959. It read somewhat oddly even then that American intervention at Dien Bien Phu in 1954 was "unfortunately" prevented by lack of the appropriate conventional forces. He then added (p. 25): "This event was the first, but not the last, failure of the New Look to keep the peace on our terms." The "New Look," one remembers, was the Eisenhower policy of reliance primarily on the nuclear deterrent, but one remembers also that Dien Bien Phu occurred only one year after the final achievement of the armistice ending the three-year war in Korea.

But General Taylor has also published his memoirs, and, as is true of the comparable product of some other retired generals, these add no luster to his reputation. In one place he casually observes that "one of the prime lessons of the Bay of Pigs" is that if we take another such "first step," then obviously "we must be prepared to go all the way!" This is in the same paragraph in which he allows himself unable to understand the significance others attached to President Kennedy's omitting from the approved National Security Action Memorandum of November 15, 1961 "formal affirmation of the broad policy commitment which his principal advisers had urged"—though what was thus conspicuously not approved was Taylor's own recommendation to send combat forces! In another place he confesses himself still unable to understand why the North Vietnamese launched the Tet offensive of 1968 in which they sacrificed so many men—as though General Giap, who had conspicuously proved himself outstanding in the planning of political outcomes for his campaigns, could not possibly have *intended* the political results in the United States that did in fact follow. In his concluding chapters Taylor reveals himself as totally lacking any comprehension of, let alone dedication to, the qualities and requirements of democracy in his own country. He recommends that in another such intervention the President should seek from the Congress "a declaration of war or emergency to silence future critics of war by executive order!" [34] One does not know at what to be more astonished, his expression of such sentiments, or his ignorance of his country's laws.

It is not clear how Taylor justifies these ideas to himself. Does he thinks Presidents are incapable of error or of reprehensible action? Or does he feel that the moment such action becomes military, and therefore "national," it must in all cases be carried through to a successful conclusion. Probably the latter. General Taylor shows himself to be at all times enormously impressed with the importance of retaining prestige, and with what he considers to be the requirements thereof. To him failure to *win* deals prestige a mortal blow. There is none of John F. Kennedy's realism about being "kicked in the can for a couple of weeks."

There was also General Earle G. Wheeler, Chief of Staff of the Army until 1964 and from then until 1968 Chairman of the Joint Chiefs. One does not have the same glowing expectations of a Wheeler that one has of a Taylor, but his reputation was nevertheless of a man of sharp intelligence. Like Taylor he had earlier reservations about a commitment to Vietnam—there *is* an old axiom in the U.S. Army concerning the inadvisability of getting bogged down in a land war on the Continent of Asia—but also like Taylor he quickly became, as we slipped into serious commitment, a high priest of the win-at-any-price dogma. His important role is also revealed in the Pentagon Papers, but there is additionally the previously mentioned article, based on interviews with the principals, by John B. Henry II concerning the immediate aftermath of Tet. General William Westmoreland had called Tet the enemy's "last gasp" effort, a sign that Hanoi had decided that "a protracted war was not in its long-range interest." Wheeler cabled him to hint that he change his language, stating that "the United States is not prepared to accept defeat in Vietnam" ("defeat" had been entirely missing from Westmoreland's conception of what had happened to him), and quickly departed

---

[34] *Swords and Plowshares* (New York: Norton, 1972), the quotations are from pp. 248 and 406.

for Saigon. There he persuaded Westmoreland that if he requested sufficient reinforcements he could shift to a really offensive strategy that would include amphibious operations against the panhandle of North Vietnam. Returning to Washington, he seems to have been considerably less than frank with Secretary McNamara and President Johnson concerning the plans he had discussed with Westmoreland. However, as we have seen, he outfoxed his civilian superiors but not the trend of events. The request by the Army for 206,000 additional troops had the unforeseen effects already related.[35]

It is necessary finally to notice still another characteristic of the military in Vietnam—their consistent and endless distortion of events on the side of optimism. One must always be ready to excuse honest errors in prediction, but in this instance it is enlightening and also sobering to compare the reports and predictions coming from military sources and those of an independent intelligence-gathering agency, the CIA. Running all through the Pentagon Papers, and strikingly apparent again in National Security Study Memorandum 1 of early 1969 (released to the press by Senator Mike Gravel in April 1972)[36] is a sharp difference between estimates and recommendations of the Joint Chiefs on the one hand and the CIA on the other, with other intelligence agencies, like that of the State Department, usually falling somewhere in between. If one also compares the military judgments with those of the more incisive and dedicated among the civilian journalists (who were not difficult to distinguish from the flock), the contrast is even more extreme. To the military the situation always looked better than it did to others, they always wanted to lay on more force, and they were always optimistic of the favorable results of doing so. Perhaps the "always" needs to be slightly qualified, but not by much. The special military views had an enormous impact on national policy, because they were believed by Secretary McNamara until the end of 1966 and by President Johnson throughout his tenure.

There is a serious lesson in this. The Vietnam War is certainly

---

[35] John B. Henry II, "February, 1968," *Foreign Policy*, no. 4 (Fall 1971), pp. 3–33. The question of just how many troops were requested by the military, and how they were to be disposed, has become a matter of contention. Hoopes speaks of the "curious, retrospective effort by the military leaders to argue that an actual request for 206,000 additional troops was never made"; *Limits of Intervention*, p. 174 n. Taylor is clearly disingenuous in denying it was made; *Swords and Plowshares*, p. 388. The best source is, as usual, the *Pentagon Papers*, Gravel ed., vol. 4, pp. 546–593.

[36] Reprinted in part in the *New York Times*, April 26, 1972.

not the first war in which the reports of the military proved untrustworthy (one recalls the wholesale and deliberate distortions of the British and French military chieftains to their respective governments in World War I). The military are committed to success and hence are too interested a party to be reliable, especially in times of difficulty or crisis. The distortion, as we have seen especially in Vietnam, starts at the lowest levels and becomes intensified at each echelon until the Joint Chiefs are reached, and the latter are hardly likely to be a disinterested forum. On occasion, as we saw in the case of General Wheeler's intervention in February 1968, the same desire to advance their interests as they see them may cause the military to adopt temporarily a pessimistic view, but interest-dictated perception and reporting are bound to be unreliable in any case. The solution is clear. One is not going to reform the military, either in this respect or in very many others. It is important to have reporting agencies totally independent of the military. If these are not available, the political leader who is the consumer of military intelligence must remember his grain of salt—though in this case the grain had better be a barrel.

The Vietnamization Policy

President Johnson's decision in March 1968 not to run for reelection that year presents about as clear a case as we are likely ever to have in the American electoral system of a President relinquishing his reelection chances (in a race that normally favors the incumbent) because the public has soured on a major policy with which he is identified. It was therefore by an aberration peculiar to the American system that he was succeeded in office not by one with clearly opposed views on the same Vietnam War issue but rather by a man if anything more hawkish than himself. We have already noted some of the words and actions of Richard Nixon that confirm this point. True, Nixon won with the slenderest of pluralities, with only 43 per cent of the vote, and through a succession of accidents. But he was in, for four long years, barring acts of God or of murderous fanatics; and, as is given to all Presidents who succeed however narrowly in winning office, he was shortly talking about his "mandate."

A mandate is always interpreted by the victor as the licence for doing what he wants to do. And, unless he has gone far out of his way to hide his true feelings, what more pragmatic testimony of the popular will does he have than his own victory? Actually, the public attitudes toward the war in the election year 1968 were not easy to determine. The opinion polls by Gallup and others had shown a steady decline in support for the war, and a majority were already registering the view that the intervention had been "a mistake." [37] President Johnson had within three years moved from immense popularity to something like the opposite, and that change was certainly tied mostly to the war. Still, the only two senators who had voted against the Tonkin Bay Resolution in 1964 lost their bids for reelection in 1968. No comparable penalties were so conspicuously visited upon senators or representatives who had staunchly supported the war. One could argue that the trend in opinion was clear and that it was beginning to move quite rapidly (there could be no doubt about the direction), but to men who had just won office or regained it, it was hard to argue against election returns.

No doubt President Nixon did have a "mandate" that gave him a good deal of latitude. On matters that evoke at the same time feelings of patriotism and of perplexity, the public wants to be led. It looks for cues from its President, especially a newly-elected one, on how it should think. But some cues wear out faster than others. Had he chosen to do so, President Nixon could have dedicated his first months in office to getting us out of the war rapidly and completely. He could have branded the intervention policy of the previous administration a grievous mistake for which he would not share responsibility. The only way to remedy so tragic and far-reaching an error, he could have asserted, was to liquidate it without delay. He could have moved decisively to do so, in any of a number of possible variations. What he did do was to move about as far in the opposite direction as he dared. Inasmuch as it was clearly too late when he took office to think in terms of turn-

---

[37] The Gallup Poll (see monthly issued Gallup Political Index Report) began in early 1965 asking periodically in identical language two questions. The first referred to confidence in the (current) President's handling of the war, and the second was given in the following language: "In view of the developments since we entered the fighting in Vietnam, do you think the U.S. made a mistake sending troops to fight in Vietnam?" Concerning the latter question, there was an overwhelmingly favorable (for the government) response throughout 1965, and a still markedly favorable response through 1966. However, about July 1967 a majority began expressing the view that the U.S. had "made a mistake," and after that the proportion expressing that view fairly steadily increased. Two outstanding papers on American public opinion and the Vietnam War are: Verba, Brody, Parker, Nie Polsby, Eckman, and Black, "Public Opinion and the War in Vietnam," *American Political Science Review*, vol. 61, no. 2 (June 1967), and J. P. Robinson and S. G. Jacobsen, "American Public Opinion About Vietnam," in W. Isard (ed.), *Vietnam: Issues and Alternatives* (Cambridge: Schenkman, 1969).

ing back towards further escalation of the war, his decision was to stand pat. On March 4, 1969 he announced: "There are no plans to withdraw any troops at this time or in the near future."

That turned out to be the wrong cue. It had been worn too thin by his predecessor, and what was left of it was abrasive. Three months later, on June 8, he stated: "I have decided to order the immediate redeployment from Vietnam of . . . approximately 25,000 men." This got a far better response. The process of "winding down" the Vietnam War was thus reasserted (counting the two-step termination by President Johnson of the bombing of North Vietnam in March and October 1968 as the logical beginning). The withdrawals continued, at a rate calculated to bring about 100,000 U.S. troops home from Vietnam—from a peak of almost 550,000—by the end of Mr. Nixon's first year in office. On November 3, 1969 the President gave a speech on Vietnam which most politicians and news analysts agreed had "effectively defused" the Vietnam War as a political issue. When one reads the speech today, it is not easy to understand how it could have had that effect. It was mostly an argument against overprecipitate withdrawal. But it also contained the promise of further withdrawals. Obviously, it was the latter point that made the most sound.

The President was credited with so favorable a public response that political opponents dared not harry him on Vietnam. That we were withdrawing at all seemed to be generally satisfactory, and no one of political eminence dared ask: But why so slowly? At the rate then current, it would take four years to bring them all home, except that there was no promise that the President intended ultimately to bring home all. Apart from frequently uttered slogans like "peace with honor," the meaning of which was never filled in, the President vouchsafed the country no hint why he felt it necessary to withdraw so gradually. The hard commitment to reduce steadily the number of troops in Vietnam was a far-reaching one, and it implied acceptance of certain conclusions about ultimate success or failure. Or did it? One would not wish to be disorderly in withdrawal or to leave an unnecessary amount of disorder behind. Still, the matter needed explanation.

An important part of the explanation is undoubtedly contained in the earlier discussed article in the January 1969 issue of *Foreign Affairs* by Dr. Henry A. Kissinger, who had just become the President's closest adviser on national security affairs and foreign affairs generally. Although President Nixon's policies must always be regarded as his own, for which he has to assume full responsibility regardless of whose advice he has accepted, it was also true that on Vietnam as on many other other matters, Nixon and Kissinger were of kindred views. Kissinger's brilliant facility at terse exposition, written and oral, would always make any intelligent person listen to him with respect, but in Nixon's case it would also usually be with full concurrence.

Kissinger's essay, entitled "The Viet Nam Negotiations" (which he submitted for publication before he knew he would hold so exalted a post and which he was then unable to withdraw in time), outlines a plan for dealing with the Communist negotiators whom President Johnson had finally brought to the conference table in Paris in May 1968. However, what had followed in Paris had been a sort of choreography, at any rate something other than negotiations. The question was how to get the matter down to business—if it could be done at all.

The first half of Kissinger's article was given over, as I have indicated, to a severe indictment of the performance of the U.S. military leaders in Vietnam. They had, he maintained, with characteristic energy and aggressiveness done all the wrong things. The Tet offensive had proved the bankruptcy of the Westmoreland strategy. The United States armed forces had now shot their powerful bolt, but in the wrong direction. All this was argued with obvious expertness and insight, and most persuasively. But the question remained: What now?

To Kissinger the failure was not even remotely a reason for giving up. Whatever the lack of justification of the original U.S. commitment to Vietnam (Kissinger curiously identified 1961 and 1962 as the years of error), "the commitment of 500,000 Americans has settled the issue of the importance of Viet Nam." He rang in strongly the issues of "credibility" and prestige; "other nations can gear their actions to ours only if they can count on our steadiness." If we simply gave up in Vietnam our foreign critics would not be mollified; they would only "add the charge of unreliability to the accusation of bad judgment." He also invoked what has since been called the "backlash" issue. "Washington was aware [prior to March 1968] that a bombing halt which did not lead rapidly to substantive talks could not be sustained domestically." One should notice that this statement could hardly be confirmed on any empirical basis.

Kissinger knew what not to seek through negotiations. The

fetish of a coalition government as a compromise was simply absurd. "It is beyond imagination that parties that have been murdering and betraying each other for 25 years could work together as a team giving joint instructions to the country." And again, "The danger of a coalition government is that it would decouple the non-communist elements from effective control over their armed forces and police, leaving them unable to defend themselves adequately."

If the United States would not negotiate a coalition government or its own withdrawal, what was left to negotiate? Kissinger's answer was, essentially, *a surrender by Hanoi*. After all, Hanoi had much to surrender for. "A prolonged, even if ultimately victorious war might leave Vietnam so exhausted as to jeopardize the purpose of decades of struggle." Also, "a country so sensitive to international currents as North Vietnam cannot be reassured by [such] recent developments" as the Soviet invasion of Czechoslovakia! But the basic point was: "No matter how irrelevant some of our political conceptions or how insensitive our strategy, we are so powerful that Hanoi is simply unable to defeat us militarily. . . . Indeed, a substantial improvement in the American military position seems to have taken place. As a result, we have achieved our minimum objective: Hanoi is unable to gain a military victory. Since it cannot force our withdrawal, it must negotiate about it." And again, Hanoi "cannot bring about a withdrawal of American forces, particularly if the United States adopts a less impatient strategy—one better geared to the protection of the [South Vietnamese] population and sustainable with substantially reduced casualties. . . . Above all, Hanoi may not wish to give the United States a permanent voice in internal South Vietnamese affairs. . . ." Then came the "Vietnamization" suggestion: "We should continue to strengthen the Vietnamese army to permit a gradual withdrawal of some American forces, and we should encourage Saigon to broaden its base so that it is stronger for the political contest with the Communists which sooner or later it must undertake."

Finally, the peroration: "However we got into Vietnam, whatever the judgment of our actions, ending the war honorably is essential for the peace of the world. Any other solution may unloose forces that would complicate prospects of international order. A new Administration must be given the benefit of the doubt and a chance to move toward a peace which grants the people of Vietnam what they have so long struggled to achieve: an opportunity to work out their own destiny in their own way."

One can understand the joy with which Richard Nixon would seize upon such a plan and clasp to his heart the person of its author. The latter, besides being also "conservative," obviously shared with himself a complete conviction of the primacy of foreign over domestic affairs. There was in the article hardly a hint of what was happening *inside* Vietnam as a result of the war or *inside* the United States. The former country was being virtually destroyed physically and culturally, and the United States was being torn apart socially and politically, but the latter malaise could be corrected with a "less impatient strategy" that would incidentally reduce casualties.

This article was written at a time when it was not so overwhelmingly clear as it was soon to become that the new President would not have the options that Kissinger was presuming with respect to postponing our withdrawal. That would become totally evident a year later, as a result of the enormously hostile reaction within the United States to the Cambodian "incursion" of April-May 1970, which was an attempt to show Hanoi that we were still very much in the fight but which had the opposite effect of making it clear to the whole world that the President was now bound absolutely to a program of steady and not too dilatory withdrawal. For that matter, Kissinger was not yet prepared (few were) for the kind of decay in the morale and fighting spirit of the American ground forces in Vietnam which was shortly to become all too manifest, and which included the "fragging" or murder of officers who stood for too much fighting aggressiveness or simply discipline. If there is one military lesson that comes out of Vietnam, it is that one does not fight with a conscript army a war that is imperialist in form even if not in purpose. No other nation has ever attempted it; and we have now shown that in a modern democracy it cannot be done—not at any rate if it needs to be a prolonged war.

However, we see in the Kissinger article why, if the President had to withdraw our ground forces, he would do so as slowly as domestic political considerations would permit. The next Presidential election was not until November 1972, which made it possible to stretch the withdrawal over a long period and yet be able to show on the appropriate date that it had been virtually completed. Actually, even by early 1971 the emphasis on keeping

American casualty rates low and the deterioration in fighting morale in American ground forces in Vietnam had resulted in their being almost totally withdrawn from a combat role. They were really serving very little function at all in Vietnam (and developing extremely serious problems of drug abuse), except for Kissinger's conception that their very presence constituted a formidable bargaining token for the United States.

A few characteristics of the Kissinger article must be observed with special care, especially everything he had to say pertaining to the *reasons why* we should adopt the stance he recommended. However perceptive and brilliant may have been his analysis of what had already happened in Vietnam, particularly with respect to the errors of our military policies, his arguments in justification of his recommened policies were of a quite different nature. Here he fell back on propositions that were vague, unanalyzed, untested, unproved, but which nevertheless enjoyed considerable currency and acceptance—in other words, clichés.

What did he mean, for example, when he said: "the commitment of 500,000 Americans has settled the issue of the importance of Vietnam"? This magisterial remark was surely not intended simply as the truism that Vietnam was important to us because we had so many men there. The context indicated clearly what he meant: that their presence there so committed our prestige as to make irrelevant any doubts about the correctness or appropriateness of having sent them there. Thus, any doubts about the appropriateness of slowing down their disengagement were equally irrelevant; their simply being there had settled the matter. But had it so? Certainly their being there had created a problem; but it had not created a justification. The problem we had created by sending them there had to be examined for many particulars. If we found that certain people had gravely compromised their very lives because of our commitment of troops, we no doubt had a responsibility to do something about it—but that was hardly likely to require continuation of the war! It was in any case invalid and even absurd to argue, as in effect Kissinger did, that an error in policy had become legitimized simply by our having perpetrated it.

We have commented earlier on such issues as "credibility" and "prestige." Kissinger was quite right in insisting that they were not hollow values. But neither should they be incantations. What *kind* of credibility did we want to preserve, and what exactly

was important to our prestige? Certainly it varies with circumstances. Why, indeed, should we be rushing about trying to prove
to nations utterly dependent upon us in any case that they could
sufficiently "count on our steadiness" to be able to "gear their
actions to ours." The one-sidedness of the relationship with
respect to the SEATO nations is total. Did we have to impress
with our staunchness New Zealand and Australia, not to mention
Thailand and the Philippines, for fear that otherwise they would
make accommodations with China? What kind of accommodations could they make that would be injurious to us? We have
already raised previously the more immediate question: Were
they and others *really* impressed with our "steadiness" by our
stubborness in leaving Vietnam? Was Israel, for example, sufficiently impressed with our steadiness in Vietnam to forget the
lesson of our having left her in the lurch concerning the Egyptian
closing of the Gulf of Acaba in 1967? She had in any case no
great range of choice among superpowers to support her.

It was truly remarkable to find our author musing on the perturbations in the hearts of the leaders in Hanoi when they considered the 1968 Soviet invasion of Czechoslovakia. Surely if they
were the kind of people we constantly charged them with being,
they would have been participants if located in Europe—like
Poland and Bulgaria. Could the Soviet action in 1968 really have
worried them? And then those concluding sentences, beginning
with: ". . . ending the war honorably is essential for the peace of
the world." The theme was Mahlerian, and contained a note of
redemption. What did "honorably" mean in this context? In
what way was it "essential for the peace of the world?" The words
were uttered as though the answers were obvious, but they were
in fact totally obscure. And this sentence was followed by the
apocalyptic warning: "Any other solution may unloose forces
that would complicate prospects of international order." The
"may" instead of the more forthright "will" was perhaps reassuring, but did he really mean *any* other solution? That takes
in a lot of territory. And what were the vaguely suggested forces
that might be unloosed to—do what? Destroy? No, merely to
"complicate,' and to complicate "prospects" at that. Was that a
reason for keeping a horrible war going virtually indefinitely?
When have the prospects for international order been other than
complicated? Kissinger must have meant "seriously worsen" rather
than "complicate," but that would still leave the United States

in the strange role of a Zeus who "unlooses forces" simply by stilling his terrible anger.

The policy of Vietnamization was only fleetingly glimpsed in Kissinger's essay, mostly because it did not really develop into a policy until his key assumptions of 1968 had been proved wrong. He had assumed that simply by correcting the technique of our negotiatory approach in Paris—by shrewdly interpreting the choreography, as it were—and also by impressing the North Vietnamese with our firm intention to stay in South Vietnam until they were ready to come round, everything would fall into place. It is no disgrace to be proved wrong in these difficult issues. However, the idea that in such negotiations our people and theirs talk past each other merely because of subtleties of discourse that our negotiators do not understand is far-fetched and by now hackneyed and outworn. The reason for the failure of the negotiations in Paris is quite simple: We wanted to negotiate their surrender and they wanted to negotiate ours, and these two positions were truly irreconcilable. Also, to repeat, we knew before Kissinger's article had been very long in print that the negotiating leverage of our mere presence in South Vietnam was a rapidly wasting one, and the people in Hanoi knew that as well as anyone.

In 1970 the word *Vietnamization* began to be heard more and more. What it seemed to mean was a relinquishment of any substantial hope of success from the talks in Paris, which were indeed more charade than talks, and a commitment to seemingly perpetual war in Vietnam, except that the ground forces would be hired by us and only the air and naval forces would be our own. However, though the Nixon Administration never filled in the details of what the concept really meant and what it hoped to achieve, we could find the answers to these questions reflected in still another document. Not prepared by Kissinger or anyone on his staff, it lacked intrinsic political importance. On the other hand, it was the only intellectual exposition of any length and depth of what Vietnamization was supposed to mean, what its justifications were, and what it was intended to accomplish. It had been more or less "commissioned" by Dr. Kissinger, and was reported to have been received by him and President Nixon with real satisfaction. At very least it gives us a clue to thoughts congenial to Nixon and Kissinger.

This paper, "An Essay on Vietnamization," was written by Dr.

Guy J. Pauker of the RAND Corporation, and was issued in March 1971.[38] Dr. Pauker is a specialist primarily on Indonesia, but his expertise in Indochina as well is considerable. As an area expert he is a good deal more than ordinarily perspicacious and, like Kissinger, he has expository gifts that make him much more than most scholars both readable and persuasive.

He opened the essay by putting himself on record as having doubted since 1955 that the policy pursued by the United States in Vietnam could succeed. The basis for his pessimism, he said, was mainly "the character of the Vietnamese anti-Communist elites." He had concluded, as a result mostly of numerous conversations with members of the Vietnamese elite over a period of fifteen years, "that the odds were low that a viable nation-state could be built without a greater degree of civic morality than was currently operative in South Vietnam."

Now, however, he had undergone a change in conviction: "Early in 1970, the author began to realize that the enormous input of American resources of the last five years may have accomplished a feat of political alchemy, namely the transformation of the government of South Vietnam into a regime that could be viable if it continued to receive massive American material aid and if it accepted as a fact of life continuing low-level Communist violence." The two "ifs" concerned matters of substantial importance (one wonders especially about the restriction to *low-level* Communist violence); but in view of our past commitments they were nothing to gag on, provided the "alchemy" was genuine and impressive. Granted that we never want to send good money after bad, we do want to be alert to an important change in the character of the investment. The alchemy would be meaningless unless we continue massive aid (for at least a decade, it later turned out). Still, things were looking up, and we would surely want to pursue the matter further.

Dr. Pauker expressed his additional conviction "that the balance of military forces in South Vietnam is constantly shifting to the detriment of the Communists." The latter conviction had been expressed throughout 1969 and 1970 by many Vietnam ob-

---

[38] I am informed that Dr. Pauker expressed his new views orally to Dr. Kissinger, who greeted them with marked enthusiasm; he had Pauker present them also to the President, and urged him to write them up. The official designation of the resulting long (93 pages) paper is as follows: "An Essay on Vietnamization," The RAND Corporation, R-604-ARPA, March 1971.

servers, though we did not know how much they were sensitive to Robert Kleiman's point cited earlier that the same picture of "improvement" would be presented if the enemy had simply withdrawn into his sanctuary. Pauker's paper was released before the South Vietnamese offensive into Laos of March-April 1971, where the North Vietnamese response surprised and dismayed many who had thought them in much worse straits than they then proved themselves to be.

When we look into the nature of the alchemy, we have to realize at once that even the best realization of Pauker's hopes might produce a regime that "could be viable" but could hardly be attractive to many Americans. It would certainly not be what we call democratic. "Vietnamization and a protracted military conflict require an authoritarian regime, based on the armed forces and on 'civic action' relations with the masses." A broadly based non-Communist regime is simply impossible. "All students of Vietnamese politics in the twentieth century are in agreement . . . that no political movement in Vietnam, with the exception of the Communist Party led from the beginning by Ho Chi Minh, has been capable of mobilizing broad popular support. . . ." We should, Pauker admonished us, "either abstain from interfering in the medieval domestic politics of Third World countries or should accept living with their unsavory characteristics when our real security interests are at stake." As an either-or proposition it was faultless, but it did not tell us why we should continue to support Thieu. Was he the best we could have, and, above all, were our "real security interests" truly at stake?

With respect to the first question, others who were comparably knowledgable about Vietnam considered Thieu's position to be basically weak, even within the Army. Thieu belonged to that generation of Vietnamese officers who had been NCOs for France, and the younger generation of Vietnamese officers considered Thieu as much a lackey of the Americans as he formerly had been of the French. He may or may not have been the best man available to us, but he was not really very good. Pauker admitted that he lacked broad support in the country, but it would be "unrealistic to seek consensus." Now let us go one short step further in realism. What Pauker was saying was that the United States had to be prepared to practice collusion in keeping Thieu in power by undemocratic means. "The Thieu regime must be able to consolidate its power not in accordance with western political standards but in line with Vietnamese experience and capabilities." It might not be too difficult to get used to that sort of thing; perhaps indeed we were too used to it already.

The basic question was, Why? Why should we have supported this government as the indispensable instrument of that Vietnamization which, as Pauker also admitted, might not succeed at all? Apart from the spending of its own resources, which ought not to be dismissed too lightly, the United States government would have to continue practicing deceit to its own people about the character of the government it was supporting and the phoniness of the democratic procedures by which that government remained "viable." It would also have to help keep a war going in Vietnam that had lasted far too long already to the enormous misery and distress of the Vietnamese people. The moral issue that had been raised so often was really pertinent here. *Why* was it obligatory for the United States to do its best to keep that war going?

After speaking repeatedly but vaguely of American security objectives in Vietnam as though they were good and true and necessary objectives, Pauker revealed that he did not believe in them at all. He made but slight appeal to the falling-domino theory. Instead, after repeated references to how much we had already sacrificed "in American lives, treasure, and national reputation in South Vietnam," he made it clear that the country he really wanted to keep from disintegrating was *the United States!* Continued intervention in Vietnam was mostly a means to that end. This is how he summed up his argument (in his Preface, where authors often do their summing up):

> The author has always believed that we should not have interfered in the struggle in Indochina. But he also feels strongly that it would now make matters worse if, in response to an unconscious urge for self-punishment, we were to forego the opportunity to achieve the major goal of our intervention and allow by default a Communist victory. The confidence of the American people in their form of government could be shaken if the sacrifices of the last six years appeared to have been made in vain. And the "lesson" of our defeat is more likely to benefit our enemies and destabilize the global political environment than to help the next generation of American policymakers avoid the mistakes of the recent past.

The key sentence was the penultimate one that reads: "The confidence of the American people in their form of government could be shaken if the sacrifices of the last six years appeared to have been made in vain." The "could" instead of a "would" is the voice of honesty speaking at the cost of making the whole argument tacky and insubstantial. Still, it was his main point. Throughout his essay he stressed our past sacrifices too often to permit any other conclusion. Whom else could these sacrifices have impressed but ourselves?

Here we see once more the so-called "backlash" theory, which was almost as important for keeping us in the Vietnam War as the "domino theory" was in getting us into it. We noticed it also in Kissinger's article, when he made that curious remark: "Washington was aware that a bombing halt which did not lead rapidly to substantive talks could not be sustained domestically." Surely the exact reverse was true. Yet Kissinger made that statement as though it were so unquestionably true as not to warrant the slightest qualification.

A much stronger statement of the backlash idea was by President Nixon himself, when he said in April 1971:

> I know there are those who honestly believe that I should move to end this war without regard to what happens to South Vietnam. This way would abandon our friends. But even more important, we would abandon ourselves. We would plunge from the anguish of war into a nightmare of recrimination. We would lose respect for this nation, respect for one another, respect for ourselves.[39]

That worthy most often mentioned in support of the backlash idea was the late Senator Joseph McCarthy, whose infamous career as a troublemaker was supposed to have been a direct result of our having let China go to the Communists. It happens there was only one Joe McCarthy, whose capacity to do harm depended on a peculiar personality that did not survive intensive television exposure. The damage he did was like nothing compared to the damage of fighting the Vietnam War. If we had had at the time a Secretary of State with the courage and integrity that anyone in that office ought to have, and which John Foster Dulles in this respect did not have, there would have been no grim retirements of good civil servants, like John Carter Vincent and others, which

---

[39] The Nixon quotation is taken from an article by Jules Witcover in the *Los Angeles Times*, May 16, 1971.

made "McCarthyism" such an unhappy and costly experience. The Republicans did not fight McCarthy because they preferred to use him politically. Moreover, there is no reason to believe that the China episode was more important in causing McCarthyism than the Alger Hiss episode (which also brought Richard Nixon into prominence). Anyway, McCarthy fretted and strutted his hour upon the stage and then was heard no more. His censure by the Senate ended his career as a troublemaker, after which his death was superfluous.

The United States had seen plenty of commotion in the streets and other kinds of anguish as a result of our intervention in Vietnam. That the John Birchers might now take up where the Weathermen left off was of course a possibility, but possibilities are endless and many others were far more worrisome. Actually, the "backlash" idea was to some degree researchable. One could examine in detail, for example, what happened in France after the termination of the war in Vietnam in 1954, and especially after the termination of the war in Algeria in 1962. The latter war stirred France deeply because of the *Algerie Française* propaganda, mostly on the part of the officer corps, and because of well over a million Frenchmen, the *pieds noirs,* in Algeria whose families had lived there for generations. These became displaced people. There were many bombings in Paris and elsewhere in France during the war, and also a "generals' revolt," involving four of that rank, in Algeria itself in early 1961. Charles de Gaulle had been returned to power in 1958 because the existing government could not cope with the commotion, thus causing the transition from the Fourth to the Fifth Republic. But once the war was ended, there was such obvious relief on all sides that all trouble abruptly ceased, and there was not another genuine political riot in Paris until de Gaulle had been in power for ten years. France is naturally different from the United States; but, nevertheless, studies of events as nearly comparable as possible to the one we are concerned about are always preferable to unfounded assertions about the catastrophes that will happen if we end a war.

About the American situation there are two questions to be asked. First, did the several Presidents most involved, specifically Kennedy, Johnson, and Nixon, pursue their Vietnam policies primarily or even largely out of concern for the right-wing backlash? Second, whether they did or not, was there a real basis for such fears in the political climate of the United States? To me the available evidence indicates a strongly negative answer to both questions. One can find a few casual remarks to the contrary on the first question, including some quoted from Presidents Kennedy and Nixon in this chapter and the previous one, but when placed in the larger context of their known remarks and behavior they appeared isolated and insignificant.

I cannot terminate this section without one more reference to the last quoted remark of Pauker. As one convinced of the reality and importance of unconscious motivations and urges, I must take strong exception to the notion that the eagerness of so many Americans to be quit of the war in Vietnam was even remotely due to "an unconscious urge for self-punishment." Naturally, there are many people involved, and each person responds to the ringing of his own particular bells of unconscious fantasies and urges. But I suspect that in a very general way these unconscious motivations had far more to do with keeping us in the war than with getting us out of it.

The Two Channels of Information

One of the tragi-comic moments in the campaign described by Townsend Hoopes to change President Johnson's mind about the Vietnam War occurred during March 25 and 26, 1968 when the Senior Advisory Group on Vietnam met in the White House to consider the advice they would give the President concerning the Army's request for more troops in Vietnam. On the evening of March 25, they listened to briefings by three men, members respectively of the State Department, the CIA, and the Army. The next day their *rapporteur*, McGeorge Bundy, delivered to the President in the presence of all of them a summary that indicated that the overwhelming majority favored getting out of the war rather than further in. The President, visibly shocked, demanded on the day following to see the three men who had briefed the Senior Advisory Group. One, unfortunately, was out of town, but the two others presented themselves. "What," the President demanded, "did you tell them that you didn't tell me?" When they replied there were no discrepancies the President insisted: "You must have given them a different briefing; you aren't telling me what you told them because what you're telling me couldn't account for the inferences they drew."

General Earle Wheeler, when he heard of the group's views,

had demonstrated a slightly more sophisticated attitude toward all briefings. Not having attended those of March 25, he stated that if the Advisory Group's views were derived from those briefings, then he would have to say that the briefers must have been men who did not know the true situation! Hoopes, in describing these events, provides an interpretation that is neither naive nor disingenuous but which may reflect an extra dose of courtesy:

> In retrospect, it was my impression that the President's sense of incongruity reflected the extent to which he had become the victim of (1) Rostow's "selective briefings"—the time-honored technique of underlining, within a mass of material, those particular elements that one wishes to draw to the special attention of a busy chief—and (2) the climate of cozy, implicit agreement on fundamentals which had so long characterized discussions within the inner circle on Vietnam, where never was heard a disparaging word. In addition, it was evident that the members of the Senior Advisory Group brought to the meeting a wider, better balanced view of America's world role, a more direct exposure to the swift-running currents of public opinion after Tet, and of course a less fixed commitment to one policy. . . . What counted was the breadth and depth of relevant experience that the Senior Advisers brought with them. Hearing the bleak facts from the briefers, whether tinged with optimism or pessimism, they reached their own conclusions.[40]

Hoopes is here offering his characteristically insightful analysis not only of a single Washington briefing but rather of some of the circumstances that may affect the whole genre. But he leaves one thing out. The "breadth and depth of relevant experience" of the Senior Advisers must surely have prepared them also to entertain the idea that the "bleak facts" they were presented with in such briefings by representatives of such organizations were highly colored and selected and thus, in effect if not in conscious intention, quite unreliable. The advisers knew, in other words, that the truth might be a good deal bleaker than the briefings allowed.

It is naturally a truism that good policy-making depends not only on clear thinking about alternatives but also on having good (that is, reliably correct and reasonably insightful) information or "intelligence." The government is therefore largely construc-

---

[40] Hoopes, *Limits of Intervention*, pp. 216–218.

ted to be an intelligence-gathering machine, not only in the organizations specifically given over to that purpose like the CIA, but throughout all its bureaucratic components engaged in operations in the field. In the case of Vietnam the representation of the United States government in the war theatre was enormous, and included not only the specific intelligence-gathering agencies but also the armed forces and the Foreign Service. The contingents in the field representing the several agencies were active both in carrying out policy and in returning reports upon which further policy decisions would be based.

President Johnson frequently assured his listeners in press conferences that if only they could see the many cables on his desk each day they would understand as he understood, and as they in his mind clearly failed to understand, what was really going on in Vietnam. It was one of Johnson's great weaknesses that he had too much faith in the accuracy and reliability of these "cables." His listeners had their own sources and channels of information, by and large the same as those available to the public in the form of news reports, articles, and books by journalists in the field, and these often told a very different story.

It has been obvious in a number of ways that the official information channeled upward and homeward from the Vietnam terrain has been generally biased and distorted, and always in the direction of excessive optimism. Many who have seen from the inside the system in operation have reported this characteristic, at least orally, to friends, acquaintances, and news reporters. Also there is a history going back at least to 1964 of high officials making very positive reports and predictions publicly that fairly soon thereafter turned out to be far too optimistic. This is abundantly revealed in the Pentagon Papers. Finally, one can make the appropriate deductions from the attitudes of officials toward reporters whose stories disturbed them.

David Halberstam, for example, in his *The Making of a Quagmire*, describes several occasions where he and other reporters would be greeted by figures like Admiral Harry Felt, then senior U.S. military commander in Vietnam, or General Paul D. Harkins, then senior Army commander there, with reproachful words, relating to some news dispatch that had recently been filed and published, such as: "Whose side are you on?" Or, "When are you going to get on the team?" Even Secretary of State Dean Rusk was not above asking such questions of reporters he encountered, frequently with considerable acerbity. When Halberstam began publishing in the *New York Times* in the late summer of 1963 the series of articles on Vietnam that won him the Pulitzer prize of that year in reporting, there was a storm of abuse from Washington. Major General Richard Stilwell in Vietnam was specifically assigned the task of "disproving" the first long article, the gist of which was that things were going badly in the Mekong Delta. That this was a correct interpretation became obvious to all within a very few months, and it was then admitted to the press by a member of Stilwell's staff.[41] There had earlier been a U.S. Embassy (Saigon) White Paper of January 1963 prepared under the direction of Ambassador Nolting for General Wheeler complaining that "The American commitment has been badly hampered by irresponsible, astigmatic, and sensationalized reporting."[42] Halberstam reports many other comparable incidents, including a suggestion by President Kennedy to the *Times* that Halberstam be replaced in Vietnam.

Such being the attitudes of officials concerning reports and reporters whom they cannot directly control, one can well imagine the constraints operating upon those they do control! The emphasis in U.S. embassies throughout the world (except, no doubt, in Communist countries) is on "stressing the positive" or ending a dispatch "on the up-beat"; but in Vietnam it has long since reached proportions worthy, if it were not so serious, of comic opera. In the Army it operates at each echelon of command, from platoon leader on up, and similarly with civilian levels of authority. An end report will therefore frequently represent an extensive exaggeration of an initial report that has already shown an undue leaning toward hopefulness or optimism.

One hears references often to the peculiar characteristics of the "bureaucratic mind," one variant of which is the somewhat better-advertised "military mind." The bureaucratic mind is that mental set which is indispensable to working in bureaucracies, especially government bureaucracies, which differ from private ones mostly in that they are larger and less conducive to mobility in and out of the organization. A military officer or a foreign service officer normally feels he is in a lifetime career for which there are no alternative employers. He also feels a strong loyalty to his organization and certainly to the nation it represents. Thus, one outstanding characteristic of the bureaucratic mind is that it

---

[41] Halberstam, *Making of a Quagmire*, pp. 191–193.
[42] Ibid., p. 30.

can take on, usually with no difficulty visible to the outsider, the entire set of attitudes favored by the organization with which it identifies itself, including the biases and predispositions known to be held at the top. The good bureaucrat is rarely in conflict with his superiors on basic policies or related principles, not simply because he is timid but because it comes naturally to him to absorb those policies and make them his own. Otherwise he would not choose that kind of life, or having done so would look desperately for alternatives. He wants to be, and to be known as, a "good officer"—foreign service, military, or other—and this means "fitting in" with a set of concepts about which his training has left him in no doubt. As an individual he may have considerable ability, and therefore be qualified to prepare for his superiors position papers that often include shrewd operational advice. That advice, however, will nearly always be confined to the best *tactics* for carrying forward the policy that he knows to be the accepted one.

If we add to this mental quality the element of rewards and punishments, which vary from subtle to quite overt, another important dimension becomes operative. If, for example, the top command in the military wants high enemy body counts, then high body counts is what it will get, for commendations, decorations, and promotions will come of fulfilling that desire and not otherwise. The same is likely to be true of all kinds of information. If the top command wants favorable and optimistic information, that is mostly what it will get.

The degree to which it will be taken for granted in such organizations that it is right to "manage" information may reach incredible lengths—incredible, that is, for those who retain some detachment in their thinking. Thus, when Hoopes and others talk about the monitoring that Walt Rostow was practicing at the very top concerning items reaching the desk of the President, they are talking only about the last link in a long chain in which the same process has operated over and over again. It was upon such thoroughly doctored information, generally overoptimistic and often quickly proved such by events, that our entire Vietnam policy was based for at least the decade following 1961.

The alternative channel of information is the public one, having outlets in newspapers, magazines, books, and television. However, while it is open to the public, it is not truly available to the policy makers. For them it is largely preempted by the mass of material that comes through official channels. The official who reads all the cables he must read will lack the time and inclination also to read through the somewhat long-winded musings of a Robert Shaplen in the *New Yorker* on, say, the displacement of peasants to refugee camps or the sleazy corruption endemic in South Vietnam. Also, the information he gets through "channels" will often prejudice him against information that is obviously conflicting, as we saw in the case of Halberstam's *Times* article. How did Dean Rusk and others in Washington *know* that Halberstam's story was "inaccurate" or "irresponsible" or any of the other things they said about it? The official channels always seem the more authentic, especially because they contain so much information that is classified. Conflicting stories outside the system are something to be fought against.

Naturally, the quality of journalists and other reporters in Vietnam has varied over a wide range, and only a small proportion have been gifted with good minds, appropriate dedication to their work, and perhaps even a degree of linguistic skill that includes competence in the native tongue. However, the exceptional ones become well known, and are certainly known to each other. They have included some like the late Bernard B. Fall, thoroughly at home in Vietnamese (as also in French, his own native tongue), who was an academic specialist in Vietnam rather than a newspaper reporter.

A story about Bernard Fall, which also involves Robert McNamara, tells something about the methods for keeping a closed mind in Washington. If there is one practically unvarying principle about the use within the government of outside experts as consultants, it is that they must be known to be friendly to that policy on which they are being consulted. They may be critical of details or of the current execution of that policy, but not of the fundamentals.[43] It happens that the one *bona fide* expert on Vietnam who had all the appropriate academic credentials for consultantship and who was known also to be thoroughly in favor of United States policies in Vietnam around 1965 and 1966 was the British scholar, Professor J. P. Honey, who was holding a chair at a Scottish university. McNamara wished occasionally to consult with him and would arrange for his transit from Britain

---

[43] This point should be utterly commonplace, yet I do not recall having heard it described before. I could, indeed, give relevant examples from my own experience both in being invited in for consultation and also in not being invited. However, a striking and certainly more important example is that of Dr. Henry Kissinger, who has served three Presidents as disparate as John F. Kennedy, Lyndon B. Johnson, and Richard M. Nixon—but in each case he was known to be basically in sympathy with the Vietnam policy being currently pursued, though often sharply critical of execution.

to Washington and return by special military aircraft. This came to the attention of Dr. Daniel Ellsberg, then of the RAND Corporation but working close to McNamara, who attempted to acquaint the latter with the fact that there was in residence at Howard University in Washington a Professor Fall, whose academic credentials and whose expertise on Vietnam were quite as impressive as those of Professor Honey, but whose opinions were sharply different. However, before a meeting could be arranged for him with Secretary McNamara, Fall's life ended suddenly on one of his frequent trips to Vietnam, when he stepped on a land mine on the highway called "The Street Without Joy," which happened also to be the title of the last book he published before his death.

The Commander-in-Chief Syndrome

"The current restraints imposed by Congress are utterly insufficient to the task," said Senator J. William Fulbright in a speech early in 1971. "All they really do is to provide the Administration with an excuse for doing anything and everything that is not explicitly forbidden—and, as we have seen, all it takes to transfer some contemplated military action from the prohibited category to the permissible is a certain agility in semantics and an extraordinary contempt for the constitutional authority of Congress." Another senator, who preferred to remain unnamed, said wearily: "What can we do? We make speeches, demand that the Secretaries of Defense and State testify, pass laws restricting the President's actions, and on it goes." [44]

Both senators were referring, among other things, to the action of June 30, 1970, in which the Senate after a seven-weeks acrimonious debate on the so-called Cooper-Church amendment, voted 58 to 37 to restrict future U.S. military operations in Cambodia without prior congressional consent. This was hailed at the time as an historic landmark; it was the first time that either house of Congress had ever acted to impose military restrictions on a President during wartime. It had perhaps had more weight than the two senators seemed to be giving it in their complaints. President Nixon did refrain thereafter from sending American ground forces into Cambodia or Laos—though the riots on the nation's campuses and the tragedy at Kent State University in Ohio probably also had something to do with his restraint. He

---

[44]Both are quoted by Elizabeth Drew in her column "Washington," *Atlantic*, April 1971, pp. 14 f.

was put further on notice that time was indeed running out on his remaining freedom of action concerning the war in Vietnam.

Nevertheless, what Senator Fulbright was saying was basically correct. As one who had been the floor manager for the Tonkin Bay Resolution of August 1964, he had had the humiliation of discovering later that there had been some measure of fraud in the way the Johnson Administration had described to the country the incident to which the Resolution was a response.[45] Perhaps even more important, he had personally assured doubting senators that the Resolution if passed would not be used as approval for sending American troops to Vietnam—as a substitute, in other words, for a congressional declaration of war. It had, however, been used exactly so, and Fulbright in 1967 heard Undersecretary of State Nicholas Katzenbach literally reprimanding members of Fulbright's own Foreign Relations Committee for ever construing the language of the Resolution to be anything other than concurrence in the President's full exercise of his war powers.

The humiliation was to be carried a long step farther by President Nixon, who, when confronted in 1970 with the clear indication that the Senate would finally vote to revoke the Tonkin Bay Resolution (only five voted against revocation, although in 1967 only five had voted for it), announced that he did not object because the Constitutional authority he already had as commander-in-chief of the armed forces was quite sufficient to his needs for carrying on the war. The phrase "commander-in-chief" ran trippingly off the tongue of this President. It seemed to please him not only to use the powers and probably to stretch them, but also to utter the words over and over again in public. No other President of recent memory has used the phrase anything like so often and with such obvious gratification. It appeared important to him as a person that he could use this phrase in describing himself. It was obviously quite important to the country as well.

---

[45] See U.S. Congress, Senate Committee on Foreign Relations, *The Gulf of Tonkin, the 1964 Incidents, 90th Congress; 2nd Session.* Also, Joseph C. Goulden, *Truth Is the First Casualty: The Gulf of Tonkin Affair—Illusion and Reality* (New York: James B. Adler, 1969). The fraudulence lay in not reporting the total circumstances under which the two American destroyers had allegedly been attacked, and especially in not reporting that one of them, the *Maddox*, had sent a message indicating doubt whether previous reports of torpedo attack were correct. Secretary McNamara, at President Johnson's request, got in touch with Admiral U. S. Grant Sharp, Commander-in-Chief, Pacific, who indicated that he had no doubt whatever that an attack had taken place—an appraisal that has to be considered in the light of Sharp's record as one of the most pronounced hawks of the Vietnam War.

And because so much that is important in our national Constitution is unwritten, we have never had and seem unlikely to get any authoritative decision, which could come only from the Supreme Court, determining the limits of the President's Constitutional powers as commander-in-chief.[46] They are what he says they are, except where Congress restricts him in the only way clearly lying within *its* Constitutional powers, which is by way of its control of the purse.

The coming of nuclear weapons had formerly convinced many people who might otherwise have been concerned about undue expansion of the President's powers that the Constitutional provision that limited to the Congress the authority to declare war was essentially obsolete. Obviously, the authority to react in the instant manner that might be necessary to a threat of enemy attack with such weapons—or at least to appear able so to react—had to be left without hindrance in the President's hands. Long before those weapons appeared, however, we had had repeated demonstrations in the history of this country that a President determined to conduct a policy entailing high risk of war can do so, and his legitimate powers as commander-in-chief also enable him under appropriate circumstances to trigger that war. All this, however, is not the same as saying that the relevant Constitutional provision is meaningless.

We have seen in a previous chapter how during the Korean War Secretary of State Dean Acheson jealously guarded the powers of the Chief Executive by urging President Truman not to seek authorization from Congress for the war actions he had already taken. That he should have still written proudly of this in a book published as late as 1969 is a little more difficult to understand. Perhaps before he died early in 1972 his pride in this matter had abated somewhat.[47]

---

[46] The Court, by long established rule, never questions the Executive's authority in what are called "political acts." Thus, when the State of Massachusetts passed a law in 1970 enjoining the federal government against sending abroad to fight in an undeclared foreign war any conscripted Massachusetts citizen, a lower federal court overturned the law as unconstitutional, and the U.S. Supreme Court quite predictably refused to review the lower court's decision.

[47] I should personally doubt it. Dean Acheson belonged to that subspecies of *homo sapiens* whose characteristics are that they are quite brilliant without being at all reflective. This quality, which accounted for his strong antiintellectual bias, was visible in his writings and especially on personal contact. For an independent and fuller expression of the same view see Alfred Kazin's review in the *New York Times Book Review* for May 28, 1972 of Dean Acheson's posthumously published *Grapes from Thorns* (New York: Norton, 1972).

There are many aspects to the problem that would not be helped by giving more authority to Congress. As Bismarck once put it, "A peace-loving prince is not so rare as a parliament full of wise men." Our own Congress, like other parliaments, can be swept by the fever of the moment to pass a declaration of war (as it was moved to pass the Tonkin Bay Resolution) and the Constitution makes no provision for the Congress to revoke a declaration of war. Such a declaration has truly the effect of being final for the length of the ensuing war, which is ended by the President.

Besides, Congress, especially the House, has shown during the Vietnam War a truly remarkable compliance with the President's wishes. The House consistently refrained from exercising those powers of restraint that, together with the Senate, it clearly possessed. The reasons are several. First, there are the members of the President's party, who even when in a minority are a large group. Their thinking tends to have the same coloration as his, but in any case they do not wish to embarrass him. Overlapping with this group and also with the opposition party are the natural contingent of hawks and fire-eaters. Prominent among these are the southern members, most of whom wear the Democratic label. House members also function with a good deal more shielding from the public gaze than do members of the Senate. Congressmen may vote contrary to the desires of their constituents with but few of the latter being aware that they have done so, unless it is an issue on which the constituents feel very strongly; those who have felt *strongly* opposed to the American intervention in Vietnam seem never to have embraced a majority of the electorate.

Also, the fact that each representative must face an election every two years is supposed to make the House conform more closely than the Senate to the will of the people. Instead, this requirement makes it conform more to the will of campaign contributors. Partly for this reason, conservatives, being usually wealthier, have traditionally made a stronger play for control of the House, while liberals have generally been more intent on supporting their candidates in the Senate. Among those the congressmen listen to, the opponents of the war have not been more stoutly vocal than those who believe in the full support of the President. In any case, the closest the House came to attaching an end-the-war amendment to any authorization bill was on July 25, 1972, when the House Foreign Affairs Committee voted such an amendment to a foreign aid authorization bill by a bare majority of 18 to 17. This amendment failed in the full House, which continued also to knock down similar votes by the Senate.

The apparent public approval of President Nixon's speech of November 3, 1969 convinced even the most determined opponents of his war policies that they had better lie low for the time being, and they subsequently also felt that he had been at least partially successful in justifying the necessity of the Cambodian invasion in the spring of 1970. In the elections of the latter year, the President had succeeded in his determined effort to purge Senator Albert Gore of Tennessee, one of the most vocal opponents of his major military policies, including the ABM, and also Senator Charles E. Goodell of his own party in New York. It would be well if politicians were more courageous in these respects, but majorities are rarely made up of courageous men. The politician who does not have an instinct for carefully rationing his courage is not likely to remain long in office.

Besides, in these matters they are contending always, or may feel they are contending, with that somewhat incalculable emotion called "patriotism." They are contending also with certain myths that many of them may indeed share, such as that the President has more information about the ongoing war than anyone else and that he also has access to the best advice, including that of the Joint Chiefs of Staff, who are themselves the objects of myths concerning their omniscience. The President of the day has also other formidable advantages, including constant and unique access to television and the press. Members of Congress are not so much excluded from such access as they are simply lacking in opportunities to claim that they have special news or announcements of importance to dispense.

Still, an important problem is involved, and not one solely of Constitutional principle. Not only is it appropriate in a democracy for Congress to have a greater share in the authority and responsibility for something as important as war; the system also works better if the public is aware of that involvement. What keeps any nation functioning as an integrated body politic, especially under the strains of war, is an aggregate of myths and beliefs concerning the unique identity of the nation as distinct from other nations, its possession of special virtues, and so on. Adherence to these beliefs is what we call patriotism, an emotion that it is not easy nor always salubrious to dissect. In many people, obviously, including members of certain well-known societies of the right, it is a purely infantile emotion, immortalized in the famous words of Stephen Decatur (which the impious G. K. Chesterton has translated into: "My mother, drunk or sober!"). In more mature people it stems from, or at least includes, an awareness of deep social need for the organization called the state, and frequently too a pride of past national accomplishment based on full understanding of the vast imperfections of the world.

Many nations have indeed functioned efficiently in peace and war on the supposition that some emperor or king or dictator was not only the appropriate repository of allegiance, faith, and authority but also the fountainhead of all true wisdom. The United States has never been such a nation. Thus, a war that can be called Truman's war, or Johnson's war, or Nixon's war is something that is definitely degraded from being truly a national war. It will not only fail to win the support necessary to an efficient prosecution of that war, which covers a wide range of elements including, for example, reasonable control over the inflationary pressures produced by war, but it will also become a deeply divisive thing in itself. No President of the United States is universally admired, some lack any fervent following, and a few are intensely disliked by large proportions of the population. The more the war is identified as being a product of his own will that he pursues for reasons known best to himself, the more will the people opt out who are supposed to fight it and support it.

When members of the United States Senate were reduced to wondering whether President Nixon had a "date certain" in his own mind for the termination of the war, and when the Senate Leader of the President's own party was publicly corrected from the White House when he offered the conviction that the President had such a date fixed in his mind—which was the experience of Senator Hugh Scott in April 1971—things had gone pretty far. At that time Senator Fulbright was complaining that the President's war objectives were a personal secret that he successfully kept from others, including the members of the Congress.

In November of that same year Congress finally passed an

amendment to the Military Procurement Authorization bill that declared it to be the policy of the United States to bring to an end "at the earliest practicable date" all military operations in Indochina, subject only to the release of all prisoners of war. Upon signing the measure on November 17, President Nixon flatly declared that the amendment was "without binding force or effect and it does not reflect my judgment about the way in which the war should be brought to an end." He indicated the amendment would not change his policies, and further admonished the Congress that "legislative actions such as this hinder rather than assist in the search for a negotiated settlement." The same Foreign Relations Committee that had sponsored the original amendment now failed to support an additional amendment to the Defense Appropriations Bill cutting off funds if the withdrawal policy were not carried out. This seemed too drastic a measure to much of that majority now opposing the war.

Six months later, on May 8, 1972, when the President risked a confrontation with the Soviet Union, if not also with China, by ordering the mining of Haiphong and other harbors and the resumption of the bombing of North Vietnam, he made no pretense of first consulting with leading members of Congress. He simply called in a few of them for a crisp fifteen-minute briefing.

We have described previously his dramatic success in this gamble, which virtually assured his reelection the following November. No doubt adding to the landslide proportions of the latter victory was the leaking, on the eve of the election, of the news that Hanoi and Washington were on the verge of agreement for a cease-fire. And so indeed, in the following weeks, they appeared to be—until December 18, when the United States abruptly broke off negotiations and resumed the bombing of North Vietnam on a scale heavier than ever. In his press conference of December 16, Dr. Henry Kissinger had said that agreement between the United States and Hanoi had been "99 per cent completed" but that the remaining 1 per cent concerned a "fundamental point." Indeed it did, because it concerned the question of whether Hanoi should be obliged to relinquish positions it had gained in the South.

The principal purpose of the President's new action, Administration officials announced, was to insure "that North Vietnamese leaders would comprehend the extent of his anger." What then happened, however, must have been a painful surprise to him.

On the one hand, a tidal wave of protest rolled over the White House, coming from the Congress and from all corners of the country, as well as from abroad. And on the other hand, our B-52s, which had hitherto been virtually immune to ground fire at their high levels of flight, began suddenly to sustain a high rate of loss to new Russian-made SAMs. On December 30 the White House announced that the bombing had been halted and that negotiations would be resumed on January 8. The cease-fire was finally signed on January 24, 1973, on terms which stipulated that "the armed forces of the two Vietnamese parties shall remain in place" and which were otherwise insignificantly different from those the President had rejected a month earlier. Obviously it was Nixon who had given way, and the magnitude of the protest played a large part in making him do so.

The cease-fire halted American bombing of Vietnam, but not of Cambodia. For a while the euphoria over the cease-fire in Vietnam—and no doubt the impressiveness of the President's still-recent election victory—muted Congressional objections. But then came a new tidal wave, Watergate, with all its associated exposures, causing a drastic plunge in the President's standing and credibility. It was also revealed that there had been a fourteen-month secret bombing of Cambodia which had begun only two months after the President had taken office in 1969 and which had involved the falsifications of flight reports. After an interruption in 1970 the bombing had been resumed openly, and it was this bombing that the Congress finally decided it must stop through its power over funding. After some passes between the President and the Congress, a "compromise" bill was signed on July 1, 1973, calling for the termination of the bombing after August 15.

For the people of Cambodia and Vietnam the war meanwhile went on. For the latter area the "cease-fire" was soon seen to mean simply a "reduced-fire," and there was no question that before long the battle would erupt again in full fury. The situation toward the end of 1973 was certainly not back in the Square One of March 1965. There had been a vast amount of destruction to the land and the people in the meantime. But concerning the prospect for the outcome, little was changed. Nor was there a government in either Saigon or Phnom Penh that we could have taken any pride in saving even if we had succeeded, as most clearly we had not, in assuring its survival.

CHAPTER

6

Changing Attitudes Toward War

And still more generous was the answer of the great Alexander to Polypercon, who was persuading him to take advantage of the darkness of night to attack Darius; "By no means, he said; it is not for me to steal a victory; I had rather complain of fortune than steal a victory."

Related, admiringly, by Michel de Montaigne, 1580.

The Count of Gondomar, able Ambassador of Philip III of Spain, arrived in the year 1613 at Portsmouth harbor to begin his long residence at the court of England. Just as Octavian, the young Count Rofrano in *Der Rosenkavalier*, must arrive in two carriages when he comes to deliver the silver rose to Sophie, so Gondomar had to arrive in not one but two galleons. In Portsmouth harbor lay the flagship of the Channel Fleet, and the English and Spanish ships exchanged equal courtesies. As soon as Gondomar had gone ashore to a ceremonial greeting, however, the English captain sent word that now he expected the Spaniards to pay customary honors, which they must have omitted through inadvertence. In any harbor of the narrow seas, he reminded

223

them, all ships were required to strike their flags and keep them lowered as long as one of his English Majesty's ships was in port, just as at sea they had to dip their flags three times, strike their topsails, and pass to leeward "in token of the King of England's sovereignty of the seas."

This point of naval etiquette was one on which the English were peculiarly stubborn. The King of Denmark's ship had quite recently been required to give this extraordinary salute; so had the Spanish squadron that had brought the Duke of Frias as special ambassador in 1604. And in the harbor of Calais itself, in the presence of the great Duc de Sully, long chief counselor and now special ambassador of Henri IV of France, a king renowned for his deeds martial as well as amorous, the vice-admiral of England had fired into the flagship of the vice-admiral of France and compelled him to lower his flag. Thus, when the Spanish commander forwarded the English demand to Gondomar and the latter sent back word that they must refuse, the English captain immediately threatened to blow the two Spanish ships out of the water.

Gondomar requested that the impending hostilities be delayed while he communicated with the King of England, to whom he sent a message describing the situation and begging, if the English persisted in their demands, that he be allowed back aboard the Spanish flagship so that he might go down with it. James I found himself in a dilemma. But, as the late Garrett Mattingly tells it, it was James's weakness "that he was too civilized a man to risk killing an ambassador and starting a war over an empty salute." [1] Gondomar thus won, in a manner giving no offense, a notable victory for his own prestige as well as his king's.

In an age when protocol mattered deeply, a war was presumably averted on an ambassador's gamble that a king whom he had not yet met and thus could not know would not press home an established point of primacy. Or perhaps it would not have been a war. All eras have had to adjust to the idea that there could be international violence short of war. Still, to fire into the warship of a monarch with the pretensions of the King of Spain and in the process to kill or injure one of his ambassadors would have been a highly provocative act, and an English sea captain, even in the absence of his admiral, was quite prepared to do it.

If that era differed from ours in its attitude toward protocol, it

---

[1] Garrett Mattingly, *Renaissance Diplomacy* (Boston: Houghton Mifflin, 1955; Penguin Books paperback, 1964), pp. 227 f.

obviously differed quite as profoundly in its attitude toward war. War was something that had to be risked not only occasionally and strictly for matters of great moment but constantly, on all sorts of issues to which dynastic pride was attached. To say that war was constantly risked is not to say that it was constantly employed, but it was often employed.[2] The reasons for the wars that did occur frequently defy any kind of rational explanation except that they fitted into the conventions of the time determining when it was appropriate that princes should go to war. However, we must leave the question of reasons or causes of war for the next chapter and devote this one to the related but distinctive question of feelings or attitudes of people toward war, and the changes in those attitudes in the western world and in what we roughly call modern times.

The crisis attending the reception of the Count of Gondomar at Portsmouth turned out to be without bloodshed, and it would therefore escape cataloging among historic wars, usually listed with their presumptive causes. But it tells us a great deal about the place of war in the scheme of things at the time, which in this respect as in so many others is very different from our time. In the process it gives us an interesting glimpse of an existing pattern about to be displaced by another and more modern one. For James surely was aware that what had been yielded to Gondomar would sooner or later have to be yielded to others. That such an extravagant claim to international deference should ever have been fixed in custom in the first place argues a special sensitivity of the English to any possible questioning of their pretensions to supremacy in the narrow seas—a supremacy that was not to be indisputably theirs for a another century.

The Institutional Character of War

Our questioning whether English insistence on their customary honors would have produced a *war*, rather than some lesser and limited act of reprisal, and the fact that our use of that word carries a particular meaning across the three and a half centuries that intervene, point up one of the most noteworthy aspects of war. This is its retention of a distinctive and recognizable insti-

---

[2] King James's decision to forego the salute in Gondomar's case may conceivably have had something to do with the unusual circumstance that Spain was not then at war. A truce had endured since 1609 in Spain's long struggle with the Netherlands and the Thirty Years War had not yet begun.

tutional character over the centuries and even millennia, despite
vast changes in all other characteristics of organized societies and
in the nature of war itself.

Although war represents human violence in its most intensive
form, it is not simply human violence. It is something else besides,
something with a distinctive and quite special configuration. The
characteristics of this configuration cover a wide variety of phenomena, including the following. First, wars have tended, since
antiquity, to have a clear and sharp beginning and an equally
clear and sharp ending, and various ceremonials have been involved both in the initiation and the termination of war. Also, in
the periods following wars, reconciliation has often been prompt
and remarkably far-reaching. It was easy enough in dynastic times
for governments that were enemies one month to be allies the
next, but we have seen very much the same thing happening also
in modern times, when whole peoples were involved. Following
World War I the degree of reconciliation between France and
Germany was imperfect enough, but following World War II it
was most extraordinary, involving not simply governments but
entire peoples. The United States and Britain have also participated in this reconciliation, and these and other former enemies
of Germany have long been joined with the latter in the North
Atlantic Treaty alliance. The same kind of reconciliation has
occurred in the case of Japan and its World War II enemies, particularly the United States, and a mutual security alliance between those two countries followed on the heels of the treaty of
peace. Even Winston Churchill's axiom that the grass grows up
over battlefields but never over scaffolds—by which he meant that
wars are forgiven but not atrocities in war—has not proved true.
A few atrocities are remembered, perhaps with morbid monuments, but most are forgotten.

Another aspect of the institutionalization of war is seen also in
the existence of a special profession—in older days an entire caste
—who are the custodians of the nation's war-making powers and
who develop the unusual skills necessary to their function. In
former times this profession of military officers was made up
almost exclusively of the aristocracy and thus enjoyed, along with
the higher clergy, almost a monopoly of honor. Even in democracies like our own it has managed to retain into modern times a
good deal of punctilio that would appear bizarre in civilian life.

There is perhaps some psychological significance in the fact that military uniforms were until quite recently means of permitting men to deck themselves out in much greater finery than seemed appropriate in civilian life, and this tradition has survived into our own times with respect to the wearing of banks of ribbons in lieu of decorations. The only other professional group organized by the state for the control of violence, the various police forces, share few of the honorific characteristics of the military profession. We also notice that while police forces generally belong to municipalities or to various other subnational entities, the military forces belong to the nation. This situation reflects the fact that the very existence of the nation-state results very largely from the overhanging threat of war, which requires in anticipation some measures of preparation against it. The political and social status of the military has varied with different eras and also from nation to nation, but even in those countries that are relatively nonmilitaristic (among which the United States ought to be included) the position of the more senior military officers has been generally a highly favored one.[3]

Remembrance of things past is always an extremely important part of our present and of our expectations about the future. The inherited traditions about war account for our present preparations for future wars and also create expectations that are in part self-fulfilling. There is indeed an opposite side to that coin which carries on one face the well-worn motto: *Si vis pacem, para bellum.* Perhaps a total and universal amnesia about war would be desirable, but there is no use in longing for it. Almost everything else about the past is more easily forgotten than its great wars, not alone because they are "newsworthy" and exciting but also because they have absorbed so much of man's energies and their social and political effects have been so great.

One observes, however, that the institutional characteristics of war have also had some benign influence, which in part offsets the evil effects. Preoccupation with the recurrence of war may tend at any one time to make it more probable, but that preoccupation has also accounted for the development of customs and codes that add up to significant success in limiting wanton destruction and violence. Effective restraints operate in the humane treatment of

---

[3] In speaking of various countries, including the United States, as being "nonmilitaristic," I am using the distinction established by Alfred Vagts and described on p. 31.

prisoners, in the avoidance of certain types of weaponry and of certain kinds of targets, and in much else. We hear so much about the violation of these restraints that we assume they are more honored in the breach than the observance. It is very difficult to give a quantitative accounting in these matters, but even if the assumption were true, there would still be a good deal of quiet but important observance. At the opening of the Battle of Agincourt, King Henry V gave the signal that French prisoners in English hands (except, of course, those of gentle blood) should have their throats cut—a detail slurred but not omitted in Shakespeare's account.[4] This act has not particularly blemished Henry's fame because it was merely the practice of his time as it was of all antiquity. In more recent times it has not been customary. Even in so savage a war as that in Vietnam, where both sides have undoubtedly slaughtered many prisoners, both sides have also managed to accumulate fairly large numbers of them—as was true also in the Korean War. There are many men alive today and joined with their families who were once prisoners of war, including those of World War II; it would be difficult to persuade *them* that modern usages, with all their shortcomings, are not an improvement over older ones.

We also notice some quite remarkable conventions about the posture that countries like the United States and the Soviet Union adopt towards each other. For one thing, each can have a terrible array of strategic nuclear armaments aimed at the other without either regarding the situation as too terribly provocative to prevent normal relations; people simply accept the fact of those preparations as normal in a world that knows war. Second, it is possible for both sides to proceed to negotiate a limitation or reduction in those armaments—calculated if not to increase security at least to save a good deal of money on both sides—while still retaining substantial forces against each other and engaging occasionally in hostile grimaces. Both situations fit a pattern to which we are accustomed and which would look quite bizarre if we were not so accustomed; both exemplify the feeling that something otherwise unimaginable is part of the human condition. The minority who reject as useless and absurd such attempts at partial control or limitation of arms are usually the young and the ideal-

---

[4] *King Henry V*, Act IV, Sc. vi, 37–39; also Act IV, Sc. vii, 66–68.

istic who simply refuse to accept the reality of war as an existing institution. Let us abolish *all* war and *all* preparations for war, they insist. The only answer to that is one compounded out of weariness and experience: 'tis a consummation devoutly to be wished, but it seems for the time being impracticable. Let us therefore not disdain attempts to moderate war's evils.

We also observe that nations can carry out many other policies that they feel necessary and which would otherwise be deemed insufferably provocative—like concluding treaties of alliance clearly aimed at some specific third party—without upsetting the peace. Because these acts also conform with familiar patterns, they can be accepted as facts of life—not desirable in an ideal world, but tolerable in the world we know.

Because our subject in this chapter is "changing attitudes towards war," we should know what kinds of attitudes we are talking about. Perhaps the most basic and primitive one has to do with whether men seek glory in war, or on the contrary have a horror of it, or whether their feeling is something in between. It is commonplace today to denounce war as evil, but we often notice a discrepancy between pronouncement and practice on the part of those in authority. It is an interesting discrepancy. If the man who is or who aspires to be President of the United States says he hates war, we may usually believe that at least at the conscious level he does, because he is expressing an almost universal attitude. But one has to go beyond this question and inquire how deeply he hates war. If he is actually presiding over the country while it is in a war and insists that he will agree to peace only "with honor," he is alluding to certain often obscure elements in his own value system affecting highly ambivalent international practice. We notice here enormous individual differences, but we should also notice equally striking historical changes. The same man with an identical psychological makeup would probably at an earlier time have had a different "trade-off curve" as between the requirements of honor on the one hand and those of peace on the other. The word *honor* was more often on people's tongues formerly than it is now, which is not to say that they really behaved more honorably; perhaps it was only that they were more rigid.

There are many who assume that even the existence of strategic nuclear weapons is no real barrier to the kind of war that might provoke their use, and these people usually justify their attitudes by broad references to history. But all sorts of attitudes and opinions can be justified by sufficiently broad references to history. The pertinent question today is: What significant changes have been going on historically that bear on the general issue of the relevance and reliability of deterrence? That is mainly why we are interested in surveying changing attitudes towards war.

Ambivalent Attitudes: Ancient to Early Modern Times

We have to disabuse ourselves of the notion that a feeling of distaste for war and of repudiation of its awful characteristics and consequences is a uniquely recent development. There are many evidences of such rejection among sensitive people in the past, but usually ambivalently, as though the sense of being appalled were coupled with a sense of the necessity of accepting that which is appalling—and even finding pleasure in it. Even this degree of ambivalence seems to be characteristic of more recent times. It seems completely missing in Greek antiquity. In Homer we see compassion for those to whom war brings personal tragedy, as in the sad leave-taking of Hector from his wife Andromache, whom he knows he will never see again and for whom he foresees a life of slavery; also in the plea of the aged King Priam to Achilles to recover the body of Hector, his son. But there is no hint of abomination for the system that makes these tragedies possible. On the contrary, the *Iliad* is dominated by commitment to the grim requirements of war and to the glorification of valor on the battlefield—and, after all, the gods themselves are fully involved.

Even in the later and more civilized Greece there is a near-total and to us truly remarkable absence of disgust or rejection concerning war. The wise and sensitive Plato, whose childhood and youth were lived through the Peloponnesian War, is passionately dedicated to exploring all aspects of the good, the true, and the beautiful, and we feel his vast respect for the rule of law and for the importance of attaining good laws, under which people can live a well-ordered existence allowing for maximum freedom of the spirit. But in his *Republic* he never for one moment assumes that war between his ideal state and its neighbors is other than inevitable, and he adds that "nothing can be more important than that the work of a soldier should be well done." In the *Laches* he explores the nature of martial valor, and we find that Socrates whom he portrays as replete with all kinds of virtue has also not been lacking in this one. The same is also true in the *Sympo-sium,* which is on the nature of love but in which Alcibiades, in a rapturous paean of praise to Socrates, his teacher, does not omit to mention the fine example the latter set as a soldier on the expedition to Potidaea, where he showed everyone how he could endure frost, fatigue, and hunger.[5]

Thucydides, the great historian of the Peloponnesian War, has much to tell of disaster, and he reports or puts into the mouths of the main characters speeches that warn of the need for caution when contemplating war.

> Take time, then, [the Athenian ambassadors warn the Spartans] over your decision, which is an important one. . . . Think, too, of the great part that is played by the unpredictable in war: think of it now, before you are actually committed to war. The longer a war lasts, the more things tend to depend on accidents. Neither you nor we can see into them: we have to abide their outcome in the dark. And when people are entering upon a war they do things the wrong way round. Action comes first, and it is only when they have already suffered that they begin to think.

The Spartan king, Archidamus, in addressing his people supports the Athenian plea:

> Spartans, in the course of my life I have taken part in many wars, and I see among you people of the same age as I am. They and I have had experience, and so are not likely to share in what may be a general enthusiasm for war, nor to think that war is a good thing or a safe thing.[6]

How well we could have used such advice in our own time! It is not the less valuable for being strictly pragmatic. So is much anti-war counsel today, but today there is often an added dimension that was lacking then: a sense of disgust and horror at something intrinsically evil.

We see the case clearly with another author of the time, the

---

[5] According to the section numbers found in the margins of the standard translation of Plato, as used by Benjamin Jowett, the more relevant sections are in the *Republic,* 373–4; all of the *Laches,* especially 181; and in the *Symposium,* 219–21. The brief quotation from the *Republic* is from the third edition, 374C; it is worded somewhat differently in the first edition.

[6] Thucydides, *History of the Peloponnesian War,* trans. by Rex Warner (London: Chaucer Press, 1954; Penguin Books, paperback), Book 1, secs. 77–80, pp. 56 f.

great playwright of comedy, Aristophanes, with his extraordinary *Lysistrata*. In it the heroine prevails upon the women of Athens to withhold their sexual favors from their husbands in order to force them to desist from making war. Despite the extremely precarious cooperation of the women, Lysistrata manages to carry off her scheme. But we see that her plea is only for a peace between the Athenians and their fellow Greeks, the Laconians (that is, the Spartans); her special point is that what is most wrong with Hellenes cutting each other up is that all the while the barbarian outside is threatening them. Lysistrata is thus hardly a pacifist. Something of the same sort is true with Euripides and his *The Trojan Women*, written in the year after the Melian massacre described by Thucidydides. It has been called "the great antiwar play of all time," but it might be more realistic to call it a dramatic commentary on the limitless penalties of defeat.

It is in Rome, the Rome of world conquest and of the triumphal arch, that we see what is probably the birth in western civilization of the idea that war is fratricide and as such inherently evil. This idea, of which only inklings had appeared earlier, was made into a coherent and vital principal by the Stoic philosophers, beginning with Cicero. Yet even before their time the Romans had developed what they called the fetial law, which demanded that war could be fought only for *res repetitae*, that is, to obtain compensation for wrongs suffered. The Greek historian Polybius tells us that the Romans on going to war were careful to find a pretext that would appeal to foreign opinion, meaning mostly Greek opinion. The restraints of such a law clearly did not prevent the occurrence of numerous wars of conquest, and it is obvious that in Polybius' time (he died about 117 B.C.) the Roman Senate was already quite cynical about the fetial law. Still, "it would be wrong to assume that it had no effect in determining the occasions on which Rome went to war." [7]

Cicero may well have been the first to develop the significant distinction between just and unjust wars, but Seneca went far beyond this conception and in effect rejected it. He poured scorn and disdain on the pursuit of military glory, on the kind of fame won by generals who were obsessed with the lust of conquest. "We are mad," he said, "not only individually but nationally. We

---

[7] W. V. Harris, "On War and Greed in the Second Century B.C.," *The American Historical Review*, vol. 76, no. 5 (December 1971), pp. 1372 f.

check manslaughter and isolated murders; but what of war and the much vaunted crime of slaughtering whole peoples?" His younger contemporary, Pliny the Elder, wrote what is probably the most famous of all the ancient diatribes on the human misery caused by war, and concluded that man, the only animal given to war upon his own kind, was not only morally inferior to the most savage beasts but lives in more disorder and violence than any animal.[8]

And what, one asks, does it matter what a few philosophers may say, so long as the mass of mankind acts either in ignorance or disdain of them, It is a good question, and the answer has to take into account all the wars of western civilization in the nearly two thousand years since Seneca and Pliny. Still, the Stoics gave not only expression but vehemence to an antiwar philosophy that has never since totally died out, and which has periodically been revived with special fervor and also with some effectiveness. They were not ineffective even in their own time. The *Pax Romana* that developed under Augustus and lasted for some two hundred years was a conscious effort on the part of the Romans to repress all strife within the vast areas they then ruled. The evidences of that design survive today in such monuments as the Wall of Hadrian, which runs across England near the Scottish border. It speaks for an intent not to plunder but to colonize, which meant to bring security as well as civilization to a land previously subject to endless forays of marauding tribes.

It was also from the Stoics that the early Christian church derived its ideal of antimilitarism, which as the Roman state decayed and the Church grew stronger survived as a minority ideal. Later the antiwar teachings of the earlier Fathers were set aside by the authority of St. Augustine, who taught that war's cause lay in man's sin and in God's answering punishment, though the punishment obviously had to be administered by other men. The latter were thus obliged to distinguish between 'just" and "unjust" wars. Naturally, the question whether or not wars were just

---

[8] Although he wrote a large study on the wars in Germany, *Bellorum Germaniae viginti* (*German Wars in twenty books*), we have that knowledge only from Pliny the Younger, his nephew and adopted son. The only one of his works that is extant is the famous *Natural History* in thirty-seven books (*Historiae Naturalis* XXXVII). His description of the German wars concern those in which he served himself, and we may be sure that his views on war were very much developed in that experience. However, the "diatribe" referred to in the text is the section dealing with man (Book vii) in the *Natural History*.

was easy to answer when the enemy were pagans and later heretics, and from the seventh century onward there was an expanding need for armed defense against Islam.

So far as the Christian world itself was concerned, the medieval church supported the ideal of the *Pax Ecclesiae*, which had its greatest effect during the period A.D. 1000 to about 1300, when the supremacy of the Church was at its peak. Pursuing the goal of the *humana civilitas*, "the unity of mankind," which is idealized in Dante, the popes did indeed strive, with some success, to suppress both local and international wars. They established the "Truce of God," originally an interdiction against Christians fighting each other on Sunday and at one period extended to cover almost half the week. It is obvious, however, that that success was limited. The latter part of that long period which we call the Middle Ages has left its mark on the face of Europe in the survival of an architecture that speaks eloquently of the place of war in the life of the community. Where every town had its wall, where villages were huddled round the fortified castle in which protection might at any time have to be sought, where every high spot, difficult of access, was for that reason chosen for the castle and its surrounding village—we can see them still throughout Europe, especially in the south—one senses a community in which war, fragmented and internecine, was the natural state of things.

The Middle Ages were also the time of the Crusades, so that those who could not find trouble enough and early death at home could seek them in the Holy Land. In these societies and cultures, poets took an approach to war that was supremely practical. War being an omnipresent condition of life and impossible of being conceived of in any other way, their one function in treating of it was to praise valor. Popes might still take some halting steps toward alleviating war's evils, like considering with special anathema (except against Mohammedans) certain weaponry when it first appeared, such as the cross-bow in the twelfth century or the gun in the fourteenth. But even in these latter instances the appeal was to valor and its just deserts, which were infringed upon by such cowardly weapons.

By the time we enter the Renaissance the popes themselves had become warrior princes, seen as often abroad as soldiers in armor as in their white robes. Julius II, familiar to us as the special patron of Michelangelo and Raphael, who commissioned among other great things the painting of the Sistine Chapel ceiling, was so addicted to battle even in his old age as to outrage his humanist contemporary, Desiderius Erasmus. The latter, in his great antiwar satire, *Praise of Folly (Encomium moriae,* 1509), makes a special target of Julius, whom he savagely indicts with "devising a way whereby it is possible for a man to whip out his sword, stick it into the guts of his brother, and nonetheless dwell in that supreme charity which, according to Christ's precept, a Christian owes to his neighbor." [9]

The humanists, believing that the human experience in this life meant much more than a simple preparation for God's mercy in the next, would naturally have to turn for their inspiration to the ancient classics. They brought alive again the thinking of the Stoics. In England especially there were four among them, though two were foreigners, whose work largely revolved round preachment against war. These were, along with the Dutch-born Erasmus, John Colet, Sir Thomas More, and the Spaniard Juan Luis Vives. Their common and central concept, as Robert P. Adams puts it, was that "war is not an action of divine 'Providence' but largely a man-made evil that can be minimized, if not wholly eliminated, in a society whose organization is rational and just." [10] This thinking was quite consciously a rejection of St. Augustine's conception of war as man's sin and God's answering justice. Erasmus and his humanist colleagues would soon be defending the true faith against the attacks of Martin Luther, but they had nevertheless shown how to ridicule an aging pope for his furious military antics in the field and to shrug off the teachings of a formidable father of Church doctrine.

The *Praise of Folly* was especially widely read by the educated of the time, who in that day included most of the princes of Europe, and one wonders why it did not have more influence on their behavior. The answer lies partly in the marvelous ability of man to compartmentalize his mind—to praise wit and wisdom while conducting himself in precisely a contrary fashion. It lies even more in the fact that like the Stoics of old, the new humanists were bucking an old and hugely powerful tradition, the

---

[9] *Praise of Folly,* trans. by H. H. Hudson (Princeton: Princeton University Press, 1941), p. 101.
[10] Robert P. Adams, *The Better Part of Valor* (Seattle: University of Washington Press, 1962), p. 4.

glamorous cult of chivalry, which made noble the pursuit of glory and the proof of manliness through violence.

An outstanding example was the young King Henry VIII, who at the time of his accession (in the same year as the publication of *Praise of Folly*) seemed to the humanists the realization of their fondest hopes. He appeared liberal, drawn to learning, gifted artistically, especially in music, and gifted also with extraordinary good looks. But Henry demonstrated at once his awareness that whatever else an English king was supposed to be, he was still a leader in war. "He must still 'venture' himself in battle, to use an old formula, and blood himself," and a contemporary could observe that Henry was "not unmindful that it was his duty to seek fame by military skill." [11]

He thus no sooner became king than he set about seeking allies for a war with England's ancient enemy, France, and after some frustrations in the matter of allies he succeeded in having his war. He had after all commissioned the translation from the Latin of an early life of Henry V, and the translator had not omitted to call upon his patron to emulate his namesake, the glorious victor of Agincourt. In 1513 when Henry was about to embark personally on a renewed expedition against France (there had been an abortive campaign the year before in which he was not present) John Colet preached a sermon to Henry and his court, "exhorting his hearers to follow Christ rather than false heroes like Caesar or Alexander and declaring an unjust peace preferable to a just war." After the sermon Henry sought out Colet in the garden of the friary to ascertain his meaning. In this confrontation Colet seems to have lost his nerve, not at all remarkable for someone who would prefer not to lose his head, and Henry was left with his conscience at rest and his spirits high. "The illustrious dean of St. Paul's had declared his cause a just and holy one." [12]

We should not assume, however, that it was *necessary* for a king to fight. Henry's father had seized the crown by force of arms from Richard III, thus ending the Wars of the Roses, but preferred as Henry VII to live cautiously at peace thereafter. And the son's great daughter Elizabeth was certainly no lover of wars. Being a woman who could not in any case "venture" herself in

---

[11] J. J. Scarisbrick, *Henry VIII* (Berkeley: University of California Press, 1968), p. 23 and 23 n.

[12] Ibid., p. 33.

battle, she lacked that particular incentive, and like her grand-father she clearly disliked both the hazard and the cost of military enterprises. The age seemed to endure with equanimity both atti-tudes, and the ambivalence, if it may be called such, was reflected in the great literature of the times.

So we see it in Shakespeare. Hamlet the reflective man admires Fortinbras the soldier even while he despises the petty aims of his campaigns of conquest. When Hamlet encounters the army of Fortinbras and inquires of one of the latter's officers where they are going, the following colloquy ensues (Act IV, sc. iv):

> *Captain.* Truly to speak, and with no addition,
>   We go to gain a little patch of ground
>   That hath in it no profit but the name.
>   To pay five ducats, five, I would not farm it;
>   Nor will it yield to Norway or the Pole
>   A ranker rate, should it be sold in fee.
>
> *Hamlet.* Why, then the Polack never will defend it.
>
> *Captain.* Yes, it is already garrison'd.

Then Hamlet soliloquizes:

> Witness this army, of such mass and charge,
> Led by a delicate and tender prince,
> Whose spirit with divine ambition puff'd
> Makes mouths at the invisible event,
> Exposing what is mortal and unsure
> To all that fortune, death, and danger dare,
> Even for an egg shell.
>
>   . . . . I see
> The imminent death of twenty thousand men,
> That for a fantasy and trick of fame
> Go to their graves like beds, fight for a plot
> Whereon the numbers cannot try the cause,
> Which is not tomb enough and continent
> To hide the slain.

Yet the lesson Hamlet derives from this is not that Fortinbras is a fool—for he seeks a legitimate goal, honor—but that he himself is by contrast a coward. He has much better reason to act but he does not act.

The historical plays beginning with *Richard II* are naturally taken up with wars either against France, where honor and glory are at stake, or in the civil strife but recently ended where the stake is the throne itself and the power attending it. The former wars are noble, the latter always evil—except, of course, when it comes to the battle in which Elizabeth's own grandfather destroys the wicked Richard III. Typically, as in *Henry V* and in the open-passages of *Henry VI, Part 1*, we see foreign war and conquest glorified simply and exclusively as means of demonstrating the greatness of the men who wage it successfully. But even in those same plays, and certainly in various others, we often find a moving scene or passage where the poet reflects on the folly and tragedy of it all—as in *Henry IV, Part 1*, where Prince Hal slays the gallant Hotspur on the battlefield and then utters an elegy over his fallen warrior-opponent:

> When that this body did contain a spirit,
> A kingdom for it was too small a bound;
> But now two paces of the vilest earth
> Is room enough:

The same play has the King speaking fretfully of "this churlish knot of all-abhorred war." It is of course civil war of which he says this, but in the utterance the distinction is dropped. The distinction then drawn between civil war and foreign war, incidentally, is pithily expressed by Francis Bacon, when he says: "A civil war is like the heat of a fever; but a foreign war is like the heat of exercise, and serveth to keep the body in health."

Shakespeare and Bacon were contemporaries of King Henri IV of France, the first and greatest of the Bourbons, who when charged by the merchants of the Paris flea market with being a miser, laughed and replied: "I am no miser; I make love, I make war, and I build." [13] Henri thus equated making war with two indubitably creative pursuits—and incidentally showed a remarkably modern psychological insight in sensing the conflict between miserliness and capacity to make love. Yet it was his counselor, the Duc de Sully, who fashioned for Henri to present to the world his "Grand Design," a plan for a European confederation that

---

[13] Among the structures he built that stand today is the world's most beautiful bridge, the *Pont Neuf* (1604) in Paris, which bears the equestrian statue of Henri IV.

was supposed to eliminate war forever.[14] The accession (1589) of this former Protestant King of Navarre to the French throne and his somewhat light-hearted conversion to Catholicism ("Paris is worth a mass") was incidentally the happy result of the fact that his predecessor and cousin, Henri III, the last of the House of Valois, was not able to make love—not to women at any rate. He was "too fond of boys to beget one," and this fact was enough to join Navarre forever to France and to end the long and fierce religious wars in that country.

In early modern times we also notice an occasional reticence on the part of inventors lest their inventions be used for evil purposes in war. Leonardo da Vinci wrote in his notebooks—which were not intended for publication—that he had devised an underwater boat the nature of which he was unwilling to divulge even in that private place, "on account of the evil nature of men, who would practice assassinations at the bottom of the seas by breaking the ships in their lowest parts and sinking them together with the crews who are in them." [15] In the sixteenth century Niccolò Tartaglia published the first truly scientific study of gunnery ballistics in his *Nuova scienzia* (1537), and explained in his preface that he had determined to keep his discoveries secret because he had decided that "it was a thing blameworthy, shameful and barbarous, worthy of severe punishment before God and man, to wish to bring to perfection an art damageable to one's neighbor and destructive to the human race," and that to concern oneself with such matters was a "grave sin and shipwreck of the soul." When, however, he saw that the enemy who appeared at the gate of his beloved Italy was the infidel Turk, he changed his mind. "In the sight of the ferocious wolf preparing to set on our flock, and of our pastors united for the common defense, it does not seem to me any longer proper to hold these things hid."

Later in the same century John Napier, the inventor of logarithms, had the same feelings about the possibility of a Roman Catholic invasion of England, and set about devising new engines of war, including a tank and a piece of artillery presumably capable of enormous destruction. These were mentioned in a manu-

---

[14] Henri and Sully would be particularly impressed with confederation as a means of avoiding war, because most of Henri's wars were among the portions of a divided France rent by religious quarrels.

[15] E. MacCurdy (ed.), *The Notebooks of Leonardo da Vinci* (New York: Reynal and Hitchcock, 1939), I, p. 25.

script sent to Queen Elizabeth, but the artillery piece was not described. When someone tried to pry the secret out of Napier on his deathbed he is supposed to have replied: "For the ruin and overthrow of man, there were too many devices already framed, which if he could make to be fewer, he would with all his might endeavor to do; and that therefore seeing the malice and rancor rooted in the heart of mankind will not suffer them to diminish, by any new conceit of his the number of them should never be increased." [16] The poet John Milton, born shortly before Napier's death, put into his *Paradise Lost* (Book VI) the conceit of having Satan and his followers invent during the civil war in Heaven the original field gun, which, as the Angel Raphael assures Adam, to whom he is relating the story of that war, will likely be reinvented by the latter's own progeny "in future days, if malice should abound."

What do these sentiments really express? Dislike of war? Yes, certainly, but specifically of the evil passions from which war stemmed, which might mean the evil passions of an enemy, especially one with the wrong religious beliefs. The war itself was only the consequence of those evil passions. Each of the four persons just mentioned was willing to lend his great talents to the prosecution of one or more wars, including Milton, who as the author of the three famous Latin tracts in defense of regicide and the three earlier papers on *The Tenure of Kings and Magistrates*, became the number one propagandist for the Parliamentary side of the civil war in England.

There was also something else involved in the protest at least of the scientists, something difficult for a twentieth century mind to comprehend. There was a tradition among scholars going back at least to Plato that considered it a corruption of the best fruits of the human mind to try to put them to practical use. The glory of knowledge *for its own sake* perhaps explains why Plato was so intent on having the rulers of states study geometry, which might be of use to an engineer or an architect but hardly to a king. Plutarch explains on the same basis Archimedes' refusal, after he had invented several very effective engines of war. to repel the siege of Syracuse by the Romans under Marcellus, to publish any description of his work. To try to put science to practical use was,

---

[16] Quoted by John U. Nef, *War and Human Progress* (Cambridge: Harvard University Press, 1950), p. 122.

in Plutarch's words, "vile, beggarly, and mercenary dross." This attitude was still very much alive in the fifteenth and sixteenth centuries. It deeply affected Leonardo in his old age, as it did Sir Walter Raleigh, a contemporary of Napier's. To "teach the art of murdering men" ("murder" means killing by methods non-valorous) was put on a par with the effort, in Raleigh's words "to enrich a mechanical trade." Both were odious, and one distaste reinforced the other. Francis Bacon was probably the first philosopher of note to challenge "the ancient position that there was something base or degrading about putting the most sublime learning at the service of material things." [17]

To the notion that it is not war that is evil but rather the sinful passions that beget it (Milton's war in Heaven was fought just as furiously by the good angels as by the bad ones, but it was Satan's envy that set it off) a remarkable challenge arose on the part of another and younger Englishman who was appalled by the same civil war that so engaged Milton. This was the great scientist-to-be, Robert Boyle, who in 1646, at the age of nineteen, after some conversations with partisans of the House of Commons, wrote in a letter from London the following:

> The greater part of men of these parts are pleased to flatter themselves with the hopes of a speedy settlement of things; but for my part, that have always looked upon sin as the chief incendiary of the war, and yet have by careful experience observed the war to multiply and heighten those sins, to which it owes its being, as water and ice, which by a reciprocal generation beget one another, I cannot without presumption expect a recovery in that body, where the physic that should cure, but augments the disease.[18]

Now this, as we have seen, was not a totally new insight in the experience of the world, nor was it even the first time some such idea had been publicly expressed. Various sensitive moralists, among them the humanists, had called war both irrational and a corruption. One obscure Frenchman had written during the French religious wars in the late sixteenth century: "How piteous a thing is war. I believe that if the saints in paradise went to war

---

17 *Ibid.*, p. 123.
18 *Ibid.*, p. 134.

they would soon turn into devils." [19] Still, Boyle's insight that war breeds more of the sin it derives from was a fresh and marvelous one for a young man to have, and it deserves as much to be called "Boyle's Law" as the principle in gas dynamics known by that name. It seems so very simple, and yet no one had stated quite so clearly before a point of view that was to become commonplace only within our own century.

New insights on the nature of man and his institutions, even when they are important and engender a following, do not change the world in a day or even a decade. Nor is it possible to trace changes in thought along a clear path in which each new step points the way inexorably to the next. The same is true of practices in the nature of war. The surrender to the Spanish under the Marquis of Spinola of the Dutch garrison at Breda in 1625—the subject of that painting of heroic proportions by Velasquez that hangs today in the Prado, in which the subjects are bowing and smiling to each other with the greatest friendliness and courtesy as though the matter at hand were anything but a surrender—stands in sharpest possible contrast to the awful sack of Magdeburg by Tilly six years later, possibly the greatest single atrocity of the Thirty Years War. Wherein lay the difference? The Dutch at Breda were surrendering after a siege lasting eleven months, yet the terms and courtesies granted them were an almost extravagant realization of the most chivalrous observances of the time. At Magdeburg the town was destroyed by fire and not less than 30,000 were slaughtered, regardless of sex or age—in the words of Schiller "a scene of horrors, for which history has no language, poetry no pen." [20] So it has ever been. The same war, the same belligerent, will be responsible for horrors in one theatre and fairly strict observance of the rules in another. If there is a decisive change in practice or common opinion, it is perceptible usually only over the longer term, and is rarely without its exceptions and backslidings. Today we have no Magdeburgs, but we do have vast destruction at cities like Dresden, Tokyo, Hiroshima, and Nagasaki, and smaller scale horrors like My Lai. Can we say that things have really changed, or are we suggesting distinctions without a difference?

---

[19] Ibid., pp. 142 f.

[20] Frederick Schiller, *History of the Thirty Years War*. Trans. by A. J. W. Morrison (London: Gell & Sons, 1912), pp. 143 f.

The one thing we can say with certainty is that this confusion among events makes it more difficult to clarify a trend in attitudes that is both meaningful and important. It is hard to do partly because the game changes. The airplane appears, and a Douhet develops a new military philosophy centered upon it. Then nuclear weapons and rocket vehicles come along, and these create wholly new conditions and new possibilities, including certainly possibilities of unprecedented evil resulting from war. But these new instrumentalities only make it more necessary to consider the changing attitudes that will determine whether as well as how they will be used, and the prospects of movement towards a consensus that may make for safety in a world otherwise grown much more dangerous.

The year of the surrender at Breda also saw the publication by the great Dutch scholar, Hugo Grotius, of a pioneering and landmark work in the development of international law, *De jure belli ac pacis*. One notices that war comes before peace in the title, and indeed in view of the times, a codification of laws affecting civilized customs and usages of war was far more desperately needed than rules pertaining to the peaceful intercourse of nations. True to his age, Grotius based his principles primarily on the "natural law." It was the law that could still be found "if God had no interest in mankind," the law that existed not only within but also apart from revealed knowledge. Men could discover it by the full exercise of their reason, and it was thus available to pagans like Plato and Aristotle who had discovered moral principles that also guided Christians. Most of Grotius' references are in fact to classical antiquity. He also sought for rules that had developed out of the most temperate observances of the most civilized states or princes in their wars with each other. Perhaps the greatest contribution of Grotius was that in offering a codification of the best rather than the common practice, he was making it possible for each belligerent to know just what was expected of him if he wished to retain good repute among other civilized Christian states, including today's enemies who might be tomorrow's friends. This book filled a felt need, and it was considered authoritative for well over a century, during which it went through many editions. It gave way only after other publications that absorbed it had come along to fill its place and to expand the range of laws considered to be binding on nations at war. The writings of distinguished publicists have remained to this day an important source of international law, inasmuch as these writers, like the best jurists, are seeking not simply to express their view on what ought to be but rather to *find* law in what is otherwise a confusion of practices and treaty obligations.

The seventeenth century saw the end of the wars of religion and of the long struggle of the Northern Provinces of the Netherlands to secure their independence from Spain, both affirmed by the Treaty of Westphalia in 1648, and also the swift decline of Spain as a great power. Even so, the latter half of the seventeenth century had its share of wars, mostly centering round the ambitions, real or imputed, of Louis XIV. The eighteenth century opened with what was to be the last and greatest of that monarch's wars—the War of the Spanish Succession, which lasted thirteen years. In the bloodiest encounter of that war, that of Malplaquet on September 11, 1709, the nations allied against France won the battle at a cost of some 20,000 men. These losses raised in England the cry of "butchery," and contributed to the fall of the Whig party—an interesting and unusual case of a "victory" in battle resulting in the political defeat of the party associated with it. It also provided an excuse for his political enemies to recall in the following year the great British commander-in-chief, the Duke of Marlborough.

The reaction against the heavy casualties at Malplaquet accorded with a new attitude concerning the conduct of battles. Already towards the end of the seventeenth century, a spirit of moderation had begun to affect the campaigns of the time. It was made feasible by the new tactics introduced by King Gustavus Adolphus, which emphasized a new kind of discipline of the troops—discipline being not a sufficient but a necessary ingredient to restraint—but it was due mostly to the conscious effort of statesmen like Louis XIV and William III, both of whom abhorred the mixing of passion with such a thing as warfare, to make the latter more humane and civilized. Being at war, they felt, should be looked upon as another opportunity to demonstrate that one knew how to comport oneself as a European gentleman should.

The new attitude is symbolized by the career of the Marquis de Vauban, whose life span was close to that of his master, Louis XIV. A soldier by profession and more than usually learned in mathematics (most officers knew some), Vauban was known as a man of humane disposition with a special interest in preserving the lives of the troops for whom he felt responsible. He became famous first for the character of his sieges, which besides being almost invariably successful were at small cost in life. He insisted on avoiding the frontal assault and relied instead on slow, methodical digging of a carefully designed system of trenches and traverses with which his sappers moved towards the bastion of the fortress to be taken. His first published work was on how to conduct such sieges: *Mémoire pour servir à l'instruction dans la conduite des sièges* (1669). Later, when Louis' interests shifted from making new conquests to holding on to what he had gained, Vauban began to design a new type of fortification, and it is mostly the latter enterprise on which his present fame rests. He was responsible for constructing or remodeling some 160 fortresses, mostly along France's eastern frontier. All of them bore the distinctive Vauban look or signature—a low profile when seen from the ground outside, and when seen from above, as drawn on a chart, a number of bastions distinguished by angular salient points or "ravelins." [21]

Vauban fortresses were not considered to be impregnable, but taking one would normally require on the part of the attacker a large commitment of time as well as greater resources and heavier costs than were required of the defender. During Vauban's era and for some decades afterwards the convention prevailed of surrendering a fortress before it was actually captured physically, provided the attacker had shown his ability and willingness to invest the superior resources and time necessary, and provided also he had made a sufficient breach in the walls to satisfy the defender's honor.

Earlier in that same seventeenth century the customary inducement to surrender took the form of refusing quarter to the garrison if the resistance was unduly prolonged. Even the gentle Michel de Montaigne had defended the practice in the following words:

> Like other virtues, valour has its limits, which being overstepped, it is in a way to becoming a vice, in the sense that it

---

[21] See Henry Gerlac, "Vauban," in Edward M. Earle (ed.), *Makers of Modern Strategy* (Princeton: Princeton University Press, 1943), chap. 2; see also Bernard Brodie and Fawn M. Brodie, *From Cross-Bow to H-Bomb* (Bloomington, Ind.: Indiana University Press, 2nd. ed., 1973), pp. 94–97.

leads to temerity, obstinacy, and madness. . . . From this consideration is born the custom that we have in wartime of punishing, even with death, those who obstinately persist in defending a place which by the rules of warfare cannot be held. Otherwise, in the hope of impunity, there is not a henroost but could hold up an army.

Among the relevant considerations, he pointed out, were "the greatness of the conquering prince, his reputation and the respect that is due to him." Still, Montaigne lamented the fact that it was the captor who was the judge of when his dignity had been offended, and ended his essay (Book I, chap. 15) by advising each man, if he can, to avoid "falling into the hands of an enemy judge who is victorious and armed."

Later it appeared inhuman in any case to deny quarter, but what developed instead was a ritualized procedure for determining the point at which the honor of the defenders permitted surrender. Under Louis XIII a commander had been forbidden to surrender a fort until a wide breach had been made in the main wall of a fort and several assaults had been repulsed. The grand monarch who was his son, however, issued in 1705 new instructions authorizing a governor of a fortress to surrender after a small breach had been made and a single assault had been repulsed. Naturally, the governor also had to be persuaded in his own mind that the attacker had the means to take the fortress, but if he was so convinced, why waste lives? Later in the century when war had moved again towards relentlessness, the famous engineer and war minister of the revolution, Lazare Carnot, said contemptuously of the earlier period: "What was taught in the military schools was no longer the art of defending strong places, but that of surrending them honorably, after certain conventional formalities." [22] It was the evaluation of a new age upon an earlier one that in this respect was more civilized. The Carnot view has with few exceptions prevailed until the present day, the obvious justification being that the attacker has not really demonstrated his ability to overcome the defender until he has actually done so—and of course fighting spirit can often accomplish wonders.

Even apart from siege warfare, armies in the field during the late seventeenth and early eighteenth centuries no longer felt it

---

[22] Quoted in Nef, *War and Human Progress*, p. 157.

necessary to throw themselves upon each other but spent a good deal of time maneuvering close to or in full sight of each other, and often did not engage at all until, at the end of the fighting season, they marched off to winter quarters. In his famous essay on the art of war, *Mes rêveries* (1757), the great Marshal of France, Maurice de Saxe, wrote: "I do not favor pitched battles, especially at the beginning of a war, and I am convinced that a skillful general could make war all his life without being forced into one." This statement was to be held much against him and against the whole eighteenth century by early twentieth century writers and teachers on strategy like Ferdinand Foch, who felt it summed up the characteristic disinclination for decisive battle by eighteenth century strategists. Actually, in the several paragraphs he wrote immediately following the statement quoted, Maurice showed that he also advocated vigorous pursuit after victory in battle, and that his disinclination was not so much against battle *per se* as against unnecessarily costly or useless battle.[23] Maurice was, like Vauban, a humane man; but where he felt engagement to be necessary or advantageous he did not shrink from it, his own great victorious battle being that of Fontenoy (1745) against the English, Dutch, and Austrians.

Fontenoy, incidentally, has achieved a certain anecdotal fame as the battle that opened with extraordinary courtesies, in the form of the French inviting the advancing English to fire first (*"Tirez-nous de là, Messieurs les Anglais"*). Actually, it seems to have been a cherished tradition in the French army, against which Maurice long battled in vain, to compel the French front rank to remain motionless while the enemy advanced towards it and fired the first volley. The purpose was not at all to display courtesy but rather to strike a fatal fear into the hearts of the enemy by this exhibition of cold courage. In one of his final reports, before his retirement, to Louis XV's war minister, Argenson, Maurice unequivocally attacked what he called "this obstinate practice," which stemmed from the victorious campaigns of the previous century. "Good God," he commented, "what a way to win a battle

---

[23] The complete *Mes rêveries* of Maurice de Saxe are contained in translation in Thomas R. Phillips (ed.), *Roots of Strategy* (Harrisburg, Pa.: Military Service Publishing Co., 1940), pp. 177–300; the passage quoted is on p. 298. The date given in the text above for the original publication of *Mes rêveries* is a posthumous one, inasmuch as the Marshal died in 1750.

when you have to pay for your laurels with so much blood." He argued that this foolish practice had nearly cost him the battle of Fontenoy. He added that it was also absurd to compel regimental officers to stand out in front of their men when volleys were exchanged. This might be impressive but he preferred to see the officers take their place in the line. It does not detract from the somewhat misguided bravery of the French to point out that the viability of their odd notions of appropriate, combat behavior depended in part on the inaccuracy and the long reloading time of the muskets then in use.

In any case, we have a pattern evolving in the hundred years or more before the French Revolution not of avoiding war but of demonstrating while fighting it all the humane restraint that is possible without compromising the objective. This was the civilized warfare of the eighteenth century, referred to sometimes as the typically "limited" war of that period, but very different in motivation as well as character from what we call limited war today. We must also remember that it is easy to exaggerate the degree to which combat was avoided. During that period there were many battles on land, especially in central and eastern Europe, some of which were extremely costly to both sides, and there were also many engagements at sea and these were characteristically bloody. It was in the middle of this century (1756) that an English admiral, John Byng, was tried and executed for "cowardice" because in encountering a French fleet he had spent so much time in maneuvering for a favorable attack position that the French had got away. As a result Minorca had been lost. Those who tried him knew he was not cowardly but nevertheless condemned him, as Voltaire put it in portraying the episode in his *Candide*, *"pour encourager les autres."* Not since then has an admiral been executed for such a reason.

In addition to the War of the Austrian Succession, the middle of the eighteenth century saw the Seven Years War (1756–1763) which had its origins in North America. In these two great wars Frederick II of Prussia waged the campaigns that brought fame to himself ("the Great") and aggrandisement to his kingdom. As a result of these same wars, however, and the great expenses they entailed, the French king, Louis XV, ceased to be called *Louis le bien-aimé* and became instead intensely hated by the populace. His grandson, Louis XVI, proceeded some four years after his accession (1774) to participate in the War of American Independence, which had the double effect for the French monarchy of bringing into being in America a revolutionary and republican regime to serve as a model for Frenchmen to emulate and also to throw the finances of the crown into such a state that the monarchy was never able to recover. Financial troubles led finally, despite real efforts at reform, to the fateful summoning of the Estates-General, which had not met in 175 years.

The eighteenth century was also the Age of Enlightenment, which had its home mostly in France and which produced such figures as the Baron de Montesquieu, *L'Esprit des lois* (1748), Denis Diderot, editor of the 34-volume *Encyclopédie* (1751–1772), Jean-Jacques Rousseau of *Le Contrat social* (1762), and Voltaire, author of many important works, including and perhaps especially that earth-shaking novelette allegedly written in a frenzied three days, *Candide* (1759).

How Voltaire felt about war is evident at almost the very opening of that wonderful little book. Candide is no sooner expelled from the castle where he grew up, for the most natural of responses to the Baron's daughter, when he is enticed into joining an army that happens to be that of the King of the Bulgarians. After recovering from a near-fatal beating for an infraction of discipline, he has the opportunity to take part in a battle between the King of the Bulgarians and the King of the Abares. Hardly more than a half dozen pages after the book opens Voltaire, with a scornful flourish of philosophical terms, describes the battle thus (it is supposed to be a satirization of Frederick II's bloody Battle of Zorndorf of the previous year):

Nothing could be smarter, more splendid, more brilliant, better drawn up than the two armies. Trumpets, fifes, hautboys, drums, cannons, formed a harmony such as has never been heard even in hell. The cannons first of all laid flat about six thousand men on each side; then the musketry removed from the best of worlds some nine or ten thousand blackguards who infested its surface. The bayonet also was the sufficient reason for the death of some thousands of men. The whole might amount to thirty thousand souls. Candide, who trembled like a philosopher, hid himself as well as he could during this heroic butchery. At last, while the two Kings each commanded a Te Deum in his camp, Candide decided to go elsewhere to reason about effects and causes.

He clambered over heaps of dead and dying men and reached a neighboring village, which was in ashes; it was an Abare village which the Bulgarians had burned in accordance with international law. Here, old men dazed with blows watched the dying agonies of their murdered wives who clutched their children to their bleeding breasts; there, disembowelled girls who had been made to satisfy the natural appetites of heroes gasped their last sighs; others, half-burned begged to be put to death. Brains were scattered on the ground among dismembered arms and legs. Candide fled to another village as fast as he could; it belonged to the Bulgarians, and Abarian heroes had treated it in the same way. Candide, stumbling over quivering limbs or across ruins, at last escaped from the theatre of war. . . .[24]

This was written by a man who had corresponded with and for a time lived at the court of Frederick the Great, whom, however, he had come to dislike and whom he depicts most abusively in his *Candide*. To the *philosophes* generally, however, Frederick stood for modernity and enlightenment, and was thus a figure to be admired. These men were primarily absorbed with questions of individual liberty and of the ultimate authority of the state rather than slaughter. Essentially they were concerned with privilege. War was a secondary consideration, a fact that no doubt reflects the situation in the eighteenth century. People could live through wars without being much engaged by them, especially if they lived in France, for by this time the battles in which France took part were usually fought outside the country. Their attitude also reflected the general decline in the heinousness of war; there were few of the horrors of the Thirty Years War of the previous century. In the eighteenth century the distinction between combatants and noncombatants, with sanctions to protect the latter, reached heights that had not been seen before and in some respects would not be seen again.

Still, war was hardly something to which the *philosophes* could close their eyes. They seemed, however, to accept the idea that in view of the despotisms that existed in Europe, it was pretty much inevitable. The theme that appealed to them most was that of the citizen army, as contrasted with armies of mercenaries, a view preached especially by Montesquieu, Rousseau, and by a con-

---

[24] *Candide* (New York: Modern Library, 1930), pp. 11.

tributor to the *Encyclopédie*, J. Servan, who in 1781 published a book on the citizen soldier and who later became a war minister during the Revolution.

Even Voltaire felt that in view of the inbred follies of man, perpetual peace was out of the question. For him as for others of the Enlightenment, war was costly foolishness, but so long as it had attained a state of moderation it could be tolerated. He was not as sanguine about the future of war as his younger English contemporary, Edward Gibbon of *Decline of Rome* fame, who thought that Europe had already become one great republic of a common high level of politeness and cultivation and that future wars within the European society could only become less serious with time.

One figure who deserves special attention was the Count de Guibert, who in 1772 at the age of twenty-nine published a book on tactics and strategy that made him an instant celebrity, *Essai général de tactique*. It was a highly innovative work, rejecting the old war of position and going well beyond Frederick to anticipate Napoleon in lauding the war of movement. However, Guibert was also an intellectual of his time, and as such he identified himself with the *philosophes*. He decried the despotisms esconced everyhere in Europe and dreamed, without much hope of seeing it, of a citizen army in a country that had thrown off despotism. Later, in 1779, he published another book, *Défense du systèm de guerre moderne*, which explicitly rejected all the innovative ideas of his first book, and which in addition took a parting shot at the *philosophes*, who seemed to him to show too much in the way of pacifist inclinations. "To declaim against war," he said,

> is to beat the air with vain sounds, for ambitious, unjust or powerful rulers will certainly not be restrained by such means. But what may result, and what must necessarily result, is to extinguish little by little the military spirit, to make the government less interested in this important branch of administration, and some day to deliver up one's own nation, softened and disarmed—or, what amounts to the same thing, badly armed and not knowing how to use arms—to the yoke of warlike nations which may be less civilized but which have more judgment and prudence.[25]

---

[25] From vol. IV, p. 213; quoted by R. R. Palmer, "Frederick the Great, Guibert, Bulow: From Dynastic to National War," in Edward M. Earle (ed.), *Makers of Modern Strategy* (Princeton; Princeton University Press, 1943), p. 68.

This, indeed, was simply giving good expression to the classical argument for preparedness. A man who has written two books on military techniques is not likely to be himself marked by pacifist inclinations, though it is not impossible. What is interesting about this statement of Guibert's, however, is that he should have thought it necessary to write it. It tells us something about the intellectual climate of the times.

At almost the other end of Europe, at Koenigsberg in remote East Prussia, the philosopher Immanuel Kant published in the last decade of his long life a small tract called *Perpetual Peace* (1795), which was quickly translated into other European languages and which was to have a considerable influence into the nineteenth century. Taking up Montesquieu's idea that the advancing spirit of commerce is incompatible with war, he added the notion that despite the undeniable evil inherent in human nature, men were becoming increasingly capable because of their cultural progress to act on behalf of moral perfection—and war had no place in his moral scheme of things.

While Kant was writing this pamphlet the French Revolution was already in an advanced stage. To that great upheaval we shall promptly return, but by anticipating its course only modestly we make contact with that last, odd spirit of the Enlightenment, Benjamin Constant. In 1813, when Napoleon had suffered his first great reverses, he published a pamphlet entitled *De l'espirit de conquête et de l'usurpation dans leurs rapports avec la civilisation européenne*. Among several leading themes was the idea that the new weapons, especially the improved artillery, had made war unnatural for human beings. With such long-range weapons, fatalities depended on pure chance. Thus, there was no longer any place for glory in war, which had become simply monstrous. Like Montesquieu and Kant he placed much faith in the new commerce as an antidote to war.

The French Revolution and Its Aftermath

We move now to that tremendous explosion in European affairs which was the French Revolution, with its contradictory after-shock, the Napoleonic phenomenon. These events had a marked impact on the conduct of war with respect to intensity, but with respect to attitudes towards war we have a deepening of that schizophrenia in the culture which divides the Montesquieus, the Voltaires, the Kants, and the Constants on the one hand from those who revel in the age-old cult of valor, victory, and glory. The latter will now for a long time have the center of the stage and make the most noise.

With respect to the conduct of war, many clichés have centered around this as around other epical events of history. There was in France in various stages of the Revolution a tremendous élan, but this was by no means automatically translated into victory on the battlefields. In the first campaign provoked by the *émigrés*, that of 1792, the French armies, poorly trained and indifferently led, suffered serious reverses at the hands of the Prussians and Austrians—which only served to inflame the revolutionary excitement in Paris. The Battle of Valmy (September 20) was hailed by the French as a victory, but it was little more than an artillery duel that the enemy commander, the Duke of Brunswick, broke off because he considered it too late in the season to attempt to press on to Paris.

The real change came in the following year, after the execution of Louis XVI, when almost all the significant powers of Europe were ranged against the French. The latter promulgated their famous Law of August 23, 1793, the first example in modern times of something approaching total mobilization. The ringing phrases of this declaration have been much quoted, but one sentence perhaps bears repetition:

> The young men shall fight; the married men shall forge weapons and transport supplies; the women will make tents and clothes and serve in the hospitals; the children will make up old linen into lint; the old men will have themselves carried in to the public squares and rouse the courage of the fighting men, to preach hatred against kings and the unity of the Republic.

Some new military leaders were also becoming visible, first Jourdan, Hoche, and Pichegru, and soon Napoleon and those who were to become his marshals. Perhaps the greatest single change that the Revolution effected on military arms is seen here, for at one stroke the age-old incubus of depending almost exclusively on the aristocracy to provide the officer corps and especially the higher commanding officers was removed. At last talent had a chance to count above all else. A new army with new leadership could and did avail itself of the best military thinking of the time —including, incidentally, some excellent contributions to tactical doctrine published in the last decade of the *ancien régime* by people like Guibert, Du Teil, and others and incorporated into the drill book issued to the French army in 1791. The new French army soon became a large and experienced one, increasingly accustomed to success. On this combination was grafted the zeal of the Revolution, and on such a combination that zeal may well have been superfluous. The zeal of 1793, the fourth year of the Revolution, was indeed a spent thing by the time Napoleon made himself emperor eleven years later. One also has to account for the fact that enemy soldiers and sailors who were not infused with that zeal nevertheless fought well when well-led, and they were led well enough and fought well enough to destroy Napoleon in the end.

The intensity and the duration of the fighting—except for the brief peace of Amiens in 1802, England was at war with France from 1793 to 1815—and the characteristic strategies of the foremost generals of the time, with Napoleon setting the pace, made for a sharp break with the custom of "limited war" observed earlier in the eighteenth century. In Spain and Portugal the fighting with partisans descended to the savagery recorded in that great but terrible series of lithographs by Goya entitled "Disasters of War." It was an era of something approaching what Clausewitz called "absolute war," and he later speculated on what this demonstration would mean for the future.[26]

Undoubtedly the wars of the Revolution were on the French side "people's wars" such as Europe had not known before. Still, it is an old and absurd cliché that holds that modern "nationalism" begins with that era. One can find evidences aplenty of intense nationalism in Elizabethan England ("This blessed plot, this earth, this realm, this England"), and with local variations the same kinds of indications are found on the Continent as well. The Parisians did not have to chop off a king's head to learn that they were French; they had known it when that king's ancestor of two centuries earlier, the Protestant King of Navarre in the wars of religion in France, had uttered on the eve of a battle the

26 Karl von Clausewitz, *On War*, trans. by O. J. Matthijs Jolles (New York: Modern Library, 1943), see pp. 498, 582, 601.

slogan: "Quarter for Frenchmen, death to foreigners." It had been remembered of him, too, and it helped him in his contested accession to the French throne as Henri IV. If nationalism was even stronger at the time of Napoleon's career, it was also strong in the ranks of his enemies. The Spanish and the Russian peoples did not take kindly to invasion, and when Nelson flew his famous signal at the opening of the Battle of Trafalgar (1805) it was not "The King expects . . ." but *England* expects. . . ."

The extraordinary military career of Napoleon, while unique in the character and role of the chief actor, looks somewhat less novel when we study the campaigns of Frederick the Great a half-century earlier. Though using different tactics, Frederick, like Napoleon, was an apostle of the offensive and of the decisive battle. He, too, succeeded in achieving a high degree of mobilization of his kingdom, fought campaigns of movement rather than of position, and repeatedly won victories over forces considerably superior in numbers. But the Prussia he started with was little more than the old Margravate of Brandenburg plus East Prussia, while Napoleon controlled the leading country of Europe, with a unified population of over 25 million, which was greater than Austria, Prussia, and England combined.

Napoleon combined extraordinary ambitions with extraordinary talents. The latter included an outstanding aptitude for the theatrical and the dramatic. He achieved wide acclaim for his spectacular successes, while beguiling attention away from his colossal failures. He demonstrated this talent early in his career as commander-in-chief when in 1798 he took an army of 35,000 men to Egypt for the conquest of the Levant. The French battle fleet assigned to protect Napoleon's communications with France anchored in Aboukir Bay in the mouth of the Nile, and there Nelson found it and destroyed it on August 1 of that year. The French army was entrapped in the area it had come to conquer, but Napoleon went on to win some showy but meaningless victories: against the Mamluks in the "Battle of the Pyramids," against the Syrians (where the French encountered plague), and against the Turks. The army was not repatriated until some preliminary agreements were reached with the British in 1801 in anticipation of the Treaty of Amiens of the following year, which England felt obliged to conclude because of famine conditions at home. Meanwhile Napoleon had returned alone to France in

1799 and carried out the coup that made him dictator of France with the title of First Consul. Meanwhile, too, the British had sent 6,000 sepoys from India under Arthur Wellesley to join with 25,000 Turks to retake Cairo and Alexandria, which fell in the summer of 1801, and Napoleon agreed to relinquish Egypt.

Later Napoleon needlessly committed his armies to a prolonged struggle in Spain and Portugal—the Peninsular Campaign (1807–1813)—where all the fundamental strategic advantages were on the side of the enemy, for the British were able to make of that campaign a classic textbook example of the advantages of command of the sea.[27] There, too, Sir Arthur Wellesley, later Duke of Wellington, demonstrated that there were also other great generals in Europe at the time. Napoleon himself in his exile years at St. Helena referred to his losses in Iberia as the "Spanish ulcer," yet there seems to have been little diminution of his fame in France at the time they were occurring. Inasmuch as Napoleon was for the most part not there personally, the attention of the French was directed elsewhere.

The losses in Spain reached their climax at the moment the armies of France were suffering one of the greatest military disasters of all time, at the close of 1812 on the plains of Russia. The *Grande Armée* of over 420,000 men, not much more than half French to be sure, was almost totally destroyed. This defeat could not be easily concealed, yet Napoleon survived as emperor for another year and a half of war, adbicating from Fontainebleu in 1814 only after the Allies had taken Paris. Eleven months later he exploited his charisma and his fanatical following among the military to return from Elba for his "Hundred Days," with terminus at Waterloo. His death in exile only six years later was also a piece of stageworthy timing, helping to preserve the Napoleonic legend as long years of remaining life would not have done. When some years later the Prince of Joinville, sailor son of King Louis Philippe, brought his remains back to France, that country indulged itself in a vast transport of emotion, quite forgetting

---

[27] The best discussion of the Peninsular Campaign from the point of view of the use of sea power is by Alfred T. Mahan, *The Influence of Sea Power upon the French Revolution and Empire 1793–1812*, 2 vols. (Boston: Little, Brown, 1892), vol. II. To use a sentence from my own *A Guide to Naval Strategy* (Princeton: Princeton University Press, 1942; 5th ed., Praeger, 1965): "Wellington's army was transported to Spain and Portugal and supplied there by the relatively easy road of the sea, while to come to grips with that army Napoleon had to send his forces over France and over the terrible roads of a hostile Spain still living in the Middle Ages" (p. 156 in the 5th ed.).

how weary it had become of him and his wars—*la guerre éternelle* —by the time he had last departed.

The subsequent cult of Napoleon was the cult of *la gloire*. The battles that were to be chiseled on the *Arc de Triomphe* in Paris and to provide names for so many of that city's streets were nothing like the actions that were to be called "battles" in World War I. A few days or weeks of quick marches, followed by a morning in which the Man of Destiny with a *coup d'œil* made dispositions on the field assuring victory that same day, were followed in turn by a peace treaty that left France expanded in influence and usually also in territories. This was heady stuff. For decisive battles of such brief duration even the most spendthrift tactics (like charging in densely packed column formation) produced over the whole campaign relatively few casualties. It was the pattern of Ulm, Austerlitz, Friedland, Jena, and other battles. Those campaigns and battles that did not conform to this pattern left no street names.

The extraordinary power and duration of the legend still want explaining. Thirty-three years after Waterloo it enabled another Bonaparte to begin a twenty-two-year career as ruler of France, first as president-dictator and then as emperor. The legend lived on even after the shambles left by the latter in the disastrous Franco-Prussian War of 1870–1871. The one certain conclusion is that, at least for nineteenth-century France, nothing succeeded like spectacular success in war, even if the end negated all the gains.

How strangely the French Revolution contrasts with the one that preceded it in America! Although the philosophic ground work was largely shared, the circumstances were totally different. The American Revolution needed a war to succeed, but the excitement of the fighting, and even of winning, did not take over the mood of the nation that emerged. The leaders of that revolution, including Washington, never regarded themselves as professional soldiers. Washington was indeed revered after the event, but the qualities for which he was esteemed and which accounted for his being selected as chairman (or "president general") of the Constitutional Convention and subsequently as first President of the new United States were decidedly not martial ones.[28] The

---

[28] See James Thomas Flexner, *George Washington and the New Nation, 1783–1793* (Boston: Little, Brown, 1969). This is the third of four volumes to date by this author on Washington.

next three Presidents, John Adams, Thomas Jefferson, and James Madison, had played no military role in the war at all. Injustices were done during and after the war to American "tories" or "royalists," but there was nothing remotely like the explosion of rage that accounted for the Terror in France, mutely recorded in the still-visible defacement of the ancient churches, with their decapitated effigies of saints. The American Revolution thus stimulated no reaction, and was therefore immeasurably more successful in preserving and then advancing the goals achieved, despite the terrible and nearly fatal flaw of slavery.

The Modern Economists and Their International Rationalism

The year of the signing of the American Declaration of Independence also saw another event little noticed at the time but important to our story. This was the publication in England of Adam Smith's *The Wealth of Nations*, which signalled the beginning of a distinctively modern conception not simply of economics but also of the purposes for which nations exist and of the means by which they must accommodate themselves to those purposes and to each other. Smith had lived for several years in France and owed much to François Quesnay, founder of the Physiocratic school of French economists. Quesnay and others of that school had urged that wars for commerce made no sense because they required such disproportionately expensive military establishments that the economic gain, if any, from conquest was always likely to be overshadowed by its cost—an idea to which Smith was bound to be deeply receptive and sympathetic.

The mercantilist economics that Smith and his followers (and a few of his predecessors) supplanted had concerned itself primarily with foreign trade and always with the interests of the producer in both foreign and domestic trade. The interests of the producer were obviously in selling goods to acquire the maximum amount of money, the most universally acceptable form of which was gold. An increase in the gold supplies of the state was also held to be an increase in its power, for gold was considered the most important resource for waging war. To Smith, on the contrary, gold was a commodity like any other, and intrinsically hardly the most important. The benefits of trade, he held, were not in putting more money into the pockets of the merchants or the coffers of the state but in increasing the supply of goods to the consumer. Enhancement of the nation's power followed almost automatically from doing so, because of the increase in total resources available in the nation and thus also in the margins available, through appropriate fiscal procedures, for the uses of the state.

But what is the purpose of power? The wartime needs of the state were indeed paramount, but Smith and his followers insisted on greater rationality both in methods of fulfilling these needs and in giving appropriate measure to them. Inevitably there was a sharper questioning of the need for war: security, certainly, but conquest of new territories—what for? With the kind of freeing of trade that these economists considered appropriate and necessary anyway, there was likely to be little economic gain and a good deal of military cost in conquering new territories and in preserving those conquests. Here is Adam Smith on the subject:

> But in the . . . management of our American and West Indian colonies, the interest of the home consumer has been sacrificed to that of the producer with a more extravagant profusion than in all our other commercial regulations. A great empire has been established for the sole purpose of raising up a nation of customers who should be obliged to buy from the shops of our different producers, all the goods with which these could supply them. For the sake of that little enhancement of price which this monopoly might afford our producers, the home consumers have been burdened with the whole expense of maintaining and defending that empire. For this purpose, and this purpose only, in the last two wars, more than two hundred million have been spent, and a new debt of more than a hundred and seventy million has been contracted over and above all that had been expended for the same purpose in former wars. The interest of this debt is not only greater than the whole extraordinary profit, which, it ever could be pretended, was made by the monopoly of the colony trade, but than the whole value of that trade or than the whole value of the goods, which at an average have been annually exported to the colonies.[29]

Smith probably erred in attributing the desire for colonial expansion exclusively to the motive of economic gain, but the value of glory obviously did not commend itself to him and his followers as worth much of an investment. In politics the school founded by Adam Smith later became known as the "Little Englanders," because of their opposition to imperial expansion.

---

[29] The quotation is from *The Wealth of Nations*, Book IV, chap. 3.

Lord North, first minister of King George III and perhaps the one most responsible for the British behavior that provoked the revolt of the American colonies, hardly even knew of the existence of his illustrious contemporary, but the example of events in North America would long thereafter be held up as a special example of the idiocy of pursuing colonial empire. Exploitation not only cost more than it was worth, but it would not work because those meant to be exploited would not permit it. At the appropriate time they would fall "like ripe plums from the tree."

A change in language marks the progress of this school. Adam Smith still speaks of the art of war as "certainly the noblest of all arts," but a quarter century later, when peace with the First Consul was first being proposed, an unnamed writer in the *Monthly Magazine* (October 1800) wrote: "As the humane and laudable policy therefore of starving the French nation cannot be realized, perhaps it would be sound policy to prevent our own people from starving by making peace." The sarcasm could be from the pen of Voltaire, but the content has the sound of the newer school. And it sees in the "art of war," which so often depends on starving out the opponent, nothing particularly noble.

In this "liberal" or "classical" school founded by Adam Smith, later to include David Ricardo and John Stuart Mill and to merge with the "Manchester School" of which John Bright and Richard Cobden were the stellar members, we have something very different from the isolated remarks of a few persons such as may or may not reflect something vital stirring in the wind. We have instead a great political as well as intellectual movement, especially important in nineteenth-century England but with great influence on the Continent as well, and flowing directly and expansively into our own time. As a political movement it brought about the repeal of the odious Corn Laws (1846), a great humanitarian act as well as one ideologically directed towards freeing foreign trade.[30] It was the intellectual inspiration of the

---

[30] The corn laws, a combination of tariffs on the importation of cereal grains and of bounties on exports, both for the benefit of English growers, dated in their modern form from the reign of William and Mary. They imposed a considerable hardship on the English poor by boosting the price of bread, a fact that reflects the subsistence level at which the poorer classes in England (as elsewhere) were living at the time. Unfortunately, the same *laissez faire* attitude on the part of the members of Sir Robert Peel's government, which helped set them against the corn laws, was in its more doctrinaire manifestations also responsible for their lack of vigor in pushing measures to alleviate the sufferings of the Irish during the potato famines of 1845–1851. See C. B. Woodham-Smith, *The Great Hunger* (New York: Harper & Row, 1962).

Liberal Party which for a century was one of the two major parties of the country. It was a party and a movement opposed to colonial expansion—though ineffectively enough to provoke the expression that the British empire grew in a "series of fits of absent-mindedness"—and it was generally skeptical of arguments justifying large preparedness measures or the need for resort to war.

Richard Cobden, who held that war is the greatest of all consumers, published shortly before his death a little book entitled *The Three Panics* (1862), which exposed the absurdity of the "invasion panics" that had seized Britain between roughly 1844 and 1853. These fears were based on the ridiculous notion that with the new method of steam propulsion available in warships and transports alike, the Channel had become simply "a river passable by a steam bridge" (the words are Lord Palmerston's).[31] England was therefore held to be open to invasion by France, which was naturally assumed to be intent upon it. In reading Cobden today one is struck with how contemporary he is in both thought and expression. Much of what he says about the notions that fanned the panics could be translated with but minor changes into our own time, when we have also had our "panics" concerning the alleged nuclear or conventional intentions and capabilities of the Soviet Union and China. In the year following the last of the invasion panics, Britain and France did indeed go to war, but as allies instead of enemies, against Russia in the Crimea. It was in his speeches in the House of Commons against the Crimean War that John Bright rose to the acme of his considerable powers as a political orator. However, though pacifist movements were already beginning to take form in Europe and America during this period, it must be noted that the opposition to war of people like Bright, Cobden, and Mill—all of whom served in Parliament—was pragmatic rather than ideological. When the Civil War broke out in the United States, all three favored the northern side, in opposition to the government headed by Palmerston; to Bright, Abraham Lincoln was a hero to be revered.

In Britain the *ancien régime* was permitted to live alongside the new intellectual and political movement, an arrangement that

---

[31] Cobden's is now a fairly rare book, but it is treated at length in my *Sea Power in the Machine Age* (Princeton: Princeton University Press, 1941; 1943 2nd ed. reprinted by Greenwood Press, 1969), chap. 4, "The Invasion Panics."

whatever its drawbacks did marvelously cut down on bloodshed and also on instability as compared with the wildly gyrating politics of France. The Crimean War (1854–1856) is a kind of watershed between old and new in England with respect to the handling of the armed forces. Being one of the most ineptly fought wars in modern times (even the "charge of the Light Brigade" made famous by Tennyson was in the wrong direction),[32] it marked the end of the period when commissions in the British army were officially bought and sold. Retention of this outdated practice had been insisted upon by the arch-conservative but prestigious Duke of Wellington, whether he was in or out of the office of Prime Minister.[33] The expiration of that system meant greater emphasis on professionalism in the British officer corps.

Romantic Nationalism and Social Darwinism

To every liberal movement there is usually a more or less equal and a decidedly opposite reactionary one, but if these two forces were all we had to contend with, life would be much simpler than it is. There are various shades and intensities of both liberalism and conservatism, but there are also schools and movements that fall altogether outside either category. It would be impossible in this one chapter to attempt to account for all the relevant ideas and schools of thought that developed in that wonderfully fecund nineteenth century and that carried on into the twentieth, but two especially deserve mention.

One is the mystique of romantic nationalism of which one copious source is Friederich Hegel. It has nothing very much to do with his dialectic method, which influenced other great thinkers including Clausewitz and Karl Marx, but it has a great deal to do with the romanticism of the era, which was more pronounced in Germany than anywhere else. We are familiar with the romantic movement in the poetry of England, led by Wordsworth, Keats, Byron, and Shelley, but Germany had its romantic movement not only in its poetry—at a time that included the greatest of all its poets—but also in its superb music and in its philosophy.

---

[32] See Peter B. Gibbs, *Crimean Blunder* (New York: Holt, Rinehart, 1960); also Edward B. Hamley, *The War in the Crimea* (London: Seeley, 1910); and Cecil Woodham-Smith, *The Reason Why* (New York: McGraw-Hill, 1954). The last-named is a highly readable account.

[33] See Michael Howard's, "Wellington and the British Army," reprinted as chap. 3 in his *Studies in War and Peace* (London: Temple Smith, 1970).

At any rate, while intense feelings of nationalism were not new there or elsewhere, it became intellectually respectable to experience and to express a kind of religiosity about those feelings, as though they were not only natural but also good and beautiful and even sublime. It is traditional to hold that this fervor developed particularly in Germany because it was still not unified into the great nation-state it was later to become, at which time it would feel itself late in the race for colonial empire and thus for its "place in the sun." Whether this was the reason or not, there was certainly going to be a special "German problem" with which the twentieth century would have some difficulties. But what may indeed have reached its acme in Germany was by no means lacking in other countries as well.

The other idea and subsequent movement, which is relevant because it served as a foil for the mystique of nationalism, is Charles Darwin's theory of evolution as set down in his great *Origin of Species* (1859). If Darwin had only not coined that marvelously arresting and illuminatng phrase "survival of the fittest" to explain how evolution proceeds, or if he had not developed an idea making inevitable the coining of such a phrase by others if not by himself, a notion that was in his mind strictly biological might not have had the consequences it did have. In the enormous excitement engendered by the basic idea of evolution, stimulated further by the contest with established religion that it unavoidably provoked, it was about as inevitable as anything could be in the realm of ideas that the notion of "survival of the fittest" would be translated into other areas for which Darwin never intended it (but where he was quite willing to see it applied). There thus developed what has been called "social Darwinism," which is the notion that those societies or nations survive that are fittest to survive, and what more obvious mark of fitness could there be than a demonstrated competence to wage and win wars?

We are familiar enough with the ancient idea, surviving somewhat battered into the present, that war has the redeeming factor that it permits the individual participant to become a greater person than he is normally, to demonstrate his otherwise hidden greatness through his valor. All the typically virile attributes, plus those that are meritorious in either sex—endurance and fortitude as well as bravery and aggressiveness—are traditionally pictured as reaching their apotheosis in war. But now we see a quite new and different and disturbing idea, that national societies, which to nineteenth-century man obviously varied in quality, also have in war their supreme opportunity to demonstrate their true worth. From that idea it is a short step to the notion that war helps to stimulate the superiority of which it proves the arbiter. It becomes, therefore, rather a good thing. At any rate, it offers compensation for its somewhat too conspicuous evils; it lets the better nations come out on top, where obviously they belong. It thus became possible for someone to say, a German as it happened (the elder von Moltke, in a letter to J. K. Bluntschli), that "perpetual peace is a dream and not even a beautiful one. . . . In [war] are developed the noblest virtues of man." And if a great nation happened to lose a war, as France did in 1871, it now felt compelled not only to regain its territorial losses but also to prove to the world and to itself that although something temporarily went wrong, it was not really in decline.

It is no doubt possible to exaggerate these influences. It is clearly difficult to measure them. However, it is extraordinary how ubiquitous the Darwinian idea became in the five decades leading into World War I. One finds it quite prominently, for example, in Walter Bagehot's classic *Physics and Politics* (1869). Bagehot is very far from being a blatant example of social Darwinism at its worst. "Military morals," he says, "can direct the axe to cut down the tree, but it knows nothing of the quiet force by which the forest grows." A wonderful statement, and worth much by way of redemption in any court of appeals. Still, as he hedges and limits the application of the Darwinian idea, he also shows his preoccupation with it, and proposes as a generality that "in every particular state of the world, those nations that are strongest tend to prevail over the others; and in certain marked peculiarities the strongest tend to be the best." He also believes in the inheritance of acquired characteristics, and he notes that cultivation in one generation leads to more cultivation in the next, which is a beautiful thing, a sublime thing, but also a bit dangerous.

In minds lacking the agility and the cultivation that Bagehot displays, the embracing of the "survival of the fittest" doctrine was a good deal less inhibited. Even someone like Captain Alfred Thayer Mahan, the great American naval strategist and historian

—the most intellectually gifted and productive military officer that the United States has yet produced—expressed alarm following the Boer War of 1899–1902 that Britain's apparently poor performance in that conflict showed a decline in the martial virtues of the British race, a matter of considerable concern, he thought, to the United States. In the speeches of politicians and of commencement-day orators, references to being the best, and being the fittest, and being on top were simply standard fare. Friederich von Bernhardi, writing in *Germany and the Next War* (1911), was confident that "war is a biological necessity of the first importance." The idea would naturally be revived with special force later under Hitler.[34]

And the romanticism was still strong. In a Memorial Day address in 1895 to the Harvard graduating class, the late Oliver Wendel Holmes expressed himself as follows:

> But who of us could endure a world . . . without the divine folly of honor? . . . I do not know what is true. I do not know the meaning of the universe. But in the midst of doubt, in the collapse of creeds, there is one thing I do not doubt, and that is that the faith is true and adorable which leads a soldier to throw away his life in obedience to a blindly accepted duty, in a cause which he little understands, in a plan of campaign of which he has no notion, under tactics of which he does not see the use.[35]

This is not the elder O. W. Holmes but the son, the same who had been thrice wounded, the last time severely, in the Civil War, and who was later to spend many years of his long life as the great and eminently reasonable justice on the Supreme Court.

In Europe there was undoubtedly a good deal more to the threatening atmosphere in the two or three decades preceding World War I than we have touched upon. There were the long years of peace—apart from the Boer involvement, Britain had not been in a serious war against a major power since 1856 in the

---

[34] See Daniel Gasman, *The Scientific Origins of National Socialism* (London: Macdonald, 1971); also Richard Hofstadter, *Social Darwinism in American Thought* (Philadelphia: University of Pennsylvania Press, 1944; revised ed. by Beacon Press, 1955).

[35] "The Soldier's Faith," *Speeches by Oliver Wendel Holmes* (Boston: Little, Brown, 1913), pp. 56–66; reprinted in Julius J. Marke (ed.), *The Holmes Reader* (New York: Ocean Publications, 1955), pp. 150 f.

Crimea, and Germany and France not since 1871. There were the usual diplomatic incidents and quarrels that every era produces but which seem to have special exacerbations in some. The omnipresent intervention of chance, good or ill, naturally presented itself in a number of intriguing ways, including the accession to the German throne in 1888, the "year of the three emperors," of a young kaiser whose own father had considered him somewhat unbalanced.

Nevertheless, in the last years of the nineteenth century and the first of the twentieth—*la belle époque* in terms of pleasure and entertainment—there seemed to have been a poison at work that had not been known before. The Europe that had known many wars and recovered from them all, that had made such spectacular progress in the industrial arts and in other arts as well, and not least in the realm of human welfare and humanitarian reform, this Europe seemed to be simply spoiling for a war. The same Lord Lansdowne, cabinet member, who in 1917 would courageously write a letter to the *Daily Telegraph* urging an ending of the war, was able to say before that war that five shillings a week for old-age pensioners would cost as much as a war without a war's benefit of "strengthening the moral fibre of a nation."

Few have captured this mood as perceptively as the British military historian, Professor Michael Howard. Reflecting on the moods of the time, as evidenced in the writings of the various super-patriots of Europe and the United States, or in the editorials, or speeches at prize-givings or the like—from which "one learns far more about the causes of the First World War than in a lifetime of reading diplomatic documents"—Howard goes on to say: "The diplomats may have been desperately anxious to avoid a war, as were the businessmen; but . . . they were about the only people who were." Then, after quoting examples from a 1909 commencement day speech by one-time Prime Minister Lord Rosebery ("by no means a martial figure") and from the concluding words of Colmar von der Goltz's best-seller, *The Nation in Arms*,[36] Howard adds:

> One could multiply such quotations indefinitely, from French, Italian, and American sources as well as from British

---

[36] 1883, 5th ed., 1913.

and German. The children of Europe were being trained for war, and war was regarded as something natural and inevitable. Why? There was the influence of Hegel and Mazzini seeeping through all European thought, emphasising that the highest morality of the individual lay in service to the state, vulgarised in a million speech-day addresses like Lord Rosebery's. There was the popular "social Darwinism" with its creed of the survival of the fittest among nations as among species. There were the technical requirements of mass armies, which coincided conveniently with these mass trends. There was an upper class which, with its status rendered precarious by industrialisation, found in military life the security, purpose and prestige increasingly denied it in civil. There was a great mass of uprooted proletariat and urbanised petty bourgeoisie, for whom national pride provided a status and fulfilment lacking in their drab everyday lives. There was the disquieting strain of primitive savagery which composers and artists were beginning to tap during the first decade of the twentieth century. There were the boiling frustrations of deepening class war. Trends like these are difficult and sometimes impossible to document, but no study of the war can be complete which does not take them into account.

Armies, Howard goes on to say, were not looked upon as "deterrents" but as "instruments for fighting a war which was widely regarded—and not by the soldiers alone—as being inevitable, necessary, and even desirable." [37]

There were indeed some contrary voices. George Bernard Shaw, in his *Man and Superman* published in 1903, has the Devil speaking thus:

> Have you walked up and down upon the earth lately? I have: and I have examined Man's wonderful inventions. And I tell you that in the arts of life Man invents nothing; but in the arts of death he outdoes Nature herself, and produces by chemistry and machinery all the slaughter of plague, pestilence and famine. The peasant I tempt today eats and drinks

---

[37] In an essay that was originally a review-article on a book on World War I by A. J. P. Taylor, published in *Encounter*, January 1964, and reprinted, slightly abbreviated, as chap. 6, "Reflections on the First World War," in Howard's *Studies in War and Peace*.

what was eaten and drunk by the peasants of ten thousand years ago; and the house he lives in has not altered as much in a thousand centuries as the fashion of a lady's bonnet in a score of weeks. But when he goes out to slay, he carries a marvel of mechanism that lets loose at the touch of his finger all the hidden molecular energies, and leaves the javelin, the arrow, and blowpipe of his fathers far behind. In the arts of peace Man is a bungler. I have seen his cotton factories and . . . machinery . . . they are toys compared to the Maxim gun, and submarine torpedo boat.[38] There is nothing in Man's industrial machinery but his greed and his sloth: his heart is in his weapons.

But Shaw's is very much a minority voice. It is doubtful that he represented anything but a small minority even among the literati. His contemporary Alban Berg, the composer, was to express even after war broke out in 1914 a very different feeling.

Yes, the war has to continue. The muck-heap has been growing for decades. . . . Believe me, if the war ended today, we should be back within the same old sordid squalor within a fortnight. . . . The war's great surprise will be in the guns, which are going to show a frivolous generation their utter emptiness. . . . How fervently I wish for peace, for the end of this intolerable horror and suffering! But I still cannot ask for this wish to be fulfilled.[39]

It would probably be the last time that anyone with pretensions to being a civilized European would express such views.

Anyway, we notice among the most civilized nations of the world during the two or three decades preceding 1914 something that looks rather like the infantile notions of *la gloire* that had marked the career of Napoleonic and post-Napoleonic France, except that there was much in it that had not been known before.

---

[38] The "submarine torpedo boat" is a reference not to a submarine vessel (which existed only in primitive form in 1903) but rather to a small, fast surface vessel then newly adopted for firing "submarine torpedoes." The Maxim gun is the British version of the World War I machine gun.

[39] Berg joined the German army in 1915, and after two months of training had a breakdown, after which he was transferred to clerical duties for the rest of the war. The quotation above is from Berg's *Letters to His Wife*, ed. and trans. by Gernard Grun (New York: St. Martin's, 1971). My source is the review of that book by Charles Rosen, *New York Times Book Review*, January 2, 1972.

In the dominant mood of 1914 people seemed to be saying: We must show the superiority of our nation and our fatherland by our willingness to suffer and die for it! The enthusiasm with which the war was greeted was not a matter of a week or a month. For the first two years of the war Britain fought with volunteer armies—Prime Minister Asquith's Liberals were opposed to conscription and his government fell on the issue only in 1916—and, as Howard points out, these troops "displayed on the Somme no less ardor than the regular soldiers who had dashed over to France in 1914 for fear of missing the fighting." It was taking longer than they had thought it would, but they never thought the casualties would be light.

> There was no cold douche of disillusion after the blood-letting of 1914 or even of 1915: it was what everyone had been led to expect. This, after all, was exactly that trial of patriotism, manliness, and endurance for which the nations of Europe had been preparing themselves for an entire generation.[40]

However, this eagerness to undergo "that trial of patriotism, manliness, and endurance" was well and truly burned out, apparently forever, before the year 1916 had run its terrible, bloody course. In 1917–1918 young Americans would show that they too had been reared on the same brew as their European cousins, but for the British, the French, and the Germans it was never the same after Verdun and the Somme. The mood is again best caught by the poets of the time. From Rupert Brooke in 1914 we hear the evocation:

> Now, God be thanked who has matched us with His hour,
> And caught our youth, and wakened us from sleeping . . .

Then a year later from C. H. Sorley, shortly before he was killed in October 1915, a vision of war that had never been seen before:

> When you see millions of the mouthless dead
> Across your dreams in pale battalions go . . .

And, after another year, from Robert Palmer, killed in 1916:

---

[40] Howard, *Studies in War and Peace*, p. 104.

Lord, how long shall Satan in high places lead the blind
To battle for the passions of the strong?

And then, after still another year, from Siegfried Sassoon, who survived, in a poem called "To Any Dead Officer":

Good-bye, old lad! Remember me to God,
　　And tell Him that our politicians swear
They won't give in till Prussian Rule's been trod
　　Under the Heel of England . . . Are you there? . . .
Yes . . . and the War won't end for at least two years;
But we've got stacks of men . . . I'm blind with tears,
　　Staring into the dark. Cheero!
I wish they'd killed you in a decent show.[41]

The Aftermath of World War I

What was surely the most savage war in history up to that time ended in a savage peace—less in the actual terms of the Treaty of Versailles than in the mood in which its terms were imposed. One sees it in the inscriptions on the monuments that still remain at Compiègne where the Armistice of 1918 was signed. In Germany the democracy of the Weimar Republic was identified with defeat and shortly, in 1923, with the French-Belgian occupation of the Ruhr and with the concommitant disastrous inflation, in comparison with which what we now call inflation looks absurdly tame. But there was recovery even from those wounds and a period in which the able conciliator, Gustav Stresemann, occupied a place in every cabinet until his death in 1929, when the Locarno Treaties of 1925 were concluded, and the Kellogg-Briand Pact of 1928 outlawing resort to war except in self-defense was quickly-accepted by all the important nations of the world including Germany. It was also the period of the hey-day of the League of Nations, which did not appear to be mortally wounded by the decision of the United States not to join.[42] But meanwhile,

---

[41] All four poems from which I have quoted are included in that excellent anthology by Brian Gardner, *Up the Line to Death: The War Poets*, 1914–18 (London: Methuen, 1964).

[42] Which incidentally was *not* the decision of his opposition in the U.S. Senate but of President Woodrow Wilson himself. He instructed his followers in the Senate to vote against the treaty containing the Covenant so long as Senator Lodge's reservations were appended—reservations that Wilson considered absolutely intolerable but which others, including the representatives of the British and French governments, considered relatively harmless. See Alexander L. George and Juliette L. George, *Woodrow Wilson and Colonel House: A Personality Study* (New York: John Day, 1956; Dover paperback, 1964), chap. 15.

in 1925, the old Field Marshal Paul von Hindenburg was elected president in place of the deceased Friedrich Ebert by a narrow margin over the candidate of the moderate opposition, who would have won if the votes of the Communist candidate had been added to his. Hindenburg's election looked harmless enough at the time, but with the time of troubles that was to come with the Great Depression, it was he who would turn to Adolf Hitler and make him chancellor in January 1933, at which time World War II became virtually unavoidable.

We do not look for new ideas or new philosophies in Hitler. What we have is a man whose pathological character formation included an obsessional paranoid commitment to certain discredited racial theories. Because he also had a certain demogogic genius (which may well have been enhanced by his neurosis) he was able to project his own fantasies onto an entire nation.[43] It mattered greatly, too, that that nation lacked democratic traditions and that its desperate economic condition from 1930 on reawakened and exacerbated the pangs of national defeat and humiliation. Even so, except for some passages in *Mein Kampf*, Hitler was very careful, both for Germans and for observers abroad, not to appear to advocate war, at least not against the West. His claims to *Lebensraum* were pointed to eastern Europe and accompanied by repeated denials that war would be necessary to obtain his wishes. He even managed to fool the Poles enough so that they were eager to share in the spoils resulting from the partition of Czechoslovakia in 1938. The rearmament that became open in 1936 was avowedly for the purpose of throwing off the incubus and penalties of defeat and for acquiring diplomatic leverage, not for war. As we saw in Chapter 2, when war did come in 1939 it was greeted in Germany as elsewhere with the deepest gloom—in sharpest possible contrast to the delirium that marked the opening of World War I.

Mussolini requires and deserves even fewer words here. Facism

---

[43] There has been much speculation by psychoanalysts and psychoanalytically trained historians on the nature of Hitler's psychic pathology. An excellent paper, which also contains a useful bibliography in its footnotes, is by the historian Robert G. L. Waite, "Adolf Hitler's Guilt Feelings: A Problem in History and Psychology," *The Journal of Interdisciplinary History*, vol. I, no. 2 (Winter 1971), pp. 229–250. A somewhat overlapping and even better piece is the same author's "Adolf Hitler's Anti-Semitism: A Study in History and Psychoanalysis," in Benjamin B. Wolman, (ed.), *The Psychoanalytic Interpretation of History* (New York: Basic Books, 1971), pp. 192–230. Recently published also is the formerly secret study prepared during World War II by the psychoanalyst Walter C. Langer, *The Mind of Adolf Hitler* (New York: Basic Books, 1972).

was an invention without originality, and the hollowness of all the bellicose fulminations and posturings during some two decades of it was amply proved in World War II, which Mussolini was prudently tardy in entering but not sufficiently prudent to stay out of altogether. The Italian people felt no quarrel with the British people and even less with the Americans, and for that and other reasons their military performance in the war was fortunately quite poor.

The dictatorship in the Soviet Union was also deeply averse to war, for the best of pragmatic reasons. Unlike the milder forms of Marxism incorporated into the various socialist parties of western Europe, the true-blue variety of Communism that came to power in the Soviet Union, and later in China, was not in any sense of the word pacifistic. Lenin's great slogan had been: "Convert imperialist war into civil war!" Stalin proved himself quite ready to use violence, internally in the purges of the late 1930's and externally in war against Finland in the winter of 1939–1940, but he did everything he could think of doing to escape a war with Hitler's Germany, going so far as to conclude with Hitler in 1939 the pact that made the war certain—against others. That Stalin was not able finally to escape the war proves only that he was making some poor bets.

Only in Japan, a nation that lived largely outside the social and cultural orbit of Europe and America, was there a government in power that cherished the use of military force as an honorable way of life. But it was a military clique that had control of the government, a clique representing a tradition for which the samurai warriors of medieval times provided the revered models. Even so, Japan went to war with the United States—in partnership with Germany and Italy—not because the Japanese loved war but because the Americans would not accede to what the Japanese considered their absolutely basic demands in the western Pacific. Thus, even they went to war sorrowfully rather than in joy. The sobering truth is that the Japanese military men who made the decision for war had no clear idea how they could win! It was a striking demonstration of faith, hope, and unclarity.[44]

The end of World War II saw the ushering in of the nuclear

[44] See Robert J. C. Butow, *Tojo and the Coming of the War* (Princeton: Princeton University Press, 1961; reissued by Stanford University Press, 1969), especially chap. 11, "The Decision for War."

age, and it saw also in the three major defeated countries so over-whelming a rejection as the world had never seen before of the dictators, cliques, and slogans that had got them involved in such individual disasters. With over a quarter of a century having elapsed since the surrenders, we can speak with some confidence of the permanency of that conclusion. It is in the strongest possible contrast with the mood in Germany following World War I, where the spirit of revanchism was not long in awakening and where the leading generals of the war were very soon again the most honored men in the realm—Hindenburg, as we have seen, being elected president less than seven years after the war's end. After World War II, however, Germany was not only substantially reduced in size but divided between East and West, and yet the Germans from top to bottom, including the military, were totally convinced that however desirable was reunification, it had to be accomplished *ohne Krieg,* "without war." An equal or greater rejection of the militaristic past occurred in Japan, being if anything favorably affected by the retention of the Emperor. There, after the signing of the peace treaty, the United States which had fought four years to disarm the country had to beg, wheedle, and press the erstwhile enemy to adopt some slight measure of rearmament.

Defeat was naturally a key reason for the new attitude, but defeat alone was not what differentiated the Germany of post-1945 from the Germany of post-1918. True, the defeat was far more overwhelming in the second case than in the first, and two in a row no doubt makes a deeper impression than one. There had also been the demonstration that the Soviet Union was far from being the weak and contemptible opponent that Hitler and some of his foreign contemporaries had thought it was, and its relative power was bound to grow. The Germans had all the reason in the world for predicating their future plans on the *ohne Krieg* assumption, and very much the same was true for Japan. But the profoundly altered attitudes in Germany and in Japan—if we fail to include Italy in this formulation it is because there no great conversion was necessary—appear to go far deeper than can be appreciated by any cataloging of relevant circumstances. The degree of reconciliation with former enemies mentioned early in this chapter is indicative of the new temper, and there are other indications as well.

273

Besides, there was the atomic bomb sitting conspicuously at the end of the path of devastation down which the German and Japanese people had been taken.

Conclusions

With this somewhat brief excursion from antiquity to the present to inquire about prevailing attitudes towards war in our western civilization, we find in general that while those attitudes changed remarkably little over the millennia, they have changed quite rapidly over the last two centuries, more rapidly in the half century since World War I, and with especial force since the coming of nuclear weapons. Where war was once accepted as inevitably a part of the human condition, regrettable in its tragic details but offering valued compensations in opportunities for valor and for human greatness—or, more recently, in opportunities for the ascendency of superior peoples—the modern attitude has moved towards rejection of the concept of war as a means of resolving international or other disputes. Especially striking is the marked fading of the pursuit of glory either as an incentive towards war and warlike acts or even as a suitable compensation for the evils of war induced by other causes. Present justifications of war and of preparations for war appear to be confined largely to self-defense—expanded by the superpowers to include defense of client states—or, in a very few instances, correction of what is conceived to be the most blatant injustice.

Because nations insist on remaining judges in their own cases, one has to retain some reservations about the effectiveness of the changes of view that we have observed since 1916. Nevertheless, a change of such dimensions, combined with the advent of nuclear weapons on top of the terrible experience of two world wars, is bound to be of the greatest significance. Certainly it greatly affects the prospects for the success of deterrence. Moreover, nations that formerly thought it quite impossible to live together in a condition of expanding nuclear capabilities have now got considerably used to it. We may not be able to predict with high confidence that the outcome of some particular rivalry will be pacific, but we can predict over the longer term a much lesser inclination than in times past to take for granted the periodic recurrence of war, certainly the recurrence of large-scale warfare. We can predict also much greater earnestness about seaching for alternatives to war.

The institution of the personal duel, with its elaborate codes defining purpose and procedures, endured for centuries and then quite suddenly disappeared from practically all societies on earth. The duel had socially and psychologically much in common with war, especially with respect to the appeals to "honor" that both involved. Strong national leaders, like Cardinal Richelieu in seventeenth-century France, tried unsuccessfully for decades to suppress it. It remained common into the nineteenth century, lasted even into the twentieth, and then suddenly became old-fashioned and ridiculous. Murder and mayhem remain common phenomena, but they are very different from the duel. They do not supplant the duel, because they have always existed along with it, just as violence in general has always existed and will no doubt continue to exist. But that violence should continue indefinitely to take the specific institutional form known as war, which involves always a far greater intensity and magnitude of violence than is likely to be encountered through more spontaneous and less formal outlets, is now decidedly questionable. This could be wishful thinking, but we are not obliged to deny important visible changes simply because they happen to be in a direction we like.

CHAPTER

7

Some Theories on the Causes of War

Sir Andrew. O, if I thought that, I'ld beat him like a dog!
Sir Toby. What, for being a puritan? thy exquisite reason, dear knight?
Sir Andrew. I have no exquisite reason for't, but I have reason good
enough.

Twelfth Night, Act II, sc. iii.

Man fought wars in remotest antiquity; he fights them still today. The fabulous changes that this span of time has seen in man's way of life and in the environment he has made for himself are pretty nearly matched by changes in the character of war itself, both culturally and technologically. Yet it persists. Why? What function does it perform? Or perhaps we should ask, what peculiar pathology remains inherent in the societies we create so that, however much altered in other respects, they continue disposed periodically to go to war?

It is hardly believable that we still do not have the answers to these questions. After so many millennia filled with so much war! Yet we have to recognize the existence side by side of explanatory theories that are radically different from each other and sometimes

276

incompatible. It tells us that at best we have only fragments of explanation. To attempt to survey them all would take us beyond our needs and intentions for this book. We shall confine ourselves in this chapter to a critical review of some of the more familiar theories on the causes of war.

Historical Approaches

Why do we need theories anyway? The historians usually tell us without hesitation why nations have gone to war in the past. May we not presume that the same or comparable reasons continue to operate today and will do so in the future, except insofar as new forces intervene, and that these new forces will surely be easy to recognize? The answer, unfortunately, is no. Though we depend critically on the work of historians, we cannot regularly accept their judgments on motivation. This is especially true with respect to the making of wars, where we see so much behavior that does not appear to be rational.

It would of course be impossible for historians to function without conceptions or theories purporting to organize if not explain human behavior. How else would an historian determine what is worth his selective attention as a putative cause of any war? He cannot fix upon particular causes for any single war unless he has some feeling for the underlying factors through which the particular ones might operate. Historians' theories may be simply "common sense" ideas adopted with little if any conscious analysis, but not on that account less binding or confining. Or they may merely reflect a traditional focus for determining what is relevant and important. One such focus is seen in the work of generations of historians who grew up in Europe and America convinced that the origins of World War I were to be found primarily in the record of pre-1914 diplomacy. In the previous chapter, however, we noted a passing remark by Michael Howard, himself an illustrious historian, to the effect that one learns much more about the causes of World War I from reading prewar editorials, speeches at prizegivings, and the like "than in a lifetime of reading diplomatic documents." [1] Howard is thus rejecting a traditional focus and in the process revealing an alternative idea or theory for determining which data are relevant and important. Yet he stands away from any systematic development or evaluation either of his own theory or of the one he rejects, apparently trusting to his instincts

---

[1] See p. 266.

and leaving the task of systematic justification to those who have more taste for it.

In this respect Howard follows the traditions of his profession, which in the main rejects the idea that generalization is the goal of history. The rejection reflects in part a suspicion that generalizations and especially theories of causation tend to confine the historian—in other words, create biases. There is plenty of experience to indicate that they do just that. Arthur M. Schlesinger, Jr. quotes sympathetically Marc Bloch's phrase about "the thrill of learning singular things." He adds, "Indeed, it is the commitment to concrete reconstruction as against abstract generalization —to life as against laws—which distinguishes history from sociology." Yet Schlesinger cannot quite bring himself to confirm the doctrine of the absolute uniqueness of events in history. He goes on:

> Even historians who are skeptical of attempts to discern a final and systematic order in history acknowledge the existence of a variety of uniformities and recurrences. There can be no question that generalizations about the past, defective as they may be, are possible—and that they can strengthen the capacity of statesmen to deal with the future.[2]

Although bias is rampant in all human thought, affecting also the professional conclusions of social scientists and even physical scientists (though in the nature of things the latter are usually more readily subject to correction), bias in a historian can often parade for long periods of time as a virtue, especially when it has a nationalistic or sectional stamp. In the latter instances recruits can be gathered to form a "school." The so-called "revisionist" explanation of the American Civil War mentioned in the first chapter, which put the blame mostly on the abolitionist "hotheads," was developed originally by southern scholars. The only thing mysterious about it was that so many northern historians also adopted their views.[3] The fact that it was the dominant American interpretation for over thirty years reminds us distressingly how unoriginal and sheep-like can be the majority of members of a distinguished intellectual guild, and historians are not alone in this. The members of the revisionist school seemed to

---

[2] Arthur M. Schlesinger, Jr., *The Bitter Heritage* (Boston: Houghton Mifflin, 1966; revised ed., Fawcett World Library, 1968), p. 91.

[3] See pp. 16 f.

feel that sensible human beings can and should separate themselves from such emotions as indignation—a puritanical attitude possibly explaining the acceptance of these views in the north— even when the indignation was directed against slavery! When William Lloyd Garrison said: "I have need to be all on fire, for I have mountains of ice about me to melt," he communicated nothing to these scholars, except possibly unreasonableness. Finally we noticed that the school existed only by virtue of glossing over, ignoring, or denying the many extraordinary cruelties inherent in slavery, let alone the monumental injustice of it—in other words, by denying or suppressing history.

There are in addition special historians' biases. One is that of assuming, unless the evidence to the contrary is specific and overwhelming, that the high policy decisions of governments are generally the product of careful, orderly deliberation that can subsequently be traced. As Schlesinger put it during his third year on President Kennedy's White House staff:

> Nothing in my own recent experience has been more chastening than the attempt to penetrate into the process of decision. I shudder a little when I think how confidently I have analyzed decisions in the ages of Jackson and Roosevelt, traced influences, assigned motives, evaluated roles, allocated responsibilities and, in short, transformed a dishevelled and murky evolution into a tidy and ordered transaction. The sad fact is that, in many cases, the basic evidence for the historian's reconstruction of the really hard cases does not exist —and the evidence that does exist is often incomplete, misleading or erroneous.[4]

The principals involved may (or they may not) go through the motions of "considering all the angles," but these motions are often perfunctory, played through on the part of highly like-minded people, and sufficiently concealed behind secrecy so that any fresh viewpoint has a difficult time penetrating. Among the more shattering revelations of the Pentagon Papers was that many grave and highly consequential decisions concerning Vietnam were made on the basis of assumptions or premises which could not withstand any kind of logical scrutiny but which were simply never challenged! Also, oral deliberations may be recorded very inaccurately or not at all.

---

[4] "The Historians and History," *Foreign Affairs*, vol. 41 (April 1963), p. 493.

The historians have indeed bestowed on us a very large proportion of the most rewarding reading we have. We should merely bear in mind that when we are told, for example, that Louis XIV invaded the Spanish Netherlands in 1667 because his father-in-law, Philip IV of Spain, had failed to pay the dowry of the daughter who was Louis's wife, thus invalidating her renunciation of her heritage (with Louis making his claim through an obscure principle called *le droit de dévolution*, which gave its name to the War of Devolution), the "real" reason may have had more to do with the young King's feeling that it was time he began making a name for himself as a leader in war. At any rate, if it was additional territory that Louis was after, it might be worth considering *why* a young man who was already ruler of the greatest kingdom in the world should have thought it worth giving up his ease and a good deal of treasure as well as other people's lives in order to gain a few more towns or even provinces.

We also have to bear in mind that whatever theory of war causation we do adopt has to be derived from historical experience and tested against a rigorous reexamination of that experience. There is no other way.[5] Other kinds of knowledge may *in addition* be vital. If, for example, we are considering a theory that lays heavy emphasis on psychological factors, we obviously derive our working insights from the clinic or the laboratory. But the testing of that theory has to depend on how well it jibes with historical fact.

Economic Theories of War Causation

The distinguished British economist, Lord Lionel Robbins, reminds us that "it would be very surprising if we were to find that there were no economic factors involved in the causation of

---

[5] In making this statement I am not forgetting that some look upon various kinds of simulation or "model testing" as a supplement to—meaning in part a substitute for—direct historical experience and the interpretation thereof. I have seen a political science doctoral dissertation, much praised by its sponsors, which purported to prove that *all* the great historians on the sixteenth century have been wrong in concluding that balance-of-power considerations played little or no part in the international politics and wars of that period. To challenge existing orthodoxy (which may itself stem from a revisionist trend in the past) may be useful or necessary and is by definition "revisionism." Its validity, however, depends on the comprehensiveness and accuracy of the history that goes into it, not on the creation of some simplified model of reality against which some selected facts of history are quite arbitrarily tested, often in a conspicuously Procrustean manner. The extent of knowledge that a competent and mature historian has acquired about his own special field is something that a non-historian can hardly begin to comprehend—as was abundantly evident in the dissertation in question.

any wars." This reminder will strike most readers as being unnecessary and in fact an understatement of the obvious. Robbins,
however, uses it to open an essay of which the general tenor is that
economic factors have been vastly overrated among the causes of
war.[6]

Certainly it was commonly sensed, long before the special contributions of Karl Marx, that people are disposed to view the
affairs of the world in terms of their own economic interests as
they see and appreciate those interests. They are obviously capable
of being moved to mighty passions in defense of those interests
—though passions, we must quickly add, also develop a life of
their own. Marx developed and systematized this general insight
into the idea of the "class struggle," which became the corner-
stone of his entire philosophic construct. But even those who reject the main corpus of the Marxian system as either disproved by
events, or outmoded by later and richer analysis and insights, or
simply repulsive are nevertheless moved by their own experience
in life to have a certain sympathy for the idea that people easily
approve what looks economically beneficial to themselves and just
as easily disapprove the reverse. Upon that sympathy it is possible
to play all kinds of tunes, and many indeed have been thus played
to wide approval. It is clear that of all the categories into which it
is possible to classify theories of war causation, those that are
Marxian or neo-Marxian have certainly had the lion's share of
attention and approval. One variant of that thought—the "military-industrial complex"—is still very much with us, entertained
by people who are not in any sense Marxians and usually anxious
not to be regarded as such.

The genuine Marxian theory of war causation need not detain
us long, because it has been of modest importance politically. The
people who have carried through revolutions in the name of Marx
in various parts of the world have been moved mostly by other
motives than the thought that they were helping ultimately to rid
the world of war. We are not talking about the old Fabian social-
ists and the modern related schools of left-wing intellectuals who
are believers in civil rights and who usually abhor war. Some of
these groups have called themselves Marxian but would not be so
regarded by Lenin and his followers. The latter, though hardly
pacific in inclination and method, have been glad to use as propa-

---

[6] Lionel Robbins, *The Economic Causes of War* (London: Jonathan Cape, 1939; reissued, Howard Fertig, 1968), p. 17.

ganda the charge that capitalist imperialism breeds war, but it has probably mattered deeply to only a few of them.

The theory developed by Marx has an explicit historical limitation. Though one can read into the Marxian philosophy a general emphasis on the "economic interpretation of history" that would seem to favor the notion that all wars are due primarily to economic causes, Marx's main theoretical preoccupation was with that particular phase of history characterized by fully developed capitalism. He was simply uninterested in what might have caused wars before that phase of history was reached, but his claims concerning the application of his ideas within that period were all-embracing. *All* important wars and important international frictions during this period were due, according to Marx, to the existence of the capitalist form of society. One perhaps detects a certain theoretical weakness at the outset, because historically one sees no conspicuous increase in frequency of wars after the onset of what Marx would recognize as "fully developed capitalism." On the other hand, there is also no obvious reason why wars should not have distinctively different causes at different phases of world history.

The Marxian theory of imperialism is often alleged to rest upon the underconsumption theory, that is, the idea that the working classes are chronically unable to consume all the goods that their labor produces and that entrepreneurs therefore seek markets abroad for the profitable disposal of the surplus goods. This urge for markets abroad is supposed to be the mainspring of that imperialism which causes intense friction and therefore war among the major powers. Actually, Marx did not clearly suggest *why* capitalism results in competitive imperialism; it was his followers who debated the reasons, and they came up with at least two radically different views. One was the underconsumption theory just noted, vigorously argued by Rosa Luxemburg in Germany and J. A. Hobson in England, and the other was the theory advanced by Lenin of "monopoly finance capital," which has to do with the struggle of capitalists to avert "the secular tendency to a falling rate of profit." As the late General Smedley Butler put it, and he was certainly no Marxist: "The trouble with America is that the dollar gets restless when it earns only 6 per cent over here. It goes overseas to get 100 per cent. The flag follows the money—and the soldiers follow the flag."

To the modern economist the underconsumption theory is without logical validity. He looks upon investment as a cost-reducing process, and sees no reason why the product of increased investment cannot be disposed of within the system in which the investment takes place, which is normally an international system in which national boundaries are fairly meaningful, but not for separating net buyers from net sellers. He also sees in the underdeveloped and poverty-stricken areas, which were the objects of imperialism of the nineteenth and early twentieth centuries, relatively poor markets for the products of a highly industrialized society. They rarely have enough to sell to acquire the needed foreign exchange. He knows also that normally it is not necessary to possess or dominate politically the sources of raw materials in order to have economic access to those materials, a fact that may have nothing to do with the underconsumption theory but which touches on the other main reason for the alleged economic benefit of colonies. By far the greater quantity of international trade has always taken place *among* the more developed countries, which provide markets for each other. Whatever distortions to normal international trade formerly obtained as a result of "imperial preference" tariff arrangements and the like did not seriously modify the proposition just stated. They happened, incidentally, most often to benefit the colonial dependency at the cost of the mother country.[7]

Before we consider further the historical proof on either side of the argument, we should take account of another school that depends entirely on the same data and which we shall call the neo-Marxian or "scandal school" theory of war causation.

The Scandal School (Neo-Marxian) Theories

Marx and his more orthodox followers, despite some individual differences in their views, sought the cause of imperialist wars in the institution of capitalism itself, and not in the personally sinister behavior of a few of its practitioners. In doing so they engaged in a kind of theoretical analysis that had occasionally the power of being intellectually impressive. Although the modern economist cannot salvage much of value from *Das Kapital,* he has to acknowledge that in the history of economic theory it was in some respects ahead of its time. We come now to a quite different school of advocates, who as a rule do not regard themselves as Communist at all and whose "theorizing" on the economic causes of war

---

[7] Similarly, the preference in its tariff schedule that the United States used to give to Cuban sugar had the result of providing Cuba with an American subsidy that was important to its economy.

is on a much lower intellectual level. They have engaged simply in a hunt for a quite special kind of scapegoat. They have rejected the notion that stupidity or chauvinism or individual psychological quirks or wrong-headed ideologies among substantial numbers of people may have accounted for most of the wars of modern times. Instead they have put the blame entirely on one emotion, that of personal greed, and have shifted primary guilt from the institution of capitalism to the individual capitalist. The latter has to be rich enough to be extremely influential politically and corrupt enough to use his political influence to advance his own profit at whatever cost to the nation.

On the theoretical level there is nothing much beyond the assumption or allegation not only that people exist who combine the requisite wealth and greed—certainly a tenable notion—but also that these people have managed through cunning and the use of their wealth to get the state so thoroughly involved in furthering their ends as frequently to risk war for their sake and occasionally to get involved in it. This process must apply also to the greatest of wars, like World War I. The second half of this assumption is a good deal harder to swallow than the first, especially because the theory implies *that there can be no other cause of comparable importance*. Actually, it would be alarming enough if we found even an occasional war in which the syndrome of personal greed and high political influence was the primary causative factor, and it would not even have to be a big war to warrant serious therapeutic attention. But one would then have to acknowledge other causative factors as at least equally important for other wars, and even more generally present, which is more than the neo-Marxian or scandal school can accept. Their own special view would suffer too much depreciation thereby. Obviously, the theory is entirely an historical one and can be tested only by an appeal to history.

There were those who professed to find exactly the proof that was necessary. Some, writing before World War I, like the Englishmen J. A. Hobson and H. N. Brailsford, and a host of writers following that war, including H. E. Barnes, Charles Beard, Harold J. Laski, P. T. Moon, Walter Millis, and Bertrand Russell presented cases that fell into a classic pattern. It ran about as follows: One or more capitalists would invest heavily in some backward area to exploit natives and create markets or to get a corner on some valuable raw material resource, and when they encountered the competition of foreign capitalists they would induce their government to support them and their venture by direct diplomatic intervention. The foreign entrepreneurs would naturally do the same, and the result would be a confrontation between governments. As Harold Laski put it in a chapter entitled "The Economic Foundation of Peace": "Men have sought a specially profitable source of investment. They have been able to utilize their government to protect their interest; and, in the last analysis, the government becomes so identified with the investor, that an attack on his profit is equated with a threat to the national honor. In those circumstances the armed forces of the state are, in fact, the weapon he employs to guarantee his privilege." [8]

That phrase, "in the last analysis," as used in Laski's remark is performing its usual function of begging questions and jumping over big issues. *Why* the government should ever become "so identified with the investor" as Laski and others allege requires some explaining, especially for a large country whose government would have to be concerned with the interests of very many investors, including those whose investments were at home rather than abroad, and also with others besides investors. The passing reference to something being "equated with a threat to the national honor" is a fleeting acknowledgment of a noneconomic factor, that is, "national honor," performing a key role in the process of a nation going to war. One might ask therefore why the sociopsychological symbol of national honor is presumed always to be subordinate in importance to the economic motive that allegedly triggers it. One answer is that people will always insist on the superior importance of that which interests them most, and it is fitting that we deal with the economic interpretationists on their own terms. The first question, therefore is: are their historical examples valid?

The late distinguished Jacob Viner, then professor of economics at the University of Chicago, became suspicious of the fact that the same well-worn cases were adduced over and over again to prove the scandal-school interpretation of the chain reaction from private investment to national crisis.[9] Under Viner's guidance, one of his graduate students, Eugene Staley, began to look carefully into the facts surrounding each of the well-known cases. The resulting doctoral dissertation, later published as the landmark

---

[8] Laski's chapter was included in Leonard Woolf (ed.), *The Intelligent Man's Way to Prevent War* (London: Gollancz, 1933).

[9] See Jacob Viner, "Finance and Balance of Power Diplomacy," *The Southwestern Political and Social Science Quarterly*, Vol. 9, no. 4 (March 1929).

book, *War and the Private Investor*, produced evidence to show that almost invariably the real situation was an inversion of the alleged pattern.[10]

One famous case, for example, was the Yalu River dispute, which was generally acknowledged to have touched off the Russo-Japanese War of 1904–1905. Laski speaks thus of that affair: "The Russo-Japanese War was, in the last analysis, the outcome of an endeavour by a corrupt Government to defend the immense timber concessions in Manchuria of a little band of dubious courtiers." [11] Staley, relying on some of his own researches into the documents plus the scholarly investigations of the distinguished American historian, William L. Langer, concluded that the Laski interpretation put the cart before the horse.[12] "Actually," he says, "the 'economic' enterprise was set up in order to forward a policy of imperial expansion in the Far East that the group already favored, and far from shaping political events to insure private gain, the members seem to have cheerfully contemplated some economic loss for the attainment of their political objectives." [13] One should remember that having to protect the private investment of a national was at the turn of the century a far more respectable front for diplomatic and even military intervention than it would be today. But in the Yalu case it was indisputably a front.

A case that comes much closer to fitting the scandal interpretation but which nevertheless fails critically to do so, is that of the Mannesmann brothers, German manufacturers of steel products. In 1906 they became interested in some iron ore deposits in Morocco, which at that time the French government was moving to acquire as a protectorate. There had already been a serious crisis over the Kaiser's speech at Tangier in 1905 emphasizing the independence of the Sultan, and the international tension had resulted in the Algeciras Conference of 1906. The French continued with their "peaceful penetration," and several incidents aggravated the tension with Germany. Leading German statesmen then decided that Morocco was not worth a serious quarrel with France.

---

[10] Eugene Staley, *War and the Private Investor* (Chicago: University of Chicago Press, 1935; reissued, Howard Fertig, 1967).

[11] Quoted, from the same chapter in the Woolf book, by Staley, *War and the Private Investor*, p. 57 n.

[12] Staley consulted the original manuscript, in English, of Langer's work, published in German in *Europäische Gespräche* (Hamburg), vol. IV (June 1926), pp. 279–322.

[13] Staley, *War and the Private Investor*, p. 57.

The Kaiser wrote on a memorandum in 1908: "The wretched Morocco affair must be brought to a close, quickly and finally. Nothing can be done, Morocco will become French. So get out of the affair gracefully in order that we may at last end the friction with France, now, when great questions are at stake." The result of this new conciliatory policy was the Franco-German Accord signed in February 1909, in which Germany recognized the paramount political interests of France in Morocco while France agreed not to hamper German commercial and industrial activity there. One clause provided that the French and German governments would endeavor to induce those of their nationals interested in Morocco to engage in joint economic enterprises there.

The Mannesmanns had meanwhile been extremely active in pursuing their interests in Morocco. Prior to the accord with France, the German government looked benignly on the activities of the Mannesmanns, but when it became clear that such an understanding was in the offing, they urged the latter to come to terms with the international association called *Union des Mines Marocaines*, which already had about 20 per cent German representation including the Krupps. The Mannesmanns, however, showed themselves stubbornly incapable of reaching an agreement with anybody, and began to inspire in Germany newspaper propaganda demanding that the Foreign Office defend the validity of their claims, thereby causing grave concern to the already unpopular Bülow government. As Staley put it in his description of this affair: "There is always a certain section of the press in any country eager to wave the flag, to demand a strong foreign policy, and to accuse a government with scruples about international obligations of abandoning the national interests in favor of foreigners." [14] Staley's quoted statement, one should add, now seems somewhat dated. The chauvinist press he is describing is much less ferocious and influential than in the past.

In 1911 the French occupied Fez, and there was another Moroccan crisis when the Germans sent the gunboat *Panther* to Agadir. The German government, now headed by Bethmann-Hollweg, felt that the inflammatory pressure from the Pan-German press was being stimulated largely by the Mannesmanns. However, the 1911 crisis ended with a Franco-German convention on Morocco signed in November of that year, and immediately afterwards the

---

[14] Ibid., p. 190.

Mannesmann syndicate, realizing that Morocco was now definitely French, finally reached an agreement with *Union des Mines.*

We see in the Mannesmann case an industrial concern fulfilling all the prescriptions of the scandal-school approach. It used its money to stir up a domestic propaganda in its favor, and in so doing played upon the patriotic fervor of the Pan-German press and of the German people. An element critically missing, however, was the support of the German government. As soon as that government decided it wanted to settle the status of Morocco with the French, it sought to cope with and contain the pressure from the Mannesmanns. It urged them to reach an agreement with the French-led international cartel, and it lent its services to assist in the negotiations. It refused, however, to convert that assistance into any form of diplomatic pressure. One should also note that the Mannesmanns were playing on a patriotism endemic in Germany and in the German press, without which they could have got very little hearing at all. One must therefore ask why the patriotism should get a lower rating in the interpretation of the affair than the greed of the entrepreneurs.

We have not the space to deal here with the several other cases detailed by Staley and others, which interested readers can of course pursue by recourse to the appropriate books.[15]

Later on the emphasis fell on the munitions makers. Walter Millis's book, *The Road to War, 1914–1917* (1935), purported to explain the United States intervention in World War I primarily on the allegation that American munitions makers had committed themselves to heavy support of the Allies on a credit basis and had then induced the Wilson Administration to protect their loans by going to war in support of the Allies. Our American Ambassador to Great Britain, Walter Hines Page, was supposed to have played an especially important role on their behalf. We know that Page, who was indeed totally committed emotionally to the British cause, bombarded Wilson with letters urging American intervention. We also know that Wilson was quite aware of and disregarded entirely his ambassador's feelings.[16] Occasionally Page

---

[15] These include, beside Staley's and Robbins' books, William L. Langer, *The Diplomacy of Imperialism, 1890–1902* (New York: Random House, 1935; reissued by Knopf, 1951, 1968) and Herbert Feis, *Europe, the World's Banker, 1870–1914* (New Haven: Yale University Press, 1930).

[16] The standard work on Wilson and on his relations with Page is Arthur S. Link, *Woodrow Wilson and the Progressive Era, 1910–1917* (New York: Harper & Row, 1954); see also Link's biography *Wilson,* 5 vols. (Princeton: Princeton University Press, 1947–1965), especially vols. 3 and 4; and Link, *Wilson the Diplomatist* (Baltimore: Johns Hopkins Press, 1957), pp. 27, 50.

did use the economic argument, as an advocate will use any argument that he feels may impress those to whom he is appealing. There is no evidence or suggestion that he was in any way associated with those who had advanced credits to the Allies or that their interests had any special claims upon his concerns. He was simply intensely pro-British, and acted out his feelings; but his views were of no significance in bringing about the United States intervention.

Nevertheless, the myth that American munition makers had played a crucial part in bringing about American intervention in World War I stimulated in 1934 the inquiries of the committee headed by Senator Gerald Nye. The object was to avert American intervention in another war—one was then indeed already brewing—but perhaps the only tangible result was to induce the head of the Du Pont family to declare that the firm so long associated with his house would no longer engage in munitions manufacture of any kind, because he did not want to spend the rest of his life proving he had not caused the war that might soon come.

We may now understand why Lionel Robbins could quote and comment upon a statement by J. A. Hobson in the following manner: " 'Does anybody seriously suppose,' asks Mr. Hobson (seriously) , 'that a great war could be undertaken by any European State, or a great loan subscribed, if the house of Rothschild and its connections set their face against it?' To which one can only answer, ruefully, that many people might seriously suppose it." [17]

The works by Robbins, Staley, Langer, Feis, and Viner, all of which were published before the outbreak of World War II, effectively demolished for serious scholars the economic and especially the scandal-school theory of war causation. What effectively destroyed it for a larger audience—at least until its recent unfortunate revival with the term *military-industrial complex*—was the advent of Hitler and subsequently of World War II. Though Hitler was in the beginning described as the front man for a number of industrialists who were indeed silly enough to subscribe funds for the National Socialist Party (some of them later had to flee Germany), this interpretation was soon relegated to the place it deserved. The whole phenomenon of Hitler and of World War II simply did not fit the economic causation theories that had been so popular; and efforts to make them fit were too sadly ludicrous to all but the most ideologically dedicated. That might have been the end of the matter except that there is something in

---

[17] Robbins, *Economic Causes of War*, p. 58.

the human soul that demands scandal-tinged interpretations of serious events. Any theory of war causation that stresses economic interests has automatically an air of scandal about it. Thus, the remark of an outgoing President warning his countrymen to beware of a nefarious "complex" fell on ground that was all too fertile.

The Complex of the "Military-Industrial Complex"

Unlike most famous words that have appeared in Presidential speeches, those in the late President Eisenhower's valedictory address that have fixed the term *military-industrial complex* into the language are of known origin. We know not only who wrote the speech but also what that ghost writer had in mind when he used those words. What the President had in mind when he accepted the same words would be much more difficult to guess.

The speech writer was Dr. Malcolm C. Moos, who was later to become president of the University of Minnesota. In a published interview some years later he told how he had become impressed with the large number of military officers in the United States who upon retirement from the services had accepted lucrative jobs in various defense industries. According not only to Dr. Moos but also to the many who find this new scandal-school approach appealing, *it stands to reason* that all these former military officers in private industries dealing with the Pentagon must exercise an influence that can hardly be in the public interest. Witness, this school argues, the tremendous outlays that go into so-called "defense," the conspicuous waste attending those outlays with their chronic "cost overruns," our idiotic and terrible involvement in Vietnam, and so on. The connection of all this with the two thousand or more ex-officers in industry is not constantly reiterated; but the whole package is nevertheless deemed to smell of evil, of greed and undue profits, and all the rest.

The "it stands to reason" kind of nonlogic apparently derives its special appeal from the fact that greed is something we can all understand, though it is something we always attribute to others. Projection, using the word in its psychoanalytic sense, is at the root of demonology. Stupidity, which is at least as common as greed, is much harder for us to place at the root of things. Rarely discovering it in ourselves, we have little basis for projecting it onto others. Actually, greed is much more circumscribed in its effects, because by its very nature greed encroaches relatively soon upon the interests of others and thus arouses their opposition. But persons, institutions, military services, and other groupings can often be stupid together and happy in their common condition without arousing the least anxiety in anybody until wide boundaries are reached.

The matter of the ex-officers in industry can be quickly dismissed. Anyone with experience in the Pentagon knows that the power and influence of the most senior officer vanish into thin air at the moment of his retirement. However prestigious and important his role has been, it is finished. The retired officer does have some acquaintance with his immediate successors (whom he has perhaps brow-beaten in former days) and he understands organization charts. He has other lore of often inestimable value. But of influence in the services he has none, and he knows it. Anyway, he is competing with brother retired officers who represent rival firms. One might surmise that while he was still an officer his behavior was possibly swayed from the narrow path of duty by the dangling before his nose of a job-in-retirement. But in respect to what important decisions could he be swayed? No such decision is made without committee upon committee sitting upon it, and checking their decisions always with higher echelons. There is no doubt room for a useful sociological study of the ex-officer in industry. However, one does not have to prove zero influence or even zero bribery to dismiss the whole issue as simply unimportant. One merely has to demonstrate that other things are vastly more important.

Anyway, how can one attribute nefarious influence to any person or group without even asking oneself how and upon what that influence is exercised? These elementary questions are rarely raised. There could be several categories of influence, each with its own objectives. One such category, which properly concerns us most, would be United States foreign policy, especially with respect to military intervention abroad as in Vietnam. What special influence does the industrial side of the hyphenated complex have upon such an intervention as that in Vietnam? The answer is, unquestionably, none. There is not the slightest evidence that the people concerned ever tried to exercise such influence, and there is no reason to suppose they would have been permitted to do so had they tried.

The evidence is perforce negative, but it is overwhelming. We live in an age in which few secrets of government are not promptly exposed to the public in what Meg Greenfield has called the "kiss and tell" type of memoirs,[18] written by ex-Presidents themselves and by an array of persons who served them in one capacity or another, sometimes on a level of considerable intimacy. With special respect to Vietnam, we also have the spectacularly leaked *Pentagon Papers*, in three separate editions. In the whole large accumulation of all these writings, nothing is more telling than the total absence of any hint that industrial or financial enterprises influenced significant decisions of government with respect to intervention abroad.[19]

So far as other areas of influence are concerned, like the size of our military budget or the selection of weapons systems, we should first notice that the connection of such questions with the subject of this chapter is indirect and perhaps remote. The relationship of the proportion of GNP spent on defense to such issues as the probability of war or to the proclivity of the state to resort to war is a matter on which asseverations abound but on which informed, careful analysis is rare. Many factors, apart from the circumstances of international politics, intervene to determine the magnitudes of the figures, including simple habit. Sudden sharp changes are more significant than absolute levels; they are likely to reflect not so much intentions as expectations, which are only in very small part, if at all, self-fulfilling. The nations that went to war in 1914 were spending about 3 per cent of their proportionately much smaller GNPs on armaments as compared with a figure of 8 to 10 per cent for the United States and the Soviet Union in 1971. Yet that datum gives us absolutely no reason for assuming that in the latter case the nations involved had a higher expectation of going to war or that they were objectively more likely to do so.

---

[18] *"The Kiss and Tell Memoirs"* was the title of her review-article on Roger Hilsman's *To Move a Nation*, *The Reporter*, November 30, 1967.

[19] With respect to the unfortunate United States intervention in the Dominican Republic in May 1965, Theodore Draper, who would be quick to spot such influence if it were there, saw no evidence of U.S. industrial or financial influence, and apparently Juan Bosch agreed with him. See Draper's *The Dominican Intervention* (New York: Commentary, 1966); Juan Bosch, *Pentagonism: A Substitute for Imperialism* (New York: Grove Press, 1968); and Jerome Slater, *Intervention and Negotiation: The United States and the Dominican Revolution* (New York: Harper & Row, 1971).

However, it is worth saying in passing that in these matters, too —that is, the overall size of the military budget and the specific choices of weapons systems—the influence on national decisions of the *industrial* side of the well-known complex has been far less than legend seems bent on attributing to it. On the basis of available evidence I am tempted to say that that influence is very close to zero, but it may reduce disbelief and take account of the possibility of extremely well-hidden evidence to settle for the idea that it is merely small. I trust that readers are not much concerned with the difference between "small" and "zero." [20]

To talk about the influence of the *military* on American policy-making in the security area, on the other hand, is to talk about something important, very important. The military may at a particular moment have common interests with particular segments of industry, as when the United States Air Force and North American Aviation (later to become North American Rockwell) had a common interest in adopting as a major strategic weapon the supersonic bomber known as the B-70 (or RB-70). However, in successfully opposing its adoption, Secretary of Defense Robert S. McNamara was not troubled by the considerable advertising propaganda and the desires and political influence of North American. It was the furious desire of the Air Force to have that aircraft that made the struggle so intense and that cost the Secretary some blood. If the interests of the Air Force and North American coincided, we ought to be clear which was the dog and which was

---

[20] I am basing these remarks in part on my own experience of over fifteen years with the RAND Corporation, whose primary role was in advising the U.S. Air Force on the selection of weapons systems. That period included some service in the Pentagon and numerous conversations with persons much closer to the business side of defense contracts than myself. If there was large-scale chicanery unknown to me, it was a better kept secret than any other I have encountered. There has been a spate of books alleging the contrary, including one by Senator William Proxmire, *Report from Wasteland: America's Military-Industrial Complex* (New York: Praeger, 1970), but all of them including Proxmire's *presume* chicanery and sordid dealings because of cost overruns and the like, which the military services are even more anxious than the companies involved to keep hidden from the public. If bad judgment and waste on the part of the military are scandalous, then there is plenty of scandal to talk about, but it is not the kind that fits the popular stereotype. Professor J. Kenneth Galbraith has also in some of his *Harper's* articles made general allegations about industrial "influence," even insinuating that some firms have used the services of appropriate female professionals for sexual seduction of buyers, but if he could prove that it really happened he would still have to prove that the investment in the ladies was not wasted on the part of the companies who put up the money. I regard these unspecified charges as representing the irresponsible side of Galbraith, whose work I otherwise greatly admire.

the tail, and in terms of relative influence it was a pretty truncated tail.

But even with respect to the military, one has to ask: What gives them their importance? They have not always had it in American affairs; in fact, they have had it only since World War II. Here at last we come to the crux of the matter—the militarization of the thinking of the American political leadership as a result of the shibboleths of the cold war and of the new-found eminence of the United States as "leader of the free world." The United States is still not a militaristic country in the sense defined in Chapter 2.[21] However, the influence on both foreign and domestic politics, not so much of military leaders themselves (though that is great enough) but of militarily oriented civilians in the bureaucracies and in high political office, has been vastly greater since World War II than ever before in United States history. If one wants to talk about the military-industrial complex, that is the issue to concentrate on. The "industrial" part of the hyphenation is totally misleading if it gives the impression that the two parts are comparable in influence.

We hear frequently about the inordinate profits of the defense industries, but one of the greatest of them, Lockheed Aircraft, has recently been saved from bankruptcy by a credit backup of $250 million voted by Congress in August 1971 by the narrowest of margins. The value of its stock had meanwhile fallen to about one tenth its level of two years earlier. Others among the larger defense firms, especially those having to do with aeronautics or space vehicles, have also fallen on lean days. Boeing considered itself in relatively good health, but its stock had declined from 112 in 1967 to 12 in 1970. Lockheed's troubles no doubt had something to do with its commercial venture, the L-1011, but it is in the government's interests as well as their own that the defense industries diversify their work and continue to develop their commercial operations. Most of Lockheed's troubles were directly traceable to the heavy penalties it incurred with the large C-5A military transport of cost-overrun fame, on which it suffered a loss of some $200 million, and with the Cheyenne helicopter developed for the Army. General Dynamics did not find great joy in its F-111 fighter contract, and some of its subcontractors suffered heavy losses from it. Boeing, which spent $25 million bidding unsuccess-

---

[21] See p. 31.

fully for that contract (the money going mostly into preliminary design of an alternative model, complete with blue-prints) undoubtedly accounted itself lucky in having lost. Later Grumman admitted to losing money heavily on its F-14 contract, which it insisted it could not fulfil without renegotiation and a steep price increase. These are among the largest of the United States defense contractors.

Obviously, the story cannot be one of unalleviated misfortune for companies engaged in making armaments to government contract. For aircraft builders especially there are vital interconnections between military and commercial work. Companies bid for defense contracts because they expect to find the work profitable and often do find it so. But there is another side to the coin; as a way of making money, dealing with the government is not necessarily better and may sometimes be worse than dealing with other kinds of consumers. It is a case of a single consumer (monopsony) with what are virtually captive suppliers. The frequent collusion of the military with the suppliers is usually due to their desire to protect the latter and keep them alive against the hard crunch of the government's monopsony position.[22]

In 1969–1970 the American stock exchanges saw their worst bear market in forty years, and this with an ongoing war in Vietnam that had not yet begun appreciably to wind down. During most of the period of our large participation in Vietnam, stock prices had consistently risen with hopes of peace and as consistently fallen when these hopes were dashed. The most precipitate and deepest fall took place during the Cambodian invasion of April-May 1970. The major defense industries tended to fall more sharply than most, and did not recover nearly as well. Peace is bullish, as it has always been, with but few and easily explained exceptions. All this may not even be important, but how can it be so consistently ignored?

American industries are certainly not without interest in and influence upon certain United States foreign policies. The whole area of foreign trade is obviously one in which many of them have an active interest. However, the war-inducing aspects of even the most restrictive trade policies are too easily exaggerated, though it

---

[22] This situation is carefully analyzed in the Ph.D. dissertation by H. T. Spiro, *Optimal Organization of the Military Hardware Industry*, U.C.L.A. School of Business Administration, March 1972.

is possible to find examples where they have worsened a bad situation. The developing bellicosity of Japan in the 1930's possibly had something to do with protectionist policies abroad, especially in the United States. The embargo on oil and scrap iron imposed by President Franklin D. Roosevelt in July 1940 had a fateful effect on Japanese decision-making from that point onward, though the act was motivated entirely and patently by political and not by commercial considerations.[23] The resurgence of protectionist practices in and pressures from the United States in 1971 and 1972 has been deeply resented in Japan, though the latter country is not without blame for its own protectionism, but these matters have nothing to do with war.

The Special Case of Oil

The special influence, however, of the powerful American petroleum industry is interesting and marginally relevant, not because it has anything to do with causing wars but because it provides an example of an economic interest being advanced by an argument that makes appeal to alleged national defense interests. It is not a unique example of its kind, but in its magnitude it is an outstanding one and therefore warrants a short digression.

The petroleum industry of the United States is loosely divided into the "internationals" and the "independents," the former being companies with large interests in foreign wells, and the latter those whose major commitment has been to oil exploration and exploitation within the continental United States. The internationals could normally be expected to be interested in freer trade for the United States, but because most of their Middle Eastern oil is marketed in Europe anyway, and also because they wish to get along with the independents in the home market, where they carry on many of the same operations, they have not seriously objected to the oil import restrictions favored by the latter. The independents, however—and the term includes some huge companies—have based their success on those restrictions, which take

---

[23] The oil embargo especially put the Japanese in a position where their supplies of liquid fuel for military use were steadily declining. This put them under the constraint of having only a limited time in which to secure a diplomatic rather than a military solution in their negotiations with the United States. By November–December 1941 they felt they could wait no longer. See Robert J. C. Butow, *Tojo and the Coming of the War* (Princeton: Princeton University Press, 1961; reissued, Stanford University Press, 1969); and Herbert Feis, *The Road to Pearl Harbor* (Princeton: Princeton University Press, 1950; reprinted 1971). In both books consult the index references under "oil."

the form both of tariffs and of quotas, the latter having been the more significant until lifted by President Nixon in 1973.

At the close of World War II it was clear that the Middle East was about to displace the United States as the major oil producing area of the world and that its potential reserves were far richer than any in this country. The American independents argued, however, that in another major war the United States military forces would again be heavily dependent on petroleum products and that it was therefore imperative to safeguard a supply that lay within American home territories. In a world that knew nuclear weapons this argument was already somewhat dubious, but more immediately questionable was the manner in which the independents proposed to maintain the domestic supply. In theory it could have been done by setting aside large domestic reserves that could have been thoroughly proved, with standby wells drilled and capped. The costs, possibly including some discreet subsidies, could have been charged off as a legitimate item of national defense expenditure.

However, the independents insisted that the *only* practicable way to assure a large domestic supply for the American armed forces was by vigorous exploitation of American oil fields stimulated by a large sale of the product, that is, by actually taking the oil out of the ground and selling it to American consumers. Only thus, they argued, could further exploration and drilling on American soil be encouraged. This meant boosting tariffs and later also imposing quotas on foreign oil, thus raising the price to the American consumer. The observation that it seemed odd to try to safeguard the American supply by using it up was scoffed at as simply naive.[24]

Now, a quarter century later, the results are in. Even with the recent Alaskan discoveries, the United States has been experiencing a sharply declining ratio of proved reserves to current production

---

[24] I am writing again from personal experience, this time as a reserve officer on the staff of the late James V. Forrestal, then Secretary of the Navy, during the last days of World War II. He asked me to prepare for him a paper on the future fuel supplies for the United States Navy. My research involved interviews with leaders of the American petroleum industry, especially among the independents. They unanimously argued the opinions I describe in the text. I subsequently published this paper under the title "Foreign Oil and American Security," Memorandum No. 23. The Yale Institute for International Studies, September 1947. See also the excellent volume by Robert Engler, *The Politics of Oil* (Chicago: University of Chicago Press, 1961; Phoenix paperback edition, 1967), especially chap. 9, "Private Profits and National Security."

—a situation quite different from that implied in the "national security" argument. Further domestic exploration is no longer commercially attractive except in off-shore areas, with their well-known aesthetic and spillage problems.

[The above paragraphs were written for the original printing of this book before the drastic rise in oil prices on the part of the formidable cartel known as the Organization of Petroleum Exporting Countries (OPEC). Though its new, some would say extortionate, pricing policies began with the "Yom Kippur War" of October 1973, the cartel includes several non-Arab states and clearly continues in being for economic rather than political interests. In any case, this catastrophic change in the international oil trading situation only intensifies the burden of the remarks above. When the cartel did not and could not exist, we wasted by forced domestic consumption the best resource for combatting it whenever it might threaten to develop. In the process the American consumer was being gulled at a rate estimated to be at the beginning of the '70's about $5 billion annually, because of the higher costs that always derive from protectionism. This industry-imposed tax was, however, destined to prove little enough compared to the extra costs that would follow the price explosion of 1973.

There is enough scandal in this story to satisfy all tastes, and there is much more to the tale than we can tell here. It is a scandal built on a totally specious strategic argument, on the part of an industry used to deploying huge sums for political leverage. In this combination it is also rather exceptional.]

The Tenacious Life of the Scandal Theories

In a book published in 1967 addressed to students of political science, a chapter entitled "The Cold Warrior's Story" presents first this lead quotation from Senator Clifford Case: "Secretary Rusk is no dope; why does he keep on saying this?" The chapter proper then opens with the following two paragraphs:

> One might ponder the official reasons Washington gives for our fighting in Vietnam, and think: These reasons are so bad that we must have fallen into the hands of fools. But one might also think: These reasons are so bad that there must be *other* reasons.
>
> The second thought is better.[25]

[25] Carl Oglesby and Richard Shaull, *Containment and Change* (New York: Macmillan, 1967), p. 7. Part I of this book, including the chapter and page cited, is by Oglesby.

What *is* the second thought, and *why* is it better? The author goes on, as he puts it, "to move the analytic focal point past the white lies of warfare politics into the ideological substrata where the less pious, more honest war reasons are embedded." These "more honest war reasons"—the "better" reasons of the introduction—naturally center on the economic greed of individuals whose will the United States government is bent on advancing. This is modern "realism," essentially unchanged over the past fifty or sixty years. It is impossible to think of the Secretary of State of the United States as a "dope" or a "fool" (or even to accept the same thought under less harsh words), but there is no problem at all in thinking of him as a knave—and incidentally as one whose knavery would also have to be quite foolish to take the form charged to him. But what grounds do we have in history for expecting a higher incidence of knavery than of foolishness? The words of the Baron Oxenstierne to his son in 1648 have been much quoted but they are still indispensable: "Always remember with how little wisdom the world is governed."

At this writing some five years have elapsed since the paragraphs quoted above were written, and a somewhat longer time since Senator Case's exclamation included therein. All the evidence that has accumulated since about why we went into Vietnam, including the notorious *Pentagon Papers*, reinforce the idea that Secretary Rusk really did mean what he was saying publicly to the consternation of Case and others. If that makes him a "dope," we can regret that the term is so inelegant—and we may regret much else besides. The same naturally goes for all the other officials included under the term *Washington,* whose official reasons for our fighting in Vietnam seemed to our author impossible of belief except under the equally impossible assumption that they were "fools."

Early in 1971 a Washington newsletter reported that the South Vietnamese government was on the verge of awarding seventeen offshore oil drilling leases, and the fat (or perhaps oil) was again in the fire. Senator J. William Fulbright addressed a letter of inquiry to the State Department which elicited the response (in two letters) that the South Vietnamese government had passed a law in the previous December authorizing exploration of its continental shelf by foreign petroleum companies, though it had not yet solicited bids for concessions. Only one American company, Standard Oil of New Jersey, had indicated any interest in such concessions. Meanwhile individuals and groups all over the country exploded in indignation over the "revelation" that American boys were dying for offshore oil! One group, called Another Mother for Peace, based in Beverly Hills, California, asked in its own newsletter: "Are the potentially rich oil leases off the coast of South Vietnam responsible for the Nixon's Administration's failure to get our sons out of Vietnam? . . . The Mothers want to know why there are 337,900 American troops in Vietnam. Are they being held there to secure the interests of Standard Oil of New Jersey, Union Oil of California, Gulf, and other American companies?" [26]

One has to notice again that the knavery, or rather monumental wickedness, which is charged or implied would also have to be conjoined with a monumental stupidity on the part of government to make the charge stick. *Why* should any administration undertake so grave a political burden for the sake of oil companies? We are not talking about mere import quotas. Campaign contributions? The thought is too preposterous. Foolishness or stupidity are rejected as possible explanations of our being in Vietnam *unless* a knavery can also be charged that makes the attendant stupidity truly gigantic. That has been the history of the scandal-school interpretation.

Secretary of State William P. Rogers asserted publicly on March 6, 1971 that possible oil deposits in the Vietnam area have "absolutely no effect on U.S. policy in Indochina." Former Undersecretary of State George W. Ball, whose credentials as a long-time opponent of our Vietnam venture were impeccable and by then well known, devoted his occasional column in a news magazine to refuting similar charges that had been made to him within recent weeks on three college campuses. His remarks are worth quoting in part:

> Just as someone once described Britain as an island founded on coal and surrounded by fish, Vietnam—these young men assure me—is a land founded on vast ore bodies and surrounded by oil. Thus our adventure in that wretched terrain of paddy and jungle—what General de Gaulle once described to me as "rotten country"—is not, they confidently assert, a misguided effort of containment, but instead a textbook example of economic imperialism, gunboat diplomacy and nineteenth-century-style filibustering.

---

[26] From article by Ernest Conine, *Los Angeles Times*, March 10, 1971.

When I have countered this thesis by declaring that in more than six years' involvement at the highest level of our government I never heard a whisper that America had a significant economic interest in Southeast Asia, my student interlocutors have regarded me with incredulity, *implying that I was either gullible or a tool of the interests*. . . . [Italics added.]

Obviously, all talk of vast reserves of copper, molybdenum and other valuable metals reposing in the subsoil of South Vietnam is moonshine. Yet it is bad luck that now, in this tenth year of our Vietnamese agony, the whole continental shelf of Southeast Asia should become the focus of an oil search. . . .[27]

We have recently had the emergence also of a revisionist interpretation of the origins of the cold war, led by William Appleman Williams and Gabriel Kolko, whose work another historian, Robert James Maddox, refers to as "abusing history." To the revisionists, President Harry Truman was not simply guilty of starting the cold war but of doing so conspiratorially for unworthy reasons, with the usually ascribed economic motives on top. One who remembers some of the post-World War I literature of the same sort may be pardoned a feeling of weariness that we must go through all this again.

There is no reason to suppose that public or even private economic interests have played *no* part in stimulating wars or in contributing significantly to other kinds of war causation. If one wants to include them under the rubric of "war," the American Indian Wars of the nineteenth century were undoubtedly stimulated in the main by the land-grabbing proclivities of the white squatter, and the Mexican War of 1846–1848 put the same kind of land-grabbing onto a public or national scale. This kind of land acquisition was different in style and purpose from the perennial contest for already settled territories that had long marked the struggles of Europe. Though the American Civil War was fought over the issue of seccession, there is no doubt that slavery was the primary source of the trouble and slavery was originally an economic issue—though by the time war came it was far indeed from being entirely or even mainly an economic issue; passions were much too inflamed for that. We could add considerably to

---

[27] George W. Ball, "An Oil Spill on Troubled Waters," *Newsweek*, May 3, 1971, p. 511.

the list, the more so as we go back in time to the seventeenth century and earlier, because economic causation, far from being characteristic of the capitalist era, seems much easier to identify in earlier times.

However, entirely unacceptable are notions such as that economic issues are a *more profound* cause of war than the issues or factors with which they may be associated, such as patriotism, or that they are more pervasively present than other factors, or more ingeniously and deeply hidden, or that one is necessarily gullible or a "tool of the interests" if he demonstrates in this area as tough-minded a concern for the evidence as he demonstrates in all other areas.[28] In short, economic causes of war are not more magical than other causes. Where they exist they are likely to be discoverable with a reasonable degree of investigation and do not need to be subsumed where the evidence tenaciously refuses to expose them. And concerning most wars of recent times, including those in which the United States has been engaged, our experience is that the harder one looks, the less one is likely to see economic causation or to be bemused by some bogus indication of it.

The Psychological Theories of War Causation

We have spoken of the strange persistence through the ages of something that changes and yet remains identifiable as war. To many this fact merely proves that there is something in human nature that requires war, or even loves war, or at any rate subtly accounts for it. On one level of assertion—for example, human nature is such as to make war possible—we are being merely truistic. However, before we go into a closer examination of these notions, we should remember that there have been some (though few) primitive cultures that do not practice or even know war. Even within our own nation-state culture there are states that for all practical purposes never engage in it—including some, like Denmark and Sweden, which were once warlike and are now no longer so. Even among the larger powers to whom war has been more "natural" there have been states that have gone without war

---

[28] One anthropologist, for example, says: "In essence, the paramount motive in civilized war is overtly economic or covertly economic through politics." He is contrasting civilized war with primitive war, and the latter he finds *not* to be especially marked by economic motive. Harry Holbert Turney-High, *Primitive War* (Columbia, S.C.: University of South Carolina Press, 1949), p. 169.

for quite long periods, forty or fifty years or more. Inasmuch as these all comprise people with presumably similar genes, whatever there is in human nature that makes war possible does not seem to compel it. Also, we should notice that where war exists it operates through many institutional and bureaucratic mechanisms that normally tend to filter out the elemental aspects of human nature. It is also obvious that other forms of human behavior comparable to war have sometimes existed for extremely long periods of time, only at last to disappear suddenly or at least to be modified out of recognizable relationship to the original custom —like the institution of duelling, with its elaborate and rigid codes. If duelling was an expression of human nature, it was confined to males and restricted mainly to the upper classes, but out of those classes it took a very heavy toll for many centuries.

Still, without certain emotional phenomena, war would be both impossible and inexplicable. Yet it is not easy to determine what these emotions are, how they are sustained, and how they interact with the relevant customs and institutions of the society. We have for example, "patriotism," which is supposed to be usually involved, but the character of patriotism varies enormously from person to person. In some it is a socially approved means of venting an underlying unconscious rage of sometimes pathological dimensions—what Samuel Johnson must have meant when he called patriotism "the last refuge of a scoundrel"—and in others simply a sense of identification, perhaps with some social implications of responsibility. Also, we know that people have operated well as soldiers of all ranks, including the very highest, who were foreigners to the countries they fought for and who therefore could hardly have been moved by patriotism.

War also seems to require a certain commitment to hostility or anger among the people engaged in it, this anger being directed at an object called the "enemy." But how are healthy and well-balanced people to sustain anger for three, four, or five years against an enemy with whom they may have had no personal encounter? And who is the enemy anyway? In World War II it could be simply "Germany," or "the Germans," or perhaps exclusively the Nazis, and maybe only Hitler. The Nazis were especially effective in helping to sustain anger in many of their opponents, particularly if the latter happened to be Jews (a minute minority among their enemies) or simply dedicated to democratic values and freedoms (still a minority, though no longer so small) . For peoples undergoing German occupation or being bombarded by German aircraft it might be easy to hate "Germans," or even that more nebulous abstraction called "Germany." But many of the people who carried on faithfully in the ranks of Germany's enemies did not feel personally threatened either by Nazi ideology or by German bombs. Very likely they did not feel much if any anger but were simply devoted to a project that captured other emotions—which could be victory for one's country, or at least avoidance of defeat.

The battlefield is always a conspicuously unhealthy place, and over the centuries much thought and care has gone into dealing with the omnipresent emotion of fear. Very different formulae have been effective. Frederick the Great thought it imperative but sufficient to drill the recruit into acting like an efficient automaton under fire and to make him fear his officers more than he did the enemy. Not flattering to the ideal of human dignity or bravery, but it worked. Napoleon relied more on theatrics. No general has been willing to dispense altogether with some variant of Frederick's formula, and much energy has therefore been devoted to conditioning men to obey their superiors unquestioningly. However, today the conditioning has been usually aimed at inducing various contraints besides fear of superiors, like pride in one's unit or in one's role, or concern with one's image in the eyes of one's comrades. All who have written on military leadership have also stressed the importance of soldiers having confidence in both their immediate superiors and in their higher commanders. But what is confidence? Is it merely a mental recognition of competence, or is it an emotional displacement of the feelings that the child feels toward the omnipotent but benign parent?

Anyway, it is useless to attempt to survey the numerous ways in which the crucially necessary psychological props are used at all levels of the command structure during wartime. In this chapter we are concerned with theories of war causation, which suggests that we are concerned primarily if not exclusively with pressures or inducements operating at the very top levels of political authority.

There is an old theory that governments have sometimes gone to war because of bellicose pressures from the populace. It is the kind of theory that so long as it is entertained at the top is bound to be to some modest degree self-fulfilling. Napoleon III declared war on Prussia in 1870 largely because he and especially his wife thought that a successful war was necessary for the survival of the dynasty. He quickly learned that where the dynasty is so shaky the penalties for a disastrous war are immediate and drastic; but how correct was he in his original supposition? Perhaps for nineteenth-century France he may not have been altogether wrong. Louis Philippe's unpopularity, leading to his overthrow in 1848, was supposed to have been due in part to his foreign policy being "dull." Nevertheless, it seems possible, even likely, that the desire for war often imputed to the populace during crises was always a myth. What were the tokens of that desire, and how was its intensity measured? At least since World War I, governments have generally acted on the supposition that the populace dreaded war. One can think of partial and qualified exceptions, like the "revolt" in the House of Commons against Prime Minister Neville Chamberlain in September 1939 when it appeared he might be reneging on his guarantee to aid invaded Poland. But the same House and the whole British people had frantically cheered the Munich Agreement of the previous October. Clearly the qualifications do not amount to much.

If the decisions for war are made at the top, then the role of propaganda, too, has to be minimized. Propaganda is a tool consciously used by governments, and they are not themselves often fooled by it. Anyway, governments that have opted to go to war generally believe in their cause, and they are able to persuade themselves as well as others that they can and must win. There are indeed and have always been critical misperceptions on the part of governments contemplating war. Professor Ralph K. White, a social psychologist, emphasizes six forms of misperception, deriving his schema especially from the confrontation of Austria with Serbia in 1914 but applying it also to other wars, especially that of Vietnam. One need merely name them to enable the reader to see that all of them are in varying degrees likely to be present in all war situations:

1. A diabolical enemy image.
2. A virile self-image.
3. A moral self-image.
4. Selective inattention.
5. Absence of empathy.
6. Military overconfidence.[29]

---

[29] Ralph K. White, *Nobody Wanted War* (New York: Doubleday, 1968; revised, Anchor Books, 1970), p. 10.

It is a good list, and our author in his book insightfully illuminates its application. Especially intriguing is the heading of "selective inattention." It was simply not possible for the leaders of the government that led Japan into war in 1941 to see that they lacked something pretty essential—a reasonably reliable plan for forcing a successful termination of the war they were about to begin! [30] Selective inattention is characteristic not only of governments deciding upon a war but also of individual persons making up their minds on any issue important to them. We can guess at one good reason for it—the influence of the unconscious parts of our psyches upon our motivation. That which we want deeply to do, we usually find good reason for doing—and miss seeing good reasons for refraining from doing it. If we are unable to see or fix our attention upon some negative consideration that is important and also obvious to others, it is because there is something within us that does not want the distraction. Governments are usually made up of like-minded persons who are likely to have deep empathy with each other even if they lack it for others. Empathy toward others, incidentally, especially if they be foreigners of a different culture, requires conscious effort, considerable knowledge, and an appropriate disposition, and this combination is likely to make the possessor suspect to fellow nationals who lack it. It is, of course, especially unpopular to show empathy for any people with whom the nation is at war.

However, though one desires to understand the usual deficiencies in thought processes that permit men, including sometimes able and brilliant men, to engage their countries in wars that are avoidable, bound to be extremely costly, and occasionally bound also to be disastrous, one senses the need also for some dynamism in the explanation. We have already spoken of "selective inattention" as probably being due to a desire to escape restraints upon what we deeply (that is, partly or wholly unconsciously) wish to do, or—to suggest the compulsion usually present in the process —something we *need* to do. The next and essential question is, what causes that desire or that need? Are there special psychological pressures that push governments toward war?

This brings us to the psychoanalysts, who offer us some theories that postulate such pressures, for these are almost by definition unconscious pressures. What is commonplace in the descriptions

---

[30] White's book does not review the case of Japan; my remarks are based on Butow's *Tojo and the Coming of the War.*

of the outbreak of wars in the twentieth century, wherever we have such descriptions in detail, is that the decision-makers seem not to want war and yet they opt for moves that bring it on. Their avowals of a preference for peace seem genuine, yet their actions clearly propel them in a direction that they say they dread. If one accepts that they are not simply lying—and even if they are one would still have to explain their wish for war—then we would appear to be in the presence of powerful unconscious motivations.

The exploration of the unconscious is the province of the psychoanalyst, who is given to comparing it with the submerged part of the iceberg. The unconscious is something that bulges and broods with memories, fantasies, and emotions that have been repressed from the conscious levels of our minds because for one reason or another they were unacceptable to consciousness. Repressed material is not available for being swayed by arguments of reason, which is one reason why so much of it remains operative that is basically infantile in origin. In the relatively healthy person the repressed emotions and fantasies are not seriously disturbing and therefore lack the dynamism to intrude markedly to compel irrational forms of behavior. We call someone neurotic, however, whose condition requires him to marshal all kinds of defenses to cope with emotions that while dynamic in their effects *continue to remain unconscious.*[31] The mode of coping may take all kinds of forms. One common example is called the "reaction formation." A type of reaction formation is seen in the person who copes with unusually high levels of unconscious rage by fitting himself into a demeanor, usually at heavy cost to himself in psychic energy, which projects pretty much the opposite of rage and which fools himself as well as others. Though he appears generally mild, well controlled, and perhaps even affable, the rage will have its way, either breaking through the defenses at critical moments or else expressing itself in focused but unreasoning hatreds and in otherwise inexplicable acts of malice. What I have here given simply as an example is obviously an exceptionally relevant one to any study of why people fight. I might add that the existence of this kind of reaction formation to mask as well as to control de-

---

[31] I stress with italics the reference to powerful emotions as well as fantasies remaining unconscious because this is the issue on which the layman who has not had direct experience with psychoanalysis usually displays the most skepticism. He finds it difficult or impossible to believe that there is a part of his psyche that powerfully guides his thoughts and emotions and yet is normally inaccessible to conscious scrutiny.

structive passions seething under the surface is much more common than the layman suspects.[32]

Freud himself was rather diffident about his own ability, and presumably that of psychoanalysis generally, to contribute anything very special about our knowledge of why men fight wars. In his "Thoughts for the Times on War and Death," contributed in 1915, when his native Austria was desperately engaged in a war in which his own two sons were officers, he speaks first of the "disillusionment" that the war had brought. "We had permitted ourselves," he says, "to have higher hopes." The two things in the ongoing war that had evoked his sense of disillusionment were, first, "the destitution shown in moral relations externally by the states which in their interior relations pose as the guardians of accepted moral usage," and second, "the brutality in behavior shown by individuals, whom, as partakers in the highest form of human civilization, one would not have credited with such a thing." But, characteristically, Freud points out that disillusionment is simply "the destruction of—an illusion." Hence, it is something to be welcomed.

"The state," Freud says, "has forbidden to the individual the practice of wrong-doing not because it desired to abolish it, but because it desires to monopolize it." And so far as the brutality is concerned, well, psychoanalysts should be the least surprised, for they know what lies underneath the transformations wrought by adaptation to society. In many, apparent goodness is merely a reaction formation. Those in whom civilizing transformations of instinct go deeper are still liable to being undone by the untoward experiences in life, and war apparently acts powerfully to induce regression.

Another symptom, Freud adds, that has astonished and shocked us is "the narrow-mindedness shown by the best intellects, their obduracy, their inaccessibility to the most forcible arguments,

---

[32] The symptoms are often visible to the person sensitized by appropriate experience or training, though he need not be a professional analyst. There is much confusion about what such an observer can or cannot notice or deduce in ordinary personal intercourse, especially if it be over a long period of time. The sensitized observer can often notice *symptoms* that would not appear as such to the untutored observer, and the former may also correctly guess what they betoken—repressed rage, for example, will show itself by fairly specific though often innocuous-looking manifestations. To get at the reasons for the rage and at all its ramifications in the total personality, however, and to get the patient himself to recognize the nature of his problems and to gain from the insight, will usually require a prolonged analysis, which should of course be conducted only by a thoroughly trained therapist.

their uncritical credulity for the most disputable assertions." But this phenomenon is even easier to account for.

Students of human nature and philosophers have long taught us that we are mistaken in regarding our intelligence as an independent force and in overlooking its dependence upon the emotional life. Our intelligence . . . can function reliably only when it is removed from the influences of strong emotional impulses; otherwise it behaves merely as an instrument of the will and delivers the inference which the will requires. Thus . . . logical arguments are impotent against affective interests, and that is why reasons, which in Falstaff's phrase are "as plenty as blackberries," produce so few victories in the conflict with interests. Psychoanalytic experience . . . daily shows that the shrewdest persons will all of a sudden behave like imbeciles as soon as the needful insight is confronted by an emotional resistance, but will completely regain their wonted acuity once that resistance has been overcome. The logical infatuations into which this war has deluded our fellow-citizens, many of them the best of their kind, are therefore a secondary phenomenon, a consequence of emotional excitement, and are destined, we may hope, to disappear with it.[33]

This is the civilized, sensitive Freud, who, however, is making no claim to originality or novelty in what he says here. It is a good expression of what we should know to be true even without his special insights. The remainder of this long essay is a disquisition on human attitudes toward death.

More famous among Freud's published thoughts on war was his open letter, published in 1932 under the title of "Why War?" (*Warum Krieg?*), in reply to Albert Einstein. However, it is a much emptier piece—surprisingly empty for Freud. He first expresses surprise that Einstein, in soliciting his views on a topic for open discussion, should choose this subject ("Why War?" thus has a double meaning). He then proceeds as though he were merely an intelligent, cultivated layman and not at all the great creator of a very special discipline that some would think highly relevant. He praises the League of Nations as an important and interesting

---

[33] Sigmund Freud, *Collected Papers*, trans. by Joan Riviere (London: Hogarth Press, 1948), vol. IV, pp. 288–317.

experiment, and warms to his subject only when he asks why people like Einstein and himself should even concern themselves with war rather than take it for granted along with many other evils that are man's lot in life. Toward the end he says: "The result, as you see, is not very fruitful when an unworldly theoretician is called in to advise on an urgent practical problem." [34] It is a justified modesty. One wonders whether it is Freud the physician and therapist speaking, who could not get greatly interested in something he felt he could do nothing about. Yet he had written insightfully on other subjects that were beyond manipulation by individual therapy.

Many of Freud's followers have been less reticent. Edward Glover, a British psychoanalyst, is known for his essays gathered and published under the title *War, Sadism and Pacifism*.[35] Here he erected no grandiose theories but made some contribution to showing how some manifestations of what we normally call group psychology, especially in matters having to do with war, are more explicable in terms of what we know about depth psychology of the individual. Another British psychoanalyst, Roger E. Money-Kyrle has done much the same sort of thing in his *Psychoanalysis and Politics* based on extended interviews with German Nazis following World War II.[36] However, there have been others of somewhat more vaulting ambition.

A theory much favored by some psychoanalysts directs attention not to the specific neuroses of individuals but rather to the universal instinctual drive known as "aggression." The psychoanalyst speaks of "normal" aggressive instincts and of appropriate expression thereof, implying that marked deviations in either direction, that is, toward excessive passivity as well as toward excessive aggressiveness, are equally indicative of disturbed ego functioning.

Dr. Konrad Lorenz, the well-known Austrian student of animal behavior, has presented in his *On Aggression* a key book on the subject from the biologist's point of view. Though not a psychoanalyst himself, Lorenz acknowledges his indebtedness to the guild, which in turn treats him with great respect. In his book he explores various kinds of animal aggressiveness, and professes to

---

[34] *Collected Papers*, vol. V (1950, James Strachey, ed.), pp. 273–287.

[35] E. Glover, *War, Sadism and Pacifism: Further Essays on Group Psychology and War* (London: Allen and Unwin, extended series 1946).

[36] R. E. Money-Kyrle, *Psychoanalysis and Politics* (London: Duckworth, 1951), see also his *Man's Picture of his World* (London: Duckworth, 1961).

find behavioral analogies in the human being, including and especially resort to war (though in characteristically Lorenzian form he finishes off with a chapter entitled "Avowal of Optimism"). The analysts, finding in their normal practice innumerable examples of what appear to be instinctual aggression, are disposed to be, with but few exceptions, sympathetic to Lorenz's views.[37]

A few analysts have recently come forth with a theory that throws heavy responsibility on something they call "filicide," which is the reciprocal of the well-known Oeidpus complex discovered by Freud. Where the Oedipus idea emphasizes the son's unconscious fear and hatred of the father, mostly because of his jealous love for the mother, filicide refers to the unconscious hatred of the father for the son, upon whom the former may displace feelings of jealousy and hostility felt at an earlier stage of life toward siblings and indeed even toward the father.[38] And what better way, they hold, of finding expression for filicide than by sending the youth out to die in a war? How often indeed has it been remarked that wars are made by the old for the young to die in!

In both these theories as well as in various others we could mention, we are dealing with phenomena that may indeed be very common or, as in the case of aggression, universal and necessary and thus important in influencing individual human behavior. That is not to say, however, that they carry us very far in explaining *war*, except perhaps in a way that we previously characterized as truistic—that is, "human nature is such as to make war possible." After all, we start out with that knowledge. If someone tells us that the Vietnam War is due to "aggression," meaning not aggression in the legal sense of one state or faction attacking another but rather unconscious aggressive drives on the part of American

---

[37] Konrad Lorenz, *On Aggression*, trans. by Marjorie K. Wilson (New York: Harcourt, Brace & World, 1966; Bantam Books, 1969). An exceptional criticism of the Lorenzian view by a psychoanalyst is found in Robert Gorney, *The Human Agenda* (New York: Simon & Schuster, 1968, 1972), pp. 113 f. As Nathan Leites has pointed out in his *The New Ego* (New York: Science House, 1971), psychoanalysts are generally careless and loose in their terminology, and Gorney's conception of what constitutes "instinctual aggression" may be somewhat idiosyncratic.

[38] Dr. Arnaldo Rascovsky appears to be the leader in presenting this view. He has written two papers on the subject, both so far as I know not yet published. They are: "Towards the Understanding of the Unconscious Motivations of War," presented to the Conference on The Role and Relevance of Psychology in International Relations, Institute on the United Nations, New York, January 10, 1970; and (together with Matilde Rascovsky) "On Filicide." These papers were lent to me by Dr. Robert Dorn of Pacific Palisades, California.

policy-makers, he tells us little or nothing about the vastly complex situation that got us involved *there* rather than elsewhere; that got *us* involved and not the majority of our allies, who stayed aloof from it; and that subsequently turned hawks into doves at highly varying rates of conversion. If we read closely the history of any of several crises, we see that the decision that could have gone for war has sometimes gone for conciliation and peace, or, conversely, that the decision for war, or for escalation as in Vietnam, has often been made most reluctantly and in obedience to convictions that owed more to outworn axioms than to emotions. We know indeed that things are not necessarily what they seem, and it is especially the psychoanalyst who sensitizes us to that understanding and who deals with it in his work. Nevertheless, it is always necessary to start out with the historical facts of any crisis as best we can—something that the therapist absorbed in his clinical work rarely has the time to do—and then see how far our overall sophistication, certainly including our psychological sophistication, can go in helping us to understand and explain them.

Human emotions, including and especially repressed emotions, make up a vitally important part of the reasons why men resort to war or, being in an obviously unprofitable war, find it so difficult to withdraw from its clutches. Emotions enormously affect perception as well as decisions and behavior, and they certainly affect the degree of rigidity we show about any of these. No doubt there is a good deal of aggression in the normal human being, especially the male human being, and just as surely there is much repressed rage among various personalities who may rise to positions of influence and power. There can hardly be any doubt that these factors are involved in the genesis of wars and in accounting for the intensity and especially the persistence with which they are usually fought.

However, it should also be obvious that war has become a poor form of outlet for human aggression and rage. It has long been too dangerous and too costly, and the intended victim is too impersonal and remote. Such feelings are more suitably taken out on tangible, visible persons close at hand, especially if the latter have a significant relationship to oneself and if their means of retaliation are limited. Also, it is more satisfying not to have the intervention of enormous policy-oriented bureaucracies to overorganize the job, which is what happens in war.

One must be especially wary of drawing analogies from the aggressive behavior of animals. The study of animal behavior as compared with that of human beings has the advantages of simplicity and of frankness of exposure. Yet until one sees the counterpart in animal life of government bureaucracies, of customs and traditions by which foreign policy and other objectives are determined and pursued, and of the ability to predict easily certain gross consequences from the reciprocal use of such instruments as nuclear weapons, we are clearly mistaken in pressing analogies too far. Animals, after all, though they live, and kill, and die, do not seem to understand death.

It is also a simple fact that different political regimes do have conflicting objectives and interests, however foolishly or shrewdly those objectives and interests have been determined. Also, while the determination of the actors to pursue those interests even through war clearly draws power from the emotions, it also draws guidance from intellectual conviction. That conviction may reflect flawed rationality, but it is not necessarily irrational in the psychological sense. One need only consider, for example, the conviction of the late Chairman Ho Chi Minh and his followers that Vietnam ought to be unified under the control of himself and his party, and that of five American Presidents that in this objective he ought to be opposed. We indeed find in such fixity of purpose on both sides expressions of aggressiveness, but to say just that adds nothing to our knowledge of the situation beyond what we know when we say simply that on both sides resolute men were involved. The world would undoubtedly have been a more peaceful place if men were less resolute (or aggressive), but in that case we should probably also still be living in the stone age—if the race had managed to survive at all. In the Vietnam situation it may indeed add a dimension to our understanding to say that while each side showed a lack of empathy about the other's resolution, a number of relevant circumstances, including the fact that Hanoi felt an enormously greater stake in the business and hence was correspondingly more resolute, suggests that the *error of judgment* was critically greater on the side of Washington. When fleshed out with the appropriate factual material, such a statement may have guidance value for the future.

Psychological theories do not easily adjust to man's considerable adjustment to the enormous changes in the character of war that have taken place in modern times and especially over the last thirty years. Nuclear weapons have clearly made a critical difference in man's proclivity for war, because almost anyone has enough sense to know that the danger they pose is extreme. There are other factors of comparable influence, including man's experience with two world wars. The general assumption is that man is "too irrational"—or too much ridden with aggression—to take account of these things, but the closer we look the more we see that he does indeed take account of them. Just as nations like Denmark and Sweden became pacific where they were once warlike because they took account of changes in the circumstances surrounding them, so too the more recent experiences of the greater powers have made the people who govern them much more cautious than they once were. If the change in their behavior falls short of what circumstances appear to demand, the reason may be that it is not clear what they should do to change more. The fact that war has suddenly become more fearsome does not mean, for example, that we should immediately yield up to our opponents everything that has been or could become a bone of contention between them and us.

It is a pertinent question whether our having a better knowledge of what emotions, hidden or otherwise, are at work during wars and during crises that may lead to war would make the least difference in our handling of the next crisis that comes along. Very likely not, though we should still like to know, partly for the same reason that we spend enormous sums to learn the age of the universe. Also, it *may* help. The diffusion and vulgarization of the Freudian insights have already had an enormous impact on our society, and while some results may shock the Spiro Agnews among us as much as the vulgarization affronts the Freudian purists, the consequences seem to include among other good things a much greater tolerance for human aberrations. Phrases like: "What is he trying to prove?" have entered the language and have meaning to all people of more than a modicum of education. They suggest an awareness of hidden or unconscious motives at work less noble than those proclaimed, a skepticism that strikes directly at the kind of posturing that has caused some of the most trouble in the world.

Still, psychoanalysis is an abstruse science. The jargon is easy to acquire (and often profitless) but not the insights and the comprehension that enable one to sense fairly the inner springs of motivation or compulsion residing in the unconscious. On the other hand, having that competence is not in itself enough to warrant sovereign judgments about the nature of war and peace. Most professional psychoanalysts are simply babies in politics, and they are especially disadvantaged because it is hard for many of them to believe that there are aspects of human behavior that they do not understand. They are generally very busy people, and few of them have thus far invested the time and effort necessary to gain some feeling for the institutional side of international confrontations. From the other side, a few political scientists and historians have managed to acquire more than a bowing acquaintance with psychoanalysis, through the appropriate reading and training and perhaps also through having contributed substantially to the income of one or more analysts. A few even use it effectively in their work. But they are thus far very few, and they are not likely ever to be many.

Except for the appearance over the years of a few biographies and biographical sketches that demonstrate real psychoanalytic insight—and biography of political leaders is unquestionably the place for the most payoff in this area—we have advanced very little beyond the positions established by Harold D. Lasswell in the early and middle 1930s with his several brilliant monographs, beginning with *Psychopathology and Politics*.[39] In some ways we have even lost ground, because what was fashionable and forward-looking in that earlier day seems to many today to be dated and somewhat threadbare. Fashions change in the social sciences and in the writing of history. Today the sound of the computer is heard in the land, and psychopathology is a little passé. Not, of course, in the real world. Psychopathology abounds all around us, including the high councils of government, but it is always a question of what kind of data one wants to gather.

Political Theories of War Causation

Let us first define "political theories" of war causation as those theories that either explain war through emphasizing the dominant sway of some political tradition—like the pursuit of maintaining the "balance of power" —or that emphasize the absence of certain political manipulations which might reduce critically the

[39] H. D. Lasswell, *Psychopathology and Politics* (Chicago: University of Chicago Press, 1930; new edition, with "Afterthoughts by the Author," Viking Press, 1960); see also his *World Politics and Personal Insecurity* (New York: McGraw-Hill, 1935, Free Press paperback, 1965); and his *Power and Personality* (New York: Norton, 1948; Viking paperback, 1962). Among the few outstanding biographies of politically important persons written with benefit of true psychoanalytic insight, two are: Alexander L. George and Juliette L. George, *Woodrow Wilson and Colonel House: A Personality Study* (New York: John Day, 1956; Dover paperback, 1964), and Fawn M. Brodie, *Thaddeus Stevens, Scourge of the South* (New York: Norton, 1959, Norton paperback, 1966).

chances of war occurring. A generation ago, some political scientists like the late Professor Quincy Wright, then of the University of Chicago, used to make a distinction between fundamental causes of war and what they called "key" causes.[40] The latter were causes that could be manipulated, and that if manipulated would presumably reduce greatly the chances of war. For example, if one assumes that arms races are of substantial though not necessarily fundamental importance in causing war, then it is obviously desirable *and possible* to control them by international agreement. A more ambitious example is the perennially recurring proposal of "world government." Again, the organization of the world into independent nation-states does not have to be proved to be *the basic* reason for the existence of war; if we could manipulate the international system to reduce importantly the autonomy of these states, we could allegedly make resort to war well-nigh impossible. In other words, economic or psychological or other theories of war causation could be substantially correct and yet be irrelevant if they concentrate attention on factors that are not manipulable. Those factors that are manipulable and also effective in preventing war give us the keys we seek.

The idea of world government has had a sturdy appeal over the years and indeed over the centuries, inasmuch as some part of the notion was contained in the "Grand Design" of Henri IV's minister, the Duc de Sully, at the beginning of the seventeenth century. In our own time we have seen it wax exceedingly strong following the two great wars of our century, resulting in the founding of the League of Nations following World War I and of the United Nations after World War II. Both these institutions proved a disappointment respecting what they were mainly supposed to accomplish, which was to prevent war. Both were quickly rejected by those who would not settle for less than the real thing, which was a union of world peoples strongly enough knit to possess at the core either a monopoly of world military power or at least enough predominance of such power to be able to impose peace even on what would otherwise be the superpowers. The idea has made strange bedfellows. One may doubt, for example whether Drs. Edward Teller and Linus Pauling are agreed politically on anything except the necessity for world government. Clarence

---

[40] See Quincy Wright, *The Causes of War and the Conditions of Peace* (New York: Longmans, Green, 1935); also the same author's *A Study of War*, 2 vols. (Chicago: University of Chicago Press, 1942), vol. 2, chap. xix.

Streit has long been the hardiest member of the class, and no amount of failure seems to daunt him.

The most important weakness of world government is that, apart from a very few persons like those just mentioned, no one seems to want it. That is, no one seems willing even to begin paying the price for having it. Nor do I wish to imply that anyone should. There are good as well as bad reasons why people do not want world government. The world is full of a multitude of different peoples, and considering how imperfectly even the most fortunate of them succeed in governing themselves, which of them would be content to be ruled in important respects by others remote in space and understanding? Hearing or reading the speeches that go on in the United Nations General Assembly can be a sobering experience. One may be perfectly willing to have in the United Nations a place where the so-called emerging nations have a chance to express their views and yet be dubious of their ability to benefit Americans through exerting a greater influence on our affairs. Yet in order for a world government to be of use in preventing major war, we have to think of the supranational government having in the net a very large and persisting influence upon its subject peoples or nations. It is a myth to suppose that important military power can be handed over to an institution that exists solely for the purpose of possessing and controlling that power. It would have to have the means, at the very least, of *exacting* the resources for the maintenance of its power, which itself implies a good deal when the ramifications are thought through.

The political forces operating since World War II have been in the main working in the opposite direction, especially with the liquidation of the great colonial empires. The member states of the United Nations have about tripled in numbers since the founding of that organization, most of the new members being newly independent nations. The wars and imbroglios of our time continue to be mostly inspired by nationalism, whether they be wars of independence as the Vietnam War originally was and as it has continued to be in the eyes of Hanoi, and as the Algerian and Biafran wars were; or they have been attempts to unify by force artificially divided nations, as in Korea or in Vietnam as viewed from Seoul, Saigon, and Washington.

On the other hand, there has also been a good deal of important unifying going on in the world, much of it without benefit of formal organization. The borders between the nations of western

Europe certainly do not have the significance they once did. The European Economic Community, or Common Market, was designed to contribute to that end, but the accomplishment seems to have proceeded independently of that design. Nations that formerly considered themselves "natural enemies," like France and Germany between 1870 and 1945, or England and France before then for some 500 years, have reached a stage where war between them is virtually unthinkable. Certainly we see none of those nations—nor either of two others formerly considered "great powers," Italy and Japan—making the slightest degree of preparation for possible war against any within this group. They also are deeply reluctant to spend much on preparations for war against the opponents designated or implied in their respective alliance treaties with the United States, a fact that has for a long time bothered the successive administrations of this country, quite possibly through our inability to recognize a good thing when we see it.[41]

Political Causation Theories: Arms Races and Efforts at Control

Arms races as we have noted, are also often charged with being a primary cause of war. Such competitions sometimes *have* exacerbated an already tense political situation, which itself has usually been the primary cause of that competition. The arms rivalry be-

---

[41] Before World War II, and certainly before World War I, no one seemed to be worried about other nations not spending enough on armaments. Quite the contrary. One might assume that the change of heart that has come upon several nations formerly considered great powers might be a matter of rejoicing, but instead the United States under successive administrations has evinced a perennial gripe that our allies were not "pulling their weight." Most of this dissatisfaction stems from particular views that our allies simply do not share with us concerning common needs and common dangers. During the Kennedy and Johnson years it was the American view that our NATO partners ought strongly to build up their conventional forces, leaving the nuclear power to us. It was the view of most of those partners that this was nonsense—that there was no sufficient Soviet threat to warrant the large additional expenditures and expansion of conscription, and that if there were, it would be our nuclear arms rather than their conventional ones that would deter the Russians. On the other hand, our European allies, especially the Germans, have attached great value to the presence of American ground troops on the Continent for reasons that have nothing to do with the views just described. As a highly visible token of American commitment to their security, it represents something of very special value that they get at low cost, no cost, or possibly even economic gain, depending mostly on the character and scope of the "offset" agreements concerning purchases that may be operating at any particular time (they have been frequently renegotiated). That is not necessarily a sufficient reason for the United States to maintain its forces in Europe at present (1972) levels. These, with their dependents, have constituted a heavy burden on the U. S. balance of payments.

tween the Israelis and their Arab enemies has aroused anxieties on both sides, as does also the fear that one of them may acquire nuclear weapons. But no one could doubt that the anxieties and the hostilities would be there anyway.

Much the same, in varying degrees of hostility, has been true of historic arms races like the great naval competition between Germany and Great Britain prior to the outbreak of World War I —the "classic" arms race of modern times in the sense that present fears about such competitions derive largely from what is generally supposed to be the history of that episode and its aftermath. With its naval laws of 1898 and 1900, Germany embarked on a large battleship building program designed to achieve not naval equality with the British, let alone predominance, but rather a navy big enough (so the Germans thought) that the British would rather be allied to it or neutral than opposed. These laws and the ensuing program undoubtedly heightened British suspicions of German intentions and therefore had perhaps something to do with Britain's declining a German alliance and deciding to join the Entente Cordiale with France in 1904, which in 1907 with the Anglo-Russian understanding became the Triple Entente.[42] However, various other factors were more important, including a German diplomacy that rejected several British overtures for an understanding and showed an addiction for creating crises like those at Morocco. Moreover, the British had for several centuries manifested a special sensitivity to what they considered their absolute need for naval predominance—a need that had certainly not diminished with the great growth during the nineteenth century of British population and industry but not of farm products. At the time in question they had written into law (in 1889) the goal of the "two-power standard," that is, Britain must have a greater navy than the combined navies of any two powers that might be allied against her.

An insistence on naval supremacy might strike others as lacking a sense of equity, but for the British it was the *sine qua non* of national existence.[43] No Continental power was remotely as vul-

---

[42] A very revealing statement why the British should not conclude the preferred alliance with Germany comprises the secret memorandum by Francis Bertie, dated 27 October 1901. Kenneth Bourne, *The Foreign Policy of Victorian England, 1830–1902* (Oxford: Clarendon Press, 1970), pp. 464–469.

[43] British consciousness of the special utility of seapower as their first line of defense goes back very nearly a millennium. Even when the invasion of William of Normandy threatened, a fleet was kept mobilized to intercept him; but storms delayed William for a month and the Saxons released the men of their fleet for pickling meat, this being the season of provisioning. The last man to invade England and

nerable to the interruption of its sea communications (Germany had defeated France overwhelmingly in 1870–1871 despite having its sea communications cut off by the French Navy at the outset). Inasmuch as all of this was well known to the powers of Europe, the Germans were asking for trouble with the British unless they either curbed their naval aspirations or came to some understanding with them on the subject. This the proud Kaiser and his cohorts were unwilling to do, the last opportunity being the Haldane mission of 1912. Even so, the British knew they could outbuild the Germans on the seas, and they would rather have outbuilt them than fought them. When the British decision for war came in 1914, the German naval pressure had surely been a contributing cause, but it seems at the time not to have occupied the thoughts of the men in Asquith's cabinet. Questions of the balance of power in Europe and the guaranteed freedom of the Low Countries were uppermost in their minds.

Thus, the classic case was also a distinctive and exceptional case, and anyway it played no unique part in bringing Britain into the war against Germany. Armaments competitions, if they are really sharp enough to warrant the term *race*, are quite complex and variable in character, and the only generalization that applies to them all is that they are likely to be costly. In some cases the pace is forced mostly by the rate of technological change, of which one of the most spectacular historical examples is the period from about 1850 to 1906 concerning naval architecture. During that period the battleship went through a continuing metamorphosis that changed it from an all-wooden, unarmored, sail-driven vessel carrying smoothbore guns mounted broadside and firing roundshot, to an all-steel, heavily armored, steam-powered ship carrying a main battery of as many as ten 12-inch rifled guns mounted in revolving armored turrets (which describes the British *Dreadnought* of 1906) and capable of firing elongated steel shells with great ac-

---

fight a successful battle against the reigning king was the Earl of Richmond, who took the crown from Richard III at Bosworth Field (1485) to become Henry VII (William of Orange's landing in 1688 to displace James II was not resisted). However, the dominant English view in medieval and early modern times was that it was the sea itself, rather than superior seapower, that served England ". . . in the office of a wall, /Or as a moat defensive to a house . . ." (the lines which Shakespeare puts into the mouth of the dying Gaunt in *Richard II*). This view was not altogether naive because it would take a good many ships, and fair weather, to land a large hostile force on English shores. Modern British naval supremacy really began with the Commonwealth and with the Restoration of 1660 and lasted about three centuries. With the end of World War II, enough relevant conditions had changed to end the purpose and the feasibility of continued British supremacy on the seas.

curacy, range, and penetrating power. Most of the change took place over a period of about thirty-five years, and included experiments with quite bizarre models.[44] Nations that did not attempt to keep up technologically, like the United States for some twenty-five years following the Civil War, found themselves with navies that were hopelessly and even ludicrously obsolete.[45] At a time of such extremely rapid obsolescence, nations willing to enter the competition at all tried to stay abreast technologically, but had little inducement to build up large forces that would certainly soon be obsolete. For the main purpose of major warships has always been, at least until very recently, to fight enemy warships, and when they could no longer do so they had had their day.

There is only a superficial similarity between that situation and the missile-nuclear race following World War II. Weapons that do not have to fight their like do not become useless because of the advent of newer and superior types. They may still be formidable additions to the stockpile, until such time as they may be routinely replaced, with the fissionable materials reused. Thus, with nuclear weapons especially, there could be a meaningful competition in quantities even while there was an extremely fast rate of change in technology. The Russians seemed content not to push the pace until about 1965, when they embarked on a program showing determination to achieve something like parity with us in strategic nuclear weapons.

Unfortunately, such a program lends itself to all kinds of interpretations in the rival country, and those with a low threshold of alarm, like former Secretary of Defense Laird, became too readily certain that what the opponent intends is not "parity" but a "first-strike capability," a phrase of Herman Kahn's meaning an ability to overwhelm and destroy the opposing retaliatory force with a surprise attack, so that the deterrence value of that force is greatly diminished or eliminated. Others, including this writer, while accepting the need to be watchful and to maintain a secure retalia-

---

[44] For the story of this metamorphosis in the warship see my *Sea Power in the Machine Age* (Princeton: Princeton University Press, 1941, 1943; 2nd ed. reprinted by Greenwood Press, 1969), especially chap. 12.

[45] Somewhere in his autobiographical sketch, *From Sail to Steam* (Boston: Little, Brown, 1907), Alfred T. Mahan tells the following story from his experiences as a U.S. ship commander on the China station in the early 1880s. A group of French naval officers making a return courtesy call paused when they were leaving his wooden ship and gazed at the smooth-bore guns with which she was still armed. One of them quoted aloud the well-known line of François Villon: *Mais où sont les neiges d'antan?* ("But where are the snows of yesteryear?")

tory force, see a situation where very wide gyrations in force levels may have little real effect on the strategic balance. We did not treat the Russians with contempt when our numerical superiority over them in strategic and other nuclear forces was very large, nor should we expect them to treat us with contempt if they managed temporarily to gain an edge on us in numbers—unless they really did achieve that first-strike capability (or the illusion of having one) that seemed to give Mr. Laird such bad dreams. There is an additional cushion, though one we should not want to rely on excessively—that with the high force levels having existed for so long on the United States side, Messrs. Brezhnev and Kosygin, or their successors, could not be easily convinced by any group of technicians that it was now possible to strike at the United States with impunity and that they should accept the risk of trying it.

Anyway, the kind of nuclear race that was going on through the 1950s and 1960s could hardly be considered to be contributing to anyone's bellicosity. In the days of American nuclear monopoly, there was some small, politically unimportant following for the advocacy of "preventive war." But as soon as the Soviet Union began to develop a nuclear stockpile, that talk disappeared. The more both sides built up, the less possibility there was that either could achieve that first-strike capability which in any case would remain uncertifiable. Thus, the strategic situation between the Soviet Union and the United States became profoundly stable. Here is a case, in other words, of an arms competition producing stability rather than the reverse, and this was so closely recognized on both sides that according to one report, the United States government during the Kennedy Administration took the initiative in communicating to the Russians certain electronic techniques (called "PAL") for better central control of deployed weapons. More weapons on both sides meant higher costs, but not provocation or any other kind of enhanced disposition to go to war. Quite the contrary was the case.

What seemed by the beginning of the 1970s to threaten the upsetting of this comfortable regime was, first, the development of theretofore unexpected accuracy of aim in long-range offensive missiles, an accuracy that in time could no doubt be adapted to the MIRV (multiple, independently targeted reentry vehicle) system, and second, the development of what promised to be a technically satisfactory ABM (antiballistic missile) system. When an offensive missile—or rather its one or more nuclear warheads, each contained in a vehicle designed to tolerate reentry of the atmosphere in approaching target—becomes accurate enough, no underground silo that it is feasible to build is likely to provide protection for the missiles of the retaliatory force.[46] Thus we find raised anew the spectre of the enemy's achieving a real first-strike capability against one's own land-based missiles. For the United States there was also the still unthreatened and very powerful retaliatory force residing in the force of forty-one Polaris-type submarines, each carrying sixteen missiles; thirty-one of these had been or were being refitted with the Poseidon missile carrying ten MIRV-type warheads. This is in itself a tremendous force, amounting to over 5,000 warheads. Still, the submarine force was always considered a backstop force, an alternative means of doing that for which the Minuteman ICBM force was the main force, and it is always good with such high stakes to maintain an alternative. Besides, there is always the possibility that the submarine will become more easily detectable. Thus, while the threat to the Minuteman force might alarm some more than others, it was definitely not something to ignore.

At this point the ABM came forward as a method of coping, at least in some meaningful degree, with the new threat to the ICBM in its silo. Too expensive and too limited or uncertain in effectiveness to be a reliable means of protecting cities, it could if it lived up to the promise of its advocates be effective in providing significant help to silo-protected underground missiles.[47] So, too, would

---

[46] The cube-root law relates to the decay of blast effect, that is, the radius of any given overpressure expands with the power of the bomb only according to the cube root of that expansion of power; for a given intensity of thermal radiation the expansion of radius is according to the square root of the increase in radiation at the source. Because of this, an improvement of accuracy is likely to be much more important against a hard-point target than an increase in explosive power.

[47] A missile in an underground hardened silo is a "hard-point target" as compared with a city, which is sprawling and soft. The city is much harder to defend for a number of reasons, especially: (a) an attacker who wishes to destroy one or more important cities probably feels he can afford to expend a substantial number of bombs for each one, which may incidentally mean he can saturate the defenses, and (b) blast effects as low as 5 psi (pounds per square inch) can do great damage to city structures, as can thermal radiation over wide radii. Thus, accuracy is unimportant and all incoming missiles over a wide area have to be intercepted; only one or two penetrating the defenses will be enough to destroy each city. Missiles in underground silos, however, are relatively easy to defend, mainly for the following reasons: (a) the attacker has to be vitally concerned about the exchange ratio, that is the number of missiles fired by him in relation to number of missiles destroyed—because he is shooting at a large number of virtually identical targets, and what matters is the result not at any one site but overall; (b) to have a true first-strike capability the attacker must be able to count on getting a very high proportion, something approaching 100 per

be a vast further buildup of offensive missiles. Either way would, however, be quite expensive. And this is where we come to the questions of mutual disarmament and of arms control.

The history of *disarmament* by mutual, uncoerced agreement is extremely lean. The Washington Naval Armaments Treaty of 1922 is one of the very few instances in modern times where important implements of war, in this instance large warships either completed or under construction, were actually destroyed or converted under the terms of the treaty. The history of arms *limitation*, both quantitatively or qualitatively, is considerably richer. There are cases where nations agreed to avoid certain kinds of armaments altogether—usually because they considered them too heinous, and also insufficiently advantageous militarily to overcome the repugnance due to heinousness—and where, without necessarily cutting back on existing strength, they agreed to limit the number and power of weapons for the future. The same Washington Treaty of 1922 plus the London Naval Limitation Treaty of 1930 are examples, as are the various treaties of The Hague and of Geneva which have outlawed various weapons like dum-dum bullets or poison gases, and more recently the treaties of 1972 between the Soviet Union and the United States limiting strategic nuclear forces.

Much has been written about arms *control*—the overall concept that includes disarmament, arms limitation, and specific guidance of future development—and a good deal of it is enlightening and useful. However, it is remarkable how much confusion there can be even among experts on the appropriate *aims* of an arms control initiative. Theoretically, arms control by mutual agreement can be for the sake of (a) greater mutual security; (b) saving money on both sides; or (c) some combination of both. Most scholars who talk and write about arms control seem to be interested almost exclusively in (a), which happens to be far the most difficult objective to achieve.

There is sometimes a reasonable case for increasing mutual security by having *both* sides spend *more* money on certain types

---

cent, of the missiles he is aiming at; and (c) because of the hardened condition of the targets, the defender in controlling his ABM system needs to fire only at those incoming missiles that are following paths that would bring them close to the silos he is defending. Thus, in defending large cities like New York, Chicago, or Los Angeles, ability to inflict an attrition rate of, say, 80 per cent of incoming missiles (or reentry vehicles) could well be meaningless. In defending a large number of hard-point targets, however, such an attrition rate would normally be prohibitive for the attacker. See also pp. 389–392.

of weaponry or installations—for example, on better passive protection in silos of deployed retaliatory missiles. During the disarmament conferences held in the early 1930s under League of Nations auspices, there was long fruitless discussion on which weapons were primarily defensive and which primarily offensive. The answer usually is—as with the case of the tank, around which much of the discussion revolved—that any given instrument can be both, depending on how it is used strategically. Tanks later spearheaded the fateful German thrust through the Ardennes in 1940, but if the French had disposed of a properly concentrated armored reserve, it would have provided the best means for their cutting off the penetration and turning into a disaster for the Germans what became instead an overwhelming victory. Even fortifications can be offensive, if their purpose is to permit economizing on troops in one area so that more may be concentrated for offensive action elsewhere. Part of Hitler's preparations for his attack on Poland in 1939 involved fortification of Germany's western frontier facing France.

It is usually difficult enough for any group of experts on either side to agree among themselves on what kind of arms control would make for enhanced mutual security. Tanks, for example, may now be headed for obsolescence because, like combat aircraft, they are becoming rapidly more costly while effective antitank weapons appear that may be carried and operated by a very few soldiers or even one. It would be difficult to get free agreement among suitably expert persons within the United States on just how many of what kinds of tanks ought to be purchased. To get such an agreement within an international group with security as the criterion would be next to impossible. It would be easy to get agreement, however, that tanks are exceedingly expensive, from which it might follow that their number could be *arbitrarily* reduced.

Rival nations engaged in arms limitation conferences have usually brought massive suspicions to the conference table, some of which may have been justified. Whole-hearted dedication to the principle of arms reduction regardless of relative military advantage is not only unknown to negotiators but probably inappropriate. Each side must thus inspect very carefully the other's proposals. In addition there are suspicions that go much beyond what is justified (inevitably a subjective judgment) because the negotiators are surrounded by technical experts drawn from the groups, military and civilian, whose entire professional experience has usually conditioned them to be (a) the most desirous among their fellow citizens for greater military power for their own country; (b) more pessimistic than most about the chances of avoiding war; and (c) more than usually distrustful of the one or more nations representing the opposite party. There has also usually been the hawk contingent at home, ready to pounce upon any "give away" of military advantage, and often succeeding in making political capital out of their posture.

In the SALT (Strategic Arms Limitation Talks) endeavor between the Soviet Union and the United States most of the conditions just mentioned have certainly applied, except that the political attitude within the United States in 1971–1972 was such as to make almost any kind of agreement in the net a political advantage to the administration that could accomplish it. The combination of disillusionment with the Vietnam War and the discovery of vast new claims on the national budget for serious domestic needs had created a new mood of national impatience with the tremendous military budgets of the recent past—just at a time when the ABM was ripe for deployment. At the same time the Soviet Union was seen to be increasing its offensive power in ICBM's, too many of which, in Secretary Melvin R. Laird's estimation, were of the SS-9 type, which are supposed to carry 25-megaton warheads. Weapons of such power could have no purpose except to achieve what Secretary Laird at one time regarded as "unquestionably" the Soviet intention: to achieve a first-strike capability.[48] Meanwhile Soviet naval power had grown apace, while the needs of the Vietnam War had necessitated postponement of American naval shipbuilding programs.

---

[48] How it is known (if it is indeed known) that the SS-9 carries a warhead with an explosive power of 25 MT must be highly classified. But if true, the information helps confirm the intelligence that the Russians do not yet have a satisfactory MIRV. It would make more sense to have a large missile carry a number of separate warheads, whether or not independently targeted, than one huge warhead of 25 MT. A weapon of such size is presumed to be intended against underground missiles in silos only because it could hardly have any other conceivable use or purpose. A huge weapon makes up for inadequacies in accuracy, but because of the cube-root law mentioned in footnote 46 the exchange in efficacy is very much in favor of getting closer to the target. The cube-root of 25 is something just under 3. Thus, for a given distance from target, a 25 MT bomb will have about three times the blast or earth-shock effect of a 1 MT bomb. Naturally, as one approaches the limit of accuracy possible at any given state of the art, increases in explosive power become more meaningful. It should be added that if the estimate of deployment of SS-9s derives mostly from the size of the holes being dug (as seen from reconnaissance satellites), the deduction is most unreliable. The extra space could be for extra concrete in the silo.

The political, economic, and technological grounds for agreement on important strategic arms limitation agreements were thus unusually favorable. The extraordinary improvement of relations with the Soviet Union since the Cuban missile crisis of 1962 had survived the ouster of Khrushchev from power in the Soviet Union. At an early stage of this rapprochement it proved possible to reach agreement on the banning of nuclear tests in the atmosphere in order to limit radioactive pollution. The banning of underground tests failed because of the American insistence for on-site inspection—which represented the influence of the technical experts, who have continued to assert that cheating on underground tests is technically feasible. This failure, however, has not been particularly serious.[49] The worsening of relations between the Soviet Union and Communist China had also greatly increased the disposition of both to seek better relations with the United States, a reason that might not have been so favorable to significant success with SALT except that China represented so poor a member of the nuclear club.

On both sides the economic factor exerted an extraordinarily powerful coercion to reach agreements that could bring about large savings. The American ABM was poised for but had not yet begun massive deployment. The official estimates for ABM costs were high enough, but the familiar cost overrun was virtually inevitable. After making a maximum effort in 1969 and 1970 to secure congressional support of that deployment, and winning in the Senate by an exceedingly close margin in one test, the Nixon Administration found itself ending fiscal year 1971 with a deficit in the national budget of $23.2 billion, the second highest deficit since World War II, and looking into two successive fiscal years, which included the calendar year of a Presidential election, in which the deficit would certainly go higher.[50] Even with the ABM,

---

[49] The fact that underground testing was not prohibited in the same convention that prohibited atmospheric testing may prove a boon if underground nuclear explosions become a means of processing underground deposits of natural gas or oil shale. Some promising experiments have already been carried out in these matters. The ban against atmospheric testing affects only the United States, the Soviet Union, and the United Kingdom, inasmuch as China and France refused to sign the convention. However, the atmospheric testing thus far done by China and France is small compared to what was previously being done by the United States and the Soviet Union.

[50] President Nixon in 1969 threw his own maximum effort into getting a favorable vote in Congress for his proposed ABM deployment, and won in the Senate by only one vote. He made a second such effort the following year, though the vote was not so close. One of the reasons he gave for advocating the ABM authorization was that it would give him more leverage in the forthcoming SALT negotiations. The treaties of

additional measures could become necessary to restore the threatened security of the land-based retaliatory force. And there were those enormous naval shipbuilding programs waiting, as well as the programs for some new-generation combat aircraft, which, as the experience with the F-14 demonstrated anew, had now become devastatingly expensive.

On the technological side, the prospects were greatly favored by the fact that the American ABM had not yet been deployed (the Russians had deployed their inferior Golash system round Moscow and Leningrad, but this still represented a minor investment). It is always immeasurably easier to get agreement to refrain from proceeding with a deployment not yet seriously begun than it is to cut back on one that has been made.[51] The MIRV was mostly water over the dam. The United States had already begun to deploy it in its Poseidon and its Minuteman III missiles, and without close on-site inspection it would be almost impossible to police it. On the other hand, so long as the bogey of "first-strike capability" could be kept under control, mutual deterrence could be accomplished just as well with x number of missiles on each side as with $20x$, with x representing a figure considerably smaller than that already achieved on the American side. Nor was it essential to be finicky about parity, though gross inferiority would be unacceptable to a nation unused to it and not economically constrained to it.

Above all, the SALT negotiations and the resulting treaties concerned a kind of war that both sides knew they could not and

---

May 1972 did in fact limit ABM deployment, but left us with a force too small to be meaningful but large enough to be quite costly. We cannot now tell how much President Nixon was affected in these matters by the record-breaking peacetime budget deficits of fiscal years 1971 to 1973. He may have been persuaded for fiscal reasons to back away from original plans for much larger deployment. As a matter both of principle and of history, it has usually proved unwise to vote in programs that are justified not on their own merits but as bargaining tokens. We had some related experience in the years before 1933 when the United States was still a high-tariff country. Tariff increases voted in allegedly for bargaining purposes usually managed to remain on the books after the bargaining was over.

[51] This is a point that Dr. Donald Brennan of the Hudson Institute persistently ignores or rejects. In numerous articles he has advocated building up an extensive ABM system while maintaining at existing levels or cutting back our offensive missile strength—and doing so by agreement with the Soviet Union who could presumably be induced to do likewise. Whatever other merit his position has, the fact that the ABM system has at this writing scarcely begun to exist, unlike the ICBM system, would seem to be at least one powerful answer to his argument. Among his many articles on the subject see "New Thoughts on Missile Defense," *Bulletin of the Atomic Scientists*, vol. 23, no. 6 (June 1967).

must not fight. Just how pervasive and deep is this realization is always in question, and it is likely that the official negotiators and their technical advisors—and some powerfully placed officials in the Defense Department—were among the small minority whose professional preoccupations induce them to resist the message.[52] We are, to be sure, obliged to be concerned with the barest possibilities if their consequences are evil enough. However, we have not yet invented the device that will prevent the recognition of "bare possibility" (the usual phrase is: "It is conceivable") from graduating forthwith into "significant probability." To ponder military problems as a full-time occupation develops fixations, and we do pay people to ponder them. Even so, the situation is conspicuously and totally different from that of the Washington and London naval conferences after World War I, where the negotiators discussed armaments of which actual use in a future war was certainly well above the threshold of possibility, and was so regarded.

---

[52] After some paragraphs reporting that Chairman Leonid Brezhnev had stressed to visiting Canadian Prime Minister Pierre Trudeau his concern with the economic drain of maintaining massive forces in eastern Europe, a news magazine added the following: "A more ominous view of Russian intentions—and one that could influence U.S. attitudes in future negotiations—is suggested by the Defense Department. Dr. John Foster, the Pentagon's director of research and engineering, has embarked on a controversial campaign to persuade Congress that the Soviets are bent not on slowing the arms race but on stealing a march. Last summer, says Foster, he and his staff were able to 'crack the code' of the Soviet research budget. For the first time, they claimed, they could figure out—through estimates and conventional analysis—how much Russia spent on space and how much on military research. They discovered that since 1968 Moscow's military research budget has kept climbing—to around $10.5 billion at present, compared with just under $8 billion for the U.S. That means, says Foster, the Russians are rapidly erasing the U.S. technological lead. The result, says the Department of Defense, could be 'just the kind of situation that is potentially dangerous: across-the-board military technological surprises.'" Then the report continues: "Foster's critics—most notably the Washington-based Federation of American Scientists . . . —contend that he is engaged in "a classical numbers game featuring selective disclosure, questionable assumptions, misleading language, and alarmist non sequitur conclusions.'" *Time*, June 7, 1971, in section headed "The World."
It is always possible that Foster is right and his critics are wrong, but the critics are certainly correct in labeling some of his points *non sequiturs*, such as that a 10.5 to 8 ratio on what each side very loosely calls research must mean that the "Russians are rapidly erasing the U.S. technological lead." It is possible we are spending our research money more efficiently, as we are certainly spending it differently, and besides, with rigged Soviet exchange rates and other problems, it is easy to exaggerate how much American-money equivalent the Russians are spending on military research. Anyway, the point is not so much whether Foster is right or wrong in this particular instance, though his bias is evident; it is that there are always John Fosters around and in positions of influence when efforts are being made to achieve arms control agreements. Foster would of course not be making his statements publicly without the blessing of his chief, Secretary of Defense Melvin Laird.

The surprise attack or first-strike capability question must always be viewed in this special light. If such a capability were truly accomplished by the Soviet Union, or by both sides (or by us alone?), it would have to be regarded as potentially very dangerous. It *might* make possible during a severe crisis what ought otherwise be regarded for all practical purposes as not possible.[53] That is one reason why we must negotiate with caution. But it is entirely mischievous to treat first-strike capability as something *easy* of accomplishment, especially with the necessary confidence in success; or as being surely within the Soviet *intention* to accomplish; or as being markedly more likely to be *used* by the Russians than by us if either of us managed temporarily to accomplish it. Americans feel certain of their superior virtue, and are confident that if we alone had such a capability—as actually we did for a fairly long time, much longer than the four years that ended with the first Soviet nuclear weapon—we would not use it in a surprise attack. Perhaps we would be forced to think otherwise about ourselves if the Russians also had that capability. At any rate, many Americans tremble at the thought of what might happen if the Russians alone had it, even if briefly. That is a situation we have not lived with yet—one in which the Russians have the capability to knock out virtually our entire retaliatory force by surprise attack and still have large nuclear forces left.[54] In theory there is a certain logic of compulsion for attacking in such a situation —akin to the old preventive war argument, except that now it would be the Russians who had the capability and who would presumably be more responsive than ourselves to the compulsion. Thus, it is conceivable (!) that a nuclear lopsidedness of the kind postulated could become a uniquely direct cause of a war, which would proceed out of the fear: kill or be killed. It would be a war caused by an arms race in which one side stumbled and had to be destroyed by the other before it could recover.

We are nowhere near such a position technically, and should be able without undue difficulty to avoid it altogether. But it would be much more costly without the 1972 agreements, and hopefully

---

[53] I have argued elsewhere and at length, that unless one can wipe out the enemy's retaliatory force fully or nearly so with one's initial strike, *there is really no suitable target to strike at.* This is of course only one of the reasons for refraining from attack, but a sufficient one. See my *Escalation and the Nuclear Option* (Princeton: Princeton University Press, 1966), especially chaps. 1 and 4.

[54] Some would hold that Albert Wohlstetter was describing such a situation in his well-known article, "The Delicate Balance of Terror," *Foreign Affairs*, vol. 37, no. 2 (January 1959). But see pp. 379 f.

additional agreements. For without appropriate agreements we should probably have had to go into a very full deployment of ABM without knowing the upper limits of what "full" means, and we should have had to do other things besides. Thus, the first purpose of SALT and other international arms control negotiations has been to maintain security *at much lesser cost* than would otherwise be the case, which probably spells out somewhat differently from *improving security*. And scholars who are professionally interested in the problem must get over the childish notion that there is something unworthy about going after international arms control agreements for the sake of saving money.[55] Huge sums are at stake, and it is all too easy to think of good alternative uses for them.

I must not, however, end this discussion of arms races and arms control without bringing under challenge a common assumption to which I have already alluded. It is relevant not only to the subject in hand but to all of strategy, so long as our purpose is to relate strategy to politics, which means to the whole political and social environment. I speak of the frequently encountered assumption that the Russians (or Chinese) are barbarians whose capacity for duplicity and ruthlessness is limited only by their cunning, and that we are something very different, much more elevated in moral tone.

It is, not remarkably, the view most persistently and vigorously advanced by those among us who might themselves reasonably be classed as barbarians, which is to say by those who lack all understanding and sympathy for foreign cultures and feel no pain for the lack, and whose relevant judgments about Russians or other foreigners who are also Communists is guided exclusively by such shabby and shopworn axioms as that the "the death of millions of their own people means nothing to them." These people usually fall into a characteristic syndrome that combines stubborn, sometimes extreme, illiberality at home with a completely contrasting willingness to spend huge sums to advance our military power. Their vast hidden resources of hostile feelings they project onto the "enemy," so that literally nothing too ghastly is put beyond

---

[55] In speaking in 1971 to two conferences of professional scholars on the subject of arms control, I made the point each time that saving money is a legitimate and worthy goal of international arms control negotiations, and probably the most feasible one. Each time there was a patent sense of shock on the part of the audience. It was clear in each case that they were meeting for the sake of saving the world, not of merely saving money.

him. They are to a degree finally right, in that we have to bear in mind that in the ranks of the opponent, too, there are bound to be some of the same kind of people, one or more of whom could rise to commanding power (for the psychological basis for it has nothing to do with the difference between capitalism and Communism) .[56]

Such people on both sides are usually uninterested in arms control agreements with an opponent for whom their distrust is total. If obliged to go along, however, their interest shifts overwhelmingly to "safeguards," because they are convinced that the other side is using the negotiations to steal a vital march. Safeguards are indeed important, but unreasonable demands in this area can easily abort an important and genuinely safe agreement.

Whether with respect to arms control or otherwise, good strategy presumes good anthropology and sociology. Some of the greatest military blunders of all time have resulted from juvenile evaluations in this department. Napoleon despised the Russian as somewhat subhuman, as did Hitler after him, and in each case fate exacted a terrible penalty for that judgment. Ferdinand Foch, as a writer and teacher of strategy before World War I, argued that only a recklessly offensive strategy suited the French soldier, whom he considered by racial inheritance a superior soldier to the German and also filled with an irresistable élan that demanded fulfillment in charges with *l'arme blanche* (the bayonet).[57] The French must have been in the same kind of mental bind at Agincourt, but there at least they had great numerical superiority. Examples could be multiplied indefinitely.[58]

We know a good deal about the Russian people culturally, and we know much about the policies and behavior of the Soviet government. That is, there are people among us who know these things, and they are willing to share their knowledge. They are

---

[56] The syndrome described clearly reflects an unconscious desire to punish, which takes a different form in domestic affairs from what it does abroad, but the two forms are compatible. The same kind of desire or compulsion to punish would have to take a somewhat modified form under a Communist regime from what it does under a capitalist one, but it would not be a radical difference.

[57] Observations of this kind are scattered through Foch's book *The Principles of War*, trans. from the original Paris edition of 1903 by de Morinni (New York: Fly, 1918).

[58] This is not to suggest that cultural differences have no effect on the respective fighting qualities of opposing armies. For a sensitive analysis of the cultural reasons for the differences in fighting qualities between the Israeli and Arab armies, see [Israeli General] Y. Harkabi, "Basic Factors in the Arab Collapse During the Six Days War," *Orbis*, vol. II, no. 3 (Fall 1967).

also willing to be consulted in preparation for arms control talks, along with other kinds of experts. For Russian culture all of them seem to have the deepest respect, and often also affection, as in the case of George Kennan. The Soviet political system is of course another matter. Because of the secrecy and controls built into the system, they would have more latitude than we for contravening the terms of an arms control treaty. Still, Dr. Ellsbergs are rare even in this country, and the Russians do have problems with defectors. The difference is not between black and white. When some of our people dwell on the terrible dangers of that first-strike capability that they are sure the Russians are reaching for and possibly achieving, they are usually thinking of a Soviet leadership made up not of men belonging to and molded by a rich old civilization but of monsters. The possibility is there, to be sure. They have had a Stalin, though the people he seemed most willing to kill with abandon were his own.[59] We have also seen a deep revulsion from Stalin, and though the Brezhnev-Kosygin regime represents in some respects a retrograde step from Khrushchev, it is a long way indeed from being Stalinist.

At any rate, though one must always take into account worst possible cases ("It is conceivable . . ."), a total preoccupation with them develops an immobility akin to paralysis. George Kennan has said that "trust" plays no real part in diplomacy, and in the way in which he meant it he was quite right.[60] We properly expect negotiations on important issues to be tough-minded on both sides, and though agreements are worthless that are not entered into with mutual good faith, arrangements that may affect our survival demand safeguards. But, as Kennan also agrees, tough-mindedness does not exclude reasonableness. As he has more recently stated:

> The cultivation of the ideal military posture will always be in conflict with any serious effort to ease international political tensions. There is no conceivable agreement with the Soviet Union, even in the field of disarmament itself and all the more so in any field involving territorial questions, which

---

[59] The standard book on the subject of Stalin's purges is Robert Conquest, *The Great Terror* (New York: Macmillan, 1968).

[60] Kennan was writing in a period when there was much loose talk of making "gestures of good will" to the Russians in order to "show our trust" in them, and his argument was essentially one of hard reasoning opposed to sentiment. The paper (still unpublished, I believe), is entitled " 'Trust' as a Factor in International Relations," Yale Institute of International Studies, delivered on October 1, 1946, mimeo.

would not involve concessions in the military field and the acceptance of new risks disagreeable and shocking to Western military planners. The ideal military posture is simply the enemy of every political *détente* or compromise; and whoever is not prepared to make sacrifices and to accept risks in the military field should not lay claim to any serious desire to see world problems settled by any means short of war.[61]

Do the Russians negotiate with us on arms control with the *intention* of cheating? It may be, but it is most unlikely. If, ultimately, with the worst possible luck monsters do make their way to the top in the Russian camp, we are not without resources for our protection. An important violation of an arms control treaty is not accomplished overnight. It takes time to carry through, and it is usually detected. When the Germans, even before Hitler came to power, began their "secret" rearmament in violation of the Versailles Treaty, the British and French knew perfectly well what was going on. They did fail to take advantage of their knowledge, even after Hitler made the rearmament open. There are several reasons for that, one being that no Hitler had ever been seen before in modern times.

Other Political Causation Theories: The Balance of Power; Alliances

I have not thus far said much about theories putting the "balance-of-power" at the top among the political causes of war, partly because so much has been said about it elsewhere, including other parts of this book. Professor Hans Morgenthau among others has been very balance-of-power oriented, considering it at once the most enduring historic reason for great nations going to war and also the only legitimate reason, short of direct attack, for a nation like the United States doing so. His opposition to our military intervention in Vietnam, which started from the beginning of that intervention, is due to his rejection of the claims of successive administrations that balance-of-power considerations were indeed involved—for the whole concept behind the so-called domino theory is akin to a balance-of-power concept (we must fight the enemy before his continuing successful aggressions make him too strong for us).

The history of British diplomacy and warfare stands out for its

---

[61] George F. Kennan, "Disengagement Revisited," *Foreign Affairs*, vol. 37, no. 1 (January 1959), p. 199.

conspicuous commitment over some three centuries to the balance-of-power idea, but Britain was surely not alone in that respect. Proof of that lies in the ease with which she found allies on the Continent when some great conqueror like Napoleon threatened. The balance-of-power conception is essentially defensive; it calls for a resistance by anticipatory action to an unacceptable diminution of one's influence or even one's independence. The tradition provides a kind of trip-wire for response, and also a warning to parties who might trip it, because its existence and also its approximate sensitivity to provocation are generally well known. When Louis XIV decided in 1700 that he would let his younger grandson accept the vacant throne of Spain, he knew it meant war with a coalition of powers headed by England, for none of them would accept an ultimate union between France and Spain (Louis tried in the beginning to give his assurance that such a union would not result, and in the end his assurance was accepted). The durability of the balance-of-power motif illustrates the importance and indeed the dynamism of certain ideas and convictions, which, whether right or wrong in terms of their applicability in particular instances, show the influence of an intellectual medium within which the much advertised psychological or economic or other drives must work.

Much the same is true of the idea that the development of mutually hostile blocs or alliances may stimulate the outbreak of wars, or at least convert into large and terrible wars those that might otherwise be small. Like the fear of arms races, this fixation also owes much of its strength in recent times to a single case, though a very impressive one. It is the manner in which two opposing networks of alliances converted within a space of one week in 1914 a fracas between Austria-Hungary and Serbia into a war that engulfed almost all of Europe, and in another month also Japan. Thus it was that the assassination of an archduke touched off a world war. The United States, which had maintained its policy of "no entangling alliances" from the time of the formal abrogation in 1800 of its first alliance, with France, entered World War I in 1917 not as an ally of the European Allies but as an "associated power," which was not quite a difference in name only because the tie was limited to the war period. If we discount the United Nations as a military alliance, the first formal peacetime alliance entered into by the United States after 1800 was the North Atlantic Treaty of 1949, something of a record for a nation that for most of this time had unquestionably the status of "great power." It certainly would not have happened except for the geographical separation from Europe.

In any case, nations do not enter into alliances out of whim. They do so—at least in the case of defensive alliances, which comprise the great majority—because they feel that their security is at stake and that the alliance enhances that security. That applies to the larger members of the partnerships as well as the smaller ones, though perhaps with less acute feeling of need. The great power is not guaranteeing the small one out of charity but, usually, out of balance-of-power considerations. Thus, in 1914 Russia went to the aid of Serbia not out of the feeling that Serbians were brother Slavs—though the influence of sentiment can be too much discounted, and certainly it made valuable internal propaganda within Russia—but because there were besides Serbia other small Balkan powers, and Russia did not want to see further Austro-Hungarian aggrandisement go unchecked. Comparable considerations ruled all the other powers that shortly went to war. Each alliance had anticipated the situation that did in fact evolve, as though each of the member nations had said: "Under such and such circumstances we will *wish* to go to your support, and it would be mutually beneficial to us and salutary to others if we formalize that commitment in advance."

When the crisis came, few if any of the governments bound to the opposing alliances wanted to see that crisis develop into war (except for Germany and Austria *vis-à-vis* Serbia) , but when it did develop only one of them, which had soured on its alliance partners, looked for reasons for staying out and easily found them. This was Italy, member of the Triple Alliance with Germany and Austria. The British deliberated deeply and reminded the French that they had refrained from making hard and fast commitments to them except for limited naval undertakings. The commitment to Belgium was unequivocal, but it was, after all, seventy-five years old. If the British had not been intent on maintaining the balance-of-power in Europe, and if they had not had that old fixation about the independence of the Low Countries, they might well have agreed with the chancellor of Germany that a guarantee so antique was but a "scrap of paper."

Alliances are usually intended to have a deterrence value, and unquestionably they have often been successful in this respect. In the nature of things such successes can rarely be registered and counted. The United States went to war in June 1950 to support the South Koreans, but if she had been allied with them in advance and had announced that she would honor that commitment, instead of doing very nearly the opposite, it is hardly likely the North Koreans would have dared make their attack. Also, we would not have known of our deterrence success.

However, steps taken as positive measures of deterrence incur the risk that the intended deterrence will fail, as it did in 1914. When the British government guaranteed Poland in mid-1939 it was not intended primarily for deterrence. The British knew they had come to the end of the road with Hitler, and they wanted to shore up the Polish will to resist if attacked. But unquestionably there was also some consideration or hope of deterrence, especially in Prime Minister Neville Chamberlain's mind, and obviously it failed.

Another danger or at least marked inconvenience about alliances is that they may outlive their usefulness and still remain in being, either because the party of major responsibility does not sufficiently recognize that times have changed or because it is an embarrassment to call attention to the fact by requesting a formal abrogation of the treaty. Despite all its traumatic experiences in Vietnam, which have left the American people with no taste for further military adventures in southeast Asia, the United States remains formally committed through SEATO to guaranteeing the security of Thailand—after consultation with the other guarantors to be sure. Would it make such a commitment now? Certainly not. Yet it would be embarrassing to seek to withdraw from the Treaty through the formal one-year notice allowed for by its terms. Also, on the part of the United States there is a kind of etiquette about alliance-making that holds that the relevant treaty must always "be strengthened," not weakened, and this is reflected in some recent scholarly discussions on SEATO.[62]

At the annual meeting of the Ministerial Council of SEATO in June 1972, the American Secretary of State, William P. Rogers, thought it necessary to defend the organization against its detrac-

---

[62] See for example George Modelski's chapter on "SEATO," in Francis A. Beer (ed.), *Alliances: Latent War Communities in the Contemporary World,* (New York: Holt, Rinehart and Winston, 1970). He has a section in the symposium, entitled "Strengthening the Alliance," as though without doubt that this is what ought to be done with all alliances.

tors, among whom was the Foreign Secretary of the Philippines, Carlos P. Romulo. William Morrison, an opposition member of the Australian Parliament, ventured the opinion that that meeting would be the last. "No one will want to perpetuate the farce," he said. Pakistan and France had already ceased to participate, and other Asian countries besides Thailand and the Philippines would have nothing to do with it.[63]

Particularly overlaid with etiquette and mythology and in addition with a large permanent bureaucracy is NATO, the superstructure built onto the North Atlantic Treaty of 1949. Some are convinced that NATO played an enormous security role in the past and still has an important constructive function to perform; others think that its role in the past was indeed very great but that it seems to lack a mission today. Still another view is that we have always exaggerated the importance of NATO—that the Soviet Union never had the slightest intention of attacking westward, and that the security of the one threatened area, West Berlin, was accomplished not by NATO but by the presence in the city of the United States as an occupying power, along with Britain and France. The official French policy, formulated under President de Gaulle and thus far continued under his successor, is that the Treaty is useful and relatively cost-free but that the huge permanent organization created under its terms is useless, costly, and obnoxious.

The French view certainly has merit. The amount of diplomatic and military energy as well as money that the United States has poured into NATO is prodigious. It is true that the kind of international strategic and other military planning and coordinating that has gone on in NATO would not be possible without the permanent organization, but this benefit is limited by the fact that it is an international bureaucracy that is doing the planning and coordinating. The inertias built into such an organization can only be imagined by those who have not experienced them. The members of this bureaucracy, military and civilian, normally become entirely committed to the continuation of the organization. In addition, NATO presents a reason that many find unanswerable why the United States has to give financial support and military aid to a country with the unsavory political leadership of Greece, a country hardly less totalitarian on the right than the Soviet Union is on the left. For much the same reason the United

---

[63] The *New York Times*, June 28, 1972.

States has long supported Franco Spain, though it is not a member of NATO. What is thus lost in moral status may not be worth very much in the hard coin of security, but the same is possibly true of the organizational benefits of NATO.

In short, while NATO may still be useful and perhaps even indispensable, the case for its being so is not self-evident, nor is it effectively subject to reexamination. Meanwhile we are either blessed or burdened with this creation of a time that was very different from our own days or at least looked very different. Meanwhile, too, we can only wonder whether there has not been too much permanency and especially too much organization built into the system.[64]

Conclusions

We have reviewed theories on the generation or causes of war, including views not quite formal enough to be called theories, which have been conspicuous in a number of distinct but related fields. I trust I have demonstrated that any theory of the causes of war in general or of any war in particular that is not inherently eclectic and comprehensive, that is, which does not take into account at the outset the relevance of all sorts of diverse factors, is bound for that very reason to be wrong. Psychology or psychoanalysis can tell us much, but we also know that decisions are made through bodies of men and bureaucracies that go to make up governments, and that besides having a special mode of operation, these governments or regimes always carry a heavy baggage of notions—which may be sensible or ridiculous—about their national interests. Similarly, while I would put the conventional view of economic causation very low indeed, especially in modern times, I should want to remember that the difference between great and lesser powers is mostly a difference in wealth and in the means for making portions of that wealth available for military purposes. This point may seem to have nothing to do with war causation, except that the nations that have been mostly responsible for making wars have been the nations that had the means

---

[64] This view I am expressing here is of course a minority one, both among relevant politicians and bureaucrats as well as among scholars. The cited book on *Alliances* contains several favorable chapters on NATO, especially that of William T. R. Fox and Annette B. Fox, "The Role of the United States in NATO." See also the excellent monograph by the same two authors, *NATO and the Range of American Choice* (New York: Columbia University Press, 1967). The total literature on NATO is by now vast indeed.

for considering themselves great powers. Thus, if we reject the storybook versions of greed and scandal, we should not throw out the baby with the bath water. Economics is certainly involved.

In a word, we should be ready to look always at the complexities in the causes of war and to be extremely suspicious of simplistic solutions. When some say that wars are due to "innate aggression," they are using words that tend more to obscure meaning than to clarify it. Aggression or aggressiveness is a common manifestation of mankind, but so are ignorance and stupidity, which are just as relevant but which as words used by themselves also mean virtually nothing.

If we ever succeeded in refining any intellectually acceptable body of theory of the causes of war, the question would still remain whether we should be able to do much about those causes. Perhaps nothing extraordinary and overwhelming. But we should certainly be able to avoid following out nostrums that we know to be wrong and possibly harmful. That could turn out to be a quite considerable advantage. It might help us to save a good deal of money in preparing against wars we really do not have to fight or should not try to fight, or to avoid conflicts that whether or not they graduate into greater wars are painful and costly enough in themselves. Vietnam, some of us think, was brought upon us by nostrums—nostrums concerning prestige, notions of containment mixed with falling dominoes, and other foolishness besides. These nostrums are essentially theories, and often have to be exposed by theoretical examination—though specific applications always demand also a close and precise attention to specific history.

Our strivings are usually more effective for being reasonably modest. If we stop thinking about curing war *per se*, and think more about avoiding particular wars that might otherwise engulf us, we are making solid gains, and we may in the process find ourselves putting our new increments of knowledge to good use. To avoid one small war is a great gain, especially because we never know in advance how small that small war is going to remain.

CHAPTER

8

Vital Interests: What Are They, and Who Says So?

It was more than a quarter of a century since the three leading monarchs of western Europe had taken up the struggle for international prestige and mastery, and all three may have thought that they now approached the climax of their careers: Henry with perhaps a final success against France and a bloody assault on Scotland; Francis with a last lunge against the Habsburgs; Charles, after years of waiting, with the crushing of Protestantism in Germany and the vindication of his Imperial authority. But over the years the cards had become so dog-eared, the players' features and tactics so familiar to their fellows that high diplomacy had to be played as it had never been played before. As a result, the three veteran rivals wove so dense a web of *détente* and *démarche*, anticipated, crossed and double-crossed with such ingenuity that it is a good deal easier now to admire their energy than to decipher their precise purposes.

J. J. Scarisbrick, *Henry VIII*

The phrase *vital interests* rolls portentously and somewhat granitically off the tongue, pregnant with meaning but nevertheless obscure. What do we mean when we call interests "vital," as distinct, say, from merely important? Who determines at any one time what those interests are for our country, and by what criteria and processes do they do so?

According to customary usage, those of our interests are "vital" that we are ready to fight to preserve. For them, in other words, we are prepared to take or threaten some kind of military action, including if necessary—and, one would hope, if sufficiently "vital"—full-scale war. Or, at any rate (one does blanche a bit here) war in the prenuclear style. What kinds of interest are vital enough to warrant full-scale war in the modern version of that term is a question that we shall have to face but that I should like for the time being to postpone. At any rate, the importance of vital interests comes not necessarily from some intrinsic quality, but rather from what we are ready to do about some infringement of them, real or imagined.

But are we not putting the cart before the horse? Why derive our definition from what we *do* about something? Surely we will not threaten war or undertake it except over issues of utmost importance! And surely any interest that does have real importance will have the support of our military power! Well, with respect to both points, perhaps not so surely. Looking back, it does not appear that all the wars that we or other nations have fought concerned issues of the gravest importance. The obverse is also true: Some international issues or conflicts of real importance are churned over and either resolved or left unresolved without anyone's thinking of resorting to arms over them. Various nations, for example, including our own, have long been involved in tariff or trade "wars" in which one side inflicts considerable economic injury on the other, sometimes deliberately, in retaliation for the latter's trade practices; yet rarely if ever have genuine military wars been fought over such issues. Even among the devoted adherents of the economic-causation-of-war cult, who direct their allegations into the weirdest corners, the common frictions over international trade restrictions are generally ignored. Why? No doubt it is to some extent a matter of tradition, perhaps going back to the days of mercantilism when all foreign trade was conceived to be a kind of conflict about which one did not use arms. The element of tradition always matters greatly. It works just as much on the opposite front, too, that is, on the determination of those things that *are* presumed to be worth fighting over.

The Subjectivity of "Vital Interests"

The United States is at any one time committed to a set of strategic policies aimed at supporting or implementing those purposes or interests that have either been explicitly designated as "vital" or are likely to be felt as such under challenge. We hear much glib talk about those interests, as if the speakers knew exactly what they are or ought to be. Yet they are not fixed by nature nor identifiable by any generally accepted standard of objective criteria. They are instead the products of fallible human judgment, on matters concerning which agreement within the nation is usually less than universal. We have seen something of the possible dimensions of disagreement on virtually all issues concerning Vietnam. In this respect Vietnam differs only in degree from various other crises over vital interests. In 1962 President John F. Kennedy considered it a vital interest that the Russians remove the intermediate range ballistic missiles (IRBMs) they had stealthily installed in Cuba. It was not clear whether it was the fact of their being there or the manner of their having been put there that disturbed him most. The President, however, made no issue over the presence in Cuba of large numbers of Soviet troops and of surface-to-air missiles (SAMs). One type of force was deemed permissible, another not. The judgment in each case was the President's, and in each case he had ample support but by no means universal concurrence. Some feared he demanded too much—or rather risked too much in making his demands—and of these a few remained thus convinced even years after the event, despite its wholly favorable conclusion. Yet at the time of the crisis others were sure the President was not demanding enough.

Prevailing conceptions of American vital interest, which are effectively those held by the administration in power, have obviously changed drastically with time, especially over the three decades since we entered World War II. We see them continuing to change before our eyes. In some instances—again Vietnam is overpoweringly in our minds—we know that if yesterday's decision on vital interests could be called back, it would be changed. And yet, we are not talking about mere gossamer. Some interests will be vital beyond any shadow of doubt—like a direct military attack, or a threat of such, upon the United States. In other instances the conception of what is vital may be subject to debate, but the debate is about something that is not trivial. That much the word *vital* assures—that it will concern convictions which may be wrong but which everyone would regard as deeply worthy of attention if correct.

Our examples in the preceding paragraphs further delineate what vital interests are about. They concern those issues in our *foreign* affairs that are thought to affect the survival or security of the nation, meaning specifically security against military attack. This language naturally applies to a nation not bent on expansion. A nation ready to resort to aggression to gain its ends is enlarging its conception of its vital interests. However, such aggression, too, has often been justified by its perpetrator on the ground of its alleged necessity to the security of the state, and this allegation has sometimes been sincerely meant. Perhaps the latter fact only reflects on the quality of sincerity, which is a fairly abundant commodity. There seems never to be any lack of self-righteousness whenever anyone uses or thinks of using military power; some of it is undoubtedly a feedback from the evocation of magic in the word *vital*. Anyway, inasmuch as the United States is clearly not now and has not for a long time been bent on territorial expansion of any kind—a posture universally approved by its citizenry—we may dismiss from our consideration of American vital interests those that are not conceived of as somehow defensive.

It is clear enough what we mean by national security when we are considering a direct military attack upon our own territories. This is normally the only kind of national security that small nations can afford to concern themselves about—though for the sake even of that restrictive interpretation of security they will sometimes join alliances that in principle require them to be concerned about other frontiers besides their own. Great nations, however, and especially what we now call the superpowers, will often be concerned with what they deem threats to their security that are more distant in space, time, and even in conception than simply direct attack upon their home territories. The main reason, of course, is that the superpower feels itself able to do something effective about a threat that remains as yet indirect or remote, which is not true of a small power except in token association with a large power.

But there is also another reason. In saying that a superpower may respond to a threat more distant "even in conception," I mean something like the following: In some situations viewed as distantly menacing or disturbing, a superpower, in considering its appropriate response, allows itself the luxury (or burden) of thinking in terms of national *responsibility* rather than simply of national peril. In so doing it will not usually acknowledge that it is departing from the criterion of self-interest fixed on security; it merely finds it convenient to broaden the terminology as it broadens its conception. The whole idea of "containment" is one convenient way of expressing and at the same time of justifying a preoccupation with affairs far from home, and of doing so ultimately in the name of national security.

Security: An Expansible Conception

Implied here also is the conception that "security" itself is a flexible term, and that for a nation like the United States its meaning is legitimately, indeed almost necessarily, expanded to something beyond simple self-defense. This country is so powerful, especially in its nuclear means, that it is almost impossibly difficult to imagine any nation wishing to attack us within our own shores—except under the panic surmise that it was anticipating an attack from us. Reserving for the moment consideration of what might move the leaders of that nation to have such feelings, we may concentrate simply on the fact that the circumstances to produce them are of a kind that must remain altogether rare and unlikely. This means, in effect, that *being already committed to maintain that kind of power necessary for the essential security just described*, the United States is in a position also to make its voice heard on conditions well beyond its shores.

This is the classic situation of the world power. It recalls a statement of Mahan's, somewhere in his writings shortly before World War I, where he calls it the "dilemma" of Great Britain that simply by possessing the minimum naval power essential to her security, she finds herself inevitably in a position to close off Germany's maritime outlets to the sea. One could neither expect the Germans to like this situation nor the British to settle for anything less. Under vastly different technological and geographical circumstances, we find ourselves in a somewhat comparable position.

Under such circumstances we see ourselves—almost automatically and yet not without significant choice—adopting the position that guaranteeing the physical security of our own shores to foreign attack is altogether too narrow a conception of what our security should mean to us. President Franklin D. Roosevelt, then emerging out of the deepest isolationism, put the case with classic eloquence in his Commencement Day speech at the University of Virginia on June 10, 1940—when Hitler's armies were sweeping across France and Fascist Italy had just joined the war at his side. Terming it a "delusion" that the United States could exist as a lone island of peace in a world of brute force, he went on:

> Such an island represents to me and to the overwhelming majority of Americans today a helpless nightmare of a people without freedom—the nightmare of a people lodged in prison, handcuffed, hungry, and fed through the bars from day to day by the contemptuous, unpitying masters of other continents.

He then announced that the United States would increase its own defense preparations and would extend to England and France "the material resources of this nation." [1]

Well, one might say, but the policy he announced on that day led us directly into World War II, which otherwise we might have avoided—and so it did. Let us not try to justify his position by saying that our being attacked was inevitable anyway. We do not know that, and there are good reasons for thinking it unlikely. But the alternative was grim indeed, for it meant a world outside our shores dominated in Europe by the most hideous and regressive of governments and in the Far East by the neo-Samurai of Japan. The bandwagon lure of victorious governments that can attribute their success to their rejection of "stale democracy" may be extraordinarily strong in a world of which far the greatest part is not ruled by democratic traditions, and we must recognize that those traditions possess even at best certain elements of fragility. How much poetic license Roosevelt was permitting himself when he said that his new view was also that of "the overwhelming majority of Americans today" is hard to say, but he was gifted in sensing the pulse of the nation and in any case the response to the speech throughout the nation was favorable. The country might

---

[1] Robert A. Divine, *Roosevelt and World War II* (Baltimore: Johns Hopkins Press, 1969), p. 31. This is the same speech in which Roosevelt used the more-often quoted sentence: "The hand that held the dagger has struck it into the back of its neighbor." I am citing the Divine book for this speech, available also in many other sources, because of Divine's brief but excellent treatment of Roosevelt's personal migration from confirmed isolationist to pragmatic interventionist. It effectively replies to a number of books whose view of the wartime Roosevelt reflects either intense "revisionist" animus on the one hand or idolatry on the other.

also have accepted a different cue, but it responded enthusiastically to this one.

Thus, Roosevelt was restating an age-old principle: Though we will not insist that the world around us be entirely to our liking, neither are we inclined to accept anything considerably worse than need be if our efforts can prevent it. This then becomes a fatefully important expansion of the concept of American security, one that considerably enlarges the domain over which we will insist that conditions be tolerable in our eyes. Though this attitude is often justified with the standard appeal that our own ultimate safety requires it, it does not depend for its major force on that appeal. It tends normally to find wide acceptance in the national community, and those final assurances are for the sake mostly of completing and solidifying the consensus by sweeping in also the more recalcitrant.

We must not be beguiled here from the realization that behind a confusion of large-sounding phrases, an extraordinarily important and far-reaching step has been taken. All our foreign *military* policy is justified in the name of our own security, and genuinely so, but at the same time our security is given a decidedly expansive meaning. I am not for one moment suggesting either that it should or should not be, but only pointing out that this is the case. We find in effect that the power of the United States, as well as its geographical location, gives the leaders of our country an opportunity of choice not available to lesser powers. Others would put it that its power confers upon the United States a large measure of responsibility, but responsibility is itself a matter of decision, hence of choice. The national leaders who involved us in Southeast Asia may or may not have been correct in their assessment that the security at home of the United States was *ultimately* bound up with the security of that area, but even the most avid interventionists among them would have had to admit that the connections were sufficiently indirect and perhaps even remote to make the decision to intervene a matter of fairly free choice.

If we look back into a past when we were not as a nation beset with such far-reaching, inconvenient, and even dangerous choices, we notice if we go back far enough—say to 1890—that there was a time when we enjoyed nearly perfect security at home without bothering to provide for ourselves any military power of consequence. This was enjoying security as a free good, or what I

347

have referred to elsewhere in this book as a condition of "surplus security," for so it appeared as compared with the conditions of other great nations.[2] However, we were not exercising very much influence elsewhere in the world either. We had the Monroe Doctrine, but no European power seemed interested in challenging it. By 1898, however, we had built a shining new fleet called the "White Squadron" and got involved in a war with Spain. This war did not have to undergo much explanation at the time or thereafter because it was safe, short, with enough of glorious victories to pay all costs, which were low and which could be charged to charity in that we freed the freedom-loving Cubans from their Spanish oppressors—thereafter letting them be ruled by their own oppressors, which indeed they seemed to prefer.[3] In the process we acquired some "overseas possessions," especially the Philippines and Puerto Rico, which we would have called "imperialism" in others but which we refused to acknowledge as making us a colonial power.

Just prior to World War I our navy had climbed to the position of third place in the world, but we still had an insignificant army. Yet we became involved in that war because we (or rather President Wilson) had insisted on taking positions about the freedom of the seas that we thought consonant with our status as a great power and which we would not have taken had we thought of ourselves as a small or secondary power. Indeed, nobody disagreed that we were a very great power, least of all the Germans. The latter took a gamble comparable to the one they had taken with the British in 1914, and again they lost. Did we go into that war because of our security needs? So it was proclaimed, and if we considered it basic to our security for our citizens to be free to travel in safety through war zones on belligerent ships—for such freedom appeared to be guaranteed by international law, whose sanctity President Wilson was bound to uphold—then we were fighting for our security.

---

[2] See p. 118.

[3] In our getting into the war against Spain, there was indeed the matter of the blowing up of the armored cruiser *Maine*, with considerable loss of life, in Santiago Harbor. The deliberate blowing up in peacetime of another nation's warship is indeed a serious matter, but one would expect it to be a matter of comparable seriousness to determine who was responsible. The United States government—or William Randolph Hearst, whose "yellow journalism" seemed at the time to be giving out the most effective cues for American responses—seemed not to care. Spain was held responsible, but it seems at this remove much more likely to have been the Cuban revolutionaries attempting to produce in the United States exactly the mood that was produced.

Subsequent to that war, with our navy now "second to none," we already had all the stance of a world power. Despite all the anathema to intervention built up by the experience of the previous war—concerning which our people had now concluded that it had not concerned our security at all—our resistance to becoming involved in World War II was gradually broken down by the realization that the world that our aloofness would permit to develop was really too intolerable. We were still far from having committed ourselves to war, however, when the Japanese made their largely gratuitous attack at Pearl Harbor and when Hitler and Mussolini pleasantly surprised their Japanese treaty partners by rushing in to fulfill their somewhat ambiguous obligations.[4] What a combination of blunders was this! One cannot forebear to point out the folly, possible even to a cunning man like Hitler, of assuming that being *almost* at war with the United States (we were then already escorting convoys half way across the Atlantic) was about as bad as being *at war* with the United States. He and the German people were soon to find out there was an enormous difference.

Following World War II, and with the arrival of the nuclear age, aloofness was clearly no longer possible. Part of the reason for this is that we could no longer feel really secure *at home* without also being very strong, especially in the new weapons. This also meant being very strong in air power, and the tradition of having a great navy was already established; the latter now was not merely "second to none" but by a wide margin the first. The other part of the reason was that those formerly great powers who had served us as buffers even while they were irritating and disturbing us with their quarrels were no longer great—leaving us to face, virtually alone with respect to meaningful power, a triumphant Communist Russia!

The Added Costs of Expanded Security

We should not obscure the fact that however large the military power required for our own domestic security, pursuing an active foreign policy—a position of leadership—is going to require

---

4 Before entering the war the Japanese decided that they would not join Germany in fighting Russia for the time being, "even at the cost of a German delay on entering the war against the United States." Robert J. C. Butow, *Tojo and the Coming of the War* (Princeton: Princeton University Press, 1961; Stanford University Press paperback, 1969), p. 327.

additional margins of military strength. The needed extra margins may or may not be large compared with the "irreducible minimum" deemed to be required even for a quiescent policy (in both instances the figures and magnitudes will be vigorously debated and in the end selected arbitrarily) , but there will be a difference. Also, recalling now our earlier remark that one can hardly imagine any nation attacking us at home unless it were anticipating a like attack by us, it is next to impossible to see how things could come to such a pass unless a serious quarrel between them and us had developed somewhere in the world concerning affairs extraneous to both our territories. Even the much-mentioned (and I think much-exaggerated) possibility that purely technological developments might make the enemy confident that he could attack us with impunity, and therefore make him feel impelled to do so for his own safety, implies the feeling in both camps that the other is a profound and dangerous enemy. Such a feeling could hardly develop except over a history of friction over third areas. Thus, the feedback from an active foreign policy must affect even the quantity and quality of our basic nuclear power, and we are left with the conclusion that being a world power is nothing that we obtain on the cheap, even when we manage to avoid Vietnams, and that it also adds at least marginally to the risk of ultimate destruction.

A superpower like the United States does have unique, though far from unlimited, capacities to influence events throughout the world. We may agree that its leaders would be remiss in their duties if they did not regularly seek to exercise that influence in a manner calculated to enhance the nation's long-term interests, meaning above all its security interests. Let us also agree that security deserves to be treated as something more meaningful than the simple defense of the territories within our own shores. The world extends beyond those shores, and Americans and America itself live in that world. We have nevertheless been made abundantly aware of the tendency of our national leaders to slip into expansive habits of interpretation concerning the real meaning to ourselves of threats that are quite remote in space and at least for the time being directed against others.

Political leaders hanker to be known as "statesmen," which requires that they be "far-sighted." To be far-sighted is by definition to see threats well ahead of the time they develop into immediate perils. Lacking the capacity for perfect or even clear-sighted discrimination among threats, one plays it safe by seeing to it that none is ignored. Every disturbance anywhere must be regarded as potentially a peril, and this kind of attitude, as we have seen, can easily be shored up by a variety of slogans purporting to rest on history, like that on the indissolubility of peace, on remembering Munich, on the terrible improvidence of isolationism, and so on.

We cannot assert that these views are wrong—simply that in the United States in the first twenty-five years after World War II the cards were heavily stacked in their favor, just as before that time they had inclined in the opposite direction, especially concerning Europe. The major reasons for this change have been reviewed, in these pages and elsewhere, over and over again—the exhilaration of a commanding victory in a very great war, for which, in addition, there could be few subsequent regrets; the atomic bomb; the shock of confrontation with Stalin's Russia, now swollen with new territories and satellites and contorted with renewed hostility; the weakness and confusion of our erstwhile allies; the fall of China to Communism and the spectre of a monolithic Communism embracing nearly half the earth's land area and half its population; the Berlin Blockade, followed shortly by the Korean War, and so forth.

In addition we must recall the conditions within the United States, which contrast sharply with those prevailing at this writing. A relatively high degree of average annual economic growth and of internal unity; no serious chronic inflation; apparent advancement in race relationships without undue bitterness (expectations were not yet outrunning performance); undisputed American technological and industrial leadership, and so on. It was a situation that both permitted and, in the view of many, obliged the eyes of the national leaders to turn outward.

The requirements for the Presidency seemed now to require as a first qualification mastery of or at least familiarity with foreign affairs. President Truman had inherited World War II and its aftermath both of triumphs and troubles, including finally the Korean War. Eisenhower had come to the world's attention as a commander of huge forces representing an international coalition of unprecedented size and unity, and had returned to the international forum as the first supreme commander of the new NATO alliance, which was also unprecedented in form and structure. Kennedy had come to power with an inaugural speech of which all the memorable phrases dealt with foreign affairs, and in a few months he was talking with de Gaulle in Paris and

Krushchev in Vienna. What happens at home, he is reported as saying to his intimates, can only hurt us, but what happens out there can kill us! Kennedy's short Administration had a much larger effect on foreign and especially NATO policy than on domestic policy. In less than three years he suffered an extraordinary humiliation and an equally extraordinary triumph in Cuba, in the latter instance facing down an overconfident and overreaching Krushchev in a manner that resulted in a clear and enduring amelioration in our relations with the Soviet Union. He was also deeply engaged with the Berlin problem, and was perforce engrossed with what was going on in Vietnam, where he considerably increased our commitment. Whether he chose it so or not, he was primarily a foreign affairs President.

His successor liked foreign affairs less and became involved even more. Lyndon B. Johnson, who could have been an outstanding success as a domestic reform President, was an unmitigated disaster not as a war President, in which he might also have succeeded, but as a *limited* war President, in which much of the national unity and the willingness to sacrifice that can be counted on in the larger tests are likely to be lacking. The Vietnam War, with all its repercussions in the United States and throughout the world, drove his reform program at once outside his capabilities and out of his mind. His successor, Richard M. Nixon, during his period as a private citizen made almost all his public statements (including articles in *Foreign Affairs* and letters to the editor of *The New York Times*) on matters of foreign affairs, and is reported to have remarked more than once that the President's job is running foreign policy while the conduct of domestic affairs can well be left to the cabinet.[5]

It is natural for those who make their careers in foreign affairs, including foreign service officers and members of the State Depart-

---

[5] Also, in Dr. Henry A. Kissinger, President Nixon selected a man whose fixation upon foreign affairs during his entire professional career has been total. For example: during the 1968 election campaign but before he had established any special relationship to Richard Nixon, whom he was then known not to admire, Kissinger repeatedly told his friends that he could not possibly vote for Vice President Hubert Humphrey because the latter would be sure to choose former Undersecretary of State George Ball as his Secretary of State. Whatever the reasons for his reservations concerning Mr. Ball—which may have had to do with Ball's distaste for our Vietnam policy—the striking fact was that in expressing this view Dr. Kissinger felt it unnecessary to offer any additional reason, despite the obvious fact that the country also had monumental domestic problems upon which the respective candidates appeared to have quite different views and capabilities.

ment, to take for granted the *primacy* of those affairs in the concerns of the nation. Even those not so inclined and having broader responsibilities will just as naturally be responsive at periods of crisis to the extraordinarily high stakes involved. But in the main, the general attitude that foreign affairs deserve prime place in the ruler's concerns are a throw-back to the days of kingship, when the order at home was taken for granted as solidly established—at near or below the subsistence level for the great majority of people—and the outstanding role of the monarch and of his chief servants was taken to be in his relations with other monarchs, both in war and in peace, though disproportionately often in war. It is an attitude that fits dubiously the United States in its present state of development—the "leader of the free world," to be sure, though far less gravely menaced from abroad than its alarmists persistently assure us, and beset at home with a restiveness caused by gigantic unresolved issues and problems. It should go without saying that the way in which we deal with these problems, or fail to do so, also has its large impact on our foreign affairs.

There is, naturally, no law or reason set down in Heaven why the United States should not accept as its responsibilities abroad various concerns well beyond those dictated by a conception of its own needs, though our constitutional structure requires that the people generally understand and agree to what their leaders are up to. In the instances both of Korea and of Vietnam, the citizenry repeatedly demanded assurance that the purpose of the interventions was indeed to enhance American security, and they repeatedly received that assurance from their national leaders, who no doubt sincerely meant it. We saw the same thing happening in the case of President Franklin Roosevelt and his assurances, but there are significant differences in dimensions between the menace posed by a Hitler on the rampage in combination with Japan and Italy, and a Ho Chi Minh reaching for the control of South Vietnam. It is a strange approach to international affairs that seeks to assert that *all* threats to the peace are all on the same plane, alike not only in character but also in magnitude of danger; but this is what some of the more doctrinaire purveyors of the "indissolubility of peace" would have had us believe.

In practice, of course, reason will intrude, and we find ourselves responding differently to the considerable range of real or suspected threats. We also find ourselves equipped with a wide range of military actions or responses for dealing with them. That range reflects varying degrees of conviction either about the essential degree of involvement of our national security or about the immediacy of the threat. The view that Communism must be contained wherever in the world it threatens to expand, especially when that expansion is by aggressive military action, will stimulate a very different American response in Central Asia from what it will in some special areas like western Europe or Cuba. When the Chinese Communists were attacking Indian outposts in the Himalayas in 1962, the Kennedy Administration contented itself with rushing arms to India by aircraft. But the response we were making at the very same time to the Soviet IRBMs in Cuba was of a different order of magnitude. When judgment is permitted to rule over doctrine, adjustments of this kind in degree of response tend to follow automatically.

The availability of variations in our responses offers some protection from the error of overreaching ourselves or of making too extravagant an estimate of the danger to our own interests of something occurring far away. However, this flexibility is at the mercy of a trap, which, too easily sprung, narrows greatly our range of choice concerning levels of response. It may hold us to much higher levels than we might in soberer moments consider wise. This trap is the fetish of "prestige," under a variety of names, forms, and guises, most of which we have already encountered in earlier chapters. As we pointed out in the case of Vietnam, prestige ought itself to be considered a variable in terms of commitment and of sanctions; but too often it is looked upon as an absolute: "The United States has committed its prestige, and therefore *must* prevail!" The whole conception of "flexible response" thus threatens to founder on the dogma of prestige. In Vietnam, what was looked upon originally as a limited and short-term commitment sucked us into something that no political leader in his right mind could possibly have chosen.

Another variable worth noting concerns the real risk estimated to be inherent in a commitment. It looks cheap and easy to offer a guarantee against aggression to a country that is in little if any danger of attack anyway. It is an old cliché that the young American republic that promulgated the Monroe Doctrine was relying upon the shield of the British navy. It is also true and perhaps equally important that by that time those countries of Europe that could still be called great powers—and Spain was no longer such—had no particular interest in expanding their holdings in the New World. Even the meddling of Napoleon III in Mexico was tentative and timid, designed more to woo and impress the Habsburgs in Europe than to win new territories for the Bonapartes, and it had the bad luck to run into its first real test at the moment when a huge and triumphant United States military power was finally liquidating the rebellion of the South. All this does not imply that the Monroe Doctrine was ineffective; it only says that the burden it had to carry was not excessively heavy.

By the same token, guarantees have often been advanced on the supposition that the guarantee itself (or alliance) would sufficiently dissuade the potential aggressor so that it would never have to be fulfilled. Undoubtedly there was much of that attitude behind the exuberance with which the Truman and Eisenhower Administrations committed the United States to all the countries originally protected by the North Atlantic Treaty of 1949 as well as by other alliances of the times. Why else should we have included Norway in that treaty, and later Turkey? Norway was much too small to be a useful ally; it has a common frontier with the USSR, but that frontier is in the far north, and the Soviet Union had never shown much interest in it. To be sure, we are talking here not about the basic justification for NATO, but rather about one idea among the mix of ideas that went into the formulation of the original plan for that alliance, and which certainly helps to account for its extension to weak, peripheral nations.

It should, however, be said about this idea that while historically it has often worked, it has sometimes failed spectacularly. It was the idea by which the principle of collective security under the League of Nations Covenant was rationalized. It was reiterated over and over again throughout the 1920s and early 1930s that if only nations would agree upon this principle, they would never have to deliver. But Mussolini in his attack on Ethiopia in 1936 showed that this was not true; after a feeble attempt at sanctions, the League of Nations security system collapsed. It was undoubtedly because Mussolini sensed the weakness of the guarantee that he was ready to flout it.

The Role of Tradition in Determining "Vital Interests"

Any reference to the Monroe Doctrine brings home to us at once the force of tradition in the formulation of vital interests. Every school child is reared on the notion, or at least was until recently, that here is an American commitment that is quite sacrosanct, and what is more the whole world knows it. No nation in the world seems to be the least bit interested in violating the Monroe Doctrine, but just in case any of them did it would be on prior notice that it was playing a very dangerous game. We have seen that other countries, too, have had their hoary incantations that are supposed to guide foreign policy makers and to make other nations tremble. These are very great advantages, but the possible penalties are also very great. The slogans that make up these traditions can easily outlive their original justification, which may itself have been largely or totally imaginary. As Lord Salisbury remarked, concerning the fear in the British Foreign Office throughout much of the nineteenth century that Russia would suddenly descend on India: "A great deal of misapprehension arises from the popular use of maps on a small scale." [6]

When Britain and France (in collusion with Israel) took military action against Egypt in 1956 because President Gamal Abdel Nasser had nationalized the Suez Canal, a response prompted no doubt by old ideas of "lifelines of Empire," they quickly discovered that the rest of the world regarded their action as anachronistic and intolerable. The pressure imposed upon them, especially by their chief ally, the United States, obliged them to desist—after which it became abundantly obvious that the transfer of control over the Canal through nationalization made no discernible difference to the general commercial or strategic interests of Great Britain and France. Apart from the quite insignificant question of the value of the shares of the company previously operating the Canal, the question of control was adventitiously exposed as being not only not vital but hardly even important. In the Arab-Israeli war of 1967, the Canal was closed altogether and remains so to this writing, but no country seems to have suffered from it unduly except Egypt itself, which lost the tariffs.

The more distant or indirect the threat that is alleged to affect our national security, the more controversial is the question whether it actually does warrant a military response, and if so, what kind. In this respect, we have witnessed—for example between 1939 and 1945, and again between 1965 and 1972—remarkable changes in the climate of American opinion concerning the range and scope of adversary actions warranting a direct military response. The first of these time frames represented a period of

---

[6] Lady Gwendolen Cecil, *Life of Robert, Marquis of Salisbury*, 4 vols. (London: Hodder & Stoughton, 1922–1932), vol 2, pp. 155 f.

United States emergence from isolationism, and the second appears (at this range) to represent, certainly not a return to isolationism, but nevertheless a distinct turning away from an attitude that incorporated a fairly ready acceptance of military intervention.

Our entrance into the Korean War in June–July 1950, after Communist North Korea invaded the non-Communist South, was a kind of action that appeared entirely appropriate at the height of the "cold war" era; but it seemed quite foreign to the mood of 1970, the era of the Nixon Doctrine,[7] when the only significant debate over President Nixon's policy of withdrawing American soldiers from Vietnam concerned the question whether the rate of withdrawal was fast enough. At this writing, it is perhaps too early to assert conclusively that the latter change represents a turning point with long-term implications, rather than merely a temporary pause. But to this writer the change appears definitely to be a long-term one. For one thing, our frustrations in Vietnam, and the resulting perturbations and divisions within the United States, have cast a new light on the real capabilities of the country for this kind of intervention, especially when it has to be based on the draft. We have also learned a good deal the hard way about the uncertainties of estimating the various kinds of risk involved (including the political risk to the President who makes the decision), and also the large total costs (including social and political as well as economic costs), as against the likely ineffectiveness of any action to shore up a partner who is weak not only materially but also politically. And most of the axioms on which the action was based will certainly no longer command the respect they once did.

To be sure, future situations will have distinctive characteristics. Still, the nation has lost a certain innocence about appraising future situations that are even slightly comparable to Vietnam, however distinctive their characteristics may be. We have also learned the wisdom of the late President Eisenhower's extreme reluctance to consider undertaking any intervention without

---

[7] Much ambiguity attaches to what President Nixon meant when he first enunciated the so-called "Nixon Doctrine" on the island of Guam in July 1969, and in his further elucidation of that doctrine in Richard Nixon, *U.S. Foreign Policy for the 1970's: Building for Peace* (Washington: The White House, Feb. 25, 1971), pp. 10–21. The basic message for our allies in the Western Pacific seems to have been that they should henceforward not depend on the kind of assistance with fighting manpower that we contributed to Vietnam, but that they may continue to depend on us for support in military materiel. But see Earl C. Ravenal, "The Nixon Doctrine and Our Asian Commitments," *Foreign Affairs* vol. 49, no. 2, (January 1971), pp. 201–217.

allies. Even though we would in any case carry a disproportionate burden, the cooperative participation of other powers, as in Korea, places the entire operation in a different moral light both in our own country and in the world outside. But in this respect, too, the times have changed. It is very difficult to imagine in the future the kind of joint enterprise in furtherance of a United Nations "police action" against an aggressor that we witnessed in the Korean War.

All this does not mean the end of American military intervention abroad. One must, however, be alive to the likelihood that we have seen the end of the kind of lightheartedness that went into American talk about "putting out brush fires" wherever they might occur. It is already becoming difficult to recall that mood, represented, for example, by Robert McNamara's request for a fleet of "fast logistic ships" (subsequently denied him by Congress) that was supposed to facilitate such fire-fighting. Among the military lessons we have learned is that *restraint in the application of force—in order to keep that application compatible with its purpose—may make the force applied ineffective for its purpose.* Thus, to grant sanctuary and to withhold tactical nuclear weapons may be utterly correct policy, but such restraints have to be recognized as being costly, possibly very costly, in military effectiveness. For the future, this is bound to mean, and should mean, not fewer limitations upon the use of force, but rather fewer occasions for applying force under circumstances requiring such restraint.

Having thus considered how variable and subjective are those interests we call vital, we must nevertheless be clear that we cannot dispense with the basic concept. Some interests are quite unambiguously vital. The perennial problem for the leaders of a superpower like the United States is to determine the outer boundaries of what is truly vital, and in more practical terms to decide—under the whole range of relevant circumstances prevailing at the time—what kinds of threat indicate what kinds of response. To be able to make these decisions even reasonably well —the proof being in the outcome—is to display statesmanship in foreign and strategic affairs.

Who Determines Vital Interests?

The persons who at any particular moment determine what our vital interests are, and how they should be defended if menaced, are naturally the political leaders of the nation. The responsibility and prerogative is centered first and foremost—by a wide margin—in the President, whose authority in these matters, at least over the short term, is awesome. In recent years one school has enormously emphasized—to a degree which this writer considers a gross distortion—the importance of the bureaucracies, which allegedly "structure the choices."[8] All the people concerned, however, including the President and his advisers, function within and derive their basic ideas from a climate of American opinion concerning the state of the world and the general conduct appropriate to the United States. Questions as to what is possible or feasible must take into account the mood of the whole population; but the guiding ideas come from that small minority who maintain an interest in foreign affairs, and especially from that portion of the latter who through special intellectual gifts or privilege of position can command the attention of others.

The ideas that spark top policy decisions stem also from the total upbringing of the persons who make them, and especially from their appreciation of those slogans that have helped to mold their conceptions of the foreign policies appropriate to the United States. There are bound to be marked individual variations in conceptual flexibility or rigidity, but we must nevertheless recognize that the high office holder is a mature man who comes to his post with a seasoning of experience and with some fairly firm convictions. Besides, he begins at once to make commitments in policy that subsequently act as constraints upon further policy decisions. Thus, we accept a certain "cultural lag" with respect to high policy orientation, which is to say that yesterday's persuasions often do govern today's decisions. Young people sense this "lag" and tend to be intolerant of it. Undoubtedly there are situations in which it results in some cost, perhaps high cost. But what is the alternative? Would policy decisions emanating from people whose convictions are not based on maturity and experience be on balance better? One who has lived through the days of Hitler, Mussolini, Stalin, and the Japanese war lords feels something that a younger generation does not concerning the aberrations that are possible in this world. That feeling or knowledge may indeed be confining and even warping; the ideal is naturally experience combined with flexibility and ability to perceive change, but the mark of that gift does not come visible on anyone's forehead.

Public declarations of high officials purporting to define the

---

[8] See above, pp. 126—130. With respect to the Presidential ascendancy over Congress in regard to war and peace, see pp. 108—112, 215—222.

vital interests of the United States often tend to be misleading, especially at the margins, for several reasons. For one thing, there is likely to be a verbal overvaluation of that which sounds moral as against that which sounds merely expedient. Thus, instead of asserting that we intend to resist the spread of Communism regardless of what kind of reactionary, corrupt, and inept regimes we may thereby obligate ourselves to defend, our leaders will declare the readiness of the United States to defend the right of free people anywhere to determine their own destinies. Whatever deception is involved tends to be in part self-deception. Policy makers share the normal human need to find their conduct, public as well as private, to some degree compatible with a generally favorable estimation of themselves.

Another reason for the misleading quality of these public declarations is, however, of a quite different order. It derives from a problem already noted—the difficulty of appraising correctly the dimensions and character of the country's true capabilities. We can within wide limits expand and restructure our military capabilities to accord with changes in the range and intensification of what are felt to be our vital interests, but important intangibles are involved that may mislead even careful students of those capabilities. For example, it has become increasingly obvious since 1965 that military forces based on conscription carry certain built-in constraints upon the decision maker. They demand, among other things, that the country must be highly united in order to insure the prolonged support of any foreign war, as it was in World War II. It was similarly united in the early stages of the Korean War, but here the staying power of that unity was much less. By the election year 1952, it was being called "Truman's War."

It has also become obvious (it was never actually questioned, but neither was it clearly enough recognized by important officials) that in a country such as ours, where free speech is inherent in the form of government, no administration has a clear field in "educating" public opinion to accept its own values, appraisals, and predictions. Its spokesmen have to contend with critics, many of whom will have credentials as impressive as anyone in power, and who have comparable access to the media in which news is reported and ideas and opinions expressed. When it comes to fighting a Hitler who has declared war on us on the morrow of Pearl Harbor, there is no problem with dissent. In subsequent war situations, however, including both Korea and Vietnam, dissent has exercised a sharply limiting restraint upon our power.

One would expect that the President and his lieutenants would at least be able to predict with some clarity and assurance their own responses to various kinds of crisis situations that might develop in the future; but the historical record suggests caution even in this limited area of prediction. Who, for example, would have forecast before World War I that a virtually disarmed America would enter that great holocaust over an issue labelled "freedom of the seas?" Certainly not President Woodrow Wilson, who expressed concern at the beginning of his term that foreign affairs might absorb an undue amount of his time at the expense of his cherished program of domestic reforms, and who at the outset of the war in Europe cautioned his countrymen to be "neutral in thought as well as in deed." Those actual German infringements of the international law of war at sea that Wilson was to find intolerable were not of great tangible importance to us. In retrospect, this manifest cause of United States entry into World War I has seemed so bizarre that many have insisted on finding deeper or more hidden causes, like those having to do with balance-of-power considerations or—especially among neo-Marxians—the usual conspiratorial interpretations stressing economic greed. Such theories, however, do not stand historical scrutiny. The President was not looking for a pretext to enter the war. On the contrary, even after receiving the intercepted Zimmerman telegram, he insisted to his cabinet on February 2, 1917 that he did not wish to see either side win in Europe and was still opposed to entering the war.[9] In his opinion, however, actual German resumption of unrestricted U-boat warfare in February 1917 left the United States no other choice. And because his own

---

[9] See Barbara Tuchman, *The Zimmerman Telegram* (New York: Viking, 1958; Dell paperback, 1965), p. 140. This was the occasion on which Wilson gave as an added reason for keeping out of the war the need "to keep the white race strong against the yellow." See also Arthur S. Link, *Wilson the Diplomatist* (Baltimore: Johns Hopkins Press, 1956), especially pp. 81–90. The curious House-Grey memorandum of February 22, 1916, to which Wilson gave his qualified approval, seems a contradiction of the above remarks because it called for American entry into the war if Germany did not accept the mild terms contained in it. However, Wilson was much more excited about the possibility of ending the war through his mediation than he was serious about entering the war. The British did not desire the mediation, and Grey's colleagues, especially Asquith, did not even wish United States entry if the war thereby had to be ended with a draw. By November Wilson was again moving toward denial of loans to the British. See V. H. Rothwell, *British War Aims and Peace Diplomacy, 1914–1918* (Oxford: Clarendon Press, 1971), pp. 34 f., 59–61.

previous actions had committed the United States to that course, and had centered national attention and emotions upon this commitment, he could carry the country with him. Another man might well have kept the country out of war—William Jennings Bryan, for example, who had resigned as Secretary of State in 1915 precisely because he considered Wilson's demands upon Germany in the *Lusitania* crisis as improvidently establishing a commitment.[10] A Theodore Roosevelt would have got us in much sooner.

Similarly, as we have seen, in January 1950 another Secretary of State, Dean Acheson, delivered a speech in New York outlining the "defense perimeter" of the United States in a way that clearly left South Korea outside it. Yet when the North Koreans attacked the South only five months later, Truman promptly committed the United States to military intervention, and Secretary Acheson was one of those who most strongly supported his doing so.[11] Were we fulfilling a vital interest? If so, why had it been not merely unrecognized but actually disavowed before the attack?

Again, President Lyndon B. Johnson was not the first but the third President of the United States to consider the outcome of the long struggle in Vietnam an American interest vital enough to warrant the intervention of some U.S. military personnel. (He was the fourth to send arms to those opposing Communist forces there.) But the decision to shift the status of such personnel from an advisory to a combat role, which also required a considerable multiplication of their numbers, was sharply distinctive, and entirely the responsibility of President Johnson. It is by no means obvious that either of his two immediate predecessors would have made the same decision.

It is also obvious that the considerations that led President Nixon to continue American participation in that war, with a slower withdrawal than his critics would have liked, were not the same that persuaded President Johnson to send combat forces originally. The difference was not so much in personal convictions as in markedly changed circumstances. In his travels in the western Pacific in July 1969, President Nixon took special care to warn some of our other allies in that region not to expect, under similar conditions, the kind of support we gave to South Vietnam

---

[10] See Louis W. Koenig, *Bryan, A Political Biography* (New York: Putnam, 1971), pp. 541–550.

[11] See pp. 59–61.

—what has since been called the Nixon Doctrine. And the following September, the Senate *unanimously* adopted a resolution that conveyed a similar warning to Thailand, concerning which (in the Senate's view) the President had apparently not been sufficiently forthright. In a subsequent visit to Thailand, Vice President Spiro Agnew told the Thais they could disregard the Senate's action, but we may be sure that they will not disregard it. Here was a sharply changing approach to the description of our vital interests—or was it in the estimation of our military capabilities?

Meanwhile, with the rapid growth of Soviet nuclear capability, the notion was gaining some currency among our European allies that the United States nuclear guarantee could no longer be relied upon.[12] Surely these critics assumed too much, and our government was right to deny the allegations vehemently. Still, in these matters how can one be truly convincing? It is difficult because the post-World War II nuclear world is totally different from any we have known before. Our political leaders give assurances in which they apparently fully believe; yet doubts cannot be stilled—possibly including their own. Everyone recognizes that total nuclear war would be an infinitely more fearsome thing than the greatest wars of the past. Everyone knows that much may hang on the identity of the President of the day, and no one can predict who will occupy that office some four years hence.

However, the question of "nuclear reliability," while not irrelevant, does not really deserve the kind of priority that the doubters automatically give it. In the confrontation strategy of the Cuban missile crisis in October 1962, the initial (and in that instance easily sufficient) American moves and postures were adop-

---

[12] Brigadier General Pierre Gallois, retired from the French Air Force, is notable for pounding home in his many writings the thesis that, under the threat of nuclear war, no ally can be relied upon. This argument, which implied a lack of confidence in the United States and in a NATO alliance that many considered to be merely the instrument of American policy, gained a substantial following not only in France but elsewhere in western Europe as well. The French used it as part of the rationalization for their nuclear weapons program, and also for their withdrawal from the organizational structure of NATO. It has since become apparent to formerly doubting Europeans that there may be many levels of tension, and even some levels of combat, without nuclear threats being seriously invoked. In any case, a strong ally is always useful to have in the face of a powerful state whose behavior is often aggressive politically even if not militarily (and sometimes even militarily, as in Czechoslovakia in 1968). Among Gallois' writings, the most important is his *Stratégie de l'age nucléaire* (Paris: Calmann-Lévy, 1960), translated under the title *The Balance of Terror* (Boston: Houghton, Mifflin, 1961).

ted without any specific reference to nuclear weapons, although with an acute awareness of their existence. Some have attributed the quick Soviet retreat to an American nuclear superiority that has since largely disappeared, though more probably it was the result of a swift Soviet reevaluation of the American mood. The Soviet Union can hardly be more desirous of war with a nuclear equal than with a nuclear superior, certainly so long as such parity is measured in large capabilities.

The degree of resolution that either side shows in any future crisis is more likely to be governed by the particular issues at stake than by the tallying of nuclear stockpiles. Spheres of influence tend to be tacitly recognized, despite explicit denials, and the disturber of the *status quo* is always out on a limb as compared with a supporter. Thus, one argument against skepticism with respect to American nuclear reliability is that it reflects a gross exaggeration of the adversary's proclivity for going to the nuclear brink. Thus far there has been none of that reckless playing of "chicken," of swift resort to brinksmanship, that filled so many of the fantasies of Herman Kahn and others in the 1960s. At any rate, crises do not start out with nuclear threats. So long as the Soviet Union has no ironclad guarantee that the United States will not use nuclear weapons, she has much to be careful about. The reverse is of course equally true.

Although my purpose has been to show that American vital interests are not to be found in objective reality but rather in the minds of men, it is necessary to repeat that we are talking not about something insubstantial but rather about what we will *fight* for. The United States at any one time does have a distinctive set of strategic policies, visible and quite firm, tied to equally visible foreign policies with their core of "vital interests," also relatively firm. These interests are rather easily identified by certain slogans, such as those expressing the need to "contain Communism" and to "resist aggression," the latter being meaningful and possibly tenacious where it also involves the former. In order to support these two interests, the United States has organized a network of alliances; and its record of dependability as an ally has thus far been above, rather than below, the call of duty. To this must be added certain important qualifications, engendered by recent unhappy experience and reflected in the currency of another slogan: "The United States cannot police the world." Still, future crises when they come may breed their own pattern of responses, and these are certainly more difficult to predict than superficial pronouncements would have us believe.

Morality Versus Ammorality in Vital Interests

We should not leave the subject of vital national interests without touching upon a matter that, when mentioned in connection with them, is often introduced for the sole reason of stressing its irrelevancy or worse. This is the issue of moral considerations, the intrusion of which into high international politics is frequently regarded by foreign policy experts as inherently mischievous, that is, as likely to cause the warping of what would otherwise be trimly correct thinking about foreign affairs. "Enlightened self-interest," they hold, is the one true guide through the confounding wilderness of conflicting appeals on the one hand and of divergent motivations on the other, and any sentiment that causes a diversion from that guiding line is likely to be not at all helpful and possibly even dangerous.

There is much to be said in favor of that conviction and a few things to be said against it—one among the latter being that it is impossible entirely to live up to it.

Like so much else in foreign affairs, the tradition of the irrelevancy of moral and related considerations on the more serious affairs of state, especially those having to do with war and the possibility thereof, has a long history, with many facets and many ambiguities. A part of the argument is summed up by Thucydides in one of his most gem-like chapters, "The Melian Debate" (Book V, chap. 7), which ends with the people of Melos paying a hideous price because they heeded the call of sentiment rather than self-interest. Inasmuch as war can be very dangerous to the state, with inordinate costs often being paid by the loser, and being itself a negation of morality in that it allows or necessitates practices to be condoned and even applauded that otherwise would be utterly repugnant and criminal, it does not appear to be a good means of dealing with evil. To attempt to cure one evil with another kind introduces intriguing difficulties into the accounting.

Also, statesmen are trustees for others. Under what moral or legal principle may they impose upon others the duties of risking or yielding up their lives, or paying in many other painful ways the costs that attend war, for anything other than the common good of the community that gives them their authority, and that most restrictively interpreted? The moral principles that incline the leaders one way or another are their own, very likely not widely shared and almost never universally shared. Our own Civil War is one of many cases in point. Lincoln favored abolition, but he went to war to "save the union," and made that the rallying cry in the North. The notion that secession was rebellion commanded far more general agreement in the North than would have been the proposition to free the slaves. It was the war itself, more than a year of it, that brought the population of the North round to acceptance of the Emancipation Proclamation—which even then had to be stated conditionally.[13] The war made the abolitionist who had been reviled in the North finally respectable, inasmuch as previous abuse of him had not prevented it; and *his* special enemies were now also the enemies of the nation, bent on its destruction. With the punitive fervor that rises with all great wars, there was general eagerness to visit condign punishment on the slaveholder, whose rebellious conduct had caused him to forfeit all claim to recompense for his lost property. Thus with the war's end, Thaddeus Stevens and his followers could push through the Thirteenth Amendment, though few had supported the war to produce that end. In short, the surgery being radical the cancer was excised, but the treatment had not been ordered for that purpose.

Even a diplomatic intervention designed to indicate hostility to certain immoral acts or behavior of the target state may, it is often held, be mischievous on the general grounds (a) that such interventions may do more harm than good to the very people we are trying to help, and (b) there may be special characteristics of the

---

[13] Proclaimed on September 22, 1862, it declared that all slaves should be free from January 1, 1863 onward in all states or parts of states that should still be in rebellion on that date. Lincoln's personal position has often been misinterpreted, largely because of his well-known letter to Horace Greeley. That he was entirely and deeply anti-slavery in his sympathies long before the war is beyond doubt, as was amply revealed in his debates with Stephen A. Douglas in 1857. That is why secession resulted from his selection as President in 1860. However, when Horace Greeley needled him in an editorial pressing for emancipation, Lincoln wrote him in a letter dated August 22, 1862: "My paramount object in this struggle *is* to save the Union, and is *not* either to save or destroy slavery. If I could save the Union without freeing *any* slave, I would do it, and if I could save it by freeing *all* the slaves, I would do it; and if I could do it by freeing some and leaving others alone, I would also do that." However, at the time he wrote this letter he had already composed the Emancipation Proclamation and had read it to his cabinet on July 22, but at Seward's urging he had agreed to withhold it until after a military victory. The driving of the Confederates out of Maryland was taken as the requisite victory. See Fawn M. Brodie, *Thaddeus Stevens: Scourge of the South* (New York: Norton, 1959; Norton paperback, 1966), pp. 158f.

situation that people far away cannot understand. Former Ambassador George F. Kennan used such arguments in late 1970 in protesting a proposed United Nations diplomatic and economic intervention against the Union of South Africa for its practices relating to racial apartheid, which practices he forthrightly condemned as "shocking and depressing." However, lest it be assumed that Kennan's was the response invariably to be expected of the experienced foreign service officer, it must be added that a very effective reply completely rejecting Kennan's views was shortly thereafter published by Ernest A. Gross, a former Assistant Secretary of State and a specialist in South African affairs.[14]

When we come to military intervention, we are talking about war, which may initially be on a small scale but which may unexpectedly graduate into a larger one. As Vietnam so abundantly proves, war easily introduces far greater evils than it may be intended to fend off, and in addition it risks failure or defeat. Vietnam also underlines far better than South Africa the difficulties of knowing who is in the right and who is in the wrong in a quarrel abroad. Even those may differ who have very considerable knowledge of the special circumstances, and people thus knowledgable are usually rare. Also, the conflicting views or principles that cause people to differ sharply concerning the situation abroad may be such as normally find a relatively easy home together within the American political framework, so that by taking our quarrels abroad we needlessly sharpen them at home. Again citing Vietnam, the vast flow of conflicting information and downright misinformation that has proceeded from that unhappy country to contribute to the unhappiness of our own—with a powerful feedback to Vietnam to perpetuate the evils there—is proof enough of these points.

Also, we may find that a government formerly (and correctly) condemned as obnoxious to us and inherently evil may nevertheless become an indispensable ally to us in a war against a more clearly evil and dangerous enemy. In 1941 we went to war against Hitler in alliance with Communist Russia, but only two years earlier the British and French had been trying, with our urging, to assist Finland against Russia in the "Winter War," something

---

[14] The statement by Ernest Gross, on the editorial page of the *New York Times* for December 30, 1970, is worth reviewing as an exceptionally good reply to Kennan's more conventional diplomatist's position presented in his "Hazardous Courses in Southern Africa," *Foreign Affairs*, vol. 49, no. 2 (January 1971), pp. 218–236.

that the Swedes happily prevented them from doing. To be sure, Hitler will long remain the classic example of the perfect enemy, in comparison with whom all other dictators become in some degree respectable and who tends to justify a war of even vast dimensions. He provides an example that may be used too much, precisely because it is too clear-cut and unlikely to be repeated.

Moralists, as Arthur M. Schlesinger, Jr. points out, "tend to prefer symbolic to substantive politics. They tend to see foreign policy as a means not of influencing events but of registering virtuous attitudes." No doubt he overstates it; moralists certainly also want to influence events. But he is right in saying that "the heirs of John Foster Dulles and the disciples of Noam Chomsky are equal victims of the same malady. Both regard foreign policy as a branch of ethics. They end up as mirror images of each other. In the process of moral self-aggrandizement, each loses the humility which is the heart of human restraint." [15]

Still, there is another side, as Schlesinger readily admits. The professional tradition against the intrusion of moral sentiment is so strong and rigid that it depends for its perpetuation on myths and on assertions that often carry a large element of exaggeration —and this fact is itself meaningful. Where precepts are habitually urged to the point of exaggeration, one has reason to suspect ambivalence, suggesting in turn the existence of strong counter-motivations.

In states at war we often see these ambivalences in acts justified in the name of "honor," though usually with curious results in terms of the normal meanings of that word. When "honor" is invoked one usually has to expect more killing rather than less— sometimes only a little more in order that a meaningless carnage may be avoided or terminated in a traditionally proper manner, and sometimes a great deal more, as when the Nixon Administration decided that "honor" required us to wind down our participation in the Vietnam War very slowly rather than very rapidly, and extra slowly with respect to aerial bombing and naval shelling. The extra lives lost were thus Vietnamese rather than American, but that, too, is presumably compatible with wartime "honor." "Honor, like charity," says Walter Goodman, "goes with

---

[15] See his "The Necessary Amorality of Foreign Affairs," *Harper's*, August 1971, pp. 72–77. One should note that in response to criticisms elicited by this article, Schlesinger in a subsequent issue disclaimed responsibility for the title, which had been chosen by the editors and which he disliked as distorting his position.

power, for the powerless are rarely in a position to exercise such virtues. Further, before one can prove himself truly honorable, he must show a capacity for dishonor, less his noble gesture be laid to some constitutional weakness." And then, "As a side effect of demolishing large sections of Vietnam, the U.S. has quite demolished the word *honor*." [16]

The same characteristics are also seen in wartime propaganda. National leaders always proudly proclaim the high morality of whatever they happen to be doing, and this proclivity becomes more marked during wartime because it is more needed. However, specialists in propaganda have long agreed that the most effective propaganda is that of the deed, and also that what one says in justification of one's acts is likely to be the more effective the more one sustains one's credibility. It is anyway pointless as well as awkward to be involved in a war for purposes that will not pass muster according to the moral consensus of our own culture. The same applies to the methods used in war.

We fought a war against Hitler in alliance with Stalin, which also happened to be in alliance with all the democracies of western Europe. But can one imagine the United States fighting a war in alliance with a Hitler? For what conceivable objective and against what more bestial kind of enemy? The impressive national unity achieved during World War II in this country meant that even the people on the conservative or right-wing of the domestic political spectrum found little difficulty in adjusting to the fact that we were allied to Communist Russia. A comparable unity would have been inconceivable if we had been fighting on the other side.

The question thus has both its intrinsic and its expediential aspects, and it is both difficult and unrewarding to attempt sharply to separate them. If one has to brand the enemy a devil incarnate, it helps if he really is one. It helps, too, if one's own goals do not show too ungainly a disharmony with the moralistic cant with which they are normally surrounded. Moreover, there is a lesser bill to pay afterwards when one is held to accounting for getting the country involved in the war. More to the point, however, inasmuch as we must determine as wisely as possible what kinds of world situations we would find intolerable as compared with those we could manage to live with, the idea that moral

---

[16] Walter Goodman, "Fair Game," *The New Leader*, July 26, 1971, p. 15.

considerations can or should be totally expunged from such a momentous weighing of alternatives is plainly absurd.

The United States is today committed to a process of granting assistance, including military assistance, to various governments, including some outside our alliance ties. This is obviously done with much discrimination. Are we so certain of our national or "vital" interests in each case as to make it a matter of moral indifference what kinds of government they are and why we feel they deserve our support?

For years the severely authoritarian government of Franco Spain has been excluded from membership in NATO, mostly because of the negative feelings of our European partners. We have nevertheless continued to give considerable assistance to Franco's regime, largely in the form of bomber-base leases, even considerably after the necessity of those leases became questionable. The suppression of democracy in Greece by a harsh rightist dictatorship caused our government for a time to suspend military assistance, but in 1971 the Nixon Administration resumed the assistance, presumably on the assumption that NATO and its needs demanded prior consideration over outraged feelings frequently restimulated by stories of torture of political prisoners—difficult to authenticate, perhaps, but equally difficult to doubt in view of the number and character of the sources. In addition the Administration sent Secretary of Commerce Maurice H. Stans there in April 1971, where he took occasion to express exceptionally warm and approving sentiments of the regime. As though that were not enough to establish a reasonable level of amity, Vice President Spiro Agnew was also sent there in the following October for the same purpose. Then in early 1972 Athens with its port of Piraeus was made a home base for portions of the Sixth Fleet, an act that, however neutral our government proclaimed it to be, was interpreted by all Greeks as an expression of support for their government.

Such decisions are only tangentially concerned with morals. If one opts for a "correct" relationship with another government—especially where it is a partner in an alliance considered important—the added cost of gestures of friendliness is indeed trivial. However, there may be other costs, some of which may reflect seriously on what appear to be moral stances taken elsewhere. Actions of this sort reveal our national priorities and help to define our national image. They incidentally also indicate the conclusion that our faith in the continuing importance and utility of NATO remains undiminished, which may reflect the fruits of continuing reassessment but is more likely to suggest simply habituation to a point of view. It is difficult to assess NATO's real utilities and capabilities on the one hand and on the other hand the real characteristics and dimensions of the threat with which it is set up to cope. Nor does our government normally try seriously to sound European attitudes on these questions. In any case, we have to weigh the fact that our behavior toward Greece and other such states does not escape the notice of the large moderate left throughout Europe and for that matter the rest of the world. In short, we are locked into a stance that inevitably has moral implications or overtones.

In 1971 the United States government also found it consonant with its vital interests to continue to send arms to the Pakistani government, a harsh military dictatorship, at a moment when the world was revolted at that government's use of American arms already in its possession to carry out in its Bengali territories some of the most horrible and bloody suppressive actions recorded in modern times. The interest pleaded was the somewhat arcane one of keeping Pakistan from falling too completely into the arms of China, with whom at that time it was virtually allied in its chronic hostility to India. Matters were not helped when, in the brief war that broke out in December 1971 between India and Pakistan over the independence of Bangla Desh, leakage to the press of views expressed in the National Security Council showed the President siding with Pakistan, a position abhorrent to most of the world, including the informed part of American opinion.

On another continent, South America, we have a long record of providing military support to dictatorial regimes, so long as they are dictatorships of the right rather than of the left. The intervention ordered by President Johnson in the Dominican Republic in April 1965 accomplished its design of suppressing a revolt aimed at restoring exiled former President Juan Bosch. Bosch had previously been ousted by the military junta then in power, the leader of which had been a lieutenant of the late infinitely corrupt dictator, Trujillo. Our objection to Bosch could not be that he was a Communist, for we made no such charge and we had previously supported him. Also, had he been a Communist he would hardly have chosen as his place of exile the United States territory of Puerto Rico. Our Administration objected to him because he was allegedly too weak and too impractical to prevent his moderately left government from being *ultimately* taken over by Communists. Meanwhile we compromised our position by a series of outright, contradictory, and quickly exposed lies concerning the Communists allegedly leading the revolt. Not a single United States casualty was sustained—from that point of view the intervention was a "success"—but the price paid was high.[17] Surely it is not altogether a matter for wonder that when official American visitors make "goodwill" or other tours of Latin America—like Richard Nixon as Vice President, and later Governor Nelson Rockefeller—they sometimes encounter manifestations of the most intense hatred.[18] Communists were no doubt responsible for whipping up those manifestations, but we had not made it difficult for them.

Subsequently, when an avowedly Marxist government under Dr. Salvador Allende Gossens took office in Chile in 1971 by strictly constitutional means, with the local military pledged to support this constitutional transfer of power, the United States did not wait for any demonstration of hostility or expropriation of American holdings but itself initiated a hostile demonstration by cancelling the visit to Valparaiso, apparently arranged by Admiral Zumwalt, of the giant nuclear aircraft carrier *Enterprise,* which was in any case passing by that port. The dismay and consternation among the Chileans, including the military who traditionally had the closest links with the United States, were visible and extreme.[19] This was bad manners rather than immorality—and very likely bad diplomacy as well. Again, it confirmed a coloration in our policy that obviously gives the lie to those of our

---

[17] See Theodore Draper, *The Dominican Revolt: A Case Study in American Policy* (New York: *Commentary,* 1968). Also Jerome Slater, *Intervention and Negotiation: the United States and the Dominican Revolution* (New York: Harper & Row, 1971).

[18] Richard Nixon described his reception in Caracas, Venezuela as one of his six crises in his book of that name, *Six Crises* (New York: Doubleday, 1962; Pyramid ed., 1968), pp. 195–252. See also Earl Mazo and Stephen Hess, *Nixon: A Political Portrait* (New York: Popular Library, 1968), pp. 165–187.

Governor Nelson A. Rockefeller's official trip, undertaken at the behest of President Nixon in 1969, stimulated hostile riots in almost every Latin American capital he visited. In Haiti he was photographed for international television enthusiastically embracing the late unlamented dictator François Duvalier. His subsequent report stressed the need for increasing United States military assistance to the governments in power in Latin America, most of which at the time were supported by military groups representing the far right. See *The Rockefeller Report on the Americas* (Chicago: Quadrangle Books, 1969).

[19] *New York Times,* March 7, 1971.

actions that we claim to be based on morality. (For example, in Vietnam "We are simply resisting aggression.") Also, it makes one wonder again why diplomatic gestures, whether favorable or negative, should be poor diplomacy *only* when they are *morally* motivated, as presumably our contrasting gestures in Greece and in Chile were not. The expropriations without real compensation of American mining holdings in Chile did come later, leading, of course, to the consideration of retaliatory measures by us. They probably would have happened in any case, even if the *Enterprise* had called with all its flags flying and bands playing. Nevertheless, the first gesture of ill feeling had come from our side, not theirs.

Why have we engaged in such policies? We can hardly justify them by our repugnance for the dictatorial form of government inherent in Communism, inasmuch as we support right-wing dictatorships that are equally oppressive and often much more corrupt. Nor can we base them on our repugnance for aggression and on our alleged vital interest in resisting aggression anywhere in the world, because it is abundantly evident that we resist only one kind of aggression. In signing the Southeast Asia Treaty (SEATO), the United States specifically inserted the reservation that it was committing itself to resist only *Communist* aggression. Is it because Communist dictatorships are always more hostile to the United States than right-wing dictatorships? That is certainly partly our doing, but in any case, why did President Nixon encourage an invitation and then commit himself so jubilantly in March 1972 to a personal visit to unrecognized Communist China? Then came the complementary visit to Moscow in the following May, with flourishes featuring the signing of a treaty a day in the great mission to halt the nuclear arms race.

The idea of rejecting moral considerations as a basis for external policies, especially with respect to military pressures or interventions, may appear thoroughly wise insofar as the attendant injunctions are mainly negative. It is a warning not to go out on crusades. Let your heart bleed for injustice; relieve human suffering where you can, including the suffering due to the injustice of others; but keep your weapons stowed. In the words of John Quincy Adams in a Fourth of July speech in 1821, "Wherever the standard of freedom and independence has been or shall be unfurled, there will be America's heart, her benedictions, and her prayers. But she goes not abroad in search of monsters to destroy." Well, one might say, but America then was a weak country. Yet that was not what Adams had in mind, for he went on to say that America

> well knows that by once enlisting under other banners than her own, were they even the banners of foreign independence, she would involve herself beyond the power of extrication, in all the wars of interest and intrigue, of individual avarice, envy and ambition, which assume the colors and usurp the standards of freedom. The fundamental maxims of her policy would insensibly change from liberty to force. . . . She might become the dictatress of the world. She would no longer be the ruler of her own spirit.[20]

Here one sees Adams, as was virtually inevitable in that day, falling back on moral principle in order to reject a policy of moral initiative.

However, where initiative abroad appears to be warranted for some other reason—which would have to mean for some reason of imputed self-interest—are we then to say that moral considerations must play *no* part in what we then decide to do or refrain from doing? This cannot but be bizarre! While morality by its very nature must finally be justified entirely on its own terms, it is not amiss to remind ourselves that especially in this world of abundant and rapid communications, any of our policies abroad that are either conspicuously immoral to begin with or likely to lapse into behavior that can be easily so labelled, whether justly or not so justly, is likely to prove quite inexpedient and ultimately self-defeating.

---

[20] The quotation of John Quincy Adams I have taken from George F. Kennan, who presented it in the Senate "Vietnam Hearings" of 1966 with the comment that he thought Adams "spoke very directly and very pertinently to us here today." *Supplemental Foreign Assistance Fiscal Year 1966–Vietnam: Hearings Before the Committee on Foreign Relations, U.S. Senate, 89th Congress, 2nd Session, on S.2793* (Washington: Government Printing Office, 1966), p. 336.

CHAPTER

9

On Nuclear Weapons:
Utility in Nonuse

I would say that only a child and an idiot does not fear war. The child because he cannot yet understand, and the idiot because he has been deprived by God of this possibility.

> Nikita Khrushchev, at Kazincbarcika, Hungary, April 6, 1964.

Nuclear war is stupid, stupid, stupid! If you reach for the push button, you reach for suicide.

> The same, on signing of the friendship pact with East Germany, June 12, 1964.

In old-fashioned Newtonian physics, before Einstein, the whole conception of "work" depended fundamentally on the creation and harnessing of movement, that is, the movement of some body relative to its own immediate environment. A body at rest did no work. To be sure, its weight caused it to push down on the surface supporting it, which meant that whatever lay below that surface must be pushing up with corresponding force to maintain the

375

state of equilibrium. Still, if there was no movement, no work was performed, hence, no energy consumed or provided. The massive weight of the Egyptian pyramids could rest on their foundations for millennia without an erg of energy being used up. Let one try to lift them by as much as a foot, however, and the situation is vastly changed. It was always difficult to grasp this notion, but we were persuaded it was true. Of course, bodies in motion through space were also in a sense in repose (everything is in motion, after all), so long as no force was acting to accelerate, retard, or deflect the course of the motion.

As in so many other ways, in politics or strategy things are quite different. Objects at rest can do enormous work—if those objects are such things as nuclear weapons. The work, though enormous, may also be subtle, so that it may not be noticed. The effectiveness of the objects may therefore be denied. That also is not new. Throughout World War I the British Grand Fleet lay for the most part in the cold, misty inlets of Scapa Flow at the far northern tip of Scotland. It sortied seldom, and only once made a real though indecisive contact with the German High Seas Fleet in the North Sea off Danish Jutland. After the war the British people asked: What good were all those battleships that had absorbed such vast expenditure? The answer, as so often happened, was most trenchantly provided by Winston Churchill, who in writing his account of the Battle of Jutland partly excused the caution of the British commander, Admiral Sir John Jellicoe, with the comment that Jellicoe was "the only man on either side who could lose the war in an afternoon." The Grand Fleet could not guarantee victory in the war but its destruction would surely have guaranteed defeat, and quickly, to Britain and all her allies. While it lay in Scapa Flow British merchant vessels could ply the seas, albeit with danger from submarines and other raiders, but German commerce was quite shut off.

The flashes of three atomic bombs in the summer of 1945 at Alamagordo and over Hiroshima and Nagasaki illuminated at once to the world that mankind had brought upon itself a deadly peril. For a time all other conclusions were quite blotted out, and even the joy of a victorious war's end was clouded over by a nagging anxiety. The scientists cried, "What have we done?" and held innumerable meetings in search of total cures. So did many others, including statesmen and politicians of various ranks, and out of some of these meetings and deliberations came the foredoomed "Baruch Proposals" presented to the United Nations in 1946. At the same time, however, there began to develop another idea, less hopeful of total cures but also less certain of total catastrophe in the absence of such cures. This was the idea of "deterrence," for which again Churchill was later to inspire a memorable phrase, the "balance of terror," which might serve finally to end war where all other means had failed.[1]

This writer in 1945 urged the idea of nuclear deterrence—which looked ahead to mutual possession of nuclear weapons by at least the two major powers—in a statement summed up in the following words:

> Thus, the first and most vital step in any American security program for the age of atomic bombs is to take measures to guarantee to ourselves in case of attack the possibility of re-taliation in kind. The writer in making that statement is not for the moment concerned about who will *win* the next war in which atomic bombs are used. Thus far the chief purpose of our military establishment as has been to win wars. From now on its chief purpose must be to avert them. It can have almost no other useful purpose.[2]

Much of the debate on atomic-age strategy since that time has

---

[1] I must be somewhat pedantic in order to anticipate the pedanticism of others and point out that Churchill never actually used the phrase "balance of terror" in his relevant speech, which was to the House of Commons on March 1, 1955, just as John Foster Dulles never actually used the phrase "massive retaliation" in his famous speech of January 12, 1954. In each case members of the press coined the phrase from words used in the speech. Churchill stated that by "a process of sublime irony" the world was facing a situation "where safety will be the sturdy child of terror, and survival the twin brother of annihilation." The relevant passage is quoted in the *New York Times*, March 2, 1955.

[2] The original paper containing this statement was published as "The Atomic Bomb and American Security," Memorandum No. 18, Yale Institute of International Studies, 1945. In expanded form it was included in the book coauthored and edited by me, *The Absolute Weapon* (New York: Harcourt, Brace, 1946); the quoted passage is on p. 76. The now commonplace idea of achieving a peaceful equilibrium through mutual deterrence was not only novel at the time but to many quite reprehensible. It conflicted with the dire predictions of renowned scientists, including J. Robert Oppenheimer, and shocked and appalled such advocates of world government as Dr. Robert Maynard Hutchins, then chancellor of the University of Chicago, who wrote a denunciatory review of the book. Some twenty-three years later Professor Michael Howard of All Souls College, Oxford, exhumed the book and wrote some very kind words about its predictions in his paper, "The Classical Strategists," originally published among the *Adelphi Papers* (no. 54) of the (International) Institute for Strategic Studies, reprinted in Howard's *Studies in War and Peace* (London: Temple Smith, 1970), and in Alastair Buchan (ed.), *Problems of Modern Strategy* (London: Chatto & Windus, 1970).

revolved around the thoughts expressed in those five sentences. Missing from them altogether is the notion of limited war, which was not to develop until the early 1950s—stimulated both by the advent of thermonuclear weapons and by the Korean War—and then there would be much debate over whether nuclear weapons could or could not be used in limited wars, or whether they could be used tactically rather than strategically. Later there would be a more esoteric debate about possible methods of limiting even the strategic use of nuclear weapons, as by using a few of them for "demonstrating resolve" rather than serious killing.[3] The latter debate would soon peter out, partly on the realization that "resolve" was not a commodity of which the United States was guaranteed a monopoly, but even more on the perception that modern nuclear weapons required more careful handling than the concept implied. There would be an American shift to "counterforce" and "no cities" strategies. There would later be a considerable official anxiety about nuclear "proliferation," culminating with but not ended by the Non-Proliferation Treaty of 1968, finally ratified and legally effected in March 1970. But the main questions would continue to concern how we "guarantee to ourselves in case of attack the possibility of retaliation in kind."

This issue contains the problem of assuring the security of the retaliatory force, and of deciding how much "second-strike capability" (the latter phrase is originally Herman Kahn's) will suffice to guarantee deterrence. Moreover, it is not acceptable to all that deterrence is all-important and that "winning" is a matter of crude and brutal irrelevance; the military, among others, have consistently refused to accept this notion. How does this unresolved question work back upon our strategy and indeed upon our entire foreign policy? Furthermore, if we talk about nuclear deterrence averting wars, what *kinds* of wars does it avert and how much can we count on its averting *any* kind? Other questions come to mind that are subsidiary to these. We should notice, however, that all of them are in part, though in varying degree, political questions, that is, they cannot be answered adequately without reference to what we might broadly call political considerations and data. But the political dimension of these ques-

---

[3] See Klaus E. Knorr and Thornton Read (eds.), *Limited Strategic War: Essays on Nuclear Strategy* (New York: Praeger, 1952). Though the older expressions of the ideas contained in this book may now seem somewhat primitive, it is essential to keep alive the principle that the launching of one or a few nuclear weapons even strategically need not and should not mean the launching of all.

tions have usually been either totally neglected or else treated in an off-hand and arbitrary manner.

The political dimension is perhaps harder to see in such questions as those concerning the security of our retaliatory forces, which would seem to be governed entirely by technological considerations. That the relevant technological considerations are important goes without saying, but they are not exclusively so. Some technicians in the camp of the opponent may be convinced, conceivably with good warrant, that with a surprise first strike they can knock out 95 per cent of our land-based retaliatory forces (we will ignore for the moment our enormous naval retaliatory power in Polaris and Poseidon missiles). Apart from the question of the intrinsic reliability of these technicians' judgment upon the reliability of their plan (that is, are they entitled with high confidence to expect those results that they may be assuming only "if all goes well"?), will their political leaders believe them or feel at all inclined to test their proposition? How dire would the political circumstances have to be to impel those leaders to test it? And how about that remaining 5 per cent, which as a result of some intrinsically minor errors in data or of mishap might easily turn out to be 20 per cent? And what really is "unacceptable damage" —to resort to that much overused and underanalyzed conception? To be sure, their own ABM *may* be sufficient to take care of most of that remaining 5 to 20 (or more) per cent, but again, how reliably? And proof satisfactory to the politicians will again be lacking. Have they in fact built and deployed that ABM? Treaties may inhibit such deployment (as they do now). As one shrewd observer has pointed out, the main differences between those who tend to favor and those who tend to oppose the erection of an ABM system lies in their differing expectations concerning the probability of a strategic thermonuclear exchange.[4] At least this view is true for the United States and we may assume for the Soviet Union as well—and this difference will affect not only *whether* one goes ahead with such a system but also *how much* of it is provided.

In 1959 an article that won extraordinarily wide attention was

---

[4] Raymond D. Gastil, in J. J. Holst and William Schneider, Jr. (eds.) *Why ABM?* (New York: Pergamon Press, 1969), p. 41. This book, sponsored by the Hudson Institute under Herman Kahn, presents the pro-ABM argument, and was the reply to the book sponsored by Edward M. Kennedy, Abram Chayes and Jerome B. Wiesner (eds.) *ABM: An Evaluation of the Decision to Deploy an Antiballistic System* (New York: New American Library, Signet Broadside no. 7, 1969).

published in *Foreign Affairs*. Its argument was not especially a novel one—that our long-range bombers in SAC, which then comprised the major part (though by no means all) of our retaliatory forces, were exceedingly vulnerable to surprise enemy attack, especially if that attack be by the missiles that were then thought to be flowing into the Soviet arsenals. However, its author, Albert Wohlstetter, made such excellent and elegant use of the data available to him as to produce a profound effect upon a large proportion of his readers, which for that journal included persons of considerable influence in the United States and abroad. The article proved especially useful in shaking up the Strategic Air Command of the United States Air Force, which had consistently refused to recognize that it had a serious vulnerability problem. Wohlstetter entitled his article "The Delicate Balance of Terror," thus, through its paraphrasis of the Churchillian phrase, inevitably throwing the emphasis on the word *delicate*.

This article, as is characteristic of so many writings on military technological affairs, took no account whatever of the inhibitory political and psychological imponderables that might and in fact *must* affect the conditions implied by that word *delicate*. Many things are technologically feasible that we have quite good reason to believe will not happen. It has in fact become abundantly clear since the Wohlstetter article was published, and indeed since the dawn of the nuclear age, that the balance of terror is decidedly *not* delicate. This assertion is based on something besides the fact that the world has not yet blown up, though in view of the enormous disparities in nuclear capabilities between powers that have been at times enormously hostile to each other—and at some periods even in active conflict through proxies—that fact is itself impressive.[5]

---

[5] American refusal even to hint at the possible use of nuclear weapons during the so-called "Berlin Blockade" of 1948–1949, and to do little more than hint at it during the Korean War beginning in 1950, at a time when we still had effective monopoly, were among the indices suggesting extreme reluctance to threaten use of these weapons even under great pressure and with near-optimum conditions for the United States. Later there developed not only the "habit of nonuse" but also a readjustment of attitudes between the Soviet Union and the United States as a result mostly of the experience of continuing to live together without war despite recurring crises and growing nuclear arsenals on both sides. Certainly there was a continuing reevaluation by each side of the psychology and motivation of the other, in general with favorable results. I have treated of this in my *Escalation and the Nuclear Option* (Princeton: Princeton University Press, 1966), especially in chapter 3, "The Relevant Image of the Opponent."

However, when we turn from questions of the security of the retaliatory force to that other matter mentioned above, whether there can be any political issue that could possibly justify to either of the superpowers an all-out thermonuclear exchange between them, we are dealing with a question that is entirely political and philosophical in the deepest and broadest sense, for it concerns the most elementary ordering of our ethical values. The military officer is entitled to his own opinion in this matter, but that opinion is worth no special consideration by others. He must be actively discouraged from attempting to impose his view by making it too automatically operative in the national defense system. His special training has usually insensitized him to some of the profounder issues involved, which is why he has been so backward in making contributions to the conceptions of restraint embodied in the whole modern notion of limited war. His relevant expertise in what is now euphemistically called "general war," which is to say unlimited war under thermonuclear conditions, is confined to the handling of the machines. It would be well if he could also tell us whether, and how, we can so order our own military efforts in the event of general war as to decrease materially the damage to ourselves; and also whether, and how, the exchange of cosmic blows can be swiftly enough terminated before all the possible blows are struck to put a meaningful limit on the destruction. On the latter issue neither the military officer nor anyone else has had much, if anything, to tell us. The problem of bringing about a quick termination to "general war" is a completely baffling one, which provides only another imperative for avoiding such war. In short, the professional military officer knows no more than the rest of us about the strategy of thermonuclear war, and he and all of us should be clear that he does not.

Fears Realized and Unrealized Since 1945

In the something over a quarter century that has elapsed since the coming of nuclear weapons, we have had some experiences that were entirely predictable and some that would have been previously unbelievable. There has also been much additional thinking about nuclear weapons and about what they would mean in war and therefore in the basic affairs of mankind. Some of this thinking has taken strange twists and turns and led down weird byways. Certain of the ideas and conclusions that seemed

clear in 1945 appear even more sharply etched today. Others have
been not so much discarded as smeared over. It would not be correct to say that today our confusion is worse confounded, but
there *has* been a good deal of confusion along the way.

I shall not here attempt an historical sketch of the relevant
events and of the thinking about them that have occurred since
1945. It has been done elsewhere.[6] I shall instead try a reassessment of where we stand today with respect to nuclear weapons,
particularly in those matters that affect the political relations
between nations.

There is at least one respect in which all our early predictions,
even those that once seemed most wild, have been more than
amply confirmed. In everything having to do with relevant technology, the guesses being made around 1945–1946 have turned
out to be short of the mark by varying degrees, depending on the
sophistication and imagination of the persons making them. The
more conservative estimates made at that time have long since
proved utterly foolish. For the major nuclear powers, which remain still the United States and the Soviet Union, the following
decisive steps have taken place. Nuclear weapons have long since
embraced thermonuclear varieties, with yields that for all practical purposes are limitless.[7] Similarly, the old question of scarcity
versus abundance has long since been answered in favor of abun-

---

[6] See the paper by Michael Howard, "The Classical Strategists," referred to in footnote 2, this chapter. Morton Halperin has written a description based on unclassified
sources of the development of thinking about limited war in his *Limited War: An
Essay on the Development of the Theory and an Annotated Bibliography* (Cambridge,
Mass.: Center for International Affairs, 1962). See also my *Strategy in the Missile Age*
(Princeton: Princeton University Press, 1959), chapter 5. Far the most comprehensive
work on the development of strategic thought in the United States since 1945 has long
been under preparation by James E. King, whose book will be published, probably
in 1975, by The Free Press.

[7] One of the Soviet shots before the treaty signed in 1963 banning nuclear tests in the
atmosphere was of a thermonuclear device that by U.S. measurement yielded energy
equivalent to 50 megatons of TNT. Moreover, the yield was "clean," that is, free of
radioactive debris in the form of fallout. The significance of its being clean is that the
same bomb or device could undoubtedly have been nearly doubled in power by
making it "dirty," that is, by surrounding the thermonuclear element with a heavy
layer of plain uranium, which is mostly U-238. With the great mass of free neutrons
released from a thermonuclear explosion, some portion of the surrounding U-238 can
be induced to fission to raise the energy yield, and it is the fission that leaves the
debris. In other words, with the same kind of thermonuclear core, a dirty bomb will
always give more yield than a clean bomb. The United States never attempted to
duplicate the Soviet giant bomb; there was no question at all that we could do so, and
thus also no point in doing it.

dance, with fissionable materials threatening to be in oversupply as concerns military uses and with the United States (and possibly also the Soviet Union) already having cut back on their production for military purposes. Warheads, including the thermonuclear varieties, have been greatly reduced in overall weight, a factor that much affects their deliverability in large numbers and their use in such configurations as MIRV and antimissile missiles,[8] and these weapons have formed what is apparently a large family of special types. The development of long-range rocketry has proceeded beyond all expectations, especially with respect to accuracy, and this has threatened a serious strategic upset by reducing the protection offered by the hardened underground silo in which land-based retaliatory weapons are housed. As a partial offset of this new condition an effective antimissile missile system (ABM) is clearly within reach if not already accomplished. Meanwhile a totally separate and thus far apparently unthreatened missile retaliatory force has taken to the seas in huge nuclear-powered submarines. All that in just over twenty-five years!

There has, on the other hand, been a somewhat surprising lack of proliferation of nuclear weapons among other powers. Besides the two superpowers, only three other nations are known to have acquired nuclear weapons, and of these only China's nuclear capability is politically as well as strategically significant. Of the smaller nations, only Israel is commonly considered to be close to having a military nuclear capability, if she does not already have it. It is obvious why that nation should be inclined to want one, though even there we see leaders of opinion who are strongly opposed.

It was once commonly predicted that many nations would have the means to manufacture nuclear weapons and that those finding themselves in that position would almost inevitably take the step of making them. The proliferation of means has gone beyond

---

[8] The original implosion bomb dropped on Nagasaki weighed nearly 10,000 lbs., to give a yield of 20 KT. This weight was brought about largely by the fact that the bomb-bay doors of the B-29 and the B-50 opened just wide enough to permit the use of a bomb of 60 inches diameter. All this available 60 inches was therefore used in molding the TNT sphere of the implosive detonator. Later it was found that much smaller spheres were quite suitable—along with other changes in bomb geometry—and it became possible to produce thermonuclear bombs of one or more megatons yield at overall weights of a third or less of the Nagasaki bomb. A nuclear bomb can now be produced within weights that it is possible for a man to carry, but it is curious that although we once worried about "suitcase bombs," the worry seems to have dissipated now that they are at last feasible.

early expectations, especially because of the dissemination of nuclear power plants from which fissionable materials can under some circumstances be easily filched.[9] However, it is now obvious that most countries that could manufacture their own nuclear weapons have thus far elected not to take that step, and the reason is *not* to be found in the alleged expensiveness of nuclear capabilities as compared with conventional military capabilities. The latter, too, are expensive. France, which was once being undiplomatically upbraided (about 1961–1965) by its American ally for "wasting" its money on an independent *force de frappe*, or *force de dissuasion* as it later came to be called, may perhaps not have acquired a very impressive nuclear force as compared with our own or the Soviet Union's, but the same money spent on conventional forces would not have produced very many modern divisions or air wings either. To President de Gaulle nuclear weapons were a badge of the great-power status that he considered essential for France, and to have spent the same money on divisions instead would in his eyes have had no utility except to please the Americans—clearly not a high-priority aim in his life.

For western Germany—the main defeated power of World War II, and still regarded with intense suspicion by some of her neighbors, including the Soviet Union—an independent nuclear capability was a political impossibility and apparently not among German desires. The same, with certain special modifications, was true of Japan, the only country in the world to have experienced their use against her. Both had signed the Non-Proliferation Treaty with reluctance, not because they wanted to proceed with a weapons program but because they did not like the symbolic status of permanent inferiority that it allotted them, especially in some of its operational terms. Similar objections had been registered by other states that had never in the past been great powers. Some were no doubt concerned with keeping their options open, and in fact the Treaty itself provides for denunciation, under

---

[9] The reason is that plutonium-239, which can be used in fission bombs, is an inevitable byproduct of the modern nuclear power plant—though the "breeder" type plants on which research is being pushed will tend to use it up. Arrangements of sorts exist for an accountability of the Pu-239, but there is also general consensus that if the managers of the individual plant are in collusion with those who wish to appropriate the Pu-239, there is little doubt of their ability to do so undetected. The Pu-239 that comes out of a power plant usually has a greater proportion of the troublesome impurity Pu-240 than the plutonium made for bombs, but it is now generally agreed that this higher proportion of Pu-240 will not make the product unusable for bombs.

some circumstances, with an uncommonly brief three-months notice. Nevertheless, in most cases the possession of nuclear weapons was felt to invite more desperate dangers than it could ever fend off. The Scandinavian members of NATO, and also Luxembourg, refused to have American nuclear weapons stationed on their territories, and their non-NATO Scandinavian neighbor, Sweden, also decided after much debate to put its defense money on an efficient air force and army but not on nuclear weapons.

Events might some day make all these countries change their minds; but for small nations living alongside a powerful neighbor that possesses huge nuclear capabilities, the considerations that had originally turned them away from the nuclear path would undoubtedly continue to be strong, or become even stronger. The Swedes for example, looking at the Soviet Union, are likely to continue to say something like the following: (a) The Russians seem to have no desire to invade us, and we will be sure to give them no cause—in any case our small but efficient armed forces, which are clearly no threat to them, would deter them from choosing that course too lightly. (b) If they do decide to invade us during a war with others, we should greatly prefer that they do not feel obliged to use nuclear weapons in the process, as they might if we possessed them and threatened to use them. (c) For us to begin now to develop nuclear weapons when the Russians have become accustomed to seeing us without them would probably be looked upon by them as unfriendly and provocative. (d) On top of all that we now have the legal obligation to desist under the Non-Proliferation Treaty.

For a much larger and potentially powerful country like Japan, the strong emotional feelings engendered by the terrible and costly defeat of World War II and the horrors of Hiroshima and Nagasaki will no doubt wear thinner with time, but they have thus far remained remarkably durable. In any case, Japan will not go back to the militaristic mentality that preceded that war and which was then already anachronistic. Among other reasons, she has had the experience of seeing how well she can fare economically and politically without foreign conquests and without a heavy burden of armaments. Yet withal, her political leaders will be asking themselves questions like the following: (a) Is the Chinese nuclear capability really a threat against us, now or potentially, and under what circumstances might it be or become so? (b) In the event we decide China is a threat, is the American "nuclear umbrella" a sufficiently reliable protection? (c) In view of the answers to the previous questions, should we continue willing to pay the price of our alliance with the United States, which often appears onerous? One can think of other relevant questions, as well as of possible situations that might be unpleasant or deeply disturbing. I am not trying here either to predict or to catalog the possibilities, but rather to establish the commonplace point that considerations other than mere technological feasibility have already made several nations come down firmly and deliberately on the side of no nuclear weapons, and these considerations will certainly continue to operate in one form or another.

New Threats to Instability

In a book published in 1966 it was possible for this writer to conclude (in the view of some too optimistically) that the old bogey of surprise nuclear attack "out of the blue," that is, out of a condition of normal peace, was gone and probably had never really existed, and that in the future "general war can hardly occur except through escalation from lesser conflicts." The statement then proceeded:

> What has happened is that the constraints to refrain from strategic nuclear attack at *any* time, including a time of fairly intense local hostilities, have become great and also obvious. . . . The chief and almost the sole incentive for moving fast in such an attack in the past, which was to destroy the enemy's retaliatory force before it left the ground, has in the last several years been sharply declining as a compelling operative constraint.
> . . . The basic physical reason [for this happy state of affairs] is the enormous and continuing improvement in the security of our retaliatory forces (and presumably also the enemy's) against attack, through the well-known devices of hardening, concealment, and mobility.[10] This improvement

[10] *Hardening* is simply another word for encasing in armor protection, and armor has historically taken very many forms. One "hardens" a missile by putting it underground in a concrete silo. Concealment of missiles in silos is considered difficult or impossible because the opponent's reconnaissance satellites are bound to pick up the hole for the silo at various times during its construction and permit its being accurately positioned on a map—thus reducing the utility of camouflage after construction. Concealment and mobility are of course the strength of the submarine-launched missile.

may indeed be threatened in the future by certain technological advances, but it need not be overturned if we remain
fully abreast of ongoing developments.

Our confidence is further increased by the fact that this
physical change has served to buttress a comparably profound
psychological change. The latter results from a greatly improved understanding, apparently on the Soviet Russian side
as well as our own, of the motivations and psychology of the
opponent. The reasons for this improvement in mutual insight are many, but the essential fact is that each side seems
to have scaled down substantially the degree of aggressiveness, recklessness, or callousness it formerly attributed to the
other—also both have now grown accustomed to living with
each other under a situation that once seemed intolerably
menacing. Stability does not thrive on illusion, but it does
help enormously to have the situation turn other than precarious.[11]

Elsewhere in the book I pointed to some of the evidence that
the Chinese Communists too had undergone their share of comparable psychological development. If they seemed (or were) a
good deal more mistrustful of and hostile to the United States
than the Russians, they were not less conscious than the latter of
the real hazards of nuclear war.[12]

What has happened since—over a period of hardly more than
seven years—would provoke many to brand at least the first part
of the quoted satement as inopportune. And indeed there has
been such a steady gain in accuracy by long-range missiles, now
augmented by MIRV, that the "hardening" in underground silos
of retaliatory ICBMs—the location of which, because of the new
reconnaissance satellites, are always known to the opponent with
extreme precision—seems to be of rapidly diminishing value for
security. The feasibility of a "first-strike capability" could be held
to be on the way back, provided one excessively discounts a number of considerations.

The quoted passage does warn that "this improvement [in se-
curity] may indeed be threatened in the future by certain technological advances, but it need not be overturned if we remain fully

---

[11] Brodie, *Escalation and the Nuclear Option*, pp. 25–27.
[12] Ibid., p. 44, including 44 n.

abreast of ongoing developments." Perhaps the warning, in which I had in mind precisely the development of greater accuracy in the offensive missile, was understated. There is a danger that one's own forces will not remain "fully abreast of ongoing developments." Remaining abreast requires money as well as alertness, and though there is no shortage of those who would strive to keep us alert with their warnings, there are always vast and constantly growing competitive claims on the national budget. Where a decade ago it was almost inconceivable that the United States would yield up to the Soviet Union anything like parity, let alone superiority, in any department of arms other than ground forces, the world around 1973 looks different.

There has also been the harrowing Vietnamese experience, into which at the height of the American fighting we were pouring at least $30 billion annually, not to mention other huge costs, some measurable in dollars and others not. Besides, the technological problems of coping with the new menace appeared more than usually difficult. Once an incoming RV (reentry vehicle, containing a nuclear warhead, which may or may not be part of a MIRV system) attains an accuracy measurable by a CEP of, say, under half a mile, there is little use in trying to solve the problem by increasing the hardening of silos in the kinds of terrain in which they are now installed.[13] Perhaps holes chiseled out of rock in steeply mountainous areas might show significantly more resistance, and perhaps we have not really explored other possibilities. The "answers" most often discussed publicly included either installing many more retaliatory ICBMs than our present (in 1973) number of 1,054, though this is now prohibited by treaty, or, more commonly, developing an adequate ABM system to be used primarily in defense of our retaliatory system, which is now also limited by treaty. In both cases the basic question seemed to be the probable exchange ratio of costs between attacker and defender, that is, how many missiles, costing how much, would the aggressor have to fire to have a *high confidence* of knocking out a

---

[13] CEP, meaning "circular error probable," is the standard measure of accuracy for any gun projectile, bomb, or missile. It refers to the radius of that circle within which will fall half the missiles aimed at its center. Note that the CEP is normally measured in horizontal projection. Thus a given CEP on flat terrain means missiles falling closer to target than the same CEP in a very steeply sloping terrain. However, if the CEP becomes low enough, the difference will cease to be important. Because of the cube-root law for blast effect noted previously (that is, blast effect increases only with the cube-root of the increase in yield), in shooting against a hard-point target there is much more payoff in increasing the accuracy of the missile than in increasing its explosive yield.

predictably high proportion of missiles of his opponent. Those who seemed to be most involved in the problem appeared usually to favor the ABM as an answer rather than merely the multiplication of retaliatory missiles.

We shall not here involve ourselves in the intricacies of the ABM debate, which was touched on in an earlier chapter and about which a great deal has already been written in books and articles easily available to the public.[14] Naturally, there is also a large component of relevant classified material. I feel obliged only to admonish the reader that there have been outstandingly competent people, highly knowledgable and intelligent, on both sides of the issue (which differentiates this issue from many others of the past), and that passions can and do run exceedingly high on the matter among people whom we should normally expect to be constrained to somewhat more objectivity, and this also on both sides. The element of "selective inattention" among those engaged in the debate is too often conspicuous.[15] On the surface the controversy seems to be concerned mainly with technological feasibilities, but a small scratch in that surface exposes the customary involvement of biases that may loosely be called political or psychological.[16] The debate is naturally made acute by the fact that

---

[14] The best two books at this writing, one pro and one con, are those symposia mentioned in footnote 4, this chapter. There have, of course, also been innumerable articles. I should also mention the section dealing with this problem in Alain C. Enthoven and K. Wayne Smith, *How Much Is Enough? Shaping the Defense Program, 1961–1969* (New York: Harper & Row, 1971), especially pp. 184–194.

[15] Which is one reason why the expert cannot be wholly trusted, though we have to listen to him. The ABM problem has been one of particular complexity, where the layman is invited to take many assertions on faith. Is it, for example, true that the atmosphere will *reliably* filter out incoming warheads from decoys? I have often been given total assurance that it will, but I remain skeptical. It is not simply a matter of having or not having access to the appropriate classified information. It is a matter of living with that information, working it through, and thinking of possible variations of design of incoming missiles that might defeat a filtering scheme. The person doing the briefing may have done that thinking, but how imaginatively? And how objectively, in view of the fact that he desperately wants to see the ABM adopted?

[16] In the following observation I tread gingerly on sensitive grounds, from the personal rather than the security point of view. But one who has had the opportunity to observe at close range over many years persons who may have a profound influence on strategic thinking and on national strategies may notice over and over again the connection between some deep-seated neurosis and a particular rigid attitude on strategic problems. Alas, I cannot venture to give specific examples. The same kind of connection naturally often exists in the case of strong political biases or leanings, especially toward the extremes of the political spectrum—as Harold D. Lasswell pointed out long ago in various books, especially his *Psychopathology and Politics* (Chicago: University of Chicago Press, 1930)—but in strategy we are dealing with instrumentalities of special power and destructiveness, often enough with a conspicuous degree of phallic symbolism, as in the self-propelled missile.

the ABM is a *new* system, which not only heightens the uncertainties about its effectiveness and its ultimate costs but also affects the issue of arms control as a means of reducing or at least keeping in check expenditures on arms. As pointed out earlier, it is always easier to reach international agreement to keep sharply in check a system of which deployment has not yet or only barely begun rather than to cut back on one that is fully deployed. Partly for that reason, in the Strategic Arms Limitation Talks (SALT) between the Soviet Union and the United States, MIRV was largely regarded as water over the dam (partly also because it would be difficult to police), but the ABM lent itself to an agreement significantly limiting its deployment.

On one important aspect of the ABM controversy both sides seemed to be in full agreement, which is that if the system made sense at all it did so much more in "hard point defense" than in the defense of cities, which are very soft. The most important hard points to defend comprised our retaliatory ICBMs in their underground silos. Thus, the ABM mission to which President Nixon gave the code name *Safeguard*, which was originally the defense of our land-based retaliatory force, including a few control points and the national control center of Washington, was far easier to justify than the proposal originally made by former Secretary of Defense Robert McNamara in September 18, 1967 that a thin ABM deployment be undertaken for defense of our cities against China. This does not mean that Secretary McNamara was ill-informed; he may simply have regarded it as a more politic approach to the initiation of a program that he felt to be largely forced upon him.[17]

The reason for the superior effectiveness of the ABM system in the *Safeguard* mission starts from the classic point that an adequate defense of one's retaliatory system is the best deterrent to the enemy's attack and thus the best protection of everything else, but it goes beyond that. In defending such hard points as missiles in underground silos, only those incoming missiles or RVs on trajectories that would bring them close to their targets need be fired against; the rest can be ignored. This could mean important economies in the use of defensive missiles, which are expensive

---

[17] See the excellent interpretation of the bureaucratic and political infighting concerning the ABM within the United States government in Morton H. Halperin's "The Decision to Deploy the ABM: Bureaucratic and Domestic Politics in the Johnson Administration," *World Politics*, vol. 25, no. 1 (Oct. 1972), pp. 62–95.

and therefore bound always to be in limited supply at any single launching site as well as overall. It also helps to keep the fire-control system from becoming overloaded. In attempting to defend cities of substantial size, on the other hand, one might in each case succeed in destroying a high proportion of incoming RVs without succeeding in saving the city. Under appropriate weather conditions such as are fairly common, a single large thermonuclear weapon exploding at high altitude might by thermal radiation alone cause a fire-storm of truly vast radius. Under poorer weather conditions serious blast damage and destruction might easily occur up to ten miles radius.[18] Thus, to say that we can hope to shoot down three out of every five incoming RVs might be virtually meaningless if we are defending an attack aimed against cities, but it may spell huge success if the target system being defended is the retaliatory force.

Naturally, the value of erecting an ABM system to defend mostly our land-based ICBMs would depend in large part on whether the land-based configuration for ICBMs was worth retaining at all. We do indeed already have our large missile submarine force, which after some thirty of the forty-one existing vessels were converted to carrying Poseidon missiles with their MIRV warheads (public reports put as many as ten warheads in each missile), were capable of firing over 600 missiles accounting for over 5,000 RVs. True, these submarines may ultimately—one might almost say are bound ultimately—to show vulnerabilities to detection that apparently have not yet become troublesome. But in these matters we have long become accustomed to the fact that each "answer" has its own reply.[19] We could, for example, build relatively cheap low-speed submarines with long-range missiles to move along our own continental shelf, as contrasted with the high-performance Trident type, though the Navy does not like low-performance ships of any kind. The introduction of

---

[18] We have noted that blast-effect radius for a given overpressure increases only as the cube root of the increase in yield, but in clear air, thermal effect increases as the square root of the increase in thermal energy. Thus the larger the bomb the more important the effect of thermal radiation compared to blast effect, so long as weather conditions do not interfere. The optimum conditions for long reach of thermal effect are: good visibility, no cloud cover or preferably the bomb exploding under a very high cloud cover, plus snow on the ground.

[19] Concerning the nineteenth century race especially between naval guns and ship-borne armor, see my *Sea Power in the Machine Age* (Princeton: Princeton University Press, 1941; 1943 2nd ed. reprinted, Greenwood Press, 1969), part III.

MIRV itself seems, superficially at least, to confuse the issue. It would appear to make the task of defending a retaliatory force much more difficult for any ABM system, and yet it would also mean that whatever portion of the retaliatory force survives is much more dangerous than before.

In any case, I do not see the United States (or the Soviet Union) on the verge of a position where its retaliatory force ceases to deter or even undergoes serious diminution in its deterrence value. The United States has now accepted so severe a limitation of its ABM deployment as to raise the question of the value of that deployment which is permitted. The Russians, too, are giving up a significant ABM deployment, so that it appears that neither side really fears a surprise knockout blow. To repeat, the technological facts alone, besides never reaching an equilibrium where we can say that all the relevant facts are in, are never by themselves alone decisive of the important issues. Our relations with the Soviet Union have progressed in a way that continues to make relatively friendly relations normal, and the change in 1972 in our relations with Communist China represented a true revolution.

This does not mean that rough weather will not again be encountered. On the contrary, one can predict with confidence that sailing in company with such partners will not be perpetually smooth—that crises, some of them no doubt quite grave, will again arise. Still, each side will be looking at the nuclear weapons of the others, at vast numbers of them, and the kind of schizoid mentality required to ignore them appears to be an attribute hard to find among people sane enough to be tolerated in high office.

What Kinds of War Do Nuclear Forces Deter?

The nuclear bomb burst upon a world that had accustomed itself to the idea that "all modern war must be total war." This conclusion was derived from World War I and confirmed by World War II. Thus, all the early talk about deterrence was concentrated upon a kind of war of which there could be no question of the relevance of nuclear weapons. War would be deterred or it would not be deterred, but only one kind of war was meant. It is worth recalling, too, that very few people could believe that under the existing state system total war—or what is now called "general war"—might be indefinitely averted through a mutual balance of terror. Considering the tribulations with the Soviet Union that followed hard upon World War II, including the Berlin "blockade," [20] at a time when that country had no atomic weapons, one should not wonder at the poor expectations then entertained for a future in which she would have them.

There was at the time, within limited circles, some talk of "preventive war," which happily faded out in the early 1950s[21]—though some expectation of it in reverse seems to be linked to the lingering fear among those who feel that the Soviet Union could some day choose that course against us. Another kind of talk that has persisted to this day raises the question in retrospect of why the United States did not use its monopoly when it had it "to ensure," as one book reviewer put it, "the triumph of peace, liberty, and the American way of life." [22]

The most open threat yet made to use nuclear weapons in a specific instance was by Khrushchev during the Suez crisis of 1956, and the immediate direct effect was not the halting of the British-French invasion of Egypt, which had already been stopped by American pressure, but a speech in Paris by our then SACEUR, General Alfred M. Gruenther, reminding Russia that the United States stood prepared to retaliate against nuclear attack against any of its NATO allies. For the most part the prevailing code has been that atomic weapons are sufficiently evident and influential in the background, without needing to be rattled to remind one of their existence.

---

[20] I placed the word *blockade* in quotes because it now seems clear—and was obvious to some at the time—that there was no such thing as a blockade, though Stalin was quite content to let us think there was so long as we did not test it by sending through a ground convoy. As Professor Adam B. Ulam points out, in connection with our fears at the time, "As a result of demobilization carried out immediately after the war, by 1948 the numerical strength of the U.S.S.R. Armed Forces had been reduced to 2,874,000 men [from 11,365,000 at war's end] . . . It hardly suggests any fear of an imminent attack or of 'atomic blackmail'." Nor, we might add, of any disposition to have a test of arms with the United States. Later Ulam mentions "Russia's formidable task of policing her satellites . . . and many factors of a similar nature which, quite apart from the atomic bomb, made any military clash with the United States simply inconceivable to a man as realistic and cautious as Stalin." See his *Coexistence and Expansion: The History of Soviet Foreign Policy, 1917–1967* (New York: Praeger, 1968), pp. 403 f., 414.

[21] At the time I was publishing my *Strategy in the Missile Age* (1959), talk about "preventive war" was still sufficiently recent and fresh enough to cause me to devote over a dozen pages to the subject; see pp. 227–241.

[22] The words are by Stephen Ambrose, in the *New York Review of Books*, November 18, 1971, pp. 41–43. However, I must add that the book he was reviewing was not at all deserving of his slighting remarks. It was that of Adam B. Ulam, *The Rivals: America and Russia Since World War II* (New York: Viking, 1971). The work of Professor Ulam is always of the highest quality, and in this book he takes special pains to expose the foolishness of the New Left "revisionists."

The Soviet Union tested its first nuclear device in late 1949, and the Korean War followed soon thereafter in 1950. In November 1952 the United States successfully tested its first thermonuclear device. When the Eisenhower Administration finally deigned to announce this fact to the world almost a year and a half later, it also revealed that the Soviet Union had itself meanwhile detonated a comparable bomb (we were not told how long after ours, but it was about nine months), and that we had also already tested a second such weapon on March 1, 1954. We subsequently also learned that the second shot had revealed the phenomenon of close-in fallout of radioactive debris, resulting in that instance in casualties to Japanese seamen on a ship, *Lucky Dragon,* which had been downwind of the shot. The label *close-in* distinguishes this kind of fallout from the radioactive pollution that reaches high into the stratosphere where it spreads round the globe to trickle slowly back to earth (partly in the noxious forms of strontium 90 and carbon 14), yet the former kind could drop lethal deposits as much as 300 miles or more downwind.[23]

Most of these facts were naturally known to people within the "defense community," including places like the RAND Corporation, long before they became public knowledge, and they had quite enough shock value to stimulate some radically new thinking about what war might be like in an age that had been visited with such monstrous weapons.[24] The first fruits of this new ferment of thinking were some new ideas about "limited war," a

---

[23] Close-in fallout results mainly from the fact that heavy soil particles swept up by the blast of any detonation near ground level will capture a portion of the much finer radioactive particles created by the fission process itself. These will not rise to any great height, and are likely to fall of their own weight or be washed down by rain.

[24] A small group at the RAND Corporation in direct contact with Dr. Edward Teller and the Los Alamos Laboratory were informed in early December 1951 that a thermonuclear device of Teller's design would be tested the following November and that it would almost certainly be successful. The task of this group was to think through some of the implications of the forthcoming weapon in order to brief the senior members of the U.S. Air Force (and, as it turned out, the Secretary of Defense) at the same time that they learned of the new development. The group comprised Dr. Ernest Plessett, then head of the RAND Physics Division, Mr. Charles J. Hitch, then head of RAND's Economics Division and currently president of the University of California, and myself. At this time my own thoughts (and resulting highly classified briefings) were drawn to the need for limiting war by avoidance at all costs of strategic bombing, confining to tactical use any resort to nuclear weapons. The "conventional war" school was to develop later. It is perhaps useful to recall, because such circumstances are bound to be forever repeated, how novel and often shocking were views that are considered commonplace and altogether natural today. The Air Force became decidedly hostile to any notions that it might be necessary to find ways of limiting war by eliminating strategic bombing.

concept that presumably had been phased out in the late eighteenth century and had conclusively expired with World War I. It is curious that it was the thermonuclear bomb rather than the Korean War that first revived this old idea in a very new guise, but that war had until then been looked upon mostly as some kind of Russian feint. However, these fabulously destructive new weapons, which besides vastly expanding the radius of blast damage over the previously known fission bombs could cause fires by thermal radiation as much as a hundred miles away, began to throw the events in Korea into a new perspective.

The Korean War finally ended with the armistice of July 1953, and Secretary John Foster Dulles presented in the following January his "massive retaliation" speech. His words appeared generally designed to warn our major Communist opponents that if there were a new aggression like that in Korea, or if the Korean War itself were resumed, the United States would not feel bound again to restrict itself to nonuse of nuclear weapons. Included with that warning was the further admonition that use of nuclear weapons meant not tactical but strategic use, against what we considered to be the homelands of the major offending powers. In fact, tactical use of nuclear weapons had until then not been much thought of. In any case, the doctrine reflected the view that nuclear weapons could deter any kind of war in which there was even a possibility of their being used, and that the United States could and would feel quite uninhibited about using them where it felt its interests were sufficiently involved, the "sufficiently" clearly being intended to mean something short of desperation.

The reaction to the Dulles speech, at first somewhat muted and then increasingly vigorous, brought out into the open and gave powerful additional stimulus to existing thought on limited war. Soon the first articles on the subject began to appear.[25] By the time Henry Kissinger's *Nuclear Weapons and Foreign Policy* appeared in 1957, there had been five years of increasingly intensive thinking about limited war, in which nuclear weapons might or might not be used tactically. The spectacular success of Dr. Kissinger's book was partly the result of its hitting the market at exactly the right time. Ideas that had been confined to a few and

---

[25] See the Halperin and the Howard publications referred to in footnote 6, this chapter. I should also mention Robert E. Osgood, *Limited War: The Challenge to American Strategy* (Chicago: University of Chicago Press, 1957), though this book contains no account of prior development of limited war thinking.

regarded by others as fairly peculiar were now ready to be accepted by a very much larger segment of the defense community and indeed of the broader public.

However, the Eisenhower Administration continued until its end to be bound by the massive-retaliation ideas to which Secretary Dulles had given expression, though the major source of those ideas was undoubtedly the Joint Chiefs, especially during the chairmanship of Admiral Arthur Radford. For Eisenhower himself these ideas had appeal mostly for reasons of economy. The common stereotype of the general as one who believes totally in the primacy of spending for national defense, at whatever cost to programs designed to advance internal welfare, no doubt has much justification on a statistical basis, but it never applied to Eisenhower. The man who during World War II presided over so much of the military application of the apparently limitless material resources of the United States seemed always to be consumed with anxiety about placing too heavy a burden upon this miraculous American economy that could accomplish such things —and this was apparent well before he became President.[26] Eisenhower was convinced that the United States simply could not afford both large conventional forces and large nuclear forces, and this naturally had to mean that the option would be for nuclear forces—a decision that then accorded well with the preferences of the armed services, especially the Air Force. General Maxwell Taylor, however, after his retirement as Chief of Staff of the Army, recorded in his *The Uncertain Trumpet* his indignant disagreement with this policy.

The coming to power of the Kennedy Administration in January 1961 meant the official triumph of the anti-massive-retaliation point of view and a swing to the other extreme. President Kennedy took as his Secretary of Defense Robert S. McNamara, who absorbed the new ideas with zest, and brought General Taylor out of retirement to be his personal advisor on military affairs and later to become Chairman of the Joint Chiefs. The

---

[26] In the autumn of 1946, General Eisenhower, then Chief of Staff of the Army, gave a closed lecture to National War College students in which the message he communicated to his military brethren was that they must forebear to ask too much for military purposes lest the economy be strained. Later, as President, he showed an aversion to inflation that must be described as phobic, with the result that the national economy remained unduly sluggish through the entire eight years of his Administration. See also his speech, pleading for welfare over guns, to the American Society of Newspaper Editors on April 16, 1953.

Administration was committed, first, to making secure the nuclear retaliatory force by introducing as rapidly as possible long-range missiles or ICBMs that could be shielded in underground silos, and second, to building up large conventional forces in order to diminish reliance on nuclear forces. One result of this two-fold surge was an increase in the military budget of some $6 billion during the first year of the Kennedy Administration. At the same time heavy pressure was put upon our allies, especially those in NATO, to build up their conventional forces to an even greater degree than we were building up ours, in order that they might come closer to sharing what we considered a more equitable proportion of the common defense burden.

The intellectuals that Secretary McNamara gathered round himself, mostly for their skills not in political insight but in the new technique of systems analysis, included a tightly-knit group out of the RAND Corporation who embraced with the fervor of religion the notion that the best and indeed the only way to seal off nuclear weapons from any possibility of use was to build up large conventional forces to operate in their stead.[27] Here, they insisted, was a new and *practical* way of coping with the existence of nuclear weapons. President Kennedy and Secretary McNamara were in total harmony with these views, and were willing to pay the price. Where the Eisenhower Administration had looked upon nuclear weapons as inescapably necessary but happily also as a means of economizing on other kinds of forces, the Kennedy-Johnson Administration looked upon nuclear weapons as necessary enough but in no way a substitute for conventional forces. Slogans soon developed to characterize the new school. One was that we must not put ourselves in a position where in the event of enemy aggression our only choice would be "between surrendering and using nuclear weapons." Another was that in the event the opponent chose to attack by conventional means alone, as this school insisted he was most likely to do, "we must not find ourselves obliged to *initiate* the use of nuclear weapons because

---

[27] These people were not in the topmost ranks of authority below McNamara, as were Roswell Gilpatric, Cyrus Vance, Paul Nitze, and others, but as acknowledged experts in the study of modern war, their thinking had much influence. I mean specifically persons like Alain Enthoven, Henry Rowen, Albert Wohlstetter, and William Kaufmann (of whom Wohlstetter seemed to be the intellectual leader, at least while they were at RAND). Charles J. Hitch, Assistant Secretary of Defense for the Budget under McNamara and a former executive of RAND, was not greatly involved in the novel thinking of the others.

of our weakness in conventional weapons." It was terribly important, in other words, to put the onus of initiation on the other side—who presumably would be so unwilling to accept it that this onus would itself act as his primary deterrence.[28]

What enemy and what situations were these people talking about? In general two quite different kinds of situations, though not necessarily different enemies. There was on the one hand interminable talk of "brush fires" outside of Europe, of which Korea had been a rather large example, and which would usually mean the use of proxies by the Soviet Union or China or more likely the combination of the two. As it turned out, Vietnam was to fullfil most of the criteria for that type of war but to depart in some critical respects from expectations about outcome—and it turned out not even to be a proxy war. But there was also a tremendous preoccupation with the European theatre.

In the scenarios that sprang up to describe the latter situation, the common characteristic was always the Soviet Union with its Warsaw Pact satellites making a surprise lunge somewhere across the line that formed the Iron Curtain, and doing so with conventional arms alone. The attack might be general along the line, intended to wipe out NATO and take over western Europe to the Pyrenees, or there might be some variation in diminished form, like what came to be known as the "Hamburg grab." In the latter instance the Soviet forces would slice around the important city of Hamburg, and then leave it to us to try to take it back—which without large conventional forces we obviously could not do unless we were prepared to start a nuclear holocaust. The "Hamburg grab" scenario was mentioned with particular frequency, not because anyone presumed to detect in the Soviet eye a special han-

---

[28] The phrases I have put in quotation marks in this paragraph are not taken from any one source but were simply expressions often used. Actually, perhaps because there was so little resistance to their views, the school I am describing committed few of their ideas to writing. One sees them expressed in the Kaufmann book described on pp. 411 f., in the annual "posture statements" put out over McNamara's signature, and in a very few articles. One source that received much attention, and which contained expressions like those I have used, was originally a speech delivered by Alain C. Enthoven before the Loyola University Forum for National Affairs at Los Angeles on February 10, 1963. The paper from which he delivered his remarks was subsequently reprinted in several books of readings, including Robert A. Goldwin and Harry M. Clor (eds.), *Readings in American Foreign Policy* (London: Oxford University Press, 1971), pp. 499–512; also Henry A. Kissinger (ed.), *Problems of National Strategy* (New York: Praeger, 1965), pp. 120–134.

kering for that particular city but because the technique described in it seemed to provide a perfect example of what needed to be guarded against.

The spirit behind the movement was at least as interesting as the arguments used to buttress it. It reminds one again of Dr. Gastil's previously noted observation that the major difference between those who favor ABM and those opposed could be found in their differing expectations about whether there would really be a thermonuclear war.[29] The real problem (it seems to this writer) has been one where we have to defend against a threat that we cannot say is totally absent, but where enemy incentive to attack seems very low. In such a case one wants to minimize expenditures. Reliance upon tactical nuclear weapons is clearly one way of doing so. We do not picture the putative opponent as trying hard to think through whether and under what circumstances we will use them, besides which he could never be sure that we would not if he attacked.

Those, on the other hand, who urged the conventional buildup in Europe appeared clearly to entertain a greater fear of Soviet attack upon western Europe than the few who did not. They feared that the nuclear deterrent would especially fail to deter a nonnuclear attack. The obverse of this fear was the hope, amounting in many to an obvious conviction, that presenting a stance of nonnuclear resistance would, if it did not deter enemy attacks, help to channel them into nonnuclear means!

Yet our government felt bound to promise our NATO partners that we would indeed use nuclear weapons rather than yield up permanently any part of their territories. Thus, the Russians were put on notice that while we much preferred to fight the coming war conventionally, we were not at all prepared to accept defeat and *would shift to nuclear weapons to avoid it.* Our allies periodically demanded and as often received reassurance that we would not wait too long to introduce nuclear weapons, tactical and strategic, into the war. At the same time we kept urging them to build up their conventional forces and also kept publicly upbraiding the French for spoiling our grand plan and wasting their resources foolishly by insisting on building up a military nuclear force of their own. They should, we held, rely on our nuclear

---

[29] See p. 379.

forces and use their resources to build up the conventional forces we desired for them.

There is no need here to recapitulate all the arguments. They are readily available elsewhere, and the issue, though not yet dead, does not have the urgency it once did. In several publications I took a somewhat isolated position against the official American doctrine and had hoped to be quit of the argument, but the issue keeps raising its head in one form or another.[30] I have been taxed by some colleagues in the field with "exaggerating" the Administration position, and indeed the statements of Secretary McNamara were varied enough to reflect some inherent ambivalence and confusion in his own mind as well as a desire to keep our allies assured that we would not shrink from threat or use of nuclear weapons if such were essential to their defense. Also, what we were saying to the Europeans was not always the same as what we were telling each other in memoranda exchanged at home. Thus, it is easy to be confused about what was really going on.

It is nevertheless clear that the Administration was missing no occasion to press the Europeans to build up their conventional forces considerably beyond the levels the latter thought necessary. Also, Secretary McNamara repeatedly indicated in his annual posture statements that he was aiming for enough conventional forces to be able to fight not just a small delaying or local action in some critical area like Berlin but rather a large conventional war, for 90 days or more, against the whole field army maintained by the Warsaw Pact Powers.[31]

Well, what was wrong with the idea? Why not by building up conventional forces get away from reliance on the rightly dreaded

---

[30] For example, Alain Enthoven in his recent book (1971) coauthored with K. Wayne Smith presents what are essentially the same arguments he put into his Loyola speech of 1963 (footnote 28). See *How Much Is Enough?*, pp. 117–164. See also my quotations from Secretary Laird, pp. 409 f. My own publications arguing against the extreme conventional buildup point of view were mainly two articles and a book: "What Price Conventional Capabilities in Europe?," *The Reporter*, May 23, 1963, reprinted in several books of readings, including the cited one by Kissinger, *Problems of National Strategy*, pp. 313–328; "The McNamara Phenomenon," *World Politics*, vol. 17, no. 4 (July 1965); and *Escalation and the Nuclear Option* (Princeton: Princeton University Press, 1966).

[31] See, for example, the direct quotations from McNamara's 1963 "posture statement" in my cited article, "What Price Conventional Capabilities in Europe?" The reference to ninety days reserves of munitions and other supplies is not contained in those quotations, but it was a bone of contention in our running debate with NATO countries for well over a year.

nuclear weapons? The main answer, no doubt, is that one cannot get away from nuclear weapons so easily. And because one cannot, their existence poses certain compensatory advantages that might as well be accepted. That being so, it also becomes relevant that a conventional buildup requires a good deal of money and increased conscription. No kind of military force is cheap. Although the advocates of conventional war capabilities kept insisting that the size of the Warsaw Pact armies had been greatly exaggerated and that the amount of extra men and money required to come abreast of them was not large, it was clear that they were talking of increases in military outlays of at least 20 per cent for most of our European allies. It was also clear to others that this was an extraordinarily optimistic estimate.

Moreover, with the selective inattention common to those who feel religious fervor about the position they urge, they refused utterly (and still do) to take into account the fact that Russians, seeing us building up our conventional forces, might find themselves inclined to do likewise. Khrushchev had in fact been rapidly running down Soviet ground forces in Europe until 1961, but stopped abruptly when he saw us moving on an opposite tack. In effect, the Soviet run-down was cited as justification for our building our forces up, because it was that run-down that made it appear feasible to match them. Besides, these American advocates betrayed no idea of the truly vast forces in tanks, artillery, and men that had been involved in the 1941–1945 war, especially between the Russians and the Germans on the eastern front.[32] They assumed that a force of thirty fleshed-out NATO divisions on the central front in Europe could stop a planned Soviet invasion by nonnuclear forces, or would at least serve to deter such an attack where our nuclear weapons would fail to deter it.

It is the last point that matters. It would be difficult to deny the utility and thus the need for spending the extra money if

---

[32] The Russo-German aspect of World War II involved at the height of the campaign 4.2 million men in 198 divisions on the German side and 6.5 million men in 530 divisions on the Russian side; from June 1941 to June 1943 the Germans lost 8,000 tanks and still held 2,300, at which time the Russians had 5,600; by November 1943 the Germans had *captured* 5 million Russians. See Albert Seaton, *The Russo-German War, 1941–1945* (London: Arthur Barker, 1971). These figures contrast staggeringly and also ludicrously with the figures treated in much NATO force planning, despite the fact that the Soviet Union with its Warsaw Pact partners has enormously greater industrial resources now than it did then.

nuclear deterrence were truly inadequate to protect western Europe against any major attack, meaning a *deliberate* attack, and *if additional conventional forces could offset that inadequacy.* But what a truly strange idea! Let us first be clear that NATO was never naked of conventional forces, and that such frequently uttered contrasts as that between "pinprick" on the one hand and nuclear weapons on the other was always pure myth. Whenever we wanted to make a show of force we seemed not to lack the forces for the purpose.[33] In part it depended on what it was we really wanted to accomplish. Dean Acheson, in a speech given in 1963 at Cambridge, England to a large international gathering, argued that NATO needed larger conventional forces in Europe —in order to throw the Russians out of East Germany! This statement got the predictable response, which Mr. Acheson found unappetizing.[34] Others have been more defense-minded, but not on that account alone more reasonable. Inasmuch as we had enough forces to take care of the demonstrations that the repeated crises round Berlin seemed to call for, and enough, too, for the "accidental" (that is, unplanned) forays of the opponent that were so often mentioned as "conceivable," for what purposes did we need more? Why especially did we need parity with the Russians and their allies in conventional forces, which they could choose to build up again—not without pain but certainly with a good deal more ease than could the parliamentary democracies of the

[33] That applies both in Europe and in the Far East. During the Matsu-Quemoy crisis of 1958 President Eisenhower was informed by the Joint Chiefs that we could not intervene effectively to save the islands for the Nationalists unless our forces were free to use nuclear weapons. This turned out to be a gross overestimation of the threat and an underestimation of our own conventional power; we did partially intervene by convoy, and successfully. In 1961 President Kennedy called up some reserves and sent some Air National Guard reinforcements to Berlin to meet what was considered a crisis there. This action was criticized privately to this writer as totally unnecessary by senior American officers stationed in Germany, and criticized publicly as unnecessary by President de Gaulle.

[34] I witnessed these events as a member of that conference. Mr. Acheson, despite his extraordinary charm and wit, tended to become testy when his views were challenged. At one point he exclaimed: "Call me anything you like but don't call me a fool; everybody knows I'm not a fool." To this the Right Honorable Harold Watkinson, former British Minister of Defense, replied: "I will not say that Mr. Acheson is a fool; I will only say that he is completely and utterly reckless." Despite this reception of his ideas, Mr. Acheson proceeded in the next month to give essentially the same speech all over Europe. His speech was published in *Adelphi Paper* (no. 5) of the (International) Institute for Strategic Studies. Much the same ideas were contained in his article published earlier that year, "The Practice of Partnership," *Foreign Affairs*, vol. 41, no. 2 (January 1963), pp. 247–260.

West, which first had to be persuaded of the need for that kind of competition?

The answer always given, with tremendous assurance, was that it would deter the Russians from launching a *nonnuclear* attack against us or our allies. In short, according to this view our nuclear forces deterred only a nuclear attack, but we needed sufficient nonnuclear weapons to deter a large nonnuclear attack. Put this way it seems absurd, but some very bright people did not so regard it. Indeed, they quite clearly believed that the very existence of a strategic nuclear deterrent made resort to limited war, especially nonnuclear limited war, more rather than less likely than it would otherwise have been—as though the potential for war existing in the world was a constant, and closing off one outlet or channel simply made the voltage flow into other, less hampered channels. However, if fear of what major war brings is greatly augmented by nuclear weapons, which it unquestionably is, *any* conflict that appears to increase the risk of such a war is bound to become less likely, not more so—and that applies to any war between nuclear powers. We cannot assume that the chances are quite reduced to zero, but neither can we assume that a conventional buildup helps to bring about that final reduction. It may work in the opposite direction.

In the special case of Europe, the premise that naturally underlay all others was that the Russians were really seriously interested in conquering western Europe, or any significant part of it, through armed attack. That premise naturally deserved to be examined by people of special qualifications. George Kennan, for one, regarded that premise as preposterous, and said so in a book first published in 1958.[35] There are of course other specialists on the Soviet Union, with somewhat varying views, but few if any of them were drawn into the deliberations of the conventional war theorists.

Alain Enthoven and others have made much of the "firebreak" idea, which holds that there is so vast and unambiguous a difference between fighting with conventional weapons and doing so with nuclear forces that both sides could have quite a go at it

---

[35] Included in his relevant words was the sentence: "We must get over this obsession that the Russians are yearning to attack and occupy Western Europe, and that this is the principal danger." See his *Russia, the Atom, and the West* (New York: Harper & Row, 1958), pp. 56–65.

with the former while remaining most reluctant to shift to the latter. Episodes like the war in Vietnam might superficially seem to bear them out, but in that case the choice for or against fighting was ours to make, and it was against a very small nonnuclear opponent where we were so sensitive about overstepping the bounds of the permissible that we did not even invade his territory! But do we really have to have thirty NATO divisions fighting desperately in mid-Europe before the Russians begin to realize that the situation is getting serious—that a dangerous "firebreak" of sorts is being approached and may be breached?

The Russians looking to the West see not only that tremendous accumulation of strategic nuclear power controlled by the United States—which somehow *might* go off if they offer the provocation that we keep saying is sufficient to make it go off—but they see also those 7,000 or more tactical nuclear weapons that we have already stationed in Europe to guard against their attack. Tactical nuclear weapons differ from strategic ones only in power, but many are reported officially to be of as much as 100 kilotons yield, which not so long ago would have been considered a fearfully powerful strategic weapon—about eight times as powerful as that which destroyed Hiroshima. We do not need repeatedly to threaten that we will use them in case of attack. We do not need to threaten anything. Their being there is quite enough. The Russians know that *no one could really guarantee their nonuse in case of a major conflagration.* If we need a greater military barrier than that, the question is always relevant: at how much additional cost? How much extra premium for how much extra insurance?

The spectacle of a large Soviet field army crashing across the line into western Europe in the hope *and expectation* that nuclear weapons would not be used against it—thereby putting itself and the U.S.S.R. totally at risk while leaving the choice of weapons to us—would seem to be hardly worth a second thought, let alone the complete reorganization and very considerable expansion of our own and our allies' military forces. Why we should have sought to encourage among the Russians an expectation that nuclear weapons would not be used in such circumstances, which would be a possible though unlikely result of a vast conventional buildup, is still another question. We are, after all, trying to deter war, all kinds of war, and not simply the use of nuclear weapons. Besides, deterring war is the *only* sure way to deter use of nuclear weapons.

It is curious that the people who were most in favor of the conventional buildup happened, as systems analysts, to be professionally dedicated to the idea that quantification *à outrance* is essential in all sorts of probability analysis, but on this issue they simply got religion. They talked in terms only of what was "conceivable." When it comes to the allocation of scarce resources, however, one wants to know how probable any "conceivable" evil really is. A commonplace idea in the insurance business, that an extremely remote contingency deserves a small premium or none at all, was here ignored. True, some contingencies would be so unutterably devastating if they occurred that we are willing to go to great lengths to reduce an already low probability as nearly as possible to the vanishing point. This surely is the major reason why we have even been discussing an ABM defense for our retaliatory ICBMs. But we simply cannot afford to apply this kind of thinking to everything that is merely "conceivable."

What ended most of this debate was not at all the triumph of pure reason but, first, the sit-down strike of our NATO allies, who after many painful meetings with Secretary McNamara and his representatives rediscovered the utility of giving lip service to ideas with which they had no intention of conforming, and second, the increasing absorption of the United States in Vietnam. In the latter affair the United States had its not-so-golden opportunity to put to use the conventional buildup to which it had committed itself, thereby sparing itself the necessity of calling up the reserves, a move that had proved so unpopular in the Korean War. Otherwise a war that became critically unpopular anyway would have achieved that condition very much earlier in time. Meanwhile too the French under President de Gaulle had effectively taken themselves out of NATO and even requested American forces ignominiously to leave France. This action served to remind our government that in the absence of a grave and conspicuous threat, some allies may finally show their aversion to being lectured at. De Gaulle might have taken this action in any case, but he was unquestionably vexed with our prolonged public hectoring on the nuclear issue. We had been telling him again and again that it was wasteful and foolish, even monstrous, for him to do what we had done.

At this writing NATO ground forces in Europe have been undergoing for some time a gradual decrease in size rather than an increase, a condition that did not await hints that the Strategic

Arms Limitation Talks might be widened to include conventional armaments.[36] Political strife between West and East having progressively diminished, there seemed to the governments concerned to be less than ever reason for keeping up conventional forces already provided. NATO, an organization in being for the sole purpose of protecting its members against Soviet military aggression, naturally had to continue with its contingency planning; but some realities are too conspicuous to evade. Having finally in 1967 adopted "in principle" McNamara's ideas about "graduated response," NATO planners found themselves in 1972 with fewer than ever conventional forces to graduate from. There can be no doubt that contingency planning had to take account of this fact by increased consideration of tactical nuclear weapons.

Our experience of the last decade could provide several themes for expatiation on the difficulties of being realistic during periods of peace for the strategies to be followed in war. But certainly the most astonishing was the refusal to credit nuclear weapons with being a potent deterrent even to limited war when that war might be between powers that possess on both sides huge stores of nuclear weapons. There has indeed been plenty of war since the nuclear age began, and the United States has accepted more than its share of it. But direct conflict *at any scale* between the superpowers has been gingerly avoided by both.[37] Quite possibly it would have been avoided even in the absence of nuclear weapons. The time period involved has been too short to prove very much, and one sees plenty of other inhibitions also at work. But one does see in the crises that *have* developed between the Soviet Union and the United States a profound awareness on both sides

---

[36] An item from London by Drew Middleton in the *New York Times* for November 15, 1971 is headed: "British Planning Bigger NATO Force." Scrutiny of this item shows that the increase planned is trivial, amounting to $260 million over three years for naval and air as well as ground forces. It is admitted that the increase is "part of the Government's answer to American criticism in the Administration and the Congress." The same report later states that the four battalions added "will ease the pressure on the British Army of the Rhine in Germany arising from the demands made by the crisis in Northern Ireland." In other words, they represent no net increase at all but a partial replacement, planned for the future, for forces already taken away for that crisis.

[37] Except for the shooting down of various aircraft. Earlier in the cold war several American aircraft that seemed to be engaged in electronic reconnaissance activities were shot down on or near Soviet coasts, and it seems likely that during the Korean War some of the MIG fighters engaged and shot down by ours were manned by Russian pilots, inasmuch as our pilots reported hearing Russian being spoken over their radio systems.

that nuclear weapons are in being and ready to go. That awareness showed itself markedly in such crises as that concerning Cuba in 1962, and played its ample part in bringing both parties back from the brink—insofar as they were ever really close to any brink.[38] Moreover, we have seen a progressively lesser tendency towards comparable "brinksmanship."

In the minds of the great majority of people, nuclear weapons are objects of unmitigated horror, and so they are—in use. We know, however, that the leaders of all the nations possessing nuclear weapons are and have long been most keenly aware of their terrible potentialities. It requires a very naive person to argue that the Chinese, for example, being both Communist and also overpopulated, would be relatively unconcerned with the destruction of millions of their people through nuclear attack, though one does hear that argument. One also hears the contrary idea expressed by some political scientists that nuclear weapons, being so obviously unfit for military use, have become effectively "decoupled" from diplomacy. They may be effectively decoupled from many kinds of problems that traditionally concern diplomatists, but hardly from problems concerning war and peace.

There is, however, one politically important group within each of the major powers that naturally finds large conventional war capabilities attractive and congenial, and this also happens to be the group that is professionally conditioned to feel a minimum of horror of nuclear weapons. To its members both kinds of force are necessary and therefore good. There was indeed a time when Admiral Radford played the Navy's spokesman in branding as "immoral" the addiction of the Air Force to nuclear bombing and in calling the B-36 a "billion-dollar blunder." The Army at that time wanted freedom to use the nuclear bomb, which it persisted in calling "just another weapon," but it was yet to discover the perplexity of finding a role for itself in a really major nuclear war. All that, as time is measured in these matters, was long ago. It was before the Korean War, when the annual defense budget was being pushed down to something like $12 billion. Today one would never speak of a whole bomber system as being a "billion-

---

[38] It is obvious that a Khrushchev who withdrew his missiles with such alacrity when confronted with United States demands that he do so not only never intended to go to war over the issue but was quite determined to avoid it. And because nuclear wars are most unlikely to break out by accident, I do not feel we were anywhere near war in October 1962. For a further discussion of that crisis see pp. 424 f., 426–429.

dollar blunder." A billion dollars would not even buy the flying prototype.

Views have changed in all the services. Today a naval officer speaks of the ship-building needs imposed upon us as a result of the Soviet naval buildup quite as though we might someday have to fight great naval campaigns comparable to those of both world wars. Drew Middleton, writing in late 1971, quotes as follows a "senior admiral" on our needs in the event of a Soviet-American confrontation over the crisis in the Near East: "It would take a thousand ships—escort vessels and merchantmen—to support our North Atlantic allies in Europe if the Russians moved. We haven't got them, escorts or merchantmen. The name of the game in anti-submarine warfare is numbers." [39] In the same article Middleton quotes senior officers of the other services in very much the same vein. Numbers and fighting morale are what count. Are nuclear weapons being considered in their views—the simple existence of those weapons, let alone their possible use? Mr. Middleton apparently neglected to ask, and his officer respondents failed to say. One would be rash to try to guess what role nuclear weapons were playing in the minds of these officers when they were speaking thus. We know that they are men who usually pride themselves on being "hard-nosed" on such matters as nuclear weapons as opposed to most civilians who are weak, and that anyone who is a "senior admiral" is no doubt proud of the Navy's great fleet of nuclear-powered Polaris and Poseidon submarines. But what does Mr. Middleton's admiral have in mind about the role and especially the effect of these submarines? Is he expecting them to deter *only* a massive strategic thermonuclear attack? Or is he stating his conception of needs for submarine escorts on the assumption that nuclear weapons are *also* being used?

Over a decade ago, Herman Kahn in his *On Thermonuclear War* spoke of the "quaint ideas" then still current among the military, including "the claim that in a thermonuclear war it is important to keep the sea lanes open." He mentions comparable ideas characteristic of the other services, and asks: "Where do such ideas come from?" His answer: "They generally result, it can be assumed, from doctrinal lags or from position papers that primarily reflect a very narrow departmental interest or which are

[39] *New York Times*, November 1, 1971.

the result of log-rolling compromises between several partisan departments of the government." He adds, too optimistically as it has turned out, "We are fortunate that on the whole these views are no longer taken seriously even by many of the decision makers who sign the papers." [40]

It is possible that in the quoted statement Kahn was correctly interpreting a trend that was later reversed. That is, officers who were at one time ready, or on the threshold of being ready, to admit that the conditions of a thermonuclear war were incompatible with the notions they had previously been advancing, subsequently became accustomed to the fact that nuclear weapons were not in fact being used even when American forces were at war, as in Korea and Vietnam. It also is likely that they have been affected selectively by the ideas of the conventional war-buildup school, that is, that they have absorbed gratefully the views that the United States would need as many ships, tanks, guns, aircraft as of yore, without necessarily accepting the basic assumption behind those views. That basic assumption is that we can have a World War III on something like a World War II scale without thermonuclear weapons being used. This is the same as saying that existing stockpiles of nuclear weapons cannot reliably deter such a war, let alone a lesser war.

Some help to our conception of what is still going on in official thinking is perhaps offered by the posture statement of March 1971 offered by Secretary of Defense Melvin R. Laird, concerning which one may assume that the Joint Chiefs of Staff had a greater hand in its preparation or at least in approval of it than they were accustomed to having under Secretary McNamara. In this statement Secretary Laird presented a "spectrum of conflict" embracing four categories of warfare, each of which allegedly requires its own special kind of deterrence. These are:

1. *"Strategic nuclear war,"* in deterring which "primary reliance will continue to be placed on U.S. strategic deterrent forces."

2. *"Theater nuclear war,"* in deterrence of which "the U.S. also has primary responsibility, but certain of our allies are able to share this responsibility by virtue of their own

---

[40] Herman Kahn, *On Thermonuclear War* (Princeton: Princeton University Press, 1960), p. 38. See also my *Strategy in the Missile Age*, chap. 5.

nuclear capabilities." (De Gaulle thus receives posthumous vindication.)

3. *"Theater conventional warfare*—for example, a *major war in Europe"* (italics added in the latter phrase) for which deterrence responsibility will be shared by "U.S. and allied forces," obviously conventional forces.

4. *"Sub-theater or localized warfare."* Here follows some "Nixon Doctrine" language.[41]

Then, on the next page, Secretary Laird adds the following:

U.S. strategic forces relate primarily to the deterrence of a strategic nuclear attack. They also serve an important role, together with theater and tactical nuclear responsible capabilities, in deterring conflict below the level of general nuclear war.

However, *as the last two decades have demonstrated* [italics added], reliance on a nuclear capability alone is by no means sufficient to inhibit or deter aggression. A sufficient nuclear capability must be coupled with a sufficient conventional capability in both our own forces and those of our allies. This conventional capability must be adequate to meet aggression in the sophisticated environment which would be expected in a conflict with the Warsaw Pact. If these NATO forces are to deter this type of aggression, they must be capable of confronting it with such capabilities as strong armor and anti-tank forces, appropriate air power for air superiority and ground combat support, strong naval forces to support NATO's flanks, and other combat support forces.

There we have it. There is really no significant difference here from the old McNamara doctrine, including the insistence that "the last two decades have demonstrated" that a "nuclear capability alone is by no means sufficient to inhibit or deter aggression." Not even to *inhibit* it, let alone deter it—and the insertion of that uncalled for word *alone*, as though we have *ever* been limited to nuclear forces alone. Then the litany continues in the style to which we have been long accustomed. What is it that the

---

[41] *Statement of Secretary of Defense Melvin R. Laird on the Fiscal Year 1972–76 Defense Program and the 1972 Defense Budget, Before the Senate Armed Services Committee, March 15, 1971*, p. 22.

last two decades have demonstrated? Simply that the United States can engage itself in a Korean and a Vietnam War and not use nuclear weapons, despite its own possession of them.[42] What has it demonstrated about Soviet aggression against western Europe? Nothing, except that we certainly cannot charge that nuclear weapons have failed to be inhibiting!

Appeal continues to a totally mythical experience. One recalls how William W. Kaufmann in his semiofficial *The McNamara Strategy* asserted in reference to the situation in Europe: ". . . the record was complete with instances where, despite the direct threats of massive or limited nuclear retaliation, forbidden actions of one kind or another had taken place." To which this writer as a reviewer felt obliged to ask, "Well, what were they?" Kaufmann went on in that vein: "But there remained a large set of aggressions which had not been deterred in the past and were unlikely to. be in the future—unless someone set the record straight by using nuclear weapons in response to one of these acts." And the reproach to those abroad who saw things differently: "It seemed virtually impossible to convince the Allies that nuclear capabilities long since had been found wanting as an all-purpose deterrent." The allies indeed had good reason to refuse to be convinced. What those terrible but avoidable failures had been Kaufmann did not specify, except for some vague references to "the crises of Berlin and Cuba." The most specific reference was: "Despite these efforts, the monstrous Wall dividing East Berlin from West Berlin went up on August 13, 1961." [43] Actually, the U.S. Administration, especially the State Department, initially greeted with some relief the erection of that wall, because they regarded as "a problem" the huge flow of refugees in the last weeks before it went up. In any case, if we had wanted to

---

[42] This does leave open the question of why the Chinese dared to enter Korea against us in October 1952 despite our monopoly possession of nuclear weapons. I have discussed this matter in my *Escalation and the Nuclear Option*, p. 111, where I lean also on the opinion of Allen S. Whiting in his *China Crosses the Yalu: The Decision to Enter the Korean War* (New York: Macmillan, 1960), pp. 134–136. The basic point is that China observed us fighting the North Koreans for four months, including periods of real desperation for us, without using nuclear weapons, and therefore had some reason for assurance that we would not use them against her forces. Whiting backs up this observation with some special evidence.

[43] See my review-article, "The McNamara Phenomenon," *World Politics*, vol. 17, no. 4 (July 1965). The quotations from William W. Kaufmann, *The McNamara Strategy* (New York: Harper & Row, 1964) reviewed there are on pp. 72, 106, 128, 258.

do something bold about that wall, it should not have required a single additional American or NATO soldier besides the considerable number we already had on the spot. The essential question was: How much did the strictly local forces affect the Russians' willingness to risk open hostilities with us—or, for that matter, our willingness to get into such hostilities with them? And the answer clearly was, little or none—unless both sides had been *completely convinced* that a quite considerable shooting war could develop on the spot without its substantially widening and incurring extremely grave risk of nuclear weapons being introduced. We know that neither side entertained any such conviction. Indeed, they gave every evidence at each critical point of being clearly convinced of the opposite.

To return to Drew Middleton's "senior admiral": we do not know whether he is restating the old-fashioned needs for keeping the sea lanes open on the assumption that nuclear weapons not only will not be used but will also fail to deter a large-scale conventional war, or whether he feels they will be used but should nevertheless not reduce seriously the need for the naval functions he wishes to preserve. What we can say, however, is that in either case the chances are overwhelming that he is wrong. I am suggesting, in other words (for what I fear is not the first time during the last quarter century), that nuclear weapons do by their very existence in large numbers make obsolete the use of and hence need for conventional forces on anything like the scale of either world war.

But how can one prove it to the satisfaction of those who make the governing decisions? Devices like war gaming are of no use in determining what deters what—though they may be of some utility in determining what operations remain feasible and necessary under certain limited and specified uses of nuclear weapons.[44] The arguments against the admiral depend mostly on a scru-

---

[44] The main trouble with simulations, including war games, in this respect is that one simply cannot reproduce in the game room the kinds of emotions, especially of fear and anxiety, that would certainly be at work in any cabinet room during a major crisis that might involve use of nuclear weapons. This is one reason for the great importance of such personal accounts as Robert Kennedy's *Thirteen Days: A Memoir of the Cuban Missile Crisis* (New York: Norton, 1969). There are of course other shortcomings as well, which make some of the more experienced practitioners of war-gaming dubious of its value as anything other than an educational tool for the players themselves, and certainly not a reliable way of deriving final answers to strategic problems.

pulous interpretation of experience, but they are also partly intuitive—as *his* arguments are entirely—and superiority in intuition unfortunately bears no external markings. Many indeed believe that in these matters superiority in intuition does have conspicuous markings, namely, a military uniform, with appropriate badges of high rank. But history, especially very recent history, suggests otherwise.

The military officer's intuition on these matters might be more trustworthy if we could rely on him to be more objective as well as more imaginative. That the existence of vast nuclear capabilities, based both on land and sea, should greatly qualify the need for the kind of capabilities that were essential in two world wars, in both of which we had, among other huge problems, that of protecting surface shipping from heavy submarine attack, would be easier for him to accept if his desires and hence emotions were less involved. He also hates to be outdistanced by the Russians in any category in which he has been accustomed to being superior, like surface naval ships. Because the case against the need for superiority in all these items cannot be finally proved, why not spend the money? One should on the other hand ask: If the Russians are making a mistake, and their record in this respect is no better than ours, why must we follow them in it?

With the senior Air Force officer we have a special consideration. To him ICBMs are not really exciting, even though they are controlled by his service. He likes craft that one must fly—very high performance aircraft requiring the special skills of the combat pilot. Thus he urges the need for a new bomber system, and he is tireless in adducing rationalizations for it. If he is right it will be by accident, for his arguments are stimulated primarily by emotion rather than reason.[45] The opportunities in limited war

---

[45] The attachment of the Air Force "rated pilot" to the vehicle that gives him that distinction is something quite special psychologically. No officer not having that rating has ever become Chief of Staff of the Air Force, and it is generally assumed that none could. However, the attachment also bears resemblance to a well-known syndrome in military history. We may remember the attachment of the cavalry man, and even the field artillery officer, to the horse; and in more recent times we have seen bomber men ridiculing aircraft carriers, and the officers of the latter joining the former in ridiculing "battleship admirals." What is a little remarkable is that bomber men find it impossible to conceive of themselves as occupying a position exactly comparable to the "battleship admirals," whose reasons for supporting their favorite craft through World War II were at least as sound as those presented by the "bomber generals" today. See, however, R. H. Kupperman and H. A. Smith, "Strategies for Mutual Deterrence," *Science*, vol. 176 (April 7, 1972), pp. 18–23.

to employ aircraft, thereby also getting a large "piece of the action," have made him forget his former abhorrence of such techniques as close support of ground forces, in which he now uses (as in Vietnam) large bombers as well as small ones, naturally with conventional bombs. Formerly he would have branded such practice a gross misuse of air power. He, too, wants to see two large and quite distinctive capabilities existing side by side, and in addition he wants to add high-performance bombers to ICBMs for strategic nuclear bombing. The Army in its turn has become very much limited-war oriented, though it has gone to some pains to prevent the Vietnam War from making too great an imprint upon its tactical habits. Korea was much more to its liking, but it wants to be freer in the future to use nuclear weapons tactically.

The main problem in having large dual forces appears to be money. We can even have a volunteer army and do away with conscription if we pay our soldiers enough. So far as concerns our allies why *not* press them (and in 1972 our government was still doing it) to contribute more conventional forces? The money spent is (mostly) theirs, and we surely do not want them to build up nuclear forces. As the issue is usually posed: Why don't they do their share?

Well, for the United States the kinds of sums we are speaking of are very large, and we see many competing home demands for the money that we did not see before the Vietnam War. Also, everything has become enormously more expensive. If a large dual capability looked too costly to President Eisenhower, what will it look like to President Nixon's successors? The GNP over time continues to rise, but nothing like so fast as does the price tag on each combat aircraft, or tank, or almost any other military implement. The F-14 combat plane, designed for use on aircraft carriers, was originally expected to cost $12 or $13 million each; the price tag in 1972 had gone to $16.8 million, which the manufacturer found inadequate to cover costs. It is not so long since an aircraft designed for the same function might cost $250,000!

We also have impressive reason for concluding that in the past we were too expansive in our security commitments abroad. Many slogans about the indivisibility of peace and the necessity for stamping out brush fires wherever they occur, especially if they are ignited by Communists, will be less acceptable in the future than they formerly were. This should have a considerable effect

414

on stated military requirements. Where our allies are concerned, some of them are perhaps oversensitive to the possibility that they are being used rather than protected—certainly a popular notion in Japan—but in any case they have shown a distaste for being pushed in directions that they consider unnecessary and even foolish. After hearing the relevant American arguments for more than a decade, those in Europe simply cannot accept the idea of a large nonnuclear war on that continent. Also, with a sharper sense than ourselves of what two world wars in the old style did to Europe, the idea of a third possessing the same period-style strikes them as having no particular advantage over anything. They are, therefore, and always have been since the nuclear age began, all-out for deterrence. Moreover, they see no reason why it should not work.[46] The Russians are not, or at least have not been for a long time, particularly bellicose or unreasonable (the matter of Czechoslovakia in 1968 they undoubtedly looked upon as an internal affair); they understand very well the potential penalties to them if they should become so.

One of the greatest costs of misreading the strategic realities of the day would be, as it always has been, that of failing to know which important diplomatic postures lie within our capabilities and which do not. In the cited article by Drew Middleton, we should recall that he was asking senior officers whether the United States could "effectively support Israel in the event of a joint Soviet-Egyptian attack." Besides the reply from the "senior admiral" that we have already noticed, there was also one from an "Air Force general," who said simply: "Forget it. With the Soviet Air Force in Egypt and the Soviet naval squadron in the Mediterranean, we couldn't get close." Now, whether or not the United States *should* take major risks with the Soviet Union over the se-

---

[46] The "they" obviously includes many different people with different ideas. The great majority of Europeans who were in relevant official positions did not accept the American ideas I have been criticizing, but some of them did. One of the latter was former West German Senator Helmuth Schmidt, who wrote a book on NATO strategy extolling the American conventional war ideas. When he became Minister of Defense under the Willy Brandt government, however, he quickly changed his mind. The army of the Federal Republic, incidentally, the largest army in NATO, has been called second in quality and effectiveness only to the American forces in Europe; but recent public reports have revealed that in morale and efficiency it is really quite poor. See, for example, "The Uncertain Trumpet," *Newsweek* October 21, 1968, pp. 54–56. A Bundeswehr general is quoted there as saying flatly, "Europe's defense rests on the American nuclear shield."

curity of Israel I shall not attempt to explore here, except to point out that there has been no conspicuous Soviet propensity to accept grave risks over the issues involved in that area, and it would be difficult to understand why they should want to. In any case it is obvious that both senior officers were giving Middleton bad advice, and would no doubt do the same for their government. With respect to the chances of getting into a conflict with the other superpower, the Soviet Union, like the United States, is always looking past local forces. It may be that a local or even an overall superiority in ships, aircraft, and other arms may be necessary to give the President of the United States backbone to face up to crises. By the same token, it could get him into trouble he might otherwise avoid. In any case, the United States surface fleet or air force is scarcely to be regarded as of pitiably small size.

The Impossible War

Toward the end of the last century, a retired Warsaw banker named Ivan S. Bloch published in six volumes, representing eight years of intensive labors, a book entitled *The Future of War*.[47] It was an extraordinary achievement, and it did not fail to gain the attention due it. A committee of officers appointed for the purpose by the Czar's Minister of War recommended that it be placed in the hands of all staff officers, and expressed the opinion that no other book could contribute more to the information of those who were to take part in the deliberations of the forthcoming First Hague Conference. It is amazing that they should have said these things, because Bloch, besides being a civilian and in addition of Jewish origins, had as a result of his intensive and far-ranging researches come out with conclusions that contradicted most of the standard predictions by contemporary professional officers. Where the latter held that any new war between the great nations of Europe would be of great violence but decisive and short, he could agree only with the predictions of great violence.

The war to come, he foresaw, would be savage beyond all precedent, with enormous casualty rates, but it would also be stalemated and therefore long. Despite the high rate of fire of modern firearms (and he was not yet taking into account the new machine guns being developed in Britain by Hiram Maxim and in Amer-

---

[47] That is the title of the American edition (New York: Doubleday & McClure, 1899). The British edition was entitled *Is War Now Impossible?* (London: Grant Richards, 1899). Both these editions were the same translation from the Russian by R. C. Long, and carry a prefatory conversation with the author by W. T. Stead.

ica by John M. Browning), the armies in the field would not (as so many were predicting) run out of ammunition. These new weapons, he said, enormously favored the tactical defensive over the offensive, and there was already plenty of experience to prove it. The slaughter would be tremendous, but it would end only with the utter exhaustion of the participants. For he did not omit to consider also the political difficulties in the way of ending such a war. "Once war had broken out," he argued, "the conclusion of peace would represent great difficulties to any government, either after failure or success. At first it would seem that the results obtained in no way compensate for the sacrifices made. . . . In the second case—that is, of failure—the stoppage of military operations without attaining the results expected might easily give rise to revolutionary movements." [48] Where Adam Smith had reassured a young friend that "there is a great deal of ruin in a nation," meaning much tolerance for strain and damage, Bloch would have used the same words to imply rather that the reservoirs of power in each nation were indeed huge but finally exhaustible.

For these reasons Bloch frequently referred to the war of the future as "the impossible war," and indeed the edition published in England carried the title *Is War Now Impossible?* Yet he was clear that the impossible could indeed happen. In a conversation with a W. T. Stead, reported by the latter in a long preface in the English and American editions, he insisted that war "has at last became impossible, and those who are preparing for war, and basing all their schemes of life on the expectation of war, are visionaries of the worst kind, for war is no longer possible." [49] However, he later says, in the same conversation:

> I do not for a moment deny that it is possible for nations to plunge themselves and their neighbors into a frightful series of catastrophes which will probably result in the overturn of all civilised and ordered government. . . . War therefore has become impossible, except at the price of suicide. [50]

Then in his own "Author's Preface" he spoke of the "great concatenation of circumstances which are the cause of armaments," and treated the possibility of its ending in the following terms:

---

[48] American ed., p. 91.

[49] Ibid., p. ix.

[50] Ibid., p. xxxi.

Such a state of affairs is unhappily still distant. It is true that the ruinousness of war under modern conditions is apparent to all. But this gives no sufficient guarantee that war will not break forth suddenly, even in opposition to the wishes of those who take part in it. Involuntarily we call to mind the words of the great Bacon, that "in the vanity of the world a greater field of action is open for folly than for reason, and frivolity always enjoys more influence than judgment." [51]

The war that came in 1914 proved Bloch to have been doubly right. It was the predictable occurrence of the impossible, and it took very much the course that Bloch outlined for it. No one else writing prior to World War I, including some who wrote late enough to take fully into account the machine gun invented by Hiram Maxim in 1883, came anything like so close.[52] Compared to the vision of Bloch the fulminations of Brigadier General Ferdinand Foch and his cohorts at the *École supérieure de la guerre* in Paris appear childish and absurd, and as it turned out their ideas served terribly to compound the destruction.[53] Though World War II was not a necessary or inevitable result of World War I, it was nevertheless a natural consequence of it; so that the real cost of going to war in 1914 deserves to be reckoned in terms of both wars and all the troubles that both produced, including some legacies that face us today and which we should be happier to be without.

Well, what would Bloch be saying today? Or what should we,

---

[51] Ibid., p. xiv.

[52] There had been some kind of machine gun dating back at least to that invented by Dr. Gatling in the American Civil War (a type of very rapid-fire machine gun called the "Gatling gun" is also used on some modern American aircraft). Napoleon III had depended heavily on the *mitrailleuse* (still the French word for machine gun) developed for him in great secrecy and used with quite disappointing results in the Franco-Prussian War of 1870–1871. Most of these depended on rotating a multi-barrelled cylinder. However, the modern machine gun required the fully integrated cartridge *plus* smokeless powder, and these became available only towards the close of the century. Both the gun developed by Maxim in England (manufactured by Vickers) and that developed a few years later by Browning in America (Colt) depended on the recoil of the discharge to reload and fire the cartridges, which were carried in long belts. The first important use of the modern machine gun was in the Russo-Japanese War of 1904–1905, and the generals who were to fight World War I had plenty of time and opportunity to be forewarned.

[53] On Foch and his school see my *Strategy in the Missile Age*, pp. 40–55.

striving to emulate him even in small part, be saying in his place? That same "great concatenation of circumstances which are the cause of armaments" is still very much with us, and now those armaments include, in very large quantities, that which we need not name again. Now we have to come to terms, as Bloch did not quite, with what is possible and what is impossible, and it does not require Bloch's careful consideration of experiments with bullets on animal carcasses to find out what is ruinous. And ruinous totally, in a way that was beyond even his powers to foresee.

Herman Kahn, in the book that first made his name a byword, set out to prove that, *provided* certain precautions were taken of a kind that he and a research team under his direction had thoroughly explored, the United States could survive a strategic thermonuclear war. By that he meant that the fatalities and other casualties, though very large, could be kept within limits that he considered tolerable, and that within a term of years that others might consider astonishingly short, say five to ten years, the country could be back to the GNP that it had enjoyed before the war. The special condition to which he attached such supreme importance was the provision in good time of adequate fallout shelters and other forms of civil defense (though he had abandoned blast shelters as unfeasible),[54] and also the storage in caves or man-made shelters of certain well-selected machine tools, the preservation of which would greatly assist in the reconstruction.

As Kahn himself said in one of his footnotes, "It is the hallmark of the expert professional that he doesn't care where he is going as long as he proceeds competently."[55] He added that that seemed to be a reasonable charge against his book. This writer fully agrees, especially concerning the competence. Unlike most

---

[54] The difference between a fallout shelter and a blast shelter is that the latter is intended to shield people inside of it from the direct blast and other effects of the bomb. It naturally requires that the people be in it at the time the bomb explodes nearby, which means that they must have warning. It would also have to be within the city, and would have to be deep and very expensive. A fallout shelter is intended only to shield the population from the radioactive debris representing close fallout, as described on p. 394. It could be on the outskirts of a city, inasmuch as survivors could repair to it even after an attack, and though its ceiling and walls (if it were not underground) would have to be thick enough to offer a good shield against radiation from fallout, they would not need anything like the strength required in a blast shelter. They would therefore be very much cheaper to construct.

[55] Kahn, *On Thermonuclear War*, p. 7 n.

other writers in the field of strategy, including myself, Kahn had the courage to explore as thoroughly as his exceptional ability and knowledge permitted the character of a "general war" with thermonuclear weapons. However, having expressed this tribute I must take part of it back by declaring that while Kahn cared well enough where he was going, he was helped along by an optimism that has in some critical respects turned out to be unwarranted.

For one thing, the precautions that Kahn deemed absolutely essential before his somewhat roseate conclusions could be warranted have not been taken and it is now abundantly clear that they will not be. For reasons that were again psychological rather than logical, the American public in 1961–1962 reacted violently against the fallout shelter program studied and proposed by Kahn and accepted by the Kennedy Administration. That program seemed for a time to be faring well in Congress, but in the face of the furiously negative attitude of a highly vocal part of the population, it collapsed and was never thereafter revived.[56] It presently appears unrevivable, and no one seems any longer interested. Second, as Kahn himself admitted frequently to his friends, his premises assumed a situation in nuclear weapons that was fast changing for the worse. His arguments, he conceded, would no longer be valid a decade hence unless there were significant and far-reaching international agreements for nuclear disarmament. That decade has passed, and with MIRV and other developments, we know he was right to be concerned by the great increase in the sheer quantity of destructiveness that would be available to both sides. As could be predicted since they began, the SALT negotiations did not produce results great enough to matter in this respect.

Third, being neither by training nor temperament sensitive to the vast psychological and emotional damage that a society like ours would suffer along with the physical devastation of a thermo-

---

[56] The extreme fury in some circles of the opposition to the building of fallout shelters by the government was certainly not a matter of logic, and one can only guess at the psychological factors that touched it off. Retaliatory missiles are far away and invisible (for most people at any rate), and their function is to *deter* war. Fallout shelters would have to be close and fairly visible to all, and they would have meaning not as a deterrent but only as a means of reducing the loss of life when the catastrophe struck. The arguments of Kahn and others that the latter aim was worthwhile not only went unheeded but even suggested that that which was not supposed to happen might happen after all.

nuclear war, Kahn undoubtedly underestimated the problems of recovery even from a war taking place under the premises he postulated. Psychologically trained people have worked on the problem, but it is difficult to do so when one cannot find any real parallels in history. Past wars and other disasters have proved the human being and his societal structure remarkably resilient, but there are limits—especially in the absence of outside help of the kind that the United States after' two world wars could give to others. One thing we may intuit with some assurance, and that is that democracy as we know it could hardly survive.

Fourth and most important, although Kahn could see reasons why this unspeakable sum of destruction might nevertheless have to be accepted rather than yield one's position on an important political dispute—the main reason being that a disposition to yield would be visible and hence tempting to the opponent—this writer can imagine no such issue that is at all likely to arise. On the simple Clausewitzian premise that we have repeated throughout this book—that a war must have a reasonable political objective with which the military operations must be reasonably consonant—we have to work back from the assumption that "general war" with thermonuclear weapons must never be permitted to begin, however much we find it necessary to make physical preparations as though it might begin. Working back from that premise is far from easy, and as I have indicated before, the idea of large-scale conventional war is simply no solution. There are requirements for a new diplomacy, the beginnings of which are in fact appearing. We shall return to this point presently—we cannot, in fact, avoid it—but we must first take up Bloch's old questions of the *possibility* of that war which must not be, and which would today and in the future really produce that national suicide of which he was indeed entitled to speak but which we now know applies to our time as it did not to his.

According to former President Lyndon B. Johnson, the foremost thought in his mind as he watched his successor being sworn into office on January 20, 1969 was ". . . that I would not have to face the decision any more of taking any step, in the Middle East or elsewhere, that might lead to world conflagration—the nightmare of my having to be the man who pressed the button to start World War III was passing." [57]

---

[57] Lyndon Baines Johnson, *The Vantage Point: Perspectives of the Presidency, 1963–1969* (New York: Holt, Rinehart and Winston, 1971), p. 566.

Recollections about such matters are, even for the best intentioned, usually unreliable, but it is unimportant whether or not these thoughts were actually coursing through his mind at that very moment. What matters is that by the time he came to write the memoirs of his Presidency, Lyndon Johnson thought that it was appropriate and therefore probable that such a thought was uppermost in his mind at that dramatic time. There could be no doubt also that by "World War III" he meant thermonuclear war, not large-scale conventional war. One tell-tale phrase confirming that fact is the one about "pressing the button." A certain few phrases, of which "pressing the button" is perhaps the most common, have long been current throughout the defense community as signifying the release of all restraints to thermonuclear war.

What we see additionally in Johnson's remark is an enormous reluctance and horror in fantasying himself taking the crucial step, and at the same time the persuasion that under some circumstances he could find himself doing it. There is something schizoid about this, which is alarming and yet hopeful, at least so long as we keep our attention on the horror and reluctance. It has certainly not been historically unusually to find an American President expressing profound distaste or hatred for war even while taking steps towards it, but a special element is present in Johnson's remark that has not been known before. Nor should we assume that it was peculiar to this one man, who was neither the most pacific nor the most bellicose of our Presidents. His successor, Richard M. Nixon, who was far from betraying deeply pacific instincts in his behavior, several times expressed confidence that once the Vietnam War was liquidated, the United States would not know war again. Undoubtedly he had nuclear deterrence in mind.

There are, naturally, those who think differently. American military officers are conditioned by all their training and their associations to believe and feel otherwise, and they can be counted upon to think of a range of evils to which a choice for thermonuclear war would clearly be preferable, and again the chief evil is the possibility of being obliged to yield in *any* confrontation. However, even they in their relevant slogans have deliberately dropped the word *win* in speaking of such a war. One hears them say, for example, that the purpose of our whole military establishment, and especially the strategic retaliatory part of it, is "to deter war if possible but to prevail if deterrence fails." The distinction between "winning" and merely "prevailing" is not elucidated, but one must be grateful even for small changes if they be in the right direction.

Still, one hears them say horrendous things. General Earle G. Wheeler, for example, former Chairman of the Joint Chiefs of Staff, remarked to a congressional committee that we should "insure that the United States and its allies emerge [from any nuclear war] with relative advantage irrespective of the circumstances of initiation, response, and termination." [58] We may assume that General Wheeler, who had a reputation in the services for being a highly intelligent officer, had weighed his words well. He had had many opportunities to do so in honing down his slogan to such a neat package. But inasmuch as "relative advantage" can also mean a small advantage, and in any case whatever distinction there may be is outweighed by the terrible words "irrespective of the circumstances . . . of termination," we may conclude that General Wheeler is willing to pay a gigantic price for an "advantage," which if meaningful at all could be really quite trivial.

To be sure, it is not only the military who speak thus. The late Senator Richard Russell, who chaired the Senate Armed Services Committee, was a highly respected member of the Senate and no doubt deserved to be remembered for other things than that exclamation, while urging the construction of ballistic missile defenses, that "if we have to start over again with another Adam and Eve, then I want them to be Americans and not Russians— and I want them on this continent and not in Europe." [59] Alas, poor Richard! Being from Georgia and an acknowledged white supremacist, he undoubtedly meant white rather than black Americans, but how could only two persons *be* Americans if there were no others left to distinguish them from? And just what moral or aesthetic superiority does the land mass of North America, or even the people on it, have to that of Europe? Or any other continent? Well, on Russell's part it was an intemperate ejaculation of an old man impatient with his colleagues, of whom he complained to some reporters that as a group they were much more reluctant to approve arms purchases than any he had known before.

There is also former Secretary of State Dean Rusk, who told

---

[58] General Wheeler made this statement in 1970 while testifying before the Senate Committee on Foreign Relations, Subcommittee on Arms Control, International Law and Organization; but I have borrowed the quotation from J. I. Coffey, *Strategic Power and National Security* (Pittsburgh: Pittsburgh University Press, 1971), p. 15.

[59] *New York Times*, November 22, 1968.

South Vietnamese Premier Nguyen Khanh in May 1964 that the United States "would never again get involved in a land war in Asia limited to conventional forces. Our population was 190,000,000. Mainland China had at least 700,000,000. We would not allow ourselves to be bled white fighting them with conventional weapons. This meant that if escalation brought about major Chinese attack, it would also involve use of nuclear arms." [60] Here was the Secretary of State appointed by that President who was eager to "put the nuclear genie back into the bottle" speaking like John Foster Dulles. At that time, to be sure, the Chinese had no nuclear stockpile; the first Chinese nuclear detonation was to occur later that year.

Also, if we go back to the Cuban missile crisis of October 1962, we find that on both sides that was no lack of clarity that if any military action began and subsequently escalated, they would at once be on the threshold of nuclear war. In his first letter to Chairman Khrushchev during that crisis, President Kennedy included the words: ". . . I have not assumed that you or any other sane man would, in this nuclear age, deliberately plunge the world into war which it is crystal clear no country could win and which could only result in catastrophic consequences to the whole world, including the aggressor." [61] In his reply Khrushchev charged the United States with pushing mankind "to the abyss of a world missile-nuclear war." [62] Robert Kennedy, in describing the situation, adds concerning the first days, "The feeling grew that this cup was not going to pass and that a direct military confrontation between the two great nuclear powers was inevitable." [63] Despite all the talk that had taken place within this President's own Administration about separating nuclear from conventional military operations—talk that had quite possibly encouraged him to face up to the issue in the first place—the prevailing considerations in the White House *during* the crisis was that a full-scale war *could* develop from their insistent demands, and that if such a war came it would be nuclear. After it was over Secretary McNamara exclaimed, in response to a question put to

[60] *The Pentagon Papers: The Defense Department History of United States Decision-making in Vietnam, Senator Gravel Edition.* 5 vols. (Boston: Beacon Press, 1971) vol. 2, p. 322.

[61] Quoted in Kennedy, *Thirteen Days*, p. 79. For fuller texts see David L. Larson, *The "Cuban" Crisis of 1962: Selected Documents and Chronology* (Boston: Houghton Mifflin, 1963).

[62] Kennedy, *Thirteen Days*, p. 80.

[63] Ibid., p. 83.

him in hearings before a congressional committee: "Khrushchev knew without any question whatsoever that he faced the full military power of the United States, including its nuclear weapons . . . and that is the reason, and the only reason, why he withdrew those weapons." [64] Whether McNamara was right or wrong, this is what the great advocate of conventional capabilities felt in his heart about the crisis just past.

What we have to conclude from these instances, and the many similar ones that could be marshalled, is that strategic thermonuclear war is indeed possible. Men who know or think they know the consequences of such war have sometimes taken steps in the direction of confrontation because they thought the latter necessary. At any rate, they could see no alternative. Perhaps the compulsions that have moved them in that direction are due to outworn habits of thinking and of action, but for the time being and at least for the generation that now holds power, they exist. That is why so many people have despaired of avoiding general thermonuclear war except through remedies that this writer, among many others, regards as utterly unavailable, like world government or complete nuclear disarmament, or ineffective for the purpose intended, like building up conventional armaments as a means of sealing off or at least critically reducing the probability of resort to nuclear weapons.

Yet, as time goes on people seem to live in less rather than more fear of what would otherwise seem to be an increasing menace. The specialists become aroused about the threats to retaliatory forces arising from the increasing accuracy of long-range missiles, and they try to communicate their alarm to others in order to get certain things done—like building an ABM—but they have to contend with a certain calm resistance that is new and that is reflected in such matters as the Senate votes on the ABM. It is an interesting phenomenon, some no doubt would argue a dangerous one, and it requires some explanation. Most important, one wants to know whether it reflects a reality or an illusion about the direction in which events are leading us.

The most hopeful part of the answer is that diplomacy seems clearly to be moving in a direction that indicates a common recognition, among those powers possessing substantial nuclear capabilities, that thermonuclear war between them is simply for-

---

[64] *Department of Defense Appropriations for 1964, Part I, Hearings Before a Subcommittee on Appropriations, House of Representatives, 88th Congress, 1st Session 1963*, pp. 30–31.

bidden, and thus also lesser wars that might too easily lead up to the large-scale thermonuclear variety. This trend shows itself in various far-reaching and significant ways. No doubt it is not moving fast enough for our comfort, and yet, it would even now take a very great deal to start a World War III—just as it took so much more to start World War II than it took to start World War I. The latter act required the brazen nerve of one half-psychotic dwarf genius, and the series of mischances that put him in the place where he could do so much damage.

A close reading of the handling of the October 1962 crisis shows at least the beginnings of the difference. Robert Kennedy's brief book on that crisis, along with several other memoirs by other participants, are intensely revealing. From beginning to end the confrontation that we call the Cuban missile crisis—the most acute crisis of any we have had since World War II—shows a remarkably different quality from any previous one in history. There is an unprecedented candor, direct personal contact, and at the same time mutual respect between the chief actors. Normal diplomatic formalities of language and of circumlocution are disregarded. Both sides at once agree that their quarrel *could* lead to nuclear war, which is impossible to contemplate and which would leave no winner. In effect they were asking each other: How do we get out of this with the absolute minimum of damage to each other including each other's prestige?

President Kennedy has the psychological advantage, not only in superiority of power, but in the fact, too, that the disturbance to security was taking place in his backyard rather than in Khrushchev's. Khrushchev also had been caught doing that which he had several times clearly promised he would not do. He had promised this directly and through his Foreign Minister, Gromyko, who only the week before had been in President Kennedy's office renewing these promises. The President made the most of this psychological advantage, but he was at the same time determined not to push his opponent too far. He dedicated himself, according to his brother, "to making it clear to Khrushchev by word and deed—for both are important—that the U.S. had limited objectives and that we had no interest in accomplishing those objectives by adversely affecting the national security of the Soviet Union or by humiliating her." [65] He also said to Robert on October 26, the day before the issue was resolved, "If anybody is around to write

---

[65] Kennedy, *Thirteen Days*, p. 126.

after this, they are going to understand that we made every effort to find peace and every effort to give our adversary room to move. I am not going to push the Russians an inch beyond what is necessary." [66]

The whole handling of the drama reflected these attitudes. The group working round the President to advise him shared and were impressed with his determination not to offend unnecessarily. The advice of the Joint Chiefs, which also had its adherents among the civilians—to strike at the missile sites and to follow up with invasion and to do both without warning—was quickly rejected. The "quarantine" idea (not "blockade," which has legal connotations of war) was invented and adopted, despite the continuing arguments of the military that it would not work. They took care that the first ship stopped, the *Marcula*, was not a Russian ship. A Russian tanker was allowed to pass. Secretary McNamara personally took over direction of these measures. This annoyed the naval chiefs who thought the details should be left in their hands, but McNamara knew very well what he was doing. There was too much at stake, and he was in direct contact with and sensitive to the wishes of the President. Meanwhile Khrushchev was given clearly to understand, as privately as possible, that time was limited and that we were deadly serious. But also he was told, in one of Kennedy's letters to him: "I am concerned that we both show prudence and do nothing to allow events to make the situation more difficult to control than it is." [67]

Despite the fact that the episode turned out so extremely well in all its subsequent ramifications—the "Cuban Trafalgar" one British writer later called it—the late President was castigated, especially by some intellectuals of the left, for having dared too much. One such writer, I. F. Stone, did so in a review-article in the *New York Review of Books* some three-and-a-half years after the event. Mr. Stone even attributed President Kennedy's action to his personal vanity, but he did not feel it necessary to speculate on what would have been the consequences had the President decided not to undertake this confrontation. Kennedy himself did not fail to speculate on those consequences. The Russians had been probing, as was their wont, and probing with a purpose. What they were doing had most immediate bearing on the situation in Berlin, but certainly elsewhere as well. The President had

---

[66] Ibid., p. 127.

[67] Ibid., p. 60.

strong reason to be confident that the Russians would not go to war over this issue. Their security was not involved as was that of the United States. Also, we knew they did not want war any more than we did, or, if it is at all possible to find a distinction, even less. Still, there was a chance. There might be an error of judgment, a wrong move. But as the President put it to his brother at one bleak moment: "It looks really mean, doesn't it? But then, really there was no other choice. If they get this mean on this one in our part of the world, what will they do on the next?" [68]

And there is the rub. With the world organized as it is, ground rules have to be established, and maintained. The United States and other governments have been slowly groping their way to finding out what those ground rules must be, and how they may be maintained without confrontations as close and as tense as the Cuban one was or at least seemed at the time. Actually, the Cuban crisis itself helped establish some of the new rules, which can be garnered from a close reading of the statements of the chief contenders. A swift upsetting "by stealth" of the nuclear status quo, Kennedy made clear, could not be permitted. And despite the fact that the United States had again and again rejected as immoral the age-old conception of spheres of influence, the same conception with a sharper and more restricted meaning began again to take hold. The fact that Cuba was only ninety miles from the tip of Florida but many thousands of miles from the Soviet Union was seen by both sides to be decisively important in determining the attitudes that both could accept. When the Soviet ambassador complained to Robert Kennedy about the American missiles in Turkey, the latter truthfully replied that the President had previously ordered them removed, that unfortunately the order had not been followed but the failure had not been reported back. The United States, he said, could not agree under duress to a *quid-pro-quo*. However, on a later meeting he added that it was the American judgment that "within a short time after this crisis was over, those missiles would be gone." [69]

But one may well ask, suppose it had been less intelligent and

---

[68] Ibid., p. 67.

[69] Ibid., p. 94 f., 108 f. On the Cuban missile crisis see also the brilliant exposition by Ulam in the cited *The Rivals*, chap. 10; also Graham T. Allison, *Essence of Decision: Explaining the Cuban Missile Crisis* (Boston: Little, Brown, 1971); and Larson, *The "Cuban" Crisis of 1962*.

less peace-minded men than President Kennedy and his immediate cohorts who had been in charge at the time, what then? The answer can only be that it might have been stickier, but by no means necessarily war. Nations do not get into desperate or suicidal wars by accident or against their will. Khrushchev had choices, including the choice of accepting humiliation if need be, and all his training as a Communist revolutionary had conditioned him to be ready to accept humiliation rather than destruction to the Russian state and the Communist homeland. Naturally, it was much better to spare him both, including as much as possible of humiliation. The reward Kennedy reaped for the United States was an immediate—and thus far permanent—change in the whole tenor of Soviet relations with this country.

Kennedy's successor, less shrewd in matters concerning events abroad and our own military, got himself deeply involved in the Vietnam War; but throughout he was careful to avoid doing the one thing that might have "won" the war for him, which was to invade North Vietnam. He was also careful to avoid as much as possible the bombing of Chinese or Russian ships in Haiphong Harbor. President Johnson had as Vice President taken part in the deliberations about Cuba. Perhaps he had learned something there, or perhaps he would have behaved the same way anyway. In any case, he took good and effective care not to expand the Vietnam War to include China or Russia.

His successor, Richard Nixon, did in fact, in the fourth year of his Presidency, drop mines in several North Vietnamese ports, including that of Haiphong; but he coupled his announcement of that mining with a restatement of his war aims, which revised sharply downward those he had expressed only a few weeks earlier. He was now appealing to his great power colleagues to understand his need to avoid humiliation. He had but recently returned from his remarkable visit to Peking, and was scheduled soon to depart for Moscow. Knowing the intense animosity between the Chinese and the Russians that had made his Peking visit possible, he was banking on the fact that Moscow would want a summit meeting more than it would want to punish him, and he turned out to be right. In any case, he was hardly risking more than the cancellation of that meeting, with all the treaty signing that went with it. The Russians were hardly likely at that time to make warlike moves against the United States simply to protect their access to North Vietnam. Nevertheless, one must acknowledge that in this case it was the Chinese and the Russians who were making the necessary accommodation to the facts of life in the nuclear age rather than President Nixon.

The latter, however, was going to Moscow partly to make sure that the Middle East crisis did not result in another confrontation between the two superpowers. The "hot line" between Washington and Moscow, which had been established shortly after the Cuban crisis, had received its first use at the beginning of the Six Days War in 1967 between Israel and its Arab enemies, when the Soviet Union came on to say she would not intervene if the Americans did not, with which agreement was established without hesitation.

All this, naturally, leaves many pressing questions unanswered. What happens when both sides are not mutually or comparably desirous of accommodation? Herman Kahn was obsessed with the notion that nations might habitually play the game of "chicken," which is to keep rigidly to collision course waiting for the other side to yield. Well, they might sometime, and we must not give up the search for all possible preventives that might be effective against such collision. The leaders of no nation will wish to risk the total destruction of their country, and one of the things we have been learning over the past twenty-five years is that there are indeed many stopping points between friction, even some measure of combat, and all-out war.

But what if another Hitler comes along? That is the question we cannot finally avoid in any discourse on this subject. How mad was Hitler, and what would have caused him to stop? Would he have dared to behave as he did if the nations around him (as well as himself) had been armed with nuclear weapons? Would the German generals have dared to let him remain in power? As it was, they almost liquidated him in time. Even if we had the answers, they would only tell us what could have happened on that one special occasion.

There is as yet no final answer guaranteed to be happy. But by the same token, we have ample reason to feel now that nuclear weapons do act critically to deter wars between the major powers, and not nuclear wars alone but any wars. That is really a very great gain. We should no doubt be hesitant about relinquishing it even if we could. We should not complain too much because the guarantee is not ironclad. It is the curious paradox of our time that one of the foremost factors making deterrence really work and work well is the lurking fear that in some massive confrontation crisis it might fail. Under these circumstances one does not tempt fate. If we were absolutely certain that nuclear deterrence would be 100 per cent effective against nuclear attack, then it would cease to have much if any deterrence value against nonnuclear wars, and the arguments of the conventional buildup schools would indeed finally make sense. But then if under those circumstances we got involved in a large-scale nonnuclear war, we might find too late that the guarantee against use of nuclear weapons was not so water-tight after all.

Naturally, the kind of situation just described is not stable. It changes with time. What I have above called a "lurking fear" lurks at present not very far in the background. Over time it might recede further into the background. That might be dangerous in the long term, but in the long term a great many other things change, too. Great nations in their diplomacy may and probably will accommodate more and more to a situation in which war, the ultimate arbiter of last resort so well known in the past, is forbidden. They probably will adopt without quite realizing it, and even less acknowledging it, a new kind of sphere-of-influence conception, and a gingerliness about letting a quarrel between them go too far. What used to be called "undiplomatic language" becomes not so much provocative as a substitute for more serious involvement, and it evolves patterns by which important messages may be communicated.

Something of the sort seems at any rate, to have been happening thus far, though the "thus far" is too short a period upon which to base any far-reaching conclusions. It really begins, as we have seen, with the close of the Cuban missile crisis, following which Soviet-American relations showed an abrupt but pervasive change from what had preceded, the most conspicuous instances being the relaxation of tensions concerning Berlin. Where the British Foreign Office, upon hearing President Kennedy's speech of October 22, 1962, "expected, to a man, that the Russians would be in west Berlin on the following day," the very reverse is what came to pass.[70] Relations over Berlin promptly eased, and stayed better thereafter. Even Khrushchev's communications became immediately sober and polite, where they had often previously been violent and rude.

---

[70] The quotation is from a statement made to me orally by a senior member of that Foreign Office only a few months after the crisis.

Chino-Soviet relations during the period since 1962 have become bitter in tone, and the border skirmishes over an island in the Ussuri River during 1969 seemed for the moment threatening. A large section of the official community in Washington was completely convinced that war would come of it, but thus far it has not. Even though the Soviet nuclear capability was enormously superior to that of China—and it was therefore the Russians who would determine whether any conflict between them would go nuclear—there seemed also to bè between them the common conception that any resolution of the conflict must be—in the German general's words concerning the reunification of Germany— accomplished *ohne Krieg.* Perhaps it helped somewhat, or even much, that the "aggressor," that is, the side demanding territories held by the other, was the party much inferior in nuclear capability; but it could not have been the whole reason.

We have seen the United States engage itself in a foolish and costly war in Vietnam, but with critical restraint with respect to anything that might involve China or the Soviet Union, and doing so despite the fact that the cost of that restraint was humiliation and military failure in Vietnam. Since then we have had the Nixon Doctrine, which if it means anything means that the United States will be more careful in the future. And the latter point reminds us of what is perhaps the most hopeful thing of all, which is that the generation that remembers Munich so vividly and grew to maturity and power during the cold war is the generation that will shortly be passing from power. The one that replaces it will not really be wiser, but it will surely be more adapted to the circumstances of the late twentieth century.

CHAPTER

10

Strategic Thinkers, Planners, Decision-Makers

If I took your gloomy view, I should commence immediate inquiries as to the most painless form of suicide. But I think you listen too much to the soldiers. No lesson seems to be so deeply inculcated by the experience of life as that you never should trust in experts. If you believe the doctors nothing is wholesome; if you believe the theologians nothing is innocent; if you believe the soldiers nothing is safe. They all require to have their strong wine diluted by a very large admixture of insipid common sense.

> Lord Salisbury in a letter to Lord Lytton, Viceroy of India, June 15, 1877.

The great Marshal Maurice de Saxe, the foreigner who became for a time the first-ranking soldier of France under Louis XV, observed in his *Rêveries* that most commanding generals displayed on the battlefield the utmost confusion, and he asked himself: "How does this happen? It is because," he answers, "very few men occupy themselves with the higher problems of war. They pass their lives drilling troops and believe that this is the only branch of the military art. When they arrive at the command of armies

433

they are totally ignorant, and, in default of knowing what should be done, they do what they know." Although these words were written over 200 years ago, they have applied perennially to the art of the soldier, and apply about as well now as when they were written.

Actually, in Maurice's time there was a chance at least for a few to bypass on their way to the highest rank the kind of irrelevant duties of which he complained. One needed only to be born in a high enough station. Maurice was himself a bastard son of the Elector of Saxony and King of Poland.[1] We may assume he never had to spend much of his career simply in drilling troops. The crowning victory of his career was at Fontenoy (1745), where the commander-in-chief of the opposing army was a 23-year-old prince, the Duke of Cumberland, son of George II of England. Another of Maurice's contemporaries was King Frederick II of Prussia, who at the time of Fontenoy had already begun the career that was to bring him the title of "the Great." These men, so long as they showed any inclination at all to be soldiers (and Frederick showed little until he was about to become king) were destined from the beginning for highest command.

But alongside those who were literally born to command, there had always been the professionals, those who took to arms as a calling. Many among these reached the highest rank. For them, too, being of high birth was a great advantage and being at least of the gentry virtually a necessity, but from the latter group came most of the professional officers of Europe over several centuries, including England's two greatest generals, John Churchill and Arthur Wellesley, and her greatest admiral, Horatio Nelson. The former two became respectively the Dukes of Marlborough and of Wellington, and Nelson became a viscount (and was also created a duke by the King of Naples) but like Napoleon's their titles came from their military accomplishments rather than the other way around. Napoleon, though of modest and almost foreign origin, found himself commander-in-chief of France's largest expeditionary force at age 26, though obviously it took the upheaval of a great revolution to hasten the pace and the reach of his promotions.

---

[1] For a good account of the life of Maurice de Saxe see Jon E. M. White, *Marshal of France* (London: Hamilton, 1962). The complete *Mes Rêveries* are contained in Thomas R. Phillips (ed.), *Roots of Strategy* (Harrisburg, Pa.: Military Service Publishing Co., 1940), pp. 177–300.

Naturally, we get a distorted view from looking only at the few military geniuses that time and the passage of many wars throws across our vision. Yet even with them we wonder: How and where did they learn the art of the general? For Maurice's complaint touches only half the problem. If the duties of junior rank were really poor preparation for those of supreme command, where did that preparation come from? The necessary gift of personal leadership we can understand. There have always been men who stood out from their fellows because of their possession of that talent, which may be inborn and which is certainly helped by favorable childhood experience, including the experience in a class society of being relatively well-born. But how did those who reached the top learn *strategy*? Given an enemy to deal with, how did one proceed to use one's army? Where did one send it and for what purpose? *Tactics* are by contrast more easily taught by precept and experience, and in the past the frequency of wars provided ample schooling. Still, the great soldier or admiral had to make his mark not only in winning battles but also in knowing how and where to move his forces so that the battles could be fought or avoided to his own and his country's advantage.

In this aspect of his art the commander received little benefit from unstructured experience or from word-of-mouth instruction. The strategic conception is more abstract than the tactical one, and each campaign and each war is or appears to be entirely distinctive, just as the campaign that led to Blenheim (1704), in which Marlborough marched from the Netherlands deep into Bavaria, was a more distinctive inspiration and accomplishment than the battle that was its culmination. There had to be in the leader who conceived and conducted it an inventiveness, a native cunning, and a tendency to reflect on the enemy's goals as well as the needs and aspirations of his allies. Meaningful parallels were usually not to be found in the leader's own experience, though he may have found them in a creative reading of history—the kind of reading that enables one without effort and perhaps only half consciously, or even unconsciously, to recall some past instance that bears in some significant way on a present problem. Certainly we know that John Churchill's famous descendant of our own time used history in that fashion. But it is clear that the earlier Churchill had never been *trained* in strategy, and he very likely had never read a book on the subject, for in his time virtually none of any consequence was current. And as Madame de Pompadour said in her *Memoirs* of Maurice de Saxe: "War was all he knew; and that he knew without learning it."

Maurice's own little book, which came after Marlborough's time, was published posthumously (1757) and it had little company or competition. Like Frederick's *Instructions to His Generals* (1747) [2] and memoranda for his successor, Maurice's book was not intended by its author for publication. Anyway, both Maurice and Frederick dwelt mostly on homely matters concerning the handling and provisioning of armies, and only incidentally and in passing made observations or contributions on what we should now consider fundamental strategy. When Karl von Clausewitz in the following century was to write the first really adequate treatise on strategy, and still by a wide margin the greatest, he paid little attention to either Maurice de Saxe or Frederick. He did, however, pay his respects to the original Renaissance source of wisdom on politics and strategy, Niccolò Machiavelli, more famous today for his *Il Principe* but also author of *Arte della Guerra* and the *Discorsi*. Machiavelli's *Art of War* had been a classic through the sixteenth century, translated into all the major European languages, but had not been forgotten in the seventeenth and eighteenth centuries. The nineteenth-century Clausewitz, who tended to scorn most other military writers, treated Machiavelli with respect because like him "he was convinced that the validity of any special analysis of military problems depended on a general perception, on a correct concept of the nature of war." [3]

Machiavelli's large contribution reminds us that there have always been some few civilians to whom the study of warfare was intriguing as something besides history, and of course we know that most military history has been written by civilians, especially in modern times. Soldiers have always cherished the image of themselves as men of action rather than as intellectuals, and they have not been very much given to writing analytical inquiries into their own art. It is obvious, too, that the required talents are very different for the two pursuits. Perhaps as a result of some defensive feeling on the matter, military men have in the past turned a certain degree of obloquy on those of their colleagues who were in their eyes too scholarly about war. A century after Clausewitz,

---

[2] Also contained in Phillips, *Roots of Strategy*, pp. 311–400.

[3] Felix Gilbert, "Machiavelli: The Renaissance of the Art of War," in Edward M. Earle (ed.), *Makers of Modern Strategy* (Princeton: Princeton University Press, 1943), p. 25.

Alfred T. Mahan would be called "a pen-pushing sailor" and would be given a bad fitness report on his last duty at sea as commander of the cruiser *Chicago* (which he may indeed have deserved). Mahan in his memoirs described himself as being in his own opinion temperamentally unsuited to the military profession, and the great writing career that made him famous did not begin until he was transferred to an essentially civilian pursuit as a faculty member of the new U.S. Naval War College.[4]

The civilian writers with something important to say have usually been well received by the professionals, who understand their own needs and also the paucity of contributions by their brethren. Some pages back we noticed the respectful attention and treatment accorded Ivan Bloch by the Czarist officers. A century earlier Nelson was supposed to have studied with deep respect a treatise on naval tactics written by an Edinburgh banker named John Clerk who had never been to sea.[5] Another distinguished writer on naval strategy—and also on naval history, which was his main field—was the British civilian scholar Julian S. Corbett, who was a younger contemporary of Mahan's and who won the latter's esteem as well as that of other naval officers.[6] Some professional military may in certain moods inveigh against "armchair strategists," by which they mean interlopers on their terrain who are not identifiable by a service uniform, but this is usually an attitude of disgruntlement concerning particular views with which they are in disagreement. Naturally, too, there are and always have been a few primitives who consider the fact of wearing or having worn a uniform the indispensable entitlement to the expression of any views on military affairs; but these are normally the ones who would never read anything of a reflective character anyway even if written by one with the most unchallengable military cre-

---

[4] See his *From Sail to Steam: Recollections of a Naval Life* (Boston: Little, Brown, 1907). His last sea duty, on the *Chicago*, came as an interlude in his work at the Naval War College, and he had already become famous for some of his publications. Rear Admiral Erben, whose flagship the *Chicago* was on this cruise and who wrote the bad fitness report, no doubt attended the festivities at Oxford and Cambridge Universities where Mahan was granted honorary degrees. Mahan's elevation to rear admiral upon retirement had nothing to do with his writings but was an honor given automatically to retiring captains who had served in the U.S. Civil War.

[5] John Clerk, *An Essay on Naval Tactics, Systematical and Historical* (London, 1790, 1797). This work was apparently deemed significant enough to be republished in Edinburgh in 1804 and 1827 and in the United States under the title *System of Seamanship and Naval Tactics* (Philadelphia, 1807).

[6] See J. S. Corbett, *Some Principles of Maritime Strategy* (London, 1911, 1918).

dentials. They are also likely to be the ones most deeply immersed in parochial service attitudes, so that if they were totally honest in their proscriptions they would include among those outside the pale all who wore the wrong *color* of uniform—or even the wrong insignia of branch within the service.[7]

The True Nature of Strategy

The role of the civilian in contributions to this field, which became so prominent following World War II, is more understandable when we reflect further on what strategy really means and what it embraces. There are a number of standard definitions, including the one by Mahan that distinguishes between tactics and strategy according to whether or not the opposing forces are in contact. Upon contact, he wrote, we have the fighting that represents the employment of tactics; prior to contact, however, or going on independently of it, we have those major dispositions of forces that will determine whether, when, and to whose advantage contact takes place. As a definition of strategy it will do perhaps as well as any other, inasmuch as the purpose of definitions is usually not to explain but to distinguish—and it helps us to get on with the real job of exploring the true meaning of the idea. I have waited until nearly the end of this book before dealing with the matter, instead of taking it up at the outset, because it will now be much easier to put across ideas that are both fundamentally important and usually neglected.

The idea stressed repeatedly in this book, explicitly and implicitly, is that which most makes Clausewitz stand out from those who might otherwise come near to being his peers and which accounted for his being impressed with Machiavelli. It is the concern with the fundamental nature of war as a branch of politics. The usual conception, prevailing today almost as much as formerly, stops far short of that understanding. It is preoccupied almost exclusively with the winning of wars, as though the latter were conceived to be something comparable to athletic contests—with, to be sure, an added ingredient of seriousness. The general has indeed been trained or conditioned to want desperately to win, and to be willing to pay any price possible to do so. It may be neces-

---

[7] Perhaps this is as good a place as any to add that my own reception by the armed services has on the whole been extremely generous over a long span of years despite my often expressing criticism of their views, though their approval was especially warm when my views coincided with theirs.

sary to let him content himself with that conception in order that he may be the best possible *fighter*, which is the skill we mostly desire of him and the one we exclusively ask of those generals short of the very top. However, there also has to be at the top, certainly in the civilian and preferably also in the military departments of the government, the basic and prevailing conception of what any war existing or impending is really about and what it is attempting to accomplish. This attitude includes necessarily a readiness to reexamine whether under the circumstances existing it is right to continue it or whether it is better to seek some solution or termination other than victory, even if victory in the strictly military sense is judged attainable.

Naturally the Vietnam situation leaps to mind. The British journalist, Henry Brandon, in a speech delivered in 1969 reported the following:

> Before leaving Saigon on one of my periodic visits to Vietnam late in 1967, I asked the leading civilians and military in charge whether a reduction in the intensity of the war, a reduction of the cost in men and material, would not be worth striving for. I thought it might help to induce a more patient and forebearing attitude towards the war on the part of the American public. . . . Not surprisingly, they all reacted alike. They said it was not their business to include American domestic opinion in their calculations; that was up to President Johnson.

The trouble was—and we do not need to endorse Brandon's particular solution, which was in fact that adopted by President Nixon, as the one most desirable under the circumstances—that no one in Washington, including the President, was ready to take up the considerations that those in Saigon were all too eager to leave to him. Instead the prevailing slogan was, as it is almost invariably: "The commander on the spot must either be given our full confidence or be replaced." This is usually translated to mean: "We must give him everything he asks for." Mr. Brandon continues:

> But foreign policy begins at home. The fact that President Johnson ignored American public opinion and disregarded the mounting opposition to the war as he fought it, forced him not only into political retirement, it also aroused deep

mistrust in government and in the military. The war was seen
by many as unnecessary; by others as immoral. It inflamed the
already restless youth and created an atmosphere conducive to
violence whether on the university campuses or in the black
ghettos. . . .[8]

Brandon was pointing to what was obviously a failure in strategy. It was a failure in the larger sense in that the results were
clearly contrary to the national interests of the United States, but
also in the narrower sense that American performance in Vietnam
was adversely affected. The fighting morale of American troops
began to decline conspicuously even before their numbers were
reduced. The question of responsibility seems clear, but only if we
make it too simple. The President was of course primarily responsible. But he could have been helped, if not by the commander in
Saigon then at least by the Joint Chiefs at home. The latter in
fact, especially the two successive chairmen of the Joint Chiefs,
Generals Maxwell Taylor and Earle Wheeler, did everything in
their power to induce the President not to moderate the intensity
of the American participation in the war. The latter not only ad-
vised against such a turn in United States conduct; he positively
schemed against it.[9] A wiser President would have ignored their
advice; more strategically minded generals would have given better advice. The latter are, however, extremely rare, and we cannot
count on their being present at the appropriate moment.

Clausewitz had learned from experience very early in his career
the importance of "the correct political basis" for any nation at
war. He had entered the Prussian military service as a *Fahnen-
junker* or ensign at the age of only 12, and in the following year,
1793, had gone with the Prussian army into France in what was
the second campaign of the War of the First Coalition. This campaign was carried on without spirit. He later noted in *On War*
that while in the previous year "a sort of chivalrous spirit" had
been enough to inspire the march into Champagne (which ended
with Valmy), now that that been used up and inasmuch as "Prus-

---

[8] From an unpublished speech delivered by Henry Brandon on December 19, 1969 to
the Eleventh Annual Conference of the Institute for Strategic Studies (now called
International Institute for Strategic Studies).

[9] General Wheeler in effect admitted as much in an interview with John B. Henry II.
See the latter's article "February, 1968," *Foreign Policy*, no. 4 (Fall 1971), especially
pp. 18 f. See also above, pp. 193 f.

sia had neither anything to conquer nor to defend in Alsace
. . . . she continued the war with very little interest." [10]

It is interesting that Clausewitz, whose whole life from boyhood
on was spent in military service and who as a scholar and philosopher was totally self-taught, should have grasped the essence of
the issue, the nexus between politics and strategy, so much more
clearly than virtually all of his peers and successors. The basic
reason one finds undoubtedly in his native intellectual prowess,
the extraordinary power and reach of his mind. However, he also
had some bitter and extraordinary personal experiences to help
him along the way.

His relatively brief life (he died in 1831 at the age of 51) covered the entire French Revolution, and his entry into the Prussian
army coincided with the beginning of the Terror. He was to be
deeply immersed in the whole vast Napoleonic cataclysm. Although he certainly did not identify with the *ancien régime*, he
soon came to look upon Napoleon (whom in his writings he always referred to as "Bonaparte") about as our own generation
looked upon Hitler—the enemy of Europe and of mankind. He
was nevertheless objective enough always to credit this detested
man with being a superlative general.

In 1805 Clausewitz saw his sovereign, King Friederich Wilhelm
III, cling to his neutrality while Napoleon in the campaign culminating with Austerlitz defeated Austria and Russia. Now facing
Napoleon alone, the Prussian king found the Emperor's new demands upon him unacceptable and foolishly declared war. In our
time the script somehow seems familiar. With an army that still
believed in the invincibility of the tactics bequeathed it by
Frederick the Great—meaning an army that had learned nothing
from the events of the past decade—this king marched off in 1806
to utter defeat and humiliation in the campaign of Jena and
Auerstädt.[11] As General Hermann von Boyen, later Minister of
War, was to write of it: "There have been few campaigns in which

---

[10] Karl von Clausewitz, *On War*, trans. by O. J. Matthijs Jolles (New York: Modern
Library, 1943), Book viii, chap. 9, p. 624.

[11] One should notice in this regard that tactics can change drastically without being
attended or forced by significant changes in weaponry. Frederick had stressed rapidity
of fire, without too much interruption for aiming, from troops pressing forward in
rigid and precise close formation. Napoleon, with smooth-bore muskets only slightly
more wieldly and accurate, had placed greater emphasis on taking good aim, even at
the cost of rapidity of fire, and had stressed relatively loose and open formation of his
troops in the attack. There was also a different use of the artillery, which was

such numerous, and often incomprehensible, blunders piled on top of each other." [12] Clausewitz, then age 26 and an *aide-de-camp* to one of the king's sons, was to write in his *Nachrichten* on the campaign a fierce denunciation not only of the tactics but also of the strategy that had led to the defeat, which he attributed partly to an outworn "pedantry" that deceived itself with "hollow phrases and false similes, like 'wing bastions' and 'active defensive' in such important matters where only the clearest and most precise expressions should be used." [13] This was already unusual insight for a young man, to see that time-hallowed and deference-evoking words may have little or no meaning. He was also experiencing the fact that defeat, however bitter, was a marvelous incentive to clear thinking.

Afterwards Clausewitz participated with his revered Scharnhorst and Gneisenau in the drastic reforms of the Prussian army, which included among changes in tactics the elimination of the requirement of nobility for officer status. Then in 1809 Austria, observing Napoleon's difficulties in Iberia, once more took up arms against him and this time made a good showing, though not yet good enough, and Napoleon added the name of Wagram to his victories. Clausewitz and his colleagues were beside themselves in despair that their king did not go to Austria's aid. But the king would not move without Russian support. Again he was left alone to face a victorious Napoleon, who now asked him to yield up Silesia or to raise the funds to pay the indemnity owing from the previous war, which Napoleon thought could be nicely done by reducing the Prussian army to 6,000 men. However, the immediate crisis was avoided by drastic new measures of taxation.

Three years later came the crowning blow. With war developing between Napoleon and Czar Alexander I, Friederich Wilhelm no longer had the option of neutrality and was forced to choose sides. He opted for an alliance with Napoleon, to whose *Grande Armée*

---

virtually unchanged technologically (though perhaps with more use of canister and grape as compared with solid round shot). Similarly, the great German breakthrough on the western front in the spring of 1918 was *not* due to the use of tanks as an answer to the machine gun (the Germans had built very few tanks) but to a new kind of infiltration tactics. Even in the Battle of the Somme in 1916 the British on a few occasions made good advances when by careful staff work they coordinated their artillery appropriately with the infantry movements; but much more often the staff work was deficient in this respect and the total result was a costly failure.

[12] Roger Parkinson, *Clausewitz* (New York: Stein and Day, 1971), p. 102.

[13] Ibid., p. 54. The full title of the *Nachrichten* referred to is *Nachrichten über Preussen in seiner grossen Katastrophe* (1888).

he committed 20,000 men, which was half his army, promising also not to augment the other half. At this Clausewitz resigned his commission and left his beloved wife to whom after long years of waiting he had recently been married.[14] Along with various others of the leading reformist soldiers of Prussia he went over to the Russians, thus becoming nominally the enemy of his own king and of that king's army, which contained his two brothers who were in the contingent assigned to Napoleon's army (though placed under Marshal Alexandre Macdonald, who did not go into Russia).

With the Russians he fought in the great campaign of 1812, in which the *Grande Armée* went to Moscow and then perished in the retreat. He witnessed with his own eyes and was torn to the core by the unspeakable horrors of this flight, including the awful scenes of the crossing of the Berezina River.[15] No one would ever have to tell him how terrible war could be. But as a true son of his times and of his profession, what he saw did not affect his acceptance of war as a fact of life. It did no doubt accentuate his feelings that the correct use of thought in the handling of it deserved a very high priority. Napoleon had caused the war and thus the suffering on both sides. He had also been guilty of a colossal strategic blunder, a large part of which had been the purely political error of assuming that simply by placing himself and his army in one of the Czar's two capitals he would cause the latter to come suing for terms. "A capital," he had said, "which is occupied by an enemy is like a girl who loses her virginity." [16] One wonders what he meant by that: that her father would be bound to rush to the defense of her honor? It would be neither the first nor the last time that a senseless or frivolous analogy would help inspire bad strategy.

It is significant that in his *On War*, Clausewitz, always scrupulously fair, defends Napoleon's strategy to a considerable degree,

---

[14] It was his wife Marie (née von Brühl), whom he married in December 1810 after a courtship lasting over six years, who after his death was to devote her few remaining years to editing and publishing his works.

[15] Clausewitz wrote to his wife: "What ghastly scenes have I witnessed here. If my feelings had not been hardened it would have sent me mad. Even so, it will take many years before I can remember what I have seen without feeling a shuddering horror." To his memoirs he confided: "I felt as if I could never be released from the terrible impressions of the spectacle. . . . in this fraction of some three days march, all the horrors of the [retreat] were accumulated." Quoted in Parkinson, *Clausewitz*, p. 194.

[16] Quoted ibid., p. 157. In this case, however, Parkinson does not give his source.

and does so on political grounds. The campaign failed, he says, "because the only means to secure success failed. . . . It was only by reaching Moscow with the force of his blow that Bonaparte could hope to shake the courage of the government and the loyalty and steadfastness of the people." He then points out: "It is permissible to judge an event according to the result, as that is the best criticism upon it, but this judgment, derived merely from the result, must not be passed off as evidence of human wisdom." This idea is startling because it is simple, correct, and rarely observed. Then he adds: "The campaign of 1812 did not succeed because the enemy's government remained firm, the people loyal and steadfast, because it therefore could not succeed." He agrees that "the result has shown that Bonaparte deceived himself in his calculations," and he concedes that he did not make sufficient provision against the failure of his major premise—that Alexander was bound to seek a peace once Napoleon got to Moscow.[17]

Because his reputation had preceded him, Clausewitz held a succession of staff posts near or at the top of the Russian command structure. He was therefore in a position to see how close to defeat the Russians had several times come, mostly because of their impatience to fight battles for the sake of honor. The idea of falling back deep into Russia before offering serious resistance to the invader did not sit well either with the Czar or with various of his generals, including his original commander-in-chief, the incompetent ex-Prussian von Phull (to whom Clausewitz had been assigned as *aide*). As he later put it in *On War*: "The most profound sagacity could, therefore, not have devised a better plan of war than that which the Russians followed unintentionally."[18] Clausewitz himself played some part in helping to establish the unintended.[19] Yet it was not until General Mikhail Kutuzov took over command that a Russian retreat deep enough to let Bonaparte take Moscow became part of their designed strategy. Even Kutuzov knew he would have to fight one full-scale battle before Moscow, though he was determined not to fight more. That battle

---

[17] Clausewitz, *On War*, Book viii, chap. 9, pp. 620 f.

[18] Ibid., Book viii, chap. 9, p. 608.

[19] Before leaving Prussia he had talked with Scharnhorst about the coming campaign, and had agreed entirely with the latter's conception that the only sound strategy for the Russians was to fall back deeply within their own territory and delay as long as possible a full-scale confrontation with the French. As an *aide* to von Phull he had tried to convey this view not only to his commander but also to the Czar. See Parkinson, *Clausewitz*, pp. 144 f.

was fought at Borodino, where the Russians lost to no purpose 58,000 casualties out of their original force of 112,000. The French, too, suffered severely in this bloodiest of battles, but so long as the Russians held to the Kutuzov strategy, theirs was a doomed army anyway.

Even when the French, after a fateful wait in Moscow of thirty-nine days, had begun their tardy retreat late in October, Clausewitz in his letters to his wife, though foreseeing the triumphant end result, was still expressing concern that the Russians might yet throw everything away. "It will be through human failings, not fate, if Europe is not saved now," he wrote, adding that if the worst happened, he would "go with the German Legion to England."[20] It may have been his native melancholy that made him apprehensive even when he saw so clearly the ruin that Napoleon had brought upon himself, but he had also grown painfully accustomed to seeing stupidity in high places. He knew of the heavy pressures upon Kutuzov, and he probably considered the cunning and wisdom of that general too good to be true—besides which the latter's place in command was always subject to the suspect will of the Czar. When, however, the French retreat began to founder in starvation and the fierce cold of the Russian winter, Clausewitz was all for pressing the attack. Despite his real anguish at the horrors he saw at the Berezina, Clausewitz, in later writing his account of the campaign, blamed Kutuzov's subordinate Wittgenstein for not being more aggressive there, where "he might have made the French loss much greater."[21] Still, the inner conflict between his undoubted compassion and something much fiercer in his nature must have contributed to the depression that seems to have deepened steadily throughout his life.[22]

Clausewitz fought the French until the Emperor's abdication of 1814, and on Napoleon's return for the "Hundred Days" took part (as a Prussian officer once again) in his fourth campaign against

---

[20] Ibid., p. 183. It is interesting, incidentally, that there seemed to be no difficulties in the way of Clausewitz corresponding with his wife throughout the whole campaign, despite the fact that she was at home in Prussia, a nominal enemy of Russia. Such a circumstance is characteristic of that period, when intercourse between citizens of nations at war often continued pretty much as usual.

[21] Ibid., p. 193. Parkinson is quoting from Clausewitz's own account of the 1812 campaign, contained in volume seven of his *Hinterlassne Werke über Krieg und Kriegsführung*

[22] For some tentative guesses at the character of Clausewitz's conspicuous neurosis, see my review-article of the Parkinson book, "On Clausewitz: A Passion for War," *World Politics*, vol. 25, no. 2 (January 1973).

the French, that which ended at Waterloo, though his own fighting on the day of the great battle took place at nearby Wavre. There as chief of staff to the Prussian Corps commander Thielmann, he played a key role in helping prevent the French Marshal Grouchy from coming to the desperately needed support of his Emperor.

For this sensitive, retiring, and deeply emotional man, who, however, knew very well the worth of his own ideas, such searing experiences, including that of the occupation of Paris afterwards, would burn deeply into his consciousness the necessary unity of war with its object.[23] He knew well enough that war was a deadly serious matter, not a game to be played for the sake of winning. Although no single author could be an adequate "guide" to us in our present problems, and not alone because the world we live in is so different from his, the startling insights that leap up at us from so many pages of his great work are still often directly applicable to our own times. There has been no one to match him since.

Although Clausewitz himself frequently speaks loosely of certain "principles" to be observed and followed—he could hardly do otherwise than seek to establish certain generalizations at least in his analytical works—he specifically rejected the notion that there could be any well-defined body of particular rules or principles that universally dictated one form of behavior rather than another. The latter idea seemed to be suggested by his contemporary, Antoine Henri Jomini, who has since been endlessly quoted for the remark: "Methods change but principles are unchanging." However, it was not until the twentieth century that various army field manuals would attempt to encapsulate centuries of experience and volumes of reflection into a few tersely worded and usually numbered "principles of war." Clausewitz would have been appalled at such attempts, and not surprised at some of the terrible blunders that have been made in the name of those "principles." [24]

---

[23] Despite his dislike for the French, Clausewitz was appalled by the vindictive behavior and attitudes of his Prussian colleagues towards the French in their occupation of Paris after Waterloo. It undoubtedly confirmed his feelings about the supreme requirement of appropriate political direction during war and its aftermath, which he developed so persistently in his *On War*. To him, satisfaction of desires for revenge was not an appropriate political motivation. Parkinson, *Clausewitz*, pp. 286–289.

[24] I have treated this matter more substantially in my *Strategy in the Missile Age* (Princeton: Princeton University Press, 1959), pp. 21–33.

In the relevant passages of *On War*, he compares war to a machine operating under great friction, or to a man walking through a dense medium like water. "In war all is simple; but the most simple is still very difficult." On paper everything is misleading. Units like battalions look uniform and their performance predictable. But they are made up of and led by men, who are anything but units, and who are subject to fear, hunger, and exhaustion. "This enormous friction which is not concentrated, as in mechanics, at a few points, is, therefore everywhere brought into contact with chance, and thus produces incidents quite impossible to foresee." Thus, he says, "theorists who have never plunged in themselves . . . are unpractical and even absurd, because they only teach what everyone knows—how to walk." Then he goes on:

> Further every war is rich in individual phenomena. It is in consequence an unexplored sea, full of rocks which the mind of the general may sense but has never seen with his eyes and round which he must now steer in dark night. If a contrary wind also springs up, that is, if some great chance event declares against him, then the most consumate skill, presence of mind and effort are required, while to a distant observer everything seems to be going like clockwork.[25]

There is more of same, which seems in the aggregate to be putting the entire emphasis on the "instinctive judgment" that comes only with practice and experience. These statements are basically opposed to any conception of tightly worded "principles" that suggest a computerized tabulation or keyboard where pressing the right button produces the right answer.

Naturally Clausewitz had heard of, or could independently have formulated from his own experience, the remark of Frederick the Great that "an ass that has been on thirty campaigns is still an ass." In his words about "consummate skill" and that "practiced judgment which we call instinctive," he was talking about that kind of talent which his own experience told him was not abundant. Besides, some countries have been fortunate enough to have avoided war for long periods. One surely does not seek war in order to give practice to one's soldiers. In any case, Clausewitz was writing a book on war, a very great book as it turned out, and its purpose, as I have said, was to provide generalizations. After all,

---

[25] Clausewitz, *On War*, Book i, chap. 7, pp. 54 f.

to say that "every war is rich in individual phenomena" and that the shrewd and capable general is ever ready to adjust to them is itself a generalization, and one of the highest importance. It helps warn the general not to be too rigid in his conceptions, especially those that in our own times he is likely to have received in the form of simple axioms in his staff college or war college courses.

It may well be that the consideration of a catalog of numbered principles (usually fewer than a dozen) with the barest definition of the meaning of each may be necessary to communicate to second-order minds (or minds too busy with the execution of plans to worry much about the specific validity of the ideas behind them) some conception of what the business is all about. Or it may help the ordinary commander to avoid the most glaring or commonplace errors; just as "the principle of concentration," for example, may help him to refrain from *unjustified* dispersions of his force. However, the commander who is capable of recognizing just as clearly the unique qualities of the situation before him as he does its likeness to somewhat similar situations covered in the textbooks will use such "principles" at most as a reminder of the obvious. In short, the catalog of principles must be recognized for what it is, which is a device intended to circumvent the need for months and years of study of and rumination on a very difficult subject, presented mostly in the form of military and political history and the "lessons" that may be justly derived therefrom —and more recently presented in other techniques as well, which we shall presently consider. However, it has to be added that in the training of the modern officer such study and rumination are not allowed for, either at the staff college level or the war college. It takes too much time, and it also takes analytical and reflective qualities of mind that are not commonly found either among student officers or among their instructors.

Besides, the military services have learned very well that what they need most in their commanders is that quality called "leadership," and in this they are quite right. Thus, officers are promoted to top command ranks on the basis above all of their demonstrated possession of leadership qualities in the command of various units, especially under combat conditions. The only trouble with this system is that that talent which is also necessary in the top leadership, that is, strategic insight, may come off a very poor second. As Louis XV said when he heard of Maurice de Saxe's death: "I am now without any general, I have only some captains remaining"; and a courtier added, concerning Lowendahl who aspired to Maurice's place: "Lowendahl's exploits are over; his counsellor is dead."

The Germans in Clausewitz's time solved this problem by distinguishing between the qualities necessary in the commander, who was expected to provide leadership and aggressive drive, and his chief of staff, who was supposed to do much of his tactical and strategic thinking for him. Clausewitz himself during his wartime career always served in a staff post, usually as chief of staff. His countryman, Marshal Leberecht von Blücher, whose role at Waterloo was a very close second to that of Wellington, was recognized by the whole Prussian army as the commander-in-chief *par excellence*. He had enormous bravery and dash, and he was certainly intelligent. But he was capable of writing the following of his relations with his chief of staff (who was Clausewitz's good friend) : "Gneisenau, being my chief of staff and very reliable, reports to me on the manoeuvres that are to be executed and the marches that are to be performed. Once convinced that he is right, I drive my troops through hell towards the goal and never stop until the desired end has been accomplished—yes, even though the officers trained in the old school may pout and complain and all but mutiny." Then, when offered an honorary degree at Oxford after the war, he said: "Well! If I am to become a doctor, you must at least make Gneisenau an apothecary, for we two belong together always." [26] Naturally, this kind of near-perfect combination would be singular in any age, and although the form continued in the German army down to World War I (being represented in the special status of the General Staff and in the relationship between Hindenburg and Ludendorff) , it would be a difficult one to preserve in the face of the normal vanity of the commander—and possibly the lack of the required talent in the subordinate.

The modern chief of staff, in the American armed services as in all others (though not the one who bears that title as the head of each service), is the executive officer of his commander, keeping him informed of developments and seeing that his orders are appropriately carried out, which may involve directing a good deal of detailed "staff work," but he would not normally be expected to do his strategic thinking for him. When Admiral William F.

---

[26] Parkinson, *Clausewitz*, p. 229.

Halsey at Leyte Gulf made the bizarre decision to throw the whole of his gigantic Third Fleet at the puny decoy force presented by Admiral Jusaburo Ozawa in the far north, thus leaving San Bernardino Strait and the American forces that had landed on Leyte unguarded against Admiral Takeo Kurita's powerful force (all in the name of the "principle of concentration"), there were subordinates in the fleet, including Rear Admiral G. F. Bogan and Vice Admiral W. A. Lee, who were convinced the decision was wrong, but their efforts to hint as much were instantly rebuffed. If any members of Halsey's immediate staff had doubts, it is not recorded. Halsey had a reputation, which he undoubtedly deserved, as a "great commander," aggressive, inspiring devotion in his men, and so forth. But at the critical moment toward which his whole career had been oriented he made a decision, at a tactical level that was also strategic, which was not only wrong but foolish, because the reasons for it were "by the book" and clearly inappropriate for the occasion.[27]

There are some today who yearn to see created a true science or

---

[27] Inasmuch as I have used this example before in other writings, I wish to emphasize that it is not because there are not plenty of other examples of misapplication of the "principle of concentration," but because this one was indeed outstanding in its magnitude and consequences and also because it happens to be a case in which my judgment about it took form concurrently with the event. At the time of the battle I was posted as a naval reserve lieutenant in the Office of Naval Intelligence in Washington, where we had the information telling us exactly what carriers and other warships remained in the Japanese navy. This information, which had proved highly reliable, told us *at the time* that the four carriers sighted with Admiral Ozawa's force were all the Japanese had left, and that except for the *Zuikaku*, the last survivor of the Pearl Harbor attack, they were small vessels converted from light cruisers and merchant vessels and of trivial military value. We also knew that the pilots left in the Japanese fleet were nothing like those our ships had encountered earlier in the war, almost all of whom had been killed. Halsey and his staff had the same intelligence, and our war experience over the previous year and a half should have confirmed its accuracy, yet they totally disregarded it. The two axioms that held their minds fast were (a) "the enemy's main force is where his carriers are"—true earlier in the war but now ludicrously wrong, and (b) "don't divide the fleet in the presence of the enemy"—an idea designed to assure superiority or minimize inferiority of one's own force against the enemy's, but totally inapplicable in this instance because of the vast superiority we enjoyed. A Third Fleet appropriately split up would have still left forces greatly superior to each opposing force, Admiral Kurita's, which issued from San Bernardino Strait, and Ozawa's. In this case the enemy's main force was that which contained his newer battleships, and that was Kurita's. Admiral Teiji Nishimura's force in the south had already been destroyed in Surigao Strait. See my review-article, written shortly after the war: "The Battle for Leyte Gulf," *Virginia Quarterly Review*, vol. 23, no. 3 (Summer 1947). There have since been many accounts of the battle, including that in the standard set by Samuel Eliot Morison, *A History of United States Naval Operations in World War II, Vol. XII, Leyte* (Boston: Little, Brown, 1958). A recent brief account which is good from the Japanese side is contained in John Toland, *The Rising Sun* (New York: Random House, 1971), chap. 22.

theory of strategy, replete with principles that are both immutable and deeply meaningful, but they only indicate by that desire a basic misunderstanding of their subject. The reasons are easy enough to see in tactics, dominated as they are by weaponry that so conspicuously changes with time. Nothing looks more quaint today than a latter nineteenth-century treatise on fleet tactics, which will most likely stress the importance of ramming! [28] With strategy, however, we expect more steadiness—and appropriately so, up to a point. We have, after all, in these pages been lauding the modernity of Clausewitz. It is, however, the kind of modernity that will not give us the answers to our contemporary problems but which, at its best, will sharpen our receptivity to appropriate insights about those problems.

To give but one example: We noted Clausewitz's explanation why Napoleon, to defeat Russia, had to go to Moscow. As it happens, the same reasoning goes far to explain the motivation for the North Vietnamese Tet offensive of 1968. But it is a similarity with enormous differences. Napoleon's effort was a total failure, an unmitigated disaster, militarily and politically. The Tet offensive in one narrow sense failed too; General Westmoreland and many others were in fact convinced that it was a complete failure. From the point of view of its political effects, however, especially upon opinion within the United States, it was a fantastic success, well worth its heavy costs to the North Vietnamese. There is no reason to assume that General Vo Nguyen Giap, whose brain child this offensive was, did not expect those losses. The gains for him, too, must have been in line with his expectations, and very likely exceeded them.

---

[28] Despite the enormous growth in size of ships' guns and thickness of armor in the years following the sortie of the *Merrimac* (or *Virginia*) in the year 1862, the fact that that ship rammed and sank the stationary *Cumberland* on that occasion, on the day before her famous engagement with the *Monitor*, made an enormous impression. This impression was augmented when at the Battle of Lissa in 1866 the Austrian flagship successfully rammed and sank the superior Italian flagship, though the latter was also practically stationary in the water at the time. There were also several accidental rammings during the next few years. Despite the failure of numerous other attempts at ramming during the American Civil War and long afterward, ramming was considered by many admirals to be the foremost offensive tactic of the ship, and the Russians even experimented with a ship that was heavily armored but without guns and that was supposed to serve exclusively as a ram. The popularity of this idea, which also was never tested in any systematic fashion, affected naval architecture at least to the end of the nineteenth century. Warships were fitted with huge beaks on the prow below the waterline—great cumbersome projections that affected the sailing qualities of the ship—but otherwise handiness was emphasized, handiness to permit dealing or avoiding a blow. See my *Sea Power in the Machine Age* (Princeton: Princeton University Press, 1941, 1943 2nd ed. reprinted, Greenwood Press, 1969), especially pp. 85–87. See also references to "ramming" in the index to that volume.

Clausewitz would have had a lively appreciation for both the similarities and the differences between the 1812 and the 1968 campaigns. We do not, of course, have to read Clausewitz to understand the latter campaign. It may be that the recognition that his comments do in fact bear upon that campaign provides us little more than a titillation of scholarly delight, just as reading in Plato some sharp insight into human nature gives us today, some 2,400 years later, a twinge of delight that is really one solely of recognition that he saw things as we do. It is not that Plato adds to our understanding; we can feel the pleasure only because that understanding already exists. In some subtle way, to be sure, education undoubtedly enhances our intellectual sensibilities, and this expanding awareness of connections between events or insights remote in time and circumstances is one of the ways in which it does so. We should not, however, press this analogy too far. We do in fact *learn* something from Clausewitz—a good deal more, I think, than we ever learn from Plato. Yet, without some measure of sensibility to begin with, the reading of Clausewitz, or of Plato, will confer neither delight nor advantage. Still, what we get from Clausewitz is a deepening of sensibility or insight rather than a body of rules, because insofar as he does offer us rules he is at once avid to show us all the qualifications and historical exceptions to them.

Strategic thinking, or "theory" if one prefers, is nothing if not pragmatic. Strategy is a "how to do it" study, a guide to accomplishing something and doing it efficiently. As in many other branches of politics, the question that matters in strategy is: Will the idea work? More important, will it be likely to work under the special circumstances under which it will next be tested? These circumstances are not likely to be known or knowable much in advance of the moment of testing, though the uncertainty is itself a factor to be reckoned with in one's strategic doctrine.

Above all, strategic theory is a theory for action. One recent critic, who with good warrant chided the "civilian strategists" of our time for not correctly anticipating the Vietnam War, did so on rather strange grounds. He distinguished between "policy prescription," which he called "the advocacy of viable solutions," and scholarship, which he defined as "the pursuit of truth." He suggested that the civilian strategists should have inclined toward the latter rather than the former, but that instead they had "fallen between the two extremes." They were, he said, "overimpressed with the potential transferability of theory to the world of action." This, after 150 years, is a sad retrogression from Clausewitz. What could strategic theory possibly be for if it were not meant to be transferable to the world of action? To turn around this critic's own words, *strategy is a field where truth is sought in the pursuit of viable solutions.* In that respect it is like other branches of politics and like any of the applied sciences, and not at all like pure science, where the function of theory is to describe, organize, and explain and not to prescribe.[29]

The New Scientific Strategists

The "civilian strategists" to whom this critic was referring are a group that evolved almost entirely since World War II, mostly in the United States, and usually associated with institutions like the RAND Corporation and a number of other organizations that have sprung up more or less in emulation of RAND. There has also been some comparable activity at a few universities, or rather it is more correct to say there have been a few individual professors scattered among the various universities who have made the study of American defense problems or of strategy their special province. The development that has been most prominently associated with the civilian strategists, though that association certainly does not characterize all of them, is what is generally known as "systems analysis," or sometimes simply "cost-effectiveness analysis," the latter term being perhaps more descriptive of the process involved.

There must always have been some kind of crude cost-effectiveness analysis in the design of military forces and their armaments. For example, a cavalryman with his horse was obviously more costly per unit to acquire and maintain than an infantry man, and there must always have been a problem involved in determining what the appropriate mix should be of cavalry to infantry —though there were times when the sheer shortage of horses decided the matter. This would ideally be determined by what the economist calls "marginal-utility" analysis, and it would apply also to determining the proper proportions of artillery to other branches of the service, and for that matter of generals to privates.

---

[29] The critic cited here is Colin Gray, whose relevant remarks are contained in his article "What Had RAND Wrought?" *Foreign Policy*, no. 4 (Fall 1971), pp. 111 ff. See also my reply, entitled "Why Were We So (Strategically) Wrong?," *Foreign Policy*, no. 5 (Winter 1971–1972), pp. 151 ff.

That does not mean that these problems are ever really *analyzed*. It would have been very difficult to do so. They were determined largely by experience and custom, and no doubt by a large measure of bias, and, as already suggested, also by circumstance. Nevertheless there was some general perception, however crude, that some correct or ideal proportion existed as a goal to be aimed for.

With the coming of the industrial revolution to armaments both of land and sea, the problem of deciding how to spend one's always limited defense funds most effectively became increasingly acute. There was, for example, a period of about twenty-five to thirty years in the latter part of the nineteenth century when changes in naval architecture were extremely rapid, especially with respect to armor thickness and the guns designed to penetrate armor. Armor grew so thick and heavy that baffling questions arose concerning where best to place it on the ship and how to design the ship to accommodate it. At the same time guns, too, were growing so large and heavy that comparable questions developed about their disposition and the appropriate numbers to carry on each ship.[30]

These problems were handled about as well as might be expected, which is not to say they were handled well. For one thing, a yearning always seemed to intrude for settling upon some customary or standard way of doing things. When, for example, the design of the battleship became relatively stabilized about 1880, it took the form of a ship with a main armament consisting of four large guns and four somewhat smaller ones (besides the much smaller "quick-firer" guns for defense against torpedo boats) and this form held for over twenty years. The eight guns of the offensive armament might consist (as in the British *King Edward* class

---

[30] This story, too, is treated at some length in my *Sea Power in the Machine Age*, especially chaps. x–xiii. In a period of exactly two decades the thickness of iron armor on British warships went from the 4½ inches of the *Warrior* of 1861 to the 24 inches (the metal in both cases being wrought iron) on the *Inflexible* of 1881. The earlier ship had carried smooth-bore guns (68 pounders) weighing 4¾ tons each and the latter 16-inch (muzzle-loading) rifles weighing 81 tons. Armor never again reached the thickness of that on the waterline of the *Inflexible* because it was already improving in quality. However, three years later, in 1884, the British had a 16¼-inch breech-loading rifle of 111 tons, which was subsequently also followed by a retrogression in calibre. During this same general period of time there was also the question of abandoning reliance on sails as a supplement to steam, the use of sails being an impediment to the adoption of the revolving armored turret. This step was finally taken with the British *Devastation* of 1873, which carried armored turrets sheltering 35-ton muzzle-loading rifles, but the development shortly thereafter in Italy of a ship carrying four 100-ton guns necessitated the building of the just-mentioned *Inflexible*.

completed in 1905) of four 12-inch and four 9.2-inch guns in two pairs of turrets distributed fore and aft. There was simply no sense in having two sets of guns so close in calibre and yet different. For this system made difficult the problem of "spotting fire" because the shell splashes from the two types of guns would usually be indistinguishable and would make range correction difficult. In addition, the custom developed of laying down simultaneously series of "first-class" and of "second-class" battleships, the latter being smaller in overall size and in the calibre of armament carried. Why was this done? Was it expected that the second-class battleships would meet only their like in enemy navies? Would not five or perhaps even four first-class battleships have been better than six ships divided into two classes of three each? To determine these questions would have required only a simple kind of operations analysis, but this seemed never to be done.[31] Then in 1906 the British solved these problems by building the *Dreadnought*, the first "all-big-gun" battleship, which in the original meant ten 12-inch guns carried in five turrets of two guns each. This was acclaimed a great revolution in naval architecture, and all battleships henceforward carried a uniform offensive armament; but why did it take so long for such a truly simple idea to make its way?

---

[31] The "second-class battleship" idea—not to be confused with the German armored ships nicknamed "pocket-battleships," like the *Admiral Graf Spee* destroyed at Montevideo, where the overall displacement was limited by the terms of the Versailles Treaty—made a strange reappearance in the years preceding World War II. The Germans built the *Gneisenau* and the *Scharnhorst*, the French followed suit with some comparable ships of the *Dunkerque* class, and the United States Navy felt impelled to enter the race with its *Alaska* class of ships, which it did not even know how to classify but finally settled on the designation "large cruiser." All these ships shared the same general characteristics: they had a standard displacement of about 27,000 tons and carried a main armament similar to that of the *Alaskas* which comprised nine 12-inch guns each. Inasmuch as these ships were no faster than the contemporary standard battleships, which carried guns of 14-inch to 16-inch calibre, and not a great deal cheaper, it is hard to see what purpose they were intended to serve. The U.S. Navy apparently had second thoughts about the *Alaska* class, and cut down the projected six to only two, which were then given a low priority in building time. During World War II the *Gneisenau*, after being only moderately damaged by air attack, was not even repaired by the Germans but dismantled instead so that its guns could be used in fixed fortifications ashore. The *Scharnhorst*, which was sent as a commerce-raider against the convoys going to Murmansk, was sunk in December 1943 off the North Cape by a British force that included one new 14-inch gun battleship, *The Duke of York*. The *Scharnhorst* could not stand up to the latter ship and could not outrun her, which indeed was completely predictable at the time she was built. The Germans, however, could at least offer commerce-raiding as a (not very good) excuse for building the *Scharnhorst* and the *Gneisenau*; the Americans could offer none at all for building the *Alaskas*.

There was also the matter of tactical lessons that seemed never to be learned, or rather which had to be learned over and over again. Cavalry charges against intact lines of infantry, which could be effective in Frederick's time, began to prove useless and costly during the Napoleonic wars, when tactics were developed to meet them. At Waterloo they were a total failure. In the American Civil War both sides learned that the proper way to use cavalry, by then exclusively a reconnaissance arm, was to exploit the horse for mobility but to do the major fighting dismounted. However, this experience had no effect on the tactics of the Franco-Prussian War, when the French especially repeatedly resorted to cavalry assaults against unbroken infantry lines, invariably with complete futility and considerable losses.[32] In World War I cavalry were not sent charging against entrenchments; nevertheless, up to 1917 large cavalry detachments armed primarily with lances were kept behind the lines in each allied offensive, ready to dash forward to exploit any "breakthrough"—which mercifully for the cavalry if not for the infantry never took place. When in 1916 Premier Lloyd George remonstrated with the British supreme commander in France, Sir Douglas Haig, for keeping so much manpower and horses unused in the form of cavalry—five cavalry divisions were being planned for the Battle of the Somme—General Joffre, who was standing by, supported his British colleague, saying that he, too, planned to use cavalry in the forthcoming battle, where again the breakthrough never came. And supposing it had come. What sort of strange visions did these commanders have: of horsemen galloping over the fields spiking fleeing Germans from the rear?

Comparable examples could be given over and over again. The most horrendous failure was that which characterized World War I, where the simple lesson provided in the American Civil War and reconfirmed in the Franco-Prussian and Russo-Japanese Wars —that direct frontal attacks on entrenched infantry armed with modern repeating hand rifles were bound to be extremely costly and usually fruitless (Ivan Bloch had stressed this point) —was not taken seriously even against strong forces armed with machine

---

[32] See Michael Howard's splendid *The Franco-Prussian War* (New York: Macmillan, 1962), especially for the accounts of the cavalry charges at Morsbronn, pp. 111 f., at Vionville, pp. 155–157, and at Sedan, pp. 215 f. Howard calls von Bredow's charge at Vionville "perhaps the last successful cavalry charge in western European warfare," but its main achievement (at considerable loss) seems to have been to enable cavalrymen to point to it for the next forty years as alleged proof that cavalry charges were not anachronistic.

guns. Modern machine guns were used effectively in the Russo-Japanese War of 1904–1905, but even in late 1915, Haig delivered himself of the opinion that "the machine gun is a much overrated weapon," and that "two per battalion is more than sufficient." By that time the British and French armies had already suffered from that one weapon untold casualties and the repulse of every offensive effort they had attempted—and worse was to come. The German machine gun more than any other weapon was to cause the complete failure of the horribly costly Somme and Nivelle offensives.

Why had not the most obvious lessons of combat experience been absorbed by commanders who were to send great new armies into battle? Because for the most part experience not personal to themselves was not really alive to these commanders, who were not students of history, even of military history, but who had absorbed an intensive indoctrination laced through with religious fervor on the merits of the offensive.[33] What was worse, in World War I the unprecedented separation of high command from front lines made it possible for the commander to be ignorant even of the experience of his own forces. When on the first day of the Somme offensive, one assaulting British division was thrown back to its starting point after terrible losses, Haig indignantly wrote in his diary that it had not even left its trenches! This kind of misapprehension of events at the front was far from exceptional.

The fact that the military have to practice only intermittently the function for which they exist means that a doctrine that is congenial can be adopted and cherished and given a dominating place in strategic planning without ever being put even to those tests that are feasible in peacetime. The British Royal Air Force after 1918 based its entire strategic policy on what it called the Trenchard doctrine of the vital role of strategic bombing (in which respect it differed not at all from the United States Army Air Forces, with the latter's open dedication to the ideas of the Italian General Giulio Douhet), but not before 1937 did the R.A.F. carry out any studies of how strategic bombing was actually to be done. When it did so it found, as the World War II

---

[33] The strange story of the exaggerated attachment to offensive doctrine prior to World War I—especially for the French, who were in part reacting to some of the alleged failures of French strategy in the Franco-Prussian War of 1870–1871 and in part responding to a kind of romanticism that succeeded in distorting, among other things, the teachings of Ardant du Picq—is described in my *Strategy in the Missile Age*, pp. 42–52. See also pp. 17 f.

Official War History put it, "that there was no clear idea what was operationally possible, what targets could be reached, how far they could be hit, what would happen to them if they were hit, or what were likely to be the casualties incurred." Or, as Marshal of the Royal Air Force Sir John Slessor was later to put it in his memoirs: "Our belief in the bomber was intuitive . . . a matter of faith." Quite the same appears to have been true of their American counterparts. Thus we learn that if the military are often too unwilling to discard an outworn idea, they will also sometimes leap to embrace without due scrutiny or testing a new idea that they happen to like.

One must remember too—and the military are by no means alone in this—that people wedded to dogmas will often continue to cherish them undiminished despite undergoing experience that to any detached observer would prove those dogmas wrong. Awkward events can be explained away as being due either to special circumstances not likely to recur or to a misreading of the evidence. In a profession arranged in rigid hierarchical order where rank means so much and where promotion is entirely at the mercy of those who write one's fitness reports, who will challenge the latters' dearest beliefs? Actually, this factor in itself is not so important as the eagerness of the younger officers, selected for their adaptability to the military virtues, to absorb and make their own the doctrines of their elders. In any profession real independence of thinking is always rare, and when it occurs is usually in some manner penalized. But the military profession provides some of the most barren soil of all for its nurture—despite, of course, frequent assertions to the contrary.

The use of scientists for assistance in making tactical suggestions goes back at least to World War I, where such distinguished British scientists as Ernest Rutherford, later to play a prominent role in the nuclear discoveries leading up to the atomic bomb, were employed to think up new ways of dealing with the German U-boats. At that time the British mathematician, F. W. Lanchester, laid the groundwork for what later became known as operations analysis, and his book, *Aircraft in Warfare* (1916), is a landmark in the field.

However, employment of scientists for advice in military decisions was carried very much further in World War II, especially in the novel field of strategic bombing. Both American and British

458

economists and others were employed in the new and exacting task of target selection for the bombing campaigns, and physical scientists were called upon to provide penetration aids for our own bombers and to find ways of thwarting enemy bombers. Then at the end the nuclear scientists showed what they had been up to all this time in the extremely secret Manhattan District Project. In fact, the prestige that the accomplishment of the nuclear bomb gave to scientists in general, at least for a considerable period of time, accounted probably more than any other one thing for the conviction of General H. H. Arnold, then Chief of Staff of the U.S. Army Air Forces, that scientists should be retained on a continuing basis in peacetime to assist the Air Force with its many tactical and strategic problems. There could have been other reasons as well, including the fact that the Germans had rather disturbingly beaten us in several important technological advances, including a jet engine which, had it been applied to fighters instead of, at Hitler's personal insistence, to German bombers, might have been enough to stop entirely the Anglo-American air offensive.

General Arnold's decision, which was soon emulated by the chiefs of the other services, was to set up outside the Air Force but supported by and closely associated with it, an organization that because of its autonomy could attract the quality of scientific personnel that could not be attracted by offers of employment within the Air Force itself. The reasons for the difference in attractiveness are several, mostly having to do with relative freedom and other working conditions, not excluding the fact that salaries did not need to be controlled by Civil Service requirements. The pecuniary consideration was, however, definitely secondary to the other. Top grade civilians are not likely to find the bureaucratic arrangements of the Pentagon setting appealing. As it happened, the people that RAND managed to attract within the first ten years or so of its existence were of an exceptional level of distinction, and also attached to RAND as consultants were some of the outstanding scientists and scholars of the day.[34]

The Air Force interest in founding RAND, which soon severed

---

[34] What is considered the standard book on RAND is that by Bruce Smith, *The RAND Corporation: Case Study of a Non Profit Advisory Corporation* (Cambridge, Mass.: Harvard University Press, 1968). However, at the time he wrote this work as a doctoral dissertation, Smith had made only one or two brief visits to RAND, which he joined as a staff member only after completing the book.

its original tie with Douglas Aircraft, stressed technological assistance. But the civilians assigned the task of organizing it introduced divisions of mathematics, economics, and social science, as well as of the more-to-be-expected engineering and physics. The inclusion of an economics division turned out to be of especially critical importance in the development of systems analysis, and the introduction of a social science division made it possible to undertake, among other things, systematic and thoroughgoing studies of the presumptive opponent or opponents of a kind that had too long been lacking from strategic studies. What we call Sovietology or Kremlinology did not originate at RAND, but it unquestionably received a strong impetus from the work done there. The same is true—to a lesser extent, however—of studies of Communist China and of other areas.[35]

However, the outstanding contribution made by RAND to modern strategic thinking was the development of systems analysis. This technique has been described in considerable detail elsewhere, and I shall here confine myself to the briefest possible description.[36] Where the older (though still continuing) operations analysis concerned itself mainly with the effort to put to optimum use equipment already in hand, systems analysis is designed especially to choose new weapons systems for the future. It is thus, unlike operations analysis, primarily a peacetime enterprise. The word *systems* indicates concern not merely with a particular weapon or vehicle, like the B-52 bomber, but with the whole system of equipment and manpower that goes into the use of that bomber,

[35] It is intriguing to speculate whether, if we had developed at RAND and elsewhere studies of Communist China with the same intensity that we applied to studies on the Soviet Union, we should ever have got involved in Vietnam to the extent that we did. Certainly one of the reasons for that involvement was the false assumption that it was Communist China that we were containing rather than merely Hanoi. This view was never shared by the few Chinese experts at RAND, almost all of whom had departed that organization by the middle or late 1960's. However, it is a well-known fact that political scientists, including area specialists, simply have not yet gained the hearing in Washington policy-making circles that has been achieved by scientists and economists. One wonders how much Secretary Dean Rusk consulted his own China experts in the State Department.

[36] Among the oustanding books on systems analysis are E. S. Quade (ed.), *Analysis for Military Decisions* (Santa Monica, RAND-387, November 1964); a revised commercial version of the preceding by E. S. Quade and W. I. Boucher, *Lectures on Systems Analysis and Policy Planning: Applications in Defense* (New York: American Elsevier Publishing Co., 1968); C. J. Hitch and R. N. McKean, *The Economics of Defense in the Nuclear Age* (Cambridge, Mass.: Harvard University Press, 1960); and especially, Alain C. Enthoven and K. Wayne Smith, *How Much Is Enough? Shaping the Defense Program, 1961–1969* (New York: Harper & Row, 1971). My *Strategy in the Missile Age* also contains a brief treatment of the subject in chap. 10, "Strategy Wears a Dollar Sign."

which may include special tankers, special kinds of ground equipment, and maintenance and manpower requirements. Everything that goes into the acquisition, operation, and maintenance over a given period of time (usually four or five years) of a fleet of B-52s comprises as a package the B-52 *system.* The analysis is usually a matter of comparison on a "cost-effectiveness" basis of one system against another, neither being yet in existence. My example chooses a system that *is* in existence, and getting quite old at that; but at one time it had to be projected, and systems being projected at this writing, like the B-1 bomber, may or may not ever come into existence (and are often highly classified).

This technique requires estimating or projecting costs for *all* the elements in each system, and also calculating the effectiveness of each system for its assigned task—and comparisons can hardly be made between systems unless the tasks assigned them are virtually identical. To put it in it simplest terms, the basic idea is that of using the (always scarce) dollar as a unit for comparing the effectiveness of one system against another. If systems A and B do the same job equally well,then the cheaper is obviously the preferable one. If system B does the job better but is also more costly, the problem is to find some way of evaluating quantitatively its superiority of performance and checking that against the increased cost. Perhaps at the increased cost it is better to shift to an entirely different kind of system.

Systems analysis is not primarily a matter of reducing overall defense costs. The goal is to get the most tactical and strategic effectiveness for one's money, but if the result also helps keep down overall defense costs, that is not an end to be despised. However, it is highly likely that overall costs will be controlled by other considerations, including and especially mere habit on fixing the number of major units required, like capital ships or divisions (with a constant upward trend in the performance and therefore cost of these units), and a tendency for the additional military items-wanted list to be indefinitely expansible and therefore always available to take up any possible slack in the budget.[37]

---

[37] Concerning habit, Enthoven and Smith have the following to say: "For a variety of political and institutional reasons, it is very difficult to reduce the numbers of major force units: divisions, air wings, and capital ships. These units are the most widely known aspect of the Services' structure; their number has remained relatively fixed for some years. (Indeed, the Navy has maintained a minimum requirement of fifteen capital ships—once battleships, now attack carriers—since the Washington Naval Treaty of 1921). The tendency has been to keep the same number of units and replace older, cheaper equipment on a 1 for 1 basis with more capable and more expensive items." *How Much Is Enough?*, p. 326. See also their comments on p. 325.

The techniques so briefly described have required in those who conduct them not only appropriate technological and scientific training but also a good deal of hard experience. In projecting the costs of a system, for example, one has to have learned how to treat the optimistic estimates of firms interested in getting a part of the contract. Similarly, in calculating the effectiveness of that system one has to also deal with "planning factors," which for a variety of reasons are likely to be either too optimistic or too pessimistic.[38] One also has to be alert for those easily overlooked qualifications or conditions that could if they intervened make a critical difference in the result. A considerable institutional as well as personal learning process has usually been required in order to develop the appropriate competence in the teams that do the work, and especially in the project leaders.

The resulting analyses are bound at best to be imperfect, but they are also likely to be far superior to anyone's simple, intuitive judgment. In the first place, the kind of intuition that might have been adequate prior to World War II—but, as we have seen, often was not—would be hopelessly inappropriate to an era marked by vast technological complexity, rapid change in the "state of the art," tremendous sums of money involved in the choices, and long "lead times" for systems about which decisions are currently being made. The last item refers to the fact that the decision being made today is for a system that may not be available for another six or eight years, at which time the entire military-technological environment is likely to be different in many relevant ways. It has not been altogether a new problem for the military, especially in the Navy, to have to think ahead technologically, but certainly the dimensions of the problem since World War II bear no comparison to those existing previously. One has to rely on specialists, on teams of technicians who will maintain an alert understanding of

---

[38] A "planning factor" is an assumption or estimate concerning some aspect of the performance of various portions of one's military machine or of the conditions under which it may be operating. For example, an estimate of bombing accuracy, measured in CEP for certain kinds of bombing under combat conditions, may be a critical planning factor, telling one how much bombing will be needed or whether it will be effective. Assumptions about weather conditions and how they will affect operations will also be planning factors. It is readily seen that any war plan or significant portion thereof involves working with a multitude of planning factors, of which some will be based on a good deal of experience and others will be sheer guesses. Some planning factors will obviously be more critical than others, but error even in the individually uncritical ones will add up to something significant. War gaming also involves using planning factors, some of which may be highly arbitrary and initially recognized to be such—though that recognition may subsequently be forgotten.

the evolving state of the art in each of several quite distinct technological fields like electronics, rocket propulsion, decoys or "penetration aids," and so on.

Also, the reasoning processes by which the conclusions are reached in any modern systems analysis are not only more detailed than anyone's intuitive judgment is likely to be but also more open and explicit and therefore more accessible to correction at any particular point where the reasoning may have gone astray. A briefing will be presented with many charts, graphs, and figures to series of audiences who will have every opportunity to challenge various assumptions or findings as they are presented.[39] Those briefed are not put in the position of being required simply to accept or reject the conclusions. There are also likely to be differences in objectivity between the officer relying on his "mature military judgment" and the technicians doing the systems analysis, even where the latter are members of a research organization supported by the same service. That greater objectivity affects many things, including the diligence with which one searches out relevant factors. The intuitive judgment has indeed in some few instances proved superior, but there can be no doubt that the systematic modern methods generally produce far more reliable results and are in many kinds of problems quite indispensable.

There is in any case a wide area left for the uses of intuition. As we have seen, systems analysis is devoted primarily to the comparison of systems intended to accomplish the same or similar missions. It is good for comparing two kinds of bombers or two kinds of missiles. It is not as good for comparing missiles with bombers. It is of no use for telling us whether the mission intended for either the bomber or the missile is worth the effort being put into it or worth doing at all. The question of ends is usually a much more important question than that of optimum means, and the systems analyst is not only without special equipment for handling the latter but may even be negatively equipped, that is, he may have a trained incapacity for giving due weight to political or social imponderables. So too, for that matter, may be the military officer.

The situation was described quite aptly in 1960 by Charles J. Hitch, then head of the RAND Economics Division and one of

---

[39] This is not to suggest that there are not also hidden assumptions and biases even in the best systems analyses—only that they are more subject to being challenged and exposed, and of course their precise places in the study will also be identified.

the pioneers in operations and systems analysis (and subsequently president of the University of California) at a conference of operations analysts. One excited participant urged that their special techniques, thoroughly computerized, be immediately adapted to the solution of foreign policy problems, whereupon Hitch dryly responded that they really appeared more appropriate to rationalizing traffic over the George Washington Bridge.

The Struggle to Control

Robert S. McNamara brought to the office of the Secretary of Defense in 1961 a mind most sympathetically attuned to the charms of systems analysis with all its charts and figures—he having been trained as a statistician, with Air Force experience in that capacity during World War II—plus a determination to exercise both the prerogatives and the duties of that office as he saw them. And he saw them in a quite different light from virtually all his predecessors, who had usually been quite content to leave "purely military judgments" to the Joint Chiefs, especially conerning equipment, insofar as the latter could be prevailed upon to come up with a common opinion.

With the help of the same C. J. Hitch, who served him as Comptroller or Assistant Secretary of Defense (Budget), Secretary McNamara reorganized the operations of the whole Military Establishment into *functions* and budgeted them accordingly. Thus, strategic bombardment, whether with missiles or aircraft, was a function that deeply involved two services, the Air Force and the Navy, both of which operated missiles and aircraft, though of very different types. The Air Force controlled the ICBMs and the long-range bombers, the Navy the Polaris and Poseidon missile submarines as well as carrier-borne aircraft (though carrier aircraft were probably no longer being accorded a significant role in a general war with nuclear weapons). The determination of the appropriate mix, especially insofar as changes were called for, should obviously not be left to competitive infighting between those two services, which had sufficiently demonstrated their propensity for such preoccupation. Actually, the Navy had originally shown only moderate interest in the Polaris submarine *because* of its "foreign" function (that is, it had nothing to do with command of the sea) but that phase had passed. Similarly, the Air Force and the Navy had often been much less avid about purchasing equipment primarily intended to enable either of them to assist the Army than they were about equipment intended for their "independent" missions—which only tells us again that the services are normally not strategy-minded but rather means-minded.

However, Secretary McNamara actually went far beyond such considerations. It was not alone the lack of objectivity among the services concerning their respective needs that was at issue. It was his opinion that the individual services could not be depended upon to make wise decisions concerning their own major weapons systems. The record seemed to show (it would be difficult to argue the contrary) that they were too eager to expend large sums in the pursuit of some extra margins of speed or other characteristic of performance concerning their ships, aircraft, or tanks—margins that might indeed have a tactical or strategic advantage but sometimes a very modest one that seemed to be hardly proportionate to the extra cost. It was not only a matter of buying the better but more costly of two types offered (which might or might not make good sense) but also of premature phasing out of an entire system of, say, fighter planes in favor of another system that promised too little advantage to justify the shift. For these and other reasons McNamara decided that it was up to him to make the important decisions concerning weapons systems choices, and this meant having available to himself the appropriate staff. Besides Charles Hitch, and initially subordinate to him, he appointed Alain C. Enthoven, also formerly of the RAND Corporation, to direct the required project. The latter was later raised to the rank of Assistant Secretary of Defense (Systems Analysis).

The military services, as could be expected, then proceeded to demonstrate that it was one thing for them to have systems analysis pursued under their own direction and control, permitting them to accept or reject the conclusions of a study as they saw fit,[40] and quite another to see it done outside their control, especially

---

[40] The Air Force, for example, gratefully accepted the conclusions of the well-known RAND base study led by Albert Wohlstetter in 1954 (see A. Wohlstetter et al., *Selection and Use of As Strategic Air Bases* [Santa Monica, RAND, April 1954]) but rejected the conclusions of the study led by the same man some years later on the means of enhancing the security of bomber aircraft at their bases. The reasons had nothing to do with the quality of the respective studies; the former fell in very well with Air Force predilections while the latter did not. The latter study, however, gave rise to Wohlstetter's well known and highly influential article, "The Delicate Balance of Terror," *Foreign Affairs*, vol. 37, no. 2 (January 1959), pp. 211–234.

when it was at the service of a strong-minded Secretary of Defense who seemed to feel no ambivalence about his own superior authority and responsibility. Enthoven and his former assistant, K. Wayne Smith, have told the story exceedingly well, at least from their own point of view, in their indispensable *How Much is Enough? Shaping the Defense Program, 1961 –1969* (1971). We need not attempt to cover any appreciable part of the same ground here. It might, however, be instructive to repeat some of their quotations of certain senior military officers, partly because those comments reveal something besides simple resentment of the civilian interloper on the issue of weapons choices. They also reveal something perennial about the frame of mind of the military officer on larger national issues.

General Thomas D. White, a former Chief of Staff of the Air Force, wrote in 1963 the following:

> In common with many other military men, active and retired, I am profoundly apprehensive of the pipe-smoking, tree-full-of-owls type of so-called professional "defense intellectuals" who have been brought into this nation's capitol. I don't believe a lot of these often over-confident, sometimes arrogant young professors, mathematicians and other theorists have sufficient worldliness or motivation to stand up to the kind of enemy we face.[41]

As it happens, the present writer can testify that General White has not always been opposed to civilians speaking out or writing on military affairs. What he objects to is a situation in which they are able to propose to those above him and have adopted decisions that he and his colleagues find obnoxious. But the statement also reveals the ubiquitous fear among the military, especially in the nuclear age, that civilians are not conditioned to be sufficiently "hard-nosed" for the needs of our times. They will be too willing to yield or back down, or to refrain from doing what it takes to win, and thus will settle for something undesirable. They lack "sufficient worldliness or motivation to stand up to the kind of enemy we face." It is a significant choice of words. Inevitably the Constitution places the President, a civilian, in a position of ultimate authority, but General White, like most of his colleagues, is clearly opposed to seeing this authority made too pervasive. And

---

[41] Quoted in Enthoven and Smith, *How Much Is Enough?* p. 78, from General Thomas D. White, "Strategy and the Defense Intellectuals," *The Saturday Evening Post*, May 4, 1963, p. 10.

he is far from being the kind of notorious hard-liner that is the next gentleman we quote.

General Curtis E. LeMay, who also finished his military career as Chief of Staff of the Air Force, expressed the following view five years later in the Preface to his book, *America Is in Danger:*

> The military profession has been invaded by pundits who set themselves up as popular oracles on military strategy. These "defense intellectuals" go unchallenged simply because the experienced professional active duty officers are officially prohibited from entering into public debate. The net result is that the military is often saddled with unprofessional strategies. . . . Today's armchair strategists, glibly writing about military matters to a public avid for military news, can do incalculable harm. "Experts" in a field where they have no experience, they propose strategies based upon hopes and fears rather than upon facts and seasoned judgments.[42]

General LeMay's statement that active duty officers "are officially prohibited from entering into public debate" is not quite true, as he should know from the attention paid many of his own public statements while he was still on active duty. There is little inhibition upon what he may say before appropriate congressional committees, which publish their hearings, and his public writings or speeches are subject to clearance procedures that are only marginally more restrictive than those applied to members of, say, the RAND Corporation. They are of course subject to some restrictions, even apart from security, as indeed they should be. It would hardly do to have active-duty officers denouncing positions taken by their own government; they have their opportunity to do so in retirement, which even for senior officers can come at a relatively youthful age, and General LeMay was exercising that prerogative in his book. Implicit in his brief quoted remark is again the fear we saw in General White, that the "pundits" will not be hard-nosed enough: "they propose strategies based upon hopes and fears rather than upon facts and seasoned judgments." Insofar as he is clearly alluding to the trials of thermonuclear war, he does not explain where in fact the military have got the "facts" and the "seasoned judgments" that are denied to the civilians who are also occupying themselves full-time on the same problems.

Finally in this connection Enthoven and Smith quote Vice

---

[42] Quoted ibid., p. 78, from General Curtis E. LeMay, *America Is in Danger* (New York: Funk & Wagnalls, 1968), pp. viii, x.

Admiral Hyman G. Rickover, whose barbs are much more explicitly aimed at the systems analysts, whom he compared to "spiritualists" and "sociologists" and whom he accused of "playing God while neglecting the responsibility of being human." He went on to say, testifying before a House subcommittee in May 1968:

> The social scientists who have been making the so-called cost-effectiveness studies have little or no scientific training or technical expertise; they know little about naval operations. . . . Their studies are, in general, abstractions. They read more like the rules of a game of classroom logic than like a prognosis of real events in the real world. . . .
>
> In my opinion we are unwise to put the fate of the United States into their inexperienced hands. If we keep on this way, we may find ourselves in the midst of one of their cost effectiveness studies when all of a sudden we learn that our opponents have ships that are faster or better than ours.[43]

One may guess that the decision that aroused Admiral Rickover's special annoyance was that of Secretary McNamara to use conventional rather than nuclear propulsion in various frigates then being built and especially in the aircraft carrier that became the *John F. Kennedy* (nuclear propulsion had already been used with great technical success in the *Enterprise*). That decision may indeed have been a mistake (in this writer's opinion, it was). But choosing the "faster or better" ship or aircraft can also be a mistake, if, for example, it inevitably means fewer ships or aircraft, as it is bound to when unit costs go up exponentially and some ceiling has to be placed on the overall budget.

By "social scientists" Rickover in this instance no doubt means economists, whose training is basic to the conceptions underlying systems analysis, but any analysis that did not include use of or resort to people of appropriate "scientific training or technical expertise" would simply be a badly done analysis. There have indeed been such analyses, both outside and inside the military services, but it is doubtful whether any done under Enthoven's supervision would have failed to include people of the requisite training and expertise. As for knowing about "naval operations," the teams doing the analyses may very well have had attached to

---

[43] Quoted ibid., pp. 78 f., from *House Subcommittee of the Committee on Appropriations, Hearings on Department of Defense Appropriations for 1969, 90th Congress, 2nd Session* (Washington: Government Printing Office, 1968), pp. 54 f.

them persons of considerable experience in such operations who may be active or retired military officers (and some civilians, too, are after all veterans of military service), but whether they did or not they would certainly fail in their duty if they did not familiarize themselves with all the relevant arguments of the Navy's own authentic experts on naval operations. Arguments that have merit can be heard or read, and understood perfectly; one does not have to go to sea to know that salt spray is wet.

In the case of the propulsion system of the *John F. Kennedy*, for example, the views of Rear Admirals J. T. Hayward and C. D. Griffin were heard both by Secretary McNamara and his aides and independently by the Joint Committee on Atomic Energy, which also published these views.[44] Their views may not have been accorded the weight they should have got, especially those of Admiral Hayward, who had been commander of the carrier division that included the *Enterprise* and who was most eloquent and also explicit in his admiration of its performance, but that can happen to the testimony of any expert, civilian or military. In any case, Admiral Hayward spoke exclusively of superior performance, not of extra cost.

Mr. Enthoven on one occasion soon thereafter (in a speech before the U.S. Naval War College) stated that everyone was in agreement that nuclear-powered warships were tactically superior to their conventionally powered counterparts, and implied that this might be especially true of carriers as well as submarines (all our missile-firing submarines are nuclear powered). He charged, however, that the Navy had not made any attempt to *quantify* the added tactical and strategic superiority in order that it might be compared with added cost. This may seem to the layman like a bizarre request: How can and why should one quantify a superiority of tactical performance? Actually, no one is asking for precise figures, but rather for some idea of whether the nuclear carrier is twice as good or only one-and-one-half times as good. If it is twice as good, would the Navy be willing to do with half the number of carriers, or would it prefer to have its presently authorized number

---

[44] *Joint Committee on Atomic Energy, Hearings on Nuclear Propulsion for Naval Surface Vessels, 88th Congress, 1st Session,* Oct. 30, 31 and Nov. 13, 1963 (Washington: Government Printing Office, 1964). Admiral Hayward's testimony is on pp. 49 f., 63 f., and is also cited on pp. 90 f. Mr. McNamara's testimony is on pp. 152–196. The cited portions make extremely interesting reading with respect to a number of factors, including not only the merits of the case but also the personality of Mr. McNamara in debate.

even if they be conventionally powered? These are not unreasonable questions, and faced with them the Navy may tend to become more measured in its advocacy and perhaps to remember that the whole concept of carrier-borne aviation has long been under fire and that it would therefore not do to have individual carriers become too astronomically costly. In this instance the Navy got its way anyway with the next or *Nimitz* class of carriers laid down, which were projected for nuclear propulsion.

Admiral Rickover's view is the simplistic one that the Navy should have the "best" (meaning highest performance) type of combatant ship that the current state of the art permits, and devil take the cost—the "devil," of course, being the civilian economy. This view has often been followed, and very often those who did so were themselves aghast at the results. For example, the Grumman Aerospace Corporation, seeing a $65 million loss in the 86 F-14s it was building under contract with the Navy, insisted it was unable to build any more unless the price per unit was materially increased. The Navy had originally intended to buy 722 F-14s, but as prices mounted from $11.5 million to $16.8 million each, the plan was reduced to 313 planes for a total of $5.2 billion. But the Navy could not have even its 313 planes unless it was willing to renegotiate its contract, which would mean, according to one report, that "the price per plane would almost certainly rise to about $20 million." [45] These F-14s, incidentally, were intended for the new carriers, and when one also considers the $600 million to $800 million cost of a *Nimitz* type carrier, then carrier aviation *was* getting extraordinarily costly and thus more vulnerable to the attacks of the critics. After all, there were alternatives. The Navy was already using the excellent Phantom aircraft, which was perhaps a fifth as costly as the F-14.

Does that mean that there is no merit to the kind of complaints quoted from officers like White, LeMay, and Rickover? The last-named, incidentally, might have had reason to complain at his own treatment at the hands of the Navy, which would have retired him as a captain if it had not been forced by congressional action to promote him to flag rank. It is to Admiral Rickover's credit that he apparently has not nursed a grievance on this score, and anyway, the whole issue is almost a digression—but not quite. His promotion was one instance of civilian intervention to overcome

---

[45] *Los Angeles Times*, financial section, January 21, 1972; article signed by Michael Getler, also printed in *The Washington Post*. See also the article by H. R. Myers on the "Navy F-14" in *Science*, vol. 176 (April 7, 1972).

what would otherwise have been an inexcusable service rigidity, considering the Admiral's exceptional contributions in his special field; and he should be ready to acknowledge the fact that other occasions for such favorable intervention can and do arise. But that does not answer the major question.

It should be noticed that of the three criticisms quoted, only Rickover's addresses itself primarily and almost exclusively to systems analysis, and on this issue there can be very little doubt who is right. Systems analysis, being absolutely necessary to certain kinds of choices, is best done by those who are appropriately trained for it and who have by dint of great diligence acquired a scarce and valuable experience in their art. It is also likely to be more effective if it is done under an authority who has no difficulty subordinating service interests to other interests of the nation. The great majority of military officers who have had official dealings with the systems analysts would probably agree with these conclusions. That some of the civilians have acted arrogantly, as General White charges, is probably true, though the perception of arrogance is a subjective one on the part of senior officers who are accustomed to a great deal of deference. These senior officers are usually willing to accord some informal equivalence of rank to civilian "men of affairs" who also appear to be of mature years, for they live in a world in which high rank normally goes only with mature age; but some of the systems analysts, including Enthoven himself when he first went to the Pentagon, have been very young men.

That the civilian analysts have had certain specific biases, institutional and personal, is also no doubt true. For example, the conviction which they clearly entertained that the services were too "performance-minded" would tend to push them in the opposite direction of occasionally paying somewhat more attention to the first word than to the second in what is supposed to be the integral phrase "cost-effectiveness." If so, it would be a simple case of overcompensation on their part for an opposite bias on the part of the military. The civilians certainly in the net brought more objectivity to their work, especially objectivity with reference to service attachment, but also objectivity with respect to the technological means by which any strategic end may be accomplished. Military officers have usually spent their entire careers perfecting their skills with respect to some *means* of war, whether those means be battleships, or carriers, or bombers, and they become deeply attached emotionally to those means. They tend to ignore or deny that the ultimate purpose of those means may perhaps be better accomplished by other means, or may even itself fade in importance. General LeMay was to the core of his being a bomber man, and as Chief of Staff he was no less interested than he had been as commander of SAC in getting a new, fast bomber for the Air Force. The North American B-70 bomber, with its Mach 3 speed, was in his eyes such an aircraft, and he left nothing undone to get it adopted as a bomber system. He took ill its rejection by Secretary McNamara and those who stood behind the latter as his advisors. No amount of mere "analysis" could have persuaded him that, especially in view of the existence of our ICBMs and submarine-launched missiles, the B-70 had too many shortcomings in range, vulnerability, and cost to be acceptable.

The much-touted "experience" that the military so commonly advance in their special claims to superior wisdom in military decisions is in this realm almost always irrelevant. Certainly senior military men possess indispensable skills acquired only through experience. Chief of these is the ability to command, to lead in battle contingents of men who may be combined into huge forces. To accomplish well such an assignment requires both experience and talent. However, when it comes to choosing major weapons systems for some future state of affairs that may be considerably different from the present—and the present may itself be considerably more different from the past than the generals are wont to allow—there often exists no military experience whatever that is relevant. That experience which is truly relevant can be effectively communicated in the form of words to those sufficiently interested and adequately informed, whether they be in or out of uniform. The methods of doing so are simply the traditional methods of learning, and are used by the military forces themselves in their various schools, service journals, and numerous manuals.

Does any military man have the *experience* to judge whether the Safeguard ABM system will work adequately to justify its cost? We remember that the Army from 1958 to 1961 pressed for deployment of Nike Zeus as an ABM system, and that two civilian Presidents, one of whom happened to carry the prestige of a five-star general, denied them the funds. In view of the characteristics of the system, it would have been a huge waste of money. We know that the civilians who conducted the World War II U.S. Strategic Bombing Surveys on the ground following on the heels of our fighting men, first in Germany and then in Japan, got a far better idea of the *effectiveness* of those great and devastating campaigns than those who directed them or flew the missions.[46] The commander got the operational experience, which was of no trifling value, but if he has not read those reports or any substantial condensation thereof, he is not as well informed about what strategic bombing can do as the civilian who has—though neither would have any solid idea of what a nuclear campaign would be like.

In terms of predictions, we have seen that those of Ivan Bloch at the turn of the century were far closer to the truth about World War I than the predictions of men like Joffre or Foch or Haig who were to direct the fighting of it. Bloch read and pondered the large amount of relevant available data; the others did not, depending rather on romantic slogans. If Lloyd George had not forced a reluctant Admiralty under Admiral Sir John Jellicoe to adopt the convoy system, Britain and France would have lost World War I before America was well into it. We could go on indefinitely in this vein. There is a long, long history on these matters, a very slight portion of which has been touched upon in previous chapters. It does not teach us that civilians are normally better informed on things military than the military themselves, or any other such nonsense. It simply tells us that there always has been and probably will always continue to be far too much pontificating and posturing on that commodity called "military judgment," which taken in itself, without supplemental inquiry and rumination, can be an extremely limiting thing. It is also to say that war is not only too important to be left to the generals but too important and far too complex to be handled adequately by any one profession. And so far as concerns responsibility, the civilian leader who has the constitutional authority and obligation to control should have no fears or diffidence about his inherent competency, given suitable advisers, to do so. Naturally, it helps to have a sharp and judicious mind, which a President or a Secretary of Defense or of State ought to have anyway, and it is always necessary to take the trouble to acquaint oneself with the problem.

The Overvaluation of Systems Analysis

The critics of the "pundits" would have been on far stronger ground if they had criticized not the handling of the systems analyses and the results derived from them, but rather the fact that far

---

[46] The United States Strategic Bombing Survey (U.S.S.B.S.) comprises 208 separate published items for the European war and 108 items for the Pacific War. There is also a British Bombing Survey. The conclusions of these and supplementary works are summarized in chap. 4, "Strategic Bombing in World War II," of my *Strategy in the Missile Age.*

too much attention was paid to what was after all "rationalizing the traffic over the George Washington Bridge." The techniques and skills generally covered by the term "systems analysis" were and remain indispensable in the choice of weapons systems, but the choice of weapons systems is not the whole of strategy, nor even the most important part of it. Supervening that area of choice are the *major* problems, perhaps not inherently more difficult but certainly less susceptible to systematic treatment and the suppression of bias: What influence did systems analysis have on the fighting in Vietnam? Practically none—and not, as some have said, because it was not tried. It simply was not relevant.

At the height of our involvement in Vietnam we were spending something like 3 per cent of our GNP on the military operations there, measured in terms of the bulge in our defense expenditures that were attributable to that war. In view of the fact that some defense expenditures that would otherwise be considered normal were deferred, the actual amount was probably something over 3 per cent. In any case it is low enough to show that mere *efficiency*, which is what systems analysis is all about, had rather little to do with the case. We used B-52s for "conventional" bombing not because they were ideally designed for that purpose but because they were on hand, not otherwise needed, and certainly of high enough performance to do the job. They may indeed have been, by sheer accident, a very good type for the purpose—quite possibly too good because of the enormous tonnage of bombs they were able to convey. What is in question, however, is not whether those bombers were appropriate for their job but whether that job was appropriate as a military goal in a war that itself may have been inappropriate to our national ends. In comparison with the latter questions, that of the suitability of the B-52 is ridiculously trivial.

The best of the systems analysts have most often been trained as economists. Economists as a group are usually somewhat more at home in the world of technology than members of other branches of the social sciences, and, more importantly, they have a theoretical training that in its fundamentals bears many striking parallels to strategic concepts.[47] On the other hand, the usual training in economics has its own characteristic limitations, among which is

---

[47] This point was developed in a somewhat ancient article by me which, for understandable reasons, has been much cited by economists. It is "Strategy As a Science," *World Politics*, vol. i (July 1949), pp. 467–88.

the tendency to make its possessor insensitive to and often intolerant of political considerations that get in the way of his theory
and calculations. He is normally extremely weak in either diplomatic or military history or even in contemporary politics, and is
rarely aware of how important a deficiency this is for strategic insight. One is often amazed at how little some of the best-known
strategic analysts of our times may know about conflicts no more
remote in time than World War II, let alone World War I or
earlier wars. It is not that they have no time for history—everyone finds time for whatever kind of study he considers important
—but rather that the devotees of a science like economics, which
is clearly the most impressive of the social sciences in terms of
theoretical structure, tend to develop a certain disdain and even
arrogance concerning other social science fields, which seem to
them primitive in their techniques and intellectually unworthy.

Thus, where the great strategic writers and teachers of the past,
with the sole and understandable exception of Douhet, based the
development of their art almost entirely on a broad and perceptive reading of history—in the case of Clausewitz and Jomini
mostly recent history but exceptionally rich for their needs—the
present generation of "civilian strategists" are with markedly few
exceptions singularly devoid of history. It could be argued that in
a world that has had to adopt itself to nuclear weapons, the reading of history may be an impediment; but not if we continue to
consider strategy what Clausewitz considered it—a branch of politics, a "continuation of politics by other means." The intellectual
leaders of that movement in the 1960s to force an enormous American and NATO buildup of conventional armaments, in order,
they thought, to circumvent use of nuclear weapons, were all systems analysts, with no basis in their training or preoccupations
for claiming special political insight of any kind.[48] This despite
the fact that they rested most of their arguments on what they
considered to be political considerations. They were trained to be
highly scientific in one area of limited application, but that did
not incline them to be comparably scientific or even worldly wise
in the larger area where ends become more meaningful than

---

[48] To avoid sounding unnecessarily cryptic, I should state that the persons I have
particularly in mind include primarily Alain Enthoven, Malcolm Hoag, Henry Rowen,
and Albert Wohlstetter. All these were trained as economists. Wohlstetter was, however, later appointed to a chair in political science at the University of Chicago, a fact
that proves nothing except the free-wheeling nature of my own alma mater.

means and where it becomes important to consider motivations and emotions as well as mechanics.

If they were nevertheless right in their contentions about the benign consequences of a conventional buildup (which were usually tied to an unwarranted belief in the unrelenting aggressiveness of the Soviet Union) it would not have been because of the special training and expertise that had made them competent systems analysts—and that had also given them the special hearing they enjoyed. Their special training could indeed have been somewhat destructive to the kind of shrewd intuition that the more intelligent layman sometimes possesses. There is nothing exceptional in that. The trained incapacity to see what the layman may readily comprehend (especially if the latter knows how to consult, but not necessarily to believe, the appropriate experts) is a common phenomenon in various professional fields. The lawyer, for example, usually comes out of his legal training firmly believing that the adversary system is the best and in fact the only way of arriving at truth in litigation or criminal law. The layman sees in it, on the contrary, mainly a contest of irrelevant forensic skills marked on both sides not by an effort to suppress bias but to exploit it and to give it the freest possible rein in one's own favor, which inevitably takes the form of corrupting the evidence. It includes efforts by each side to select the most biased jurors, but biased in the right direction. It is the exact opposite of what the scientist is trained to believe, and usually manages to live by, at least while engaged in his own special field. Similarly, in systems analyses dealing with the effects of nuclear strategic bombing, it has been customary to leave totally out of consideration the psychological and social effects of such bombing, or the fears anticipating those effects—simply because they could not be quantitatively handled—and it has often proved to be a small step from leaving such items out of consideration to implicitly denying their importance.

For all his immense and fruitful efforts at rationalizing procurement for the armed services, at insisting on budgeting by functions rather than by services, and all the rest—including above all a marked enhancement of the meaningfulness of civilian control —Secretary Robert McNamara was just as avid in 1964–1965 as any other member of the Administration to get us involved in Vietnam. Under the circumstances prevailing at the time, this attitude does not set him apart from others. Having no ideas different from those of the military about how the operation should be handled, he had to let the latter do it their way, except for imposing certain important restraints upon them. That he realized before many of his colleagues did, and certainly before President Johnson (if the latter ever did), that the whole episode had been a terrible blunder is a tribute to his general intelligence and also his humanity. Meanwhile he had raised to levels of chief importance matters of computation that he later discovered were of lesser importance. That he realized it fully is reflected in the fact that it was he who directed that the Pentagon Papers be prepared. It really did not matter very much who made the TFX, or F-111 as it was later designated, or even if it was made at all. It did not even matter so much that he saved the country the several billions of dollars that might have been spent on a B-70 system. It mattered a good deal that this inherently honest man went along with the sorry business of the Tonkin Bay Resolution and all that followed from it.

Secretary McNamara held the office more than seven years, his successor held it less than one, yet Clark Clifford put his heart and his effort into a goal that was of far greater consequence both to his office and to his country than any that McNamara undertook to accomplish. He turned the President and thus the country around on Vietnam, changing our direction from deeper involvement to that of deescalation and ultimate withdrawal. It was not his fault that the President who took office from the election that soon followed chose to move much more slowly along the path of withdrawal than Secretary Clifford thought necessary or wise. The latter was no longer in a position to influence policy. However, in terms of their individual net accomplishments, Clifford may well go down as a more significant Secretary of Defense than McNamara. True, Clifford came to office at a later date, when the fact of failure in Vietnam was obvious to almost all, but his instincts and his talents were for grappling with the larger problem, the one that really mattered.[49] His prior service suggests that he

---

[49] Townsend Hoopes relates how, when the order came from President Johnson to find means of raising the 206,000 additional men requested by the Joint Chiefs after the Tet offensive of 1968, the outgoing Secretary McNamara's instinctive response as an old organization man was to "manage the problem," to try whittling down the numbers while conforming with the request, whereas Clark Clifford's response was to begin questioning what the expectations of the military were concerning the future course of the war if these men were given to them. See Townsend Hoopes, *The Limits of Intervention* (New York: McKay, 1970), pp. 163 f.

would probably have been equally accomplished in his relations with Congress and with our allies as he seemed to be in his forensic skill in the White House. These were areas in which McNamara did not shine. The latter was often clumsy with Congress.[50] Also, he had waged in public the futile and sterile campaign to make President de Gaulle cease and desist from making nuclear weapons.

Anyway, we are not here interested in determining historically which of these men was better in the post or would have been better if given equal opportunity. The Secretary of Defense is not the only one responsible, or even the one chiefly responsible, for determining our strategic policies. Any holder of the office is likely to be selected for a variety of reasons, including many that have little or nothing at all to do with the considerations we have been emphasizing here. The Secretary of State, too, has or should have something to do with these matters, and both he and his defense colleague are working as the servants of a President who has, always, the ultimate responsibility. What is important for any holders of these offices is to get their priorities straight. All I have been trying to say in these paragraphs is that a decision to commit or not to commit forces to a certain enterprise is likely to be of far greater moment than a decision to buy or not to buy a particular kind of weapons system.

How we select or train a person to exercise good strategic judgment in the broad terms I have laid down is another matter. The President is selected by the voters on grounds that are generally irrelevant to our inquiry, and he chooses his Secretary of Defense according to lights and desires that are peculiar to him. We come back to the particular atmosphere prevailing, and we also come back to the generals and admirals who are the full-time operators in this area. Although the main message of this book has been one that stresses the importance of civilian control and urges the civilians who do control to keep clear in their minds *why* they do so, we still have to pay more attention to the traditional custodian of the nation's security. He is not the only full-time worker in that field—all civilian workers in the defense community are that, too —but he is the only full-time worker, meaning careerwise as well as in length of day, who is likely to achieve high authority and

---

[50] A good example is to be found in his testimony in the cited hearings on the nuclear versus the convention-powered aircraft carrier; see footnote 44, this chapter.

responsibility. The Nixon Administration may retain a Kissinger; the one that follows may neither find nor wish for any such person.

The Military

General of the Army Omar Bradley once told some civilians that he had been in the Army for over forty-seven years but that he had never observed anything that might be called "the military mind"! This remarkable statement bears out what anthropologists have long known, that to observe a culture or subculture in all its dimensions one must have not only the opportunity to observe it closely over a long period of time but also the detachment of being an outsider. So far as that distinctive subculture was concerned that we call the Military Establishment, General Bradley had ceased to be an outsider too long ago and at too early an age.

Other professional groupings, too, will also have their distinctive way of looking at things. I have remarked on the lawyer's special appreciation of adversary proceedings as a way of approaching truth. The doctor and the university professor, too, can usually each be counted upon to have views distinctive to his profession that will often not be shared by laymen. These distinctive attitudes, which may affect fundamental value judgments, will often be held in common by a wide range of personality types—though the demands of the profession will itself impose certain limits upon the kinds of persons admitted to the practice of it.

The military are like the other professions in these respects, only much more so. They are more so mostly because the profession is more limiting in the personality types it accepts and advances, and also because it is much more demanding in conformity and more confining in the kind of character development it furthers. Its members, for example, must be both able and eager to accept discipline and obedience in matters great and small, and yet at the same time must cultivate the capacity to command. When one adds to these demands the special requirements of command responsibility under combat conditions, toward which all else is pointed, the pattern of the mold is becoming psychologically intricate. To accomplish these and other aspects of their senior personnel needs, the services emphasize and pursue a distinctive way of life aided by separation from the larger community. The uniform and the salute, as well as the many other distinctive forms of

479

military courtesy and observance between members of the profession, are intended to promote *both* the habit of obedience and of conformity and also the consciousness of separation.[51]

However, this is not the place for a general sociological analysis of the military profession, American or any other, upon which a good deal of work has already been done.[52] We must confine ourselves to the issues relevant to the basic subject of this book.

The soldier (I here use the word to mean an officer of any military service including the Navy, and I shall usually be referring to one senior enough to be influential) will of course be varied in personality, character, and intelligence. These variations will be apparent enough to the outsider, and even more so to the insider. A psychologist or psychoanalyst may be drawn to speculate on the qualities of character that have caused a person to be drawn to the military profession (or perhaps even to writing books on military affairs), and he may find some dark significance in the fact that that profession deals ultimately in the controlled, socially approved use of huge violence and of its special instruments, which now include nuclear weapons. However, in view of the many accidental ways in which people become committed to the profession, and also the youthful age at which the commitment is usually made, we should acknowledge that it is too easy to go awry in such

---

[51] A military friend whom I had got to know well at the U.S. National War College and who was later retired from an important command of the Air Force as a four-star general told me once that before World War II it would have been impossible for him to be on such friendly terms with me, a civilian, without its being remarked upon by his seniors and having an adverse effect upon his promotion. At least times are changing.

[52] The number of titles of scholarly works that one might mention in this connection is by now quite large. I shall content myself (and, I trust, the reader) by calling attention to the leadership, in the field of sociology, of Morris Janowitz, whose outstanding work is probably *The Professional Soldier: A Social and Political Portrait* (New York: Free Press, 1960). There has been a much larger amount of work done in the field of civilian-military relations in government, and here one should perhaps mention first the work of Samuel P. Huntington, *The Soldier and the State: The Theory and Politics of Civil-Military Relations* (Cambridge, Mass: Harvard University Press, 1957); also, on the basis of a closer personal experience than Huntington's, Adam Yarmolinsky, *The Military Establishment* (New York: Harper & Row, 1971). One should not, however, forget the sensitive journalist who has made contact with the military and has done a good job of reporting it. One recent and especially rewarding example is Lewis H. Lapham, "Military Theology," *Harper's,* July 1971. Another is Ward S. Just, *Military Men* (New York: Knopf, 1970). Nor should one omit to mention that extraordinary excoriation of his own profession by a former chief of staff of the Marine Corps, General David M. Shoup, "The New American Militarism," *Atlantic,* April 1969. There are also many excellent modern biographies of military men, though these, of course, deal with the more outstanding members of their profession.

speculations. On the other hand, we do have to observe that only those become soldiers who are *not repelled* by the considerations just mentioned. This means that, especially in peacetime, a significant slice of youth is not included.

Much less speculative, however, is the pattern of character traits that the services seek to nurture and encourage and by which the process of selection upward is ruled. The traits we have mentioned as applying to all recruits to the profession are few, and embrace too many people to be especially distinctive. During periods of major war we find that a great many civilians find the military way of life congenial, at least for a time, and not only fall to with great gusto in following the "customs and traditions" of whatever service they find themselves in but fail even to see anything remarkable about the emphasis placed on them. The important aspects of selection, however, are with respect to preferment to high rank.

We ought first to consider the role of individual native intelligence, insofar as the possession of it is apparent to those who do the promoting. It is sufficiently apparent in view of the several service schools that candidates pass through who are destined for high rank and the many fitness reports they will have got on the way. I consider it first because to most people the phrase "military mind" connotes a certain lack of intelligence, as does also its cognate conception, "bureaucratic mind." It is no doubt true that when it becomes really conspicuous as such, the "military mind" or "bureaucratic mind" is usually performing stupidly. But it is not always that conspicuous, and in its more subtle guise the military mind can also be a very sharp mind.

Certainly a reputation for high intelligence is a positive factor in promotion. However, the high or exceptional intelligence must not be at the cost of other traits, which because they are deemed at least commensurate in importance with intelligence really outweigh it. An officer who is considered brilliant but somehow lacking in service loyalty, or too willing to use his brilliance for criticism in a manner construed to be negative or destructive, or who is lacking in various other of the recognized military virtues may as well pack up his things and go elsewhere. He will not rise very far.

One thus has to say about intelligence that it is important but not first, and any trait that is placed somewhere other than first on the hierarchy of values may in particular instances be found pretty far down the course. Faculty members of universities that aspire to outstanding rank know that they must place scholarship first in the traits they seek both in recruitment of new faculty and in promotion. To put scholarship first means necessarily not merely to downgrade but often to disregard all kinds of characteristics of life style or of political beliefs or whatnot that military services would certainly not disregard. Talent, in short, has to be cherished for its own sake or it will too easily be missed entirely. The military know that as well as anyone else, but the talents they are chiefly seeking are not intellectual. It follows that officers sometimes get a reputation for being "brilliant" who in a more intellectually demanding milieu would not have that reputation. It also follows that some officers will reach very high rank on the basis of various qualities that may include judiciousness, but who would not be called brilliant by anyone. It is obviously impolitic or impolite to give living examples, but the history books are full of them.

The qualities that are considered first in importance we have already mentioned in passing, and we need do hardly more than recapitulate them here. There is always an important emphasis on loyalty, and the objects of this loyalty are multiple and perhaps deliberately vague. Loyalty to the country of course, but if that were all there was to it there would be no need to emphasize it so much. It does not tell us why officers have a much better chance of reaching topmost rank if they are graduates of their respective service academies, as is undoubtedly the case, and inculcation of loyalty is one of the reasons. In the Navy, to be a graduate of Annapolis is practically a *sine qua non* for reaching flag rank, let alone the office of Chief of Naval Operations. In the Army and the Air Force, to be a graduate of the appropriate academy is less a requirement for reaching flag rank, and there have even been chiefs of staff of both the Army and the Air Force who were not graduates of West Point. But there is no doubt that it helps greatly to be a graduate of the respective academies (which now includes the Air Force Academy at Colorado Springs) and it is not because anyone thinks that cadets or midshipmen get a better education at those institutions, which academically they certainly do not. It is partly élitist custom, no doubt, but it is also because at each stage of their careers where reassignment or promotion is at question the graduates of these institutions can be counted upon (so one guesses) to have been inculcated with and to have absorbed the right spirit and the right attitudes about their profession and about their service. This incidentally means that two institutions, and soon it will be three, of quite indifferent academic qualifications have an extraordinary incidence of famous men among their alumni.

The "right attitudes" include a special devotion to duty, which is indeed no empty phrase and which can be most impressive to the person who first encounters it. They include a deep awareness of the loyalties owing both to one's commander and to one's subordinates, and the loyalty to one's service that should be second nature. The latter cannot be too much stressed overtly, because it is obviously a form of parochialism, but the officer who is really objective about his own service as compared with the sister services is not going to rise to high enough estate to make that objectivity of much service to the nation. That means that if the Navy is currently committed to aircraft carriers as its "capital ships," the naval officer destined to get on will automatically believe in carrier aviation. He may in fact be a submariner and therefore a great believer in that arm as well, but he will not publicly depreciate the aircraft carrier—nor privately either, except with utmost discretion. The Air Force and the Army will have their own special domains of sacred belief. That does not mean that there will not be heated professional debate in the service journals and in the various staff schools and war colleges, debate that sometimes argues the need for change; but it will be circumscribed debate, stressing "positive values" rather than criticizing dogmas as outdated. An article in an Army journal may well stress the need for more helicopters and better use of them and similarly with tanks, but it is far less likely to question whether new antitank devices have not made the tank obsolete. That would not look at all good if a congressional appropriations committee got hold of it.

The officer with the qualifications and ambition to attain high rank in any of the services knows that the path is mainly through posts of command. A naval officer will want to command a combatant ship of a size appropriate to his rank. This gives him his opportunity to prove he can run a taut yet happy ship. If his experience in command includes combat duty, and if he performs well under fire and shows aggressiveness within his orders, he is on his way. He will shift periodically from sea to shore duty where he will have some specialization, but he must not become too narrowly specialized. He will naturally get assignments to the right schools at the appropriate times, which at the highest levels will include either the Naval College at Newport, Rhode Island or the National War College at Washington, D.C., after which nothing stands in his way for the top posts except the competition of a few with almost identical qualifications.

Much the same is true in the other services. An Army officer will command a platoon, and then a company, and so on up. At one time it was considered necessary to be qualified as a paratrooper, and middle-aged colonels broke legs making parachute jumps. At about the same period—after the Korean War ended and before that in Vietnam had heated up—some service in Korea was considered essential for advancement, even though the battle fronts were quiescent. Colonels would leave their families to seek service for some two years in that dreary and far-off post. It was not really a matter of choice. To be a West Pointer and to have chosen the Army as a career means to have committed oneself to doing all the things necessary to becoming a general. It was a part of what is meant by doing one's duty.

During the height of our Vietnam involvement, career officers were circulated through that theatre as though it were another service school, one of special opportunity. It is certain that our actual military performance in Vietnam suffered thereby. But it was regarded as a good opportunity for the younger officers who had not seen war elsewhere to get combat service on their records, and perhaps to win distinction in that role. Like other schools, it was an occasion for some to learn and for others to evaluate them —not so much on what they had learned as on how well they had taken to the process. After all, a military officer who has not seen combat is still a large question mark. If there has been no opportunity, that is that; but opportunities that occur must not be thrown away.

In the Air Force one must have learned to fly an airplane. There are other kinds of flying ratings, like that of bombardier or navigator, but these are not command positions. The pilot is. Every chief of staff since the Air Force was formed has been a rated senior pilot, most often a bomber pilot. If he had proved himself in war, like General LeMay, who after helping lay waste to Germany set Japan on fire, and who after the war organized the Berlin air lift and later took over SAC to make it a finely honed instrument always highly conscious of its wartime mission and always combat ready, then there was nothing but to make him chief of staff at the appropriate time, even though he was not a West Pointer but merely an engineering graduate of Ohio State University. In any case, command is the word, and within sharply ordained limits, tough aggressiveness is the desired style.[53]

A man who has distinguished himself in staff positions is still a staff officer. He may become SACEUR (Supreme Allied Commander, Europe), nominally a command post but in essence a diplomatic one. General Alfred M. Gruenther, a genuinely brilliant man, could rise to that post, but he could not become chief of staff of the U.S. Army. The same was true of Air Force General Lauris Norstad, also deserving his reputation as a brilliant officer, even though he had once held the command post of USAFE (United States Air Forces, Europe). He was deputy to one SACEUR (Gruenther) and then became SACEUR himself—but never chief of staff of the U.S. Air Force. There had not been enough command assignments on the way up, and his rival at the time was LeMay. Later he got into difficulties with the Kennedy Administration at home because of his partial differences with them on their then new ideas of "graduated response"; he was highly conscious of his role as an allied commander as well as an American one, and his outlook at the time corresponded more with European views than with the novel American ones. President Kennedy showed just how much an allied commander Norstad was by abruptly retiring him without consulting our NATO allies, despite his great popularity with the latter, and replacing him with the somewhat older and now somewhat tarnished (as a result of the Bay of Pigs episode) former Chief of Staff of the Army and later Chairman of the Joint Chiefs, General Lyman Lemnitzer. No one thought Lemnitzer was being promoted.

A member of the Joint Chiefs, though he may have the mislead-

---

[53] How *visible* in external manners and mannerisms must be the desired toughness seems to vary with service and even more with nationality. My casual observation has been that British officers of all services are generally milder of mien and of habit, including manner of speaking, than their American counterparts, though considerable latitude is accepted among the latter. As an indication that we are dealing with a real subculture, however, and not merely a profession, I am obliged to mention that I have never observed in any other group besides the military such a tolerance of bragging, especially among senior officers. That is not to say that most senior officers in the American armed forces are braggarts, but I have indeed met a good number that were such. Moreover, it seemed not to be noticed or at least remarked upon by their fellow officers. It may be that bragging is a way of assuring oneself that one is really entitled to the high rank one holds and to the extraordinary deference that goes with it.

ing title of Chief of Staff or Chief of Naval Operations (misleading because he is not a staff officer but a commander or director) is, together with his colleagues and with the Chairman of the Joint Chiefs (always a former chief of one of the services, with the job rotated among the services) at the acme of his profession. He is directing one of the great services of the United States Military Establishment, and he is in Washington where the power is. He is by law one of the President's military advisers.

Now the man who has risen to the top finds himself with new concerns, political and diplomatic. He is not simply directing the Army or Navy or Air Force. He is consulting with his colleagues and advising his civilian superiors, the Secretary of Defense and the President (the secretaries of the Army, the Navy, and the Air Force are considered as having administrative roles but not as being in the chain of command). He is advising them on matters having to do with the goals and ends of peace and of war. For this he has certainly not been trained—unless a nine month survey course in international and other political affairs at one of the war colleges can be considered such training.[54] However, he has absorbed ideas and convictions and biases all along the way, and these are a large part of his working capital.

We have already in previous pages got some idea what these convictions and biases are like. Having been trained as a soldier, with all that that implies with respect to steeling one's mind against contemplation of all the immediate effects of using instruments of great lethality, and having also consorted all one's life with people of like training and disposition—with the important added factor that demonstrated toughness in combat is itself a highly favorable mark for preferment—our Chief of Staff is one who shares with his colleagues a great belief in the efficacy of force in dealing with recalcitrant peoples or regimes abroad. This

[54] As one who helped set up the U.S. National War College by serving on its faculty for the first year of its existence, and who later served on its Board of Advisers—as well as having given lectures there and at the other war colleges—I feel I can say with confidence that the training afforded at that level is by no means adequate to the needs described. It is undoubtedly a valuable training, and visibly raises the horizons of the officers who pass through it; but as far as changing their basic attitudes is concerned, the training is too brief, too casual, comes too late in life, and keeps the military consorting with each other (as well as with a few selected civilians on the faculty and from other branches of government). A few officers are sent to civilian universities for graduate training in various fields, including political science and allied subjects, but on the small sampling I have witnessed these seem usually not to be selected for flexibility of thinking, which might indeed make difficult their return to their respective services.

486

is what he means by being "hard-nosed," and this is why he distrusts the civilian who intrudes into affairs a proboscis that is not similarly armor-plated.

Robert Kennedy complained of this characteristic in his vivid account of the top-level consultations during the Cuban missile crisis of 1962. When the idea developed that blockade rather than immediate military action could be a suitable first step:

> The members of the Joint Chiefs were unanimous in calling for immediate military action. They forcefully presented their view that blockade would not be effective. General Curtis LeMay, then Air Force Chief of Staff, argued strongly with the President that military attack was essential. When the President questioned what the response of the Russians might be, General LeMay assured him there would be no reaction.[55]

LeMay may well have been right, but on no basis of special knowledge or insight that the President could not fully share. We notice in this critical instance not only the disposition to use maximum force at the outset, despite the existence of milder methods that did not exclude the more forceful ones later if they should prove necessary (and with nothing lost in the wait), but also the equally common tendency among the military to give without hesitation assurances that are well beyond their qualifications and knowledge.

Of a later meeting, Kennedy remarks, "Certain statements were made as accepted truisms, which I, at least, thought were of questionable validity. One member of the Joint Chiefs of Staff, for example, argued that we could use nuclear weapons on the basis that our adversaries would use theirs against us in an attack." [56] It has to be added that, apart from the advocacy of nuclear weapons, the military were not the only ones present arguing for direct military action at the outset. Some of the civilians did likewise, including former Secretary of State Dean Acheson and various members of Congress, including not only the late Senator Richard B. Russell of Georgia but also Senator J. William Fulbright of Arkansas. However, it was the military who were unanimous and insistent, and of course their advice carried extra

---

[55] Robert Kennedy, *Thirteen Days: A Memoir of the Cuban Missile Crisis* (New York, Norton, 1969), p. 36.

[56] Ibid., p. 48.

weight and affected the others. It took special courage on the part of President Kennedy to resist it.

As the crisis moved along its course and it began to appear at one meeting that while Khrushchev was still wrestling with our demands there was a good chance that he might yield to them, the time now being Saturday, October 27:

> The Joint Chiefs of Staff joined the meeting and recommended their solution. It had the attraction of being a very simple next step—an air strike on Monday, followed shortly afterward by an invasion. They pointed out to the President that they had always felt the blockade to be far too weak a course and that *military steps were the only ones the Soviet Union would understand.* [Italics added.] They were not at all surprised that nothing had been achieved by limited force, for this is exactly what they had predicted.[57]

I have italicized certain words because they are so often heard at staff and war colleges and in military circles generally (and of course elsewhere as well). It reflects a primitive outlook upon our opponent, who naturally respects us for our power just as we respect him for his power. But that is not the same as saying that *the application* of force is the only thing he will understand. It is hard to think of any generalization of comparable breadth that would not apply equally to the United States as to the Soviet Union, which, obviously, is not to deny that the two countries are very dissimilar in several important political and sociological respects.

At that moment word came in that one of our U-2 pilots, Major Rudolf Anderson, Jr., had been shot down and killed. There was now tremendous pressure for making an attack at least on the SAM sites on the very next day, but again the President pulled back. "We don't attack tomorrow," he said, "We shall try again." [58]

The next day the crisis was ended. Khrushchev had agreed to remove the missiles. The American military had responded impressively in their preparations and in their military conduct, but the recommendations of their leaders had left the President profoundly disturbed:

> But he was distressed that the representatives with whom

---

[57] Ibid., pp. 96 f.
[58] Ibid., pp. 97–101.

he met, with the notable exception of General Taylor, seemed to give so little consideration to the implications of steps they suggested. They seemed always to assume that the Russians and the Cubans would not respond or, if they did, that a war was in our national interest. One of the Joint Chiefs of Staff once said to me he believed in a preventive attack against the Soviet Union. On that fateful Sunday morning when the Russians answered they were withdrawing their missiles, it was suggested by one high military adviser that we attack Monday in any case. Another felt that we had in some way been betrayed.

President Kennedy was disturbed by this inability to look beyond the limited military field. When we talked about this later, he said we had to remember that they were trained to fight and to wage war—that was their life. Perhaps we would feel even more concerned if they were always opposed to using arms or military means—for if they would not be willing who would be? But this experience pointed out for us all the importance of civilian direction and control and the importance of raising probing questions to military recommendations.[59]

The importance of the latter point had indeed been dramatized by the previous Cuban experience, the Bay of Pigs episode of eighteen months earlier, from which President Kennedy had derived so much instruction. His experience was missing on a later occasion, but a good substitute was provided by someone who had undergone comparable instruction. In autumn 1967 when Secretary McNamara began openly to question the utility of continuing bombing of North Vietnam and a subcommittee of aging and hard-bitten Senate war hawks weighed in with the usual stale advice that "logic and prudence requires [sic] that the decision be with the unanimous weight of professional military judgment," McGeorge Bundy, now out of the government, came back with the following in a letter to the *Washington Post*:

> First, the Senators appeal not to evidence but to authority. They set up a group of generals and admirals against Secretary McNamara, and their position is that the generals and admirals are right simply because they are professionals. The Subcommittee does not demonstrate the military value of the

---

[59] Ibid., p. 119.

course it urges; it simply tells us that the generals and admirals are for it . . . Nothing is less reliable, in hard choices of this sort, than the unsupported position of men who are urging the value of their own chosen instrument—in this case military force. We must not be surprised, and still less persuaded, when generals and admirals recommend additional military action—what do we expect them to recommend? [60]

Still, we have to ask: What really drives them in that direction? Mr. Bundy had himself previously advocated the action he was now denouncing. He had been for the application of force, including the bombing; he had now become satisfied it had not worked and was supporting Secretary McNamara in securing a reversal of policy. But the military had not budged from their original position. Why not?

We have at various times in the preceding pages noticed the military officer's extreme dedication to the idea of *winning*, to the notion of victory for its own sake—as distinct from such questions as what is sought through victory or whether it will be worth the price paid for it tactically or strategically. This attitude, I suggested, puts war in the same category as an athletic contest, where the whole purpose is to win.

The military officer directing combat knows he is playing a much deadlier game than exists on any athletic field because his men are killing and being killed, and the niceties of sportsmanship are quite suppressed. Still, it is true in battles as in athletic contests that winning requires not only the means but also the ardent will to win, and the combat officer has been instilled with this will. The kind of military history he has read has stressed those heroic episodes, especially among historic captains of his own nation, where the will to win has conquered over considerable odds. The United States Navy cherishes among the items that dot its history such utterances as: "I have not yet begun to fight." "Don't give up the ship." "Damn the torpedoes, full steam ahead." The Army has its own list, and cherishes one particularly inelegant phrase confined to the word "Nuts!" In each of these cases the will symbolized by the utterance did in fact produce victory. There would not be much point in remembering similar utterances that were a prelude to defeat, unless the remark deserved to

---

[60] Hoopes, *The Limits of Intervention*, p. 89. The Bundy letter was published in *The Washington Post*, September 11, 1967.

be commemorated for the kind of extraordinary heroism that under slightly better circumstances would produce the desired victory.

Still, there is more to it than that. Military traditions do allow for surrender under "honorable conditions," which over the years have been redefined through the recounting of various relevant episodes. These stress those circumstances when further resistance is utterly hopeless. Lee's surrender at Appomatox detracts nothing from the mystique of his legend—but for how long had he contended against hopeless odds! Certainly, too, it is in the best military tradition for a clearly inferior naval force to flee from a superior one—so that it may live to fight under better conditions —unless particular circumstances call upon it to sacrifice itself, as for example, to protect a convoy.

Attacks by inferior forces against superior ones are not ruled out by any means, but the commander of the former should know what he is about. An advantage of spirit, of skill, of discipline, or of surprise may well make up for inferiority in numbers and has often done so. Shakespeare has glorified one such battle, that of Henry V at Agincourt, which was less a triumph of the long bow than of discipline over the lack of it. Nelson and his opponent at Trafalgar, Admiral Villeneuve, completely shared the conviction that the former had the superior force despite his lesser number of ships. The Japanese naval foray at Leyte Gulf, on the other hand, had more of the color of ceremonial sacrifice. They could hardly hope to accomplish their nominal goal, but there was no longer much reason left for attempting to preserve their fleet. This begins to verge on misdirected heroics, of which history offers sufficient examples; but how can one inculcate the necessary spirit of aggressiveness and of contending shrewdly against odds without some spilling over into the idealization also of the hopeless gesture? It is not an area conducive to cultivating sharp distinctions.

The military commander is also deeply imbued with the importance of that prestige which his success in arms brings to his nation. If a war has not been going well, a victory will cheer up a depressed population at home. When Admiral Jervis in 1797 with fifteen ships-of-the line caught up with a Spanish fleet of twenty-seven off Cape St. Vincent, he remarked: "England has need of a victory." With the help of a subordinate named Nelson he produced a spectacular one too, as that same Nelson, now in command, did a year later at the Nile. Such victories have also brought forward allies, or kept wavering ones from deserting. In our own time some of us remember the great boost to British morale that came in May 1941 when the mighty *Bismarck*, after quickly destroying the *Hood*, one of two British capital ships that had intercepted her, was herself brought to bay four days later and sunk. For the British, something was again put right in the world, and the United States, still nominally neutral, was by no means dissuaded by this victory from giving the British further aid.

However, distinctions between rational and irrational prestige-seeking may be difficult to clarify and maintain. Also, the military commander may too readily confuse the prestige of the nation with that of his own forces. The defeat of the French forces in Vietnam tended to be viewed by their senior officers mostly as a blow to the French professional Army, coming as it did so hard on the heels of that army's defeat in World War II. This accounted largely for the fury of the *Algérie Française* movement that was shortly to follow, where the Army felt itself once again being called upon to proclaim itself defeated. De Gaulle was obliged to make very much of the fact, not altogether imaginary, that a *military victory had been won* against the Algerian rebels, despite which France was freely granting the Algerians their independence! But when does the pursuit of prestige turn into the accomplishment of the opposite? The United States' staying on in Vietnam following 1968 was clearly a matter of preserving prestige, yet staying on and on made for less and less prestige, and surely the military were not the best judges of when and how speedily the transition was occurring—though they were certainly not the only bad judges.

We see that the whole training of the military is toward a set of values that finds in battle and in victory a vindication. The skills developed in the soldier are those of the fighter, and not of the reflecter on ultimate purposes. Under particular circumstances it may be considered unwise to fight, but it is rarely looked upon as ignoble; and is there any other test of unwisdom except the probability of losing? All this is fitted into a simplistic vision of the world and of what makes it function. The enemy—especially if he represents a somewhat different culture and is thus by definition barbaric—understands nothing but superior force. He understands it more clearly if it is applied than if it is merely threatened. In terms of strategic purposes, there is a particular phrase that comes easily to mind and that seems to cover a broad range of issues. It even has the prestige of deriving from Clauze-witz: *The purpose of victory is to impose one's will on the enemy.*

Now this is something that is easy both to express and to under-stand. How much better than trying to negotiate from a position of no particular advantage with people trained to be wily and deceptive! And those are the people, one is reminded, who have announced over and over again that their aim is to dominate the world! Well, in their eyes, so have we, in terms that to us sound defensive but which have created NATO and SEATO and a vari-ety of other alliances and which have brought us to wage war in Korea and Vietnam, on the very doorstep of China. Yet there has been a strong feeling among the American military that our whole international position has indeed been too defensive. As everyone knows, in the long run the defensive always loses.

As one officer in the audience put it to General Eisenhower when the latter was addressing the Naval War College on October 3, 1961, in the same year that he had relinquished the Presidency of the United States: "General, the Grand Strategy of the United States, NATO, and the Free World is a defensive one. In view of the Communist doctrine of World Domination should not the Grand Strategy of the United States and the Free World be changed to a more offensive one to protect our rights and values?" To this the General responded that he thought in the moral field it should be, but where the physical requirements for offensiveness included surprise attack with nuclear-armed missiles, he could not see where such offensiveness was compatible with that democracy which it was our main goal to preserve. Not a bad answer! A LeMay would have shown more thunder.

In the audience sat another five-star veteran of World War II, Fleet Admiral Chester Nimitz, whose only question of General Eisenhower was the following: "General, we frequently have heard that wars are too important to be left to the Generals and Admirals. Do you agree with that?" [Laughter]. At this Eisen-hower fell back on what was essentially Plato's notion that when kings are philosophers and philosophers are kings, then states will finally be well run. What he said in conclusion to a rather long reply was the following: ". . . if we can make sure that all of our officers are growing up to understand the problem of the citizen and the citizen leaders as well as his tactics and strategy in the purely military field, then I say the generals and the admirals ought to be, while subordinate to their commander-in-chief, running the war, rather exclusively."

It is perhaps too bad we cannot give all our top generals and admirals the useful training of being a President for eight years, but considering the deep convictions of some of them, it would be hazardous to try. Admiral Nimitz was one of the mildest of the men who held high military office in World War II, and it comes with a bit of a shock to hear *him* asking that leading question of General Eisenhower, which indicated very clearly that he was very far from being reconciled to those famous words of Clemenceau in 1918—which in turn were merely an echo of the conception of Clausewitz.

Other American senior generals have written books to express their hair-raising views, especially the SAC galaxy: LeMay, whom we have already quoted briefly, but whose whole book is alive with terrors, and his successor as commander of SAC, the late General Tom Power, whose looks and words were as grim as those of his chief, and whose book, which he published after his retirement, comes close to outdoing LeMay.[61] Then there was that other Air Force four-star general, Nathan Twining, former Chief of Staff of the Air Force and then Chairman of the Joint Chiefs. Twining, unlike LeMay and Power, was always mild of mien and soft spoken, but when he finally let go after his retirement in 1960 with his own book, then LeMay and Power were really outclassed.[62] It was not merely the "anti-nuclear intellectuals" and the usual "arm-chair strategists" who were betraying the country and our liberties. Even many service people had succumbed to their intellectual seductions. The latter phenomenon was somehow due to insufficient defense expenditures: "It was the shortage of resources, and how these limited resources were to be divided up, that really caused service interest in the idle philosophy of limited war."

I cannot make a comment on the LeMay-Power-Twining school better than that contained in the last three paragraphs of a brilliant review of the Twining book by Jeremy J. Stone:

The book underscores, in every outraged and undisciplined paragraph, the achievement of Secretary McNamara in gain-

---

[61] General Thomas S. Power, *Design for Survival* (New York: Coward-McCann, 1964).

[62] General Nathan F. Twining, *Neither Liberty nor Safety* (Holt, Rinehart, and Winston, 1966).

ing effective control of the Department of Defense. General Twining and his associates possess rigidly over-simplified opinions that reflect decades of isolation from political life; they have a natural self-confidence and determination that is heightened by military training and protected by military deference; and their commitment to their views is no less total than the dangers they perceive. It is quite a feat to ride herd on men like this.

It is hard to avoid the impression that Twining's views are the product of cold war battle fatigue. Drafted by his early sense of patriotism, instilled with an overriding concern for his country, ordered to search the horizon for the enemy, surrounded by men similarly charged, frustrated by the inexplicable (if not ominous) opposition of civilians, alarmed by the unpredictable speed of technological change, and conscious of the irrevocable pace of any future total war, General Twining has come to believe that the Test Ban Treaty is unilateral disarmament and to defend the case for two preventive wars against the Soviet Union and against China.

We have asked of him, not only that he think the unthinkable throughout his adult life, but that he take a deep personal responsibility for avoiding it. We have made him a watchdog, using his exaggerated fears to guard our society. In this important function, he served his country for 44 years in the most demanding offices. When he asserts defiantly that his ally Dr. Teller "lived and still lives in a real world—not a dream world," we ought to feel a measure of responsibility, and of compassion, for a man we asked to live apart in a terrible world that never was.[63]

The compassion is well warranted, and so is the note of caution. One could say that soldiers have always been like that, from antiquity to modern times. After World War I it was fashionable to quote the German generals, Colmar von der Goltz and Friederich von Bernhardi, and later Erich Ludendorff, who was to glorify "total war" in a book by that name (and to take part with Hitler in the Munich putsch of 1923). But now the phenomenon is ours, and in two real respects it is worse. One of the things that is new is a sense of frustration. The German firebrands like von der Goltz

---

[63] Jeremy J. Stone, "The General Faces 'Reality,'" *New Republic*, vol. 155, no. 18 (October 29, 1966). Mr. Jeremy Stone is not to be confused with his journalist father, I. F. Stone.

and Bernhardi were certainly not speaking of a "world that never was." They were not out of tune with those around them. They may have helped to create the world they warned of, but they also had accessories aplenty to share the blame. There was indeed bound to occur some day another war to which their warnings would seem not at all disproportionate. The other and major difference is of course nuclear bombs, and part of Twining's fury is directed particularly at the fact that some people are trying to defuse them. The other side of the coin is that the Twinings, the LeMays, and the Powers belong to a passing generation. The new generation of officers is growing up in a different environment— well, somewhat different. Yet the civil hand must never relax, and it must without one hint of apology hold the control that has always belonged to it by right.

INDEX

497